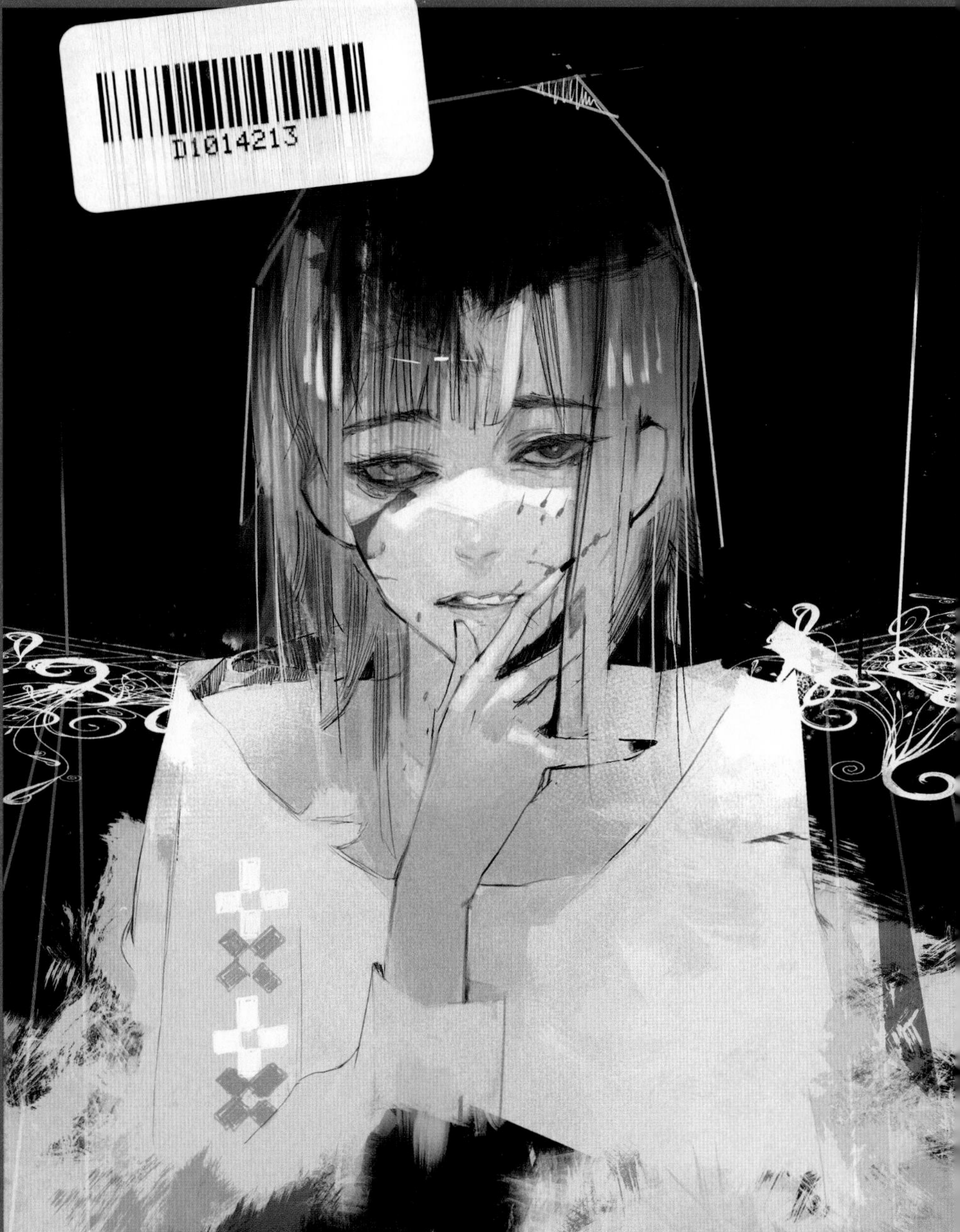

TOKYO GHOUL:re

9

東京喰種

SUI ISHIDA

TOKYO GHOUL:re 9

東京喰種

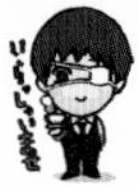

CONTENTS

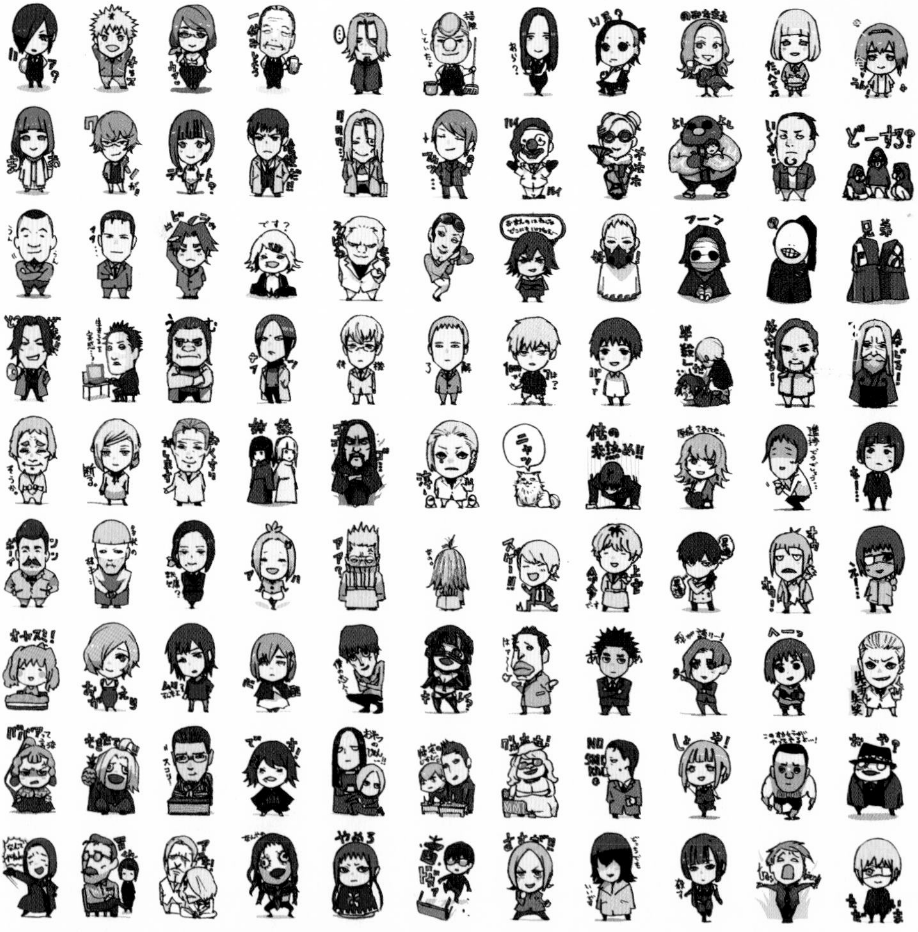

*See page 42, 62, 118, 156 and 194 for translations.

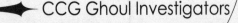

CCG Ghoul Investigators / Tokyo Ghoul : re

The CCG is the only organization in the world that investigates and solves Ghoul-related crimes. Founded by the Washu Family, the CCG developed and evolved Quinques, a type of weapon derived from Ghouls' Kagune. Quinx, an advanced, next-generation technology where humans are implanted with Quinques, is currently under development.

Mado Squad

Qs (Quinx): Investigators implanted with Quinques. They all live together in a house called the Chateau along with Investigator Sasaki.

● Ken Kaneki
金木 研
Previously known as Haise Sasaki, a CCG investigator and the Qs mentor. A half-Ghoul who succeeded Kisho Arima as the One-Eyed King.

● Kuki Urie
瓜江久生
Rank 1 Investigator
Quinx Squad leader and its most talented fighter. His father was killed by a Ghoul and Urie seeks vengeance. He has demonstrated leadership since Shirazu's death.

● Saiko Yonebayashi
米林才子
Rank 2 Investigator
Supporting Urie as deputy squad leader while playing with her subordinates. Very bad at time management and a sucker for games and snacks.

● Toma Higemaru
髭丸トウマ
Rank 3 Investigator
Discovered his Quinx aptitude before enrolling in the academy. Looks up to Urie. Comes from a wealthy family.

● Ching-li Hsiao
小静麗
Rank 1 Investigator
From Hakubi Garden, like Hairu Ihei. Skilled in hand-to-hand combat. Came to Japan from Taiwan as a child.

● Kori Ui
宇井 郡
Special Investigator
Became a special investigator at a young age, but has a stubborn side. Formerly with the Arima Squad.

● Juzo Suzuya
鈴屋什造
Special Investigator
Promoted to Special Investigator at 22, a feat previously only accomplished by Kisho Arima. A maverick who fights with knives hidden in his prosthetic leg.

● Toru Mutsuki
六月 透
Rank 1 Investigator
Become an investigator after his parents were killed by a Ghoul. Assigned female at birth, he transitioned after undergoing the Quinx procedure. Struggling with the lie he has been living with...

● Akira Mado
真戸 暁
Assistant Special Investigator
Mentor to Haise. Takes after her father. Determined to eradicate Ghouls. Investigating the Aogiri Tree. Concerned about Fueguchi.

● Shinsanpei Aura
安浦晋三平
Rank 2 Investigator
Nephew of Special Investigator Kiyoko Aura. Unlike his aunt, who graduated at the top of her class, his grades were not that great.

● Matsuri Washu
和修 政
Special Investigator
Yoshitoki's son. A Washu Supremacist. He is still skeptical of Quinxes. Deputy commander of the Rushima Operation.

● Kisho Arima
有馬貴将
Special Investigator
An undefeated investigator respected by many at the CCG. Killed at Cochlea by the One-Eyed King.

● Nimura Furuta
旧多二福
Rank 1 Investigator
Former subordinate of the late Shiki Kijima. Has many secrets.

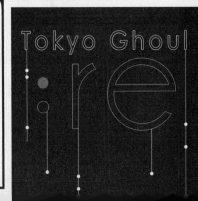

Tokyo Ghoul :re

Tokyo Ghoul :re ● Ghouls

They appear human, but have a unique predation organ called Kagune and can only survive by feeding on human flesh. They are the nemesis of humanity. Besides human flesh, the only other thing they can ingest is coffee. Ghouls can only be wounded by a Kagune or a Quinque made from a Kagune. One of the most prominent Ghoul factions is the Aogiri Tree, a hostile organization that is increasing its strength.

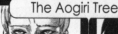

The Aogiri Tree

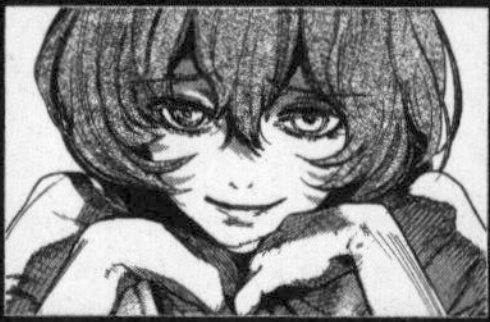

● Eto/Sen Takatsuki
エト／高槻泉
Founder of the Aogiri Tree. Also a remarkable author with many fans. Revealed herself as a Ghoul after announcing her final novel.

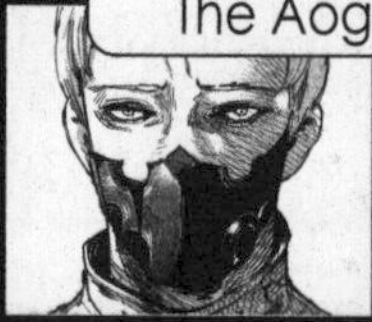

● Tatara
タタラ
A leading member of the Aogiri Tree. Related to the former head of the Chì shé lián. A Chinese Ghoul.

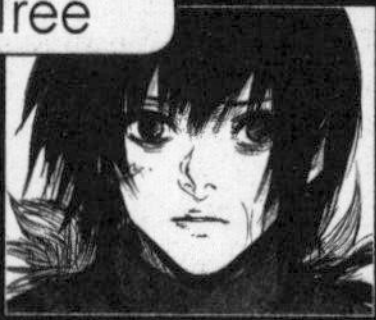

● Ayato
アヤト
A leading member of the Aogiri Tree. A Rate SS Ghoul known as the Rabbit.

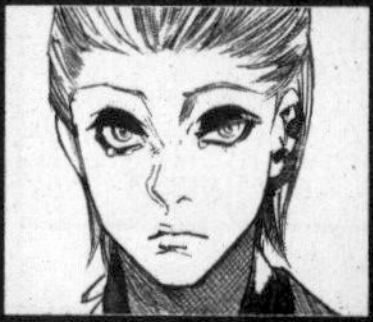

● Naki
ナキ
Member of the Aogiri Tree. Current leader of the White Suits. A Rate S, but frequently loses control.

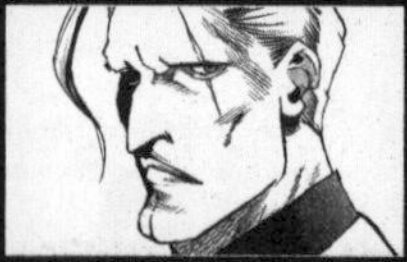

● Shosei
承正
Member of the Aogiri Tree and the White Suits. Joined after being beaten by Naki during Jason's leadership.

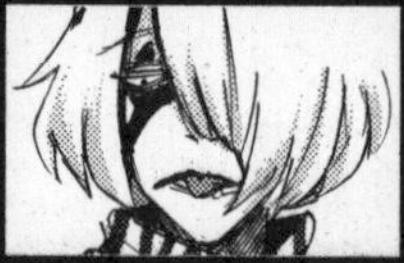

● Hohguro
ホオグロ
Member of the Aogiri Tree and the White Suits. Joined after tying Shosei.

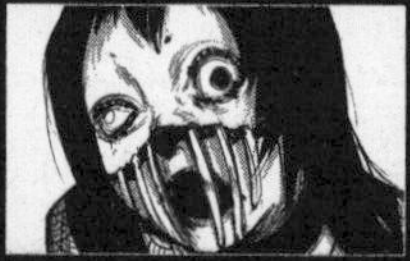

● Shikorae
死堪
Member of the Aogiri Tree. Was detained in Cochlea, but escaped after the Aogiri assault on the complex.

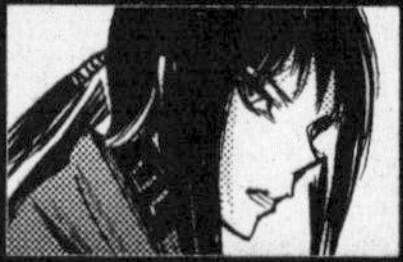

● The Grave Robber
墓盗り
Member of the Aogiri Tree. Protégé of the Bin Brothers. Somehow has experience using a Quinque.

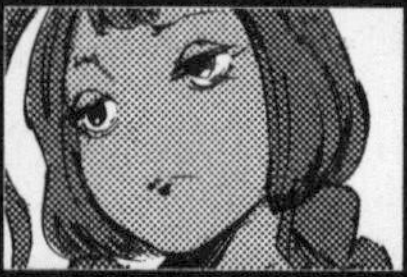

● Miza
ミザ
Member of the Aogiri Tree. Controlled the 18th Ward as the head of the Blades. A.K.A. Triple Blade.

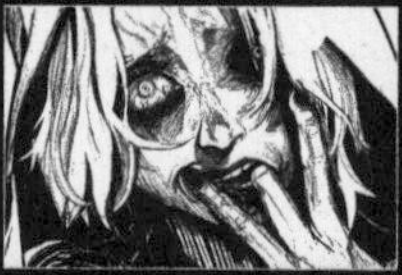

● The Owl
オウル
The current incarnation of Ghoul Investigator Seido Takizawa. Overwhelmingly powerful.

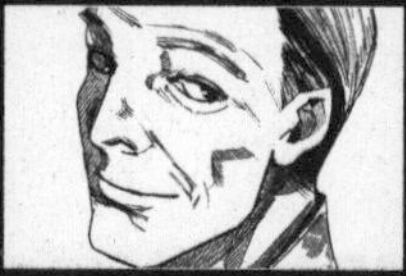

● Professor Kano
嘉納明博
Medical examiner for the Aogiri Tree. Researching how to create artificial half-Ghouls.

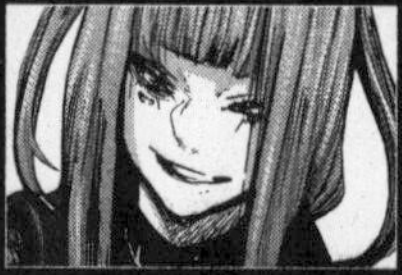

● Kuro
クロ
Underwent Kano's Ghoulification procedure, like Ken Kaneki. Absorbed her twin sister Shirona into her body.

So far in :re

T ● K Y ● G H ● U L

The CCG, determined to bring down the Aogiri Tree, discovers their stronghold on Rushima Island and begins an investigation. Meanwhile, Sen Takatsuki reveals herself as a Ghoul after releasing her final novel, *King Bileygr*. The myth of the One-Eyed King has created a deep divide between humans, Ghouls and the CCG. Haise, assigned to defend Cochlea, attempts to free Hinami but is stopped by Arima. After fighting Arima to the death as Ken Kaneki, he ascends the throne as the One-Eyed King. At the same time, the situation on Rushima Island continues to unravel...

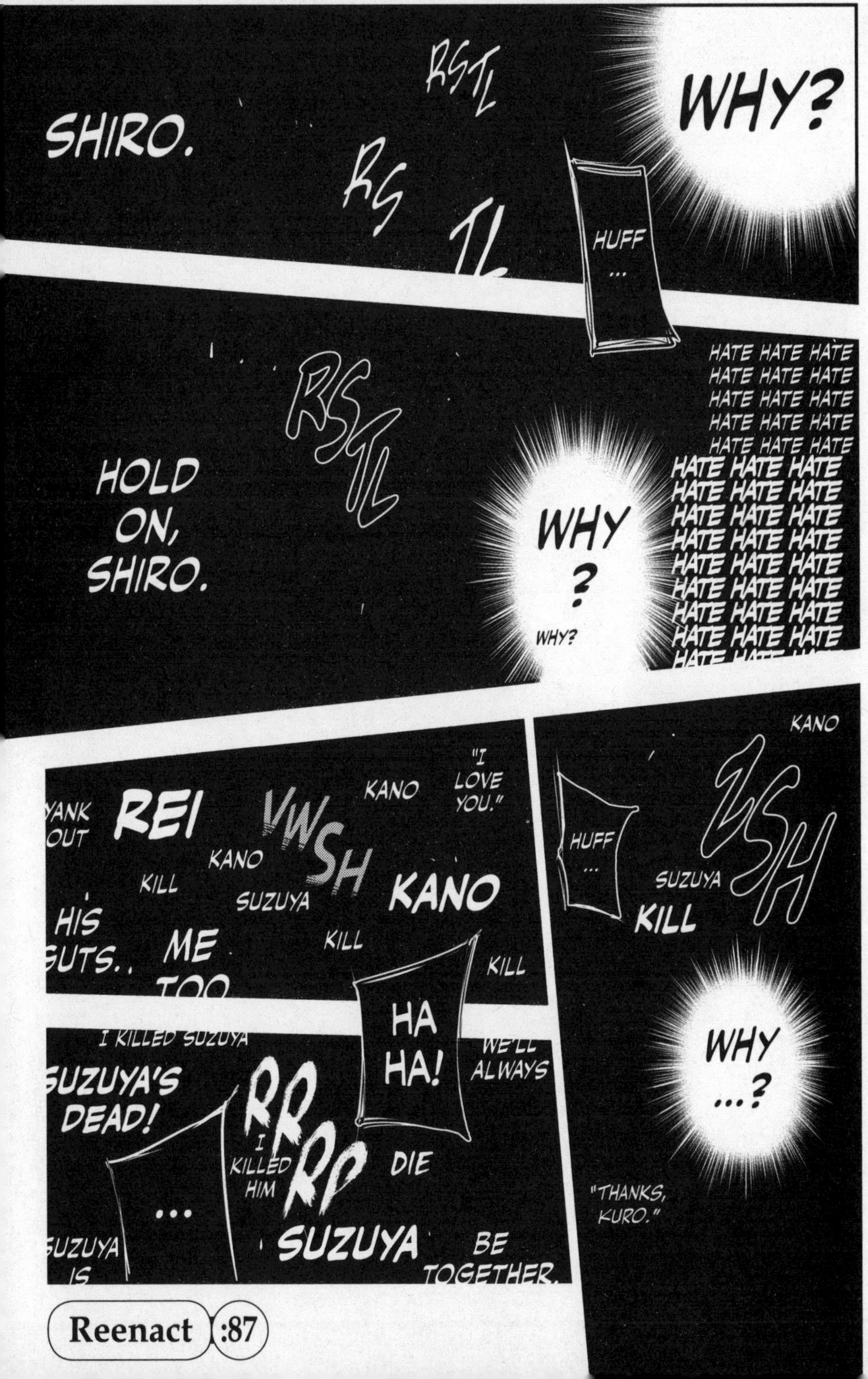
WHY?
HUFF ...
RSTL
RS TL
SHIRO.
HATE HATE HATE
HATE HATE HATE
HATE HATE HATE
HATE HATE HATE
HATE HATE HATE
HATE HATE HATE
HATE HATE HATE
HATE HATE HATE
HATE HATE HATE
HATE HATE HATE
HATE HATE HATE
HATE HATE HATE
HATE HATE HATE
HATE HATE HATE
HATE HATE HATE
HATE HATE HATE
WHY ?
WHY?
RSTL
HOLD ON, SHIRO.
KANO
VSH
HUFF ...
SUZUYA
KILL
WHY ...?
"THANKS, KURO."
"I LOVE YOU."
KANO
VWSH
KANO
KILL
KILL
SUZUYA
KANO
KILL
REI
YANK OUT HIS GUTS..
HA HA!
DIE
BE TOGETHER.
SUZUYA
RRRP
I KILLED HIM
I KILLED SUZUYA
SUZUYA'S DEAD!
...

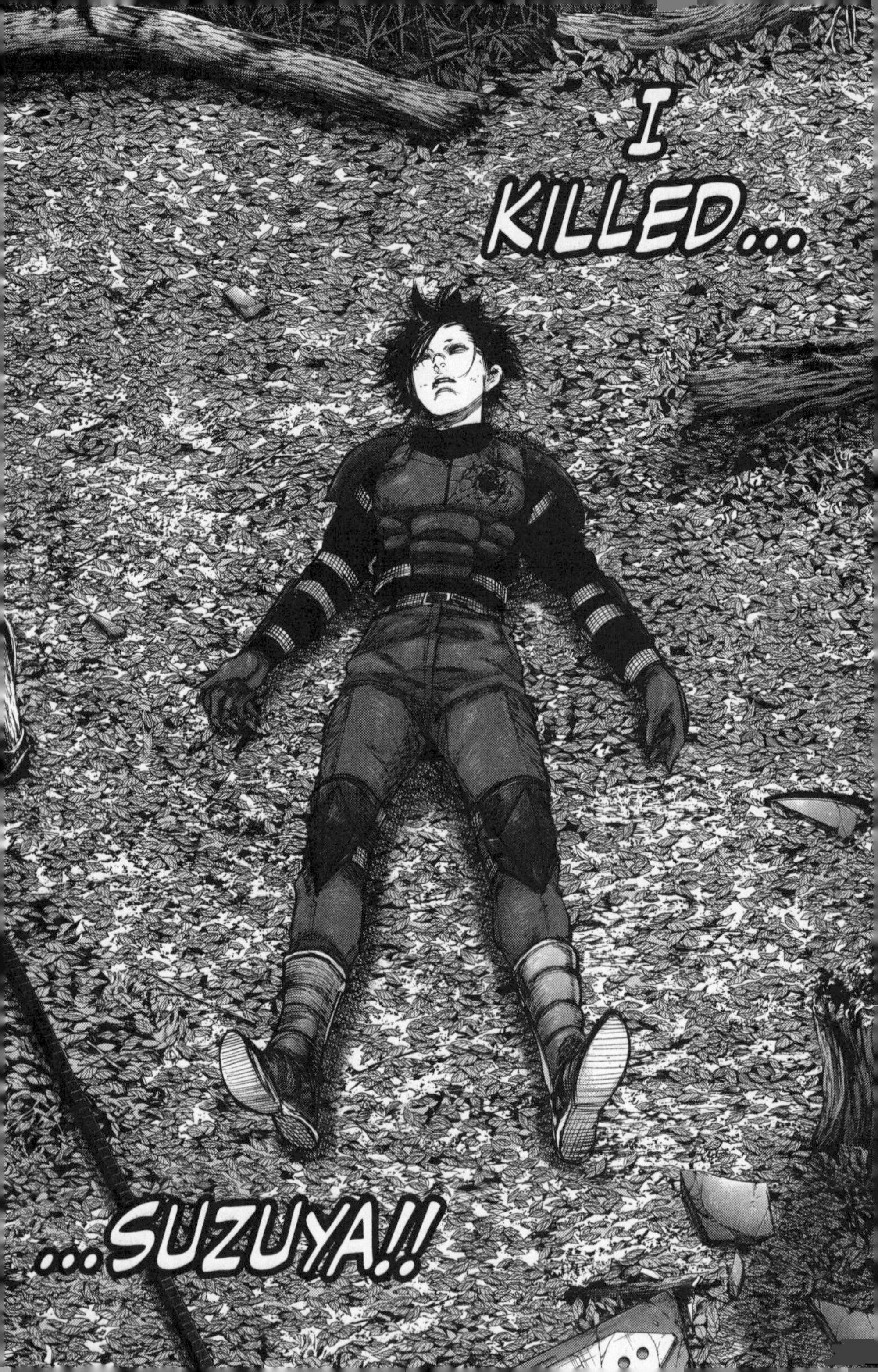
I KILLED...
...SUZUYA!!

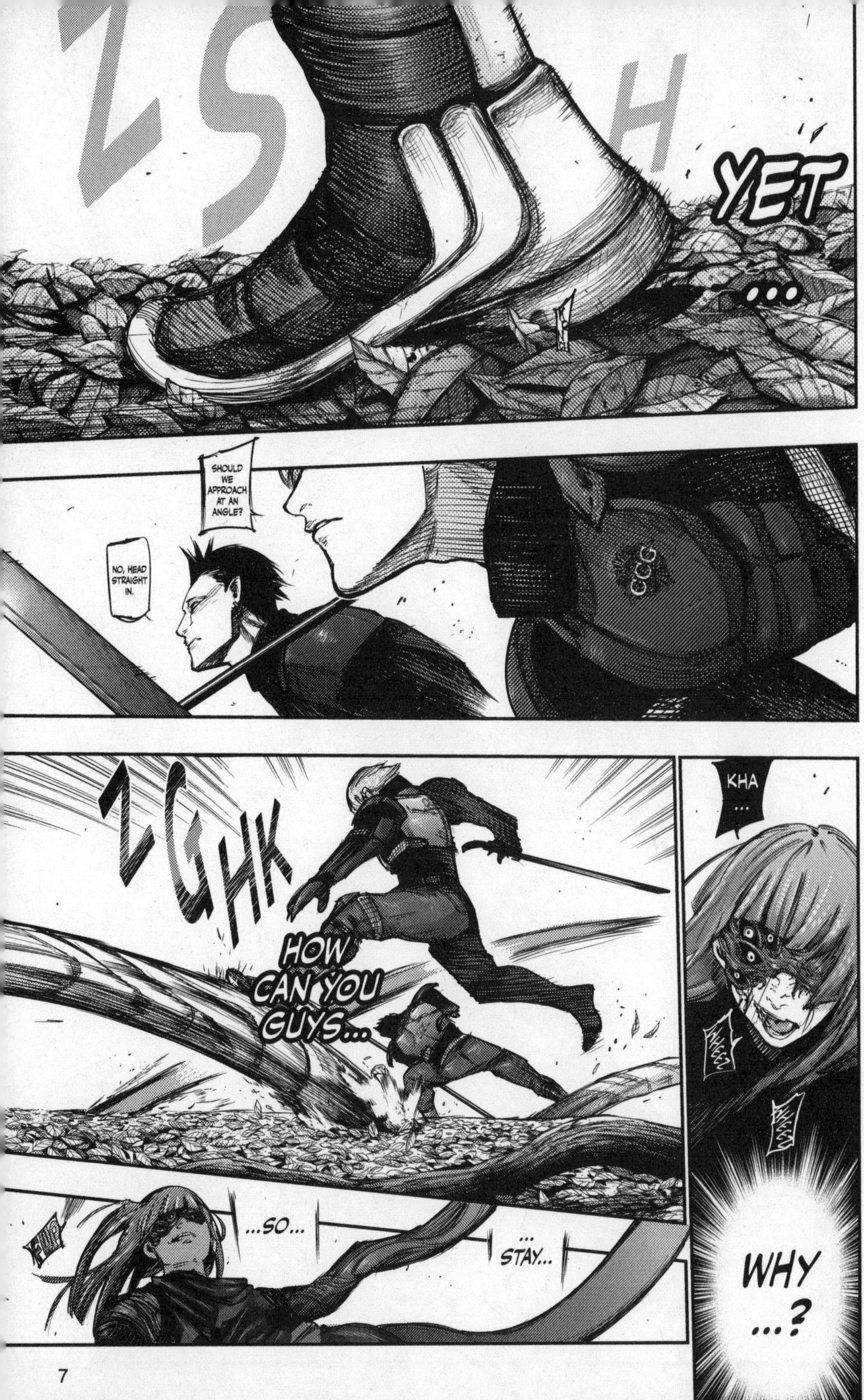
ZSH
YET...
SHOULD WE APPROACH AT AN ANGLE?
NO, HEAD STRAIGHT IN.
KHA...
WHY...?
ZGHK
HOW CAN YOU GUYS...
...SO...
...STAY...

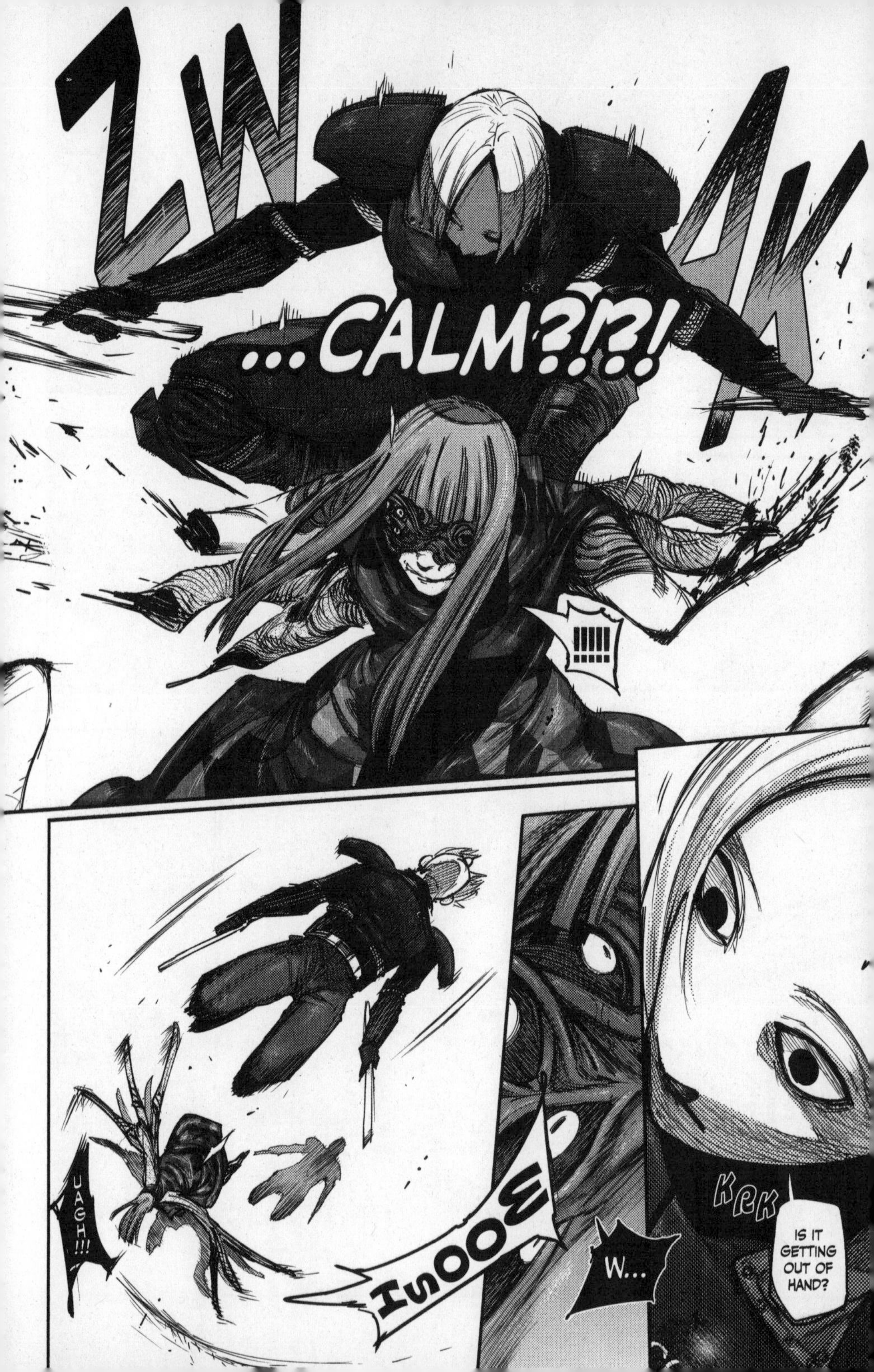
ZWAK
...CALM?!?!
!!!!!!
KRK
IS IT GETTING OUT OF HAND?
W...
SWOOSH
UAGH!!!

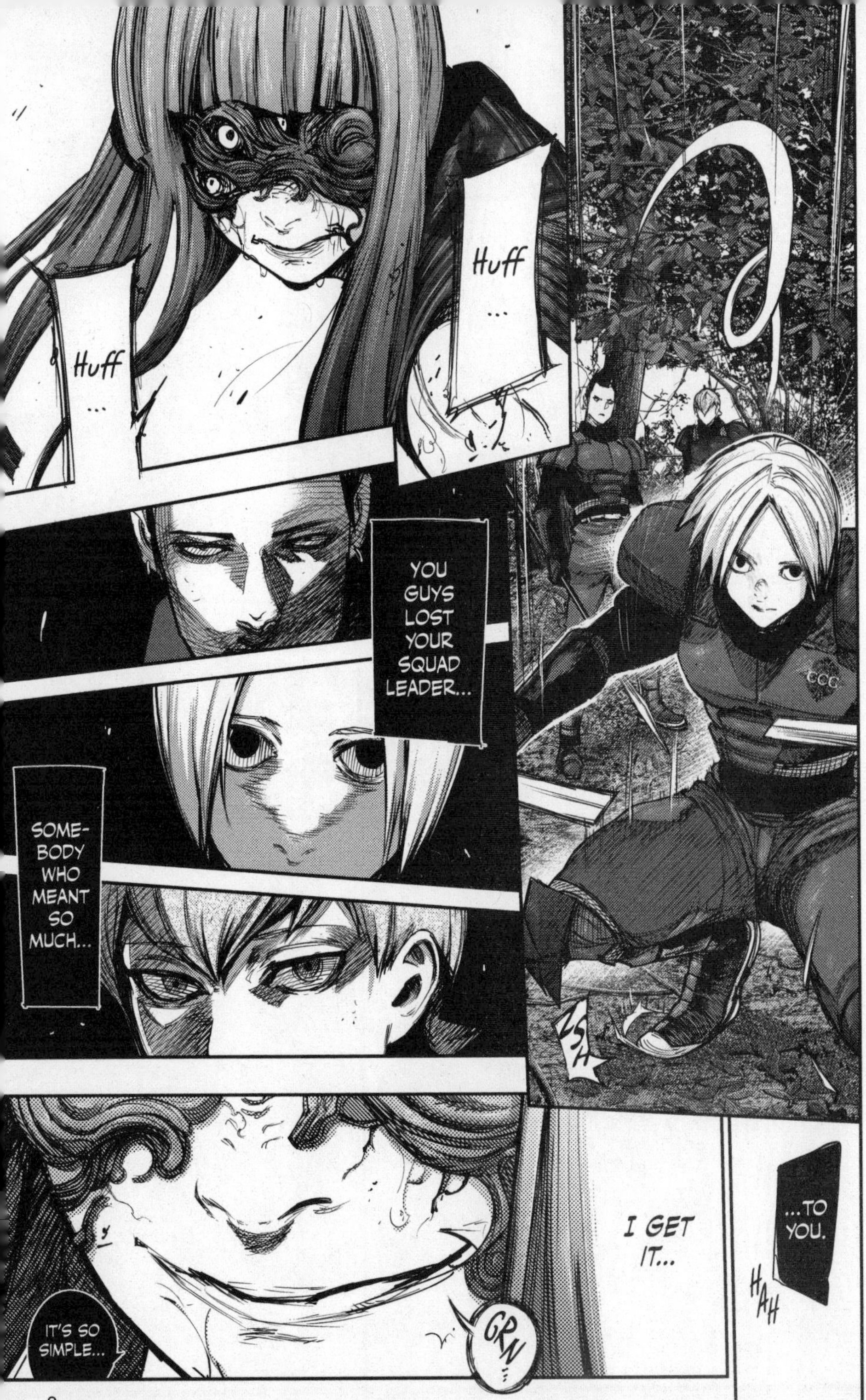
NSH
Huff ...
Huff ...
YOU GUYS LOST YOUR SQUAD LEADER...
SOMEBODY WHO MEANT SO MUCH...
...TO YOU.
HAH
I GET IT...
GRN
IT'S SO SIMPLE...

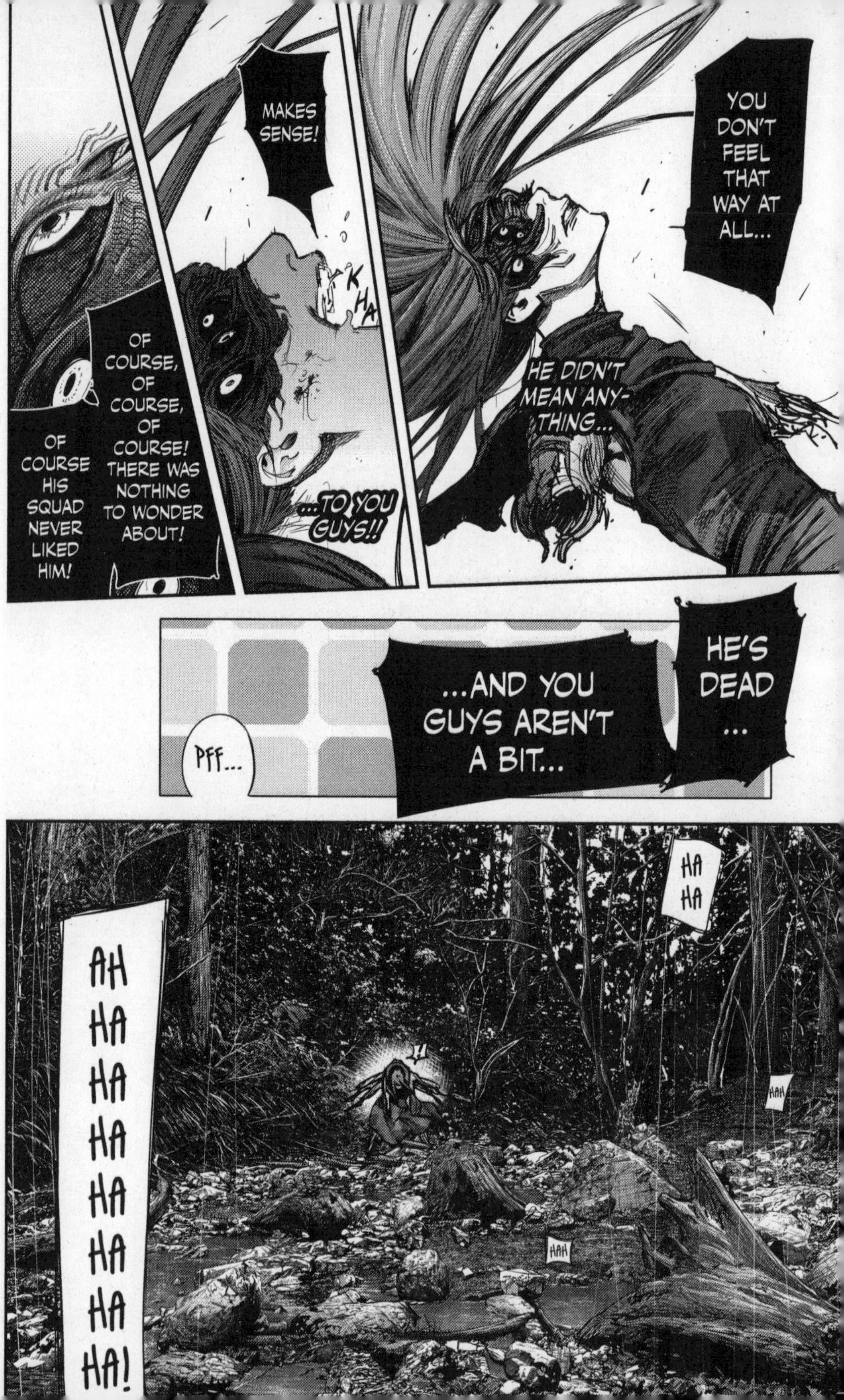
YOU DON'T FEEL THAT WAY AT ALL...
HE DIDN'T MEAN ANYTHING...
MAKES SENSE!
KHA HA
...TO YOU GUYS!!
OF COURSE, OF COURSE, OF COURSE! THERE WAS NOTHING TO WONDER ABOUT!
OF COURSE HIS SQUAD NEVER LIKED HIM!
HE'S DEAD...
...AND YOU GUYS AREN'T A BIT...
PFF...
HA HA
AH HA HA HA HA HA HA HA!
HAH
HAH

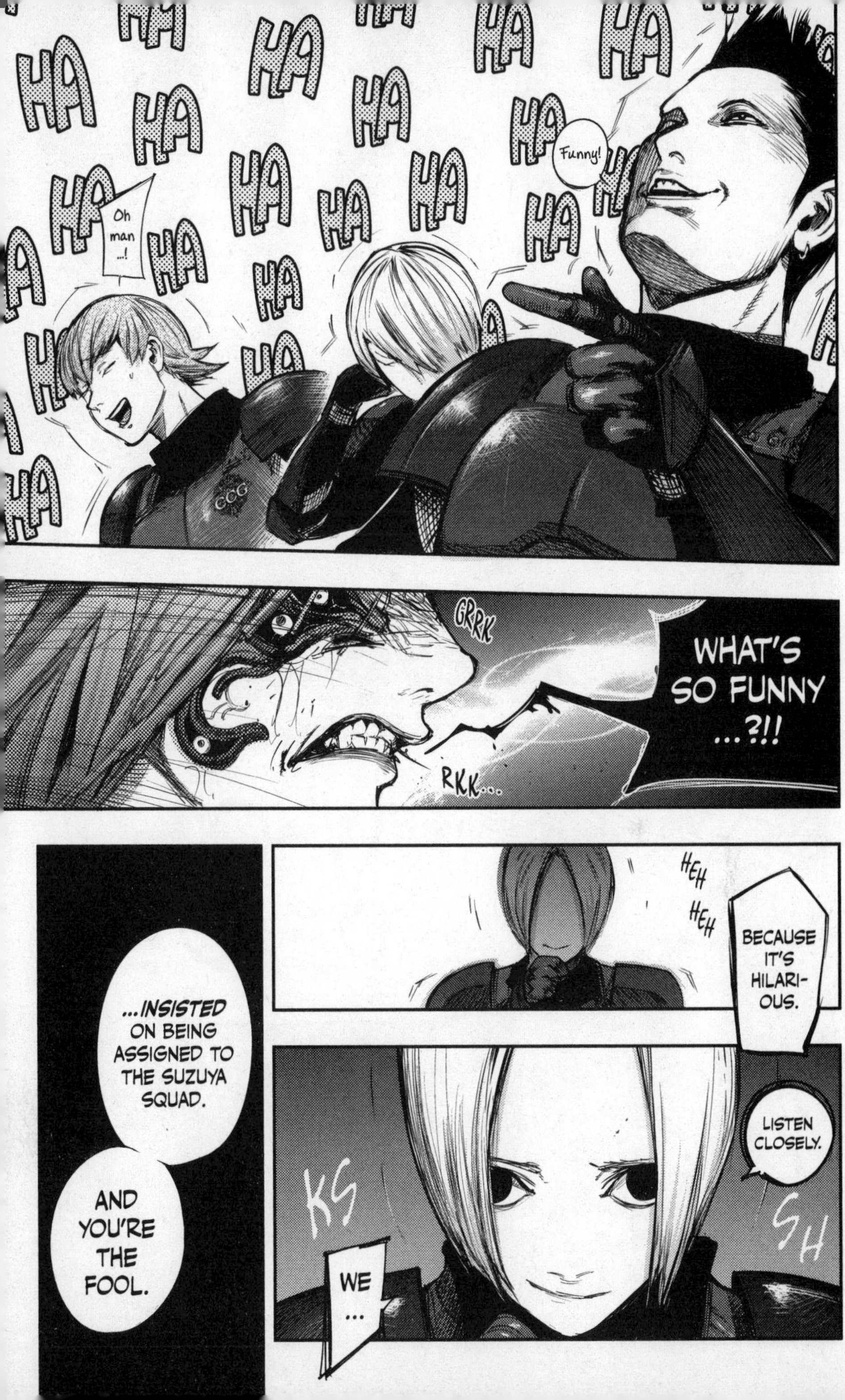

HA HA HA HA HA HA HA HA HA HA HA HA HA HA HA HA HA HA HA HA HA
Funny!
Oh man ...!
WHAT'S SO FUNNY ...?!!
GRRK
RKK...
HEH HEH
BECAUSE IT'S HILARI-OUS.
LISTEN CLOSELY.
SH
KS
WE ...
...INSISTED ON BEING ASSIGNED TO THE SUZUYA SQUAD.
AND YOU'RE THE FOOL.

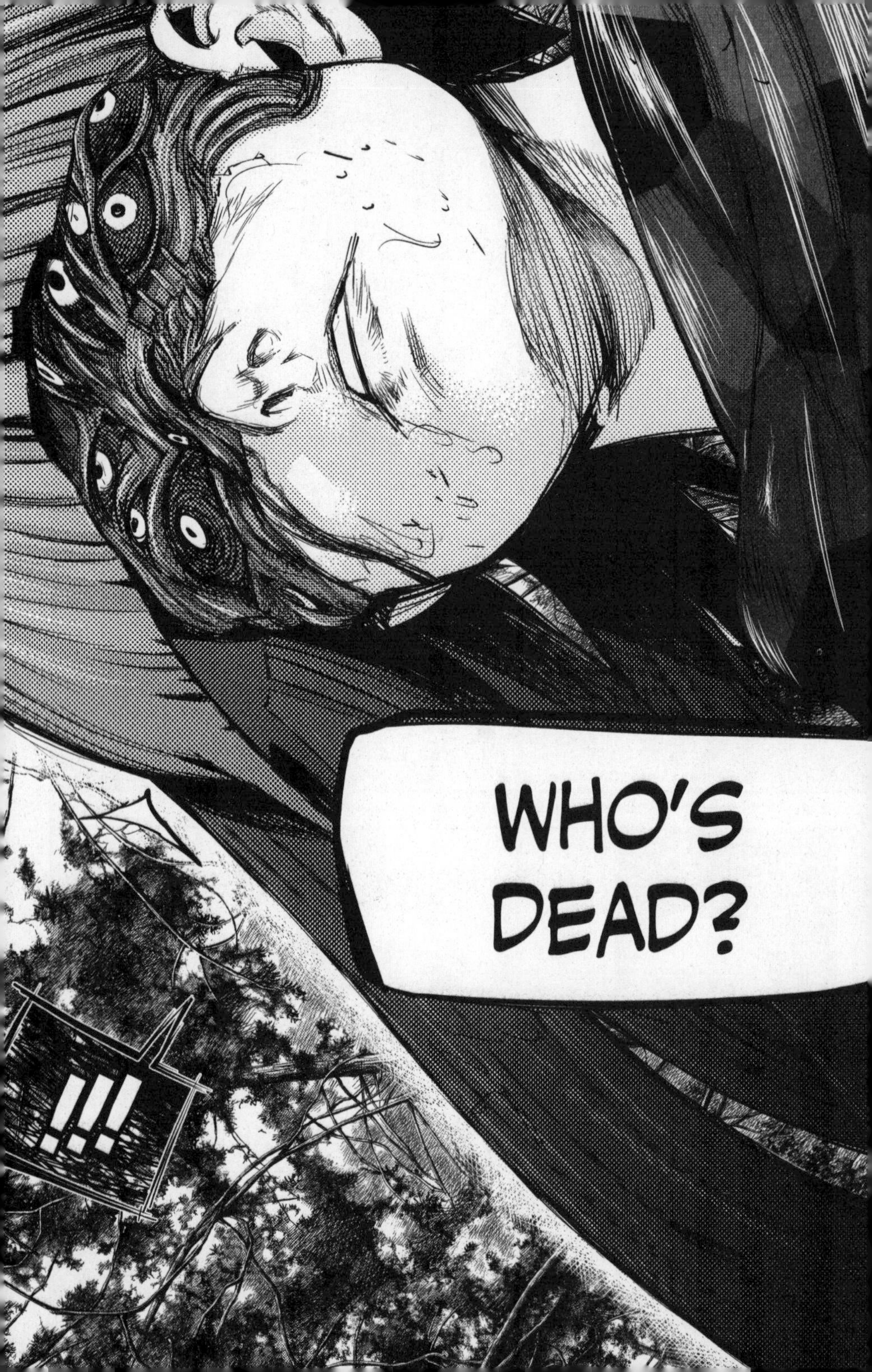
WHO'S DEAD?
!!!

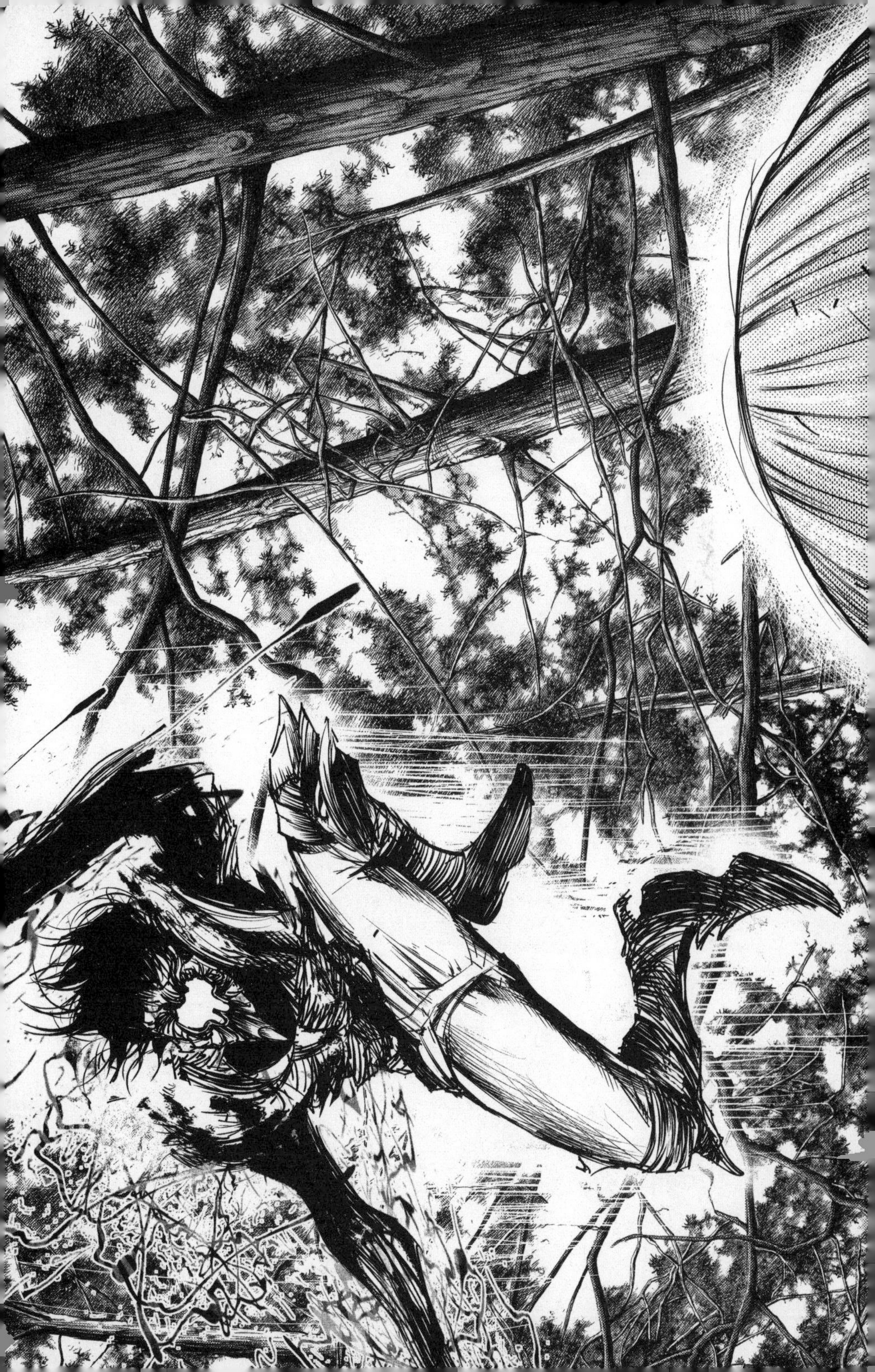

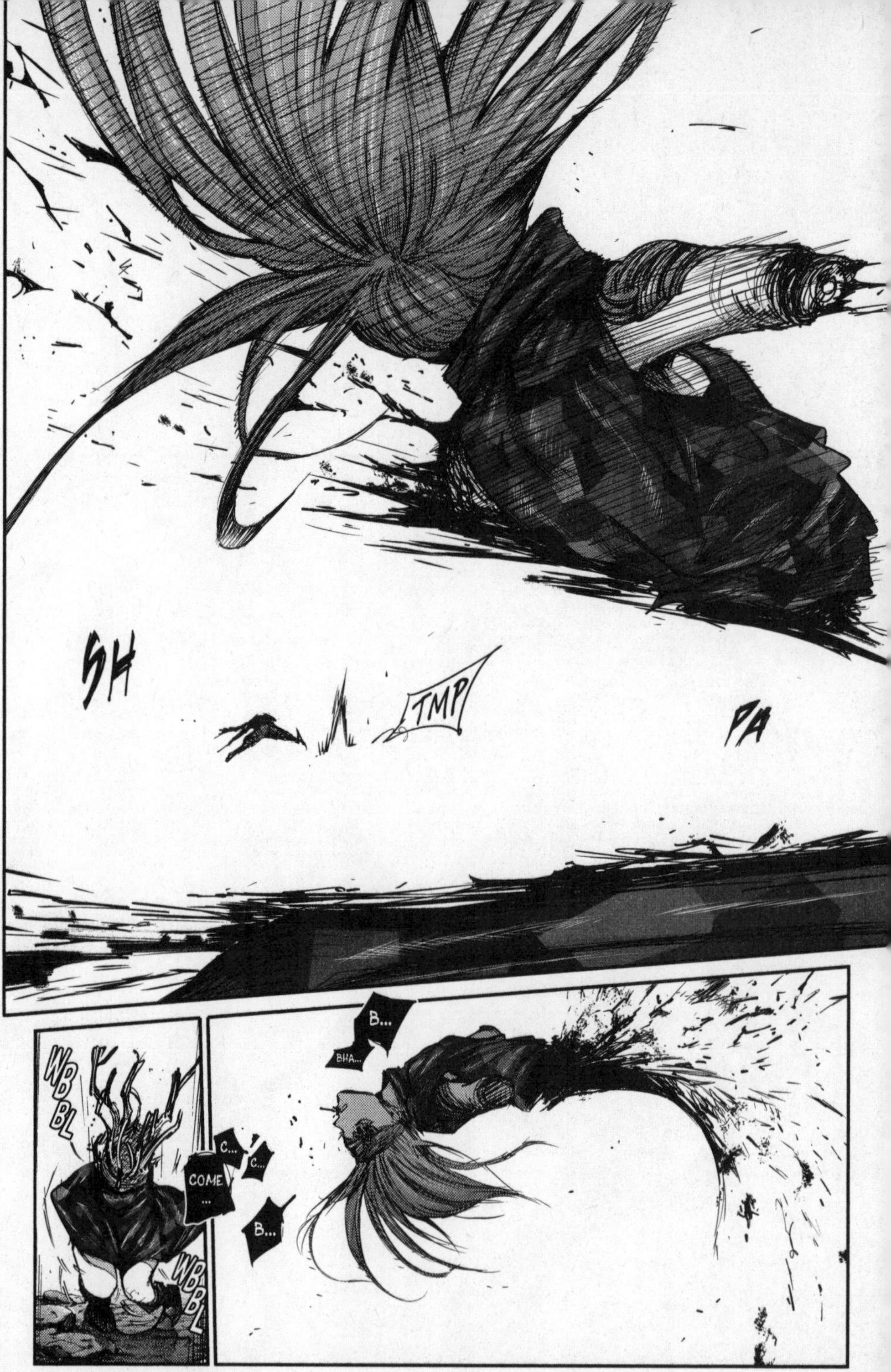
PA
TMP
SH
B...
BHA...
C...
C...
COME...
B...
WBBL
WBBL

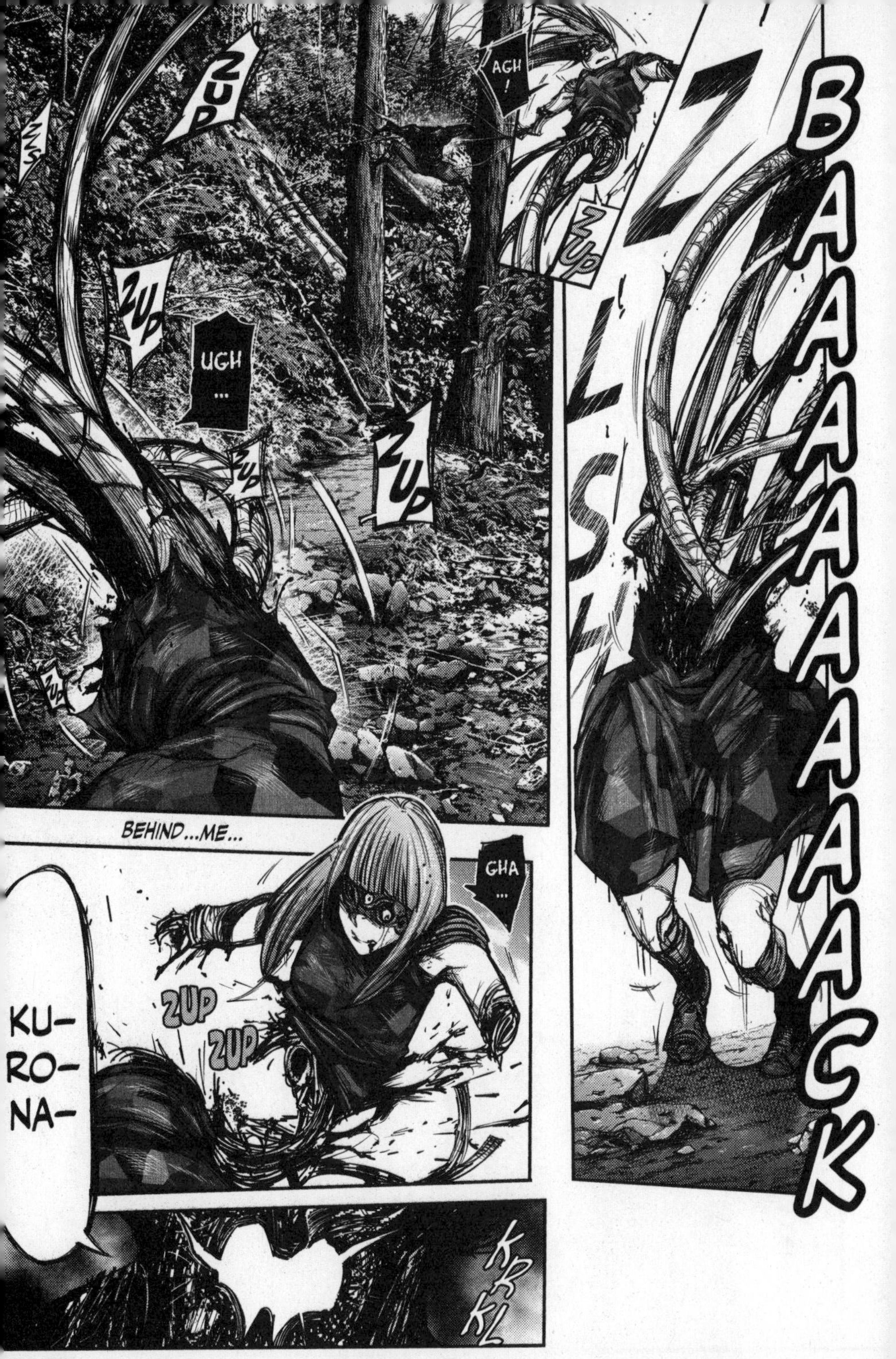
AGH!
ZUP
ZLSH
BAAAAAAAAAACK
ZUP
ZNS
ZUP
UGH...
ZUP
ZUP
ZUP
BEHIND...ME...
GHA...
ZUP
ZUP
KU-RO-NA-
KRKL

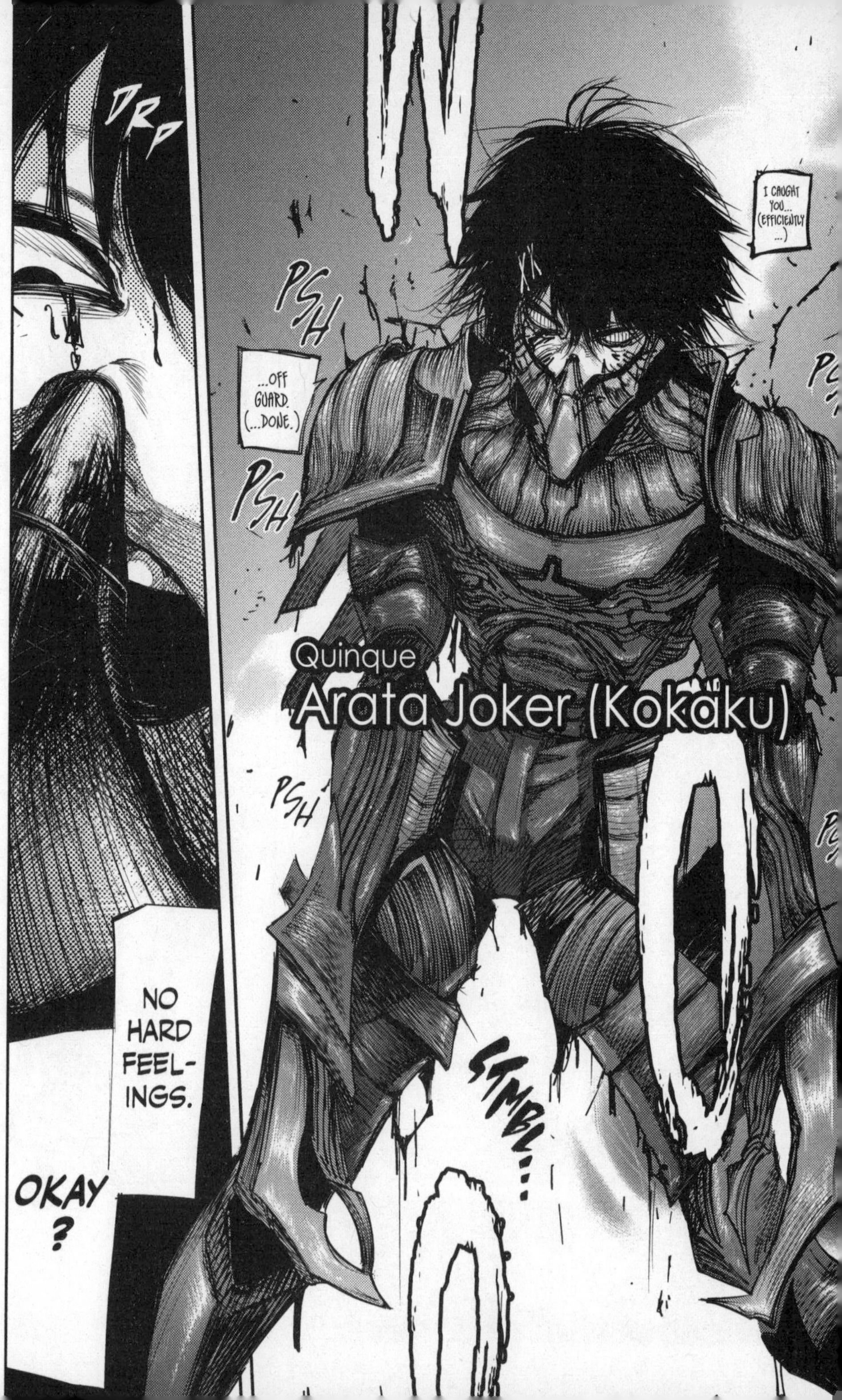
I CAUGHT YOU... (EFFICIENTLY ...)
PSH
...OFF GUARD. (...DONE.)
PSH
Quinque
Arata Joker (Kokaku)
PSH
CRMBL...
DRP
NO HARD FEEL-INGS.
OKAY?

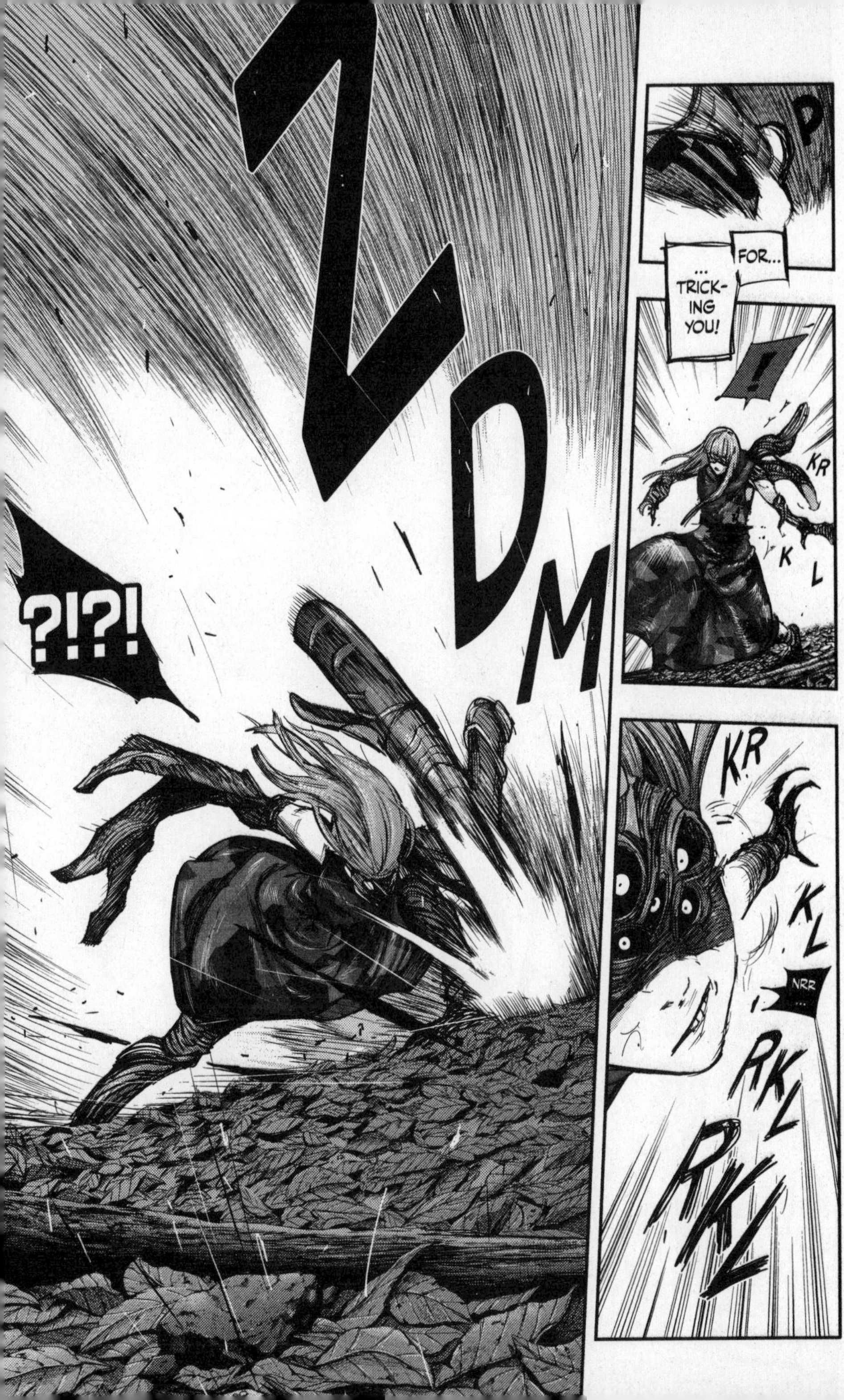
FOR...
... TRICK- ING YOU!
!
KR
K
L
KR
KL
NRR ...
RKL
RKL
ZDM
?!?!

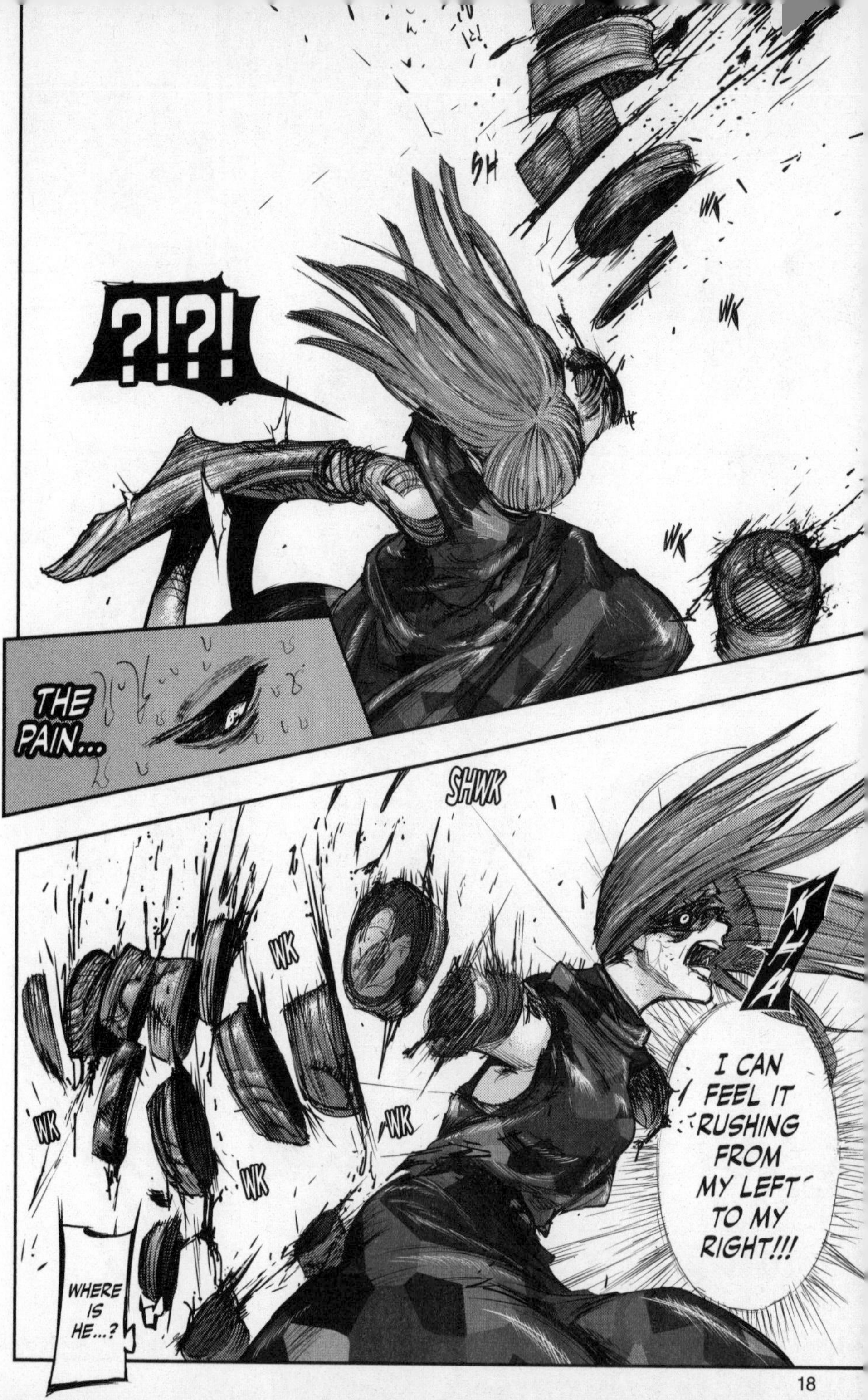
SH
WK
WK
?!?!
WK
THE PAIN...
SHWK
KHA
I CAN FEEL IT RUSHING FROM MY LEFT TO MY RIGHT!!!
WK
WK
WK
WK
WHERE IS HE...?

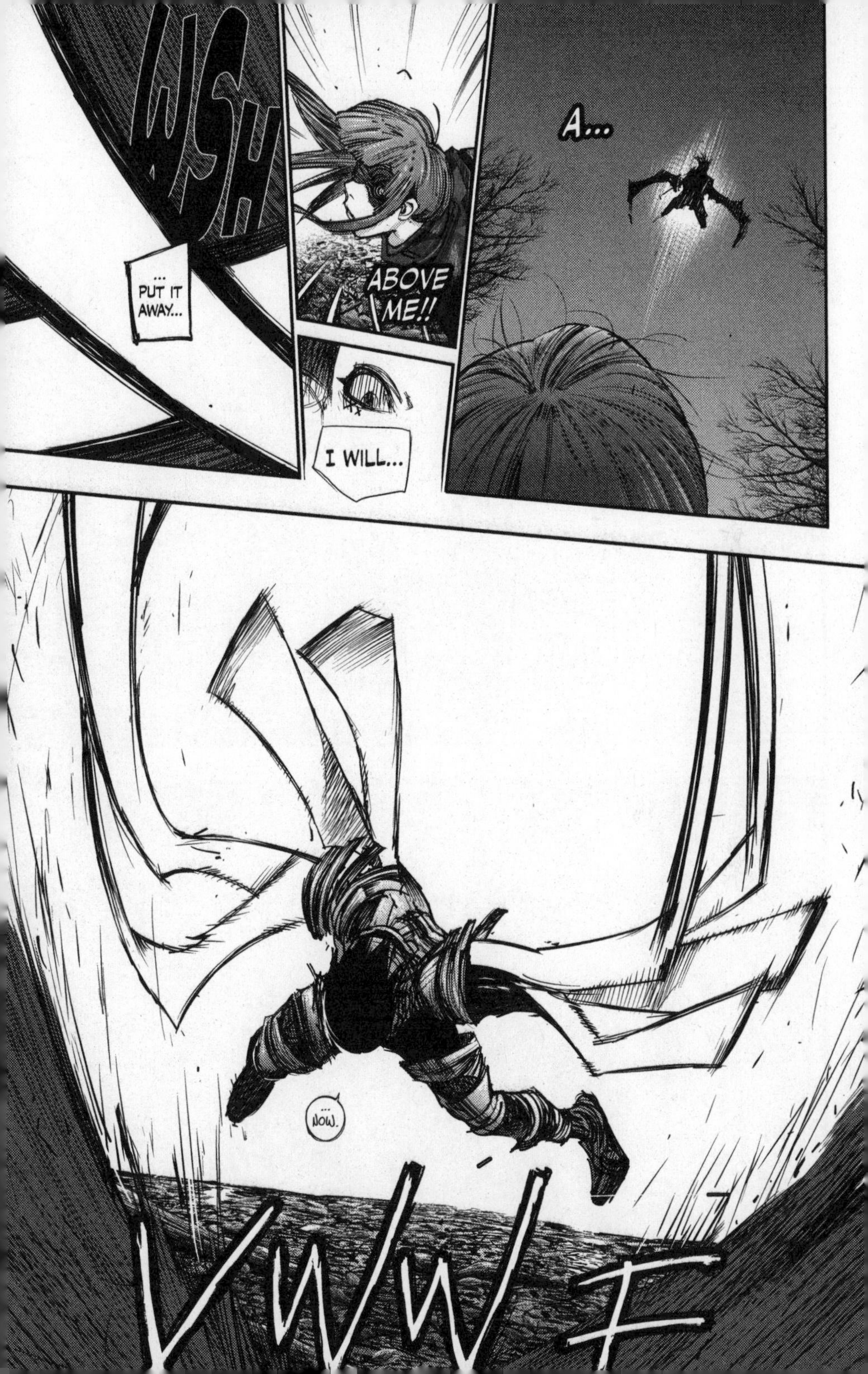

A...
ABOVE ME!!
I WILL...
WSH
... PUT IT AWAY...
... NOW.
VWWF

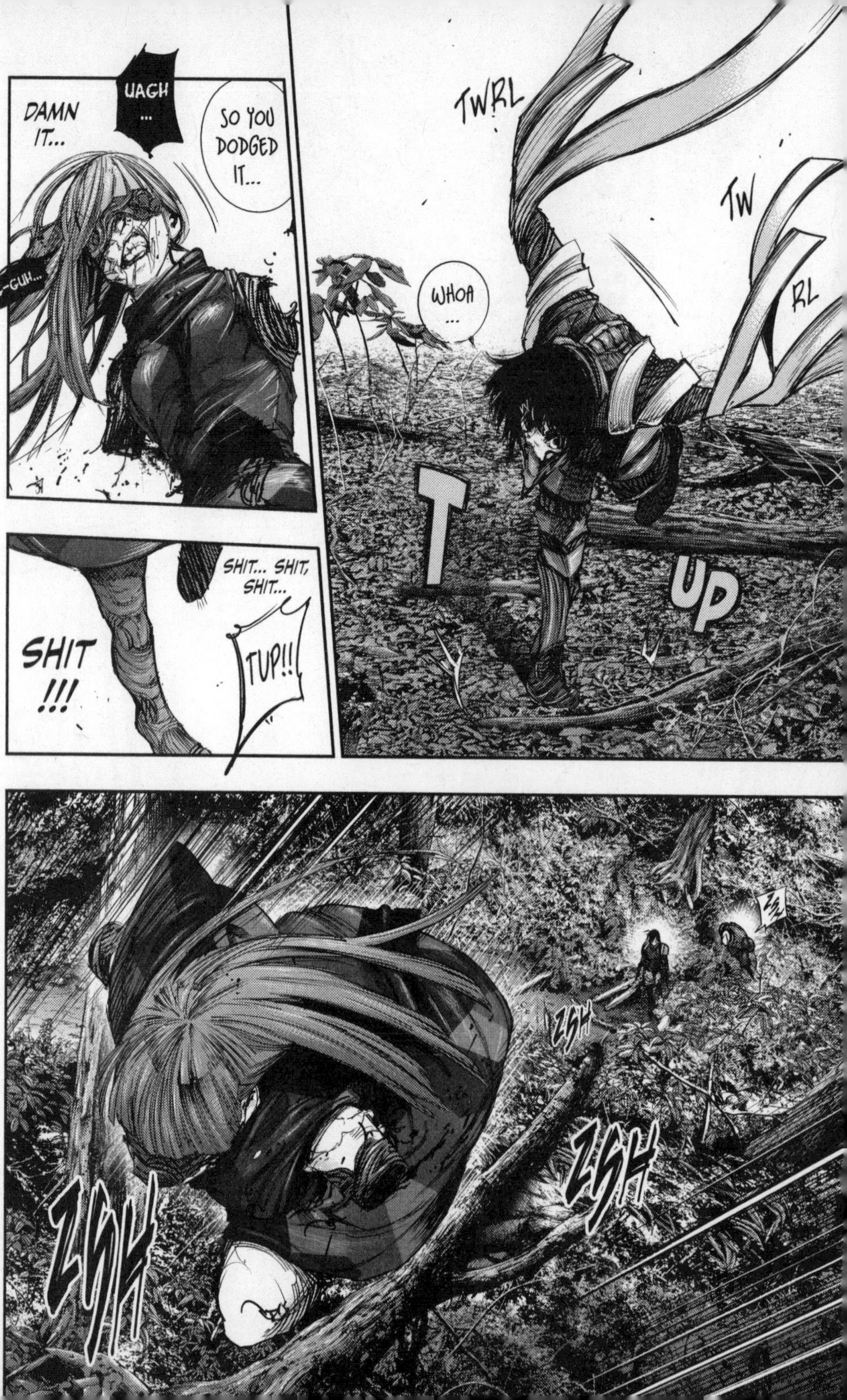
TWRL
TW
RL
WHOA ...
T
UP
SO YOU DODGED IT...
UAGH ...
DAMN IT...
G-GUH...
SHIT... SHIT, SHIT...
TUP!!
SHIT !!!
ZSH
ZSH
ZSH

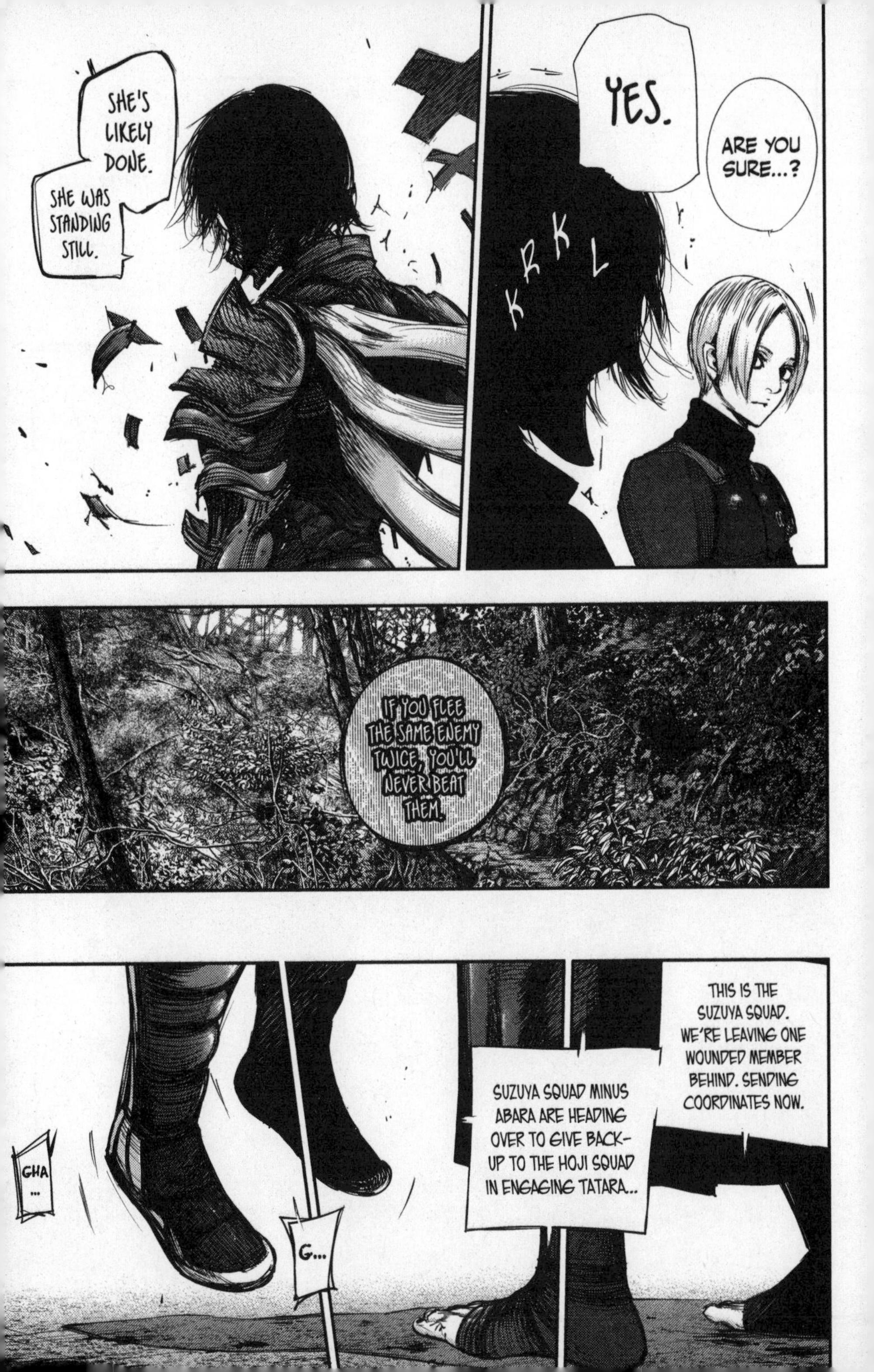
ARE YOU SURE...?
YES.
KRKL
SHE'S LIKELY DONE.
SHE WAS STANDING STILL.
IF YOU FLEE THE SAME ENEMY TWICE, YOU'LL NEVER BEAT THEM.
THIS IS THE SUZUYA SQUAD. WE'RE LEAVING ONE WOUNDED MEMBER BEHIND. SENDING COORDINATES NOW.
SUZUYA SQUAD MINUS ABARA ARE HEADING OVER TO GIVE BACK-UP TO THE HOJI SQUAD IN ENGAGING TATARA...
G...
GHA...

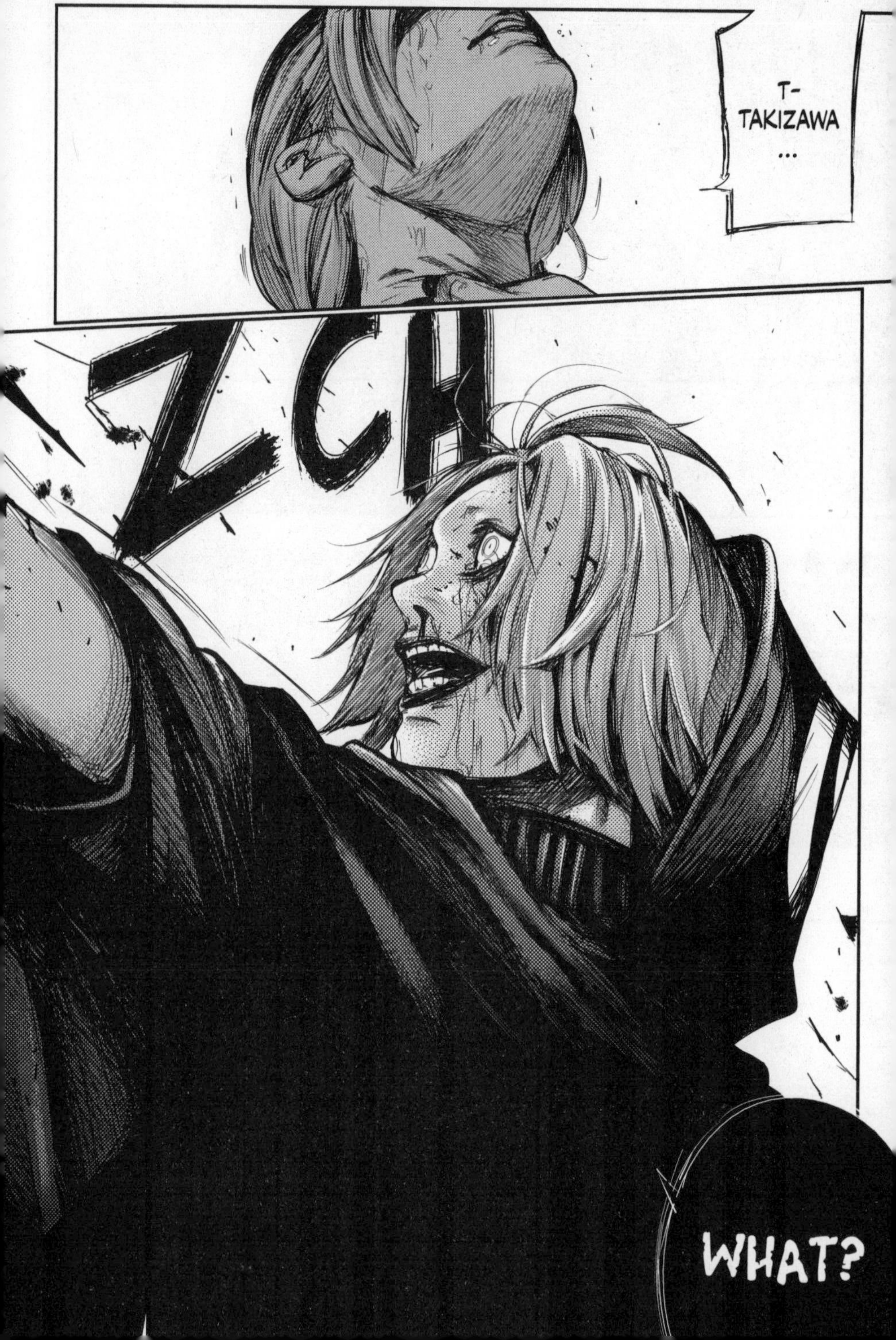
T-
TAKIZAWA
...
ZCH
WHAT?

Relief :88

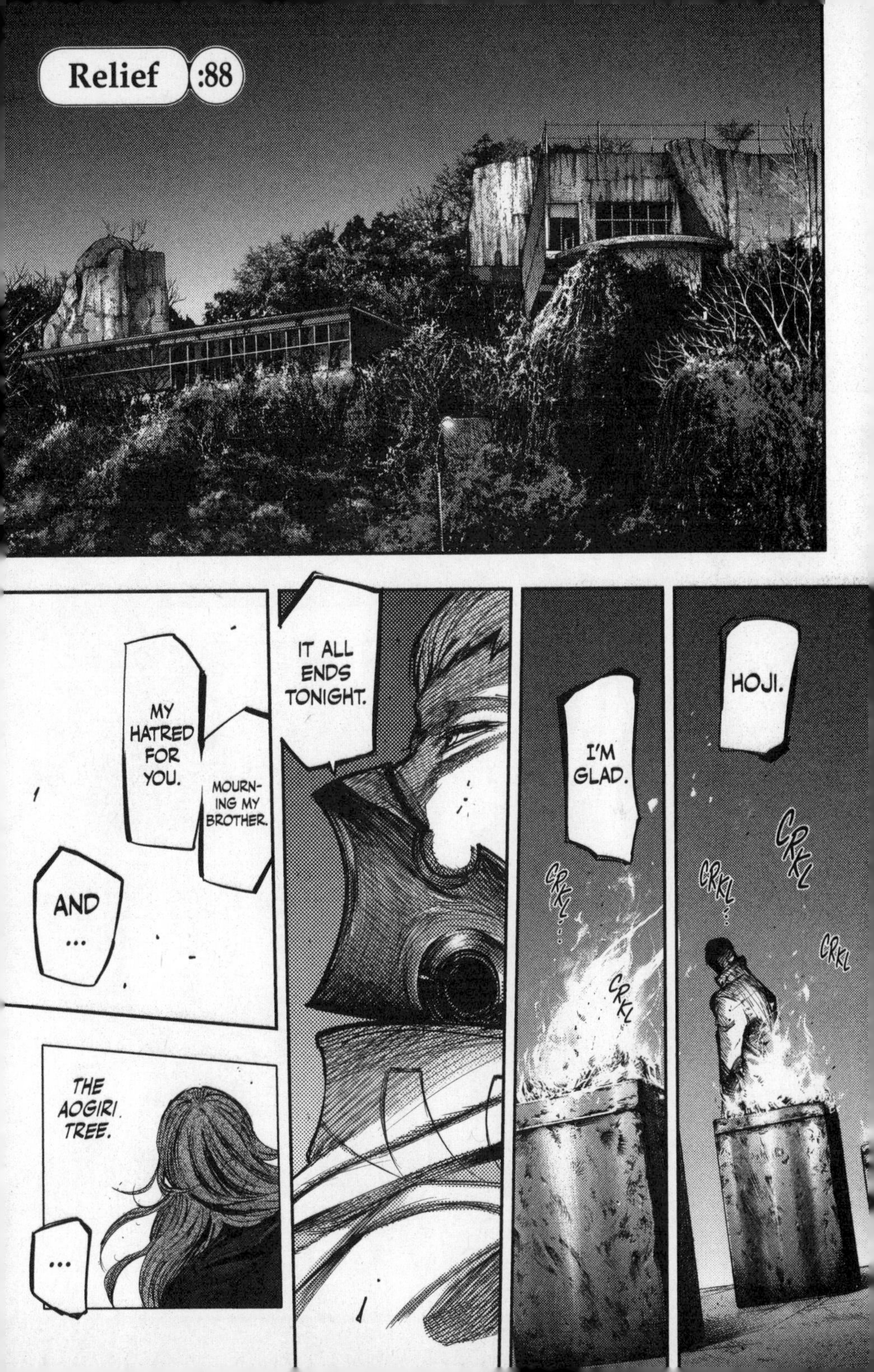
HOJI.
CRKL
CRKL
CRKL
I'M GLAD.
CRKL
CRKL
IT ALL ENDS TONIGHT.
MY HATRED FOR YOU.
MOURNING MY BROTHER.
AND ...
THE AOGIRI TREE.
...

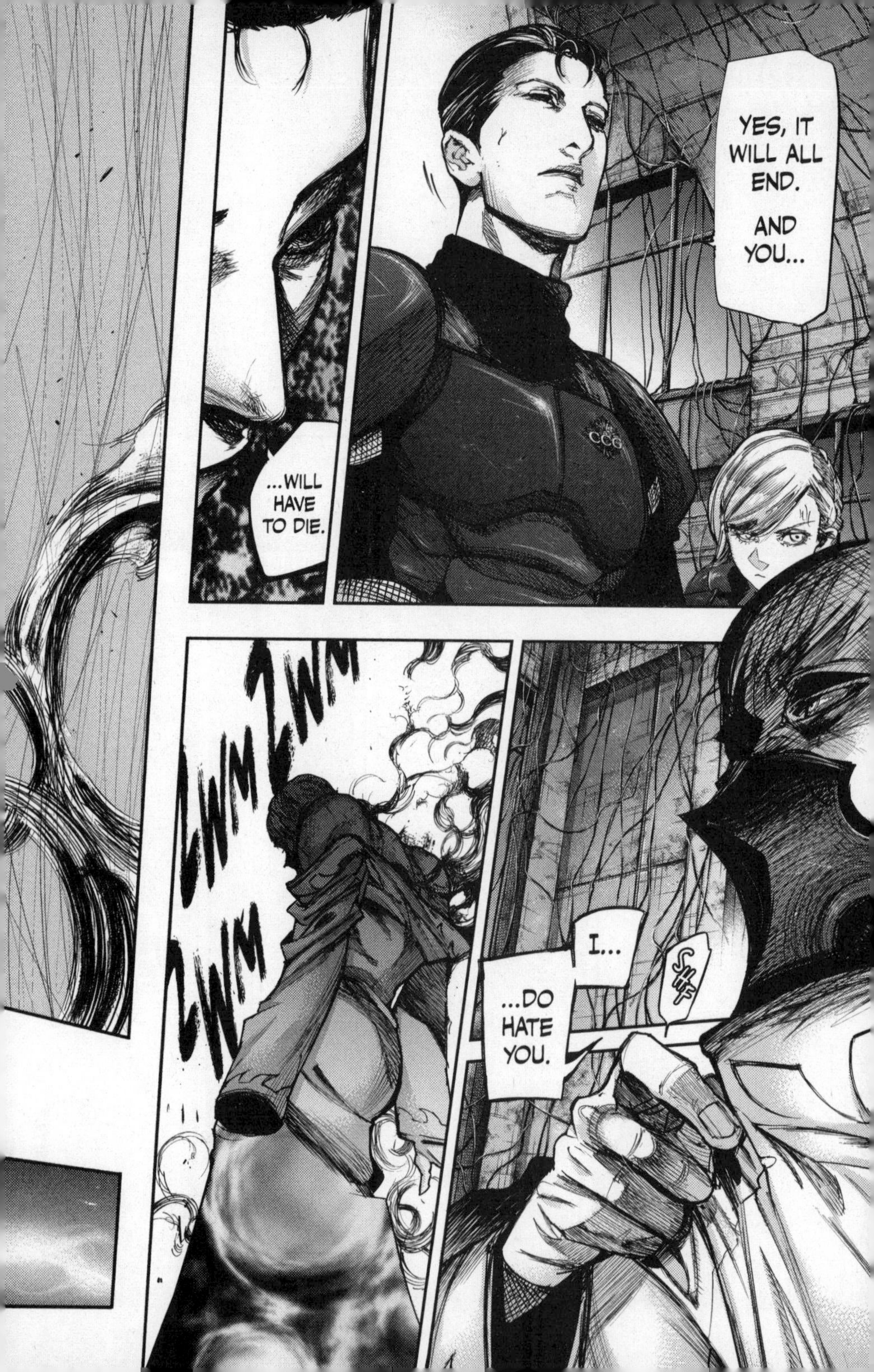
YES, IT WILL ALL END.
AND YOU...
...WILL HAVE TO DIE.
I...
...DO HATE YOU.
ZWM ZWM
ZWM

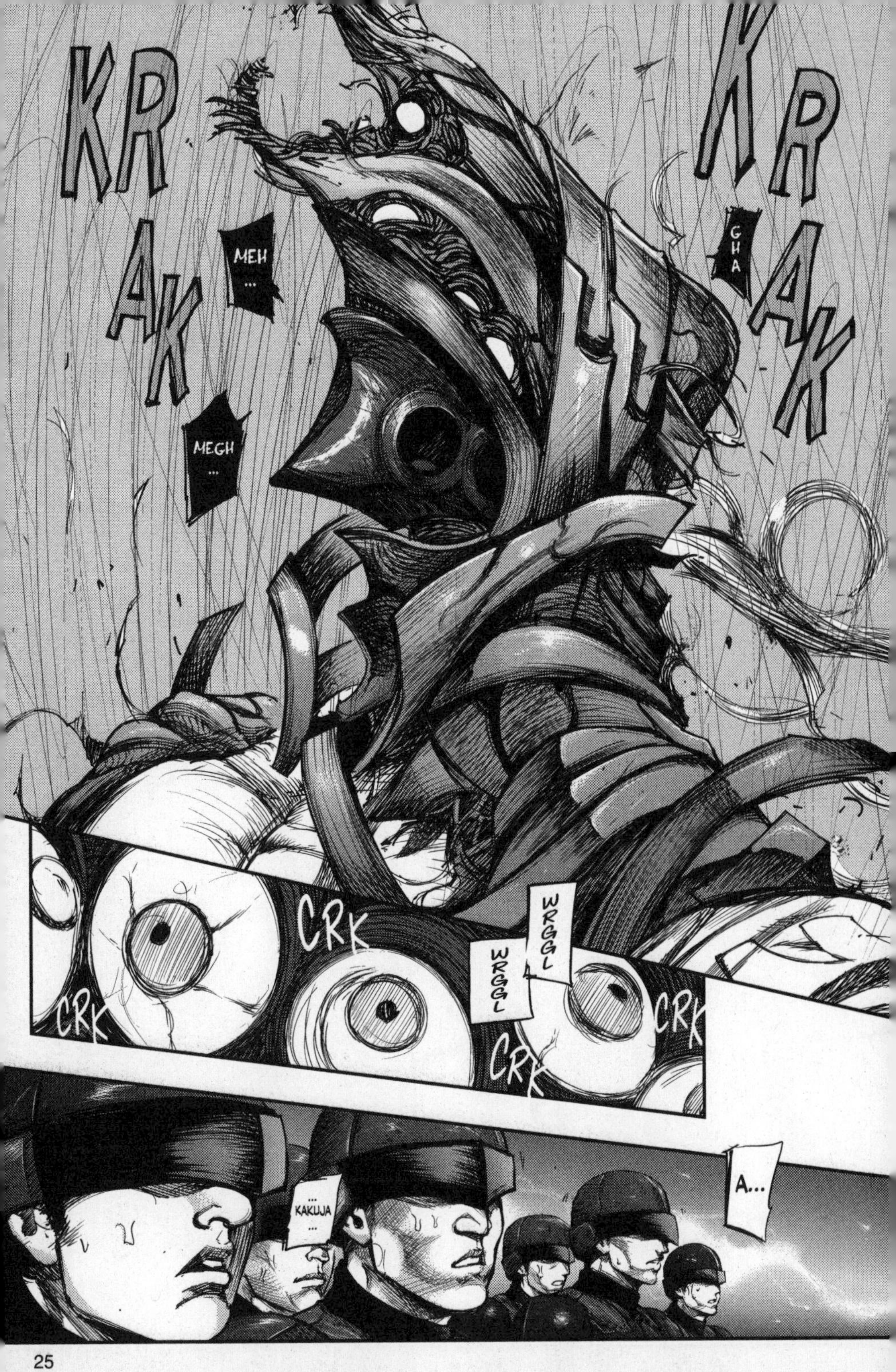
KRAK
GHA
MEH...
KRAK
MEGH...
CRK
WRGGL
WRGGL
CRK
CRK
CRK
A...
...KAKUJA...

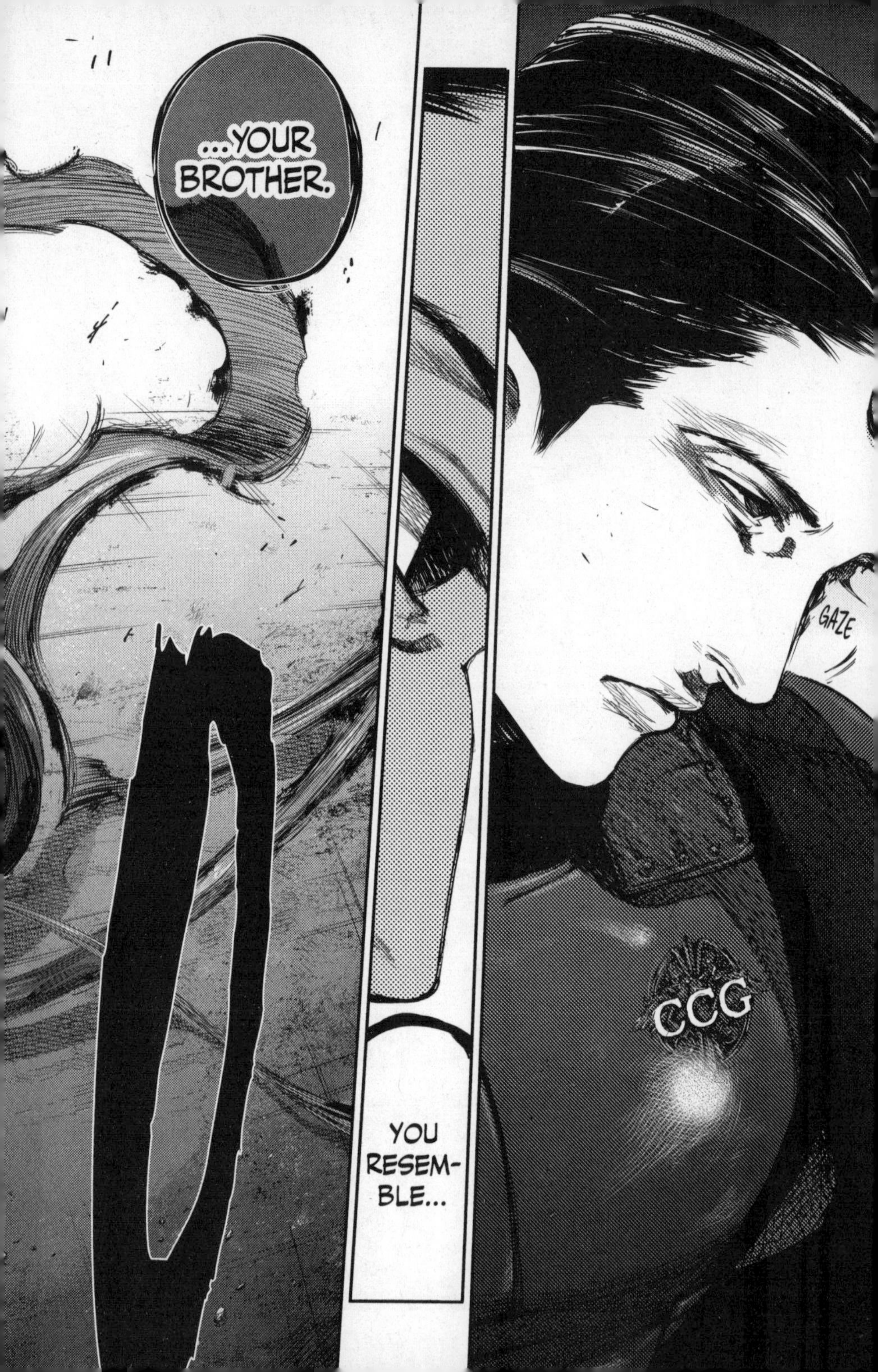
GAZE
CCG
YOU RESEM-BLE...
...YOUR BROTHER.

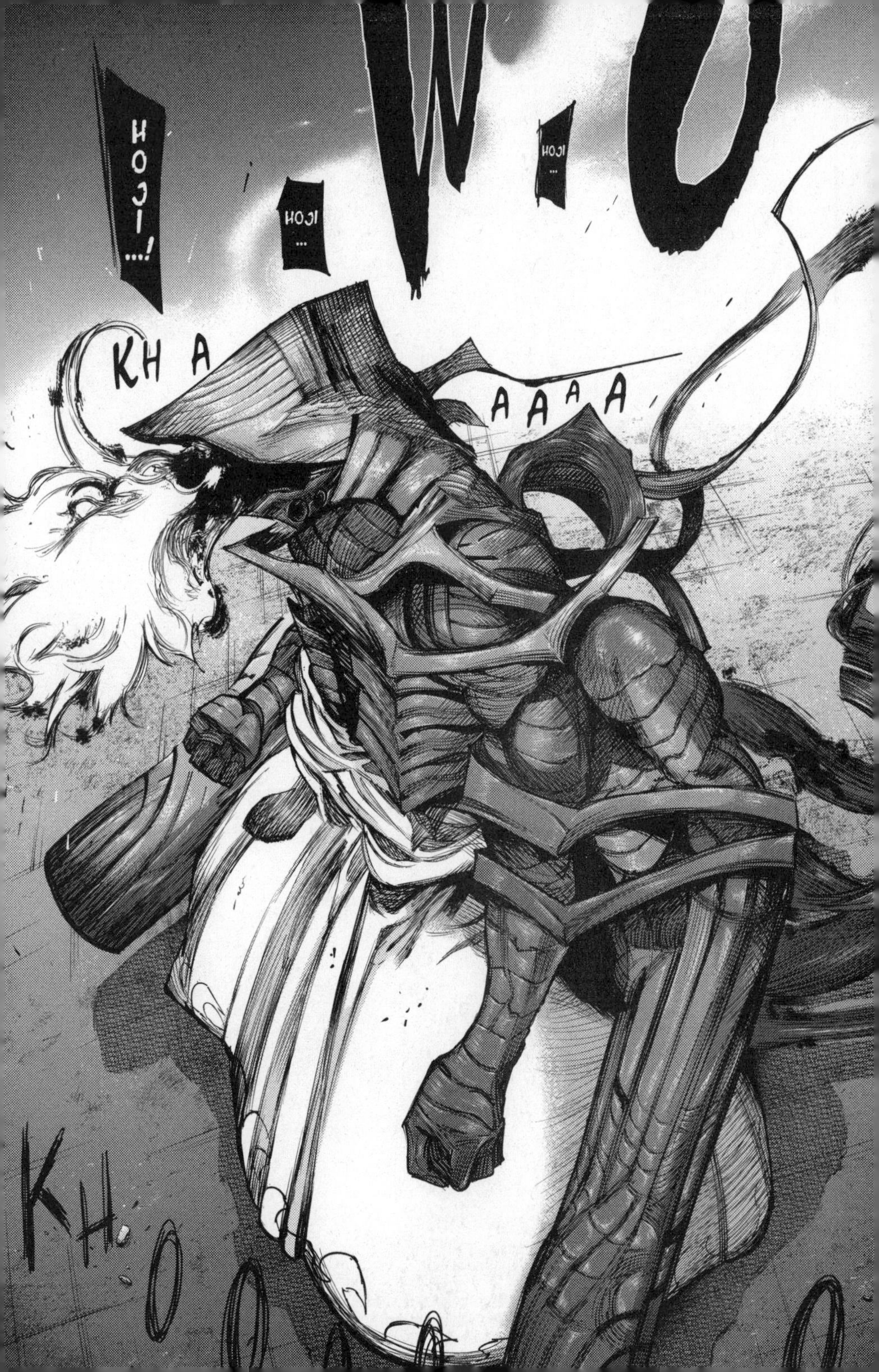

HOJI...
HOJI...
HOJI...!
WO
KHAAAAA
KHOOOO

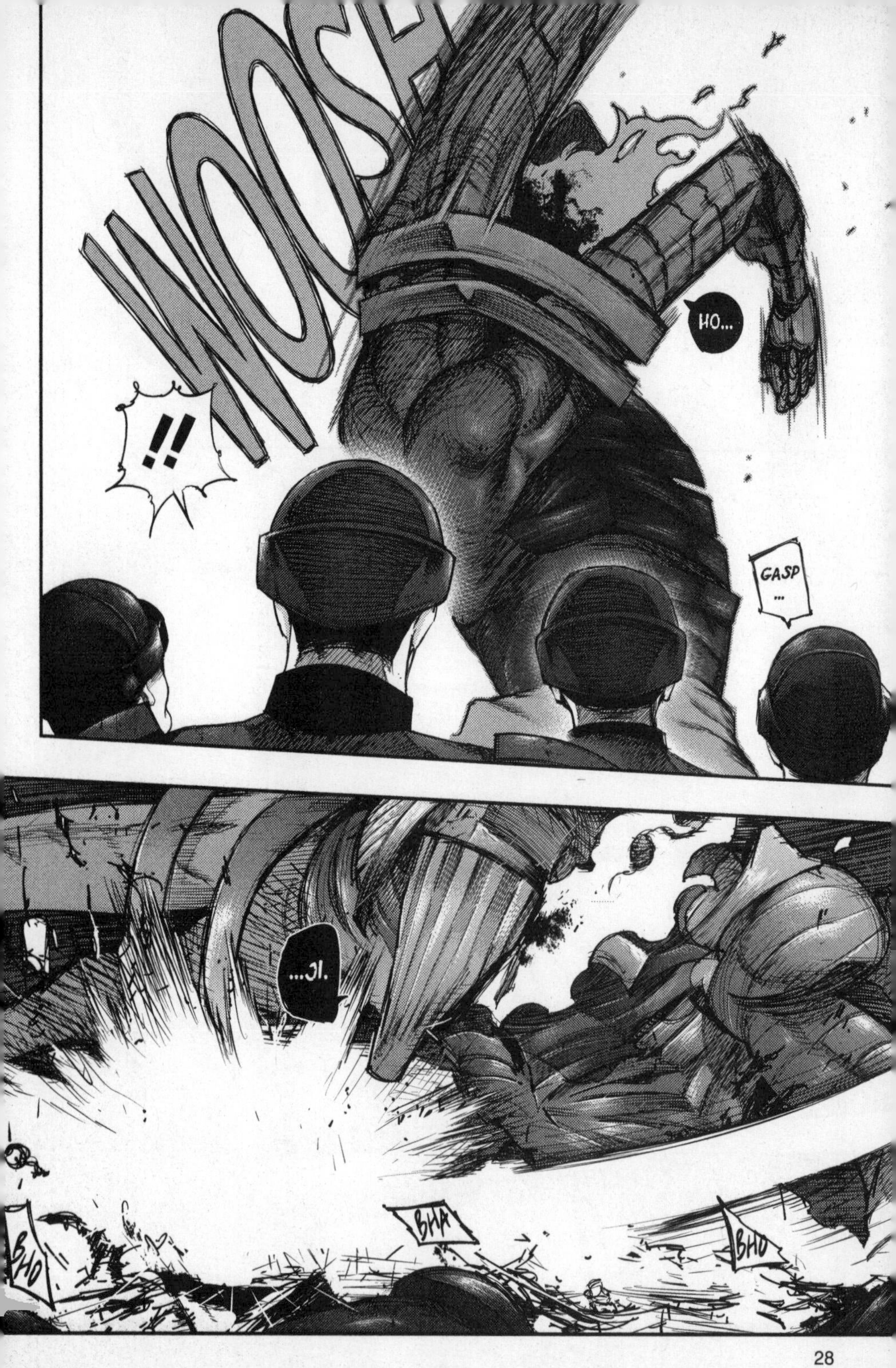

HO...
WOOOSE
!!
GASP ...
...JI.
BHO
BHA
BHO

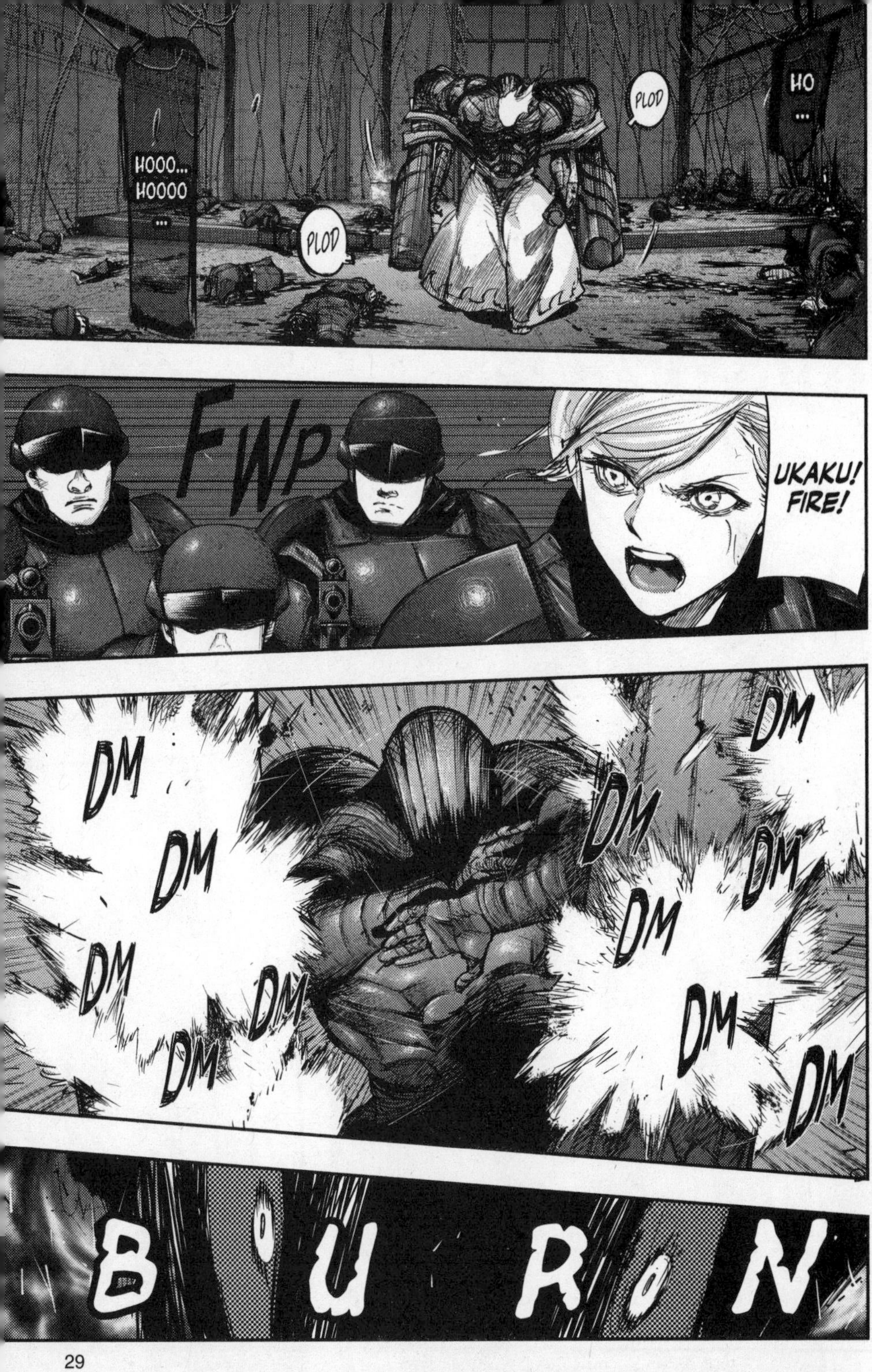
HO
...
PLOD
!
HOOO...
HOOOO
...
PLOD
UKAKU! FIRE!
FWP
DM
DM
DM
DM
DM
DM
DM
DM
DM
DM
DM
DM
BURON

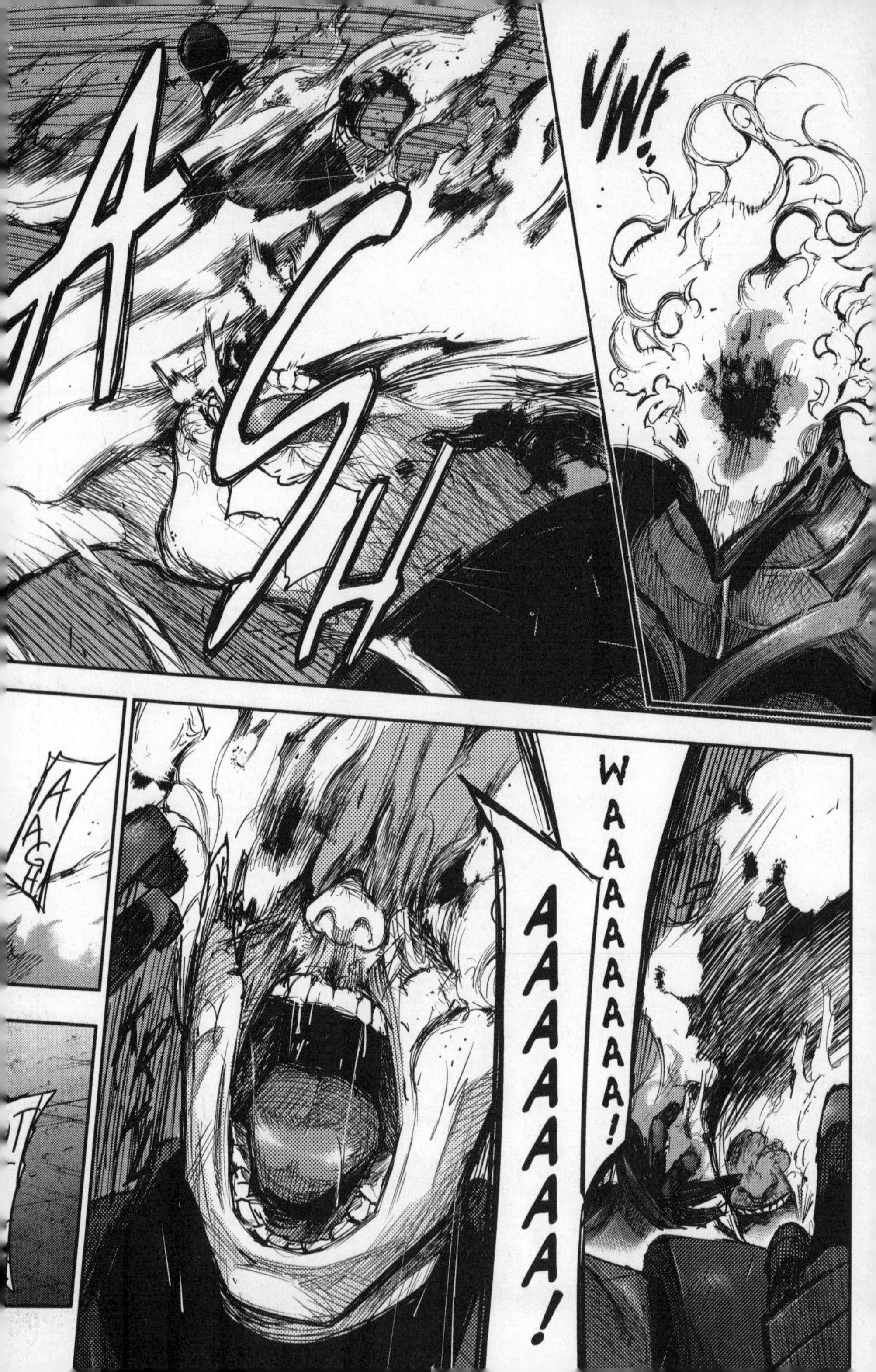
VWF!
GASH
WAAAAAAAA!
AAAAAAA!
AAGH

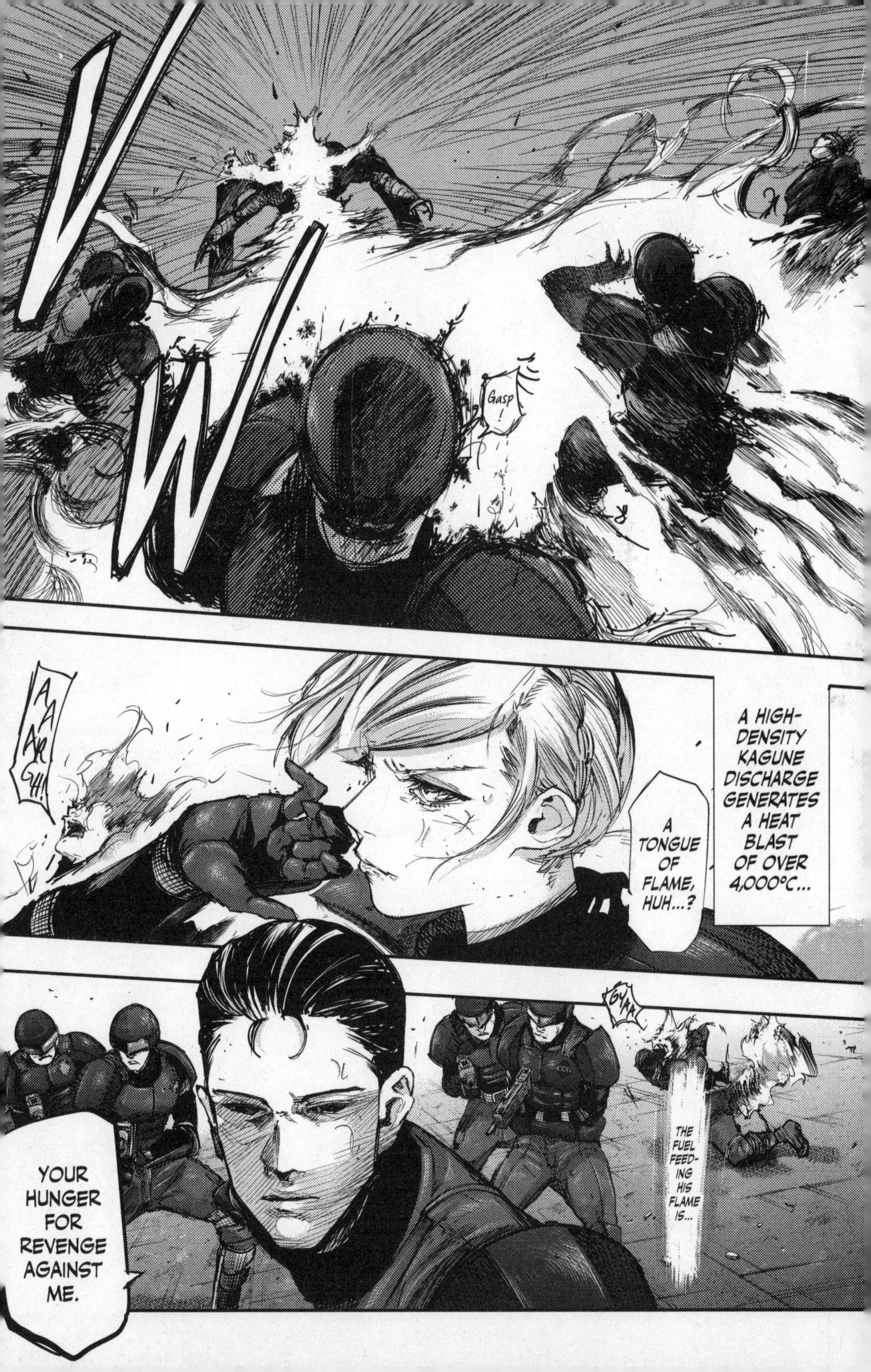
Gasp!
A HIGH-DENSITY KAGUNE DISCHARGE GENERATES A HEAT BLAST OF OVER 4,000°C...
A TONGUE OF FLAME, HUH...?
AAAARGH!
GYAA
THE FUEL FEEDING HIS FLAME IS...
YOUR HUNGER FOR REVENGE AGAINST ME.

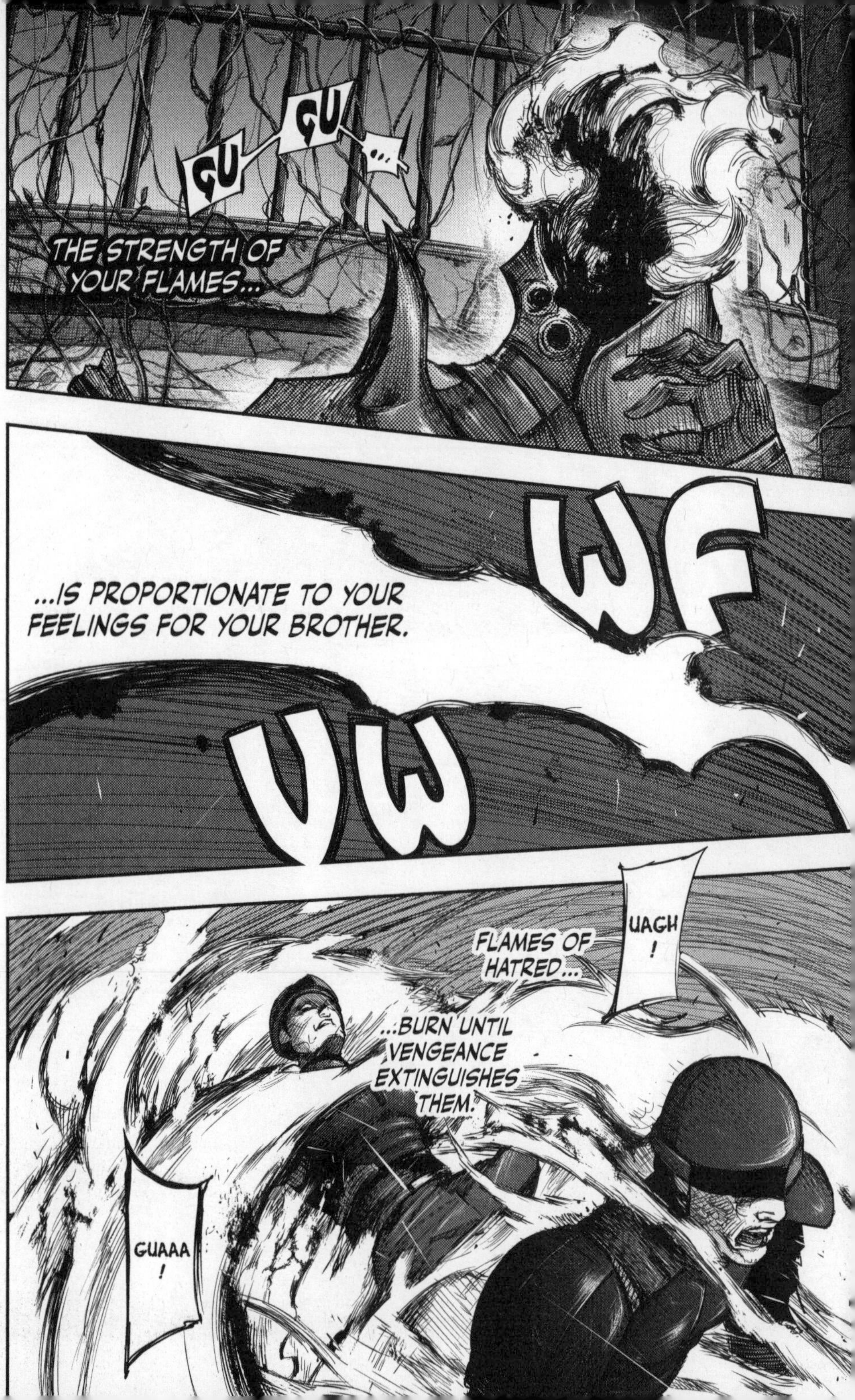
GU GU ...
THE STRENGTH OF YOUR FLAMES...
WF
...IS PROPORTIONATE TO YOUR FEELINGS FOR YOUR BROTHER.
VW
UAGH!
FLAMES OF HATRED...
...BURN UNTIL VENGEANCE EXTINGUISHES THEM.
GUAAA!

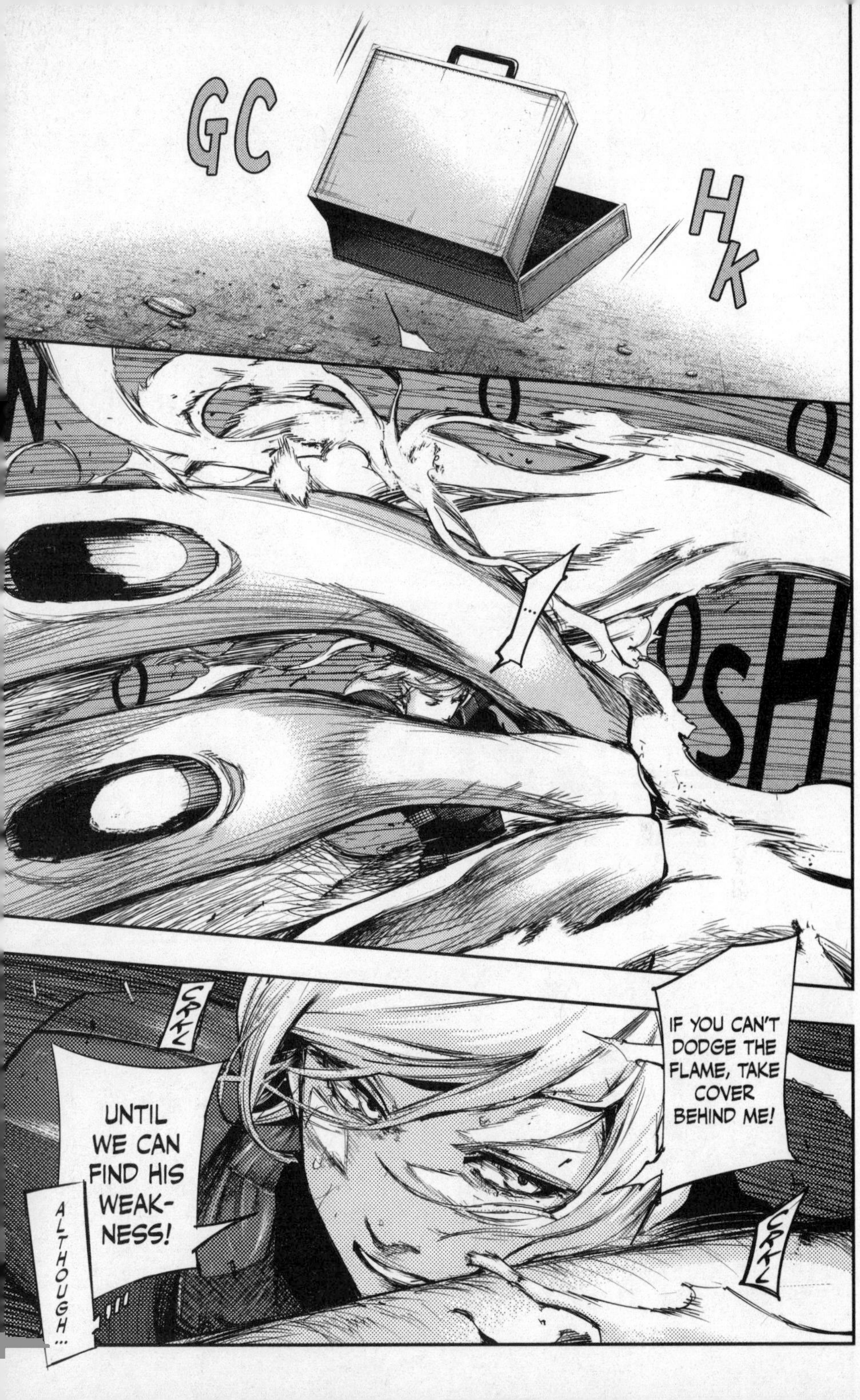
HK
GC
...
IF YOU CAN'T DODGE THE FLAME, TAKE COVER BEHIND ME!
CRKL
UNTIL WE CAN FIND HIS WEAKNESS!
CRKL
ALTHOUGH...

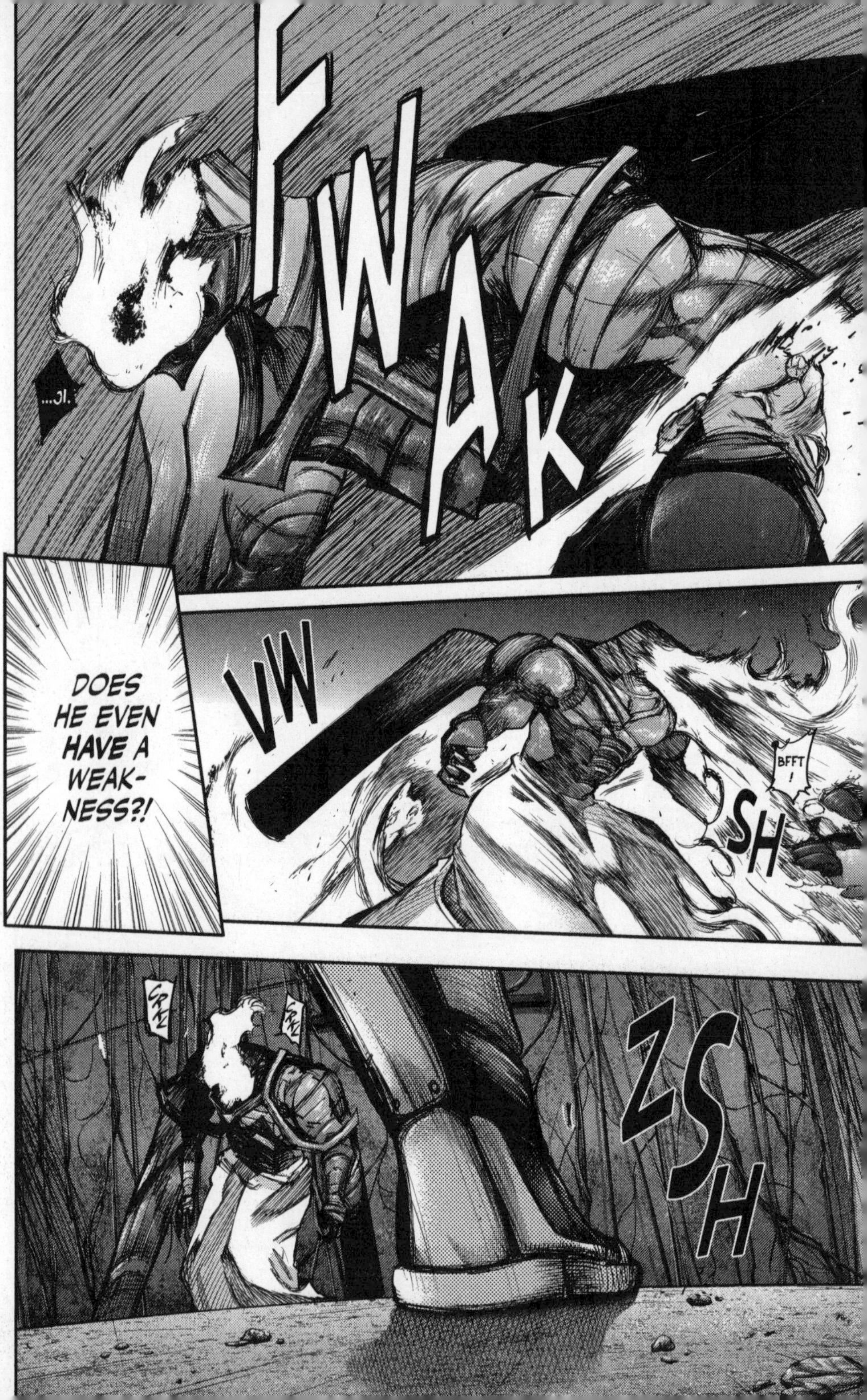
FWAK
...!!
BFFT!
SH
VW
DOES HE EVEN HAVE A WEAK-NESS?!
ZSH
CRKL
CRKL

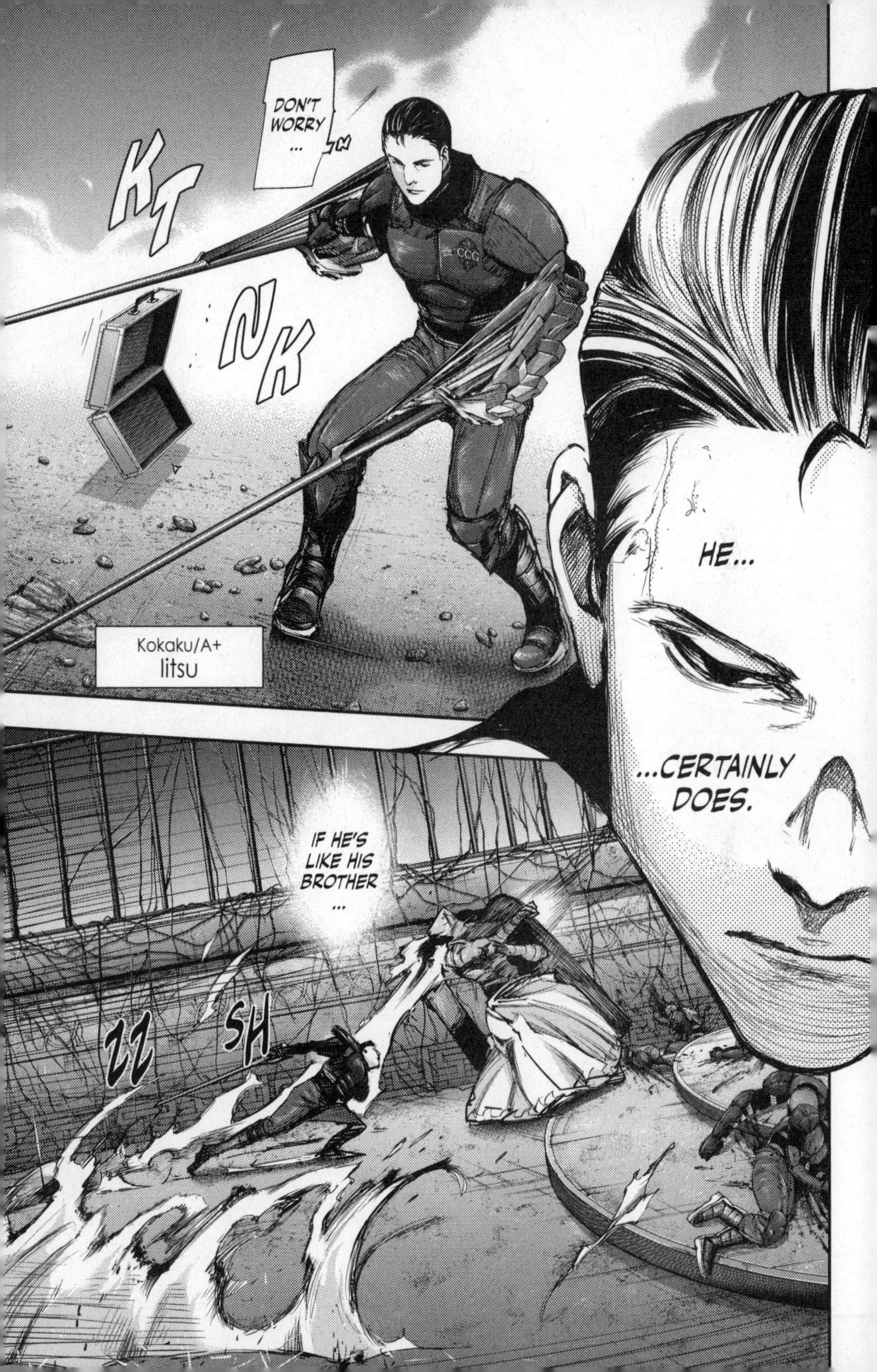
DON'T WORRY ...
KT
NK
Kokaku/A+
Iitsu
IF HE'S LIKE HIS BROTHER ...
SH
ZZ
HE...
...CERTAINLY DOES.

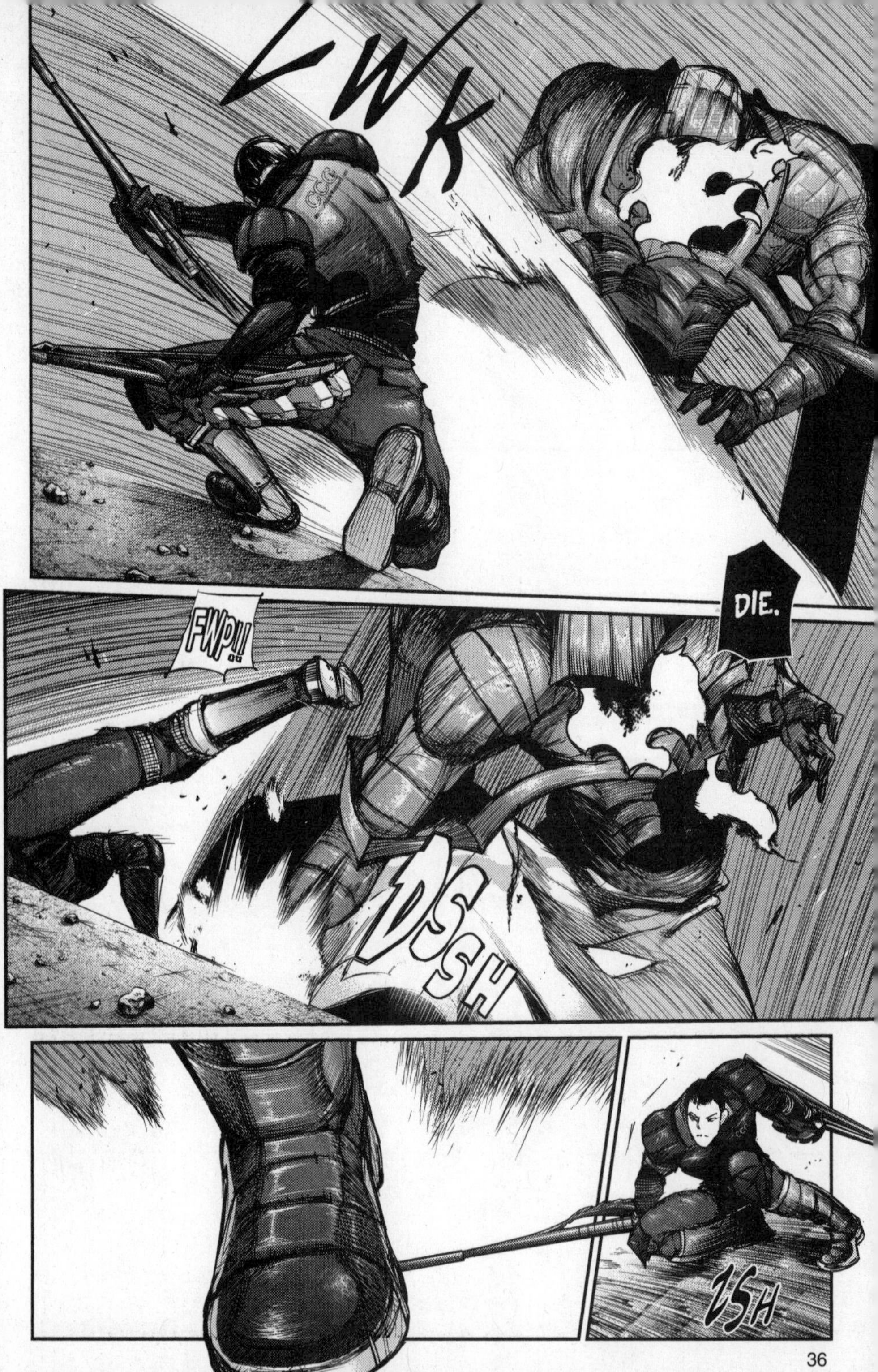
DIE.
FWP!!

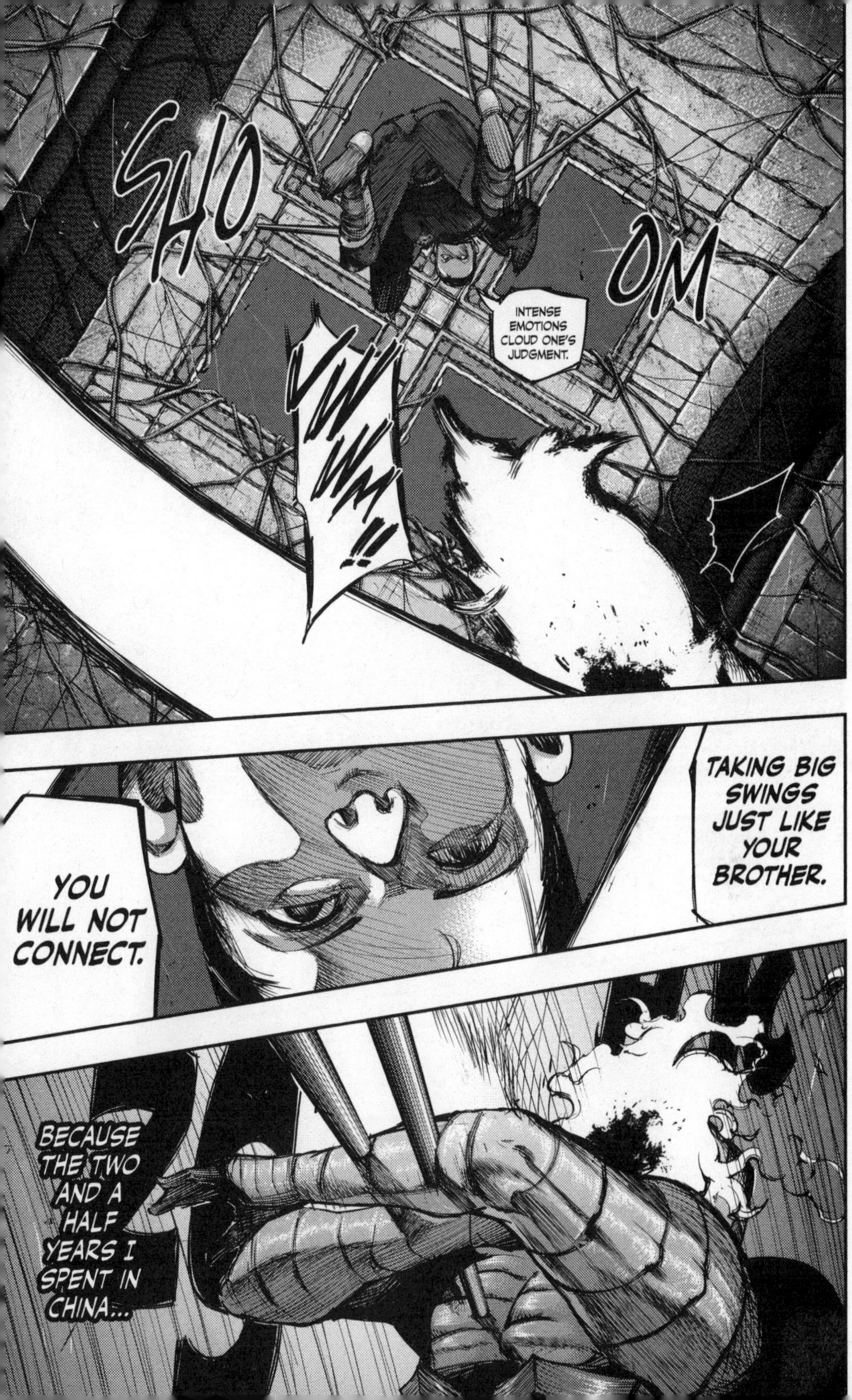
SHO
OM
INTENSE EMOTIONS CLOUD ONE'S JUDGMENT.
VWWM!!
TAKING BIG SWINGS JUST LIKE YOUR BROTHER.
YOU WILL NOT CONNECT.
BECAUSE THE TWO AND A HALF YEARS I SPENT IN CHINA...

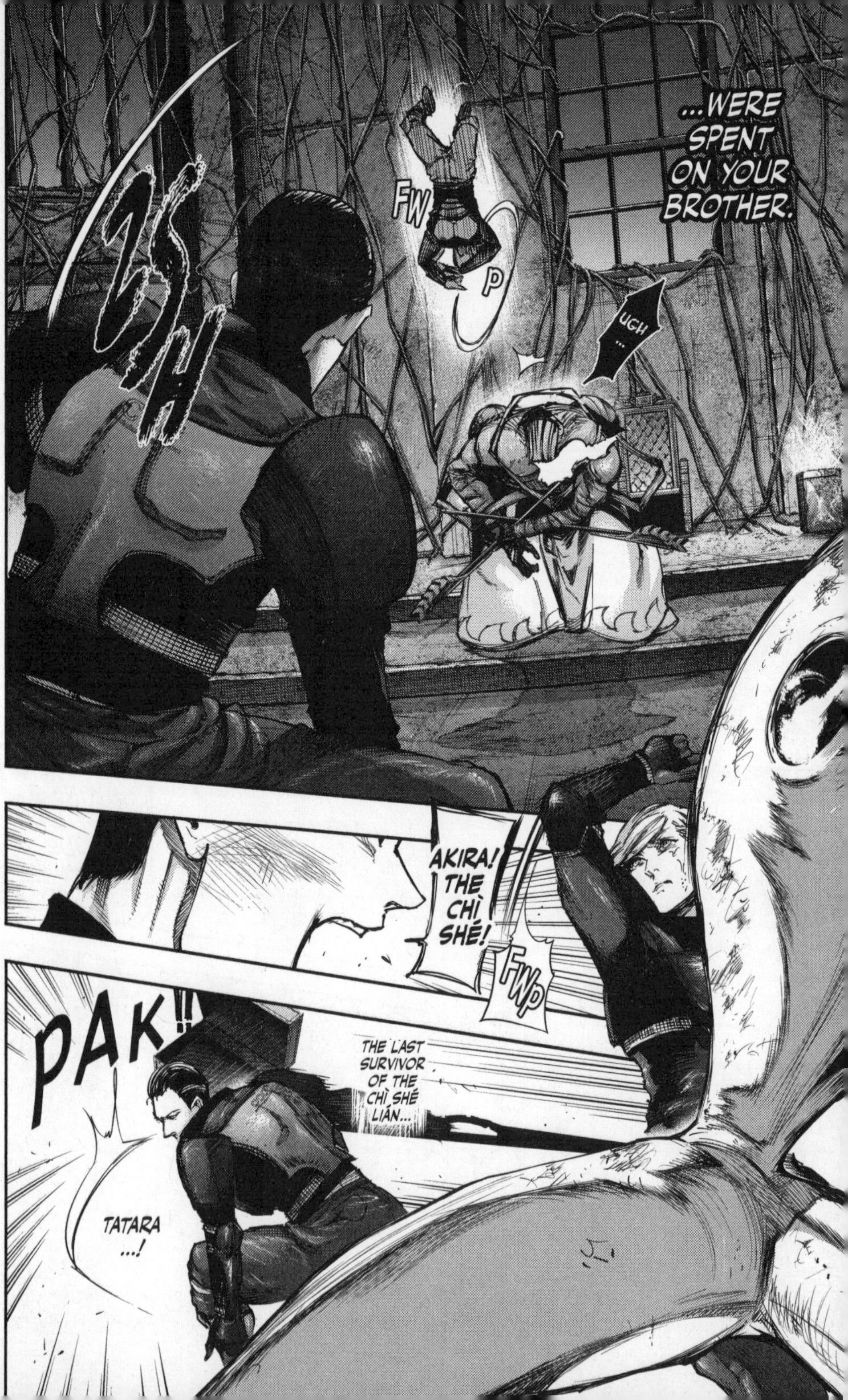
...WERE SPENT ON YOUR BROTHER.
FWP
UGH ...
ZSH
AKIRA! THE CHÌ SHÉ!
FWP
THE LAST SURVIVOR OF THE CHÌ SHÉ LIÁN...
PAK!!
TATARA ...!

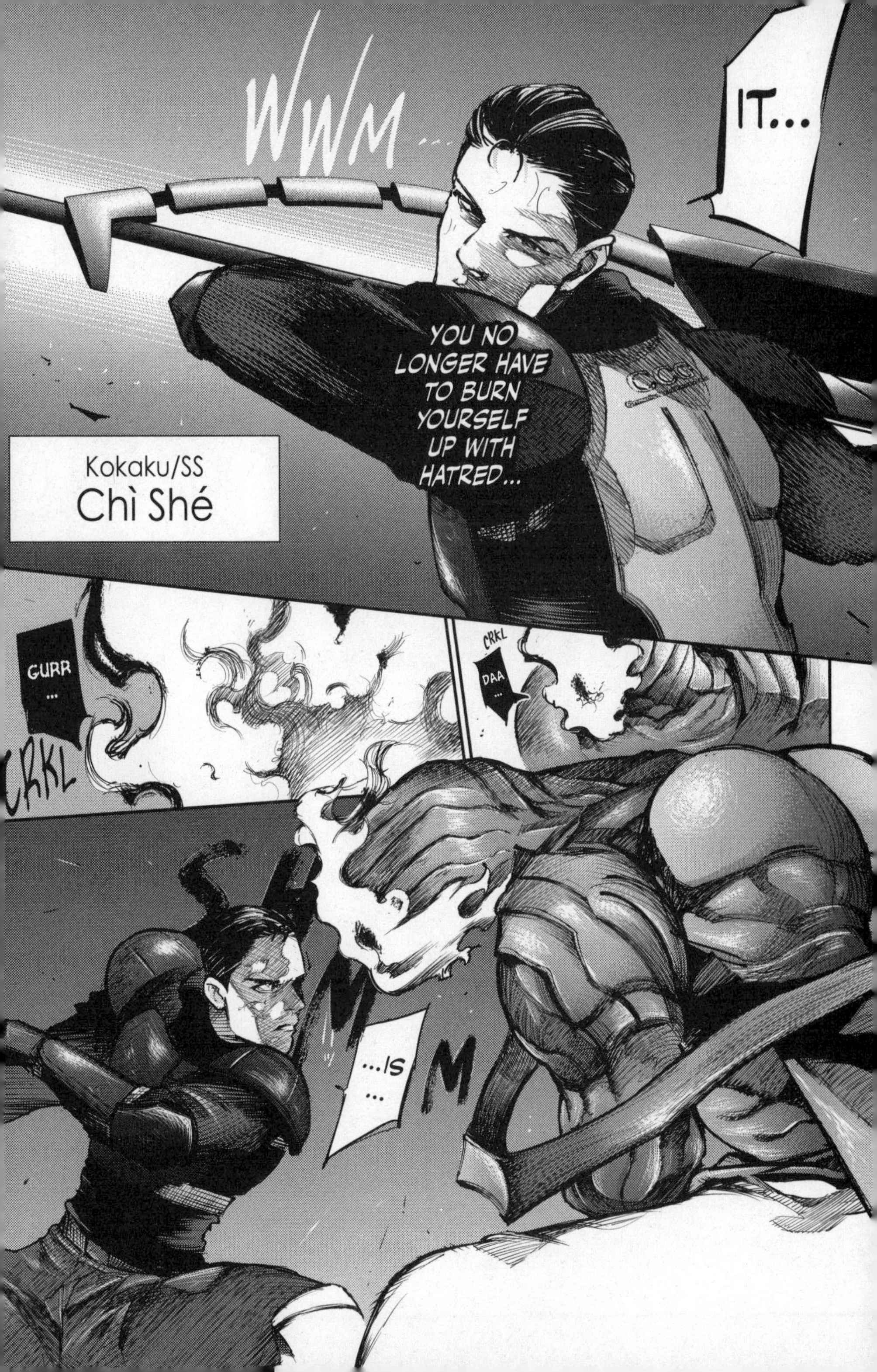
IT...
WWM...
YOU NO LONGER HAVE TO BURN YOURSELF UP WITH HATRED...
Kokaku/SS
Chì Shé
CRKL
DAA...
GURR...
CRKL
...IS...
M

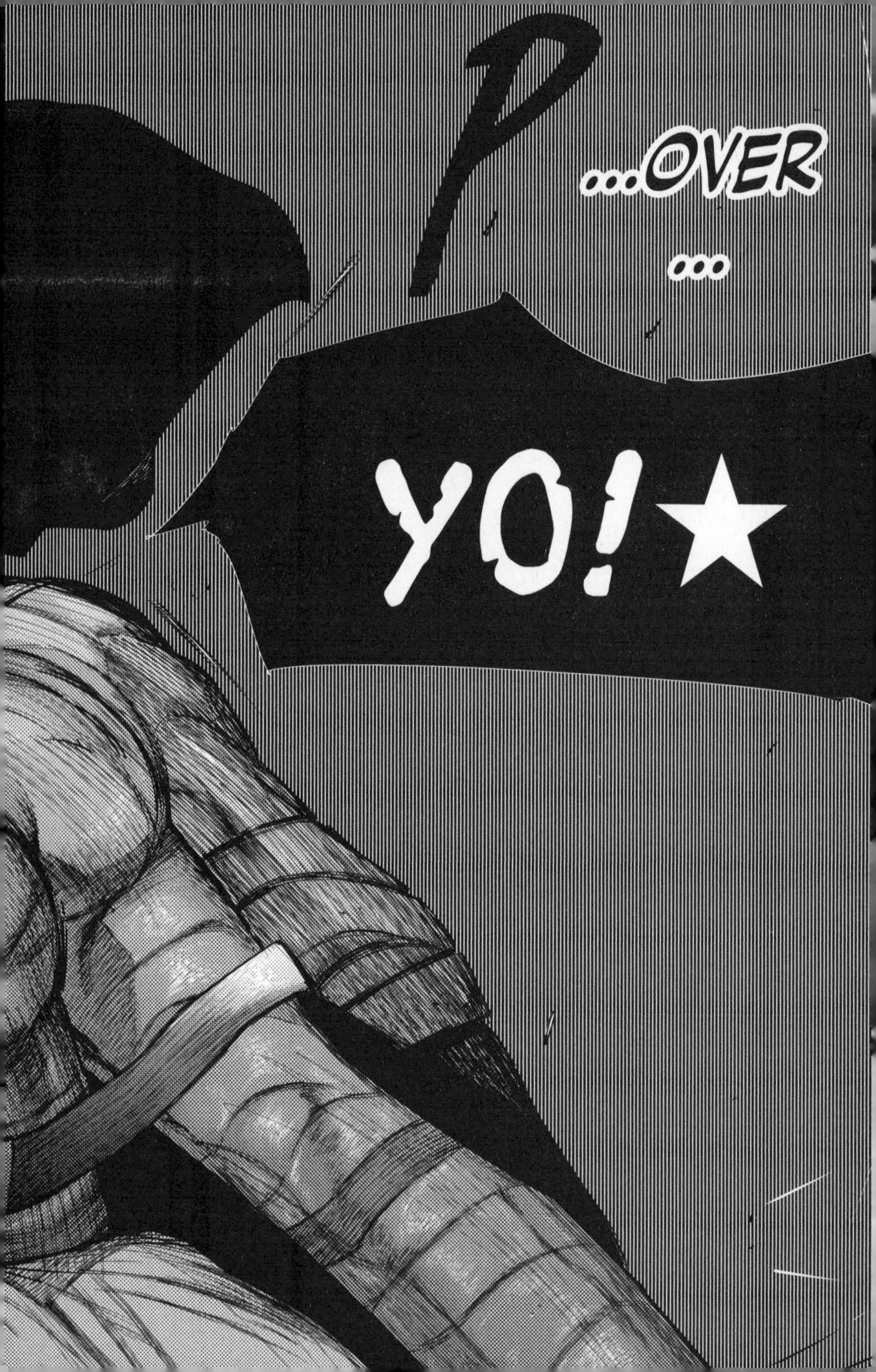
...OVER
...
YO!★

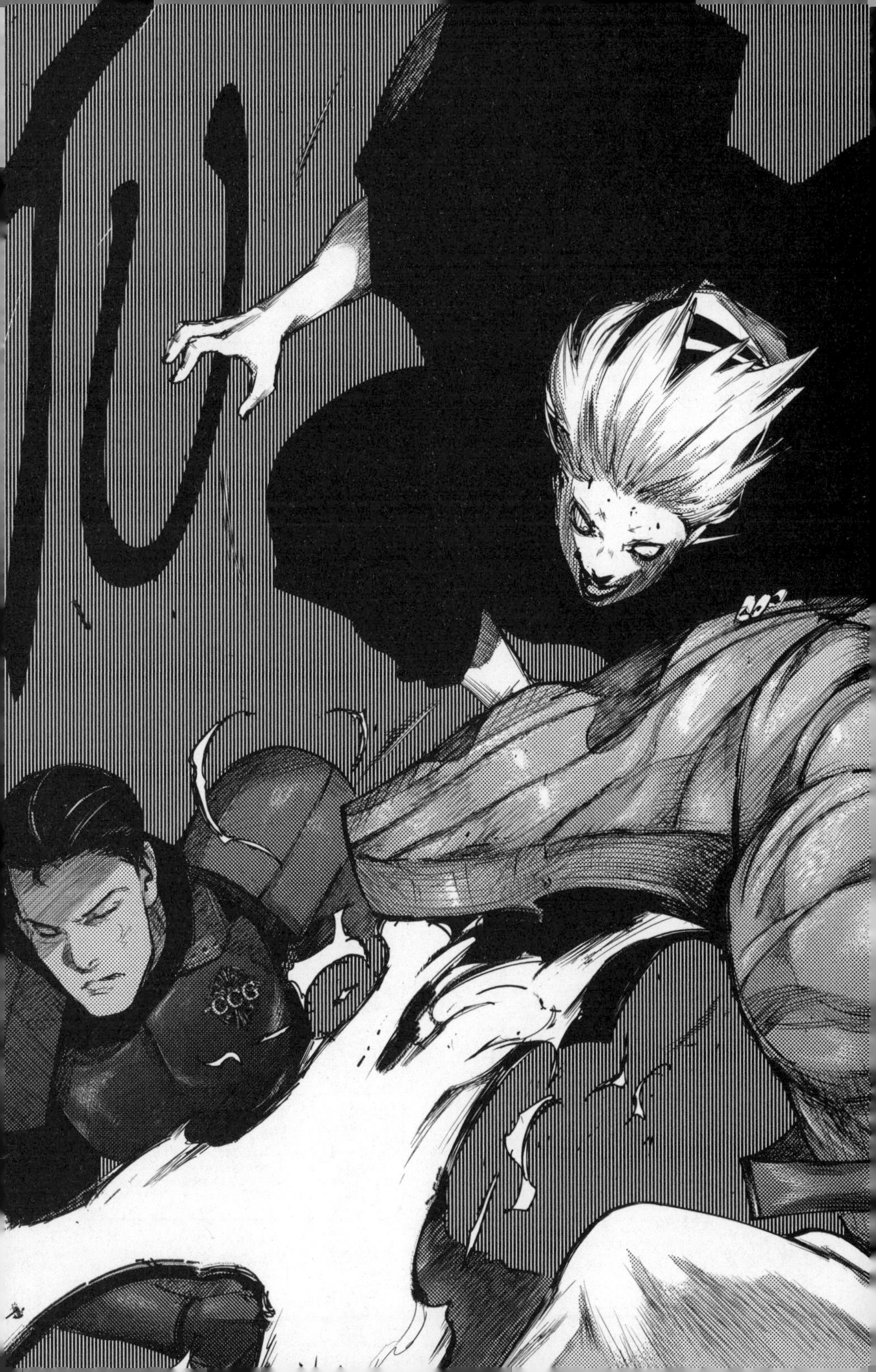
CCG

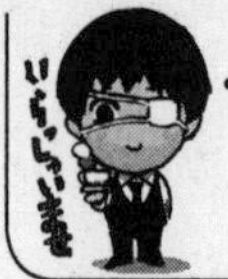

"Welcome!"

Main character

I often draw his eye patch on the wrong side.
(I made a mistake in the 100th chapter stickers.)
Mutsuki may have something to do with it.

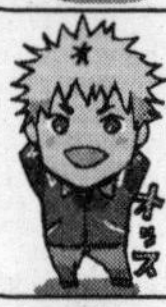
オッス

"Yo."

Hide

I think Kaneki would be even more miserable if Hide wasn't around.

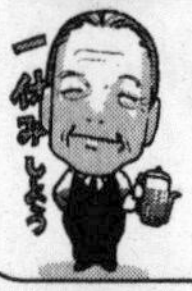

"Take a break."

Mr. Yoshimura

I got to practice drawing wrinkles thanks to Mr. Yoshimura.

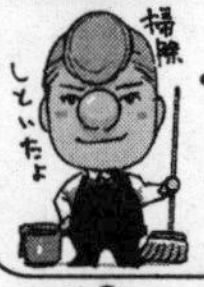

"I cleaned up."

Koma

I came up with the sequence where he fights as Devil Ape in volume 13 soon after his character was created.

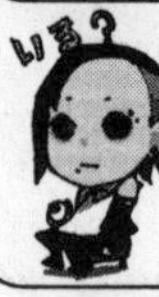
いる?

"Want one?"

Uta

He has a lot of hobbies incorporated into him.

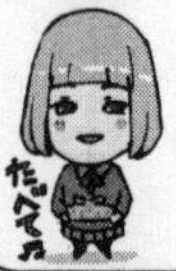

"Eat."

Yoriko

I think Touka liked going to school because of Yoriko. Revealed in the novel that her last name is Kosaka.

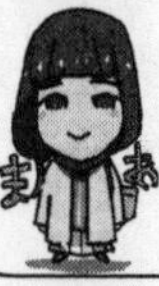

"Aw!"

Ryoko

A character name that screams "scheduled to be killed" even now.

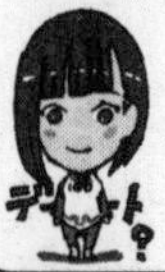

"A date?"

Kimi

A strange character whose face ends up looking like other female characters if I don't concentrate.

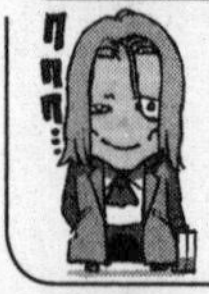

"Ku ku ku..."

Mado

The basis of investigator characters. I like him.

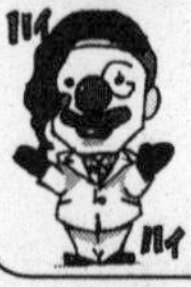
ハイ
ハイ

"Yes! Yes!"

Sota

I obsessed over his hairstyle.

*100 icon stickers were included in the *Weekly Young Jump* issue in which the 100th chapter of *Tokyo Ghoul :re* appeared.

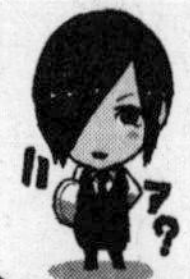

"Huh?"

Touka

I love this haircut on women. Although I've rarely seen anybody with it.

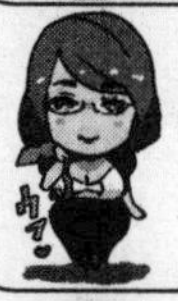

"Heh."

Rize

Whenever I'm asked "Who's your favorite female Ghoul?" I always answer "Rize."

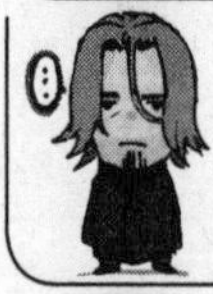

"..."

Yomo

A versatile character.

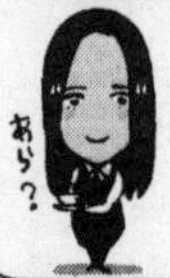
あら?

"Oh?"

Irimi

I like her sarcasm.

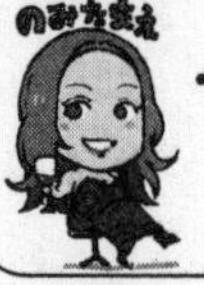

"Drink up."

Itori

She has a mole on her left breast.

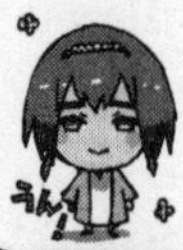

"Okay."

Hinami

Lolita.

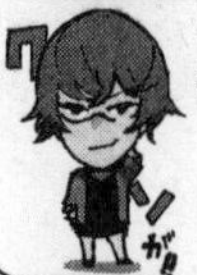

"Asshole!"

Nishio

There's a story behind the creation of Nishiki. Hope I can tell it someday.

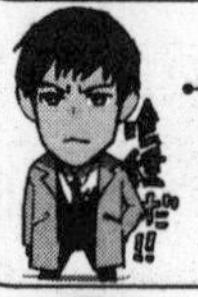

"Ghoul!"

Kotaro Amon

I used to call him Taro Komon (Anal Taro). But I put him on a cover so I hope he forgives me.

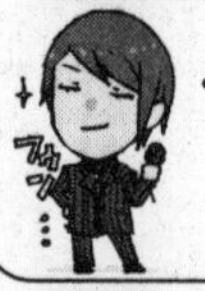

"Hmm..."

Shu

First appeared with Chie Hori ten or so years ago in a piece I submitted to a contest. His bangs keep getting longer.

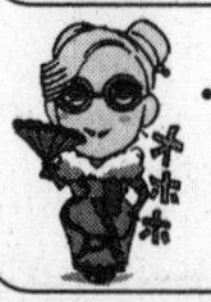

"Ho ho ho!"

Madame A

I think she's doing fine.

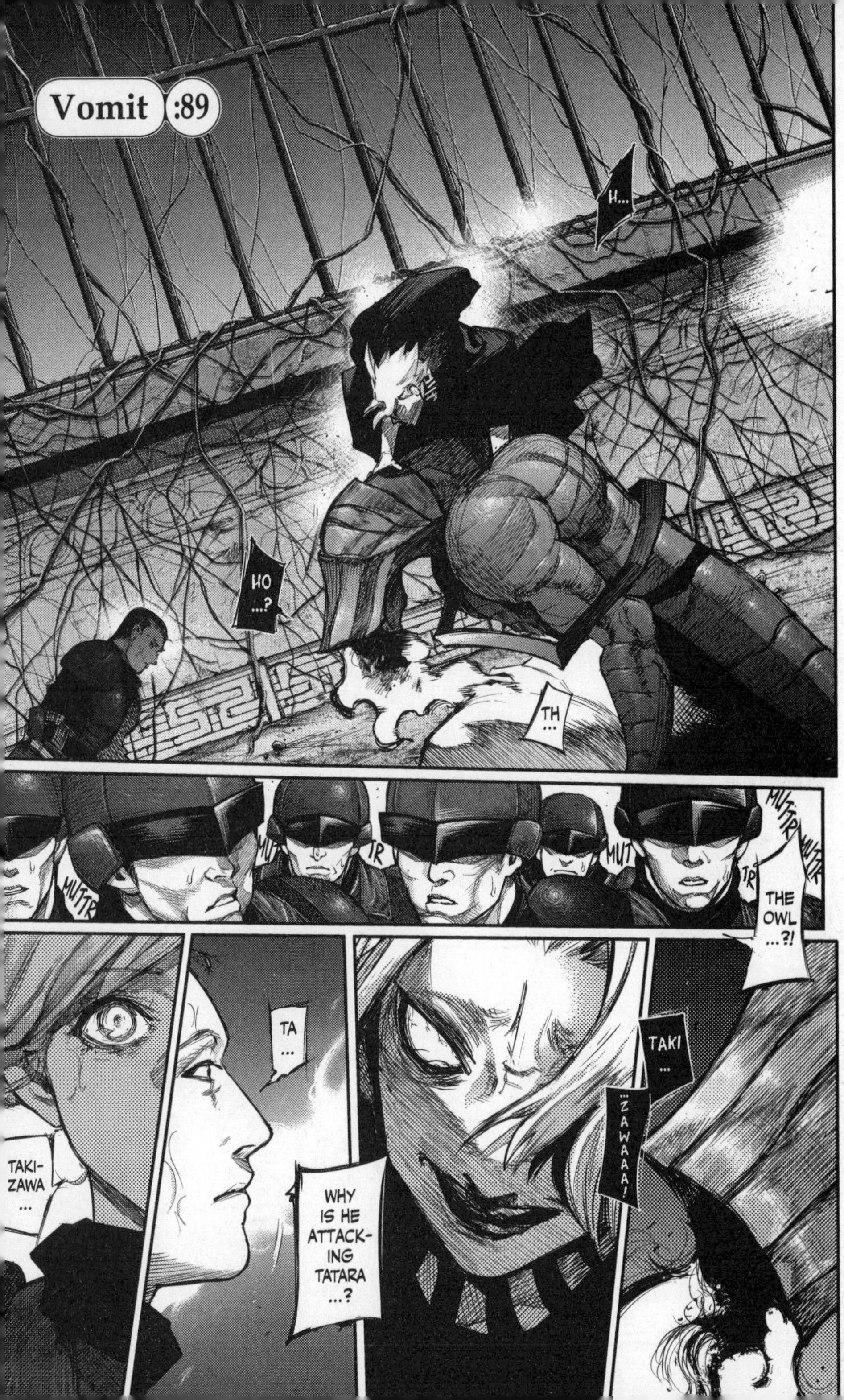
Vomit :89
H...
HO ...?
TH ...
MUTTR MUTTR
TR
MUT
IR
MUT
MUTTR
THE OWL ...?!
TAKI ...
...ZAWAAA!
TA ...
WHY IS HE ATTACKING TATARA ...?
TAKI-ZAWA ...

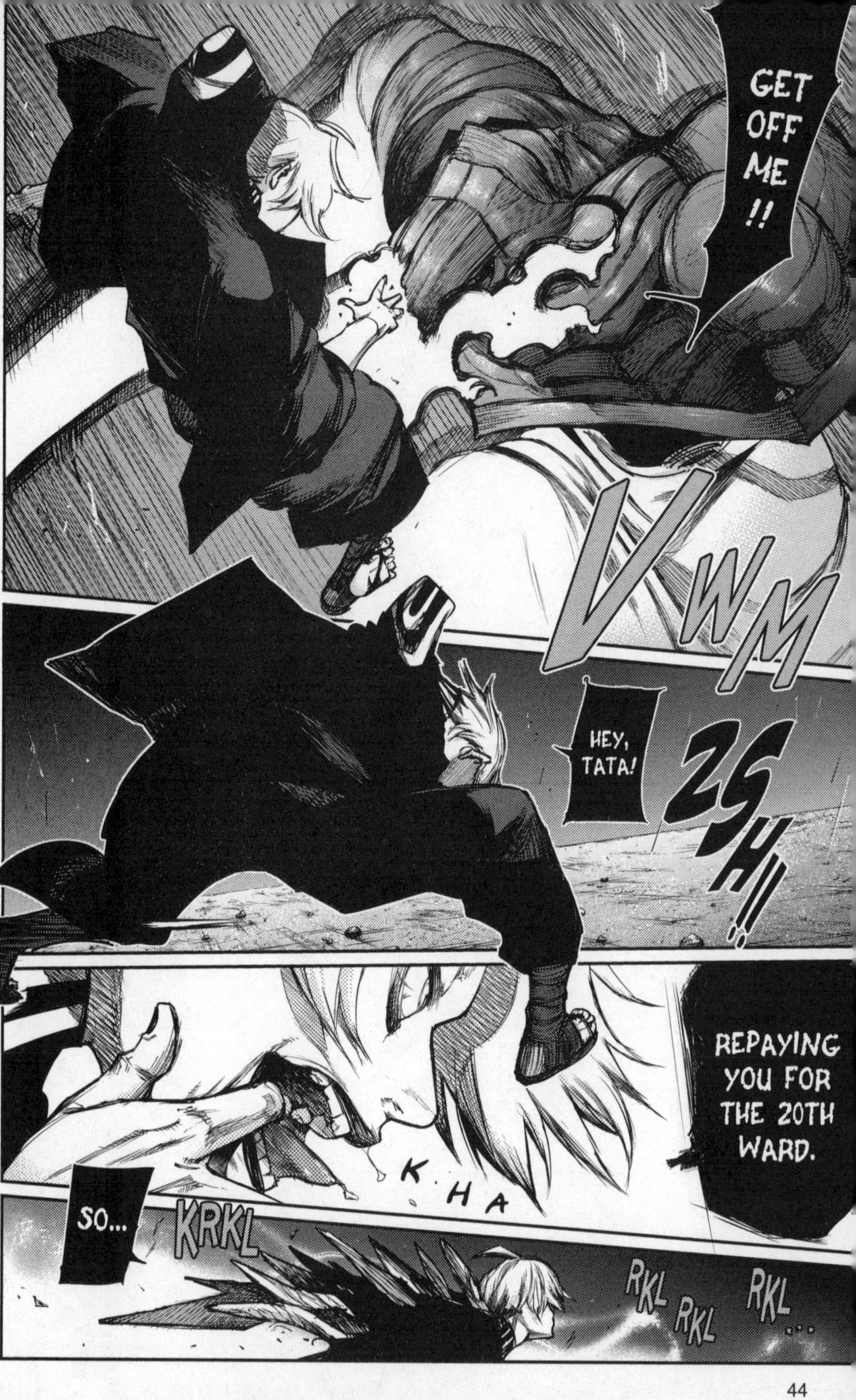
GET OFF ME !!
VWM
HEY, TATA!
ZSH!!
REPAYING YOU FOR THE 20TH WARD.
KHA
SO...
KRKL
RKL RKL RKL...

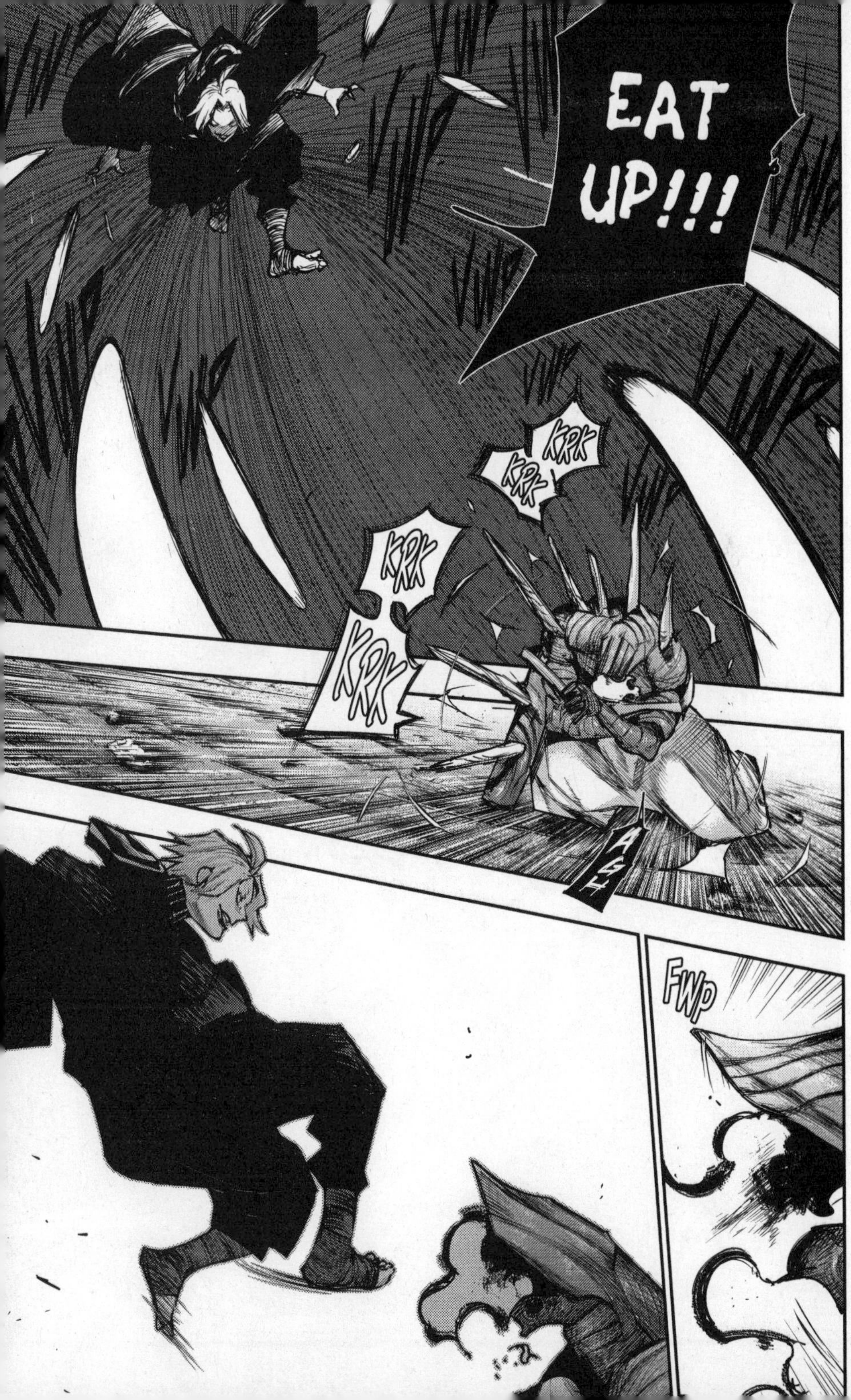
EAT UP!!!
KRK KRK
KRK KRK
AGH
FWP

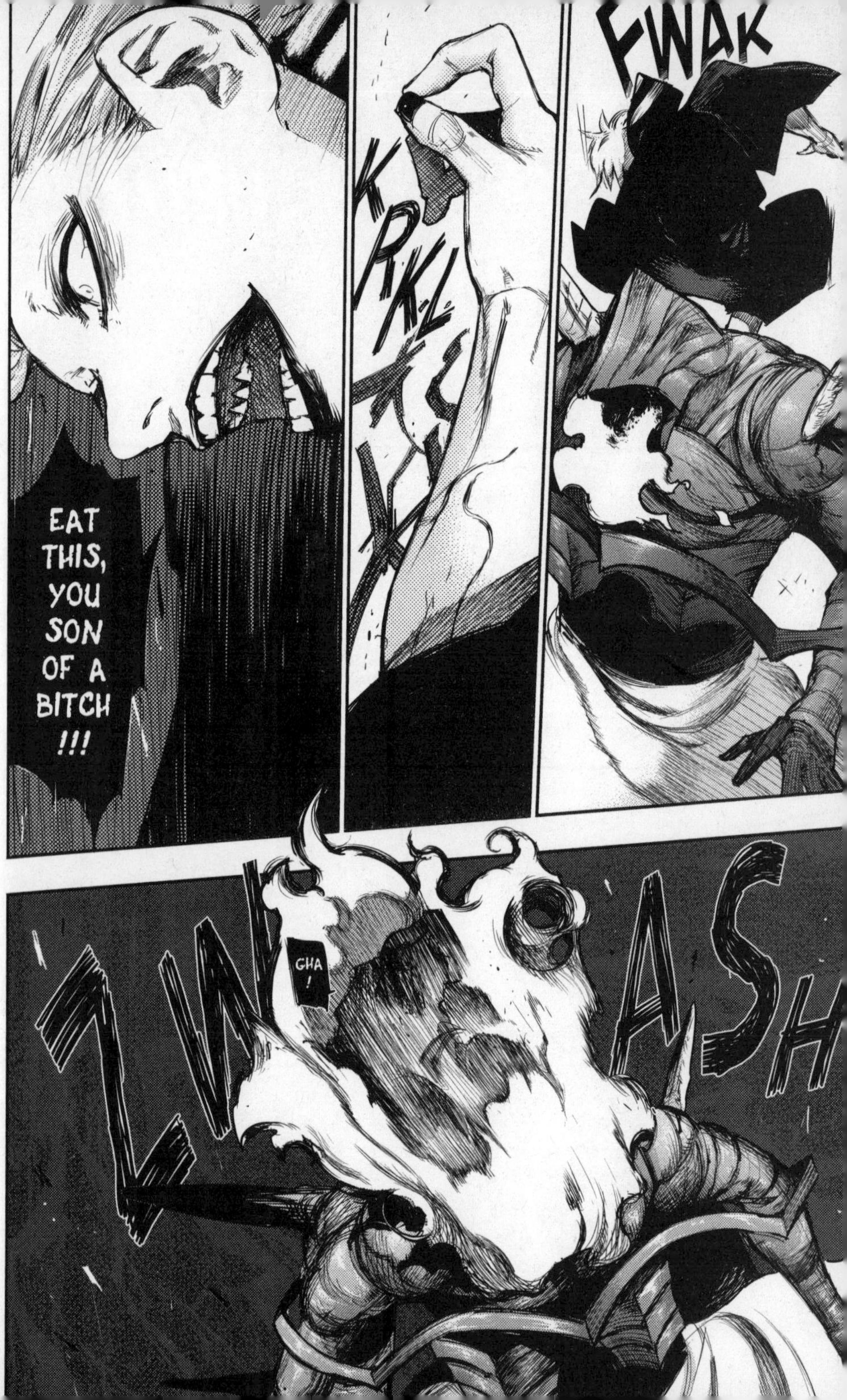
FWAK
EAT THIS, YOU SON OF A BITCH!!!
ZWASH
GHA!

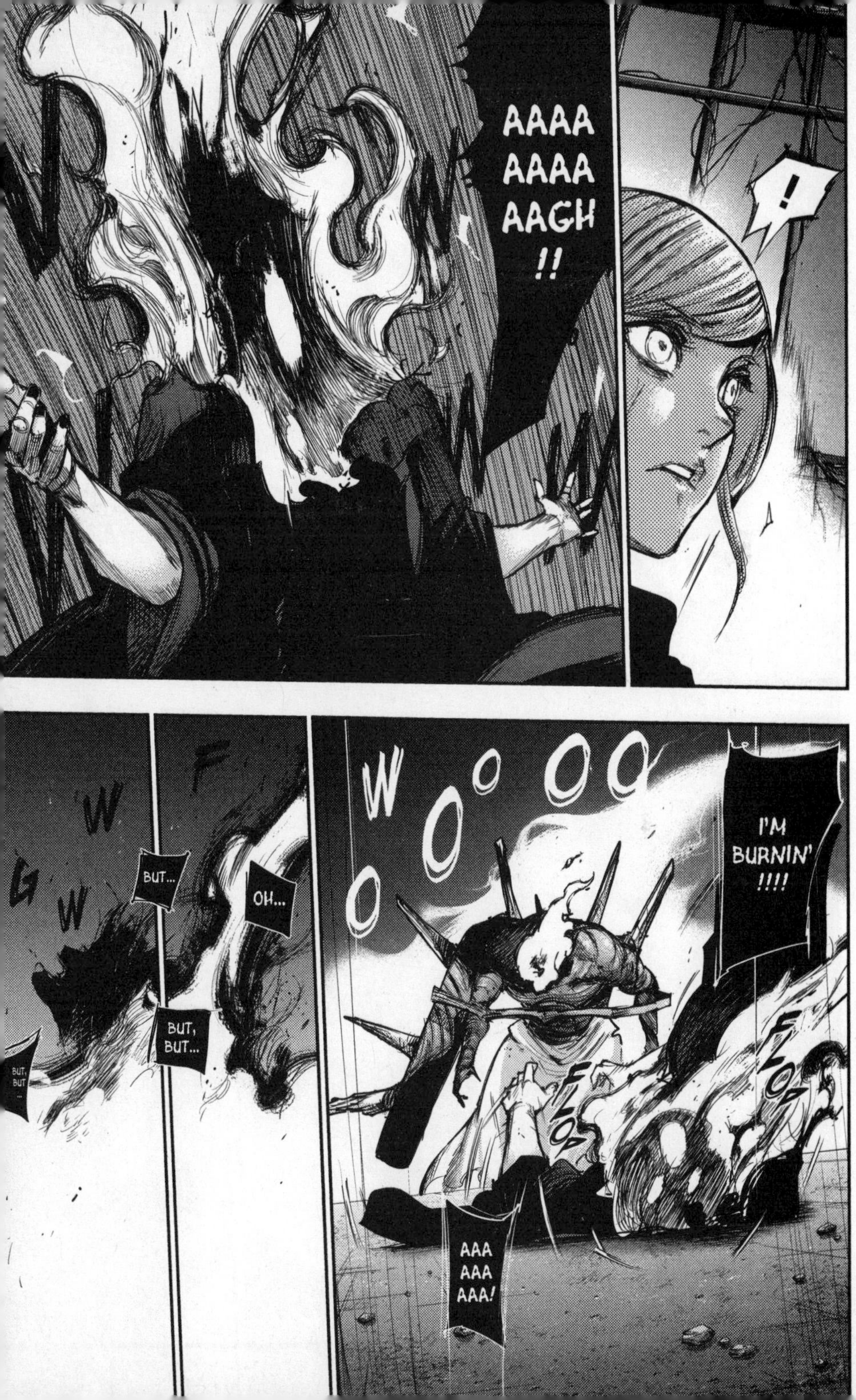
!
AAAA AAAA AAGH !!
I'M BURNIN' !!!!
AAA AAA AAA!
OH...
BUT...
BUT, BUT...
BUT, BUT...

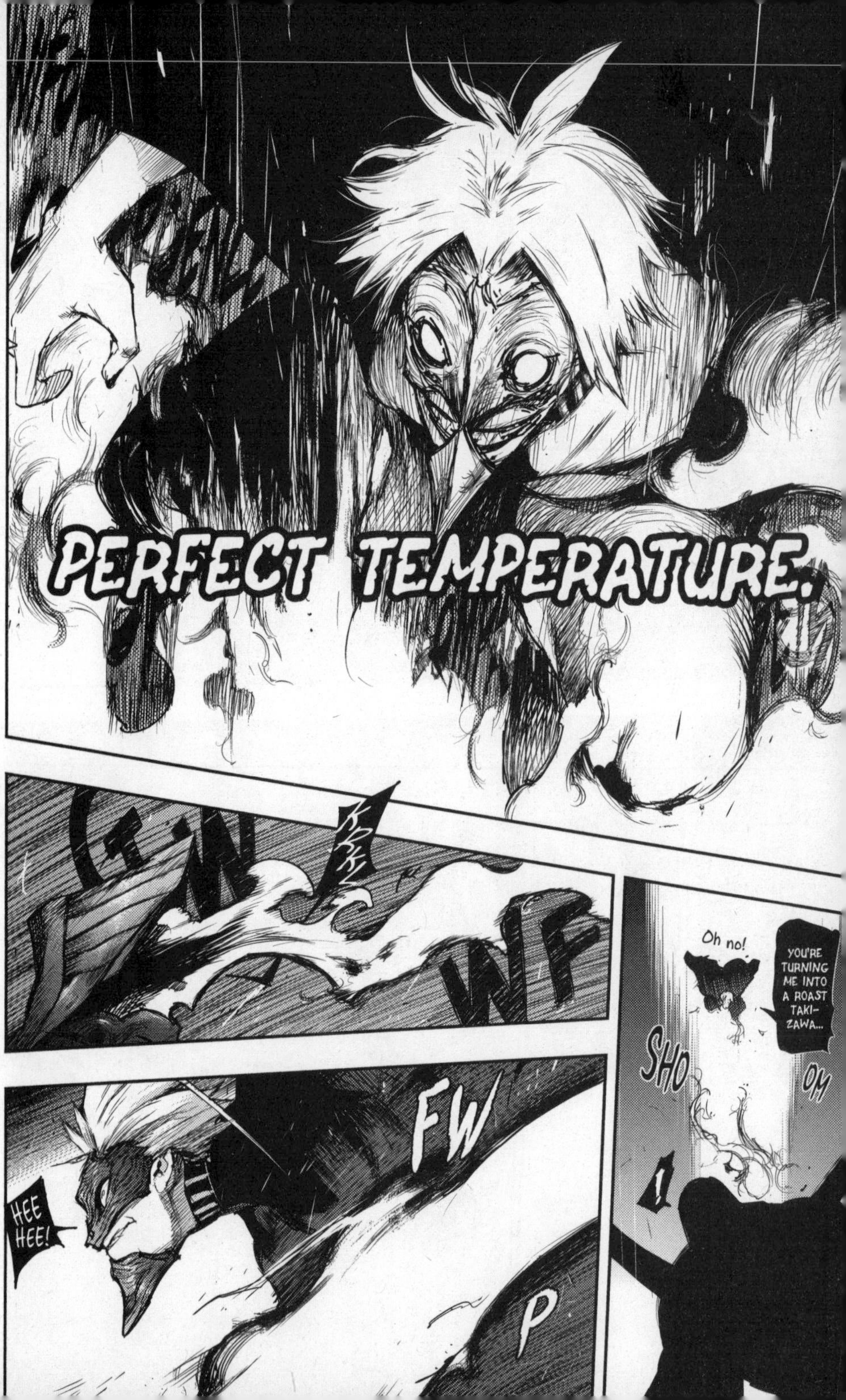
PERFECT TEMPERATURE.
Oh no!
YOU'RE TURNING ME INTO A ROAST TAKI-ZAWA...
SHO
OM
WF
FW
HEE HEE!
P

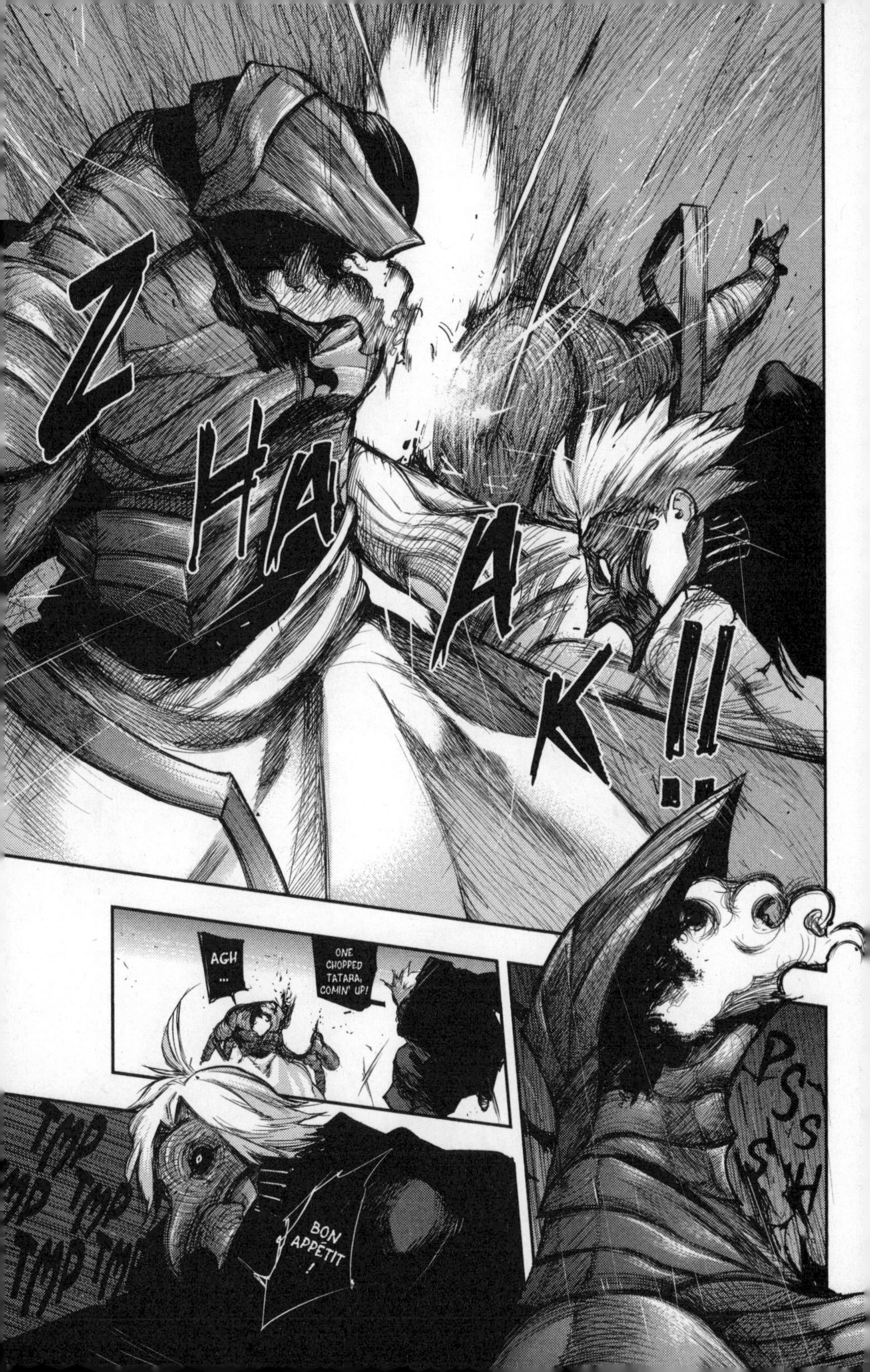
ZHAAK!!
PSSSH
ONE CHOPPED TATARA, COMIN' UP!
AGH...
TMP TMP TMP TMP TMP TMP TMP
BON APPÉTIT!

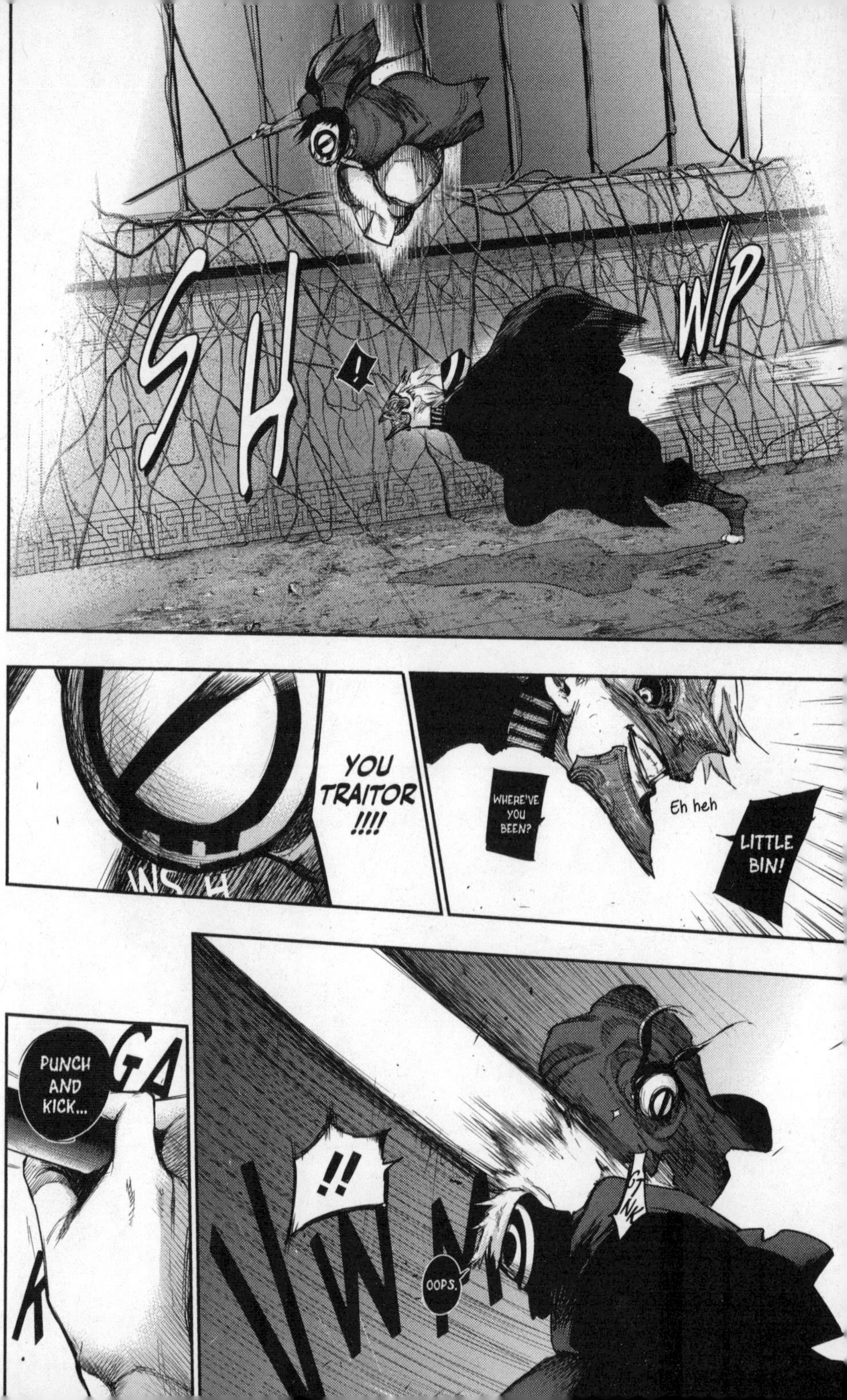
WP
!
SH
Eh heh
WHERE'VE YOU BEEN?
LITTLE BIN!
YOU TRAITOR!!!!
!!
OOPS.
PUNCH AND KICK...
GA

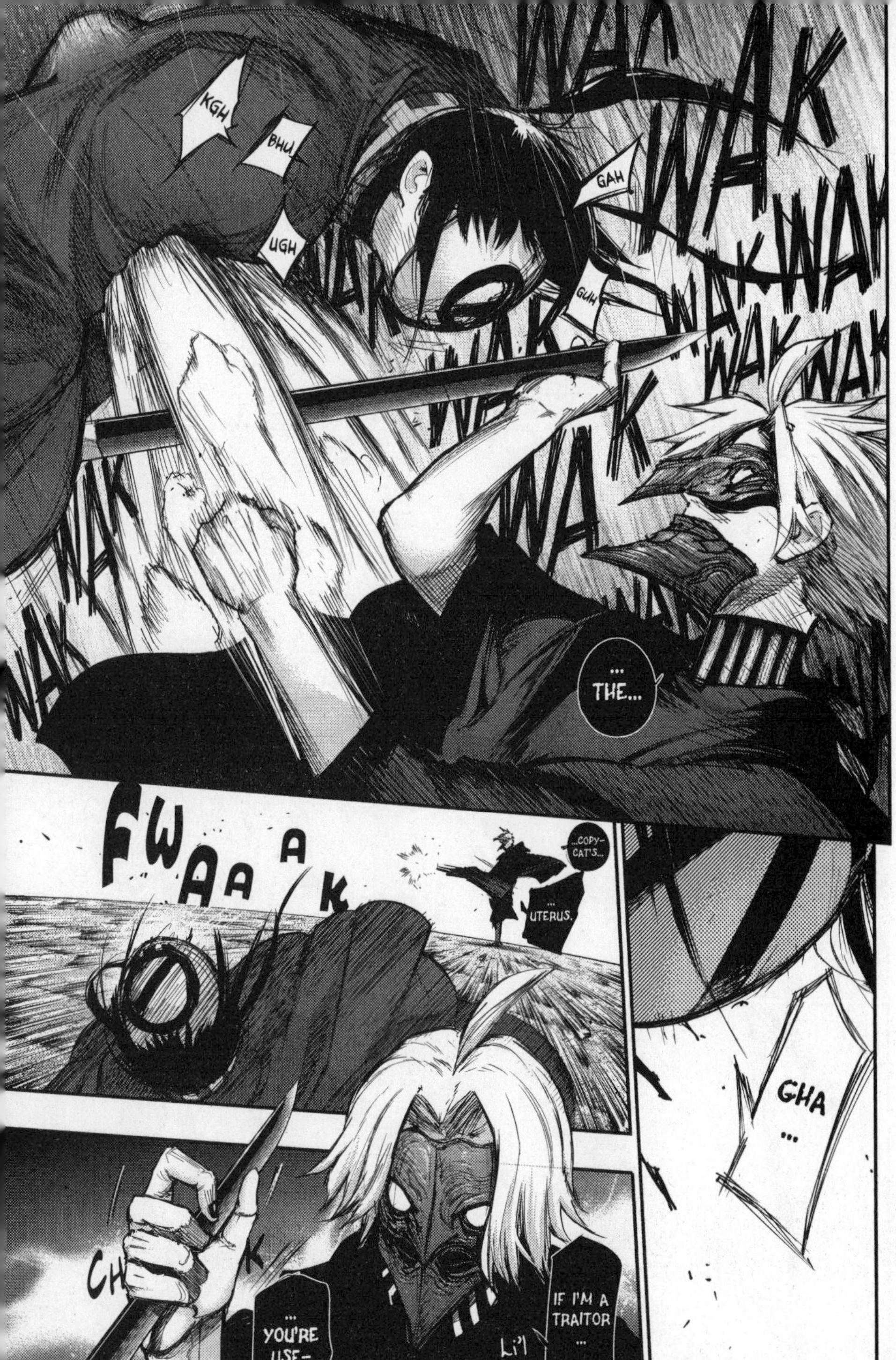
WAK
WAK
WAK
GAH
KGH
BHU
UGH
GUH
WAK
WAK
WAK
WAK
WAK
WAK
...THE...
GHA...
FWAAAK
...COPY-CAT'S...
...UTERUS.
CHAK
IF I'M A TRAITOR...
Li'l Bin...
...YOU'RE USE-LESS.

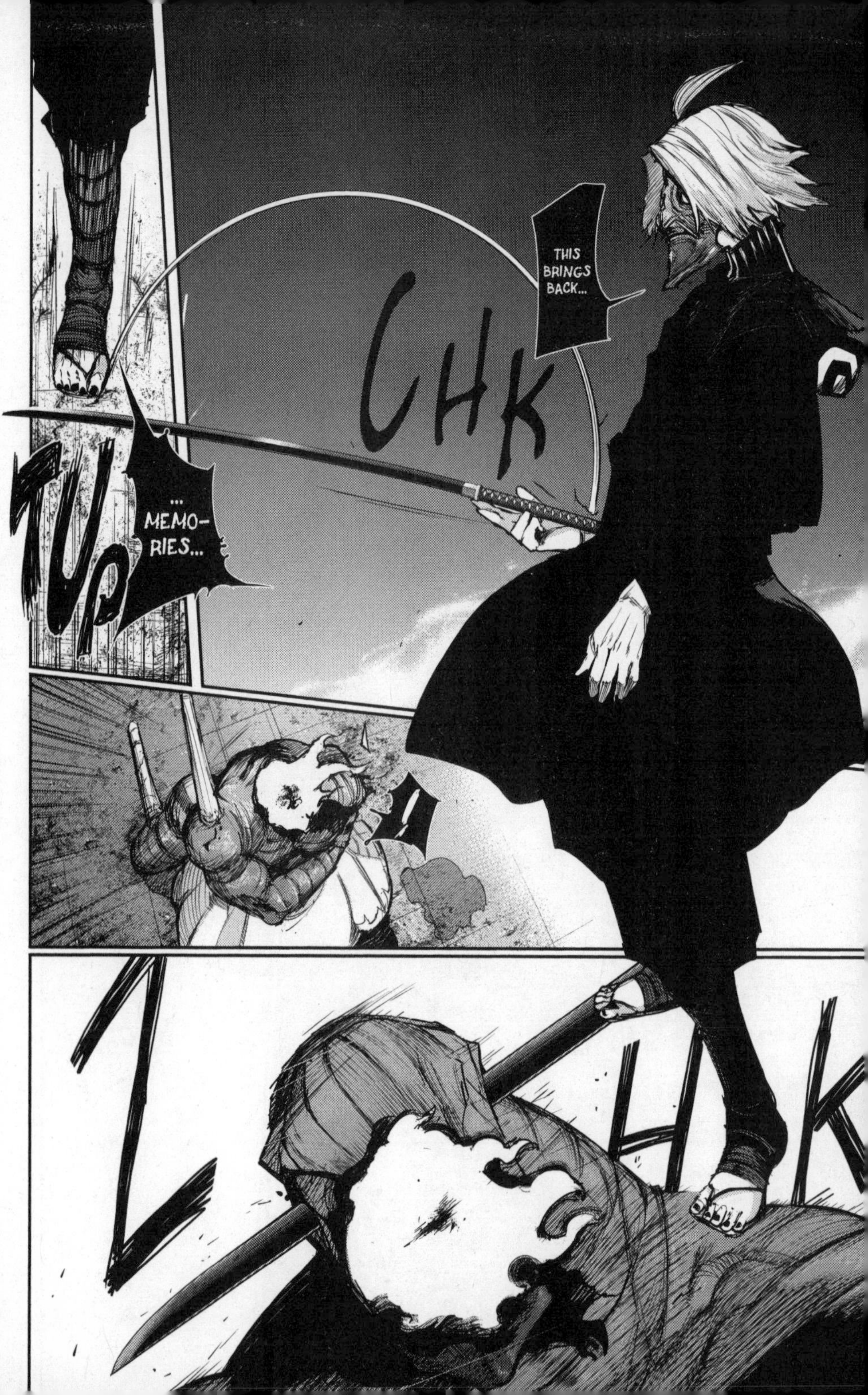
THIS BRINGS BACK...
CHK
...MEMORIES...
TUP
ZHK

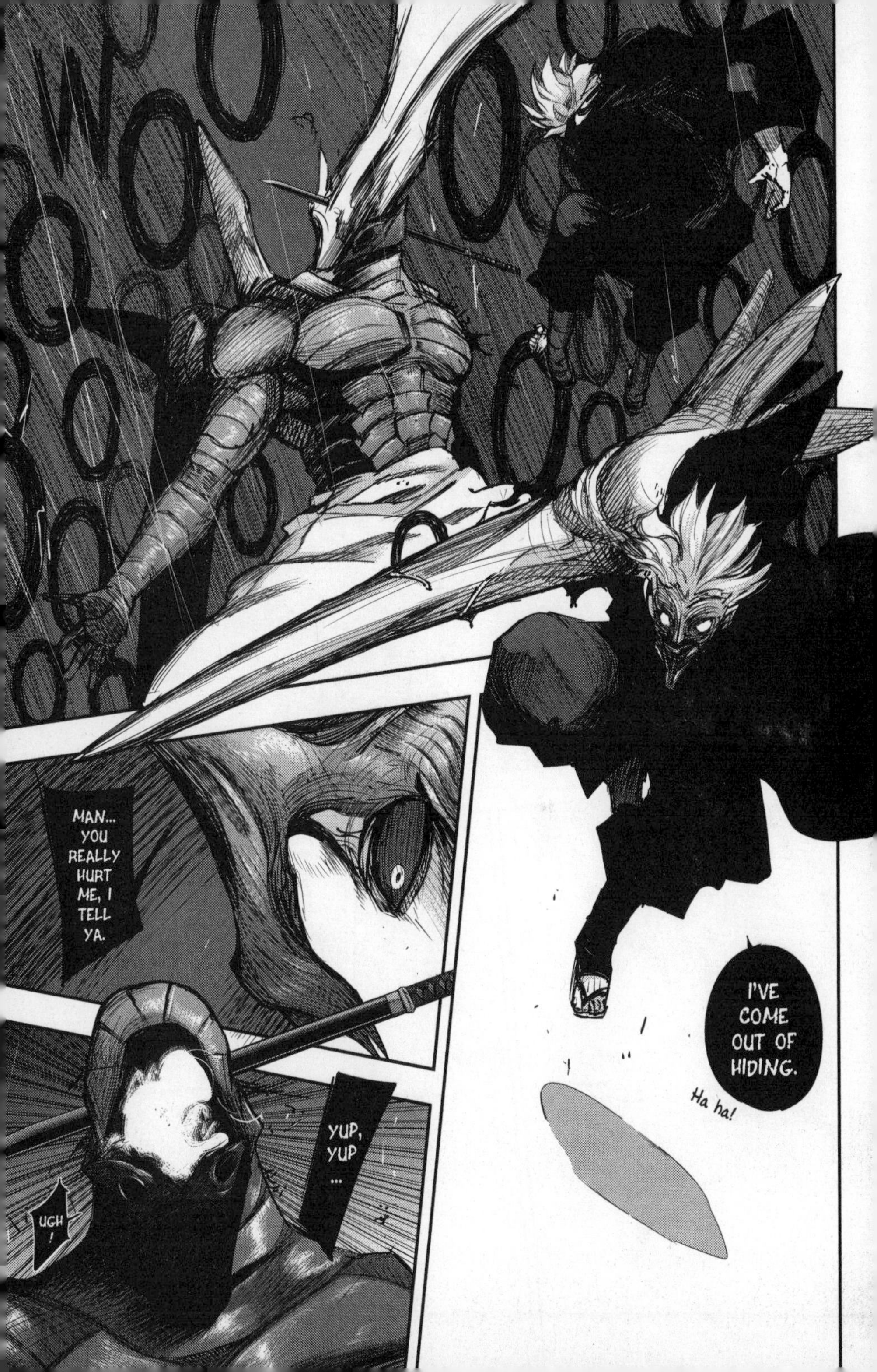
I'VE COME OUT OF HIDING.
Ha ha!
MAN... YOU REALLY HURT ME, I TELL YA.
YUP, YUP ...
UGH!

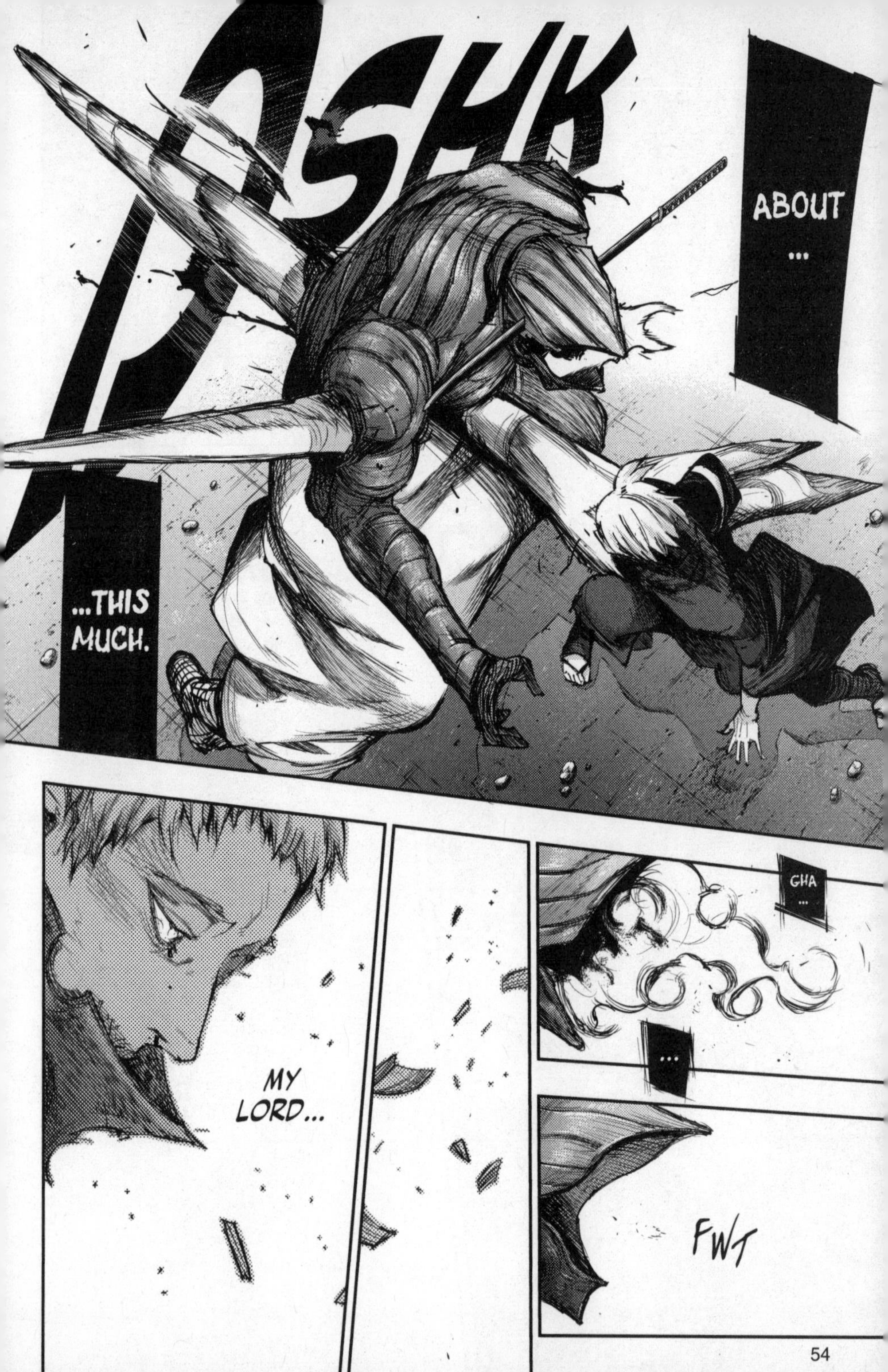
DASHK
ABOUT ...
...THIS MUCH.
GHA ...
...
FWT
MY LORD...

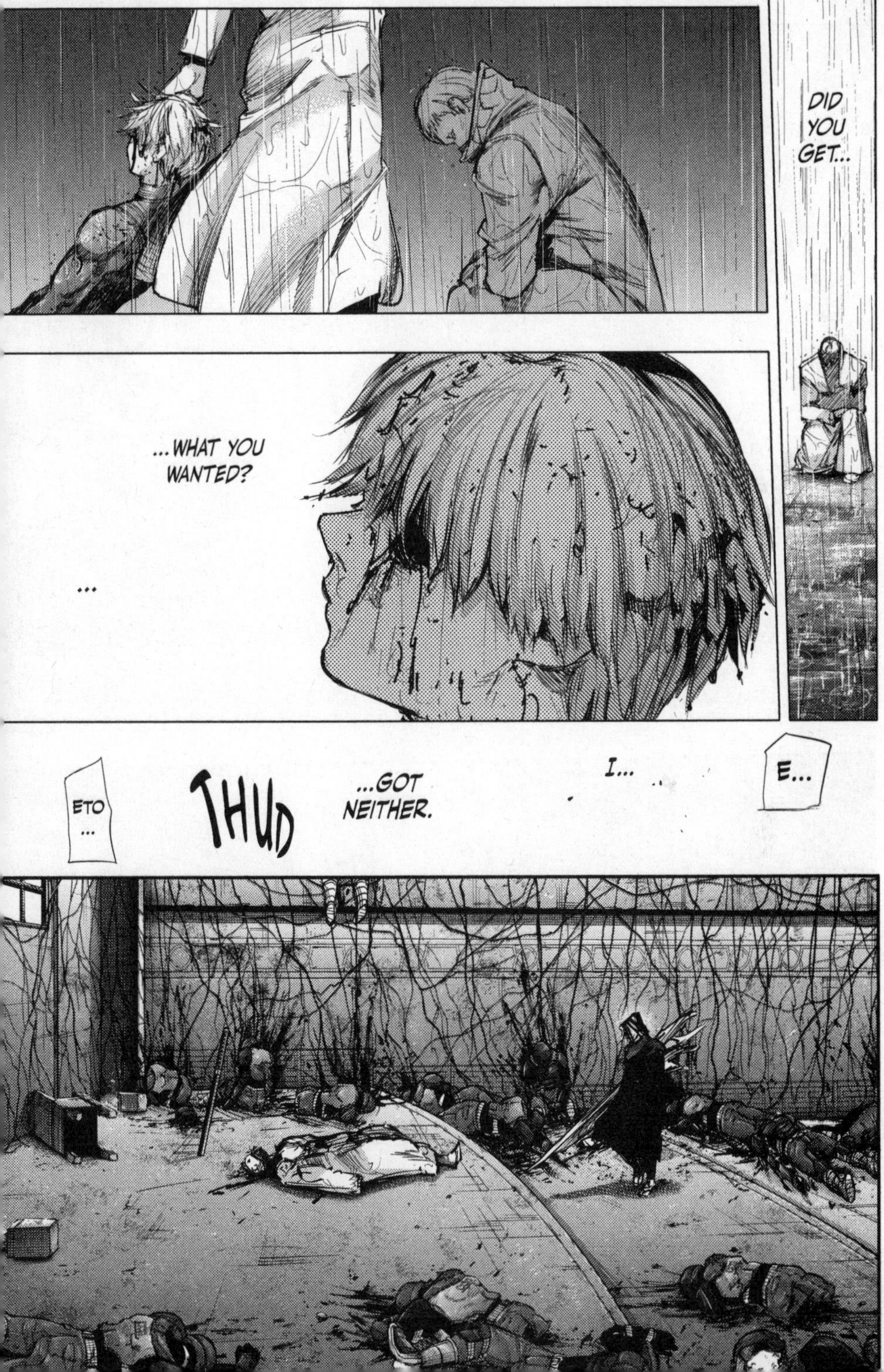
DID YOU GET...
...WHAT YOU WANTED?
...
E...
I...
...GOT NEITHER.
THUD
ETO ...

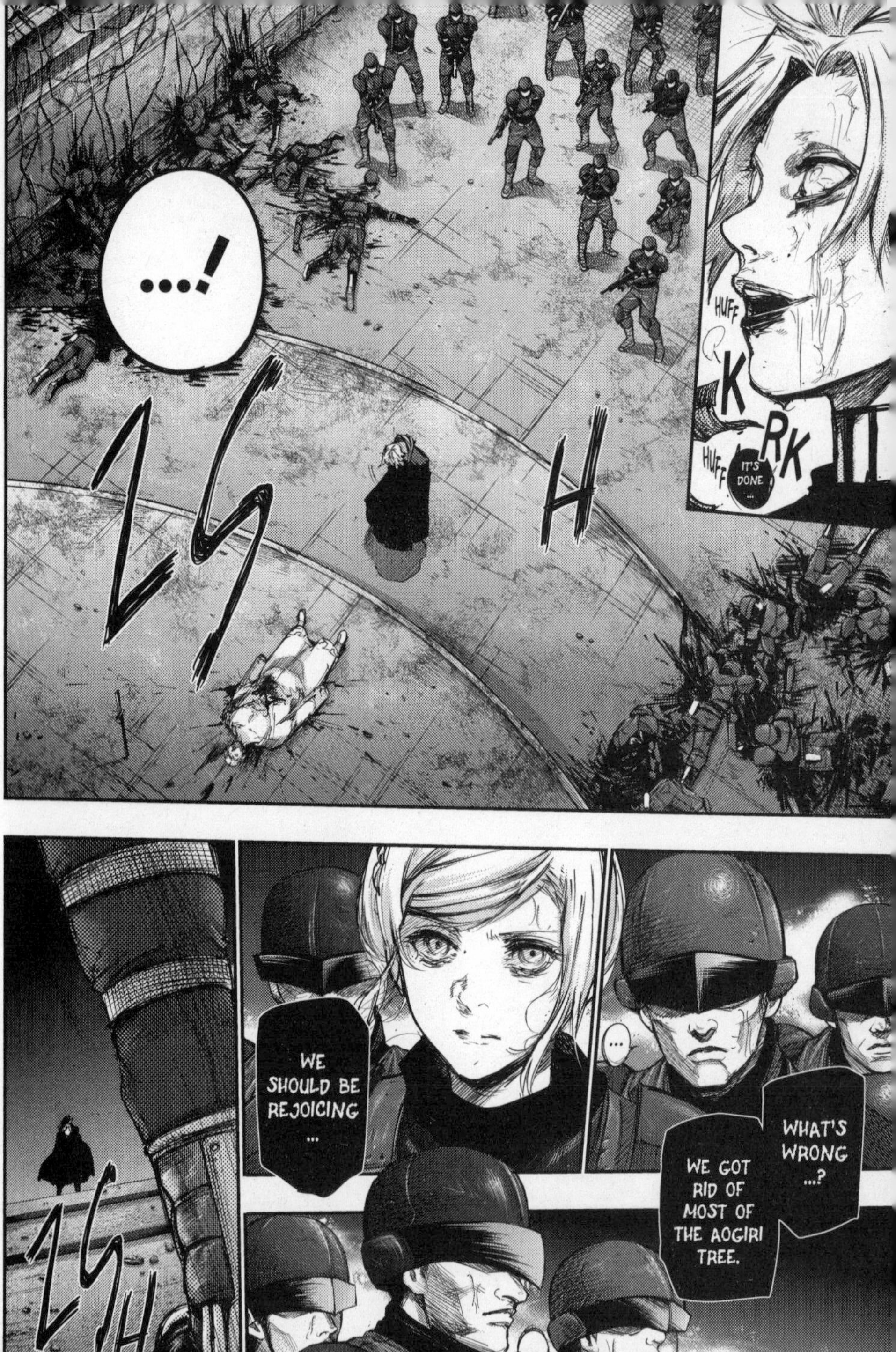
HUFF
KRK
HUFF
IT'S DONE ...
...!
ZGSH
...
WE SHOULD BE REJOICING ...
WHAT'S WRONG ...?
WE GOT RID OF MOST OF THE AOGIRI TREE.
...
ZGSH

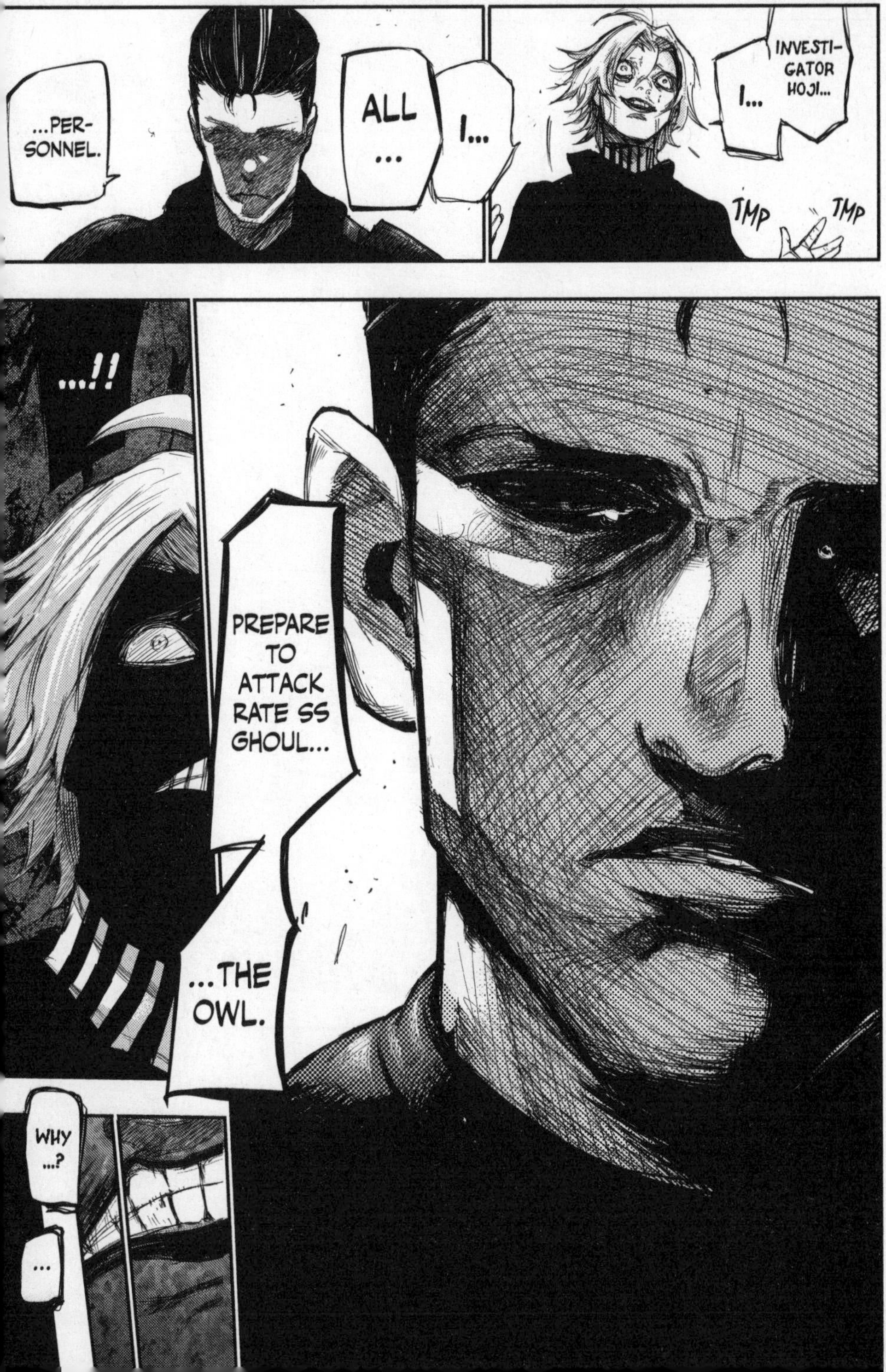
INVESTI-GATOR HOJI...
I...
TMP
TMP
I...
ALL ...
...PER-SONNEL.
PREPARE TO ATTACK RATE SS GHOUL...
...THE OWL.
...!!
WHY ...?
...

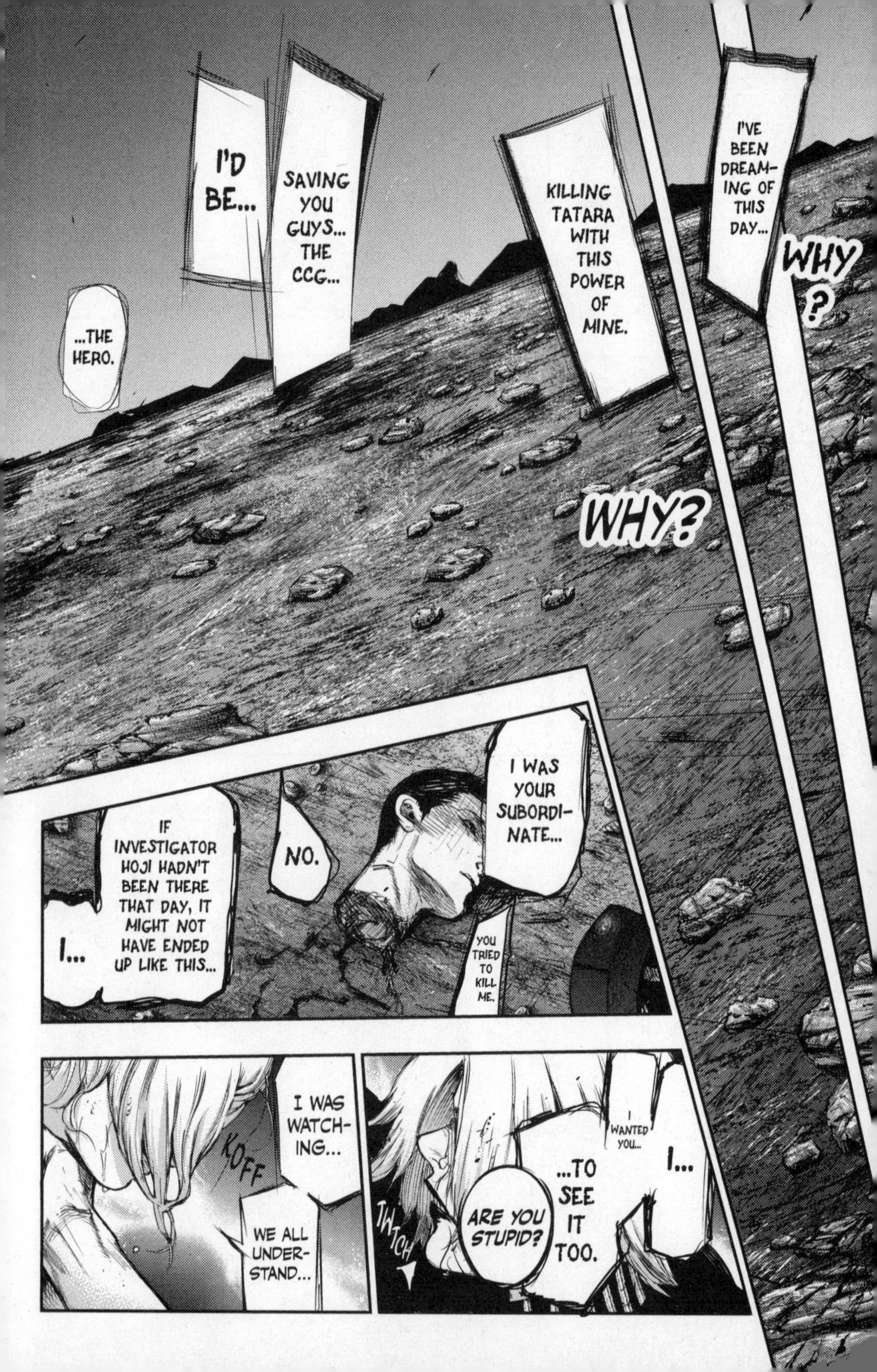
I'VE BEEN DREAM-ING OF THIS DAY...
WHY ?
KILLING TATARA WITH THIS POWER OF MINE.
SAVING YOU GUYS... THE CCG...
I'D BE...
...THE HERO.
WHY?
I WAS YOUR SUBORDI-NATE...
YOU TRIED TO KILL ME.
NO.
IF INVESTIGATOR HOJI HADN'T BEEN THERE THAT DAY, IT MIGHT NOT HAVE ENDED UP LIKE THIS...
I...
I...
I WANTED YOU...
...TO SEE IT TOO.
ARE YOU STUPID?
TWITCH
I WAS WATCH-ING...
KOFF
WE ALL UNDER-STAND...

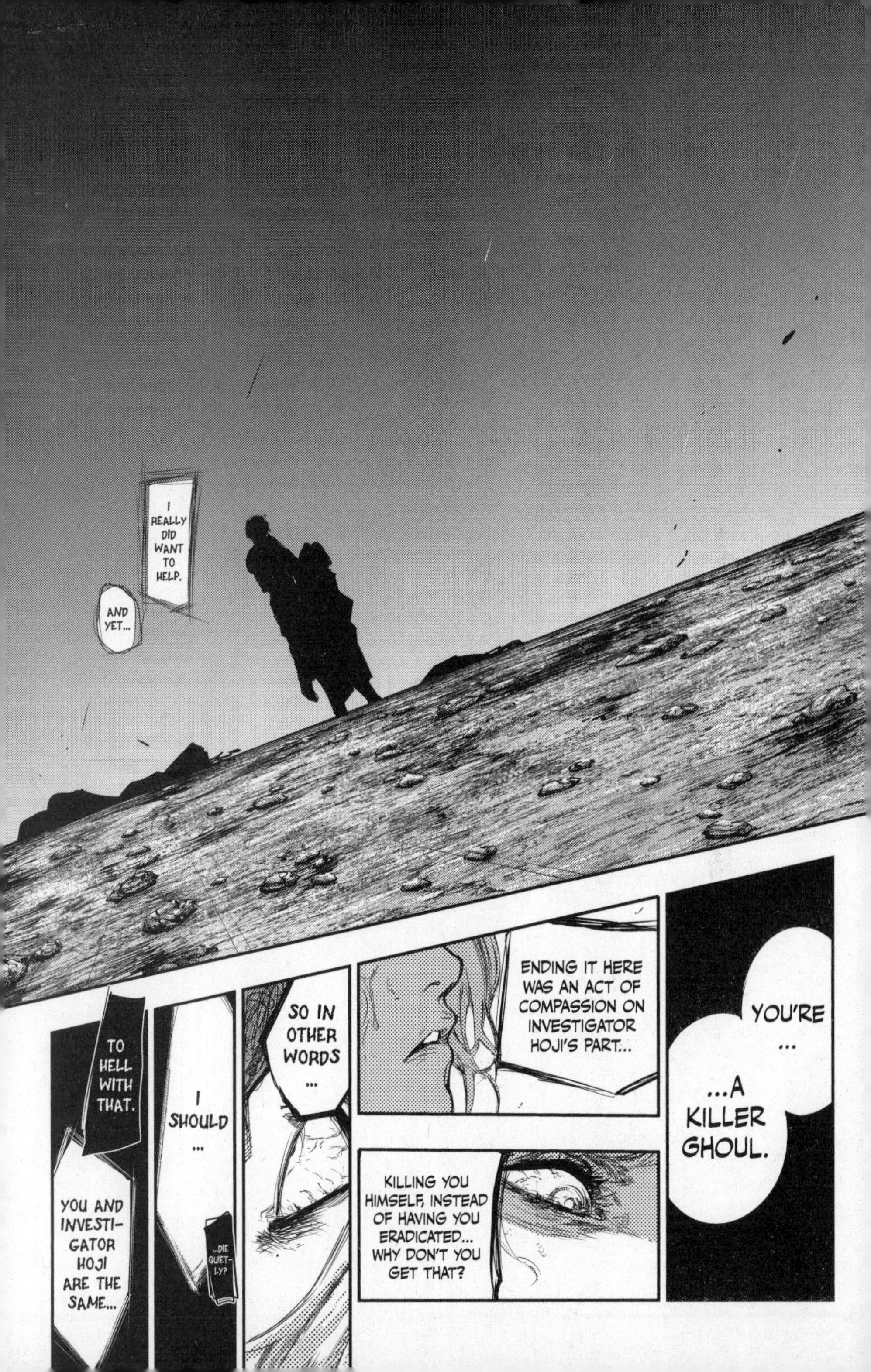

I REALLY DID WANT TO HELP.
AND YET...
YOU'RE ...
...A KILLER GHOUL.
ENDING IT HERE WAS AN ACT OF COMPASSION ON INVESTIGATOR HOJI'S PART...
KILLING YOU HIMSELF, INSTEAD OF HAVING YOU ERADICATED... WHY DON'T YOU GET THAT?
SO IN OTHER WORDS ...
I SHOULD ...
...DIE QUIETLY?
TO HELL WITH THAT.
YOU AND INVESTIGATOR HOJI ARE THE SAME...

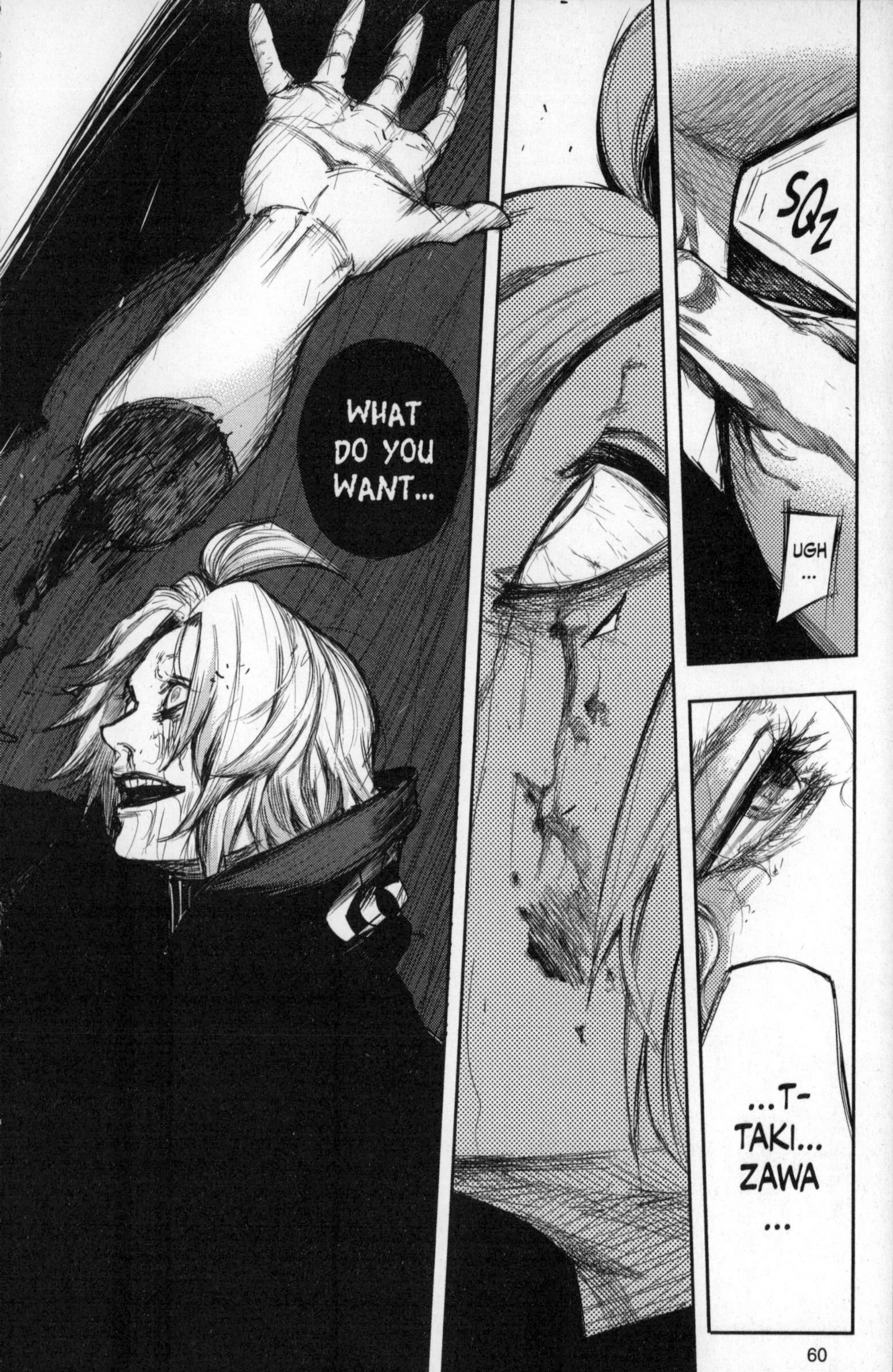
SQZ
UGH ...
...T-TAKI... ZAWA ...
WHAT DO YOU WANT...

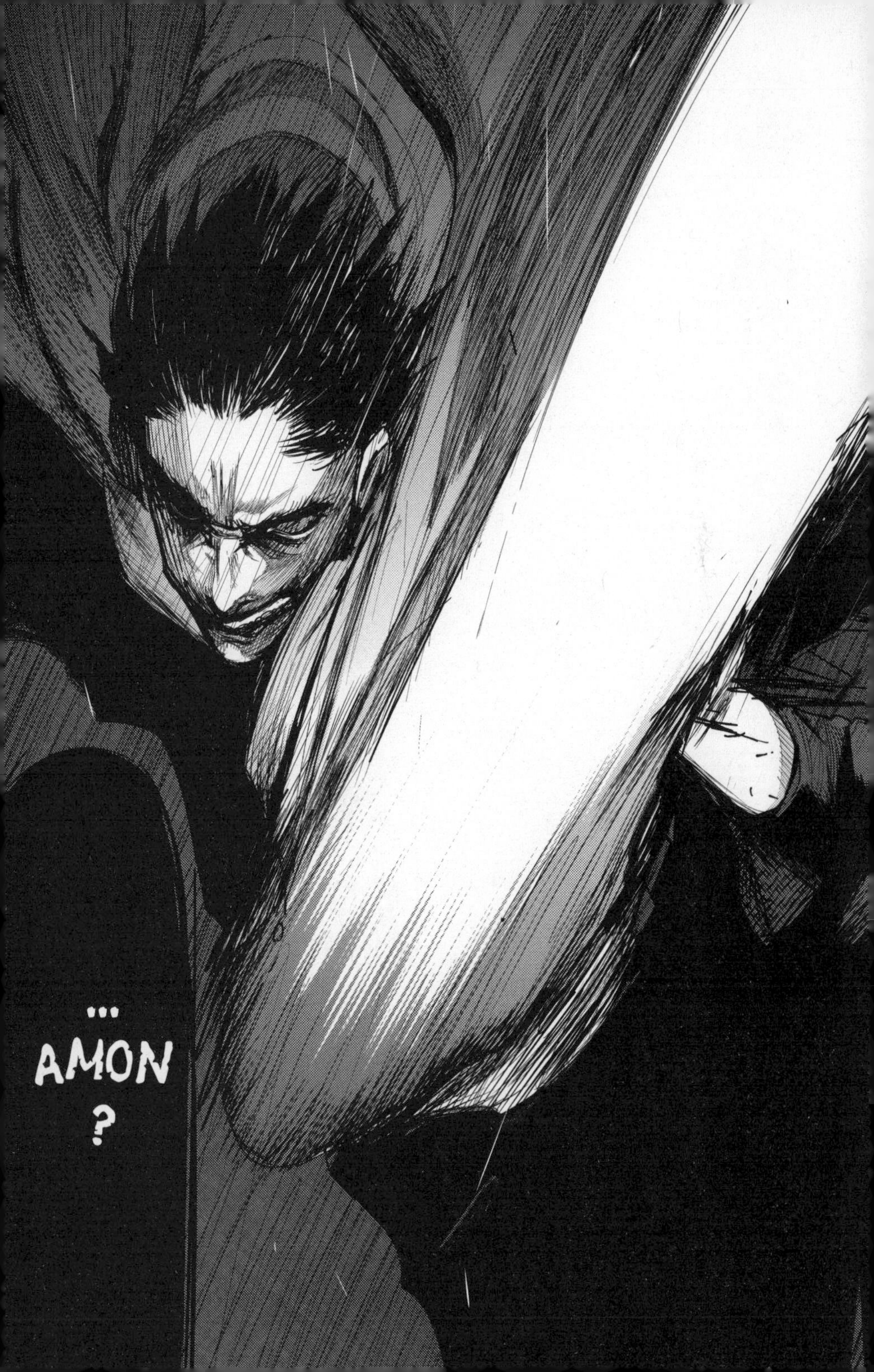
...AMON?

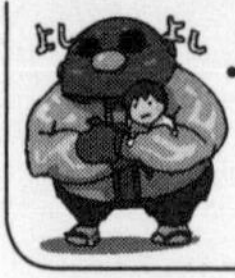
よしよし

"Good boy."

Taro

Huge.
I think he's three meters tall.

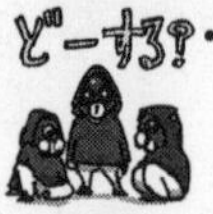
どーする?

"What d'you wanna do?"

Ichimi, Jiro, Sante

I'm sure you know, but Jiro's a woman.

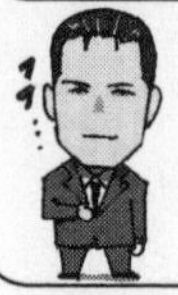

"Huu huu..."

Hoji

You see characters like this in the Gundam series...

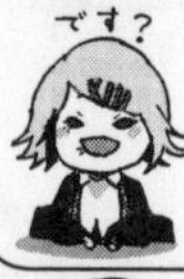
です?

"Yes?"

Juzo

The term "body stitching" didn't come up on internet searches before I used it in the story. I think *Tokyo Ghoul* was the first time it was ever used.

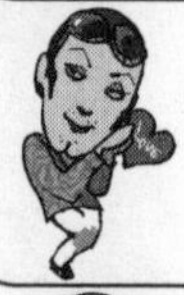

Nico

I like the three brothers in Crayon Shin-chan.

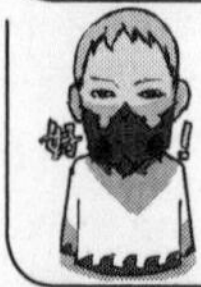

"I like...!"

Tatara

I think his hairline got higher.

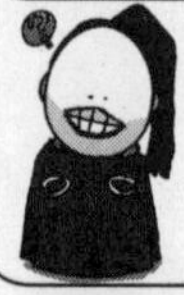

"?"

Noro

I knew there would be casualties in order to kill this character. That's why volume 5 ended up the way it did...

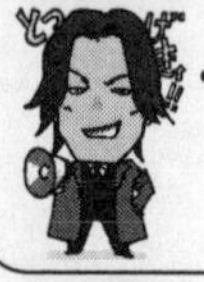

"Charge!"

Marude

I was into the Aibo series at the time. I think that influenced me.

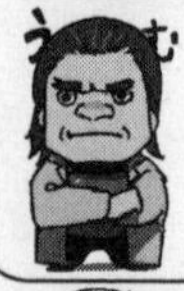

"Mmm."

Iwaccho

He can fall off a roof and be fine.

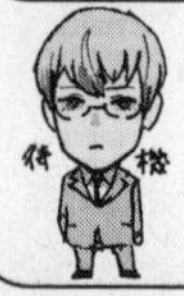

"Stand by."

Arima

His setting is "main character/ aftermath."

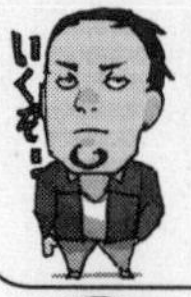
いくぞ!

"Let's go..."

Banjo

I call him Banjoi in my mind because of Tsukiyama.

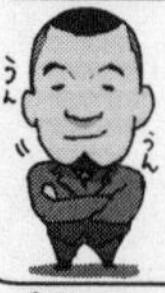
うん
うん

"Uh-huh, uh-huh."

Shinohara

An import character from a *Tokyo Ghoul* prototype. He was initially supposed to be Kaneki's nemesis, but it didn't turn out that way in the story.

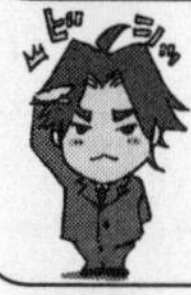

(Salute)

Takizawa

He was still in high spirits here. If he were a dog, he'd be a corgi.

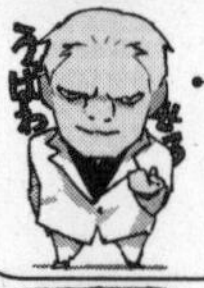

"Let me take it!"

Yamori

I think there was a character like him in *Crayon Shin-chan*.

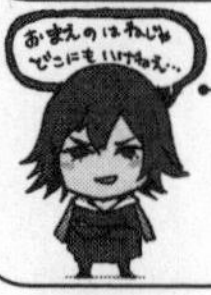

"You won't go anywhere with your wings."

Ayato

He looks like Touka, but it's easy to differentiate them when I draw them.

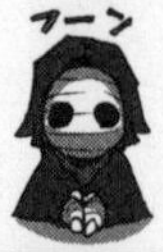
フーン

"Hmm."

Eto

Must get stuffy in there.

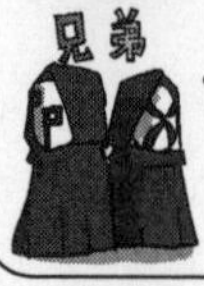
兄弟

(Brothers)

Bin Brothers

Why are they Bin again...? I think I had a reason...

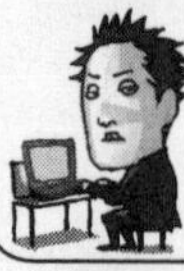

"I feel alive...!"

Mabuchi

I sometimes drool when I'm concentrating too.

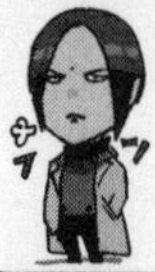

"Hmph."

Misato Gori

My illustrator friend created this character.

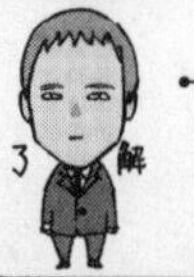

"Roger that!"

Take

Did he look like an eggplant when he first appeared?

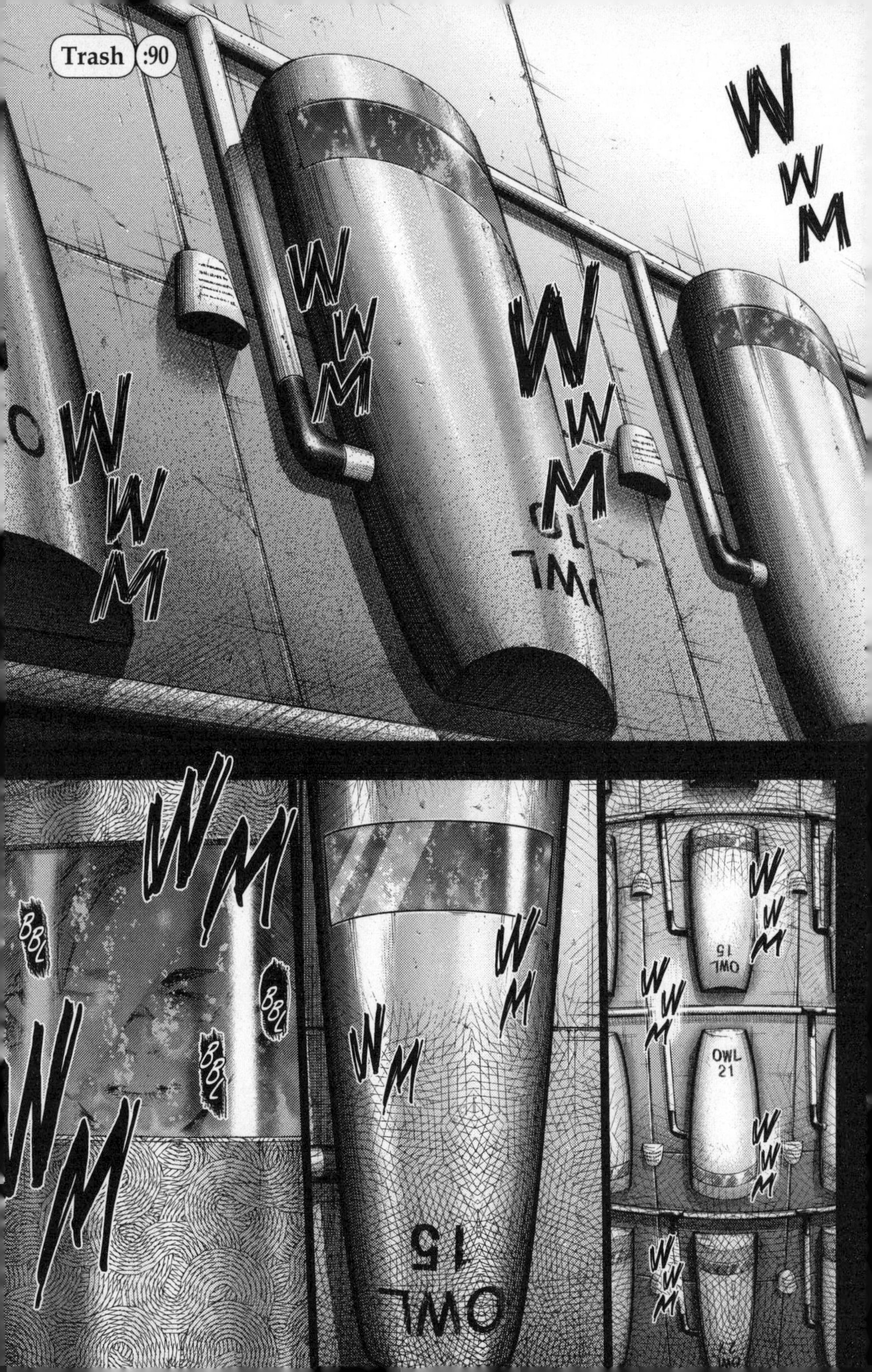
WWM
WWM
WWM
WWM
WWM
OWL 21
WWM
WWM
WWM
WWM
WWM
WWM
BBL
BBL
BBL

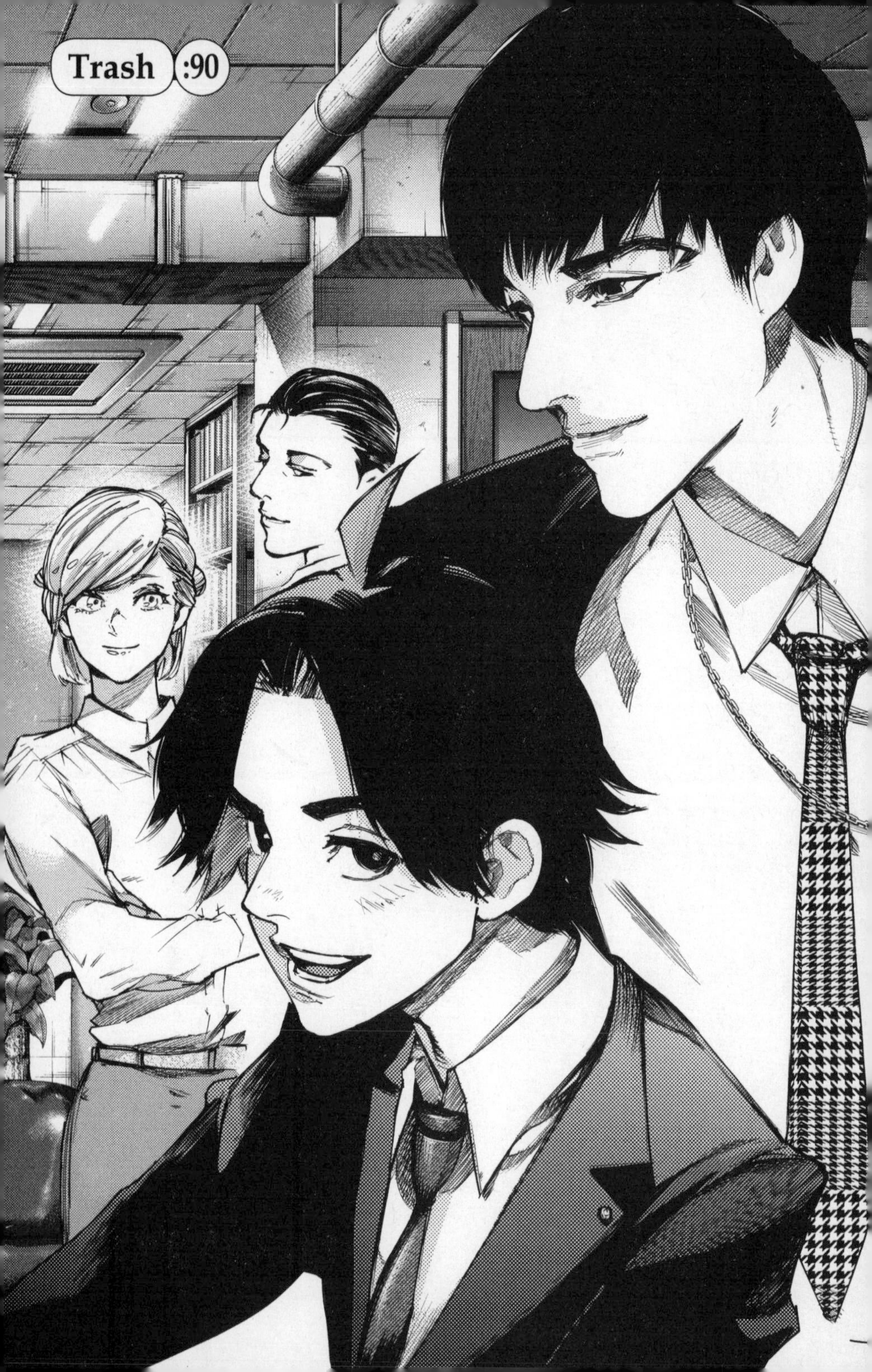
Trash :90

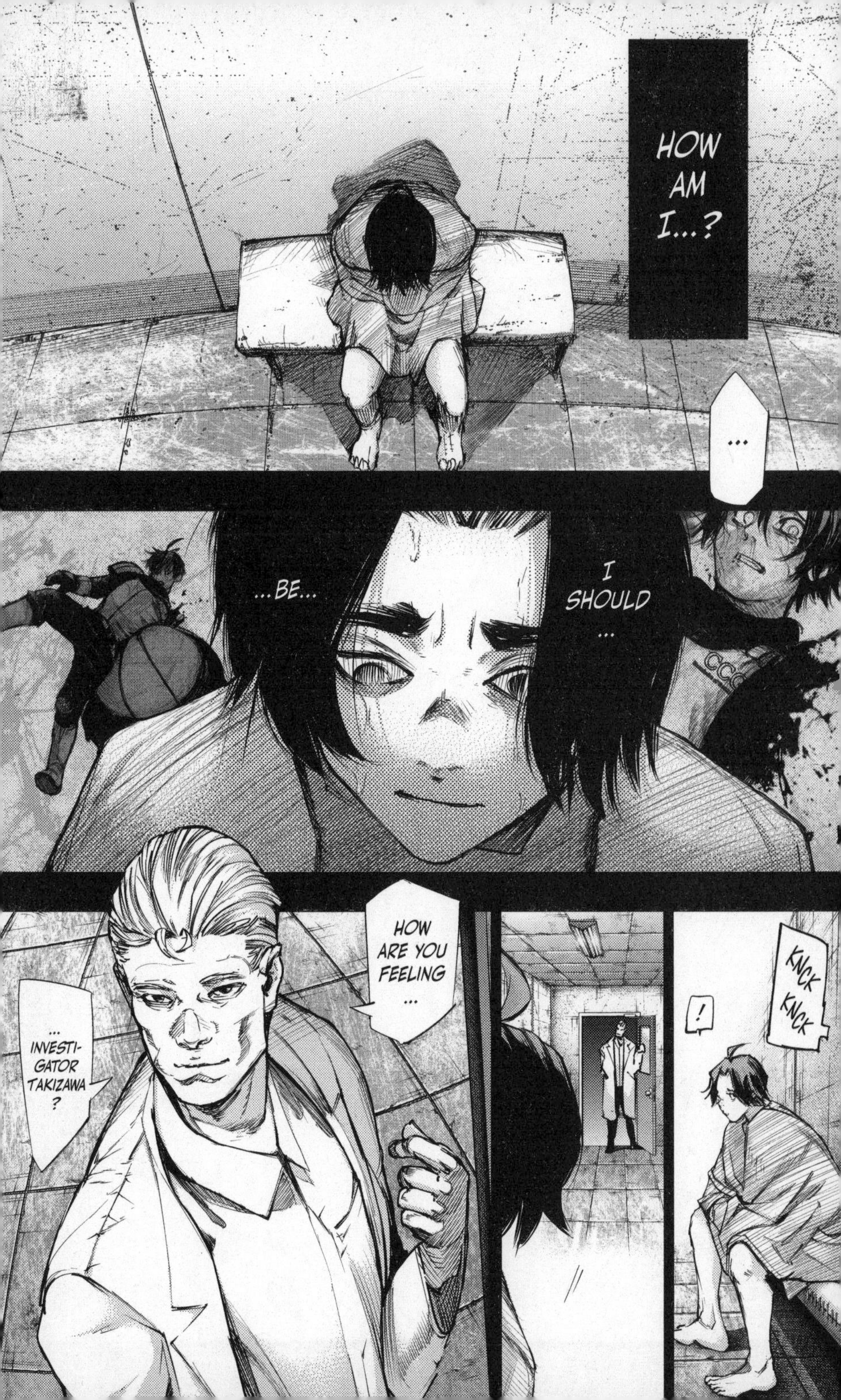
HOW AM I...?
...
I SHOULD ...
...BE...
KNCK KNCK
!
HOW ARE YOU FEELING ...
... INVESTI-GATOR TAKIZAWA ?

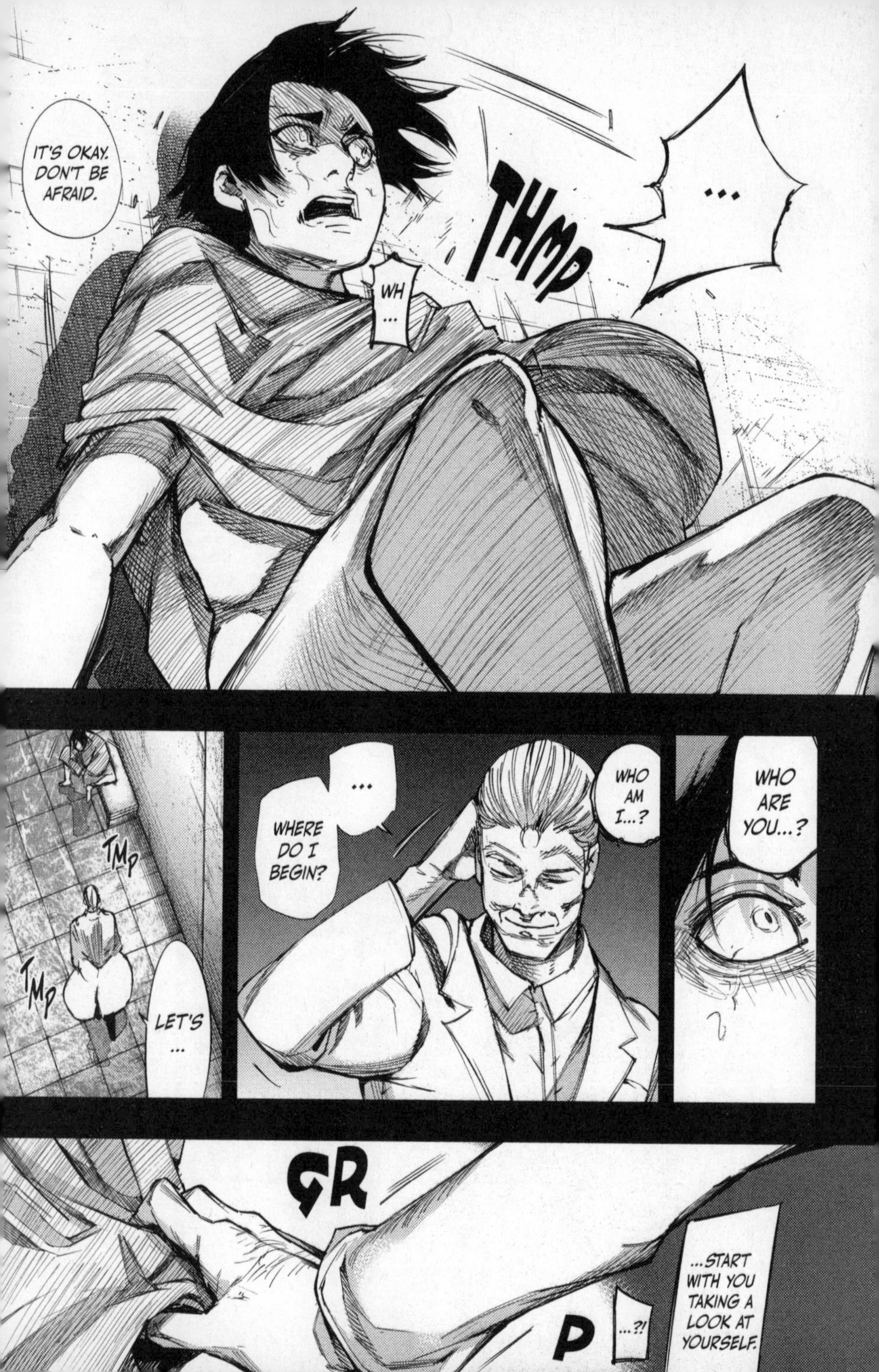
...
THMP
WH ...
IT'S OKAY. DON'T BE AFRAID.
WHO ARE YOU...?
WHO AM I...?
... WHERE DO I BEGIN?
TMP
TMP
LET'S ...
...START WITH YOU TAKING A LOOK AT YOURSELF.
...?!
P
GR

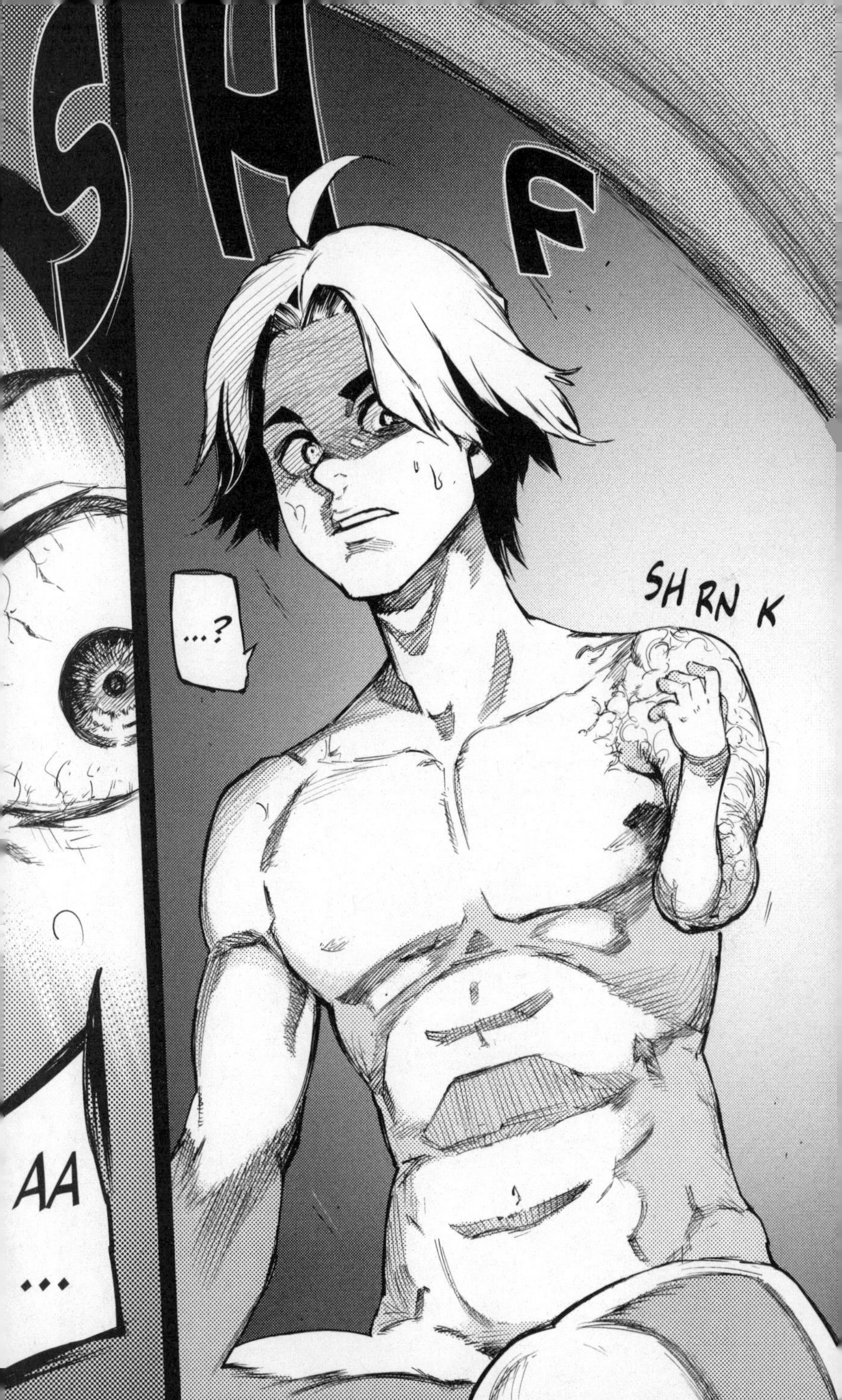
SHF
...?
SHRNK
AA
...

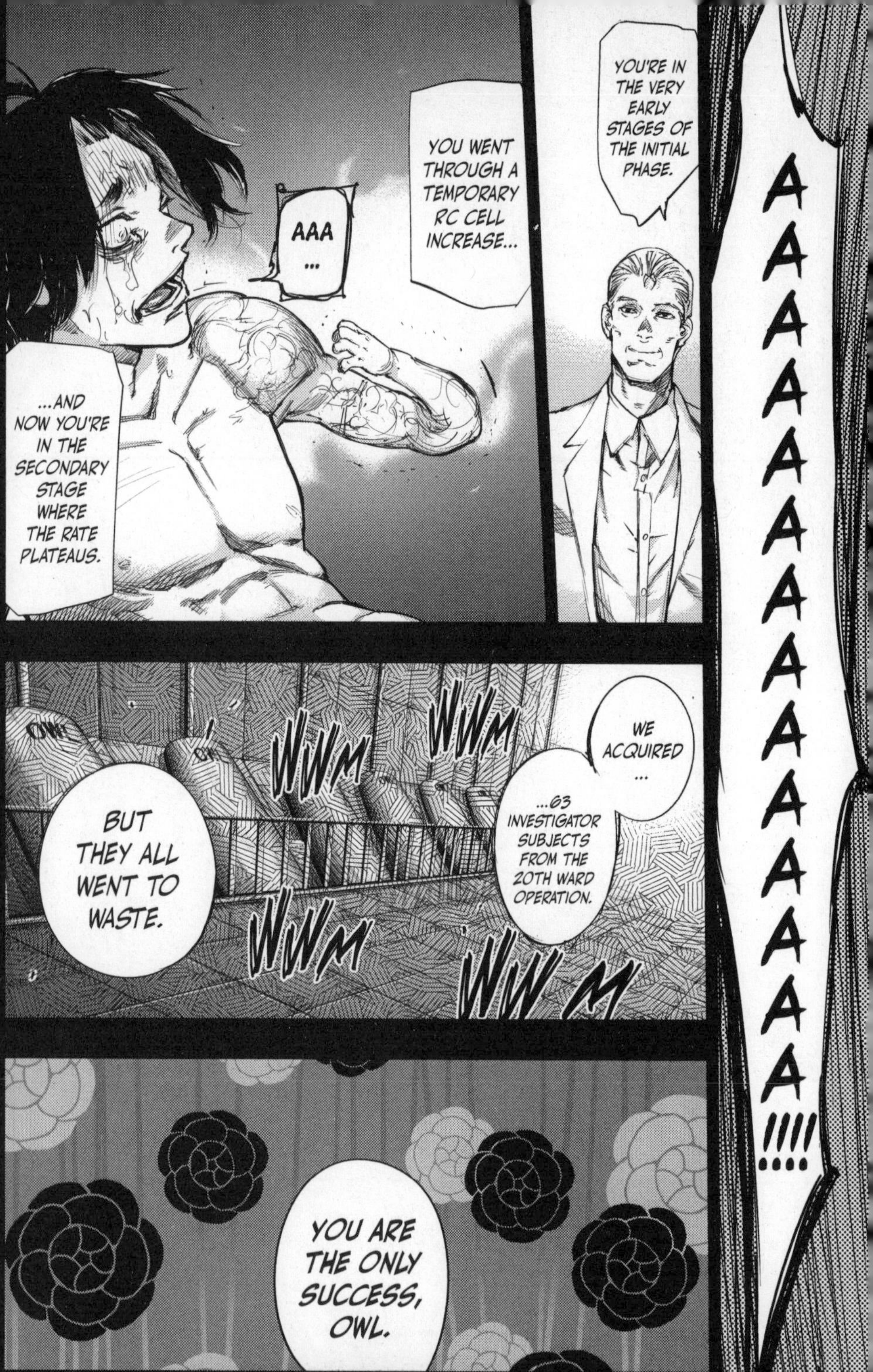
AAAAAAAAAAAAAAAA!!!!
YOU'RE IN THE VERY EARLY STAGES OF THE INITIAL PHASE.
YOU WENT THROUGH A TEMPORARY RC CELL INCREASE...
AAA ...
...AND NOW YOU'RE IN THE SECONDARY STAGE WHERE THE RATE PLATEAUS.
WE ACQUIRED ...
...63 INVESTIGATOR SUBJECTS FROM THE 20TH WARD OPERATION.
WWM
WWM
BUT THEY ALL WENT TO WASTE.
WWM
WWM
YOU ARE THE ONLY SUCCESS, OWL.

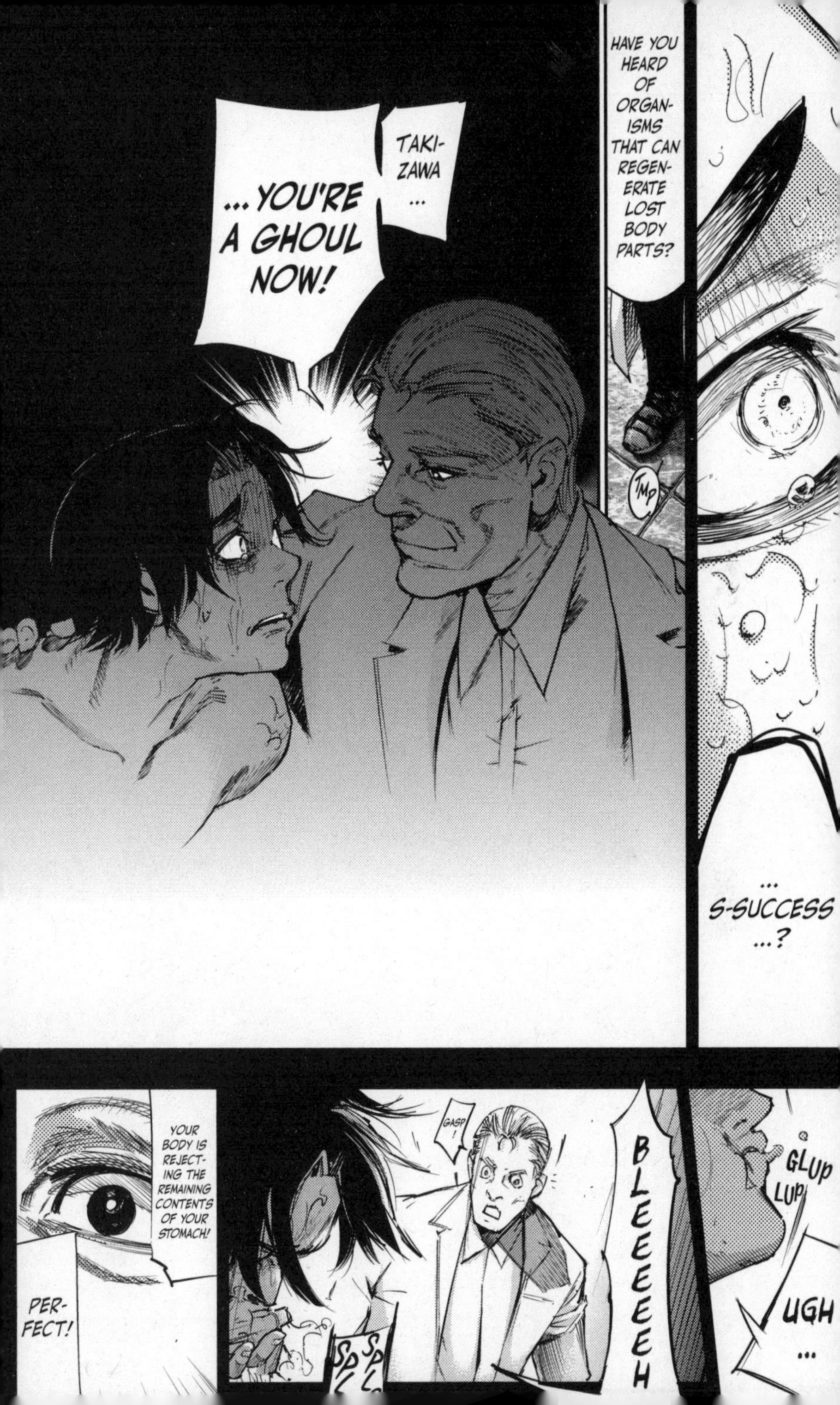
... S-SUCCESS ...?
HAVE YOU HEARD OF ORGAN-ISMS THAT CAN REGEN-ERATE LOST BODY PARTS?
TMP
TAKI-ZAWA ...
...YOU'RE A GHOUL NOW!
GLUP LUP
UGH ...
BLEEEEEEH
GASP!
SPL SPL
YOUR BODY IS REJECT-ING THE REMAINING CONTENTS OF YOUR STOMACH!
PER-FECT!

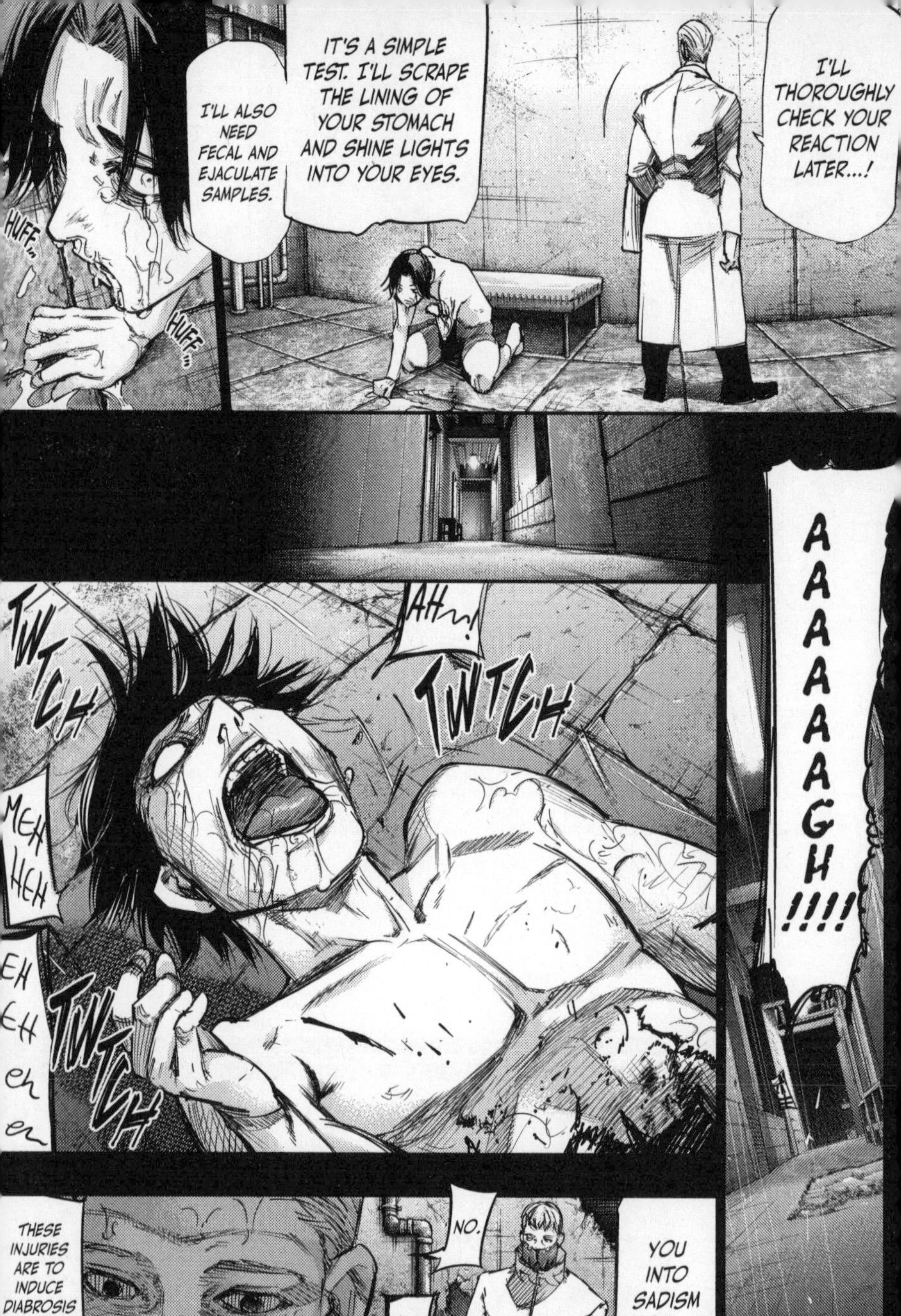
I'LL THOROUGHLY CHECK YOUR REACTION LATER...!
IT'S A SIMPLE TEST. I'LL SCRAPE THE LINING OF YOUR STOMACH AND SHINE LIGHTS INTO YOUR EYES.
I'LL ALSO NEED FECAL AND EJACULATE SAMPLES.
HUFF...
HUFF...
AAAAAAAAGH!!!!
AH~!
TWITCH
TWITCH
MEH HEH HEH
EH EH eh eh
TWITCH
YOU INTO SADISM TOO...?
NO.
Ugh...
CRK
CRK
THESE INJURIES ARE TO INDUCE DIABROSIS OF THE RC CELL VESSELS...

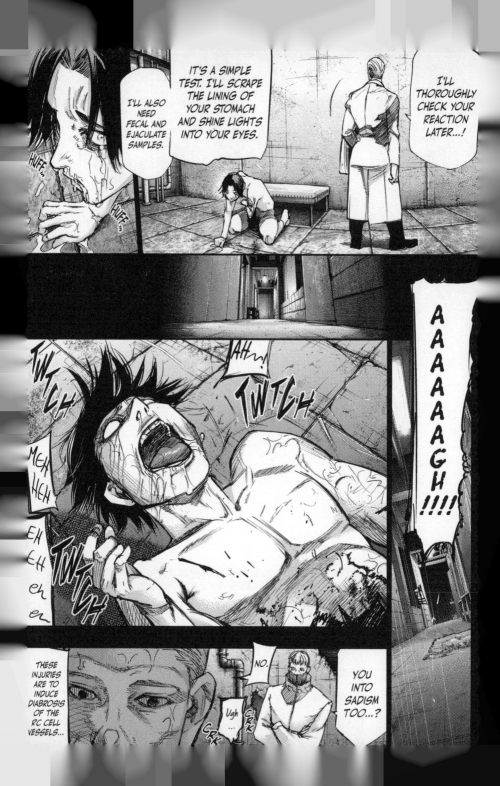

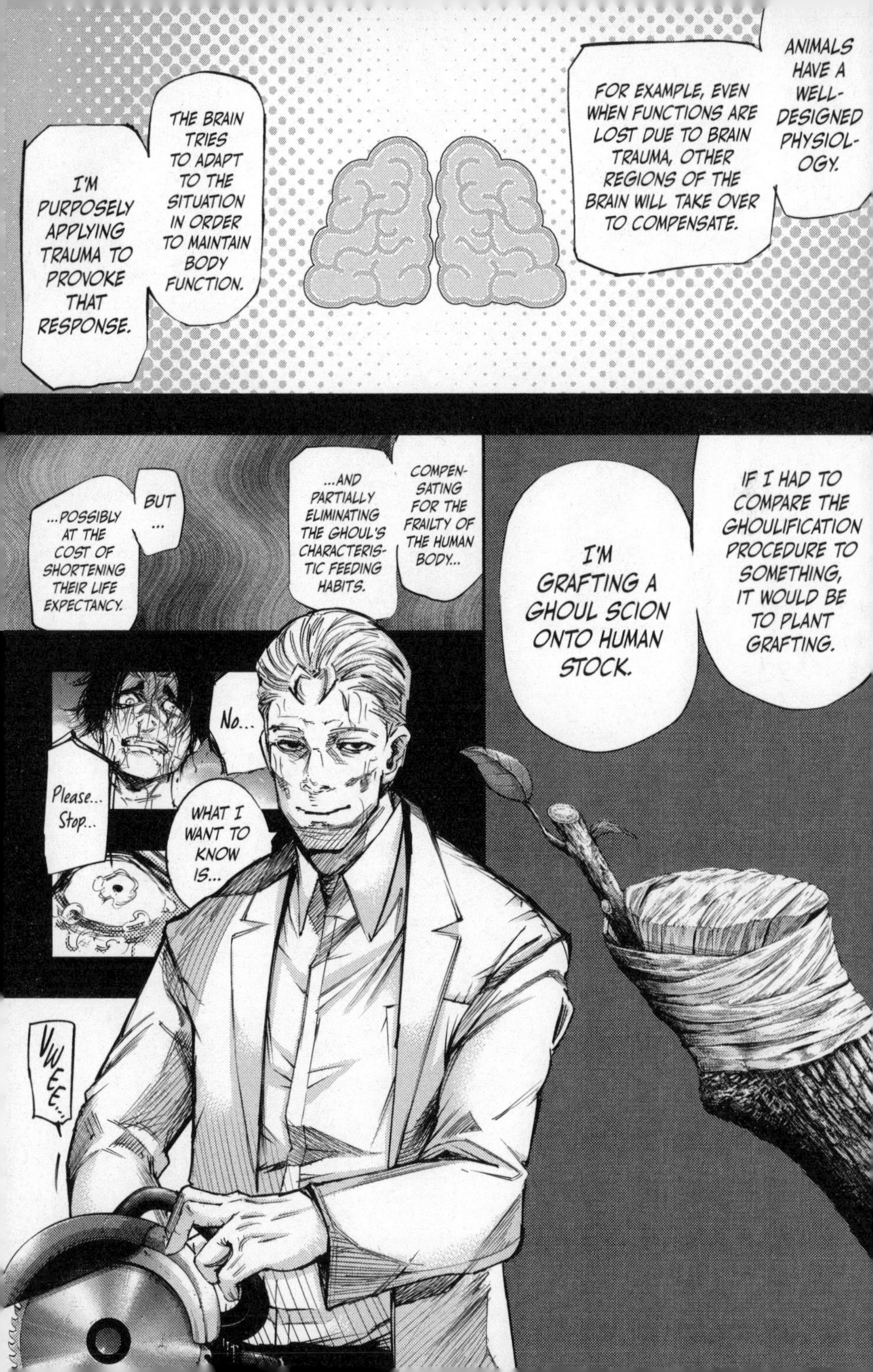
ANIMALS HAVE A WELL-DESIGNED PHYSIOLOGY.
FOR EXAMPLE, EVEN WHEN FUNCTIONS ARE LOST DUE TO BRAIN TRAUMA, OTHER REGIONS OF THE BRAIN WILL TAKE OVER TO COMPENSATE.
THE BRAIN TRIES TO ADAPT TO THE SITUATION IN ORDER TO MAINTAIN BODY FUNCTION.
I'M PURPOSELY APPLYING TRAUMA TO PROVOKE THAT RESPONSE.
IF I HAD TO COMPARE THE GHOULIFICATION PROCEDURE TO SOMETHING, IT WOULD BE TO PLANT GRAFTING.
I'M GRAFTING A GHOUL SCION ONTO HUMAN STOCK.
COMPENSATING FOR THE FRAILTY OF THE HUMAN BODY...
...AND PARTIALLY ELIMINATING THE GHOUL'S CHARACTERISTIC FEEDING HABITS.
BUT...
...POSSIBLY AT THE COST OF SHORTENING THEIR LIFE EXPECTANCY.
No...
Please... Stop...
WHAT I WANT TO KNOW IS...
VWEEE...

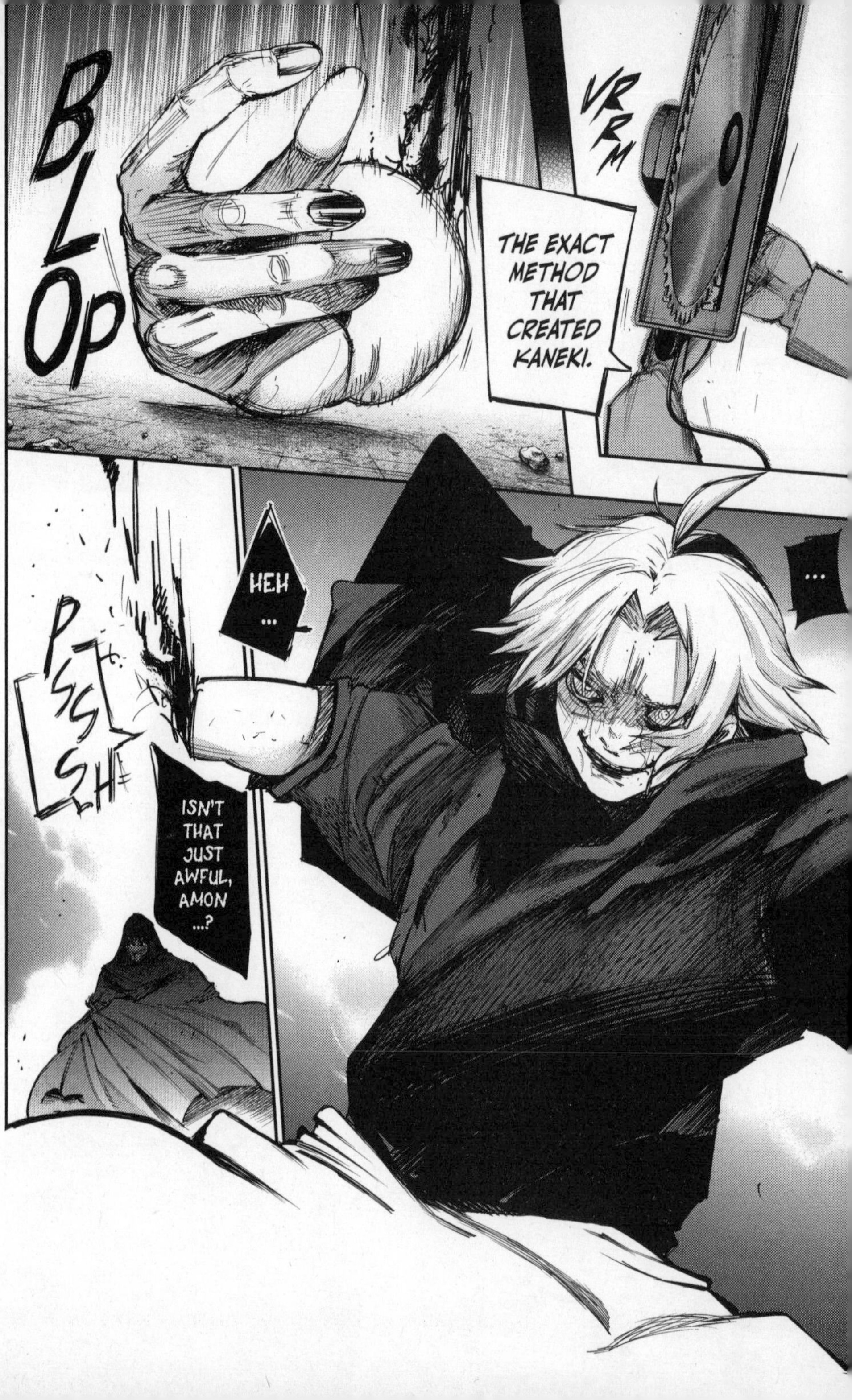
VRRM
THE EXACT METHOD THAT CREATED KANEKI.
BLOP
...
HEH ...
PSSSH
ISN'T THAT JUST AWFUL, AMON ...?

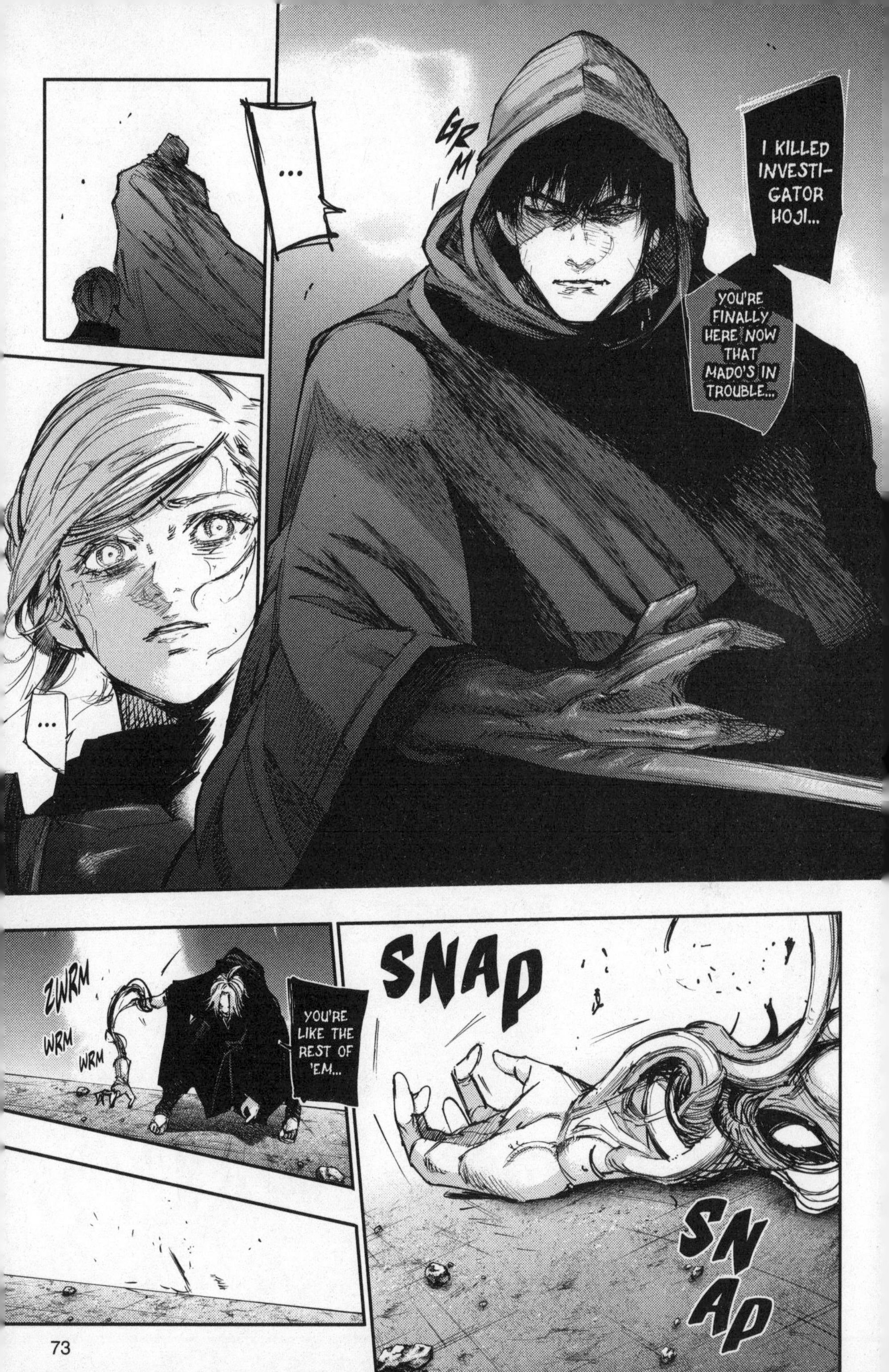
GRM
I KILLED INVESTI-GATOR HOJI...
YOU'RE FINALLY HERE NOW THAT MADO'S IN TROUBLE...
...
...
SNAP
SNAP
ZWRM
WRM
WRM
YOU'RE LIKE THE REST OF 'EM...

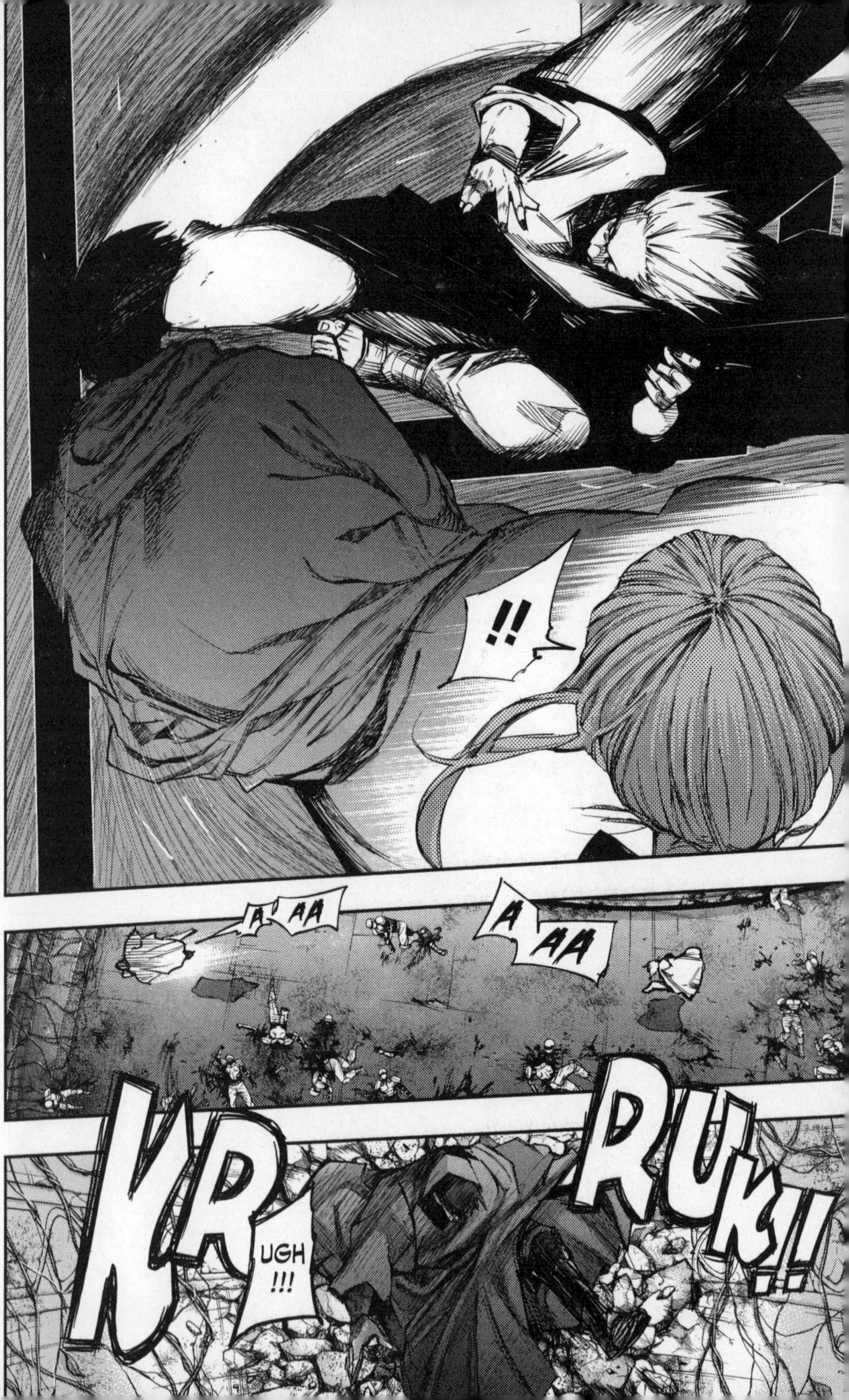
!!
A AA
A AA
KRRUK!!
UGH !!!

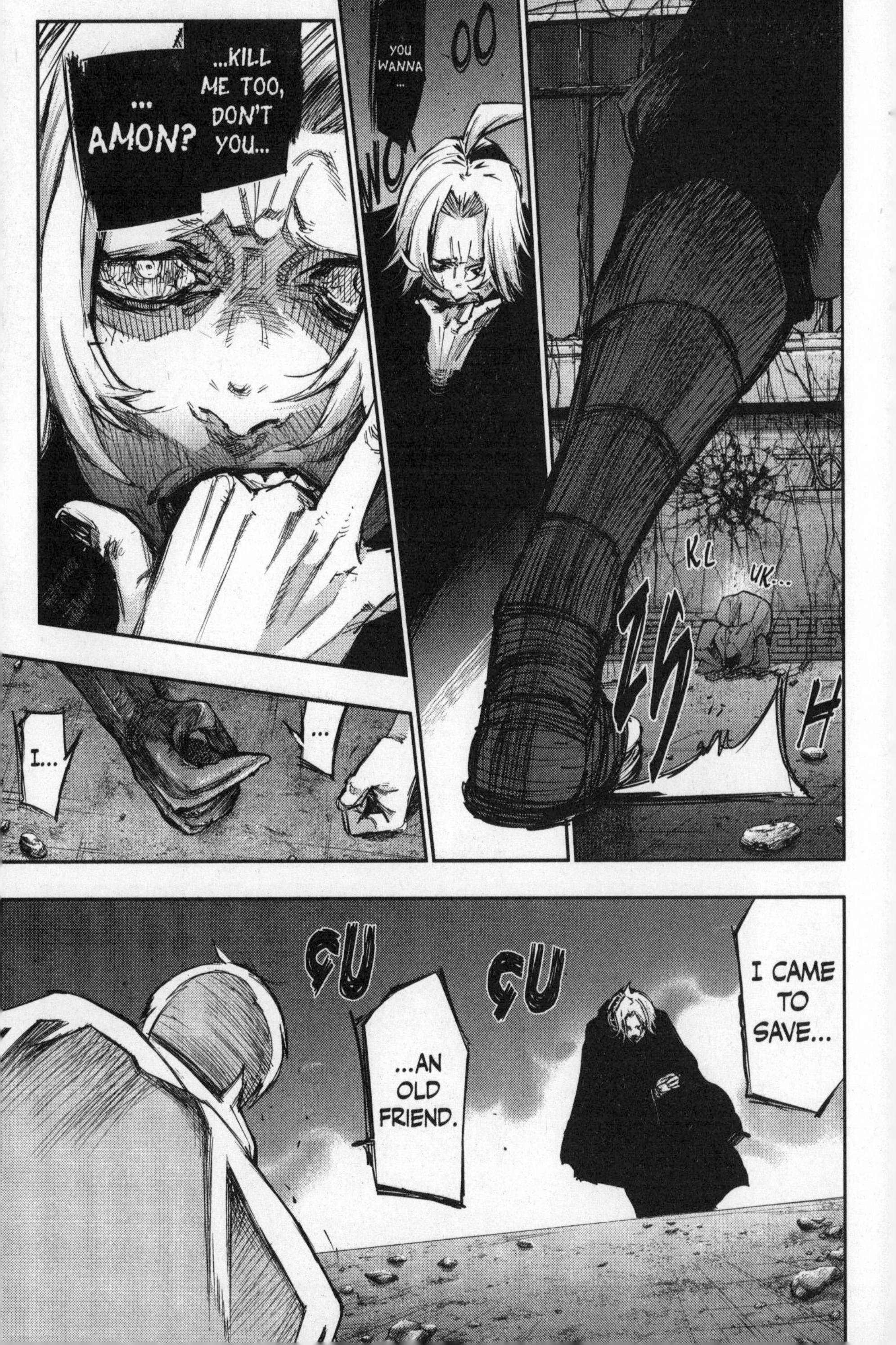
KL
UK...
ZSH
H
OO
WO
YOU WANNA ...
...KILL ME TOO, DON'T YOU...
... AMON?
...
I...
I CAME TO SAVE...
GU
GU
...AN OLD FRIEND.

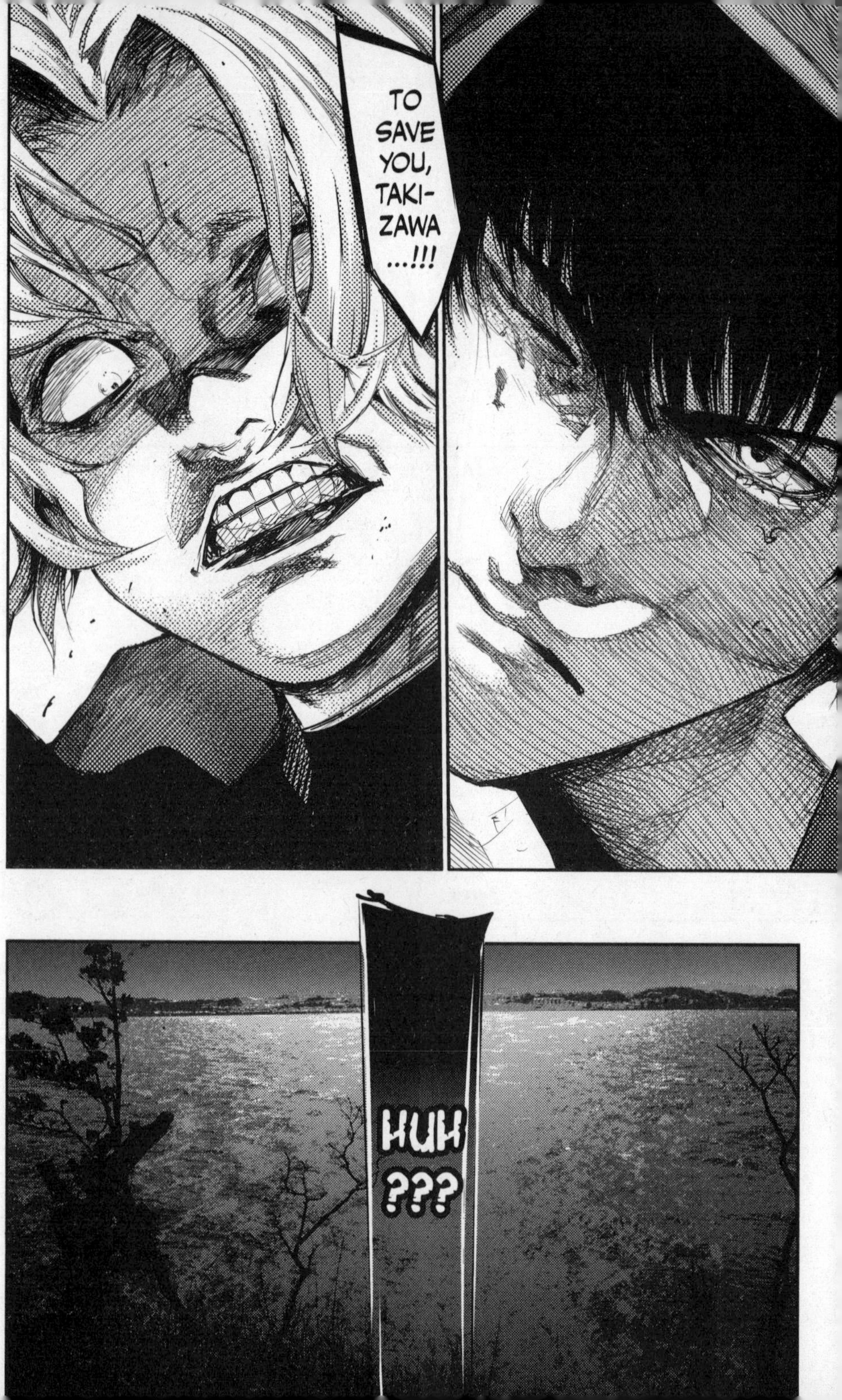
TO SAVE YOU, TAKI-ZAWA ...!!!
HUH ???

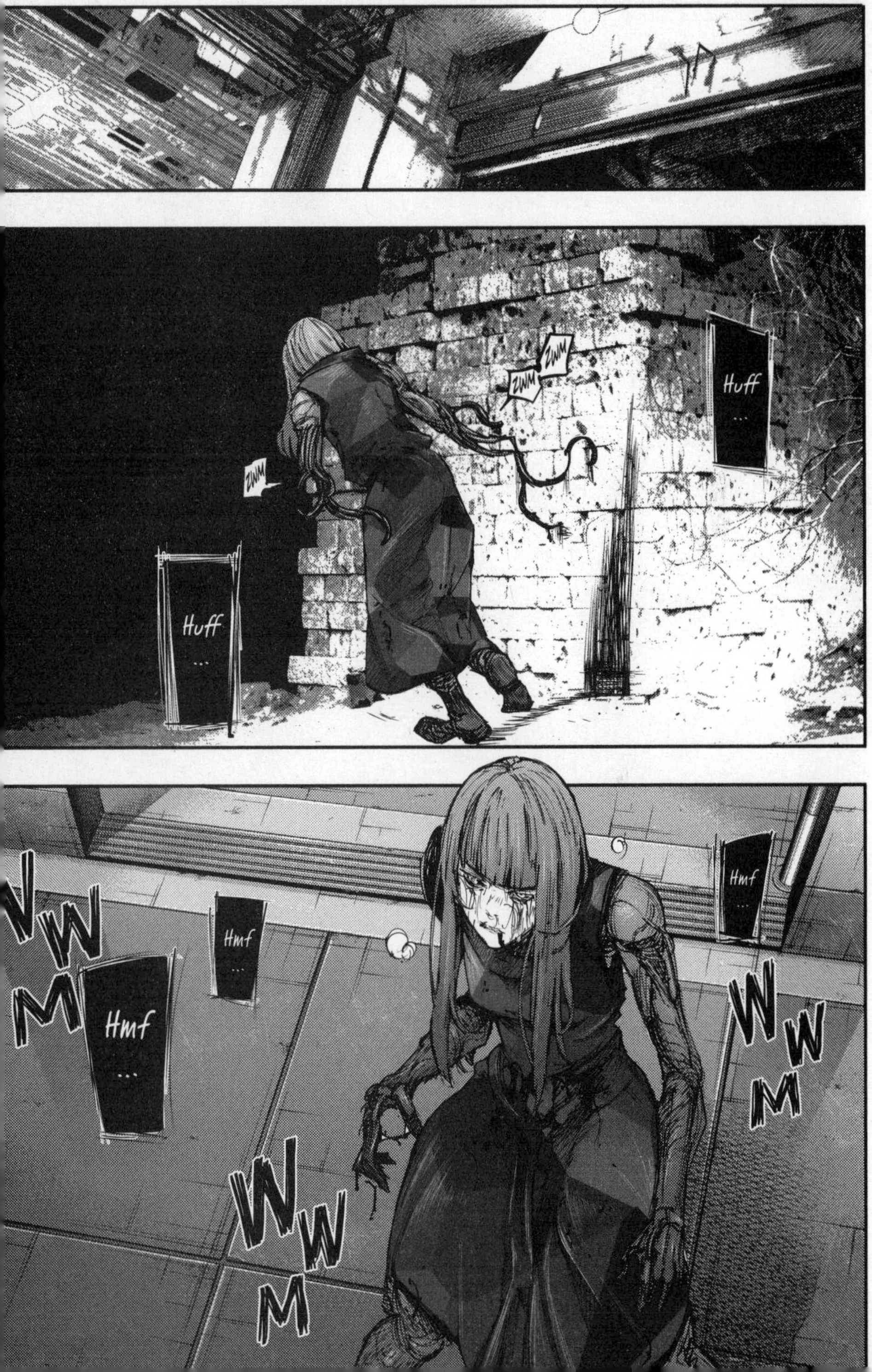
Huff
...
ZWM
ZWM
ZWM
Huff
...
Hmf
...
WWM
Hmf
...
WWM
Hmf
...
WWM

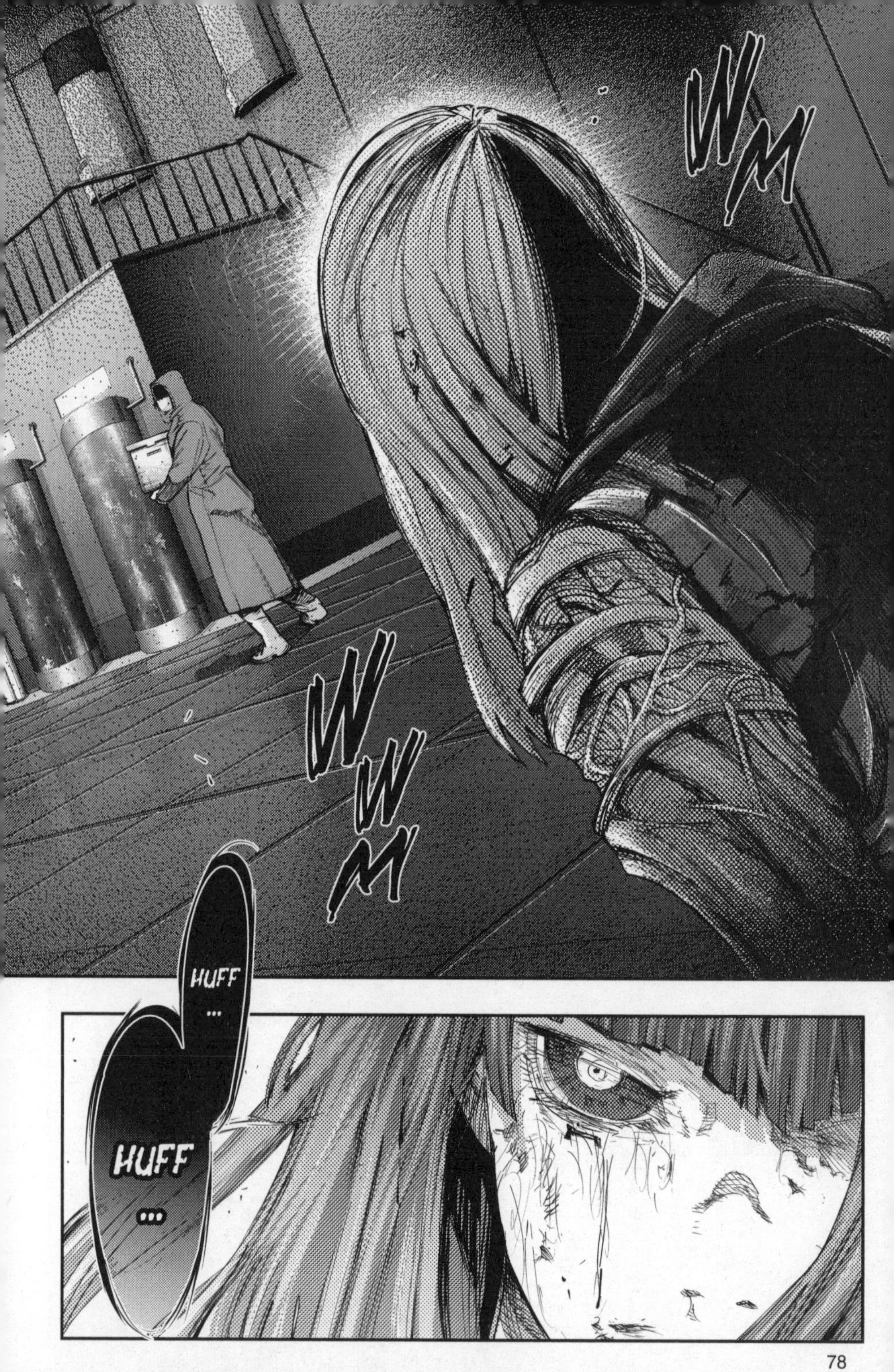
WM
WWWM
HUFF...
HUFF...

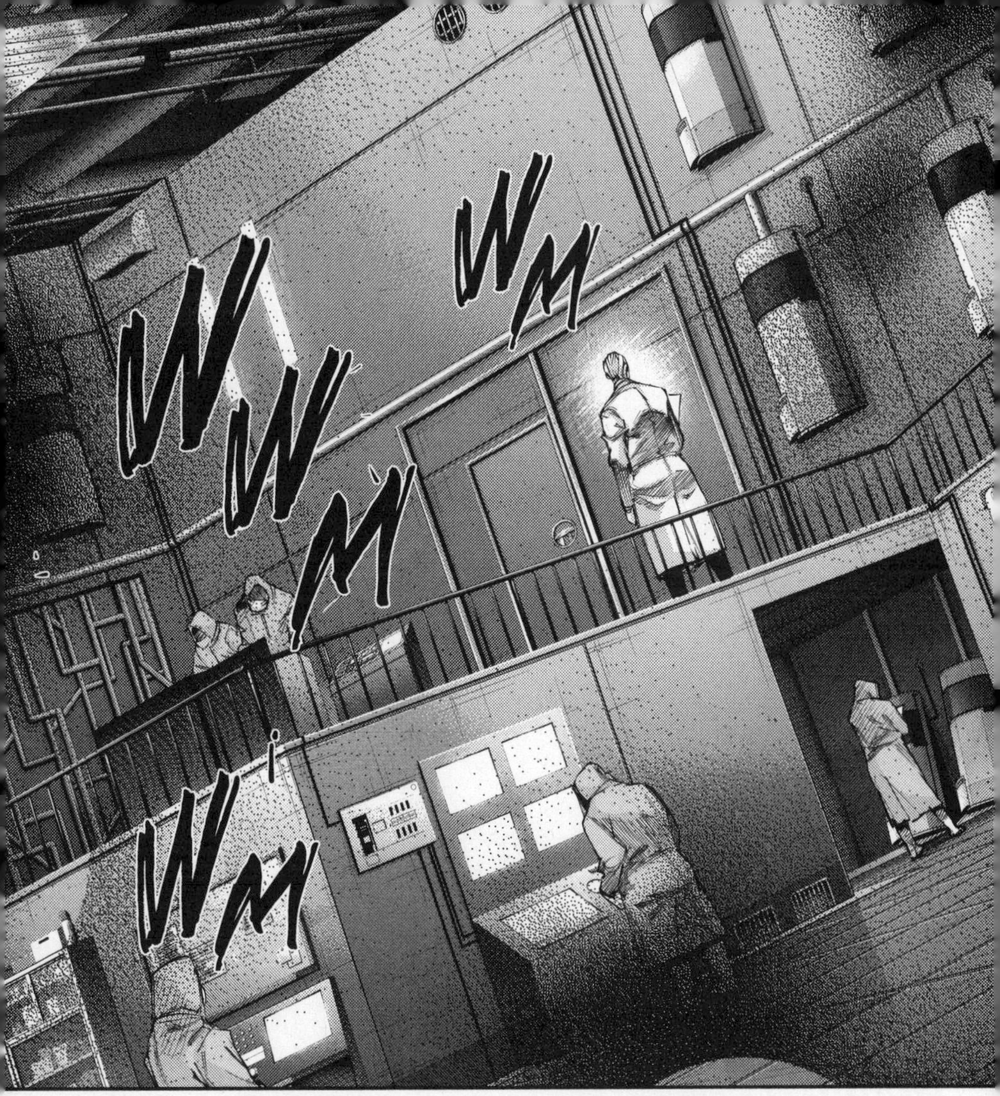
WWM
WM
WM
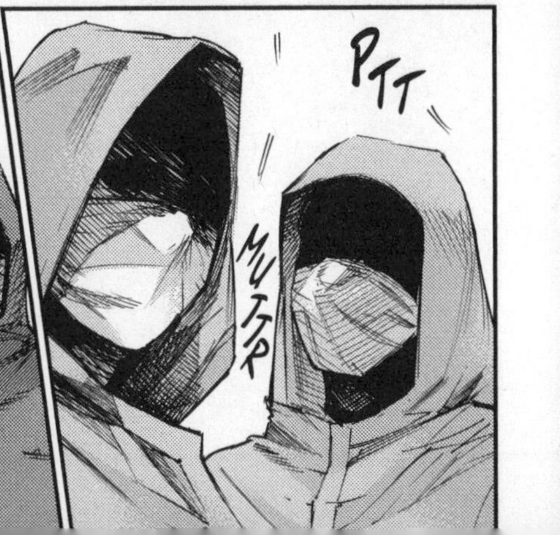
PTT
MUTTR
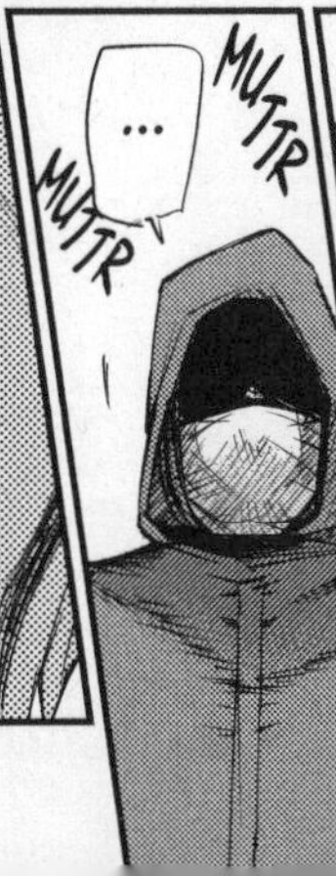
MUTTR
MUTTR
...
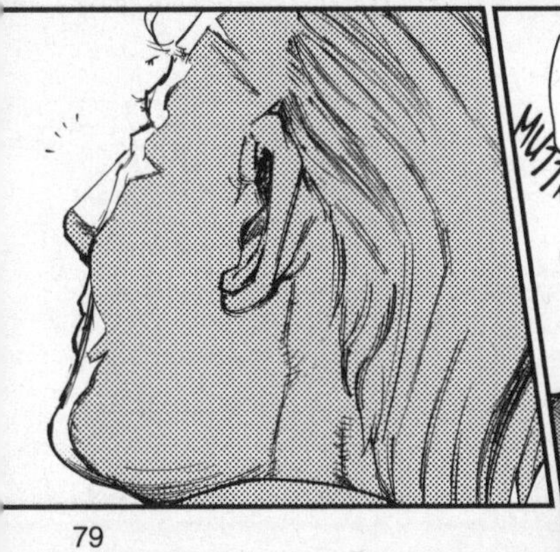

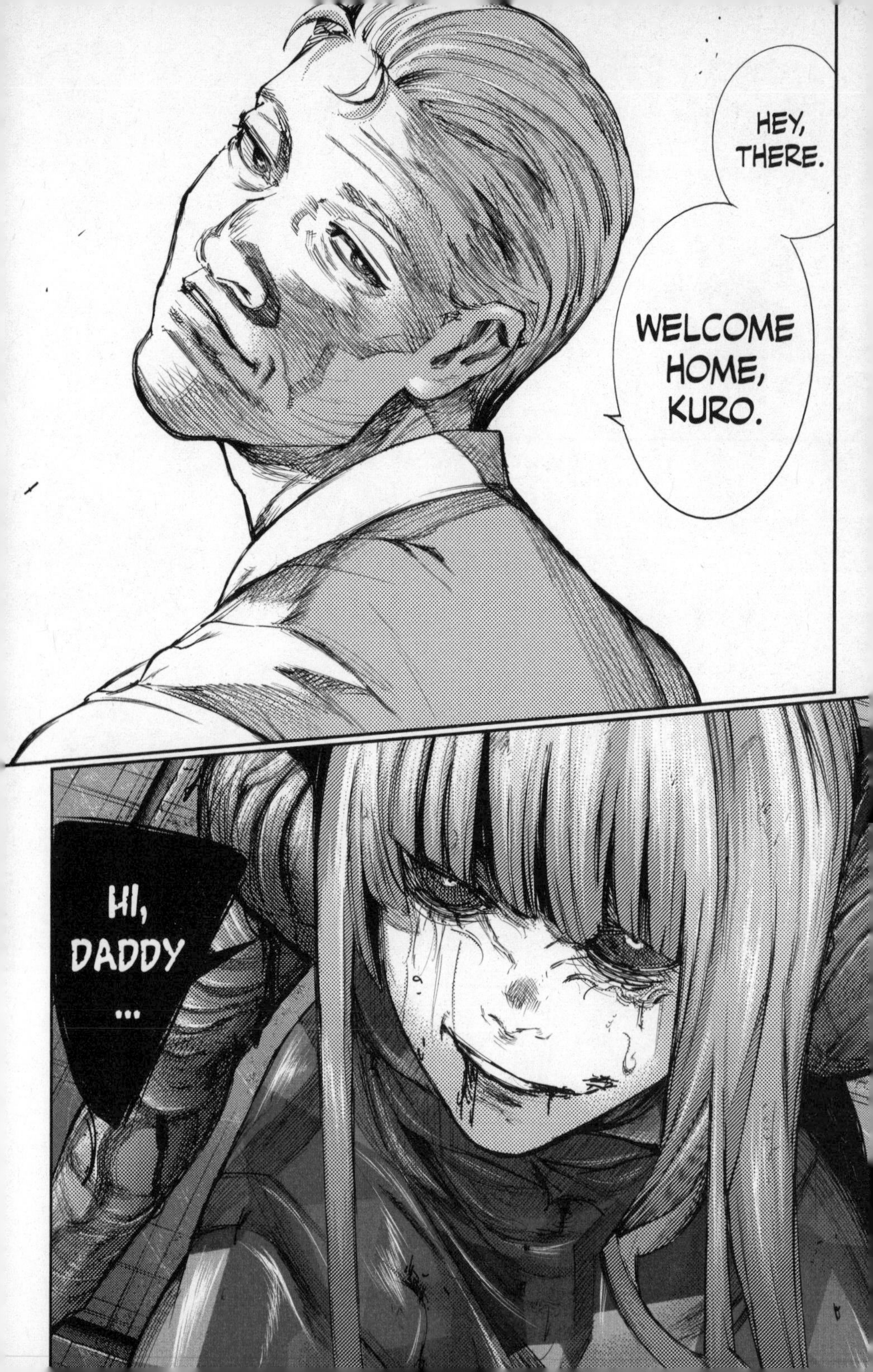
HEY, THERE.
WELCOME HOME, KURO.
HI, DADDY ...

Hunger :91

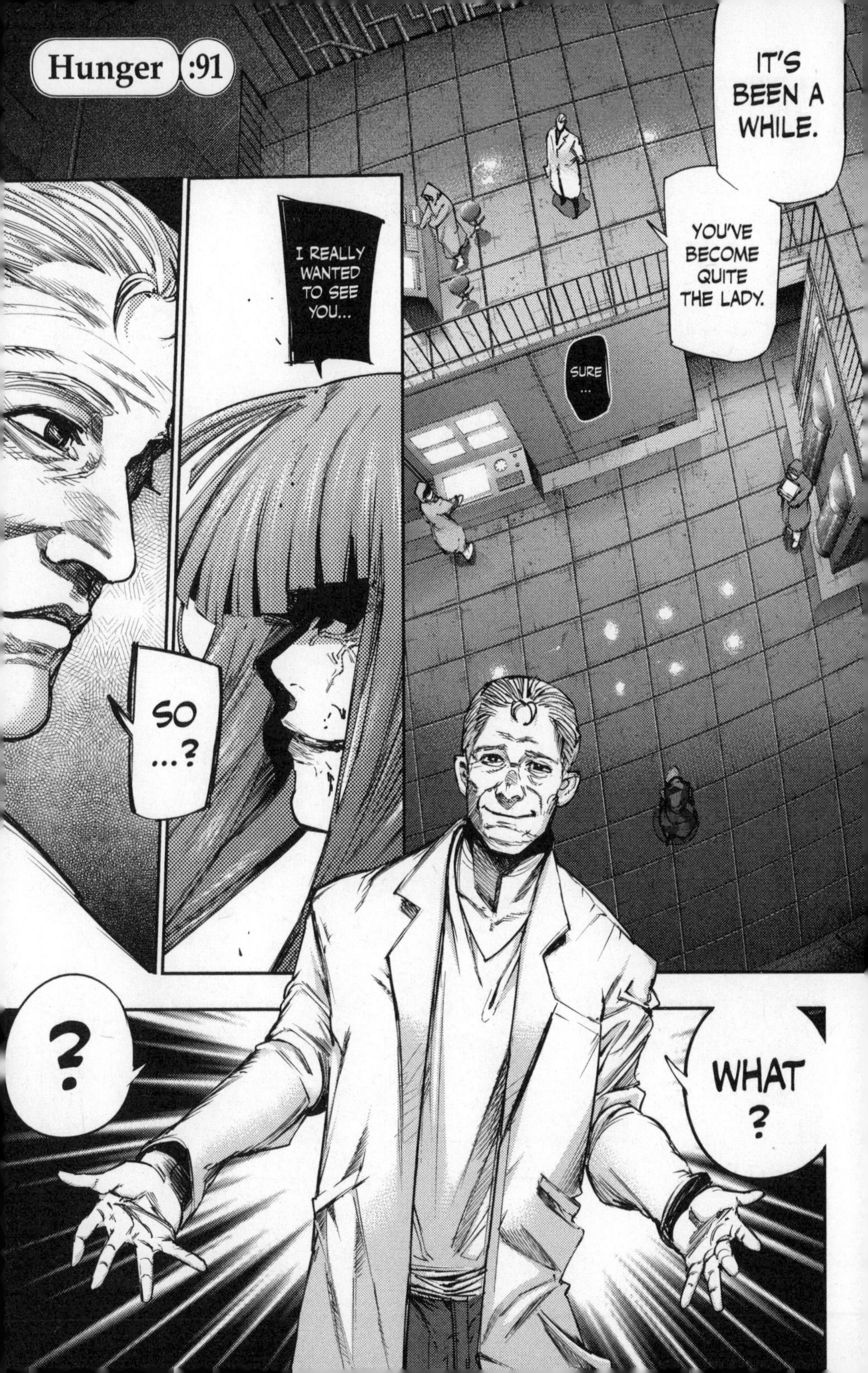
IT'S BEEN A WHILE.
YOU'VE BECOME QUITE THE LADY.
SURE ...
I REALLY WANTED TO SEE YOU...
SO ...?
WHAT ?
?

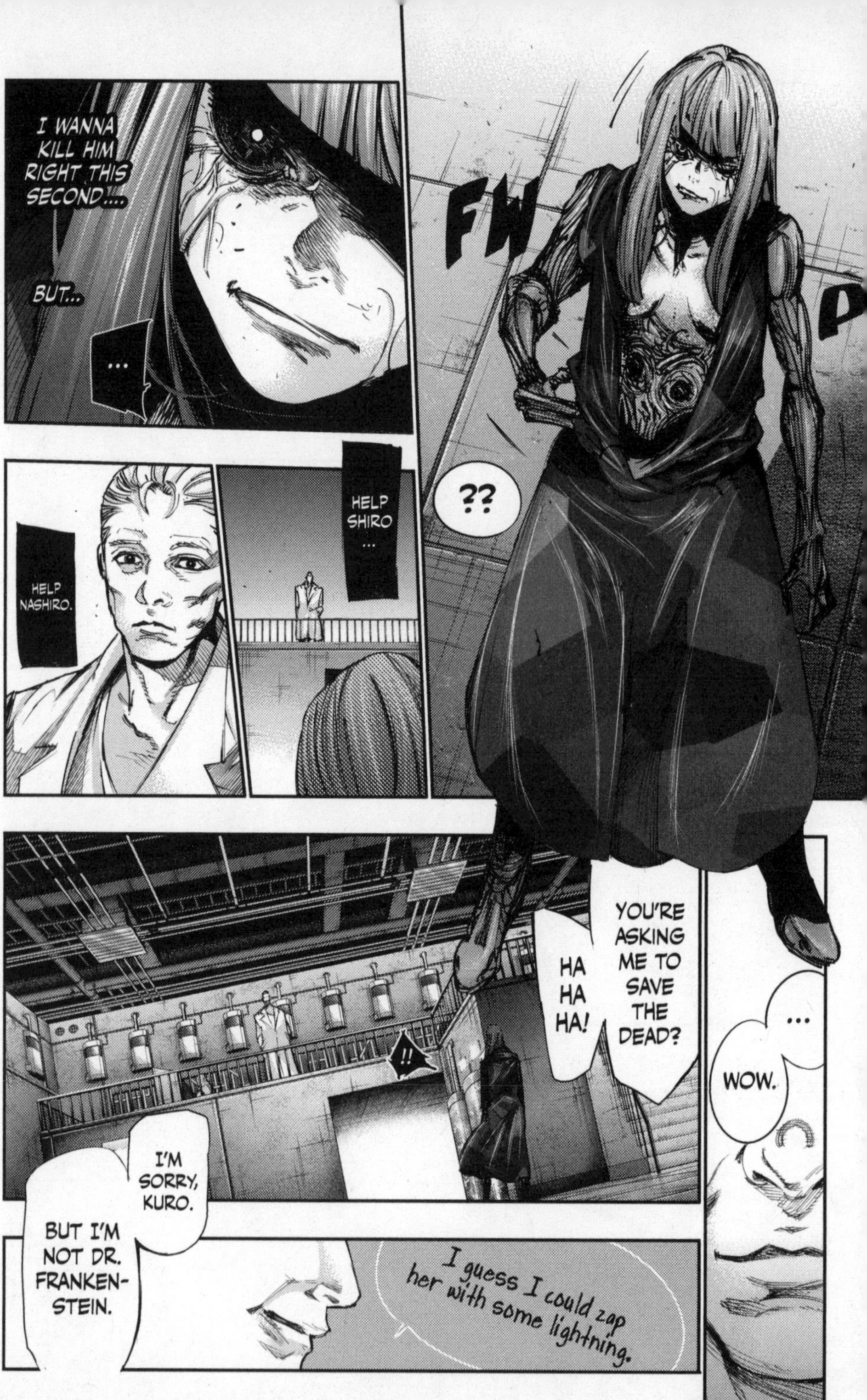
FW
P
??
I WANNA KILL HIM RIGHT THIS SECOND....
BUT...
...
HELP SHIRO ...
HELP NASHIRO.
...
WOW.
YOU'RE ASKING ME TO SAVE THE DEAD?
HA HA HA!
!!
I'M SORRY, KURO.
BUT I'M NOT DR. FRANKENSTEIN.
I guess I could zap her with some lightning.

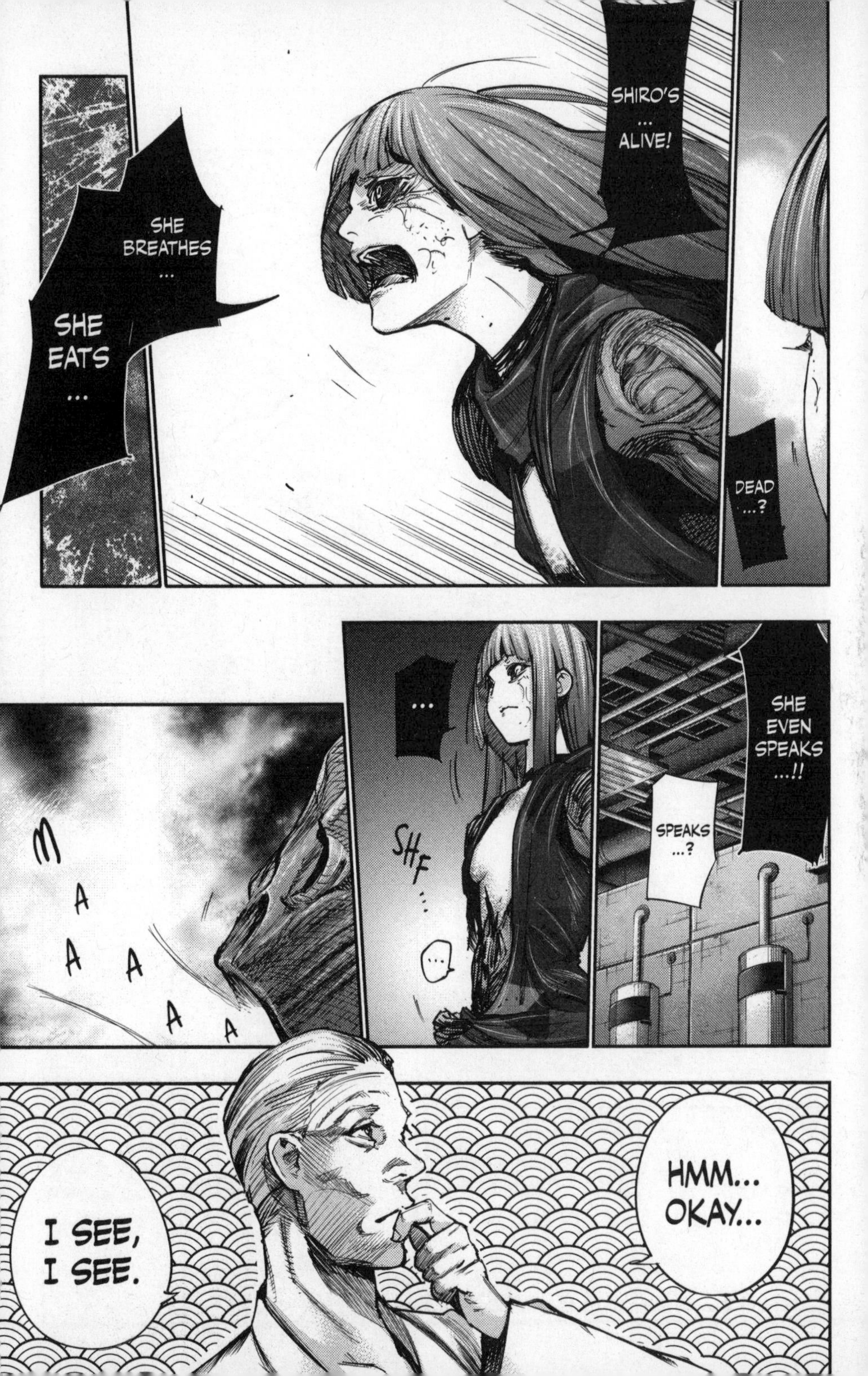
DEAD ...?
SHIRO'S ... ALIVE!
SHE BREATHES ...
SHE EATS ...
SHE EVEN SPEAKS ...!!
SPEAKS ...?
...
SHF ...
...
MAAAAAA
HMM... OKAY...
I SEE, I SEE.

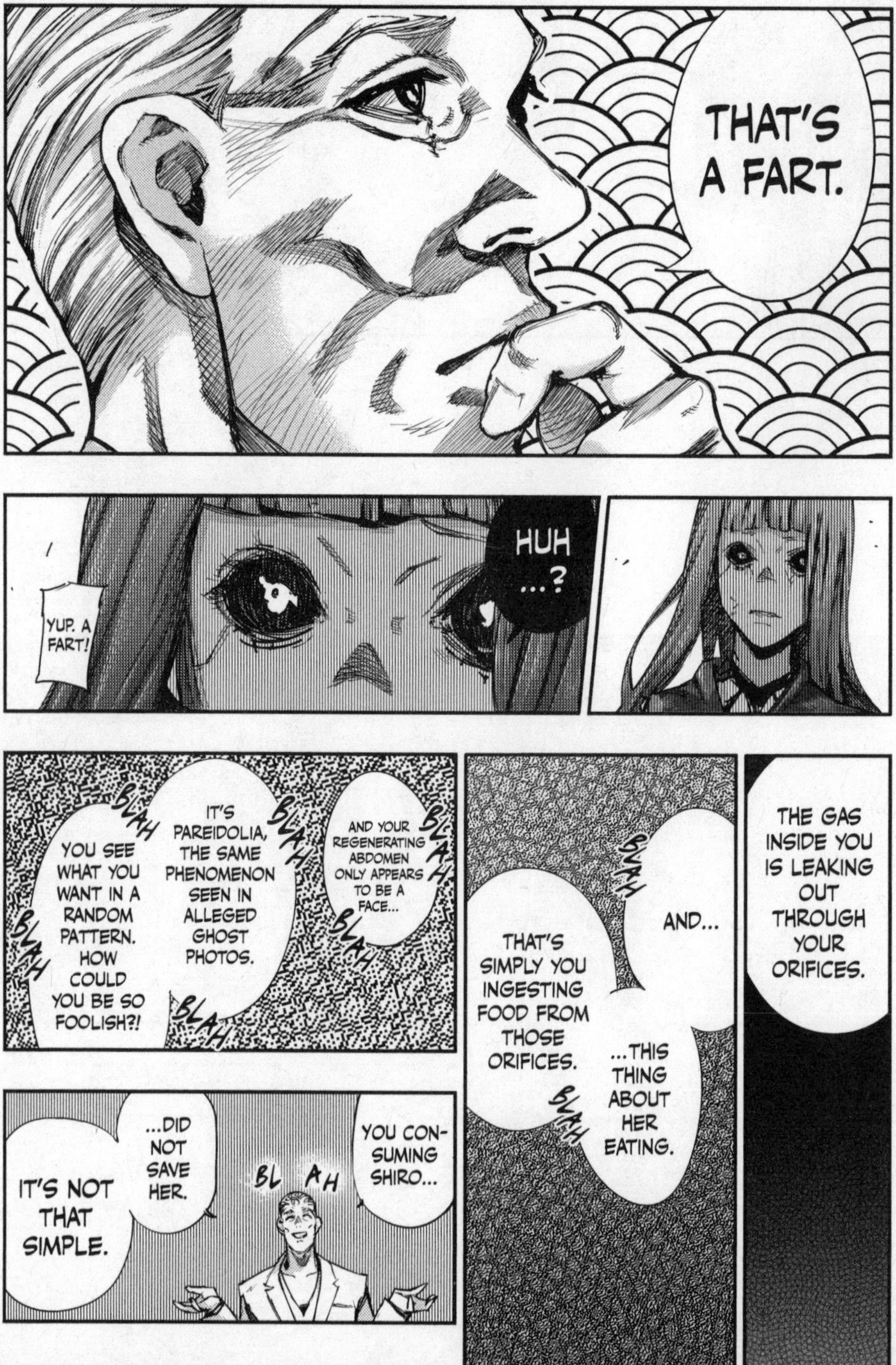
THAT'S A FART.
HUH ...?
YUP. A FART!
THE GAS INSIDE YOU IS LEAKING OUT THROUGH YOUR ORIFICES.
BLAH
AND...
THAT'S SIMPLY YOU INGESTING FOOD FROM THOSE ORIFICES.
...THIS THING ABOUT HER EATING.
BLAH
BLAH
AND YOUR REGENERATING ABDOMEN ONLY APPEARS TO BE A FACE...
BLAH
BLAH
IT'S PAREIDOLIA, THE SAME PHENOMENON SEEN IN ALLEGED GHOST PHOTOS.
BLAH
YOU SEE WHAT YOU WANT IN A RANDOM PATTERN. HOW COULD YOU BE SO FOOLISH?!
BLAH
BLAH
YOU CON-SUMING SHIRO...
BL AH
...DID NOT SAVE HER.
IT'S NOT THAT SIMPLE.

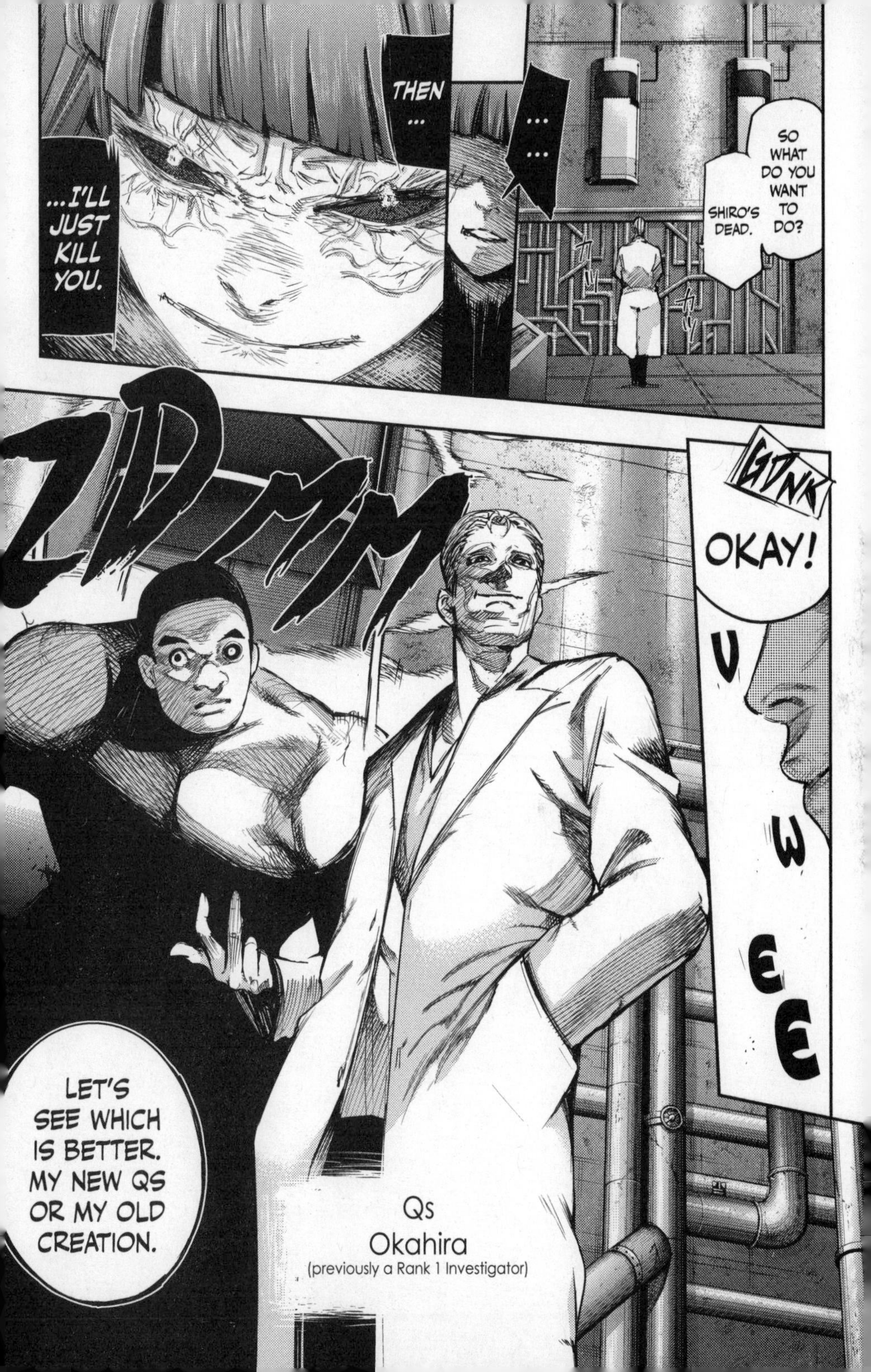
SO WHAT DO YOU WANT TO DO?
SHIRO'S DEAD.
......
THEN...
...I'LL JUST KILL YOU.
GONK
OKAY!
VWEEE
ZDMM
LET'S SEE WHICH IS BETTER. MY NEW QS OR MY OLD CREATION.
Qs
Okahira
(previously a Rank 1 Investigator)

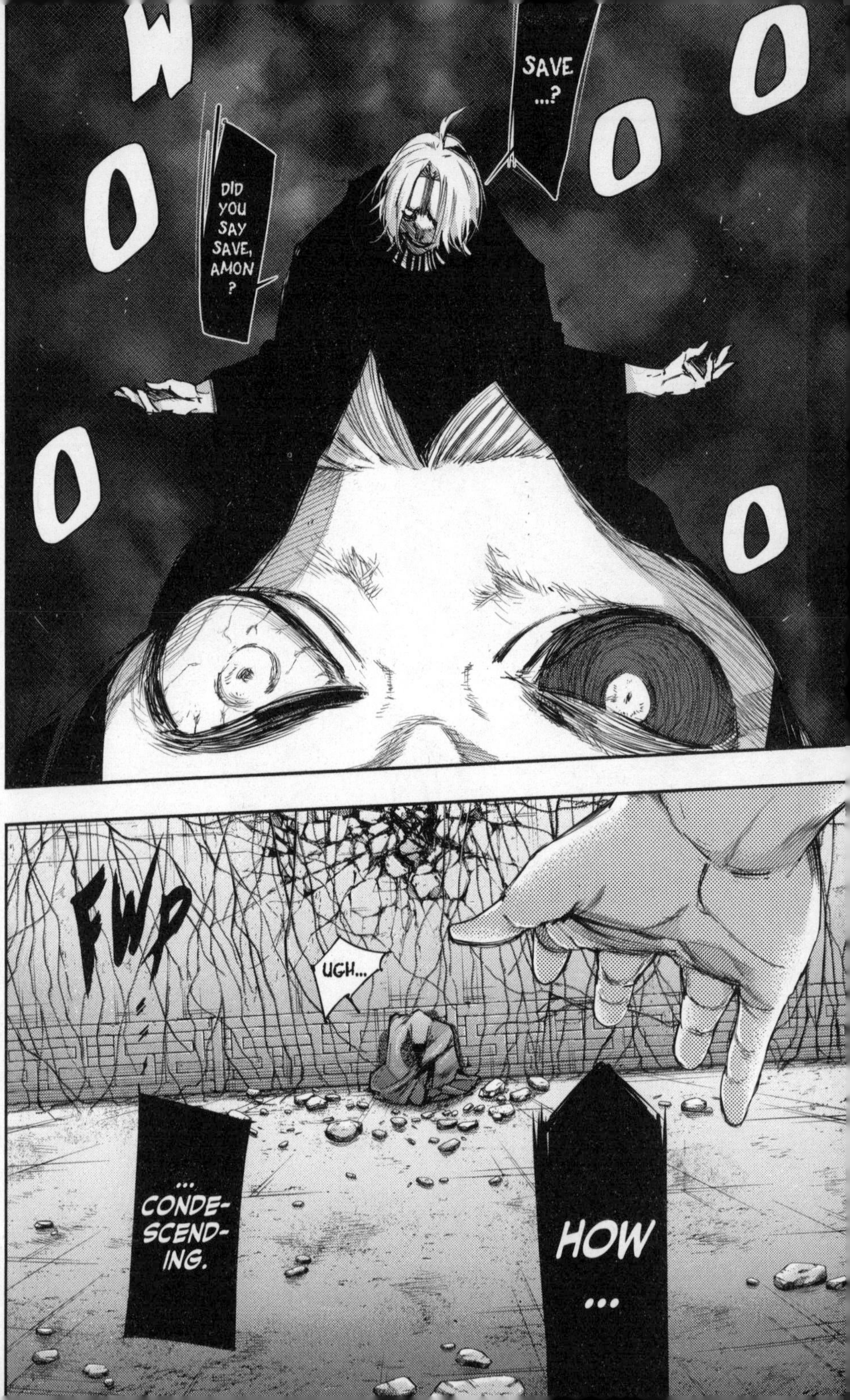
WOOOOO
SAVE ...?
DID YOU SAY SAVE, AMON ?
FWP
UGH...
HOW ...
... CONDE-SCEND-ING.

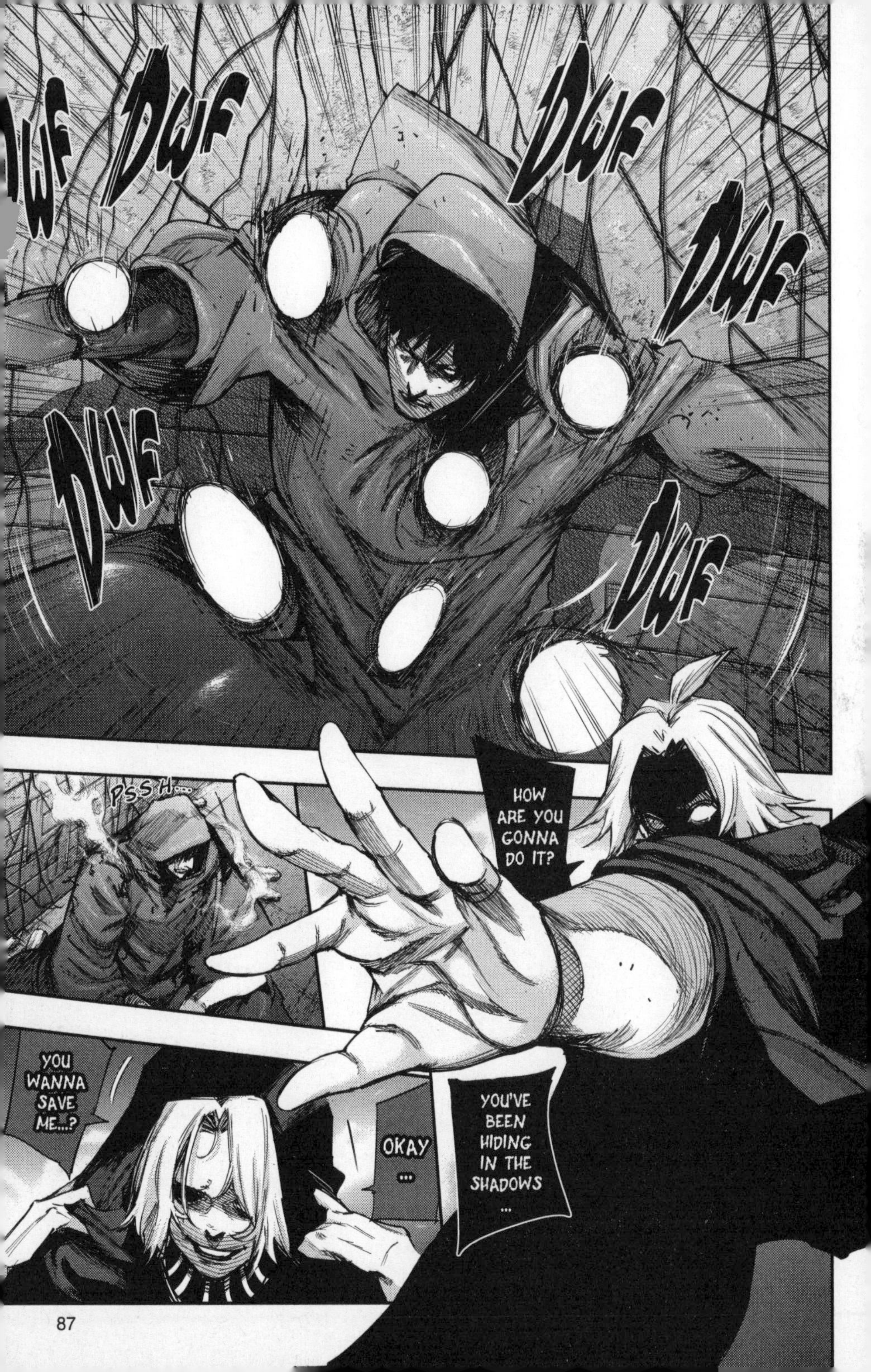
DWF
DWF
DWF
DWF
DWF
DWF
HOW ARE YOU GONNA DO IT?
PSSH...
YOU'VE BEEN HIDING IN THE SHADOWS ...
OKAY ...
YOU WANNA SAVE ME...?

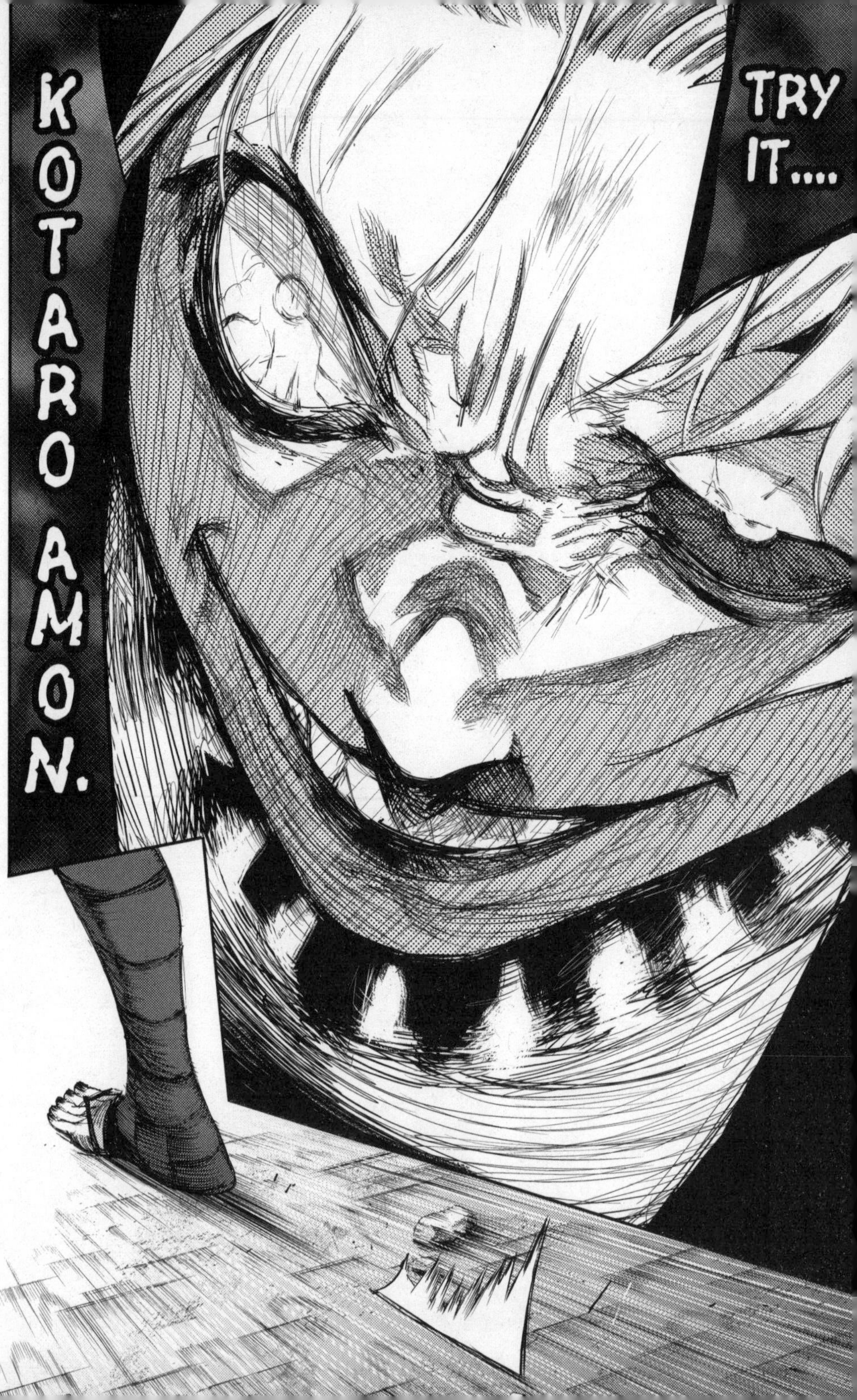
TRY IT....
KOTARO AMON.

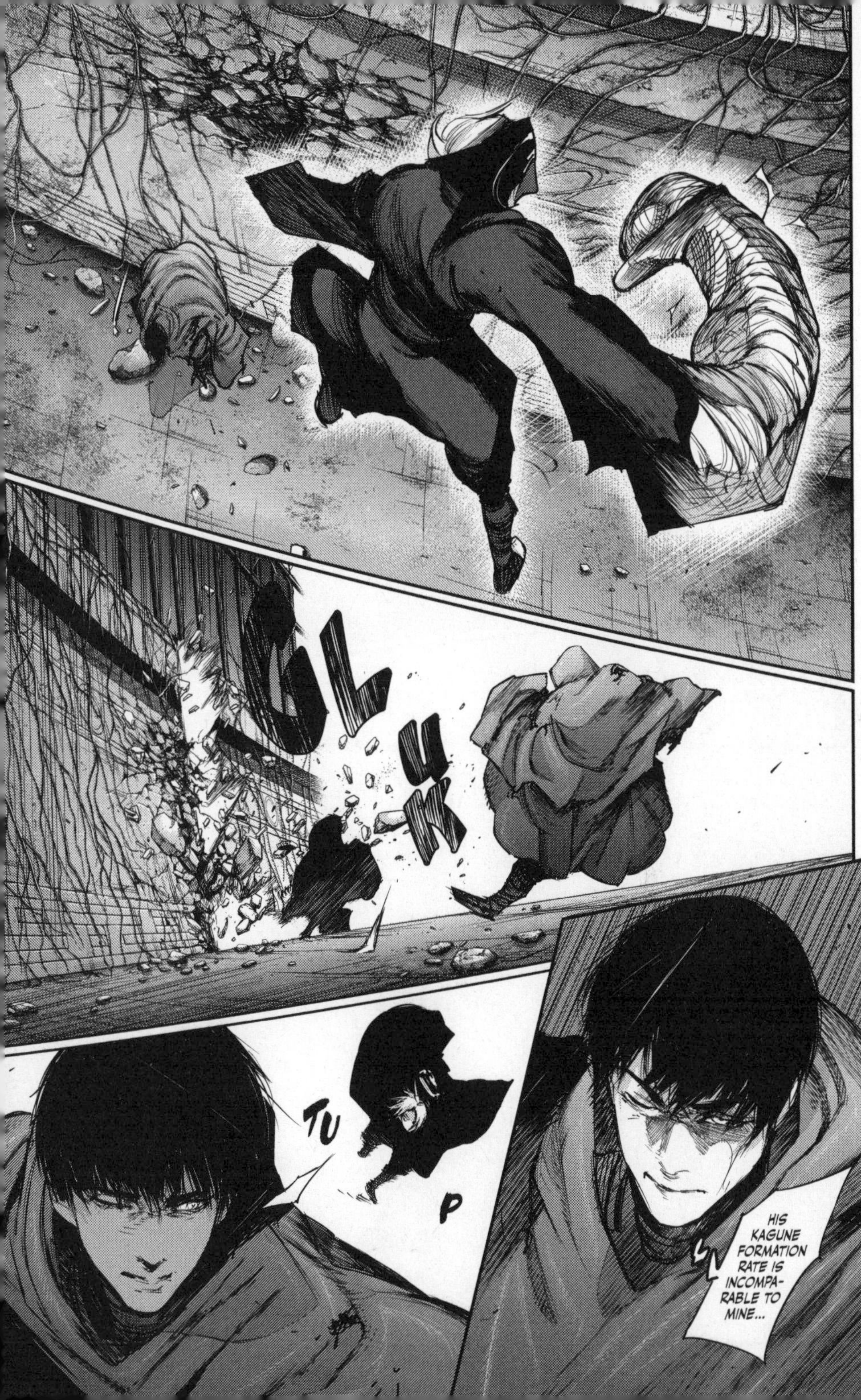
ULUK
HIS KAGUNE FORMATION RATE IS INCOMPA-RABLE TO MINE...
TUP

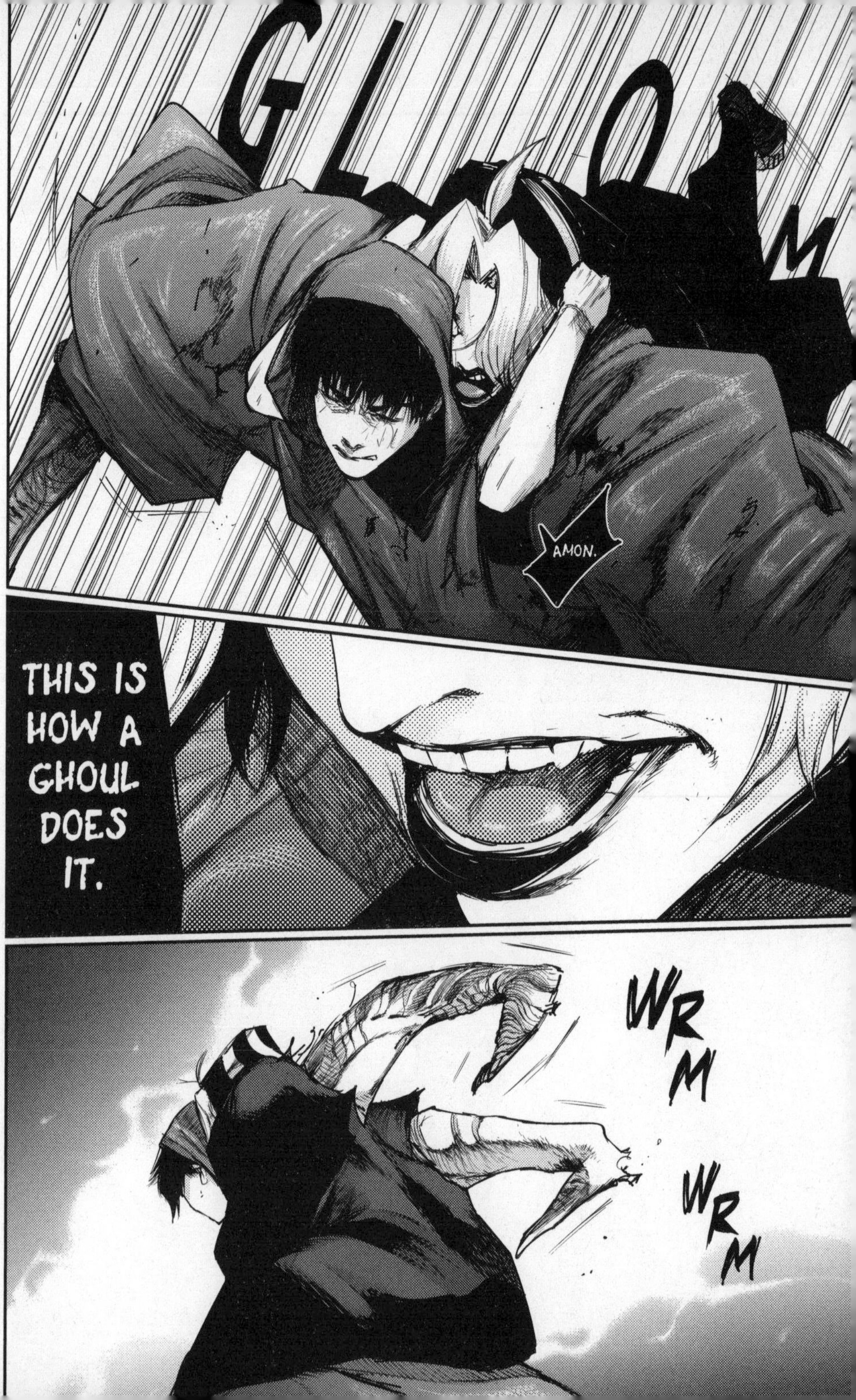
GLOOM
AMON.
THIS IS HOW A GHOUL DOES IT.
WRM
WRM

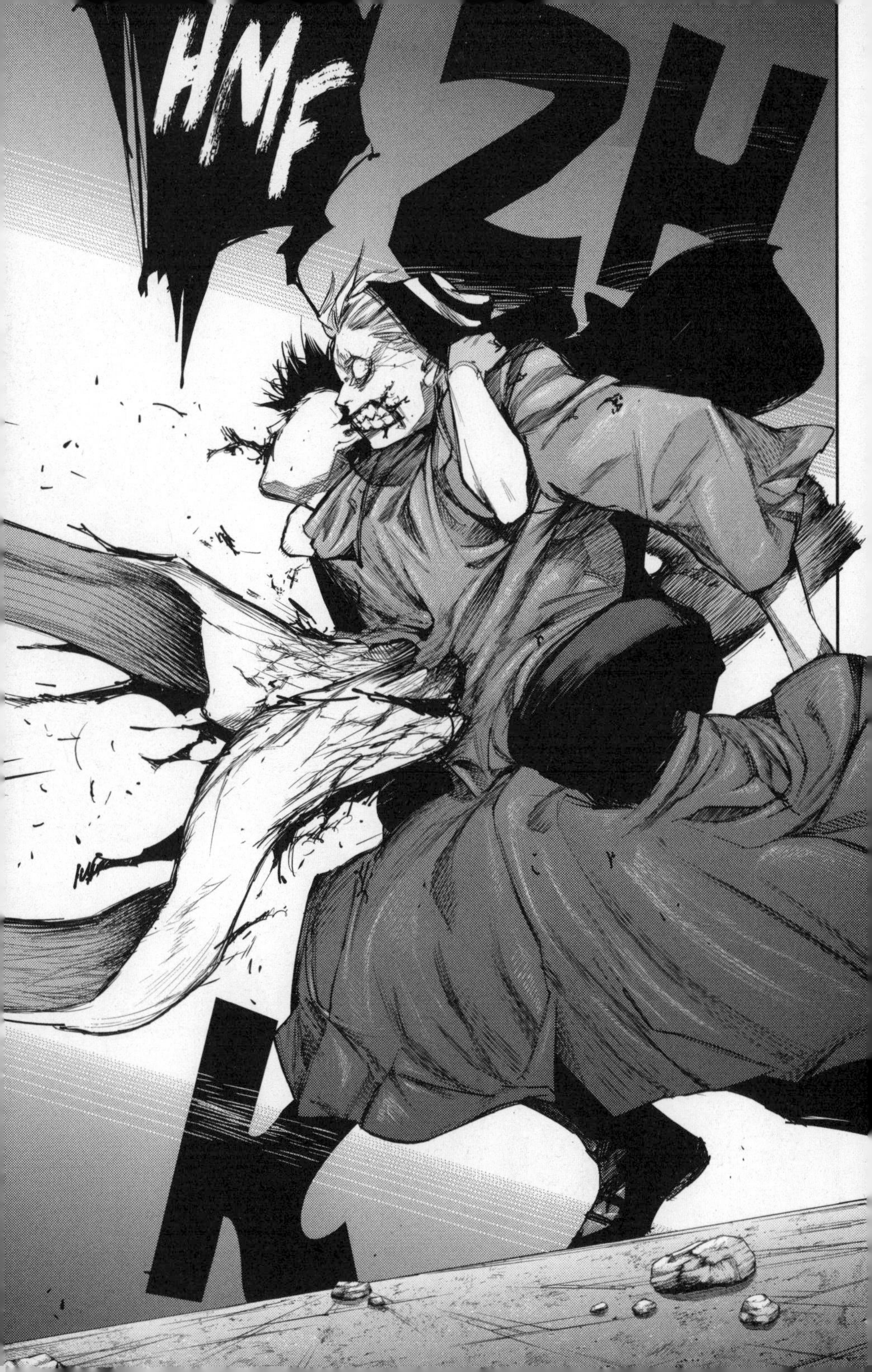
ZH
HMF

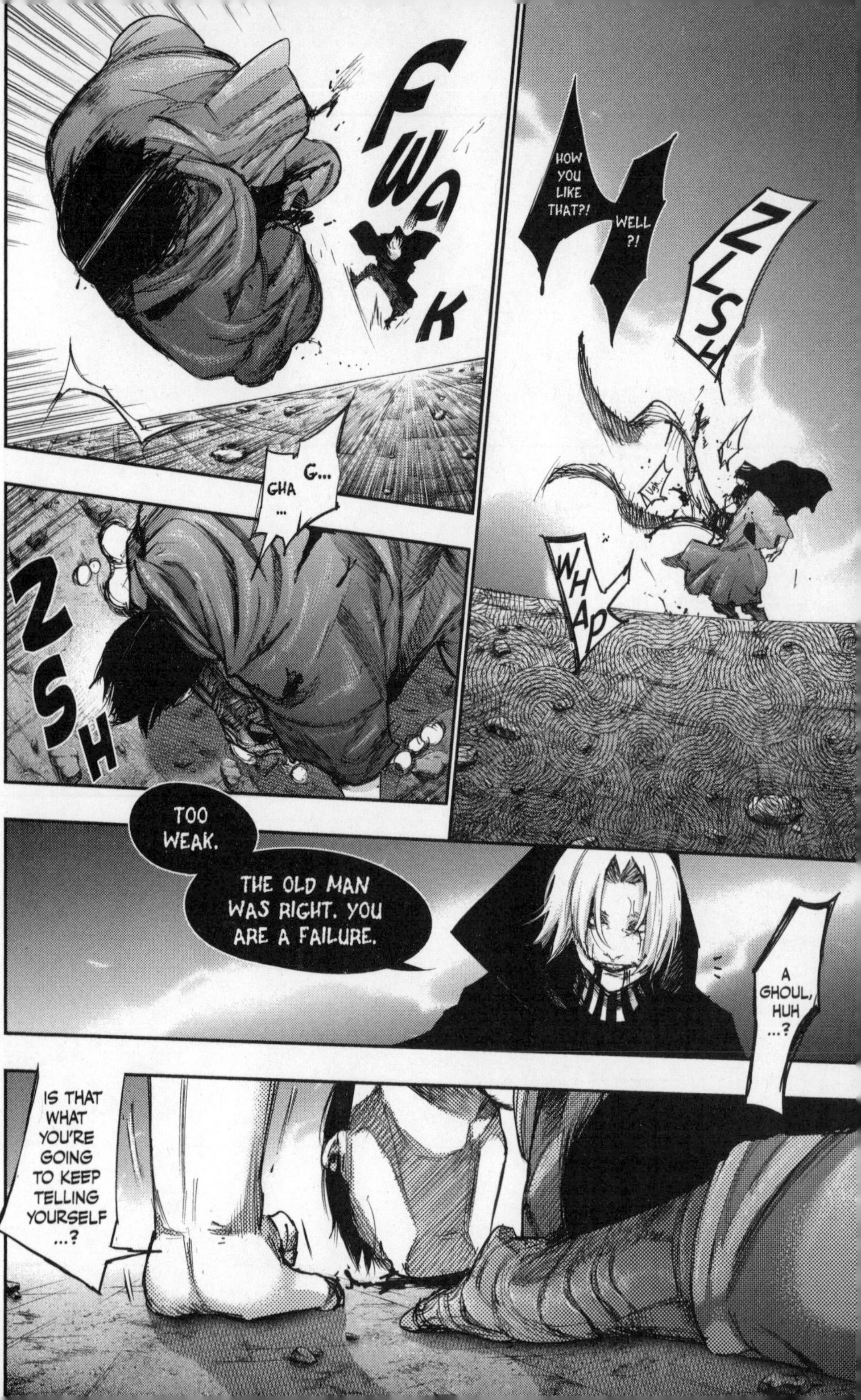
HOW YOU LIKE THAT?!
WELL?!
ZLSH
WHAP
FWAK
G... GHA...
ZSH
TOO WEAK.
THE OLD MAN WAS RIGHT. YOU ARE A FAILURE.
A GHOUL, HUH...?
IS THAT WHAT YOU'RE GOING TO KEEP TELLING YOURSELF...?

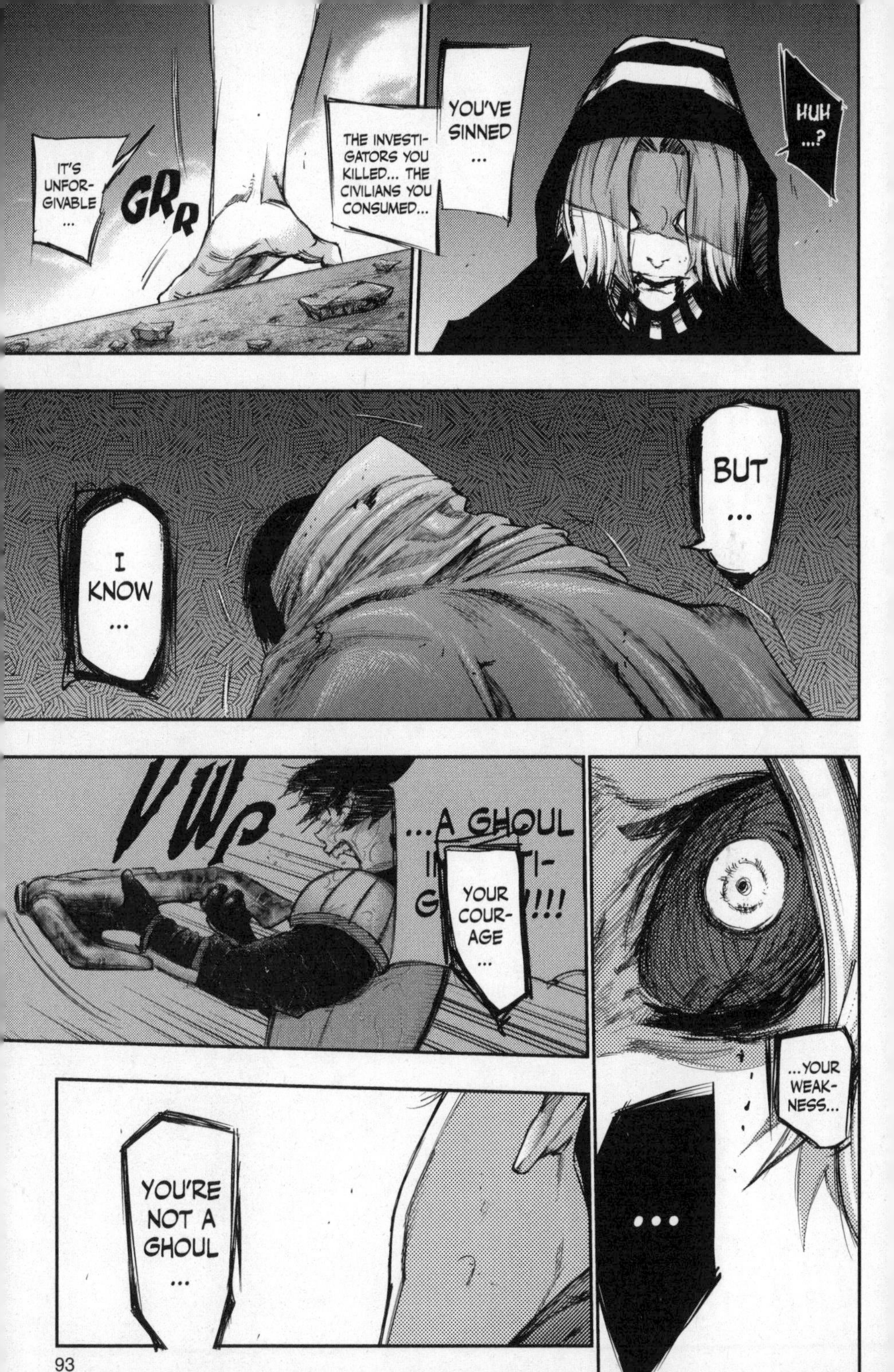
HUH ...?
YOU'VE SINNED ...
THE INVESTIGATORS YOU KILLED... THE CIVILIANS YOU CONSUMED...
IT'S UNFORGIVABLE ...
GRR
BUT ...
I KNOW ...
...YOUR WEAKNESS...
...
VWP
...A GHOUL
IN TI-
G !!!
YOUR COURAGE ...
YOU'RE NOT A GHOUL ...

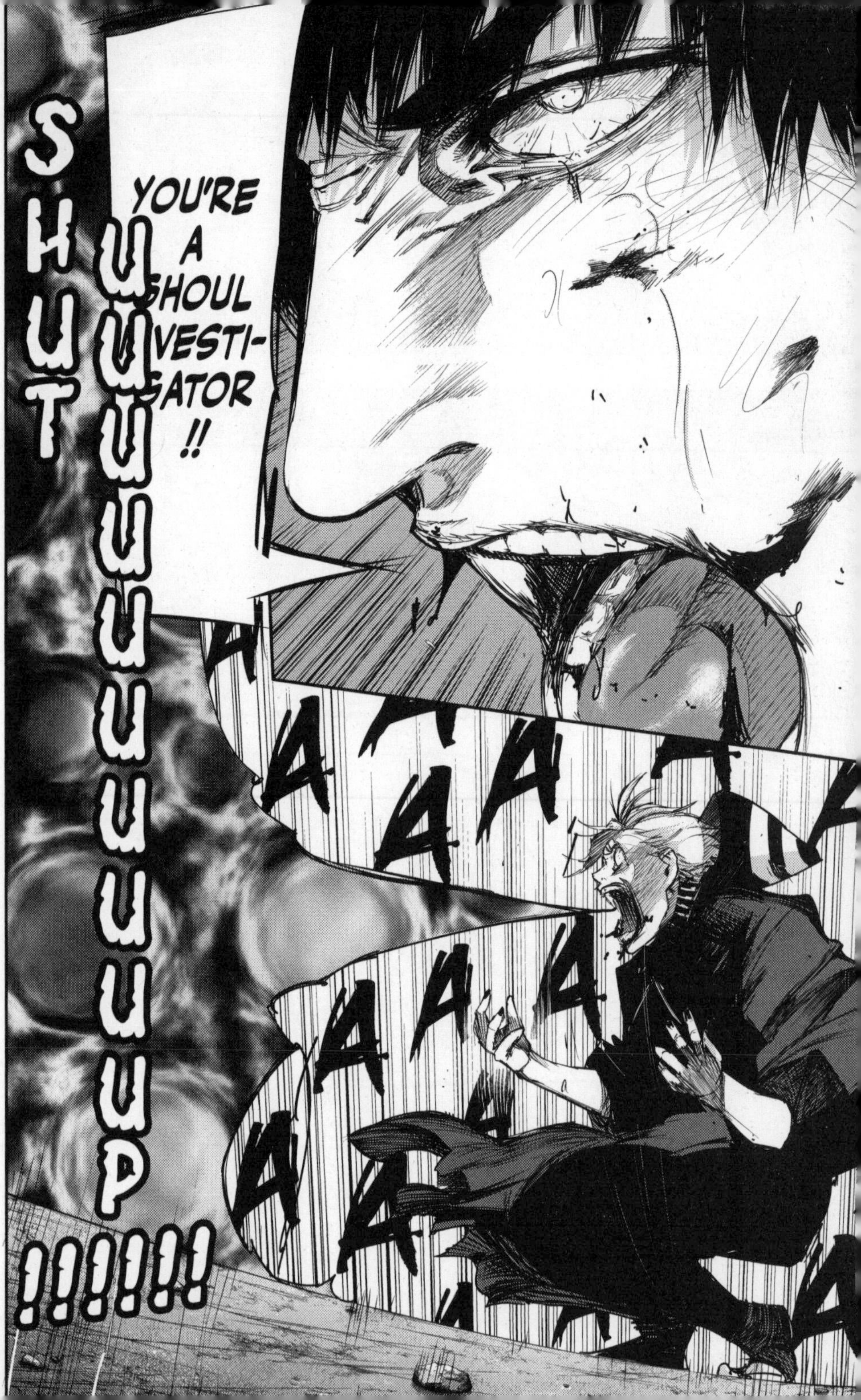
YOU'RE A GHOUL INVESTIGATOR!!
AAAAAAAAAAAAAAAAAA
SHUT UUUUUUUUUUUUUUUUUP!!!!!!

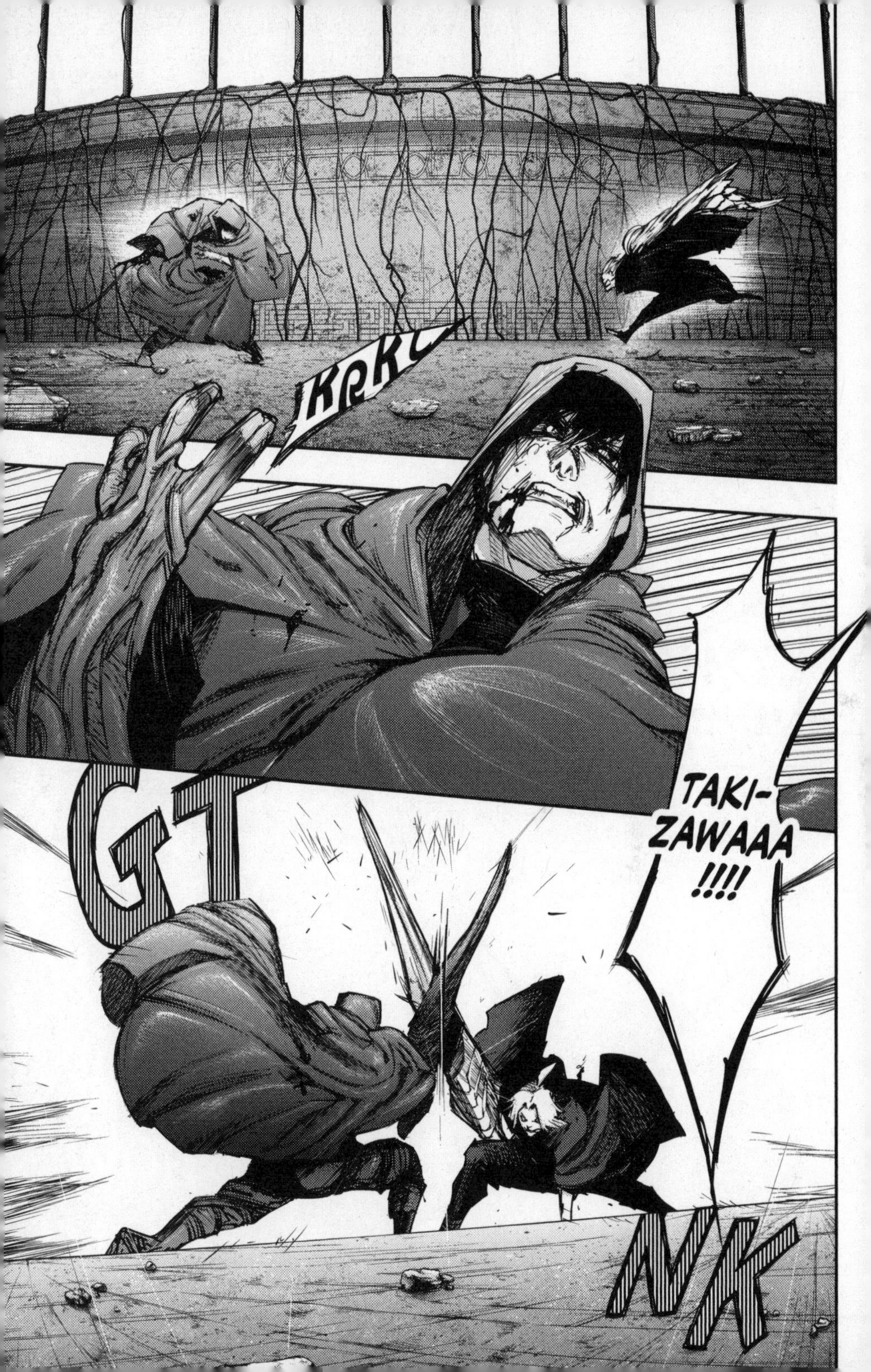
KRKL
TAKI-
ZAWAAA
!!!!
GT
NK

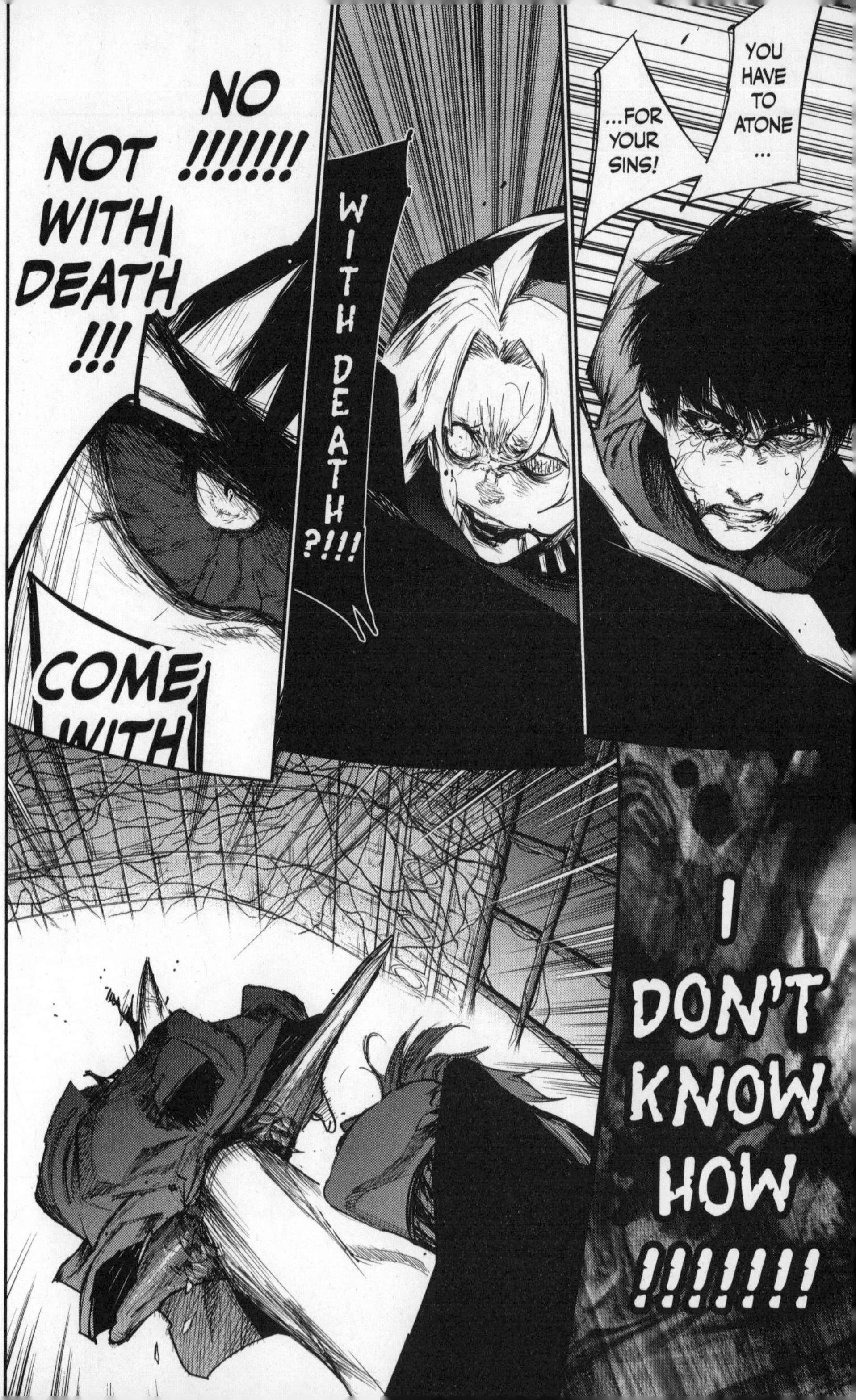
YOU HAVE TO ATONE ...
...FOR YOUR SINS!
WITH DEATH ?!!!
NO !!!!!!!
NOT WITH DEATH !!!
COME WITH
I DON'T KNOW HOW !!!!!!!

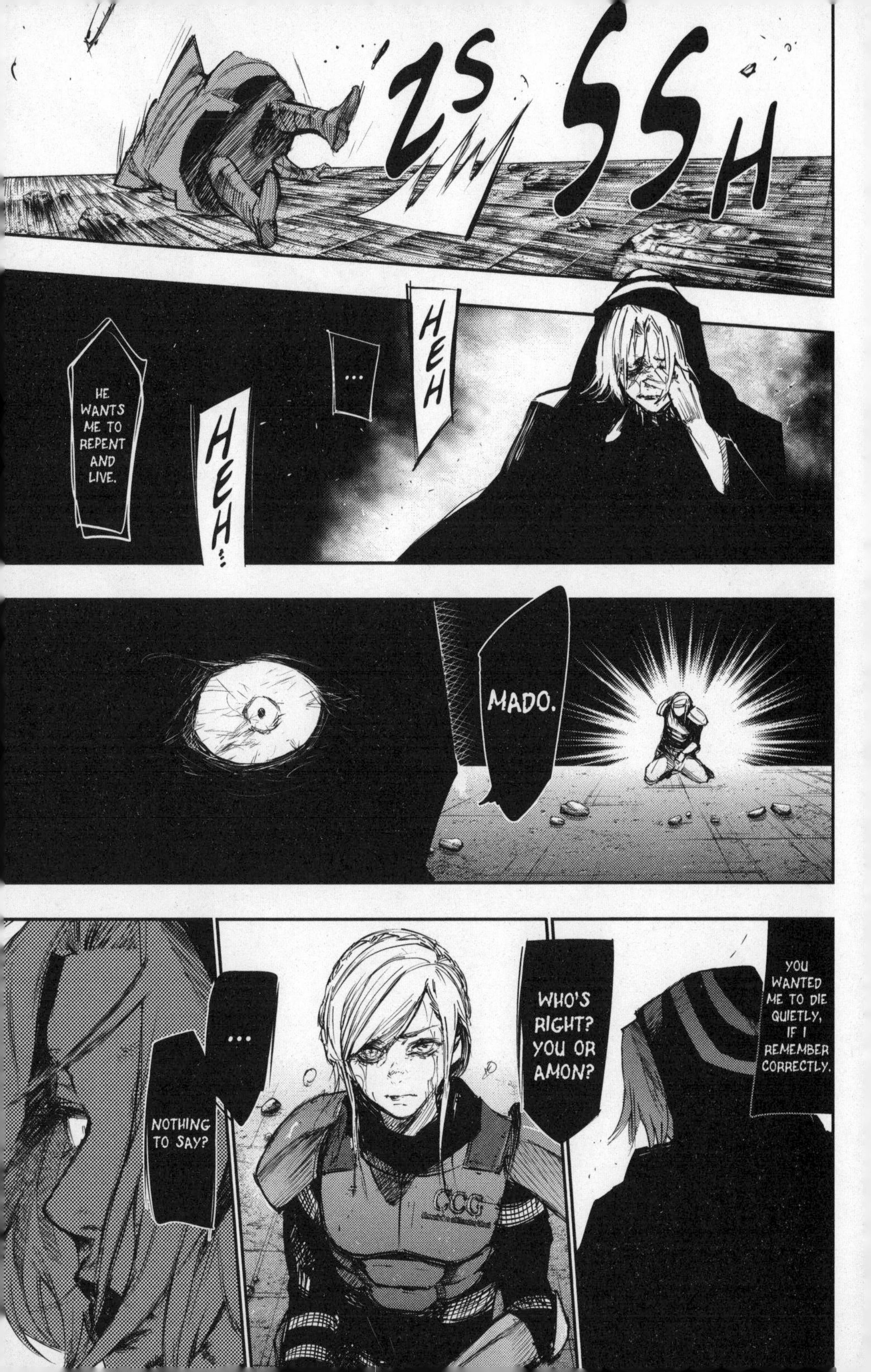
ZSSSH
HEH
...
HEH...
HE WANTS ME TO REPENT AND LIVE.
MADO.
YOU WANTED ME TO DIE QUIETLY, IF I REMEMBER CORRECTLY.
WHO'S RIGHT? YOU OR AMON?
...
NOTHING TO SAY?

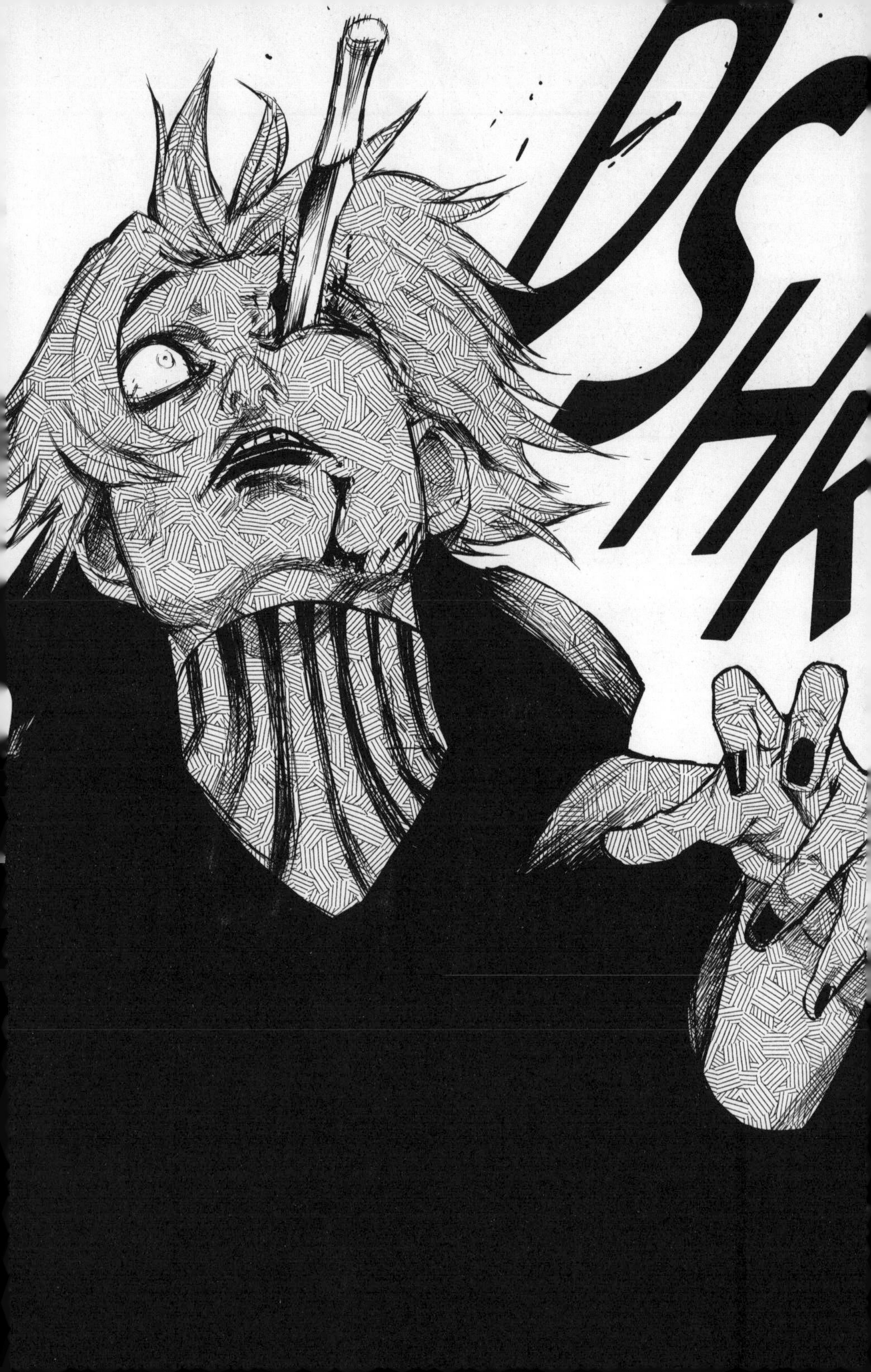
DSHK

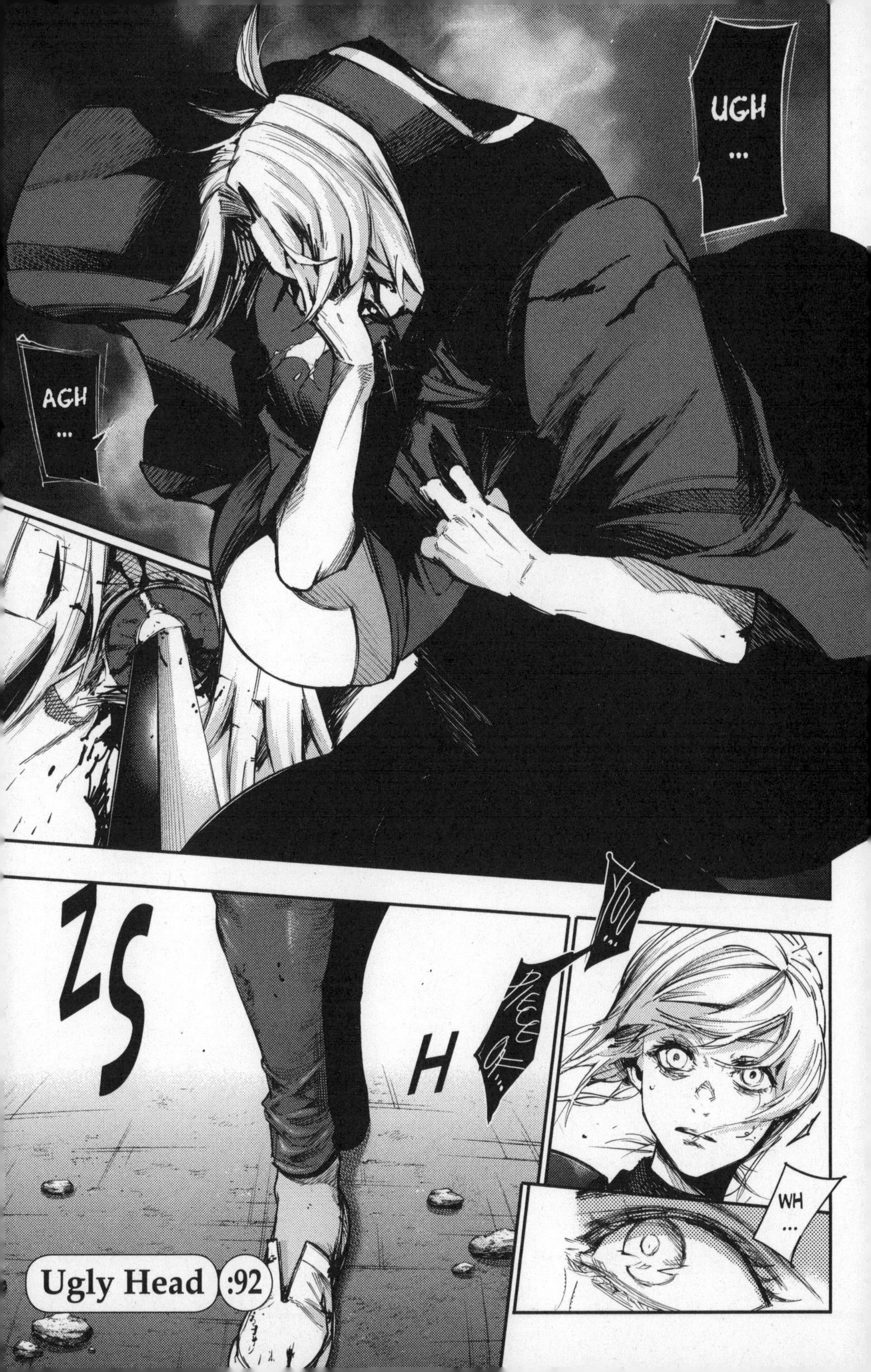
UGH ...
AGH ...
YOU ...
PIECE OF ...
WH ...
ZSH
Ugly Head :92

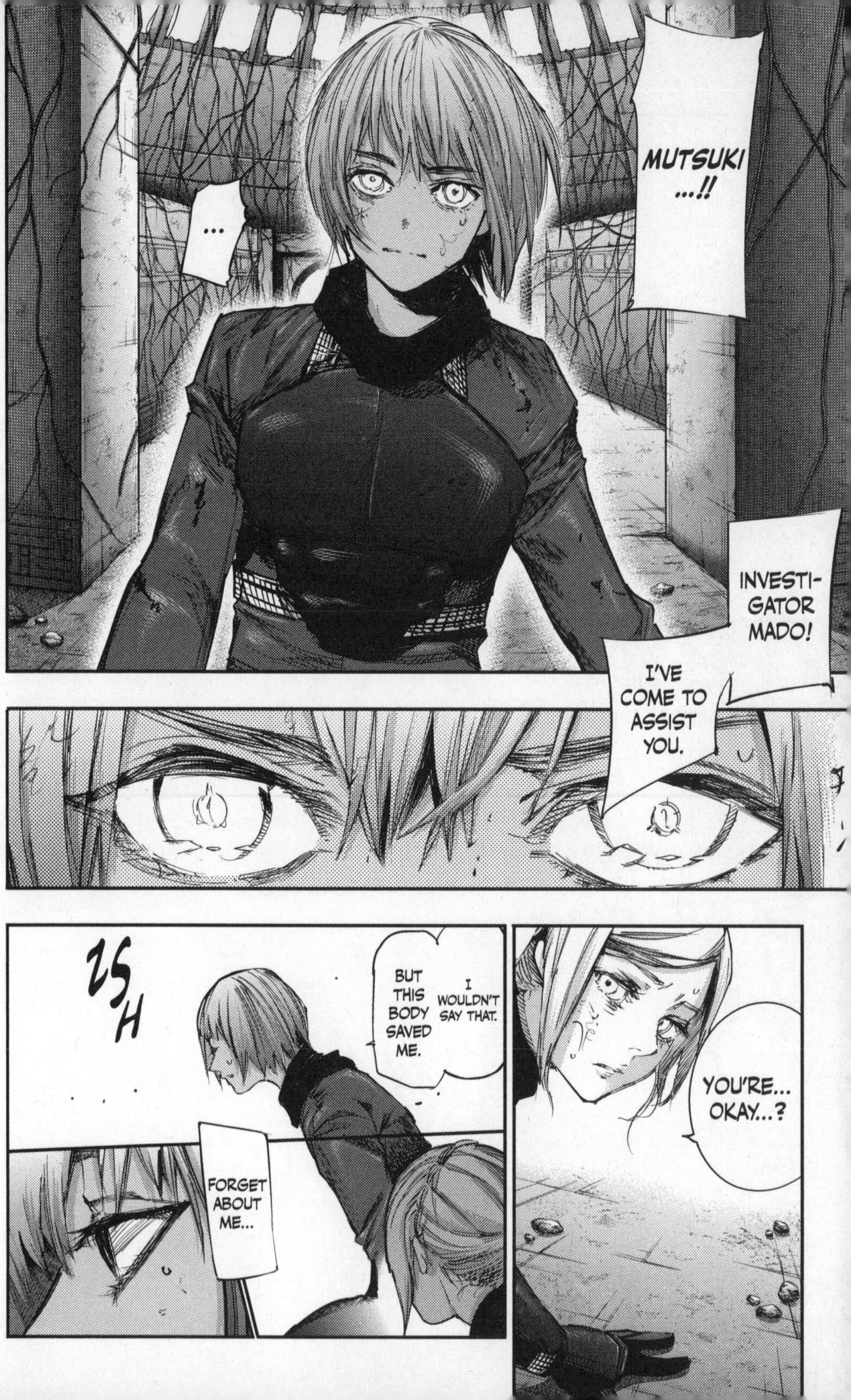
MUTSUKI ...!!
...
INVESTIGATOR MADO!
I'VE COME TO ASSIST YOU.
YOU'RE... OKAY...?
I WOULDN'T SAY THAT.
BUT THIS BODY SAVED ME.
ZSH
FORGET ABOUT ME...

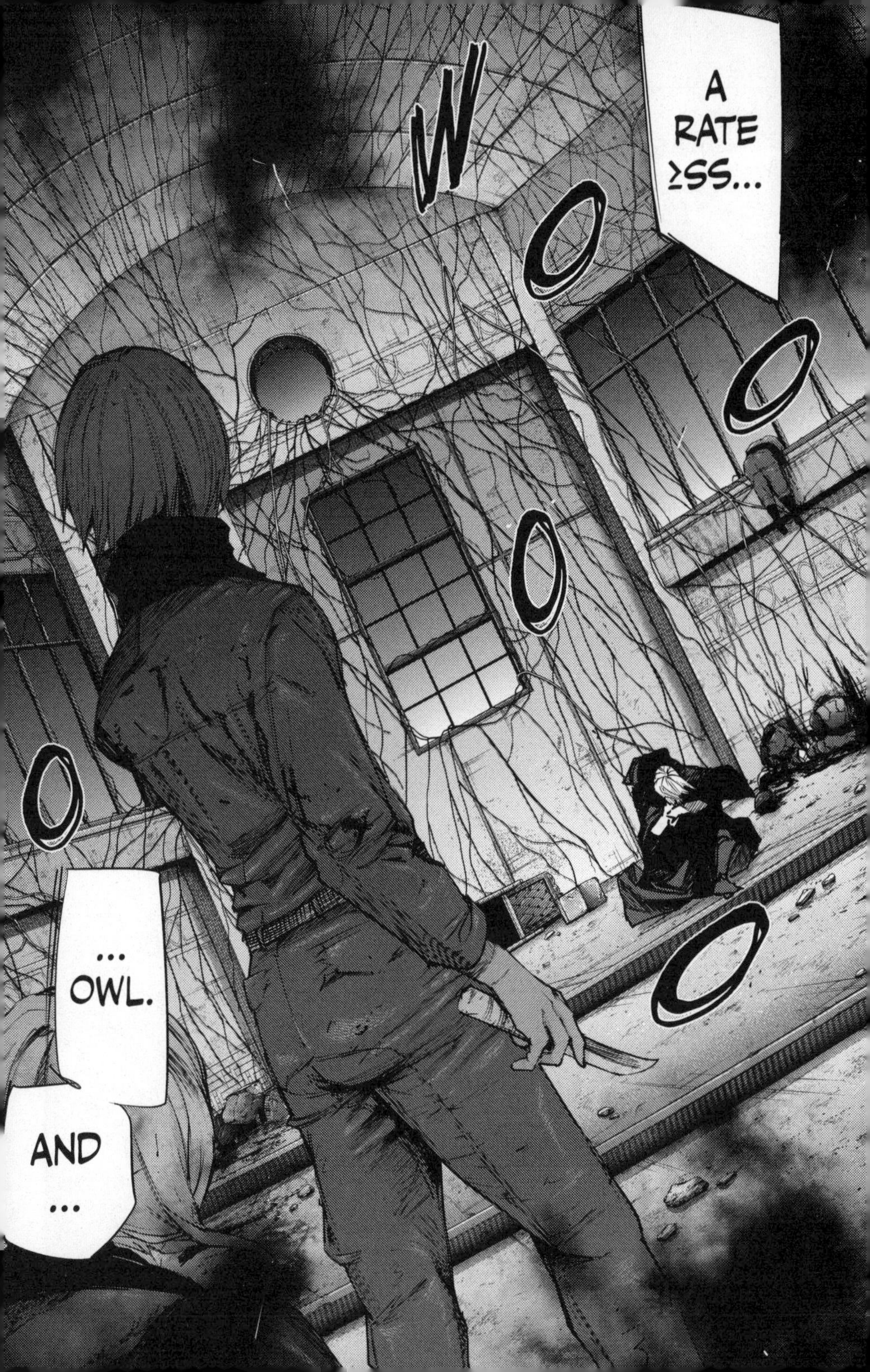
A RATE SS...
WOOOOO
... OWL.
AND ...

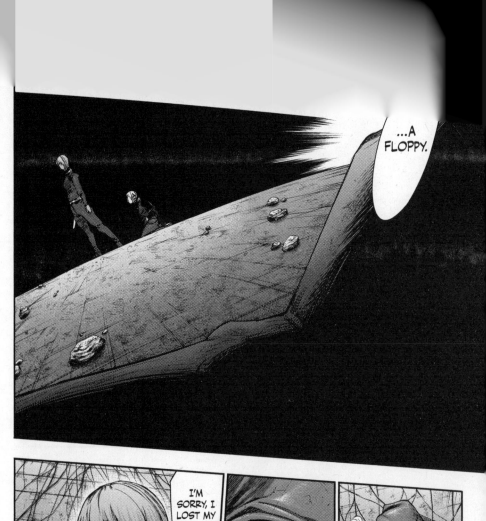

...A FLOPPY.

I'M SORRY, I LOST MY COMMS...

IS SUPPORT EN ROUTE?

YEAH...

THE SUZUYA SQUAD AND...

Huff

Huff

Huff

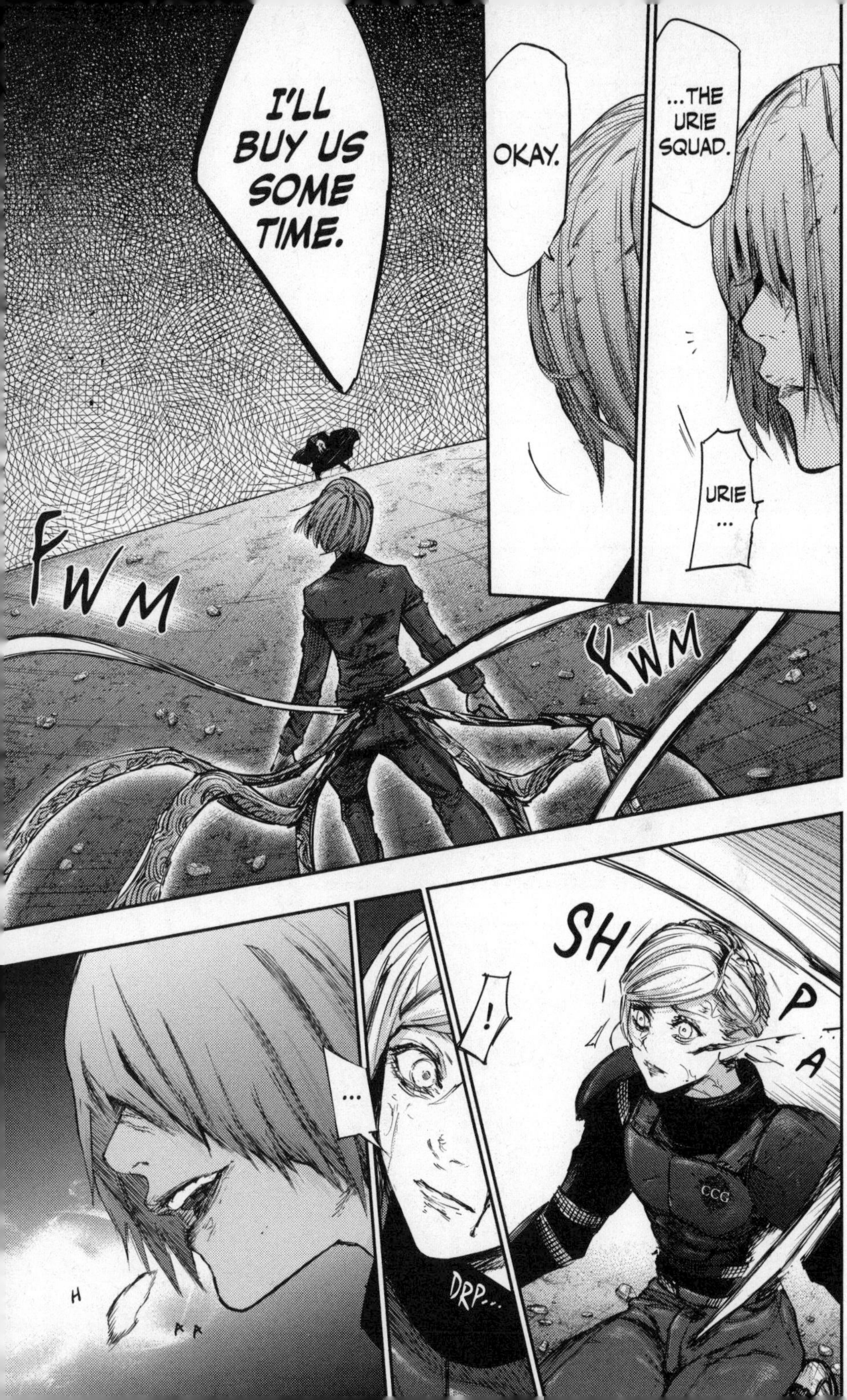
...THE URIE SQUAD.
URIE ...
OKAY.
I'LL BUY US SOME TIME.
YWM
FWM
SH
PA
!
...
DRP...
H AA

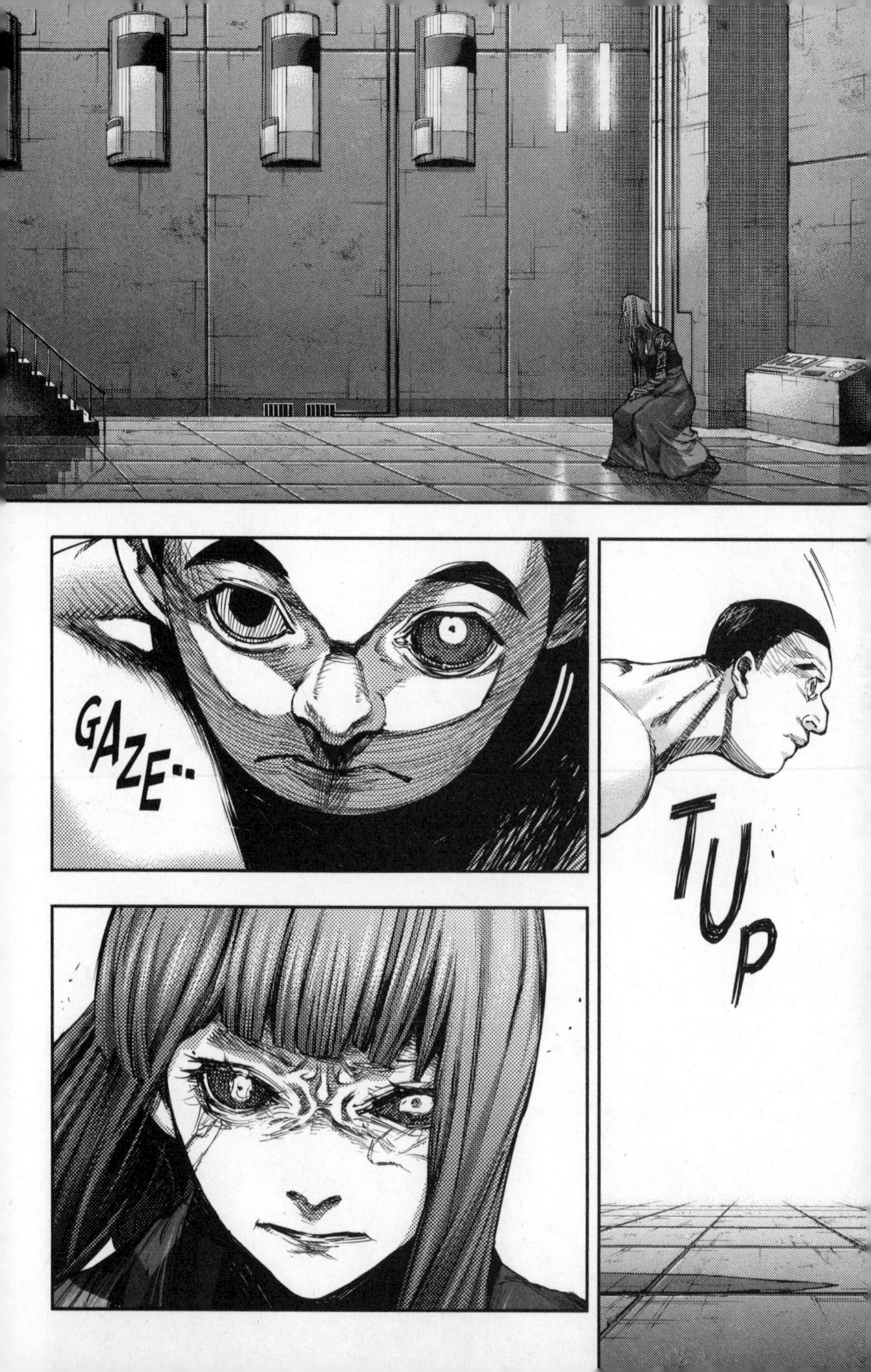
TUP
GAZE..

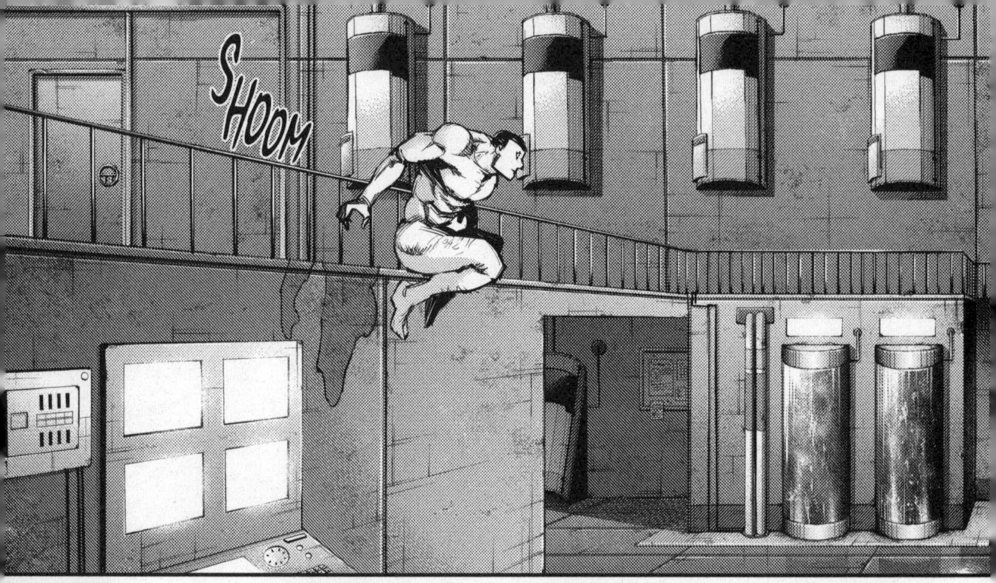
SHOOM
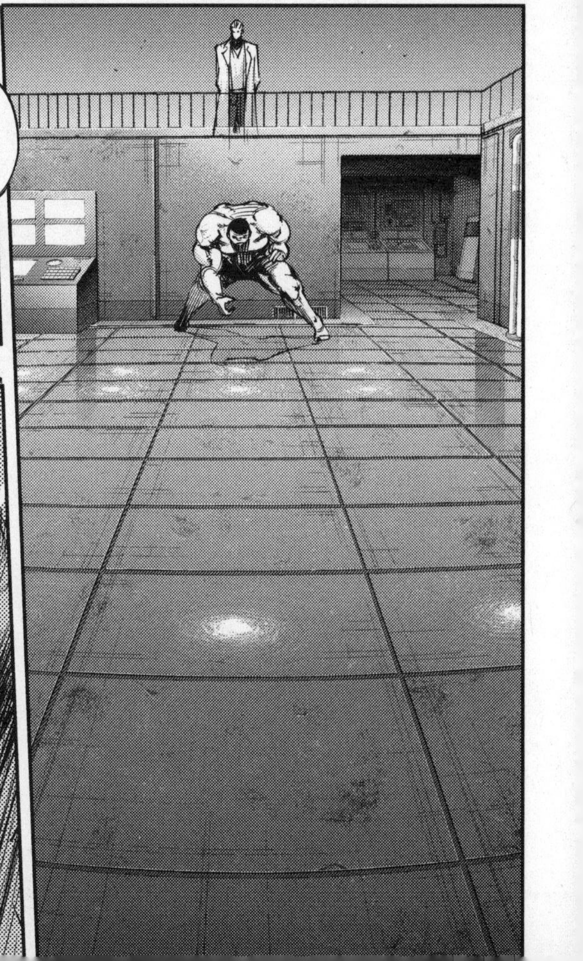
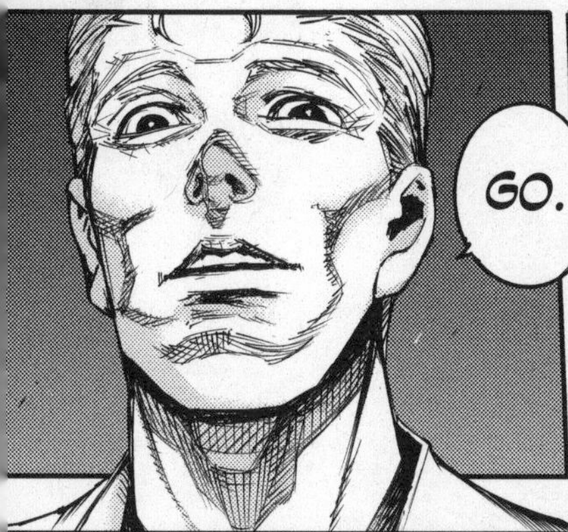
GO.
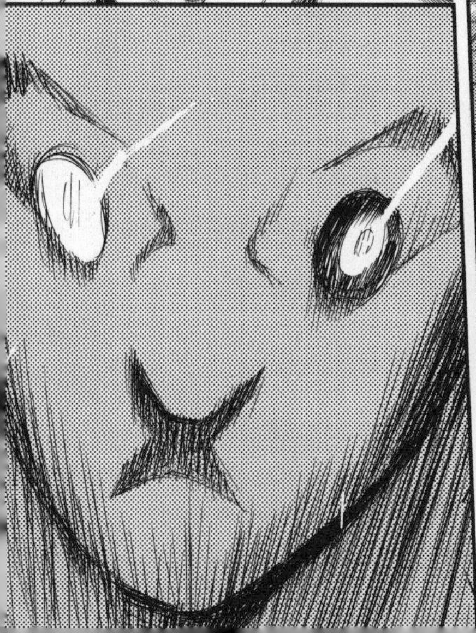

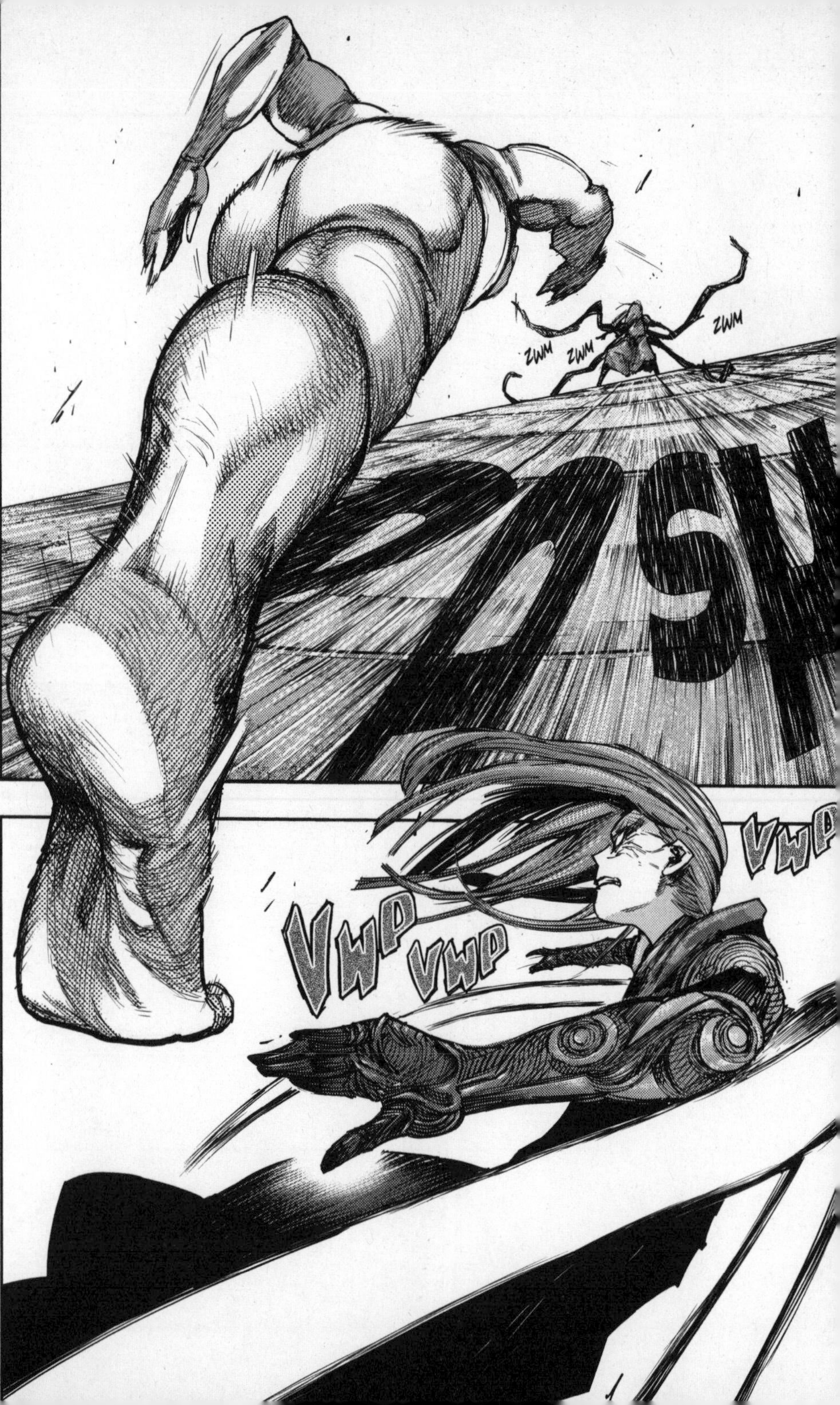
ZWM
ZWM
ZWM
VWP
VWP
VWP

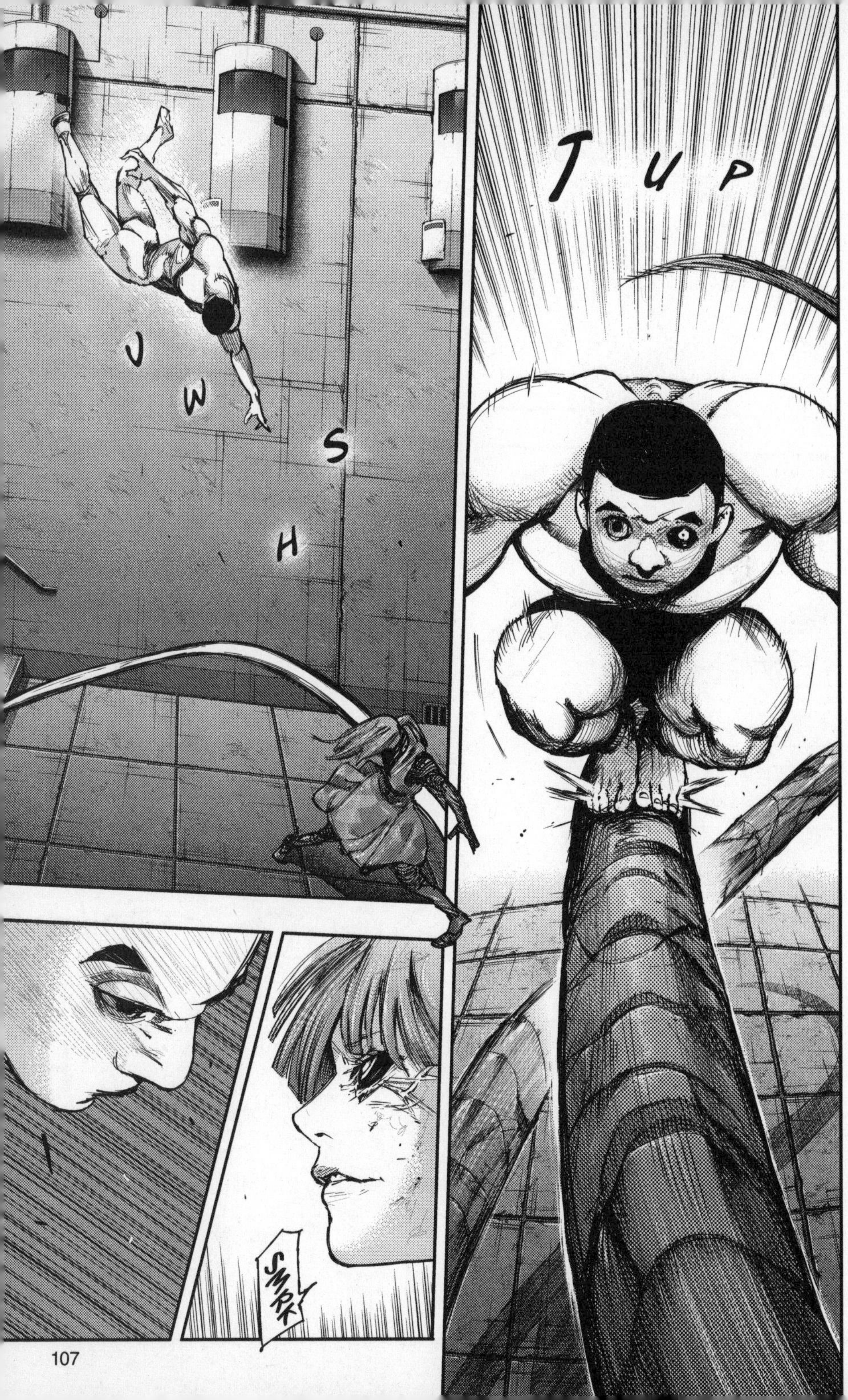
TUP
JWSH
SMRK

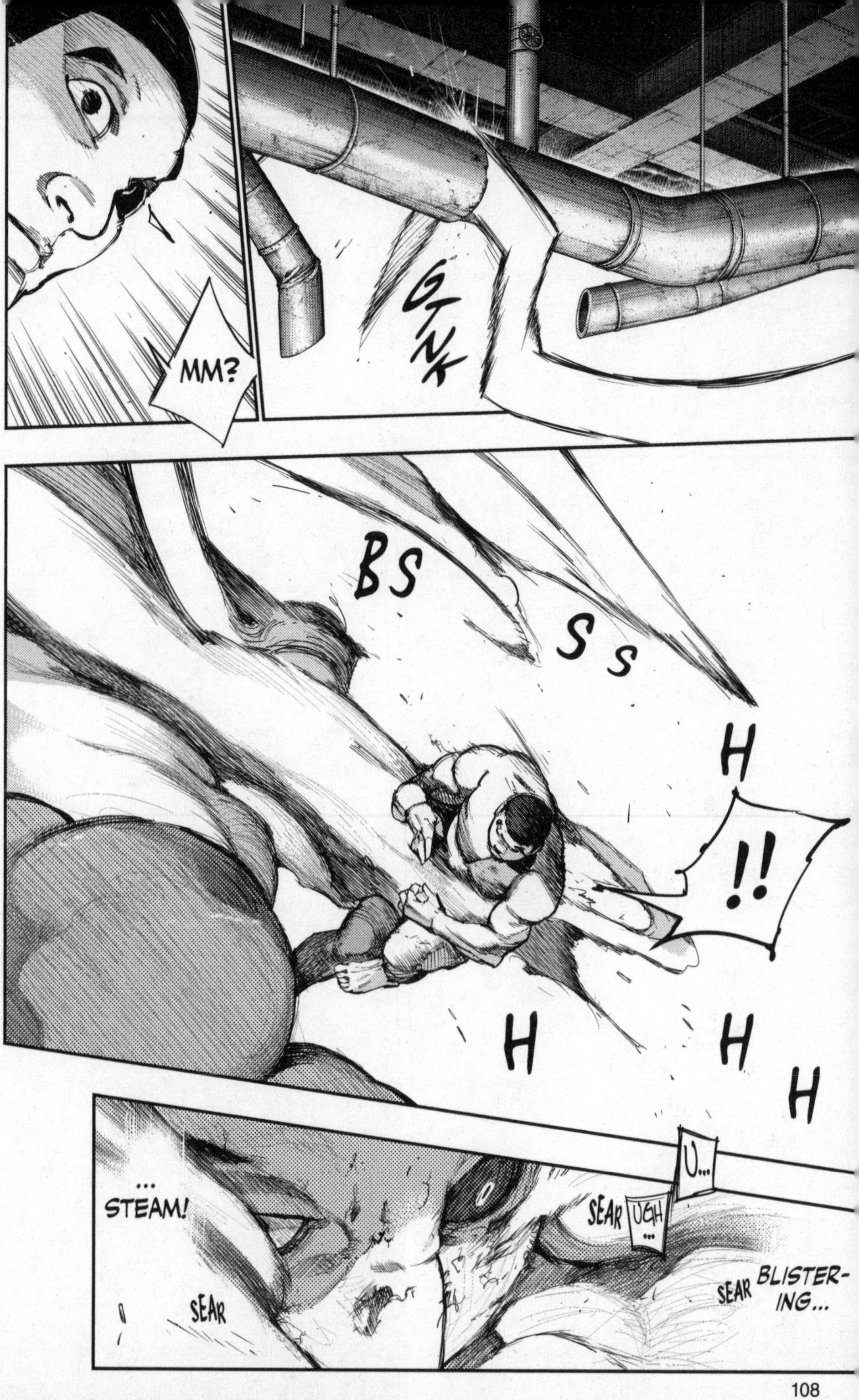
GINK
MM?
BS
S
S
H
!!
H
H
H
U...
UGH...
SEAR
SEAR
BLISTER-ING...
SEAR
... STEAM!

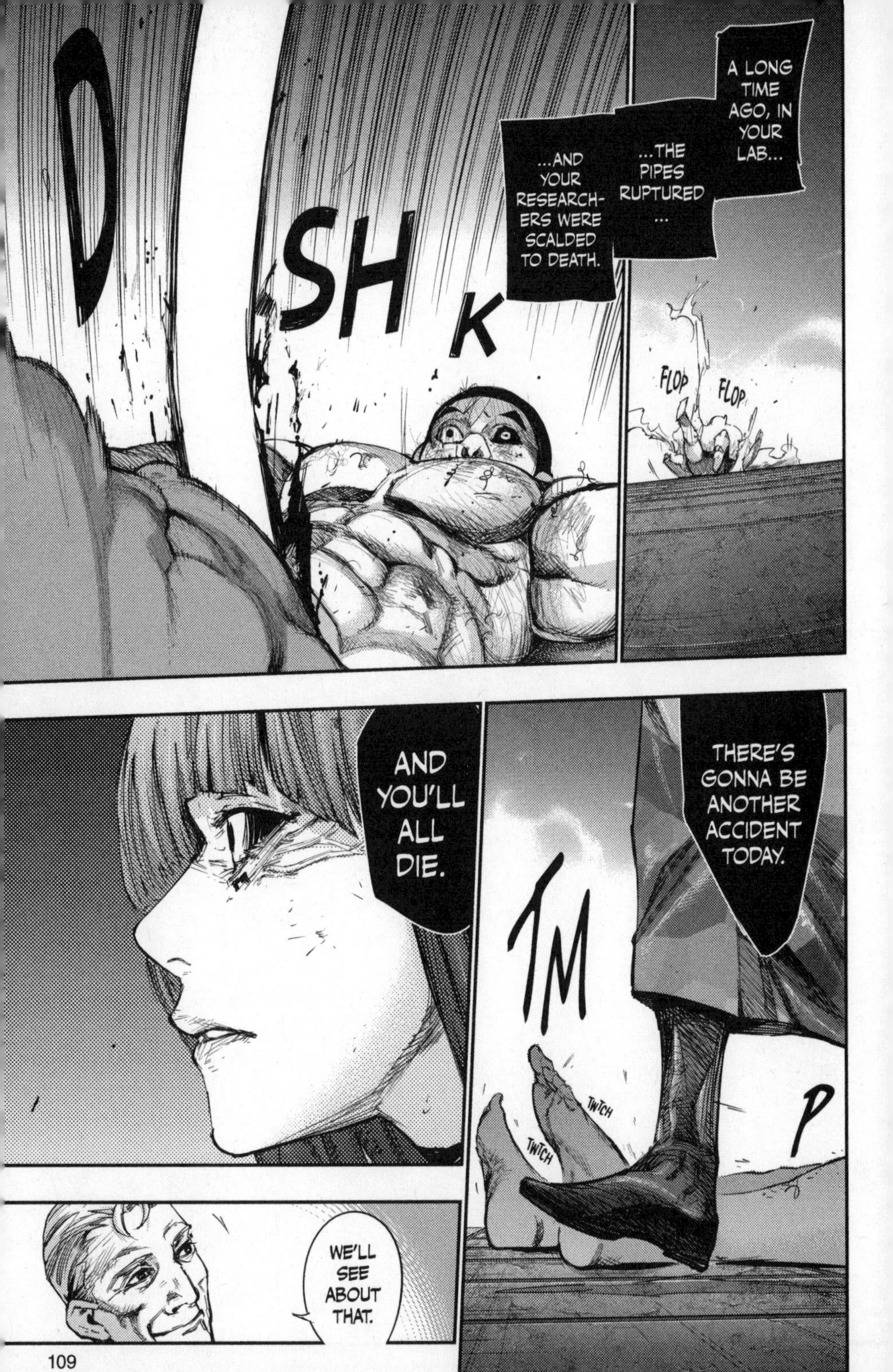
A LONG TIME AGO, IN YOUR LAB...
...THE PIPES RUPTURED ...
...AND YOUR RESEARCHERS WERE SCALDED TO DEATH.
FLOP FLOP
D SH K
THERE'S GONNA BE ANOTHER ACCIDENT TODAY.
TM P
TWITCH TWITCH
AND YOU'LL ALL DIE.
WE'LL SEE ABOUT THAT.

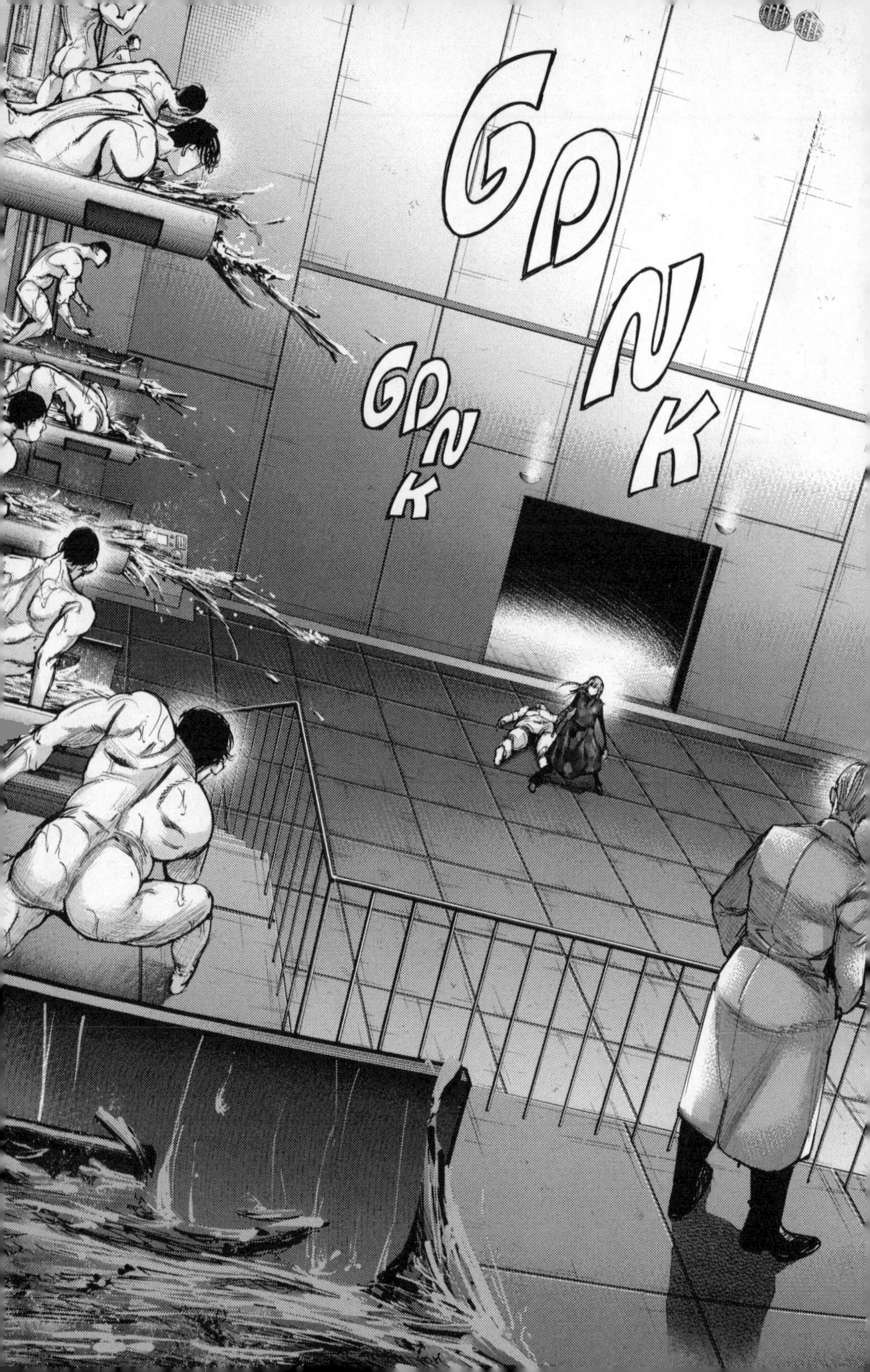
GONK
GONK

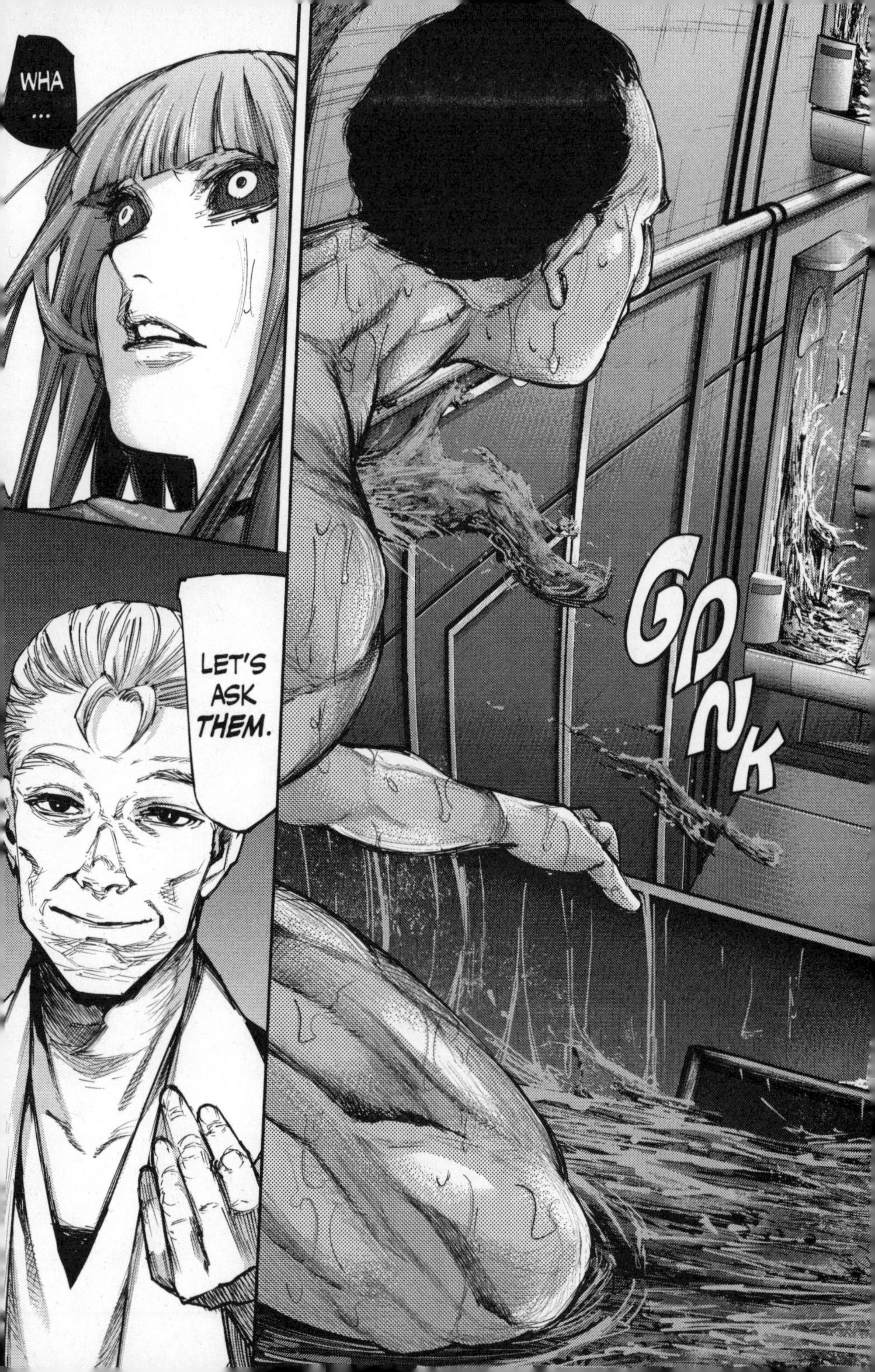
GONK
WHA ...
LET'S ASK THEM.

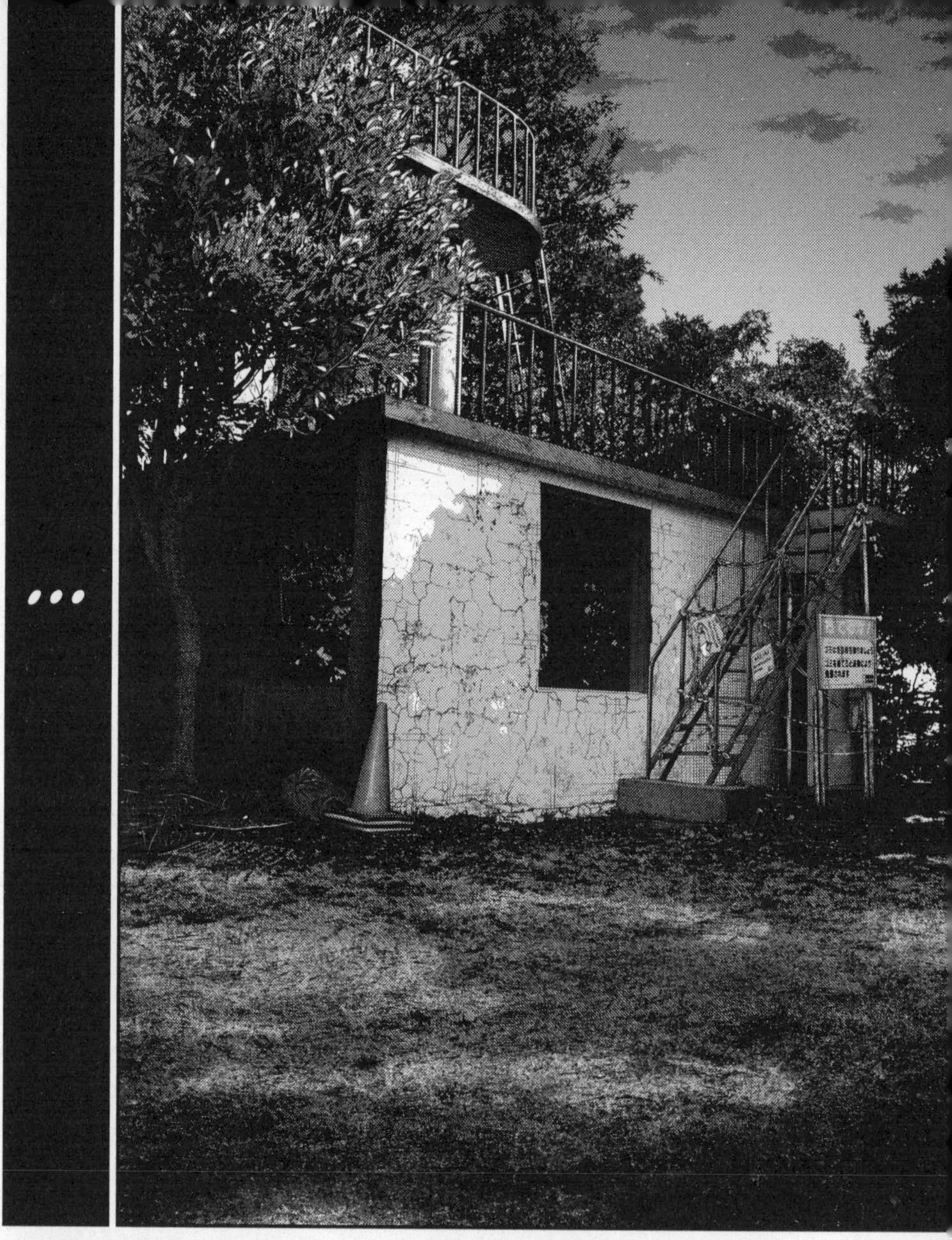
...
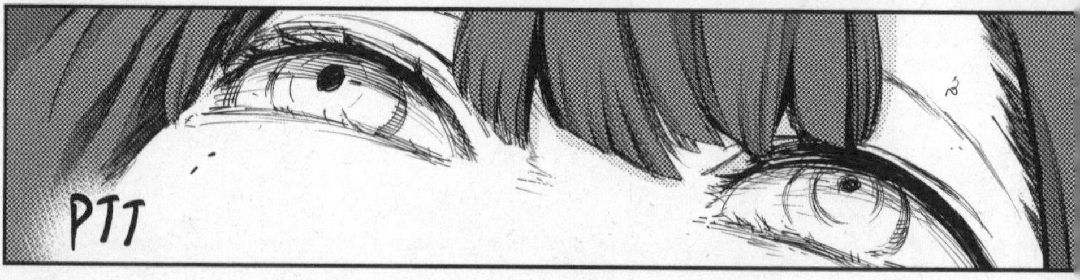
PTT

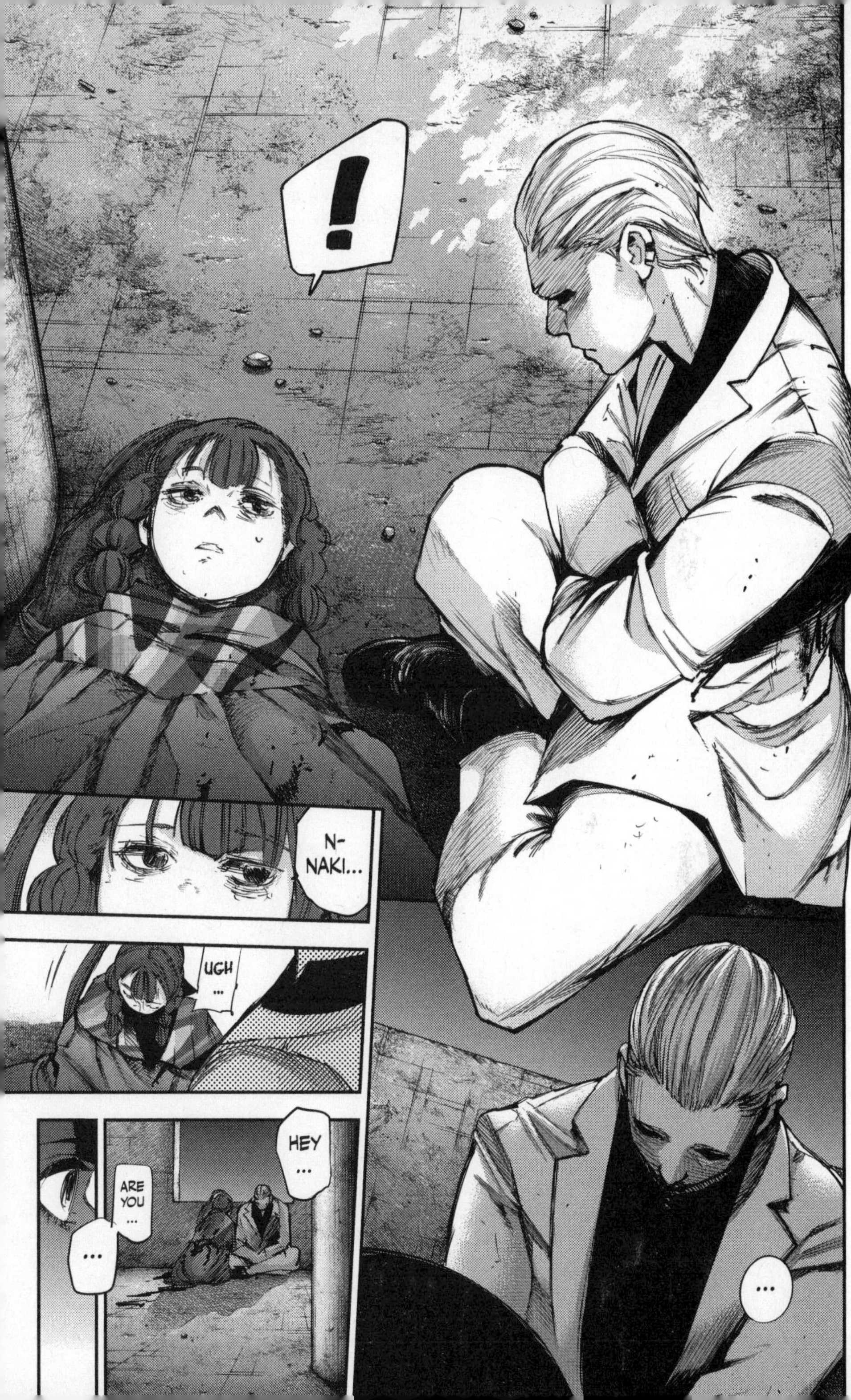
!
N-NAKI...
UGH...
...
HEY...
ARE YOU...
...

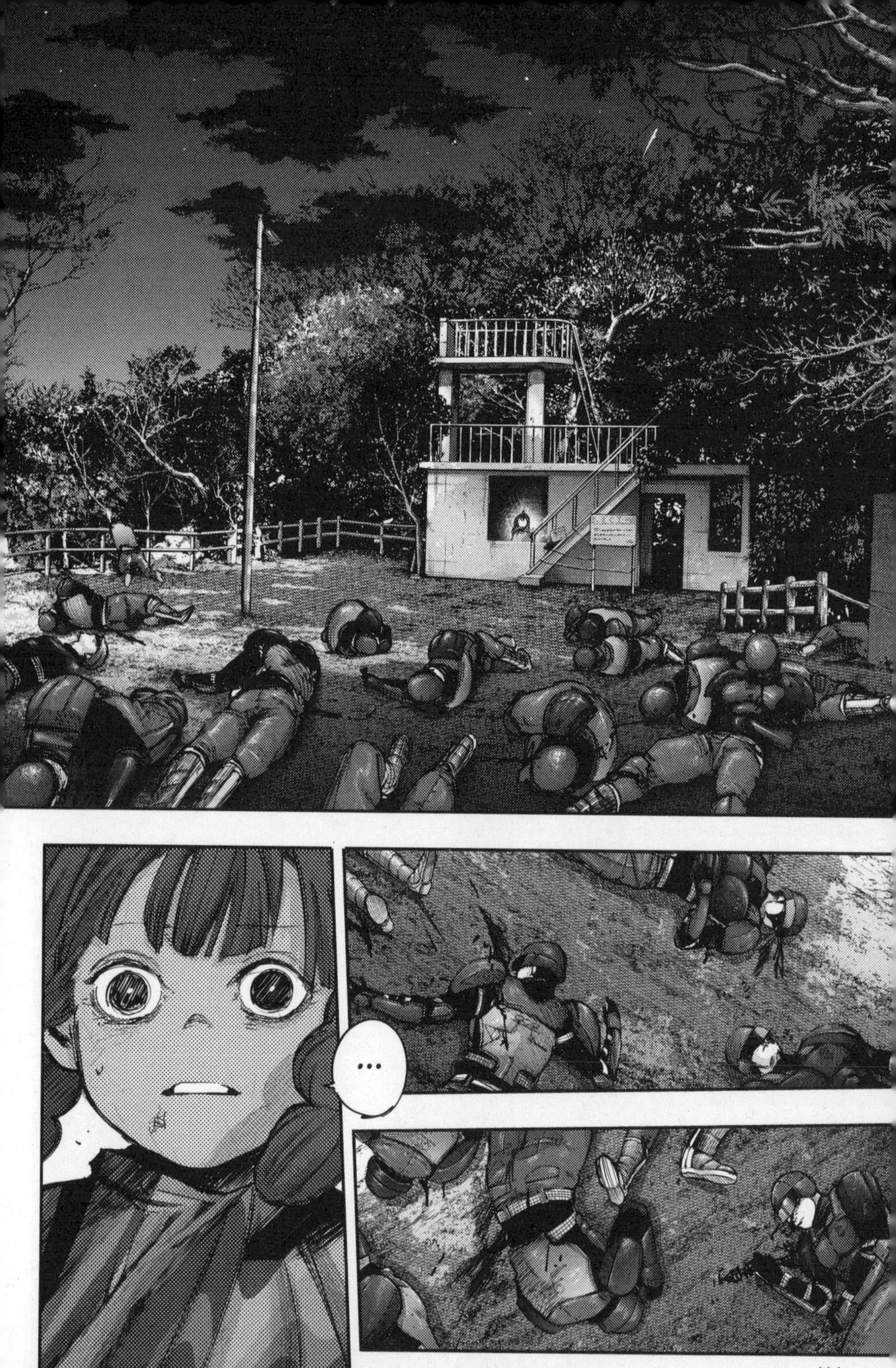
...

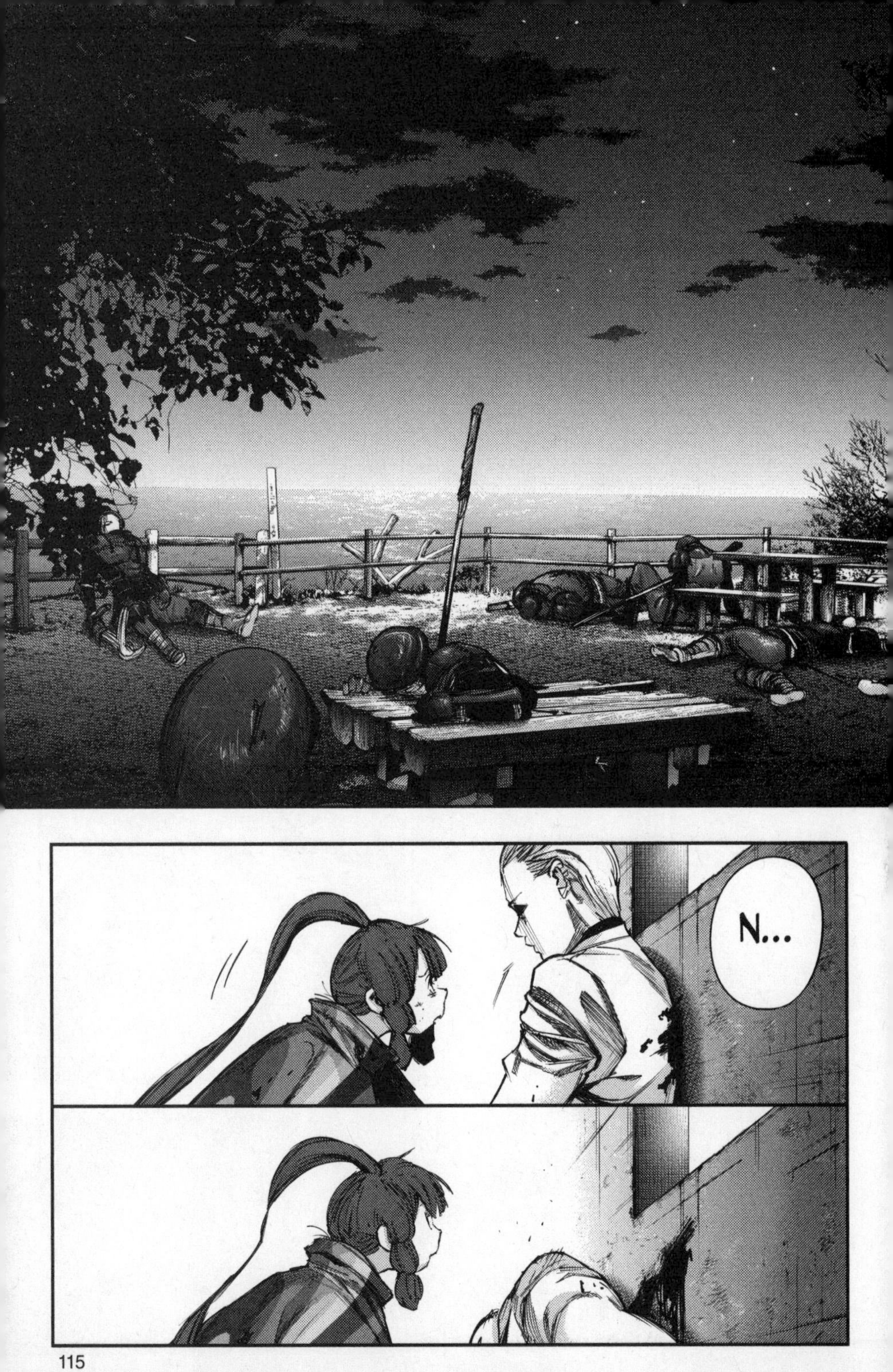
N...

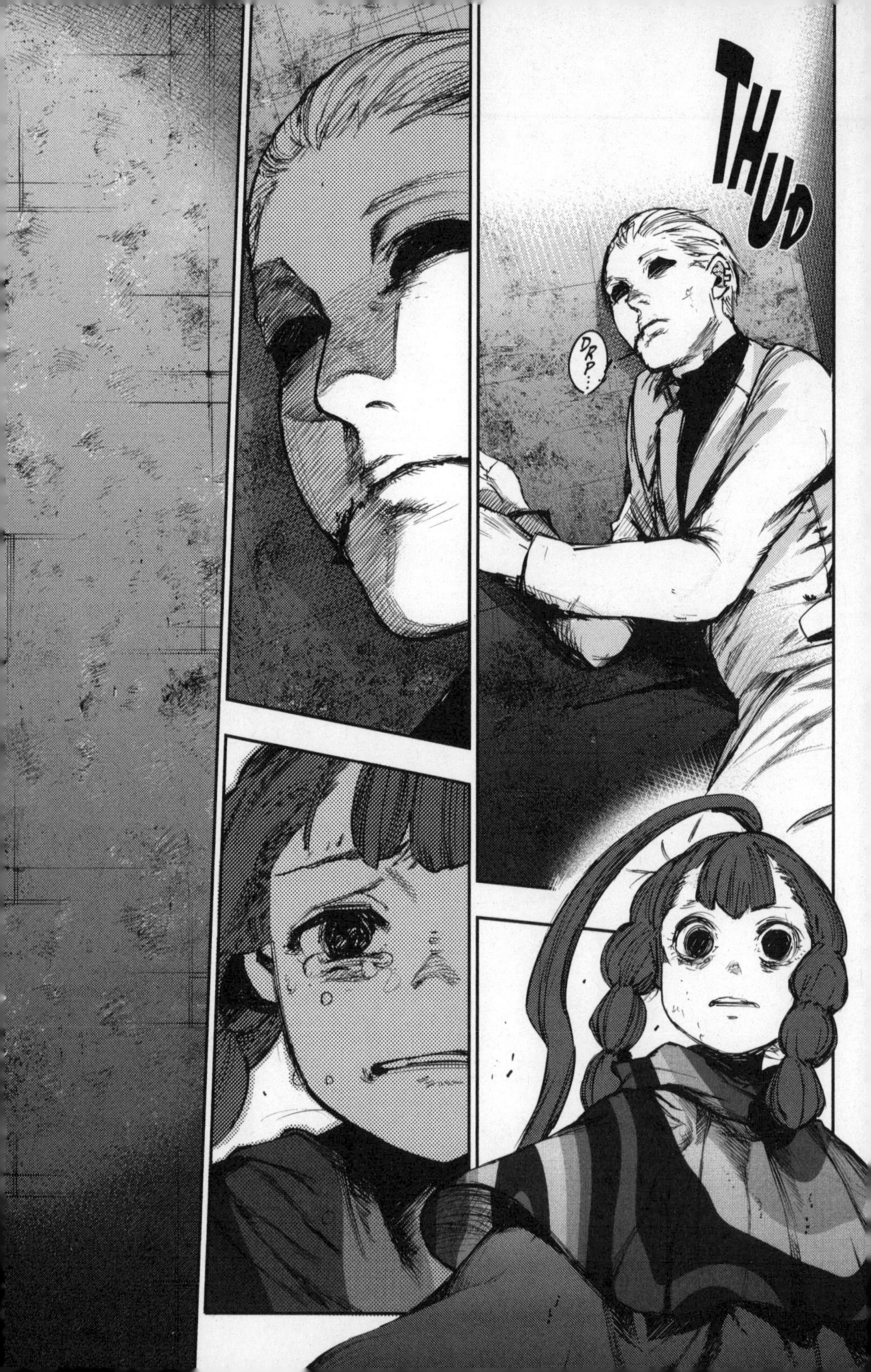
THUD
DRP...

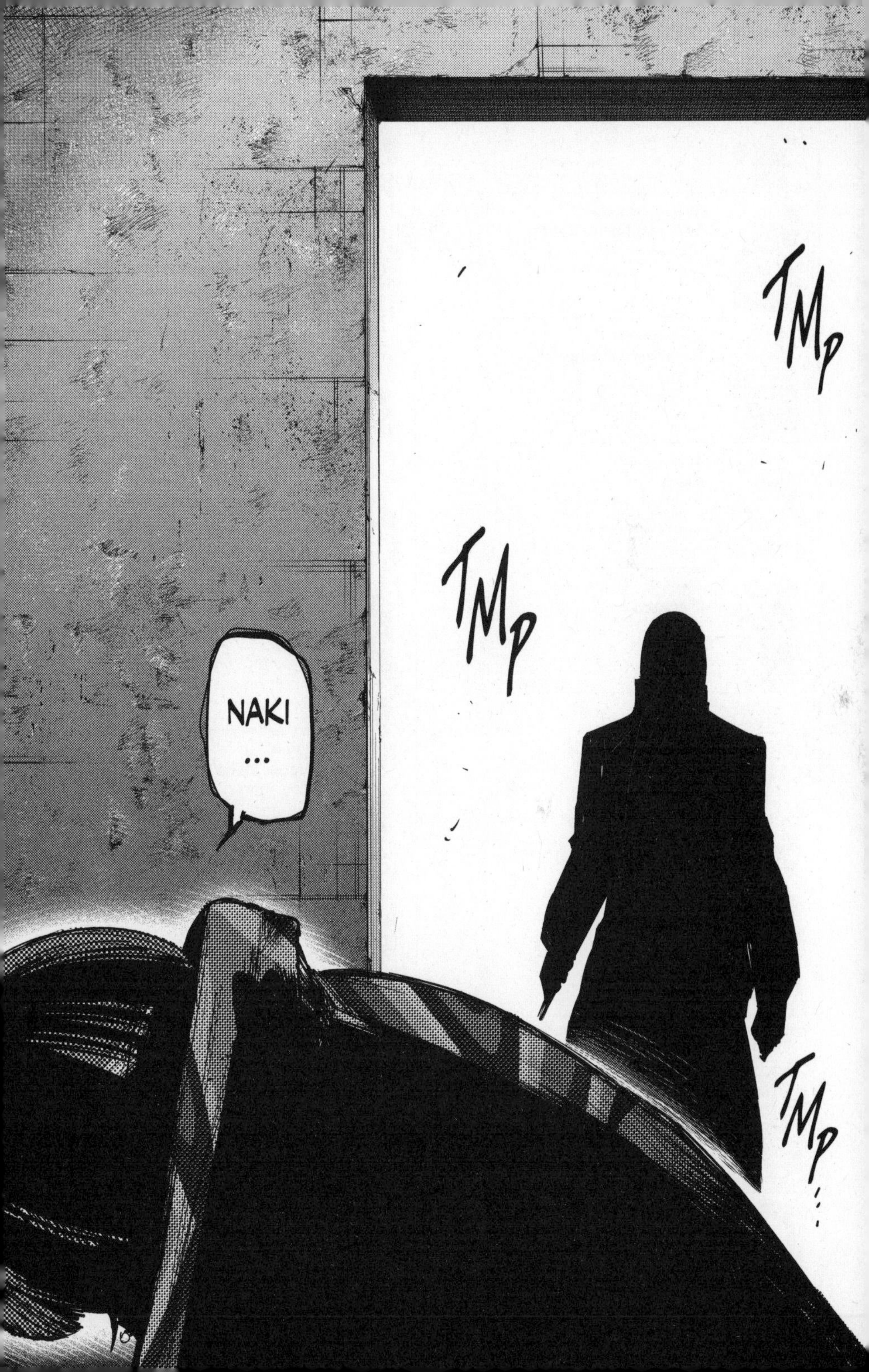
TMP
TMP
TMP
NAKI
...

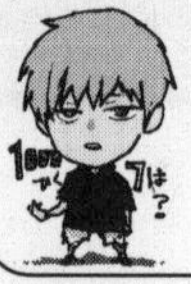

"What's 1,000 minus 7?"

Kaneki

He must've been in a bad place mentally.

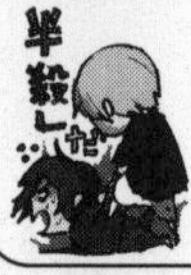

"Beat him half to death."

Beat him half to death.

He didn't have to kill him.

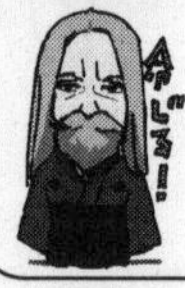

"I order you!"

Tsuneyoshi Washu

Old man.

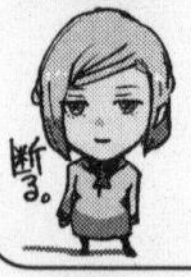
断る。

"I refuse."

Akira

I've always liked women with her personality. Although I wouldn't want to know her personally.

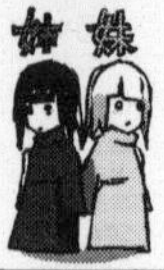
姉 妹

(Older sister Younger sister)

Shirokuro

The fact that they're twins is mystical.

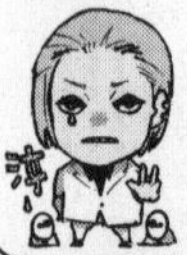

(Tears)

Naki

I wanted to keep an adversary in a white suit.

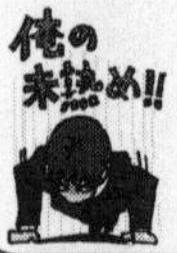

"You damned fool!!"

"You damned fool!!"

I used the wrong character for "you" when making these stickers. I was the fool.

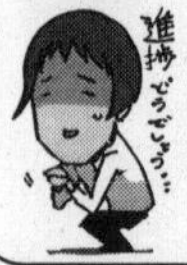

"How's it progressing?"

Shiono

My editor seemed to like him so it pained me to turn him into paté.

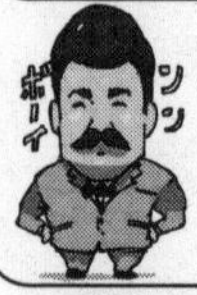

"Mm, boy."

Mougan

He adds depth to the frames. He can also make it stifling.

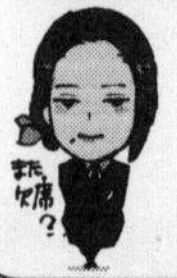
また欠席?

"Not present again?"

Aura Kiyoko

I was surprised when I calculated her age.

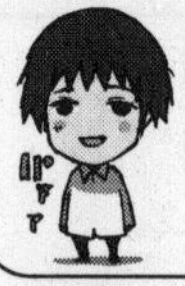

(Glow)

Arata

As a child. Doesn't really look like him. I think I wanted him to look like Kaneki.

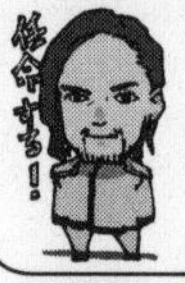

"I appoint you!"

Yoshitoki Washu

I wanted him to have chiseled features and a beard.

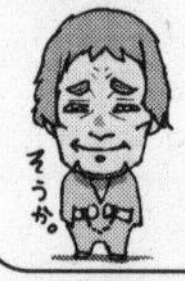
そうか。

"I see."

Donato

I had the same friend design him.

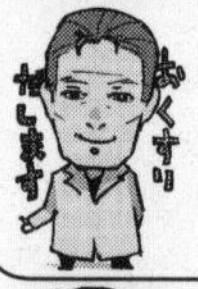

"I'll give you a prescription."

Kano

He made careless miscalculations before we edited the comics. He has a mischievous side to him.

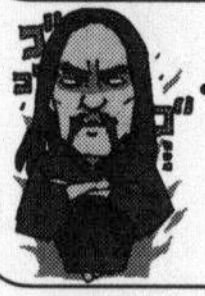

(Krkrkl...)

Shachi

Kaneki punisher man.

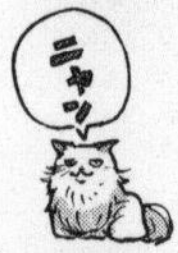

"Meow"

Maris Stella

Her name means "star of the sea" or "Venus." JAXA has a Venus Climate Orbiter called "Akatsuki."

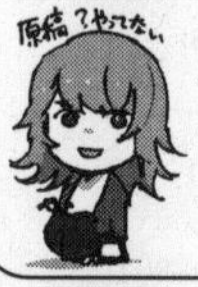
原稿?やってない

"The script? I haven't done it."

Sen Takatsuki

I'm sometimes asked if she's a reflection of myself as a writer, but I don't think she's anything like me.

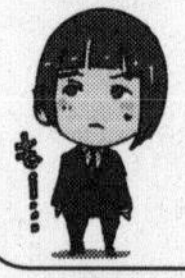

" C'mon..."

Ui

He used to be cute.

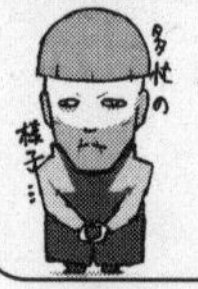

"You seem busy..."

Warden Haisaki

Avant-garde haircut.

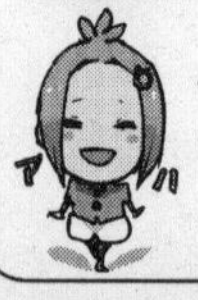

"Aha"

Roma

Uta is wearing her hair clip in the volume 12 bonus manga.

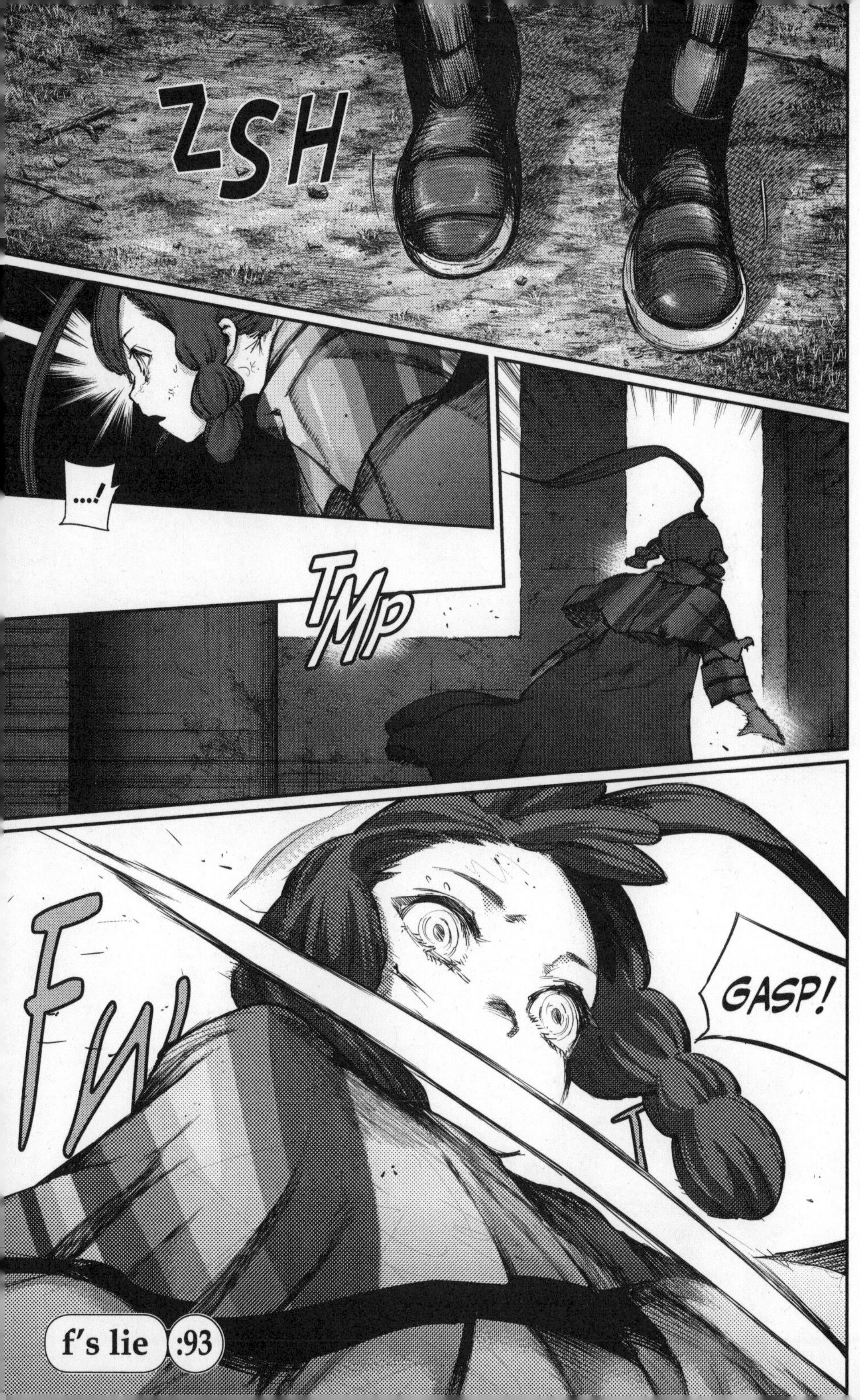
ZSH
TMP
...!
GASP!
FW

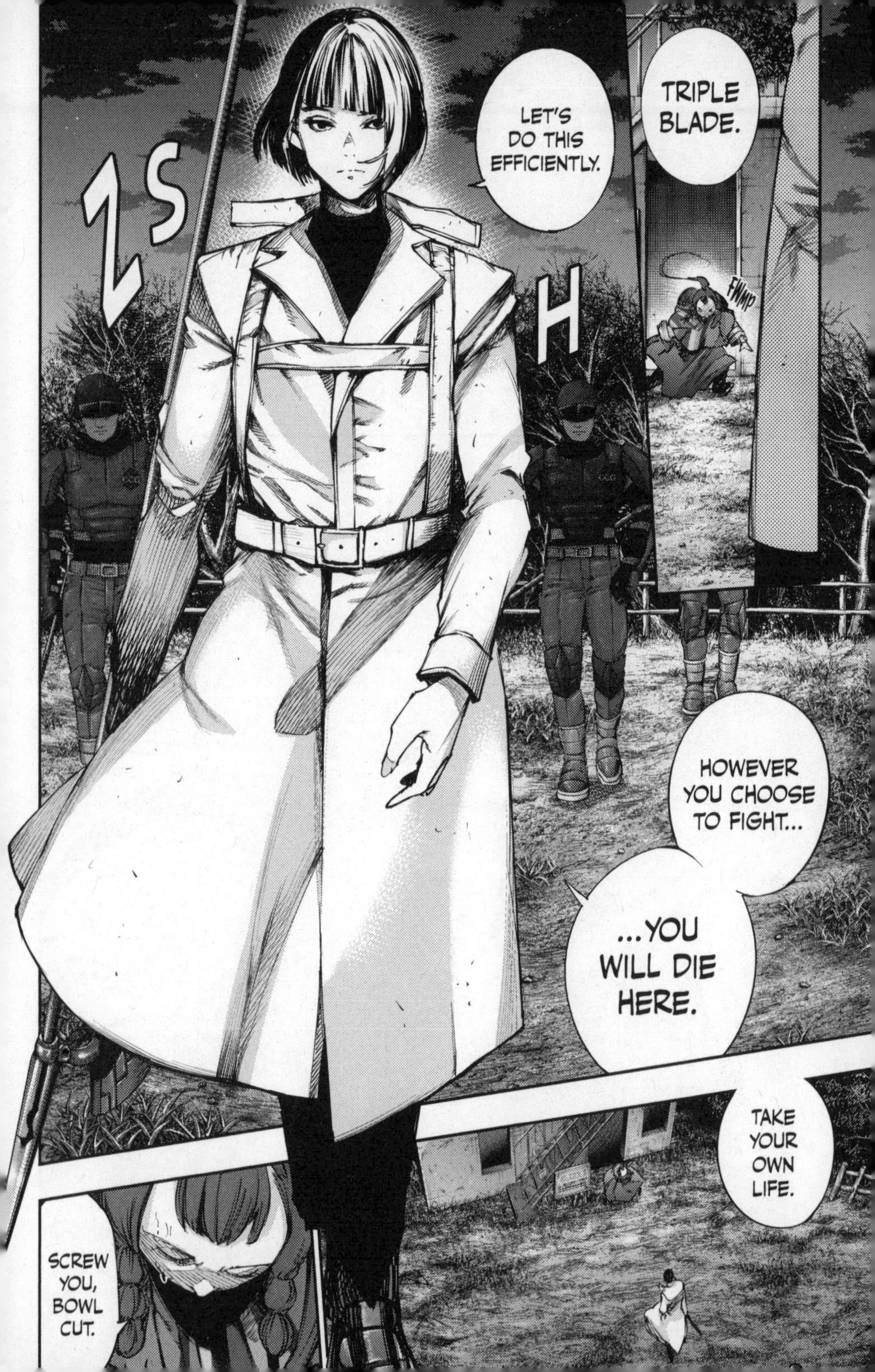
TRIPLE BLADE.
FWMP
LET'S DO THIS EFFICIENTLY.
ZSH
HOWEVER YOU CHOOSE TO FIGHT...
...YOU WILL DIE HERE.
TAKE YOUR OWN LIFE.
SCREW YOU, BOWL CUT.

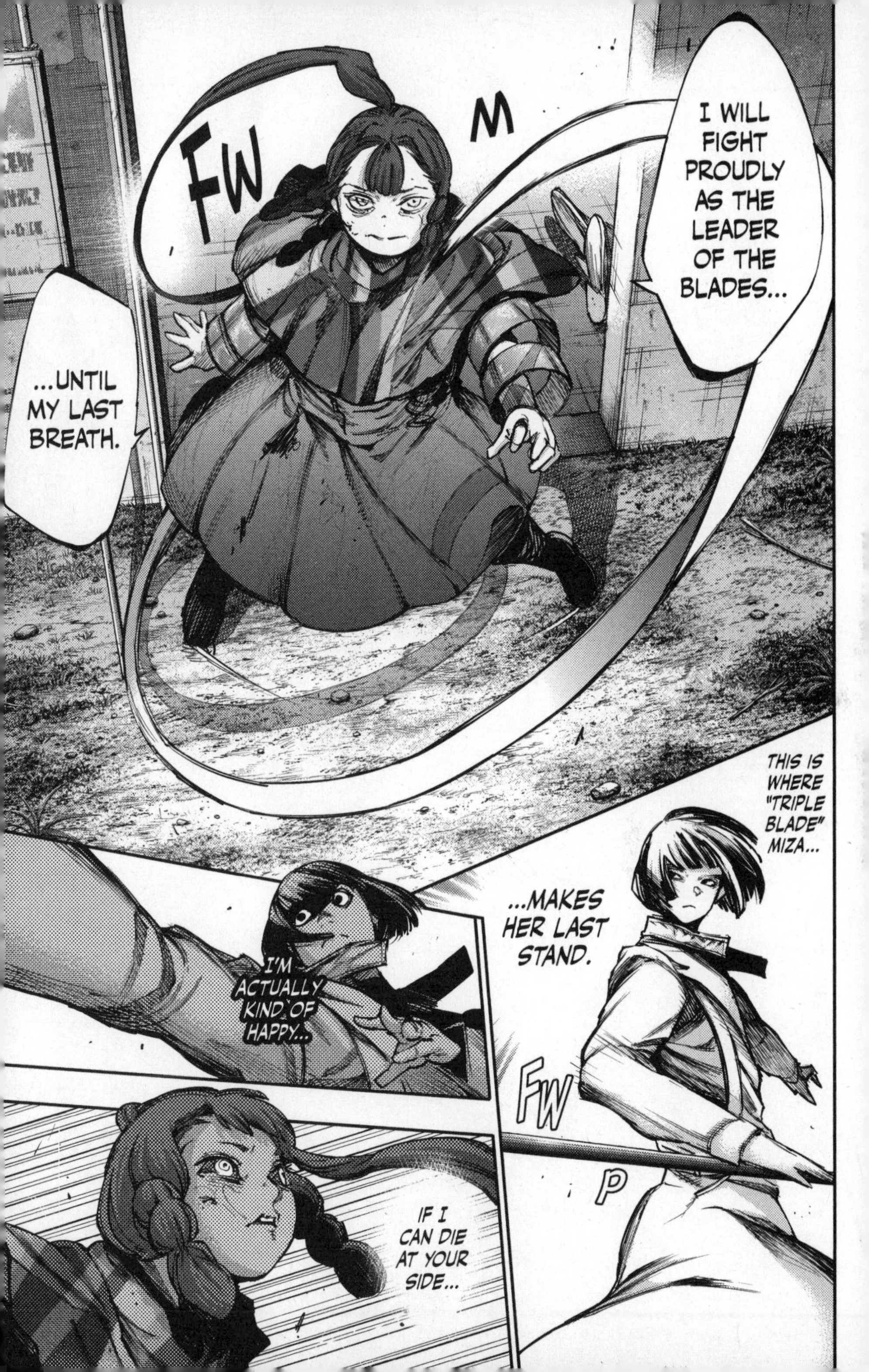
I WILL FIGHT PROUDLY AS THE LEADER OF THE BLADES...
FW M
...UNTIL MY LAST BREATH.
THIS IS WHERE "TRIPLE BLADE" MIZA...
...MAKES HER LAST STAND.
FW P
I'M ACTUALLY KIND OF HAPPY...
IF I CAN DIE AT YOUR SIDE...

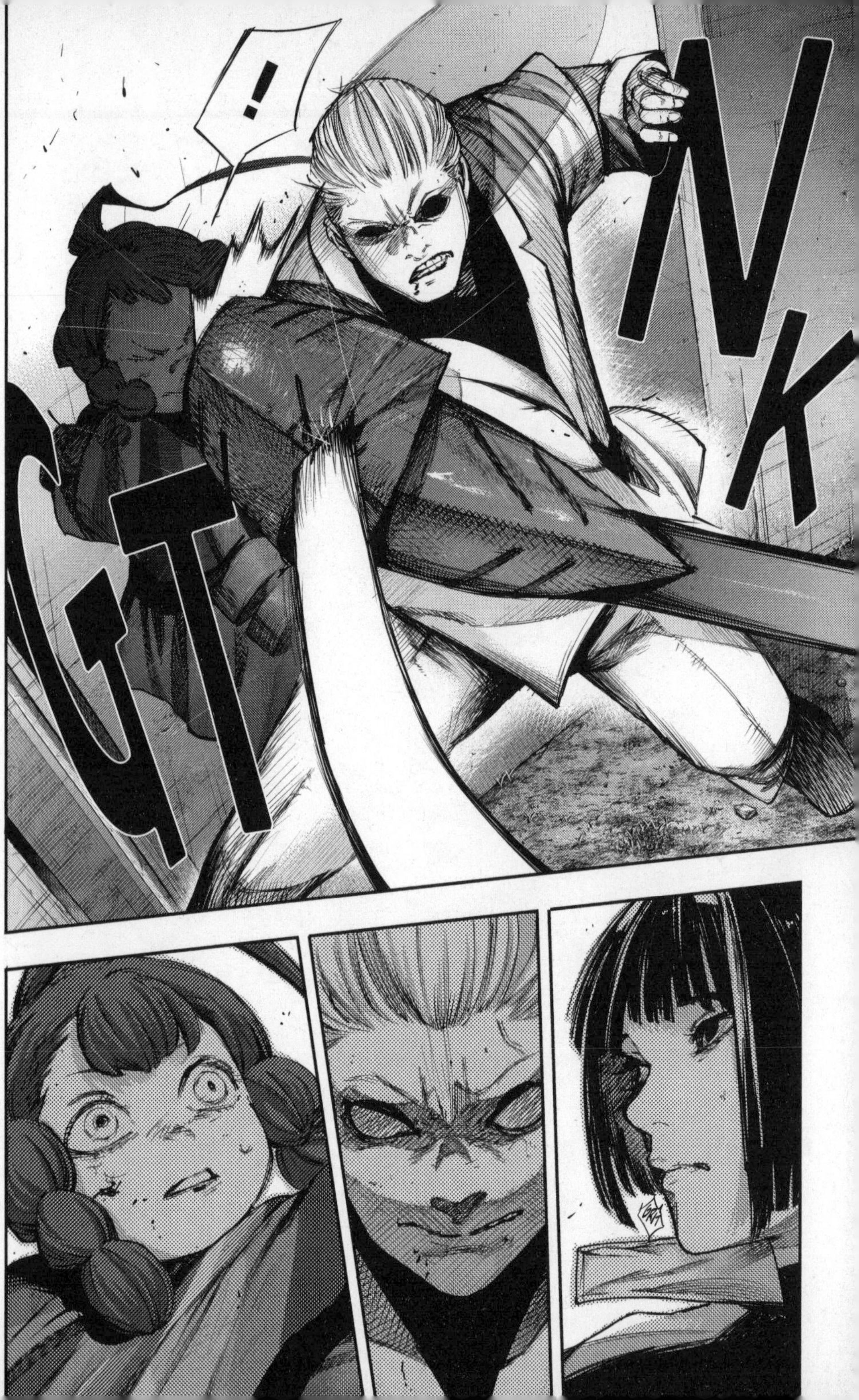
!

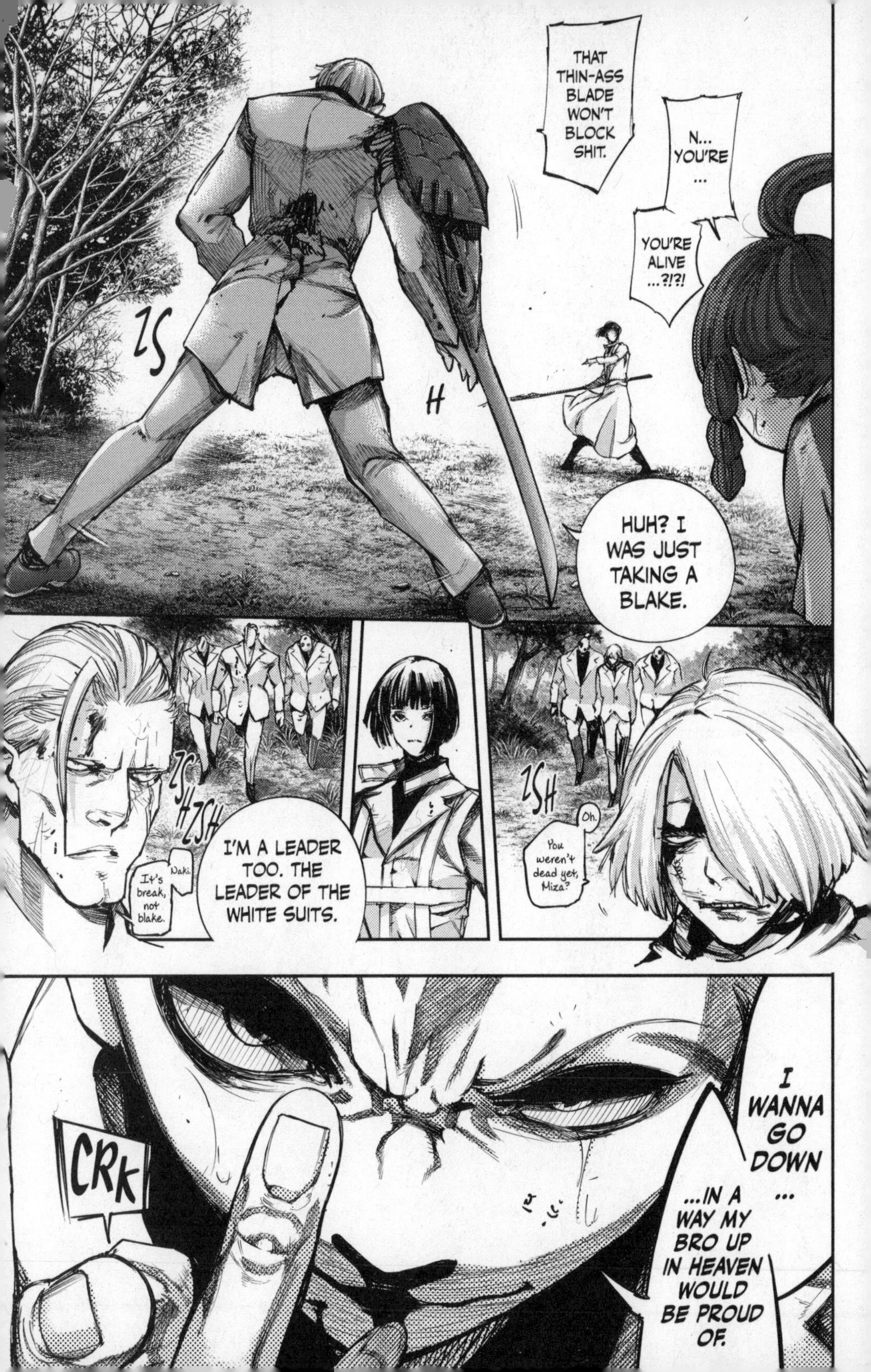
THAT THIN-ASS BLADE WON'T BLOCK SHIT.
N... YOU'RE ...
YOU'RE ALIVE ...?!?!
HUH? I WAS JUST TAKING A BLAKE.
ZS
H
Oh.
You weren't dead yet, Miza?
ZSH
I'M A LEADER TOO. THE LEADER OF THE WHITE SUITS.
Naki.
It's break, not blake.
ZSHZSH
I WANNA GO DOWN ...
...IN A WAY MY BRO UP IN HEAVEN WOULD BE PROUD OF.
CRK

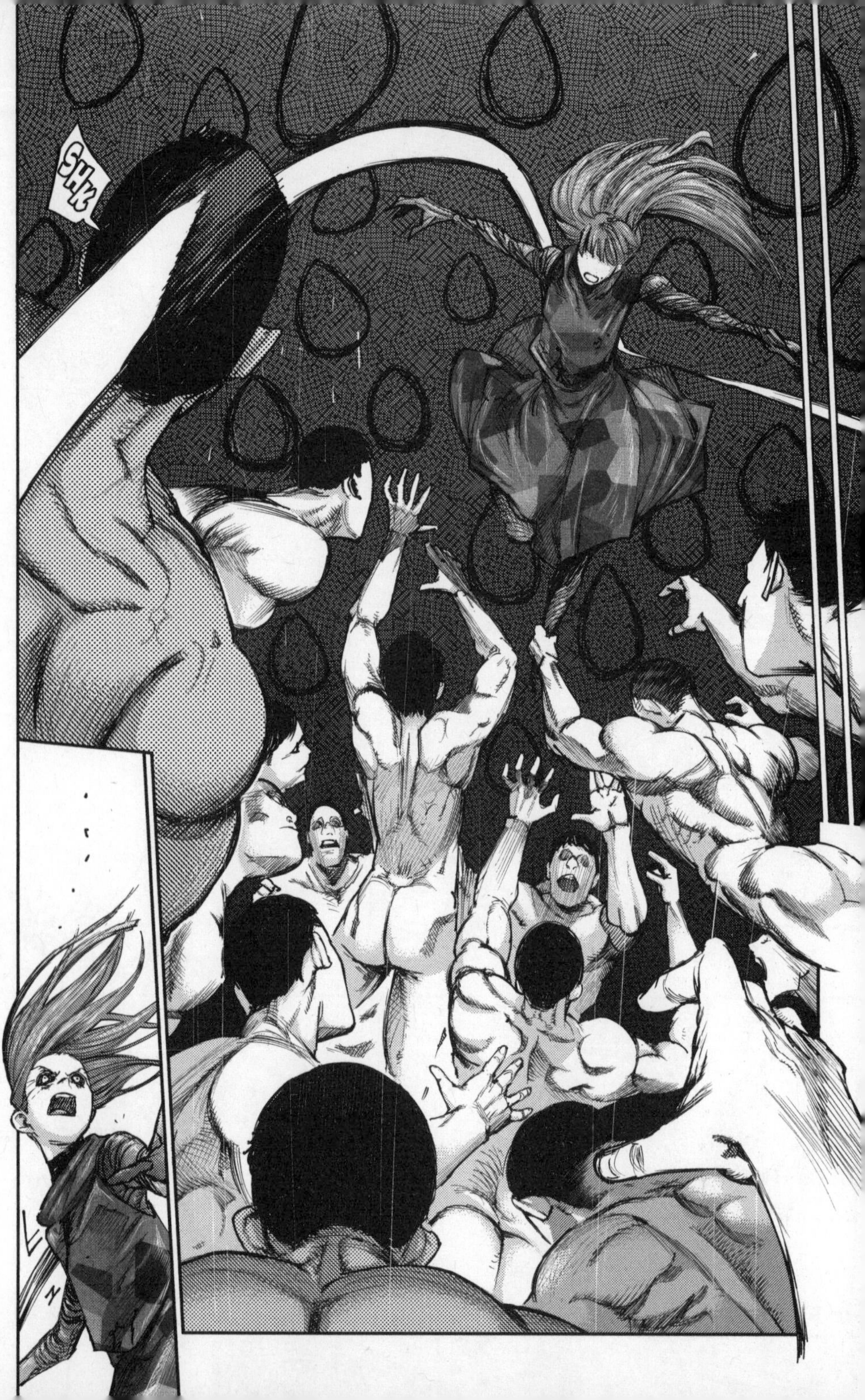
SHK

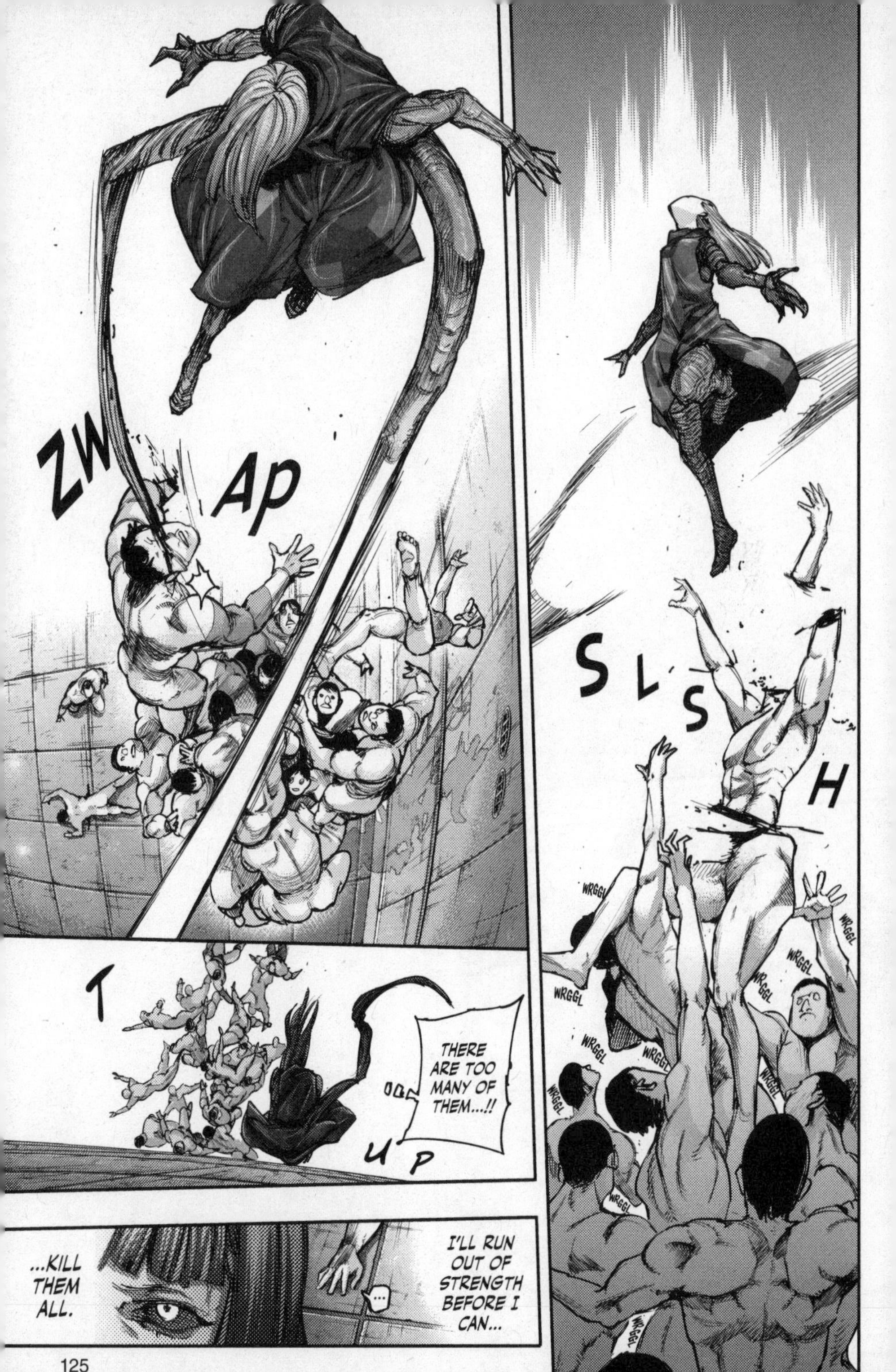
SLSH
WRGGL
WRGGL
WRGGL
WRGGL
WRGGL
WRGGL
WRGGL
WRGGL
WRGGL
WRGGL
ZWAP
T
THERE ARE TOO MANY OF THEM...!!
UP
I'LL RUN OUT OF STRENGTH BEFORE I CAN...
...KILL THEM ALL.

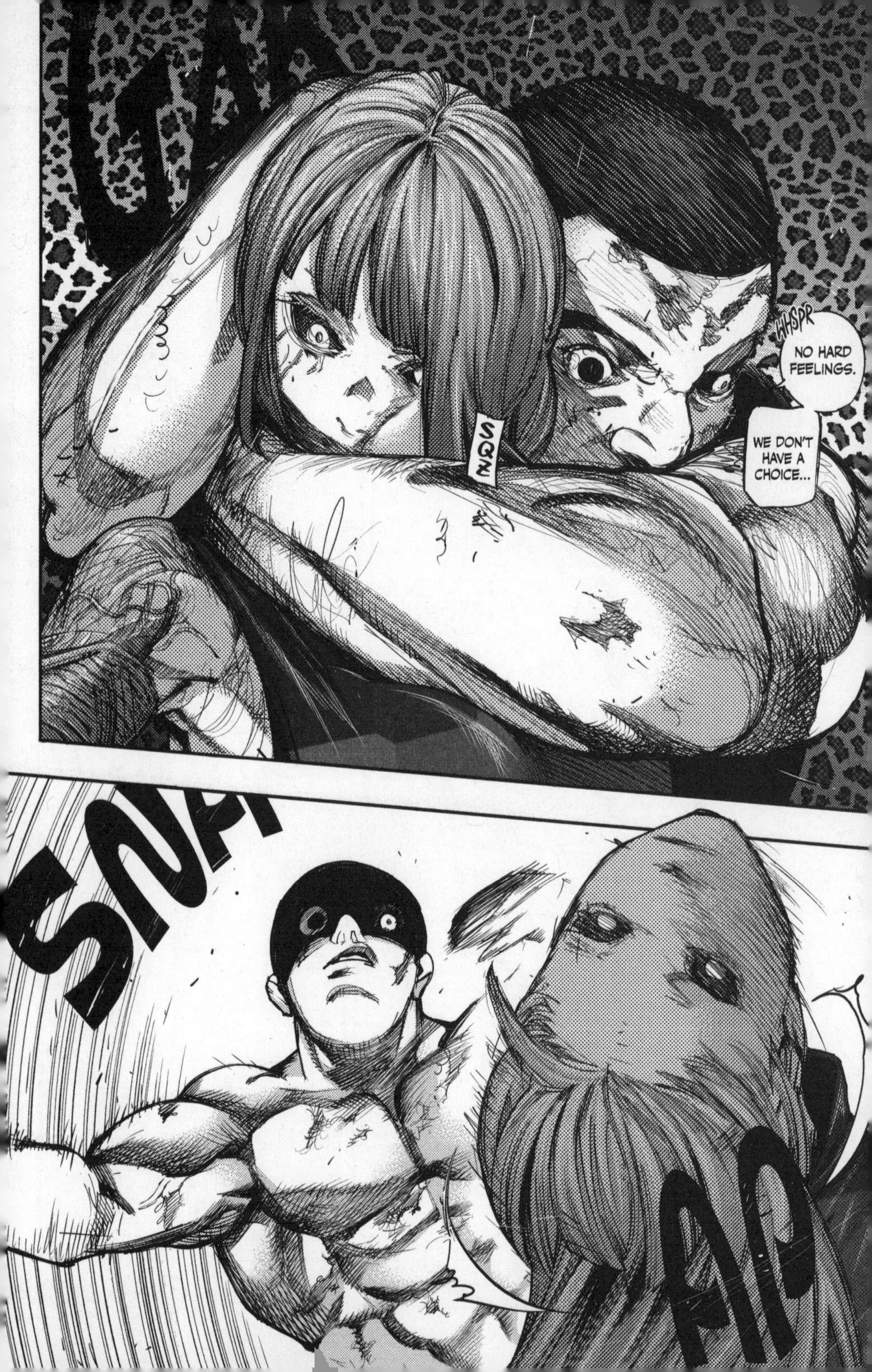
WHSPR
NO HARD FEELINGS.
WE DON'T HAVE A CHOICE...
SQZ

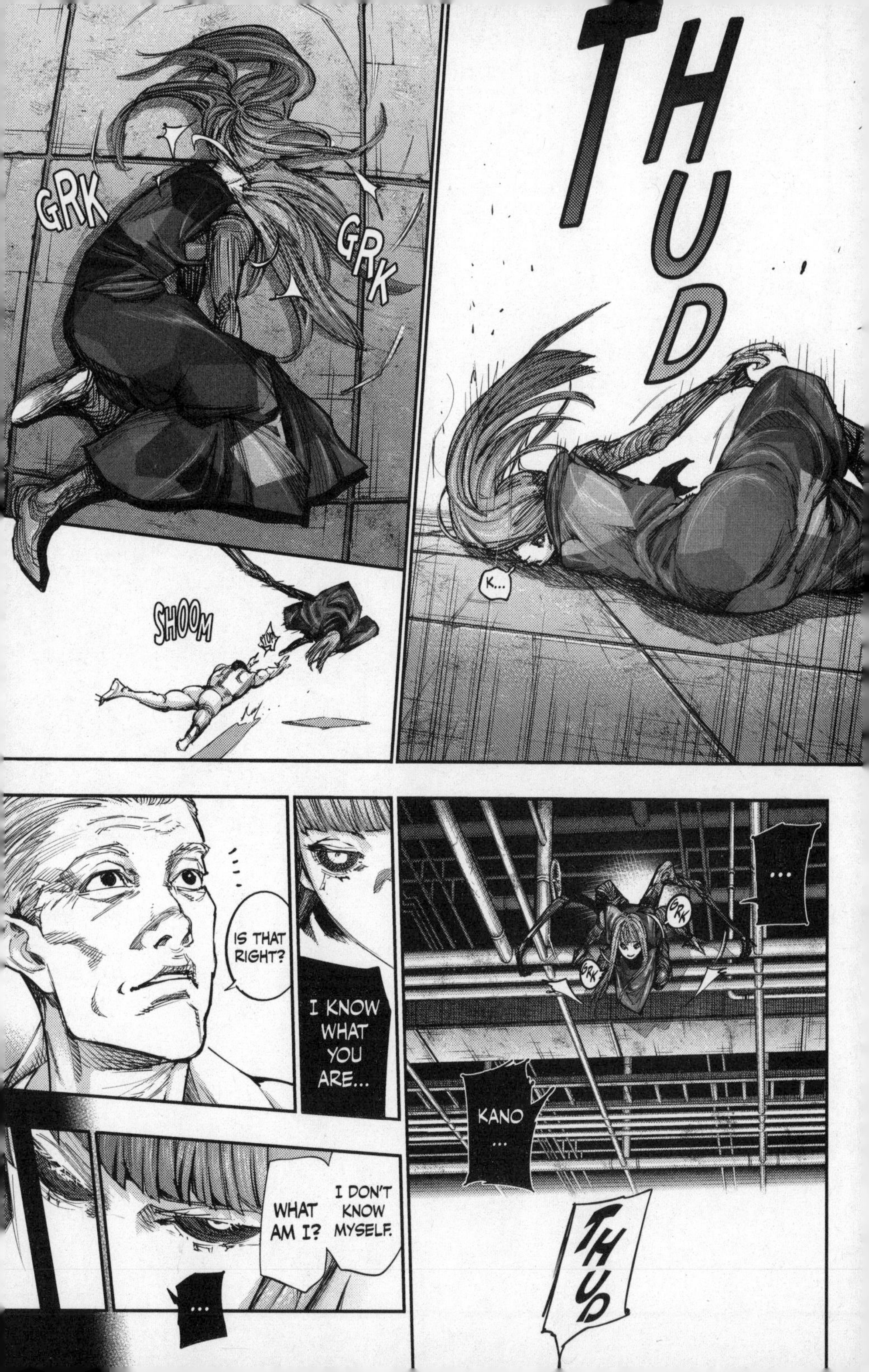
THUD
K...
GRK
GRK
SHOOM
...
GRK
GRK
KANO ...
THUD
I KNOW WHAT YOU ARE...
IS THAT RIGHT?
I DON'T KNOW MYSELF.
WHAT AM I?
...

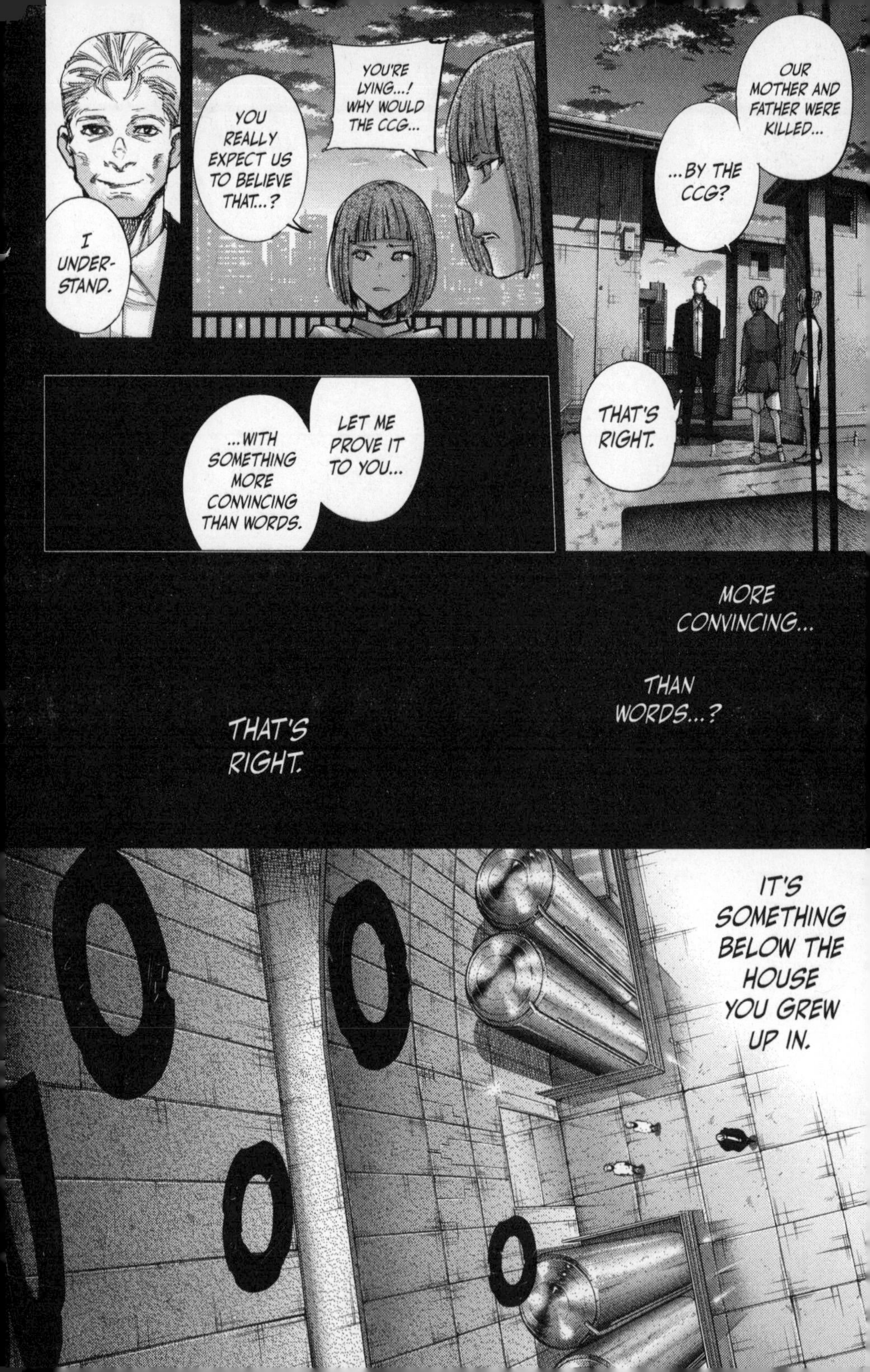
OUR MOTHER AND FATHER WERE KILLED...
...BY THE CCG?
THAT'S RIGHT.
YOU'RE LYING...! WHY WOULD THE CCG...
YOU REALLY EXPECT US TO BELIEVE THAT...?
I UNDER-STAND.
LET ME PROVE IT TO YOU...
...WITH SOMETHING MORE CONVINCING THAN WORDS.
MORE CONVINCING...
THAN WORDS...?
THAT'S RIGHT.
IT'S SOMETHING BELOW THE HOUSE YOU GREW UP IN.

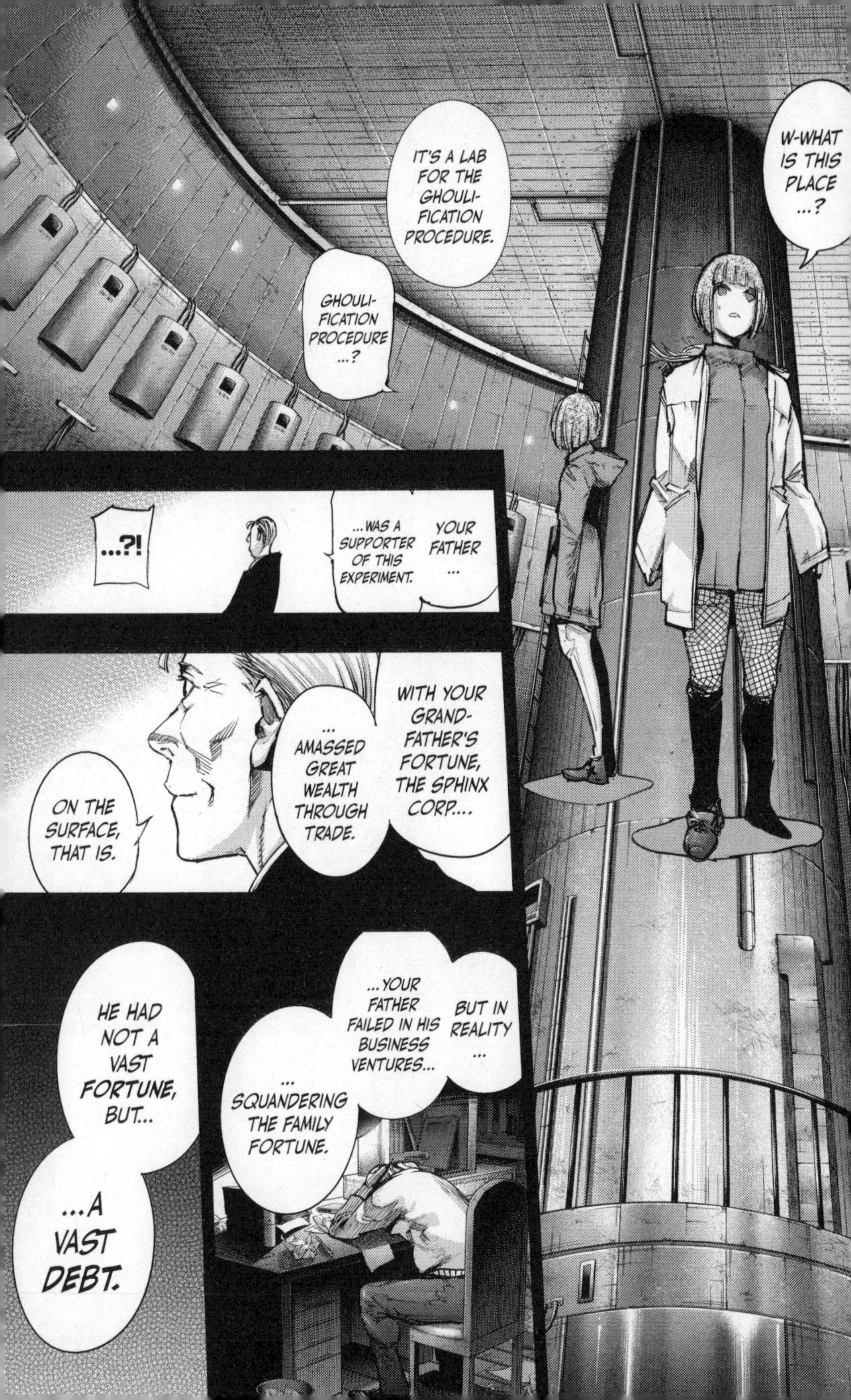
W-WHAT IS THIS PLACE ...?
IT'S A LAB FOR THE GHOULIFICATION PROCEDURE.
GHOULIFICATION PROCEDURE ...?
YOUR FATHER ...
...WAS A SUPPORTER OF THIS EXPERIMENT.
...?!
WITH YOUR GRANDFATHER'S FORTUNE, THE SPHINX CORP....
... AMASSED GREAT WEALTH THROUGH TRADE.
ON THE SURFACE, THAT IS.
BUT IN REALITY ...
...YOUR FATHER FAILED IN HIS BUSINESS VENTURES...
... SQUANDERING THE FAMILY FORTUNE.
HE HAD NOT A VAST FORTUNE, BUT...
...A VAST DEBT.

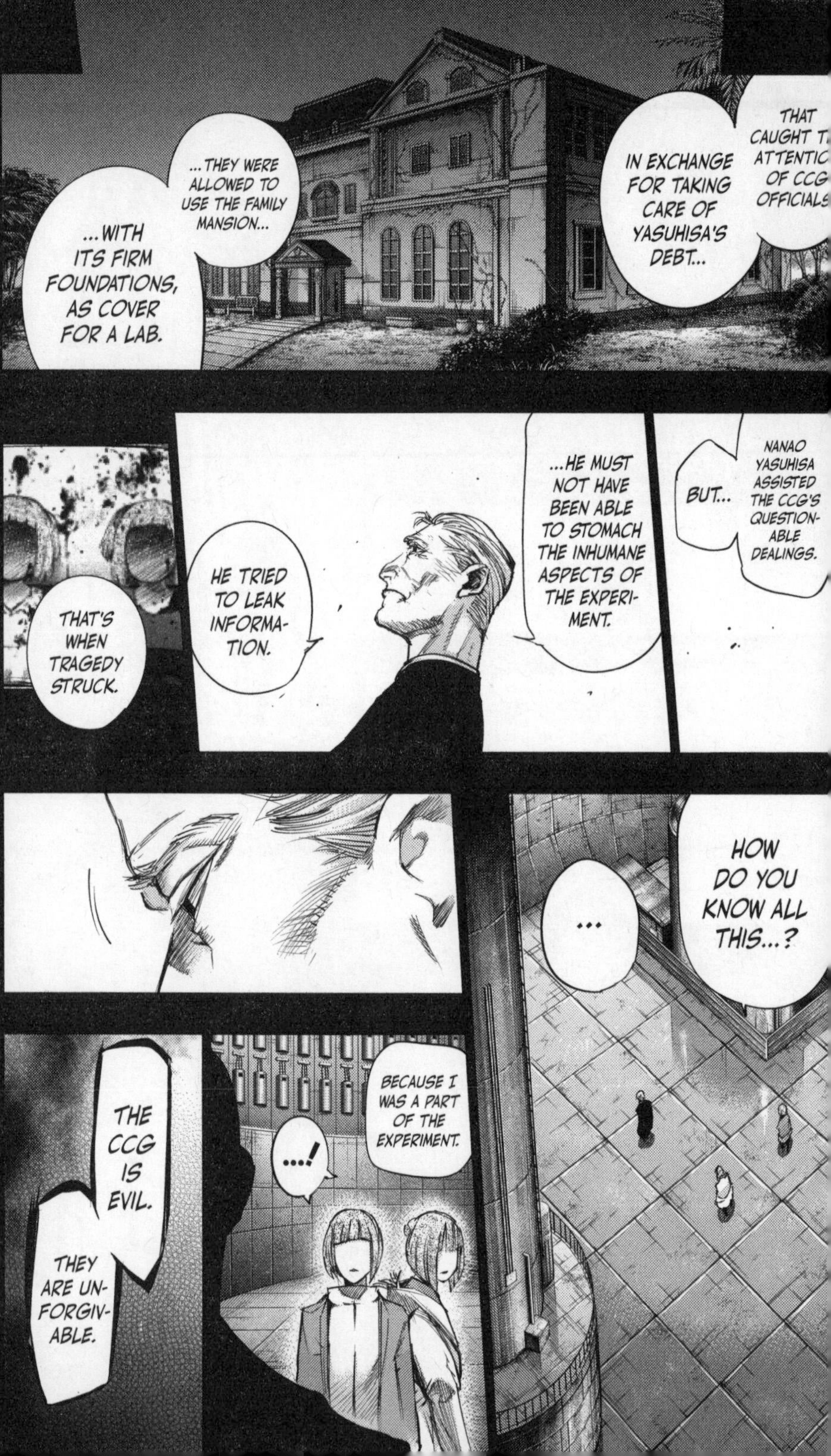
THAT CAUGHT T ATTENTIC OF CCG OFFICIALS
IN EXCHANGE FOR TAKING CARE OF YASUHISA'S DEBT...
...THEY WERE ALLOWED TO USE THE FAMILY MANSION...
...WITH ITS FIRM FOUNDATIONS, AS COVER FOR A LAB.
NANAO YASUHISA ASSISTED THE CCG'S QUESTION-ABLE DEALINGS.
BUT...
...HE MUST NOT HAVE BEEN ABLE TO STOMACH THE INHUMANE ASPECTS OF THE EXPERI-MENT.
HE TRIED TO LEAK INFORMA-TION.
THAT'S WHEN TRAGEDY STRUCK.
HOW DO YOU KNOW ALL THIS...?
...
BECAUSE I WAS A PART OF THE EXPERIMENT.
...!
THE CCG IS EVIL.
THEY ARE UN-FORGIV-ABLE.

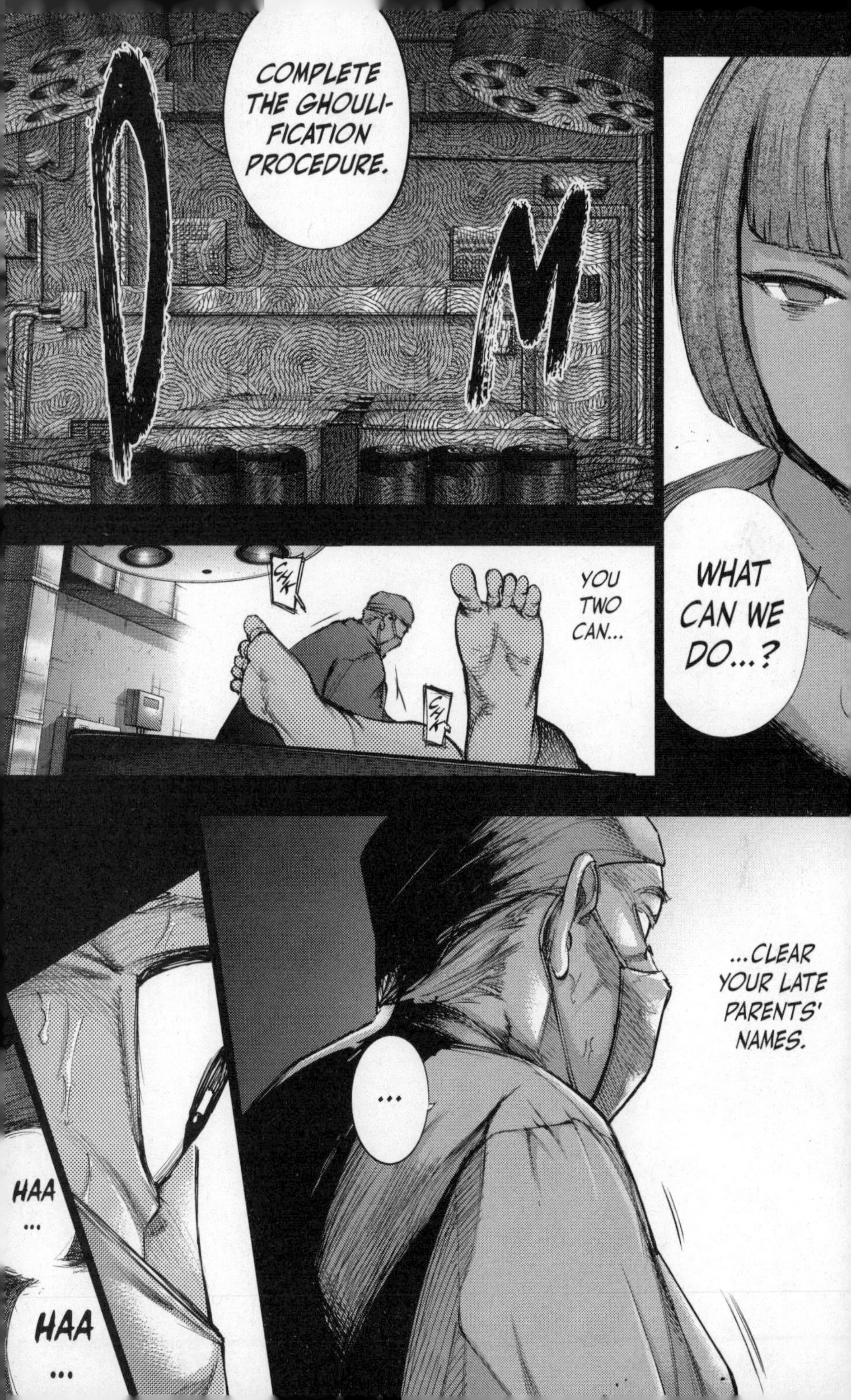
WHAT CAN WE DO...?
COMPLETE THE GHOULI-FICATION PROCEDURE.
CHK
YOU TWO CAN...
CHK
...CLEAR YOUR LATE PARENTS' NAMES.
...
HAA ...
HAA ...

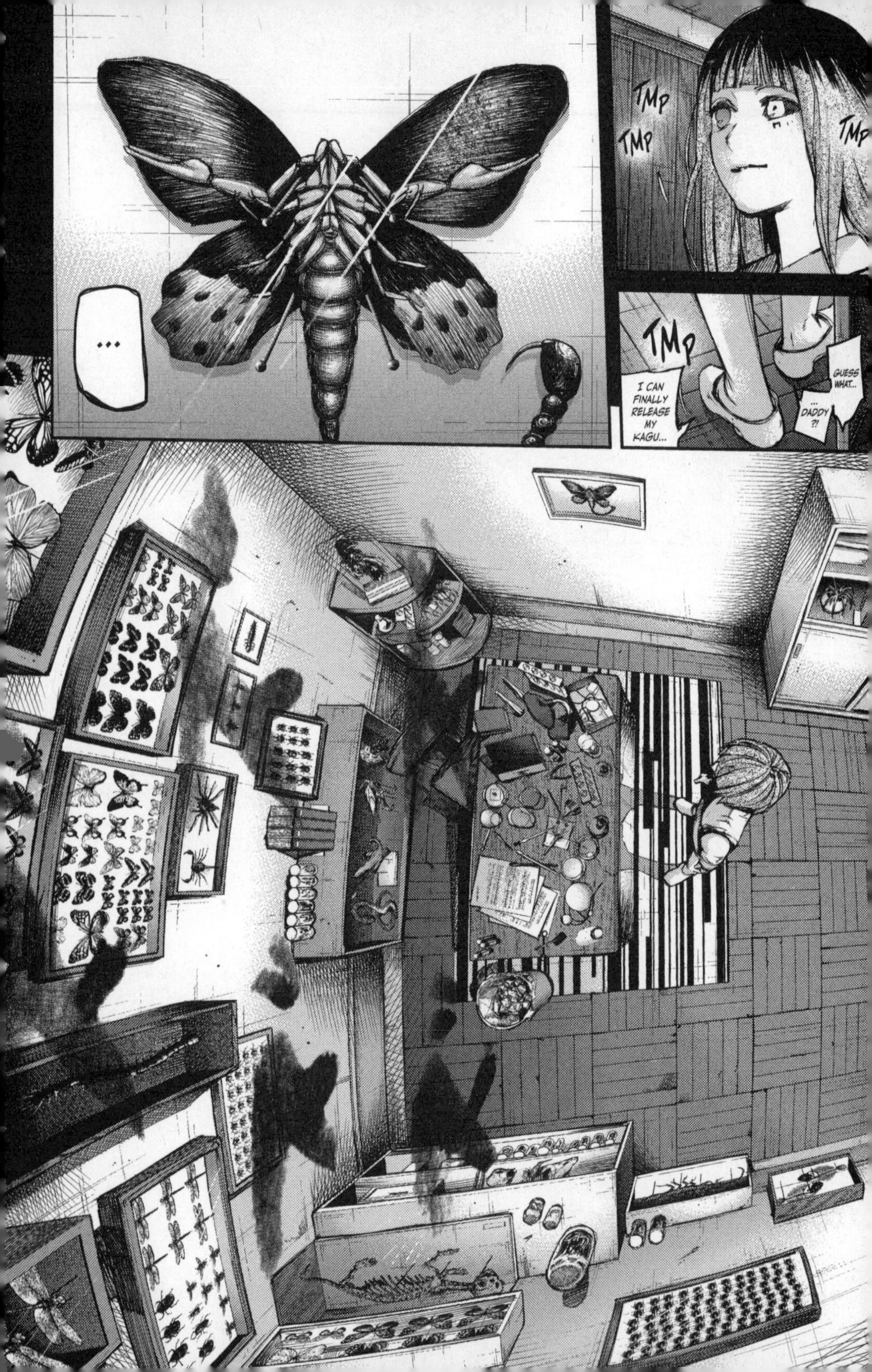
TMP
TMP
TMP
TMP
GUESS WHAT...
... DADDY ?!
I CAN FINALLY RELEASE MY KAGU...
...

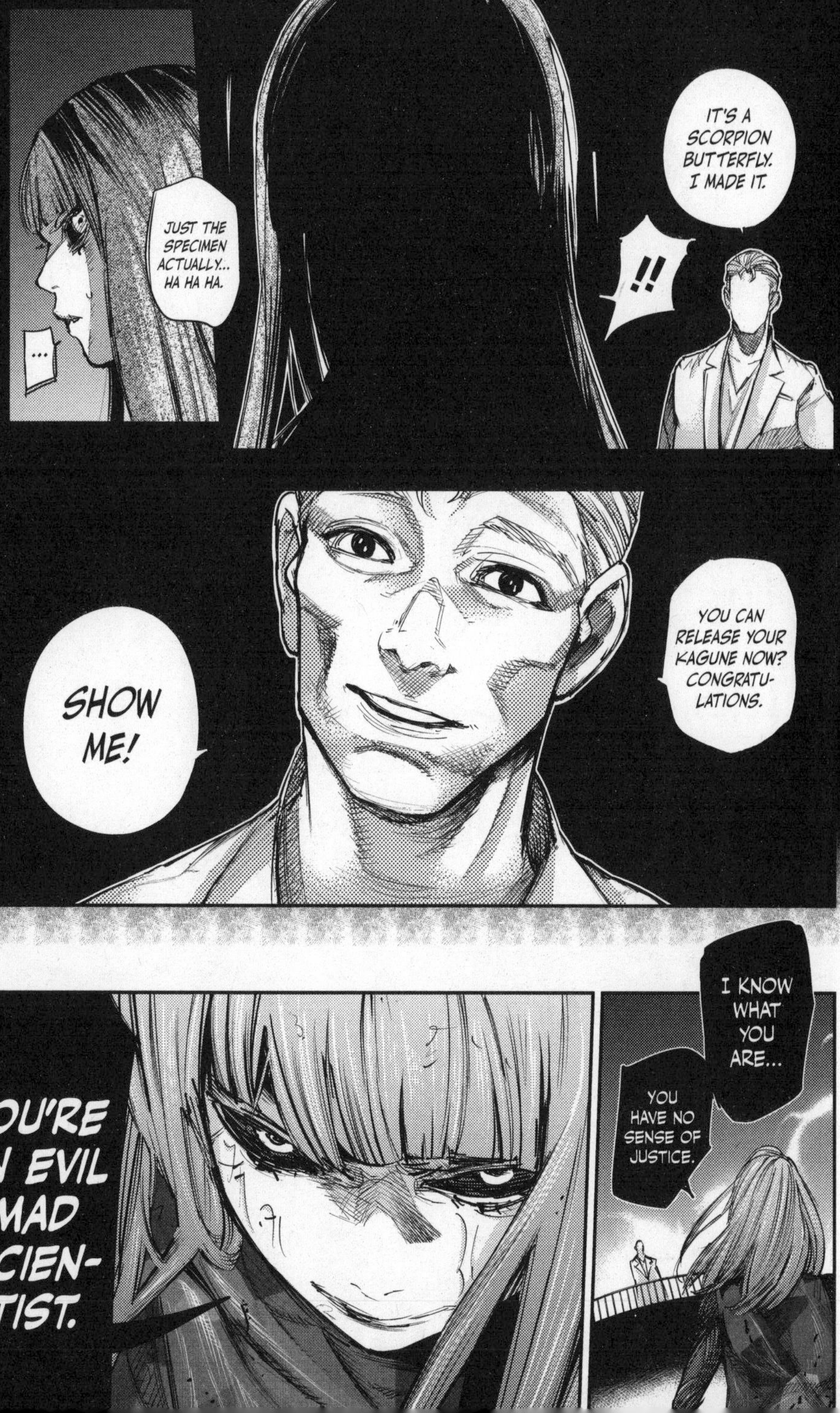
IT'S A SCORPION BUTTERFLY. I MADE IT.
!!
JUST THE SPECIMEN ACTUALLY... HA HA HA.
...
YOU CAN RELEASE YOUR KAGUNE NOW? CONGRATU-LATIONS.
SHOW ME!
I KNOW WHAT YOU ARE...
YOU HAVE NO SENSE OF JUSTICE.
YOU'RE AN EVIL MAD SCIEN-TIST.

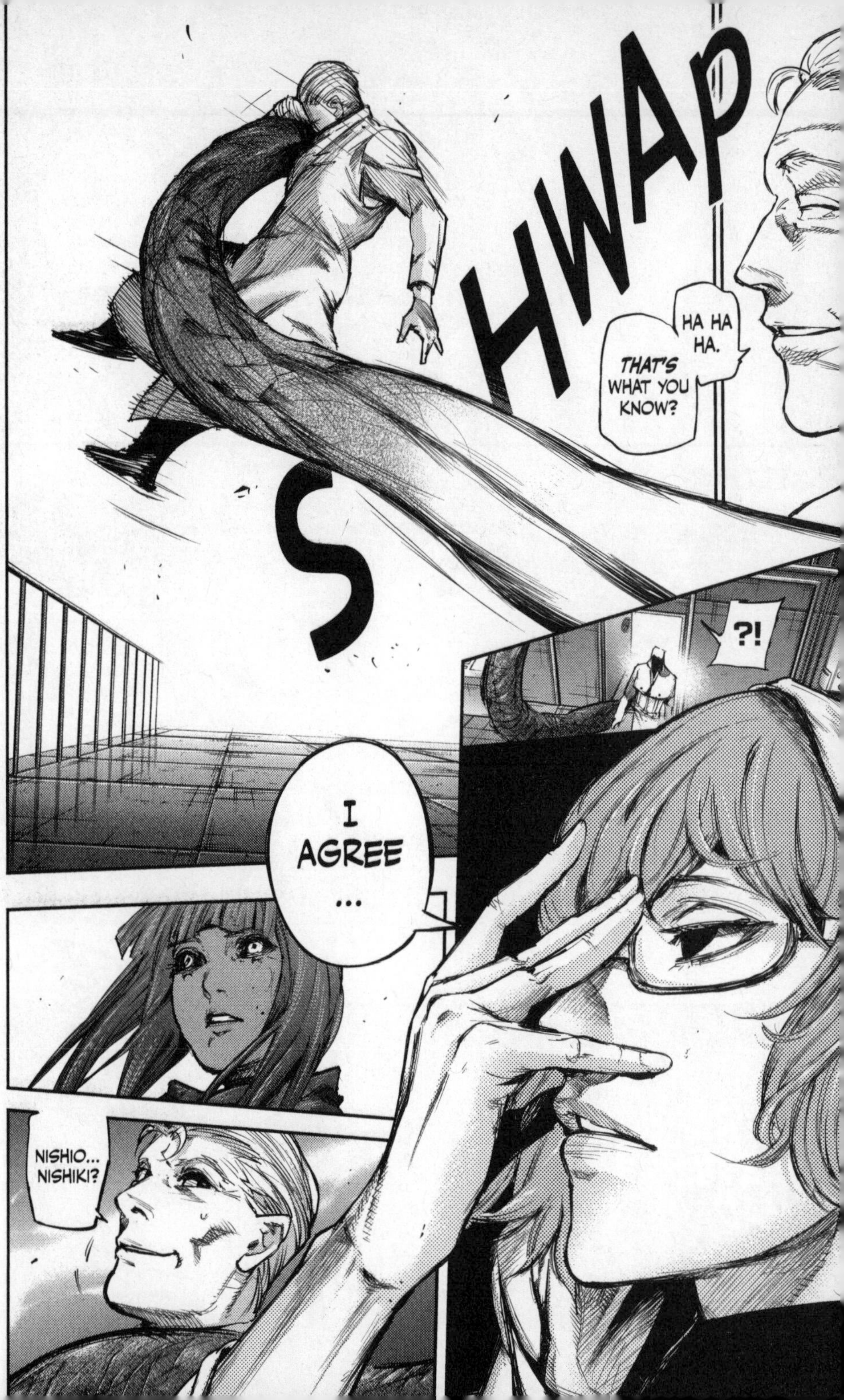
HA HA HA.
SHWAP
THAT'S WHAT YOU KNOW?
S
?!
I AGREE ...
NISHIO... NISHIKI?

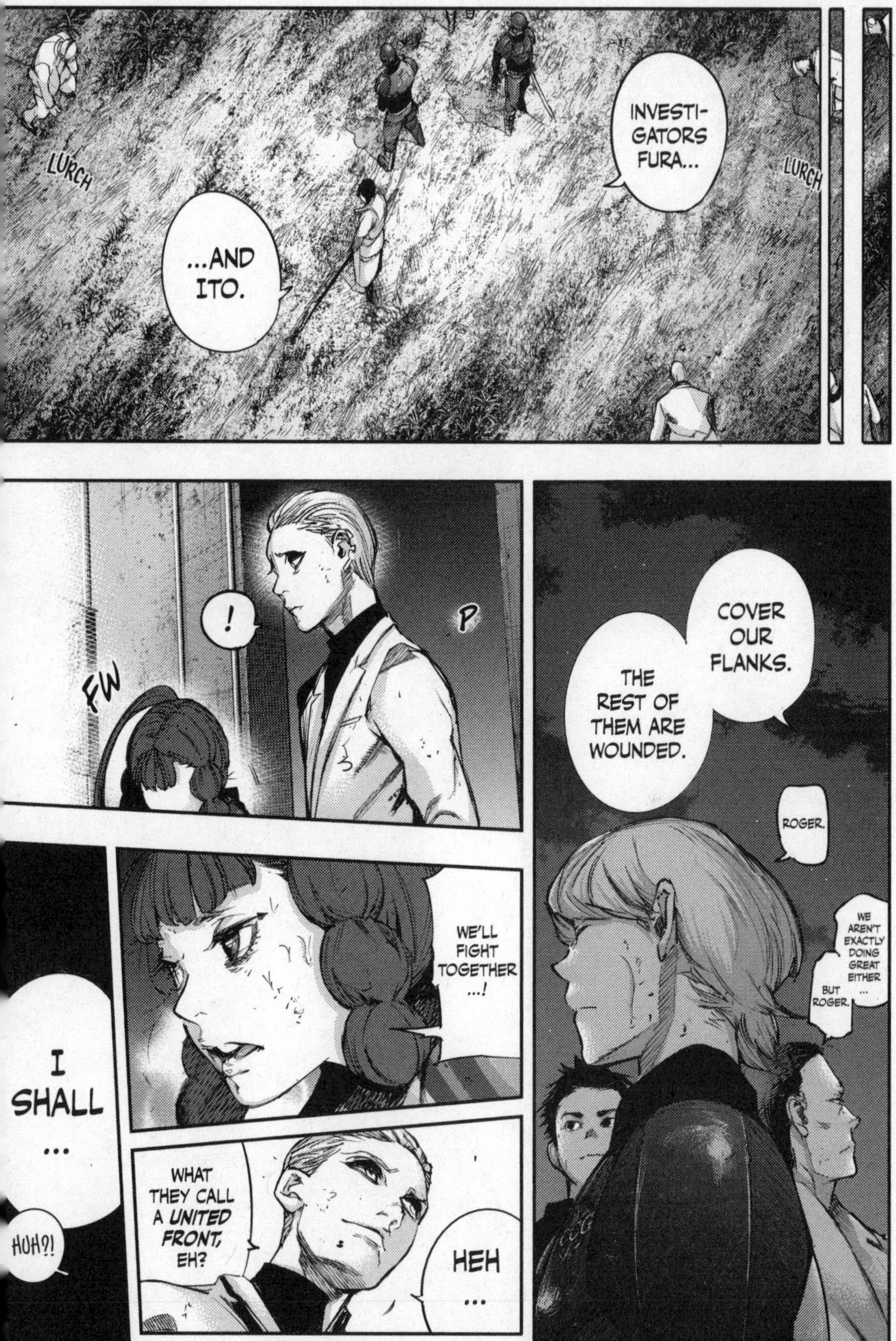
LURCH
INVESTI-GATORS FURA...
...AND ITO.
LURCH
COVER OUR FLANKS.
THE REST OF THEM ARE WOUNDED.
ROGER.
WE AREN'T EXACTLY DOING GREAT EITHER ...
BUT ROGER.
P
!
FW
WE'LL FIGHT TOGETHER ...!
I SHALL ...
HEH ...
WHAT THEY CALL A UNITED FRONT, EH?
HUH?!

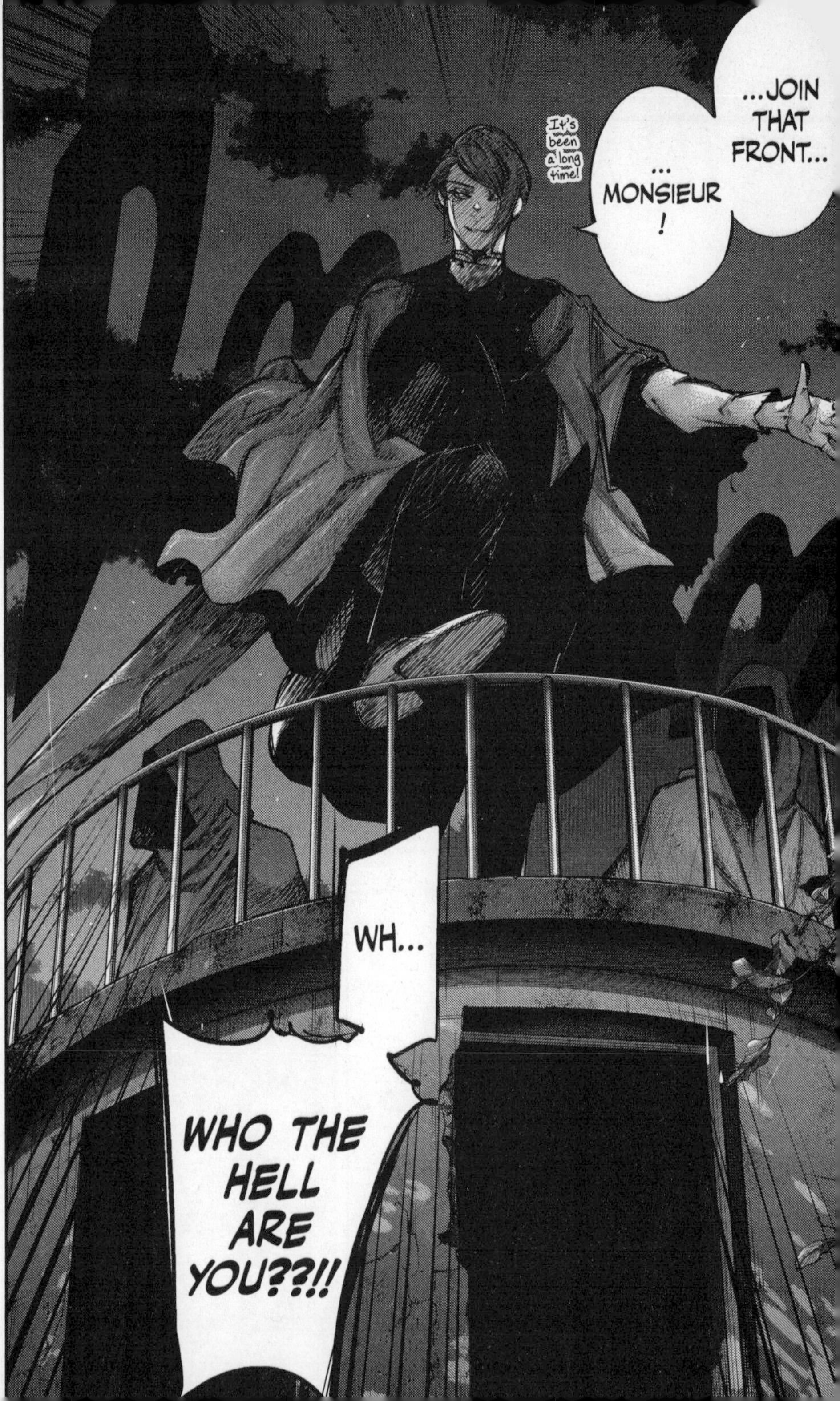
...JOIN THAT FRONT...
... MONSIEUR !
It's been a long time!
WH...
WHO THE HELL ARE YOU??!!

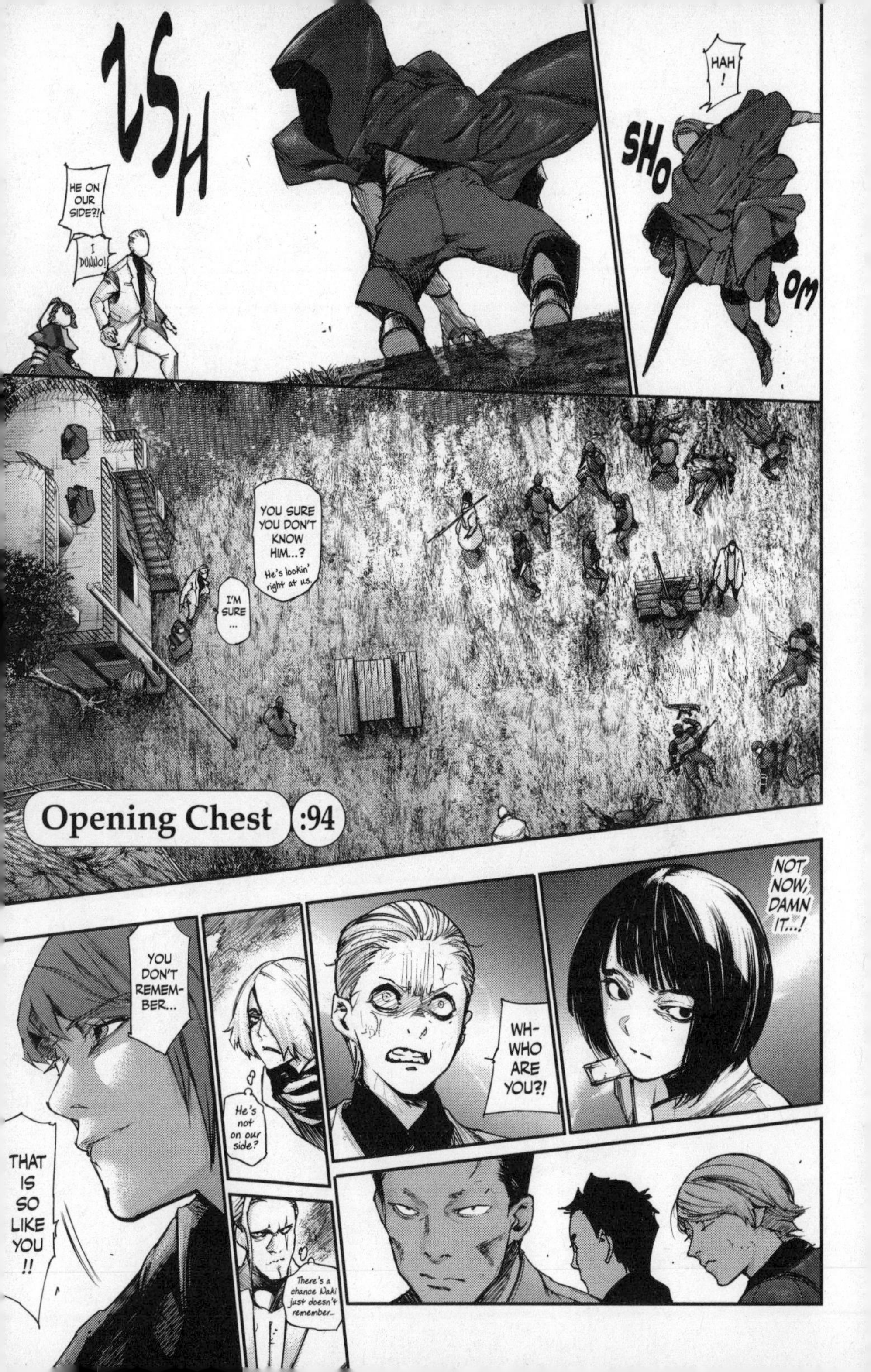

HAH!
SHO
OM
ZSH
HE ON OUR SIDE?!
I DUNNO!
YOU SURE YOU DON'T KNOW HIM...?
He's lookin' right at us.
I'M SURE...
Opening Chest :94
NOT NOW, DAMN IT...!
WH-WHO ARE YOU?!
He's not on our side?
YOU DON'T REMEMBER...
There's a chance Naki just doesn't remember...
THAT IS SO LIKE YOU!!

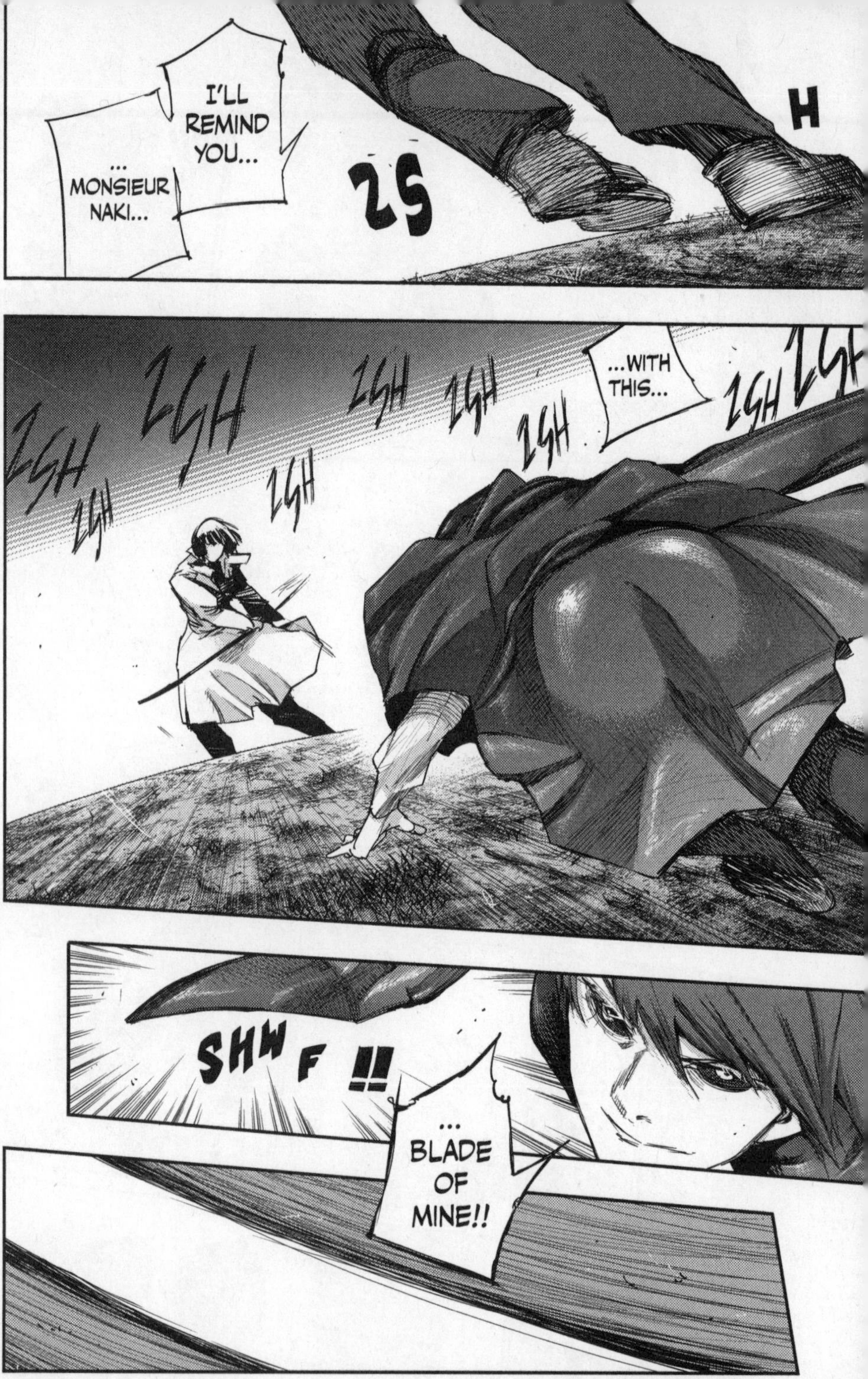

I'LL REMIND YOU...
...MONSIEUR NAKI...
ZS
H
ZGH
ZGH
ZGH
...WITH THIS...
ZGH
ZGH
ZGH
ZGH
ZGH
ZGH
SHW F!!
...BLADE OF MINE!!

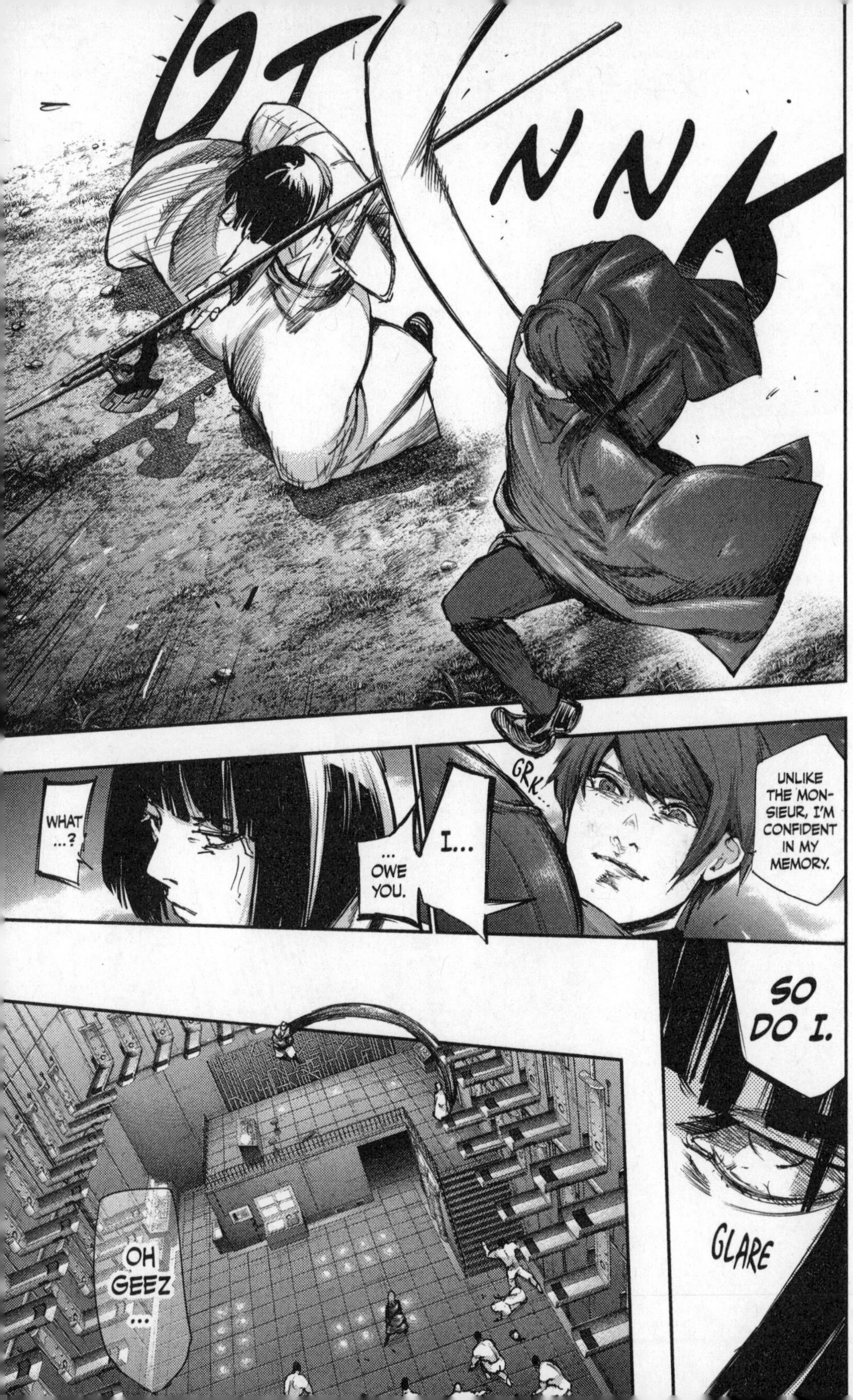
DTNNK
UNLIKE THE MONSIEUR, I'M CONFIDENT IN MY MEMORY.
GRK...
I...
...OWE YOU.
WHAT ...?
SO DO I.
GLARE
OH GEEZ ...

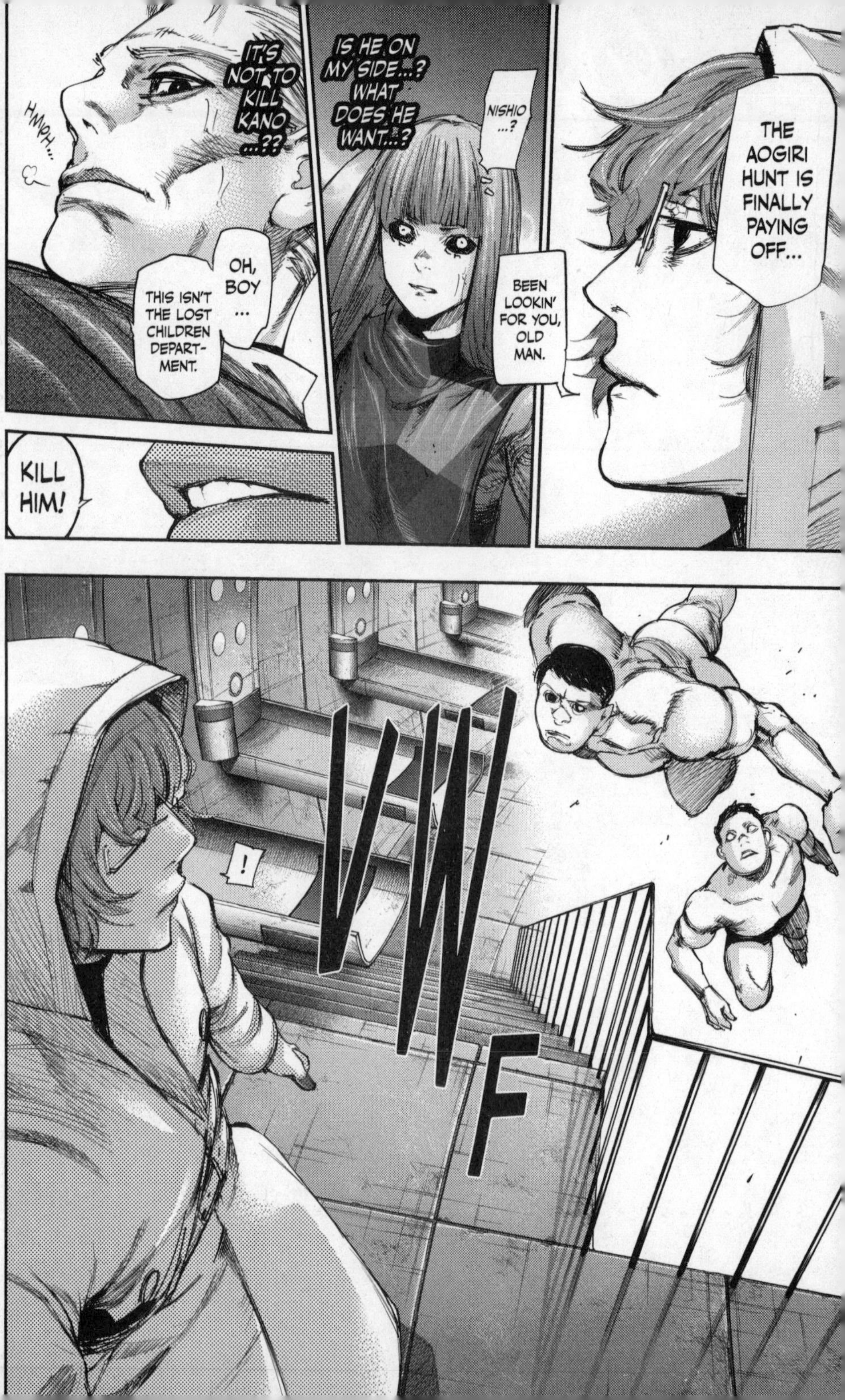

THE AOGIRI HUNT IS FINALLY PAYING OFF...
BEEN LOOKIN' FOR YOU, OLD MAN.
IS HE ON MY SIDE...? WHAT DOES HE WANT...?
NISHIO ...?
IT'S NOT TO KILL KANO ...??
HMPH...
OH, BOY ...
THIS ISN'T THE LOST CHILDREN DEPART-MENT.
KILL HIM!
!
VWF

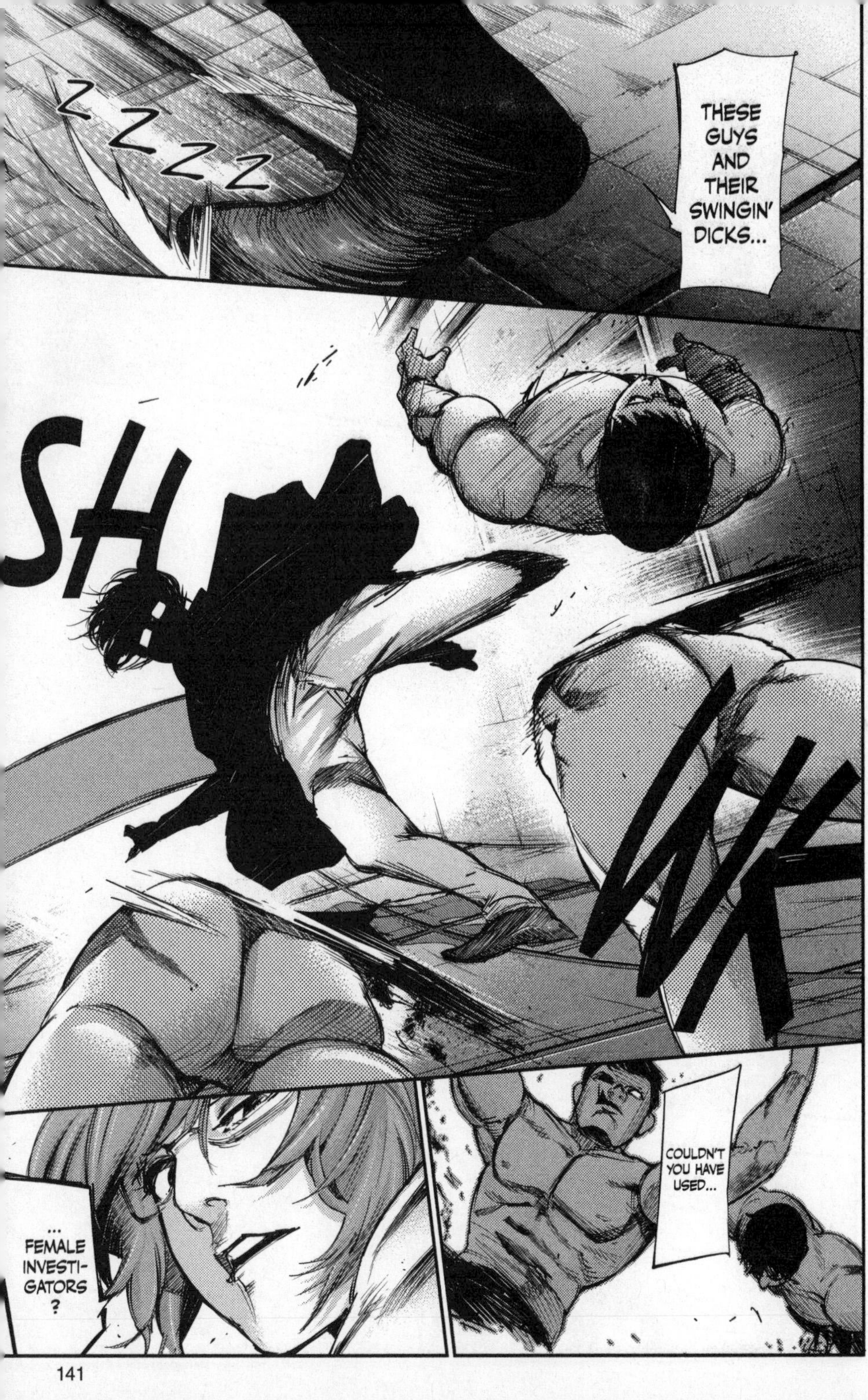
ZZZZZ
THESE GUYS AND THEIR SWINGIN' DICKS...
SH
WK
COULDN'T YOU HAVE USED...
...FEMALE INVESTI-GATORS?

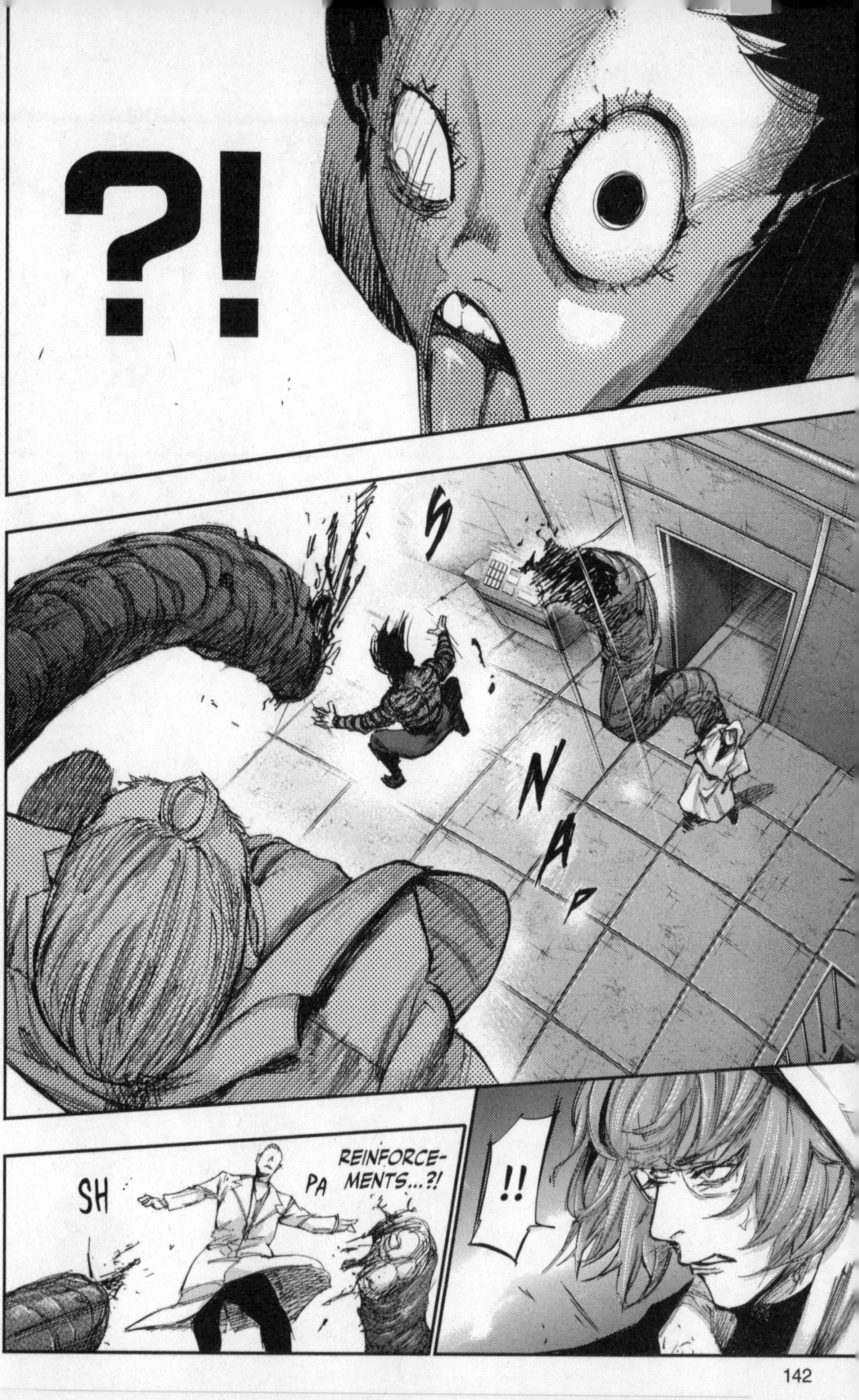
?!
SNAP
!!
REINFORCE-
MENTS...?!
PA
SH

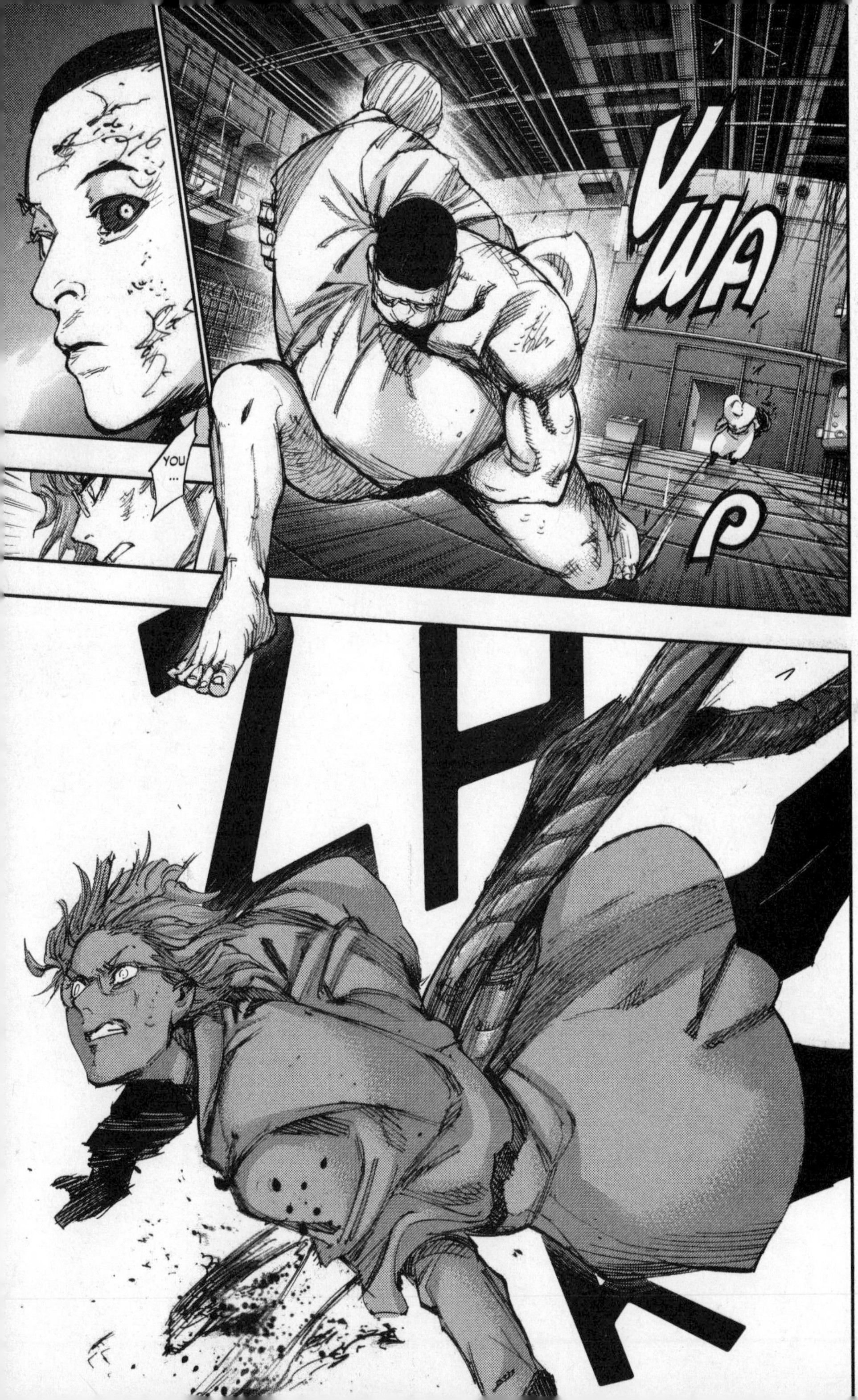
VWA
P
YOU ...

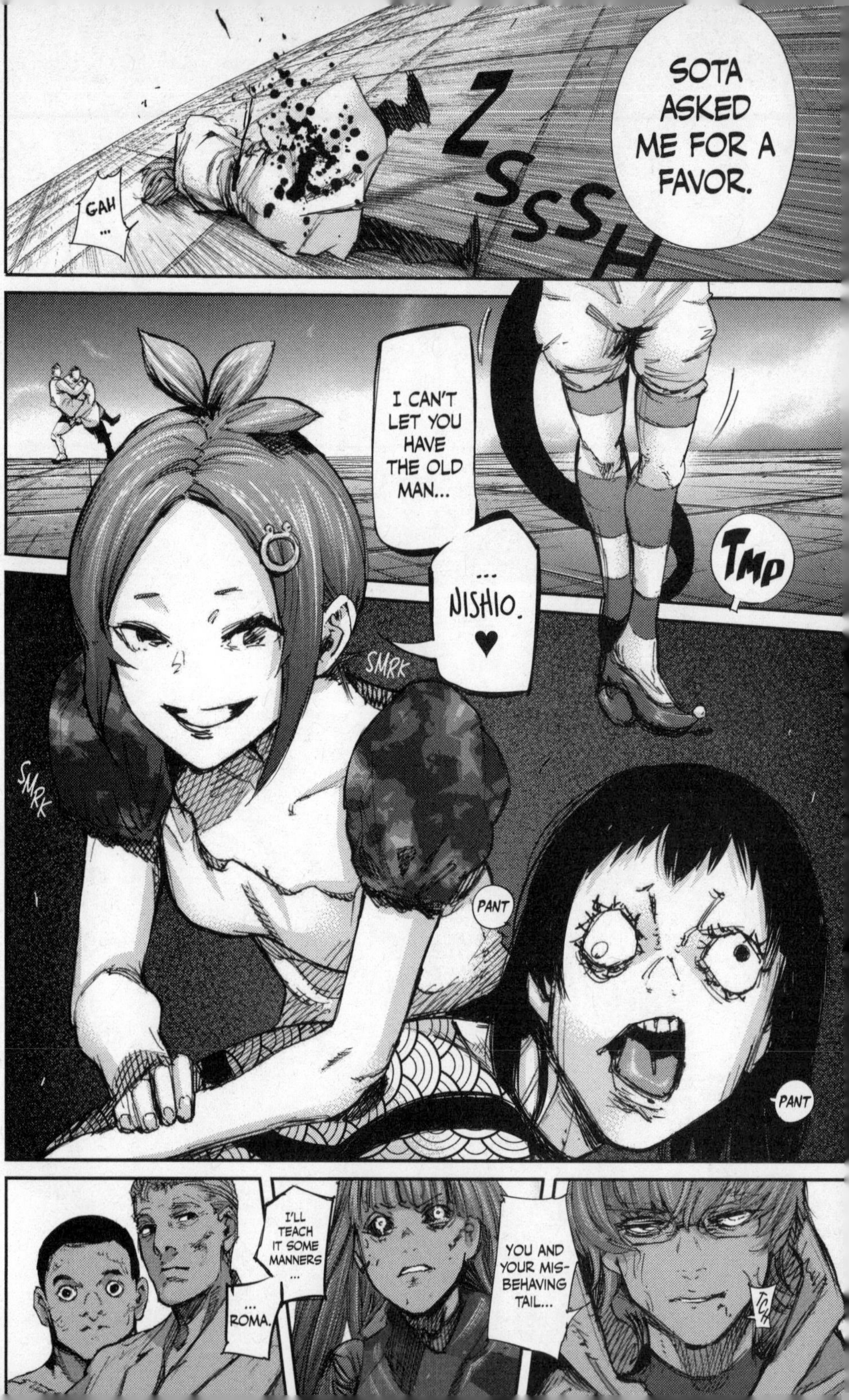
SOTA ASKED ME FOR A FAVOR.
ZSSSH
GAH ...
TMP
I CAN'T LET YOU HAVE THE OLD MAN...
... NISHIO. ♥
SMRK
SMRK
PANT
PANT
TCH
YOU AND YOUR MIS-BEHAVING TAIL...
I'LL TEACH IT SOME MANNERS ...
... ROMA.

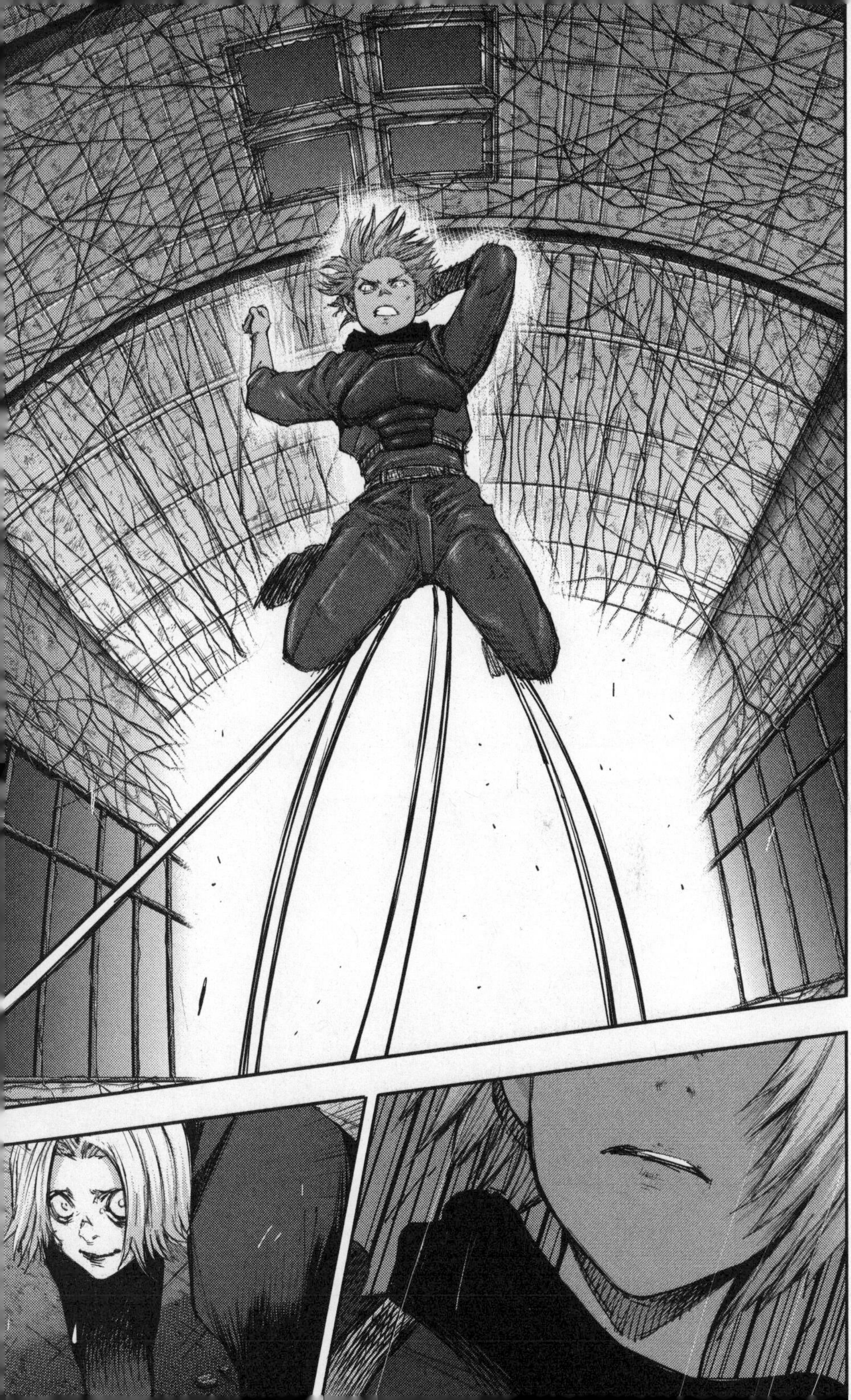

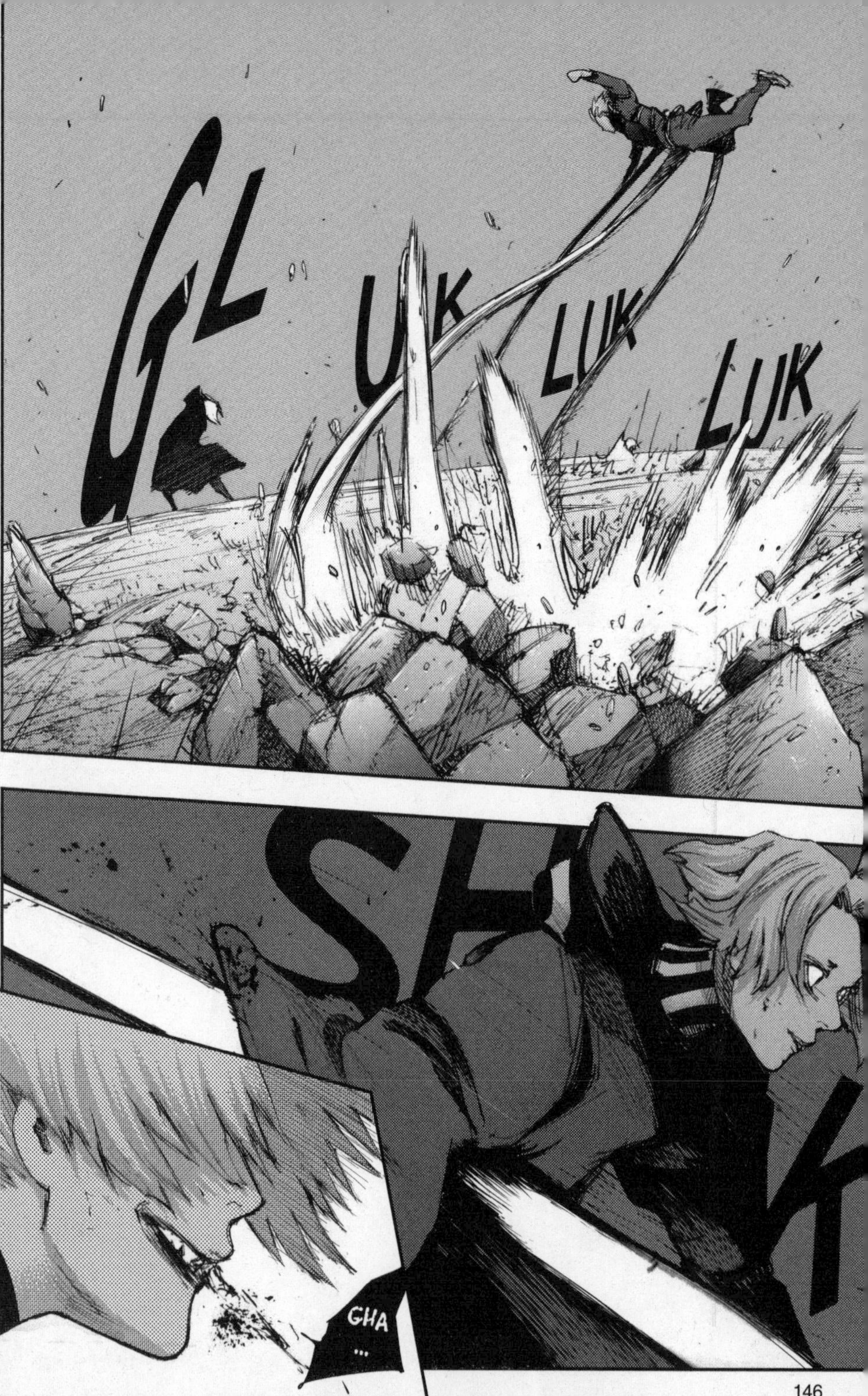
GLUK
LUK
LUK
SH
K
GHA ...

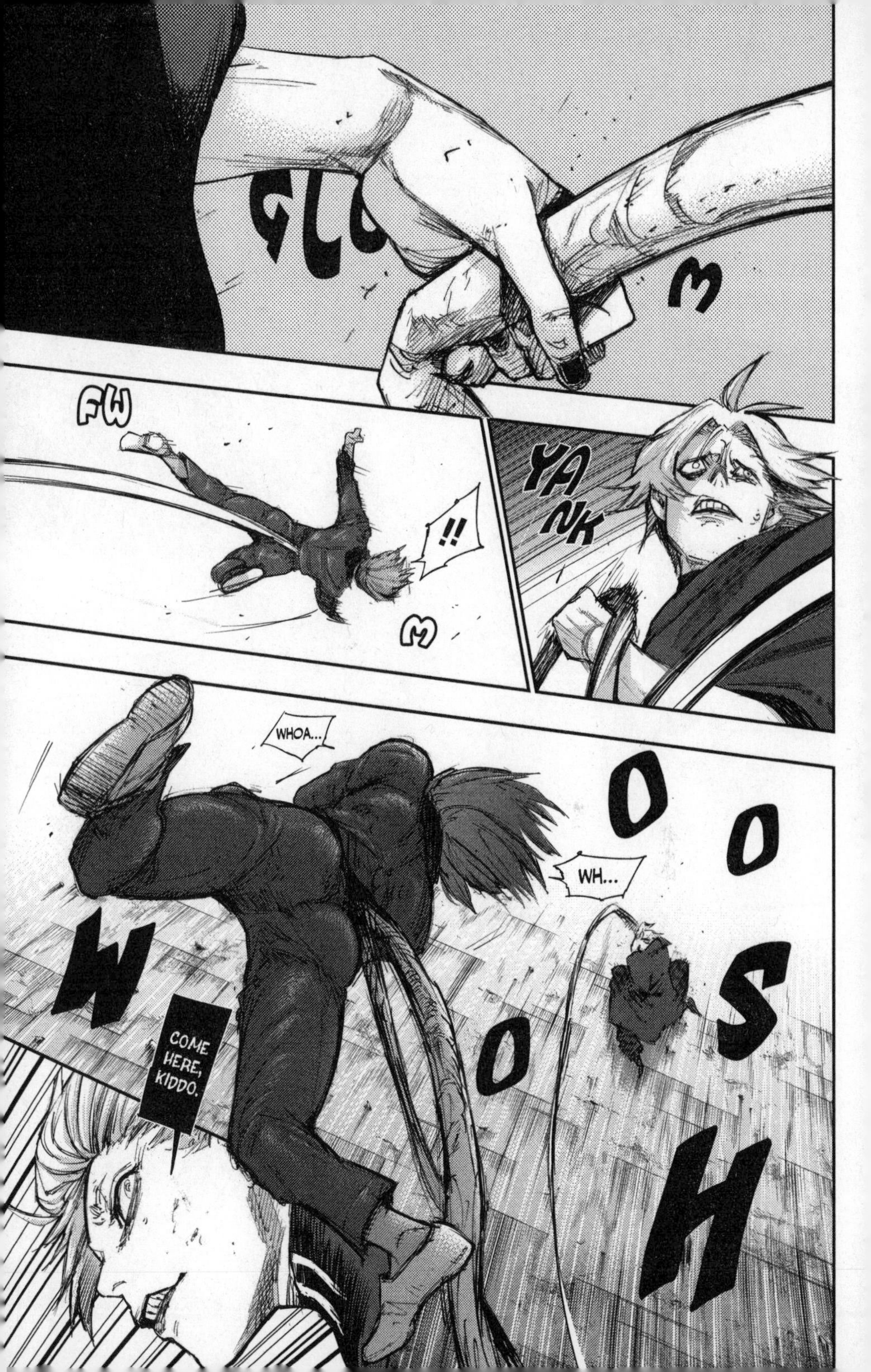
GLO
M
YANK
FW
!!
M
WHOA...
WH...
WHOOOSH
COME HERE, KIDDO.

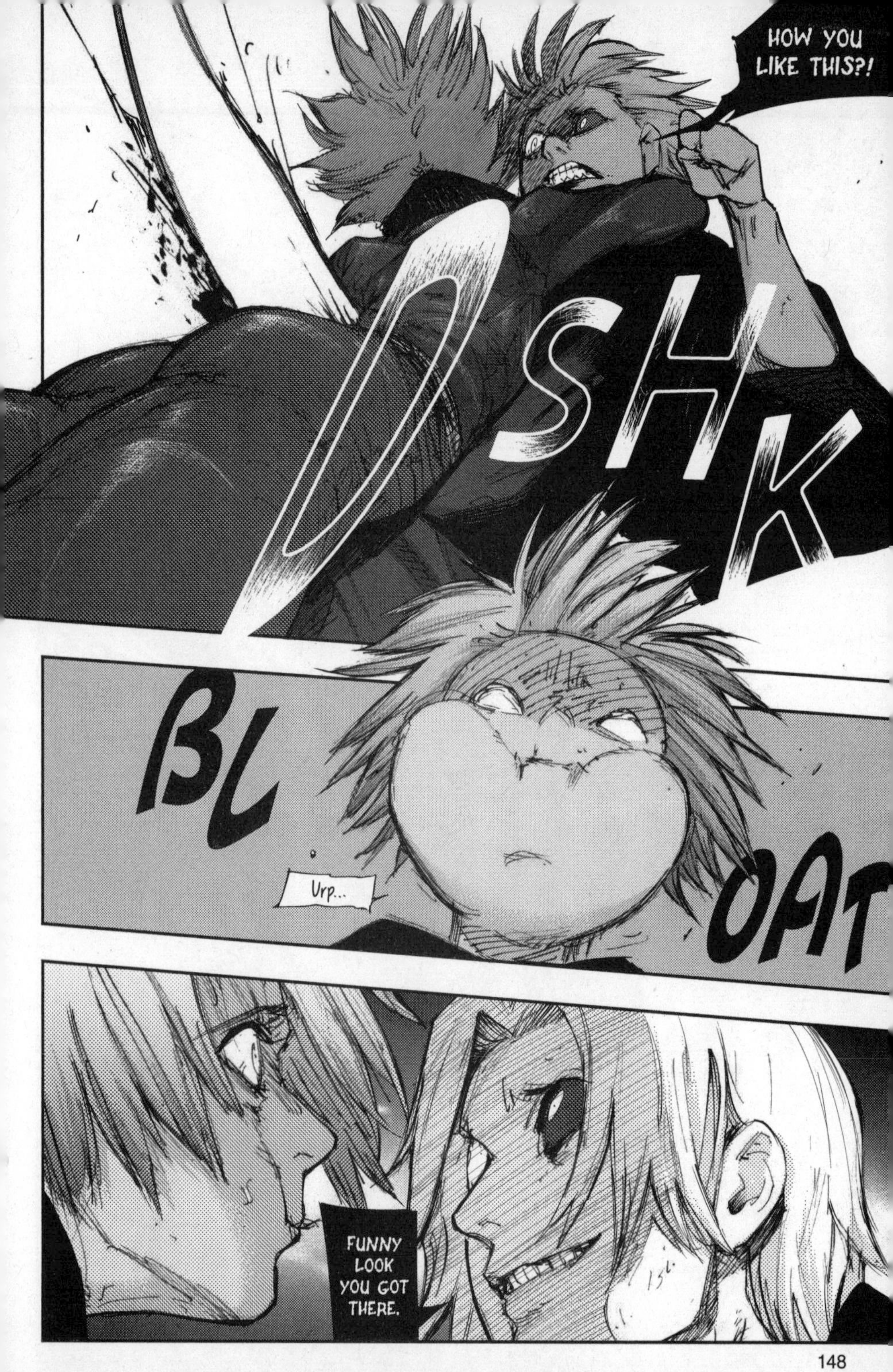
HOW YOU LIKE THIS?!
DSHK
BLOAT
Urp...
FUNNY LOOK YOU GOT THERE.

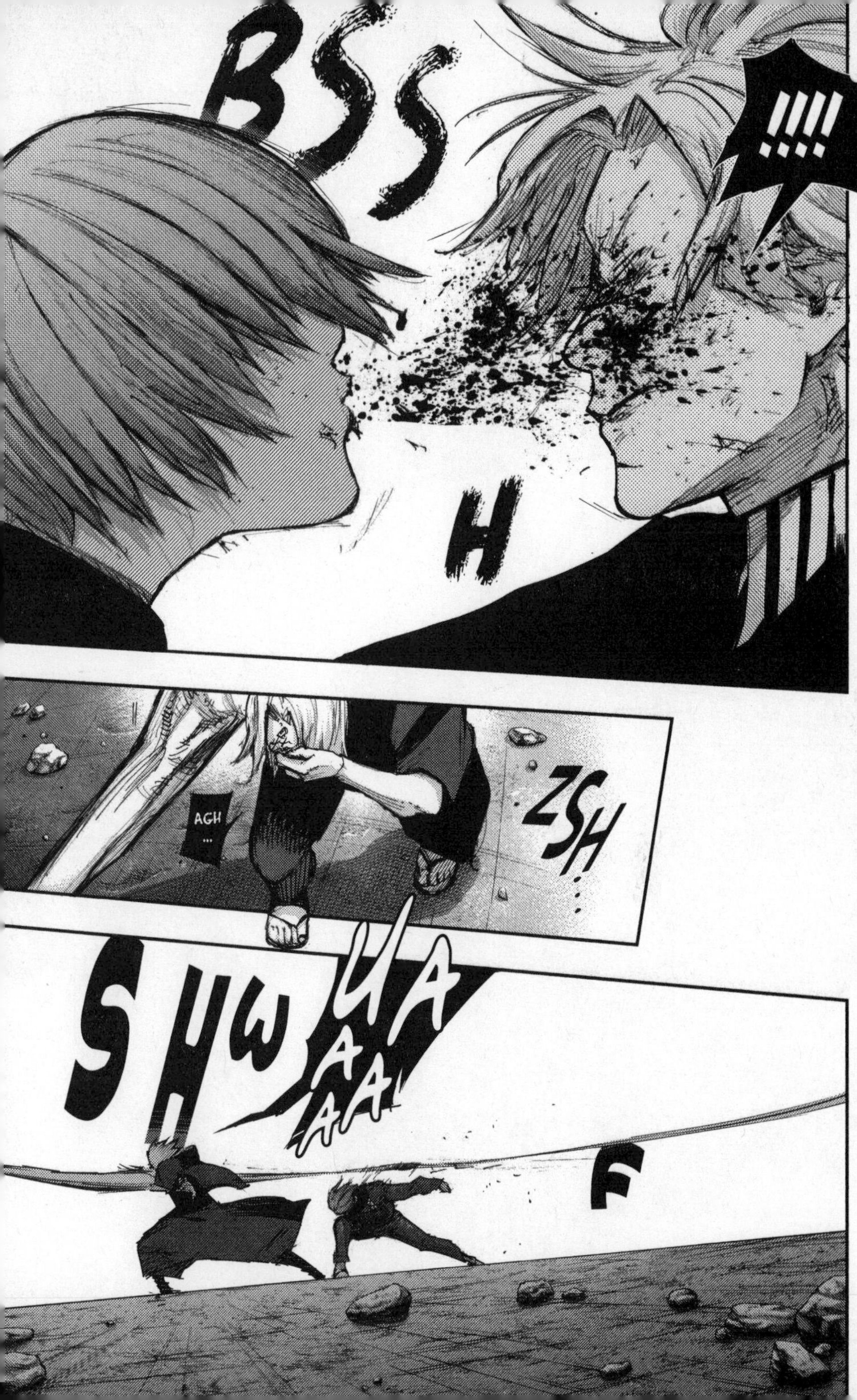
!!!!
BSSH
ZSH
AGH...
UAAAAA
SHWF

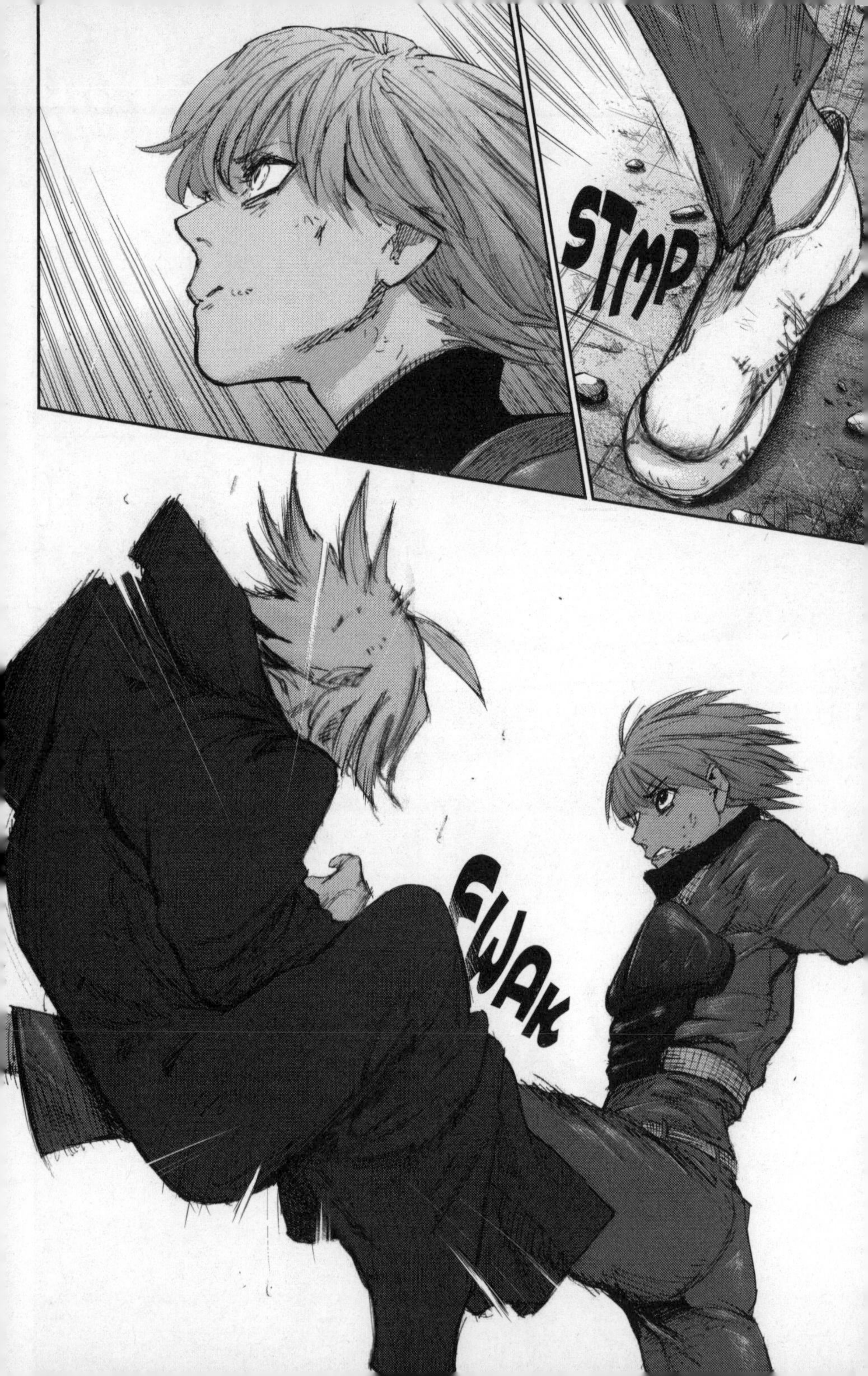
STMP
FWAK

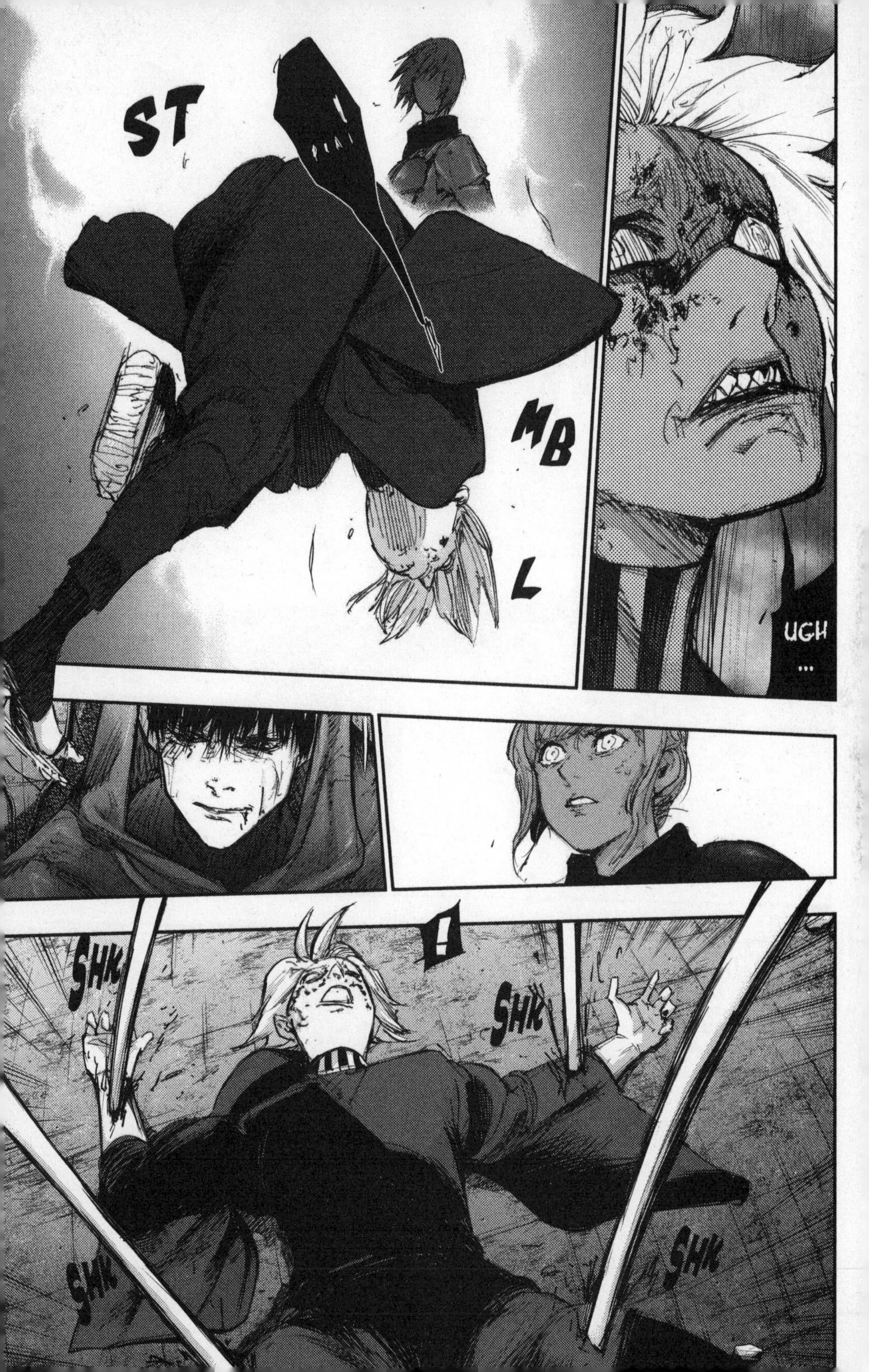
UGH ...
ST
MB
L
!
SHK
SHK
SHK
SHK

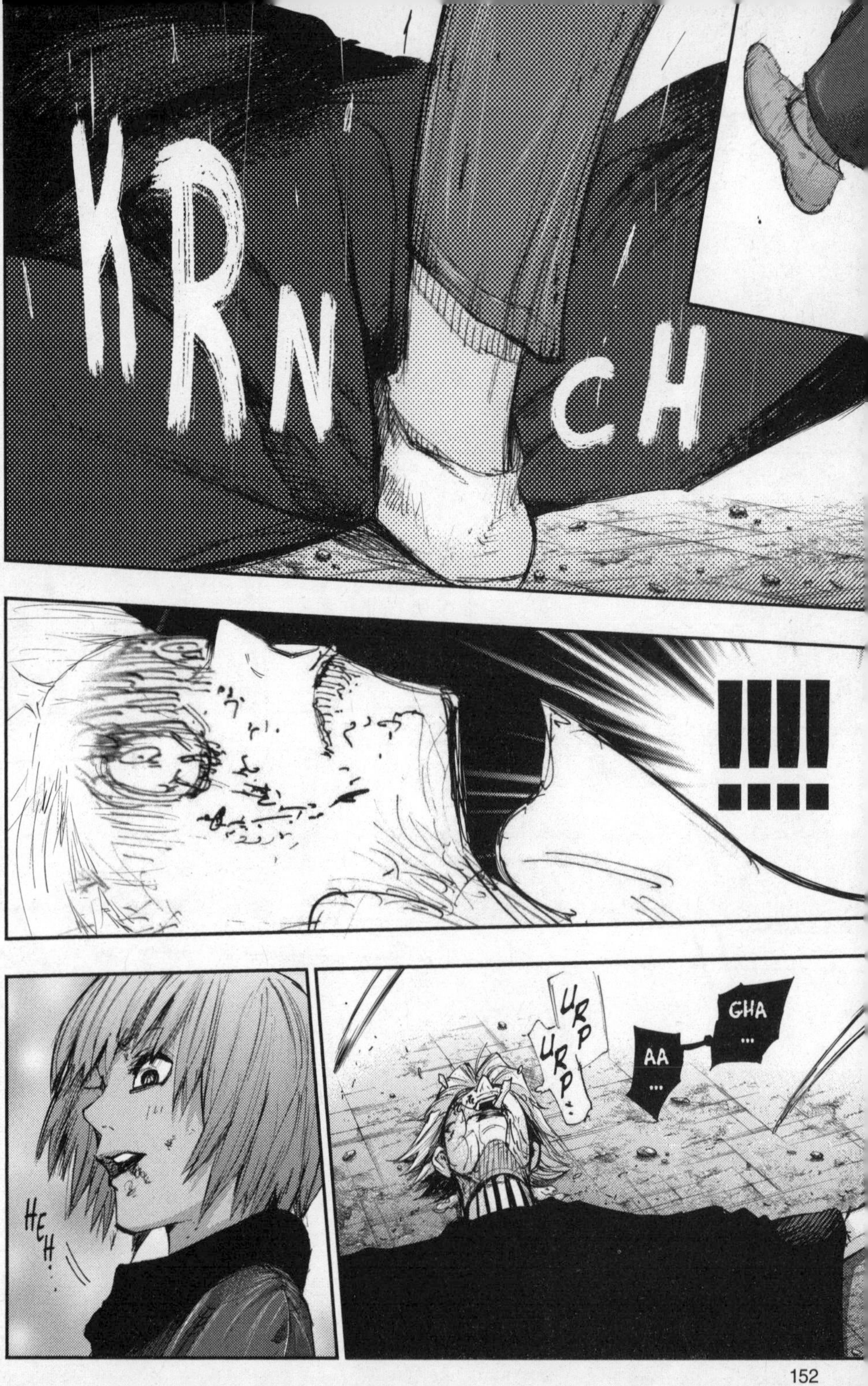
KRNCH
!!!!!
URP URP...
GHA...
AA...
HEH!

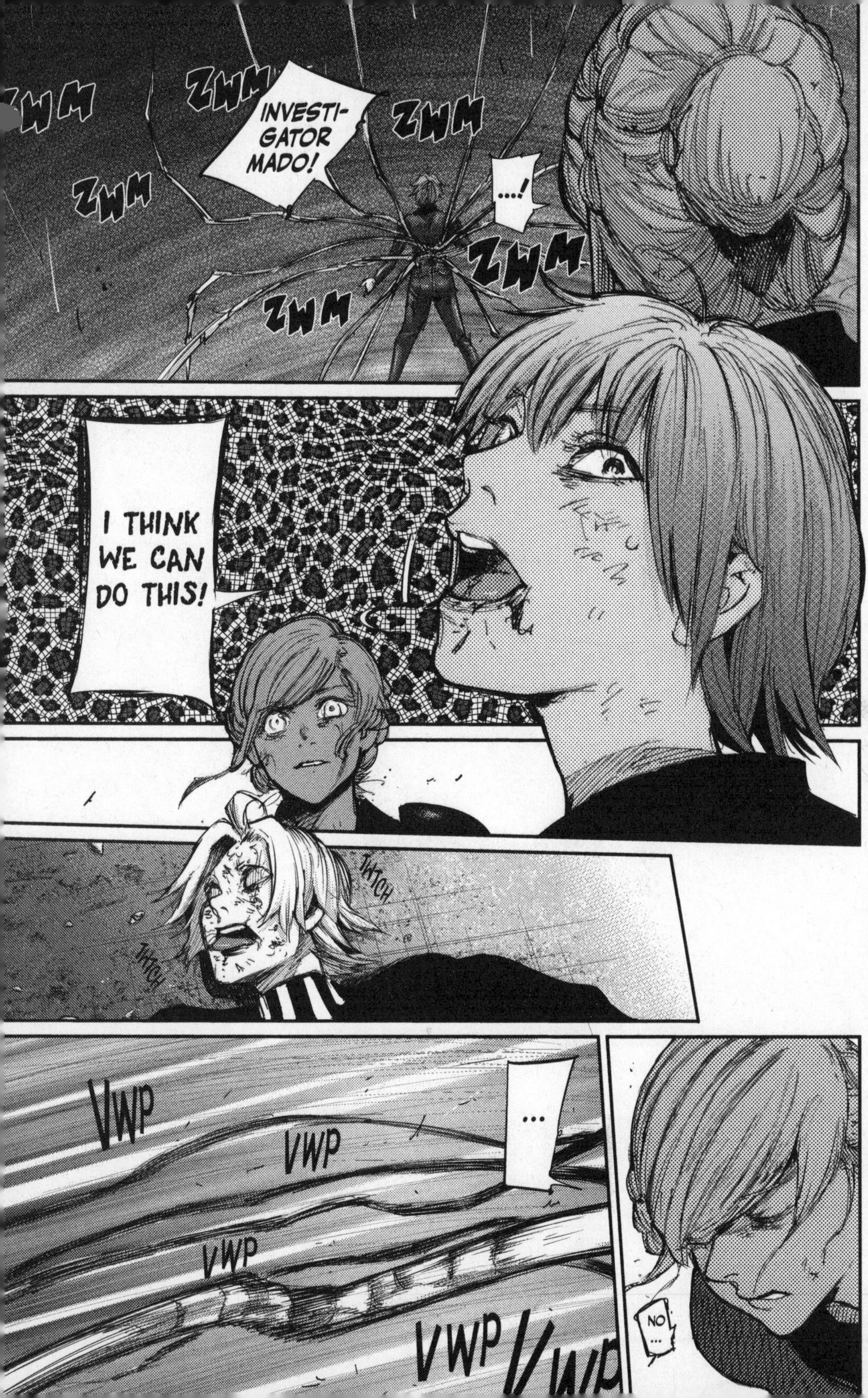
ZWM
ZWM
INVESTI-
GATOR
MADO!
ZWM
ZWM
...!
ZWM
ZWM
I THINK
WE CAN
DO THIS!
THTCH
THTCH
NO
...
...
VWP
VWP
VWP
VWP

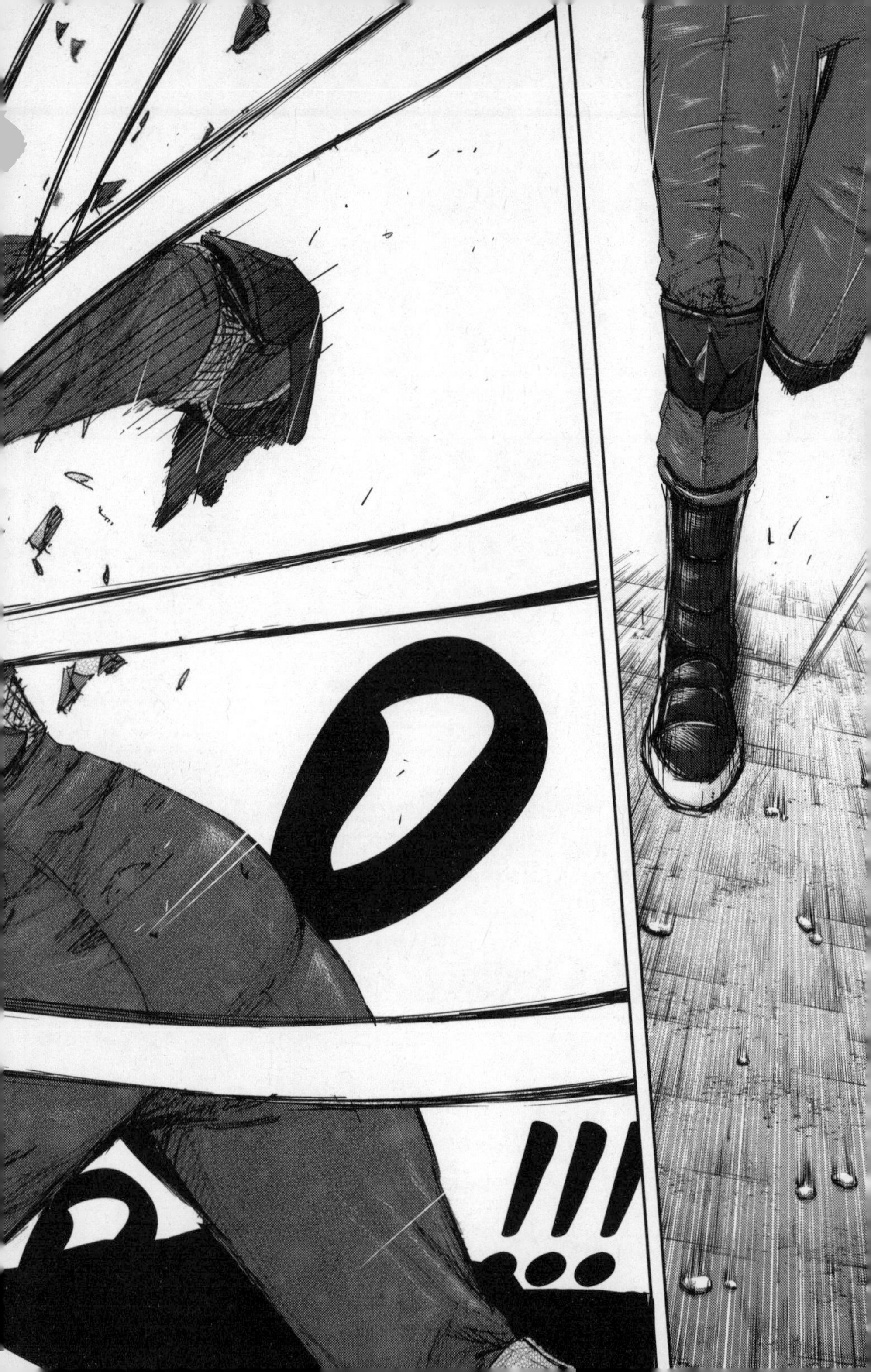

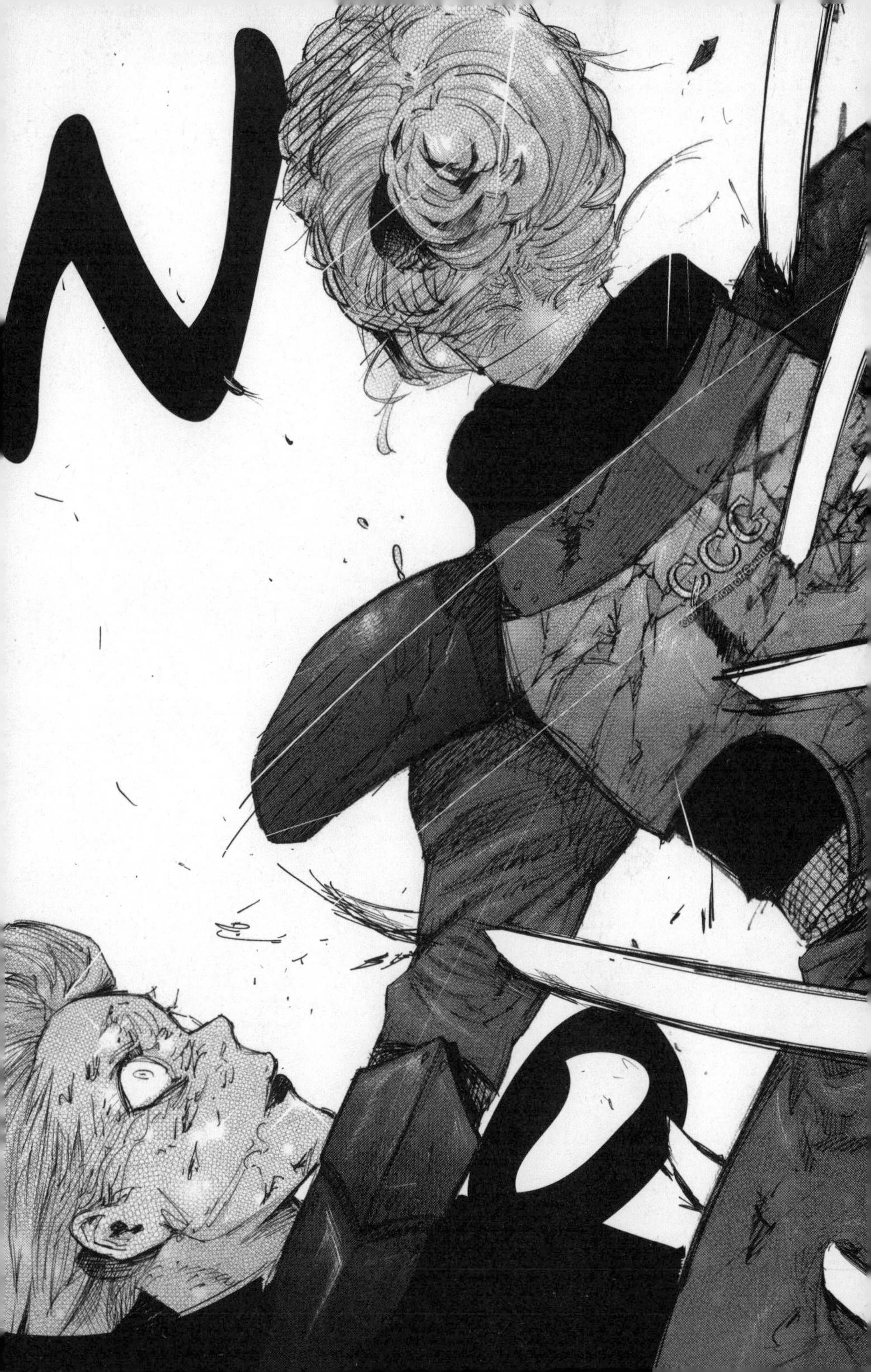
CCG

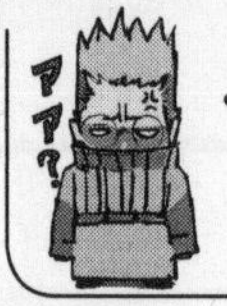

"Huh?"
Chu Hachikawa
Named after Hachiko the dog.

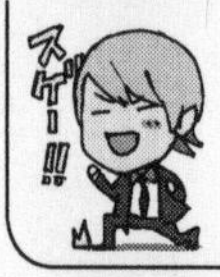

"Wow!!"
Kuramoto Ito
I had a strong desire to name him using two last names.

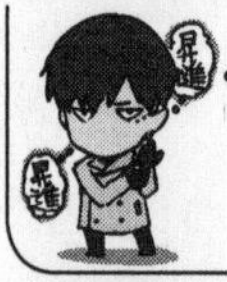

"Promotion, promotion."
Urie
I find myself cheering for him.

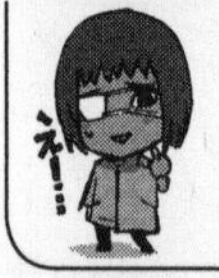

"What...?"
Mutsuki
One of the reasons I mess up eye patches.

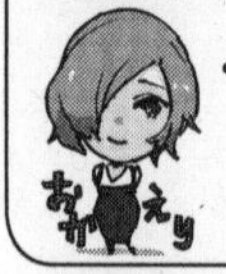

"Welcome back!"
Touka
Wish she would go back to having black hair cuz it takes time drawing her now.

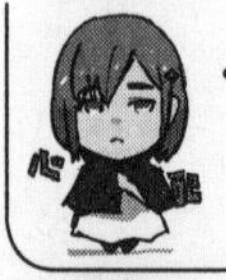

(worried)
Hinami
Just when I thought she was beginning to resemble her mother, she's looking more like Kimi. I'm in a bind.

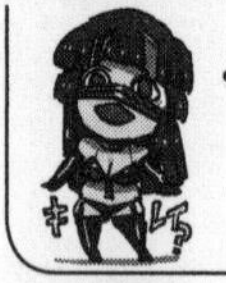

"I'm pretty?"
Nutcracker
Cute.

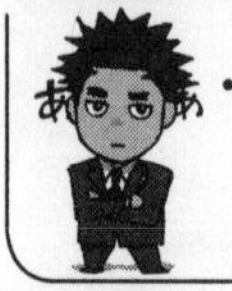

"Yeah."
Takeomi Kuroiwa
I think he's a good kid.

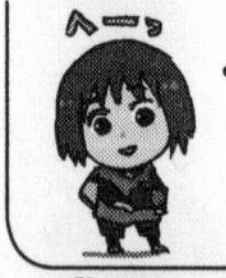

"Really?"
Chie Hori
Like Tsukiyama, she's one of the oldest characters. She's an easy character to write because she doesn't lie.

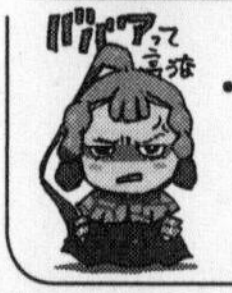

"Don't call me a hag."
Miza
The oddest haircut in this distorted world.

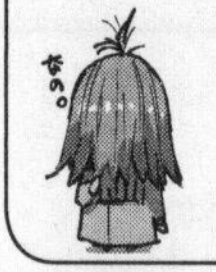

"So..."
Hogi
Named for *hoki* ("broom").

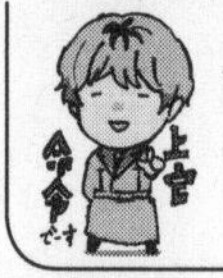

"That's a direct order."
Haise Sasaki
Looking at him makes me think of all the things that life brings.

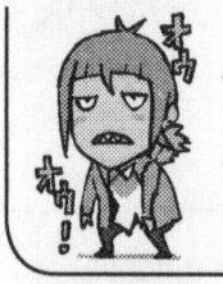

"Yo, yo!"
Shirazu
I dreamed about him when his final chapter was approaching. In my dream, while I was talking to Urie and the Qs, he was staring at me from a distance.

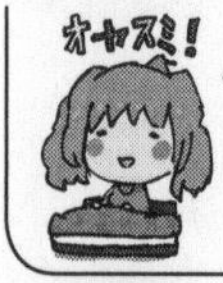
オヤスミ!

"Goodnight!"
Saiko
She was asleep the entire time in :re volume 1.

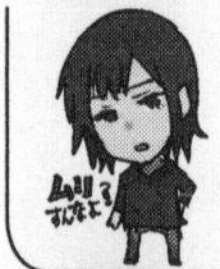

"Don't push yourself too hard."
Ayato
I'm glad he got taller.

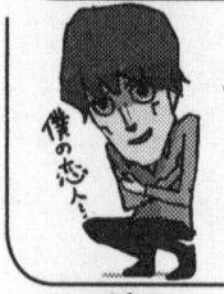

"My lover!"
Torso
Towada said there are people like him around us, but I don't think so.

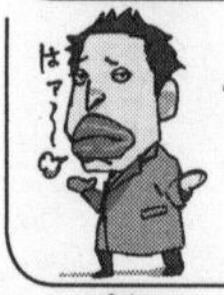

"Sigh..."
Shimoguchi
You're cute too.

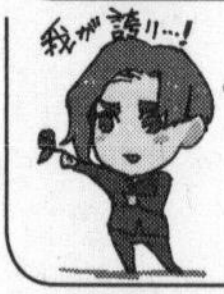

"My pride...!"
Kanae
May be a companion character to Mutsuki.

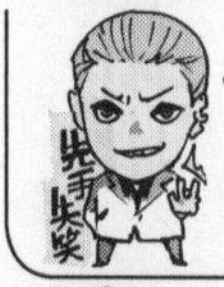

"Early bird gets the word."
Naki
Naki, more than Yamori, seems to be developing the White Suits as an organization.

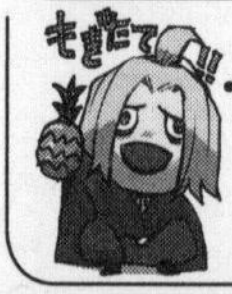

"Freshly picked!!"
Takizawa
I like his appearance. Like he could make an appearance in *Siren*.

Am :95

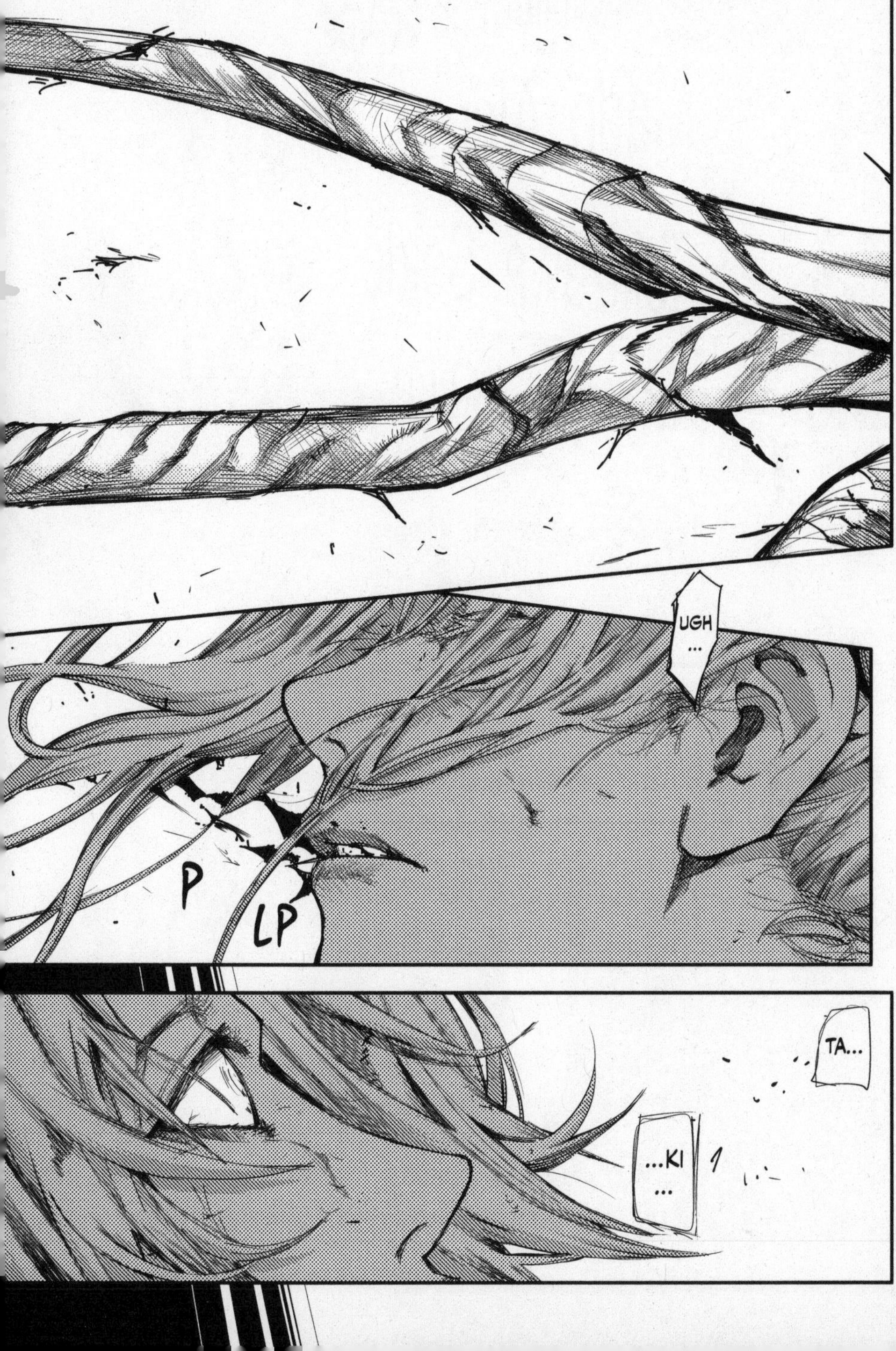
UGH...
P
LP
TA...
...KI...

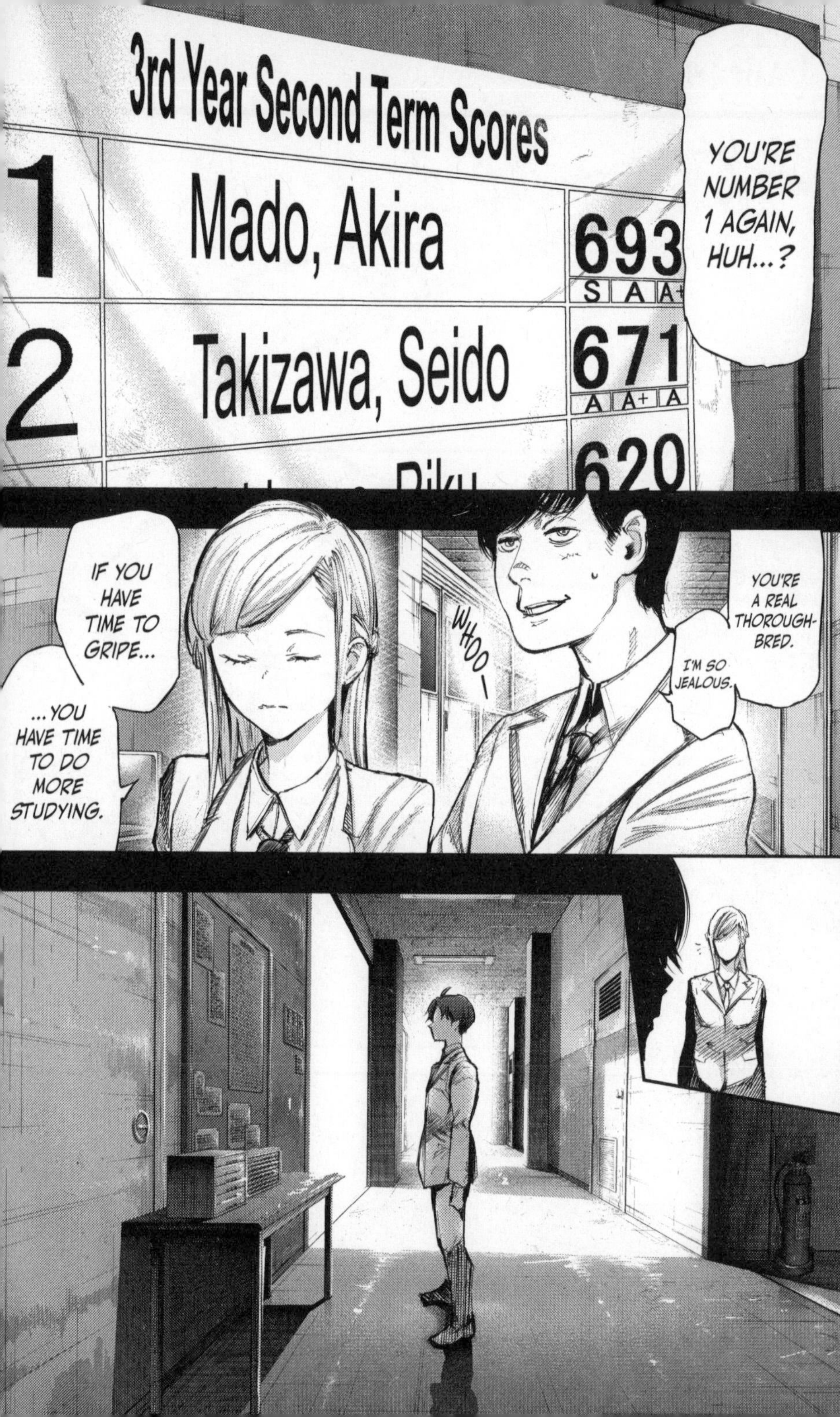
3rd Year Second Term Scores
1 Mado, Akira 693 S A A+
2 Takizawa, Seido 671 A A+ A
620
YOU'RE NUMBER 1 AGAIN, HUH...?
YOU'RE A REAL THOROUGH-BRED.
I'M SO JEALOUS.
WHOO—
IF YOU HAVE TIME TO GRIPE...
...YOU HAVE TIME TO DO MORE STUDYING.

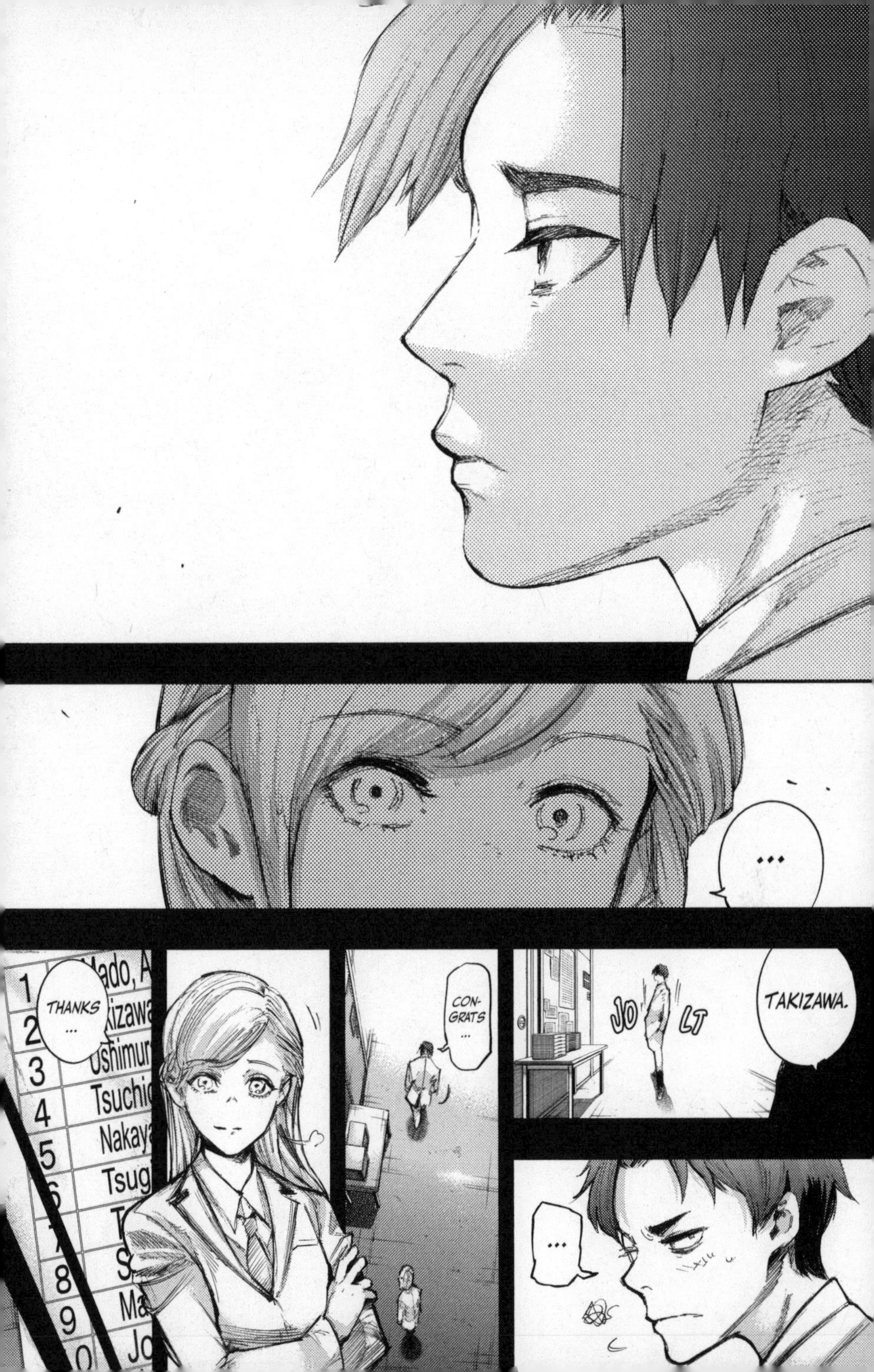
...
TAKIZAWA.
JOLT
...
CON-GRATS...
THANKS...

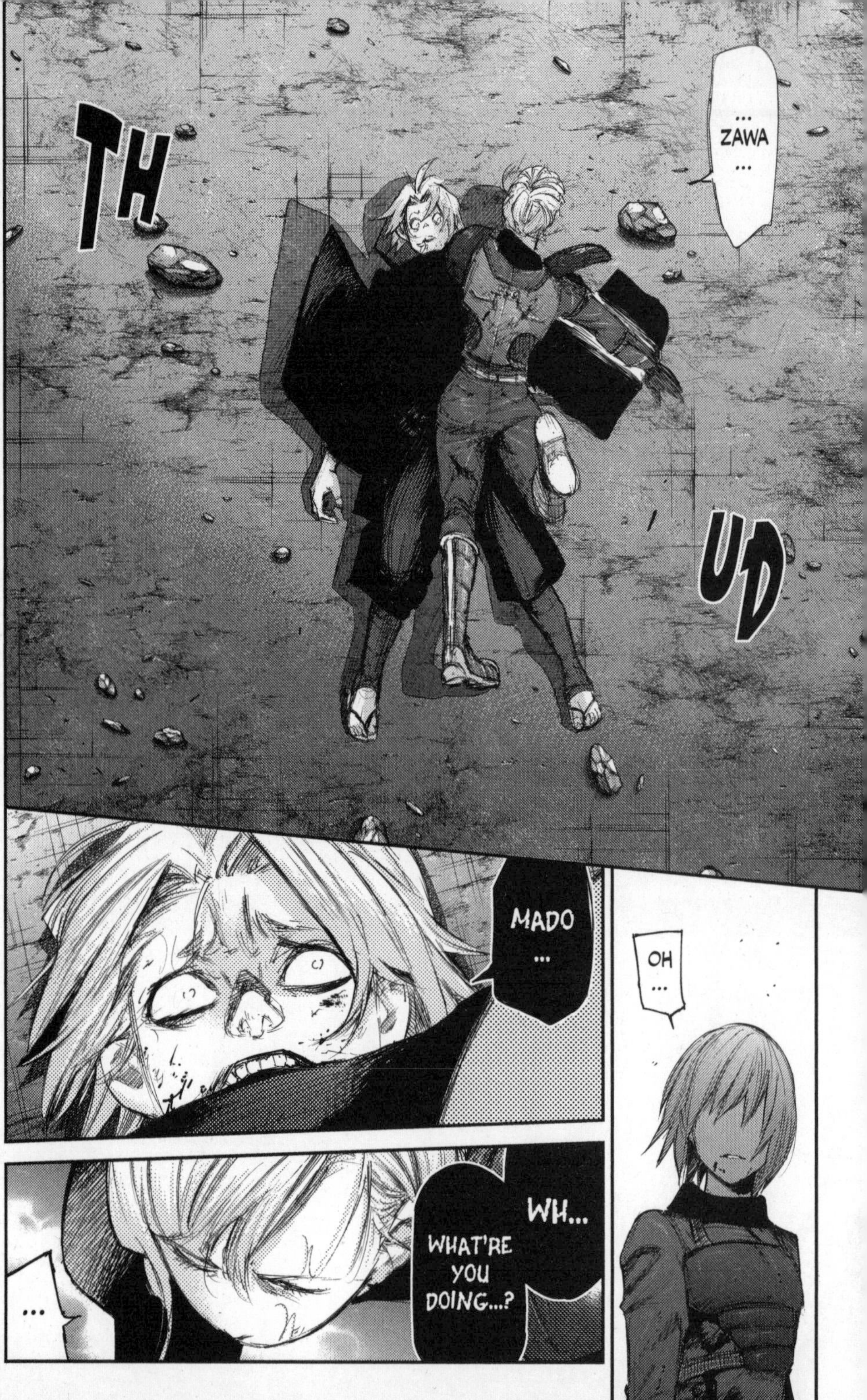
... ZAWA ...
TH
UD
OH ...
MADO ...
WH...
WHAT'RE YOU DOING...?
...

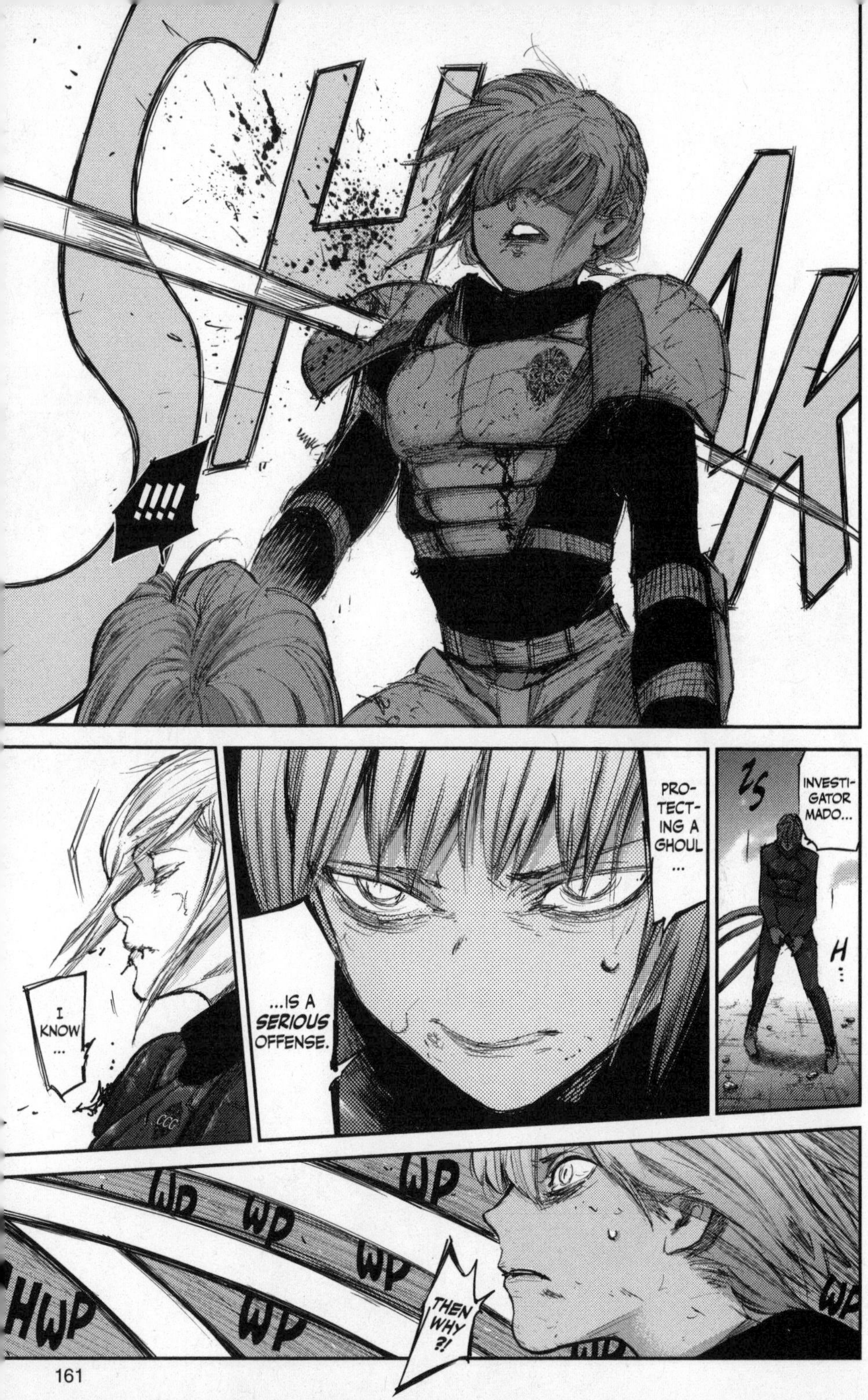
CHAK
!!!!
ZS
INVESTI-GATOR MADO...
H...
PRO-TECT-ING A GHOUL...
...IS A SERIOUS OFFENSE.
I KNOW...
WP WP WP WP WP HWP WP WP
THEN WHY?!

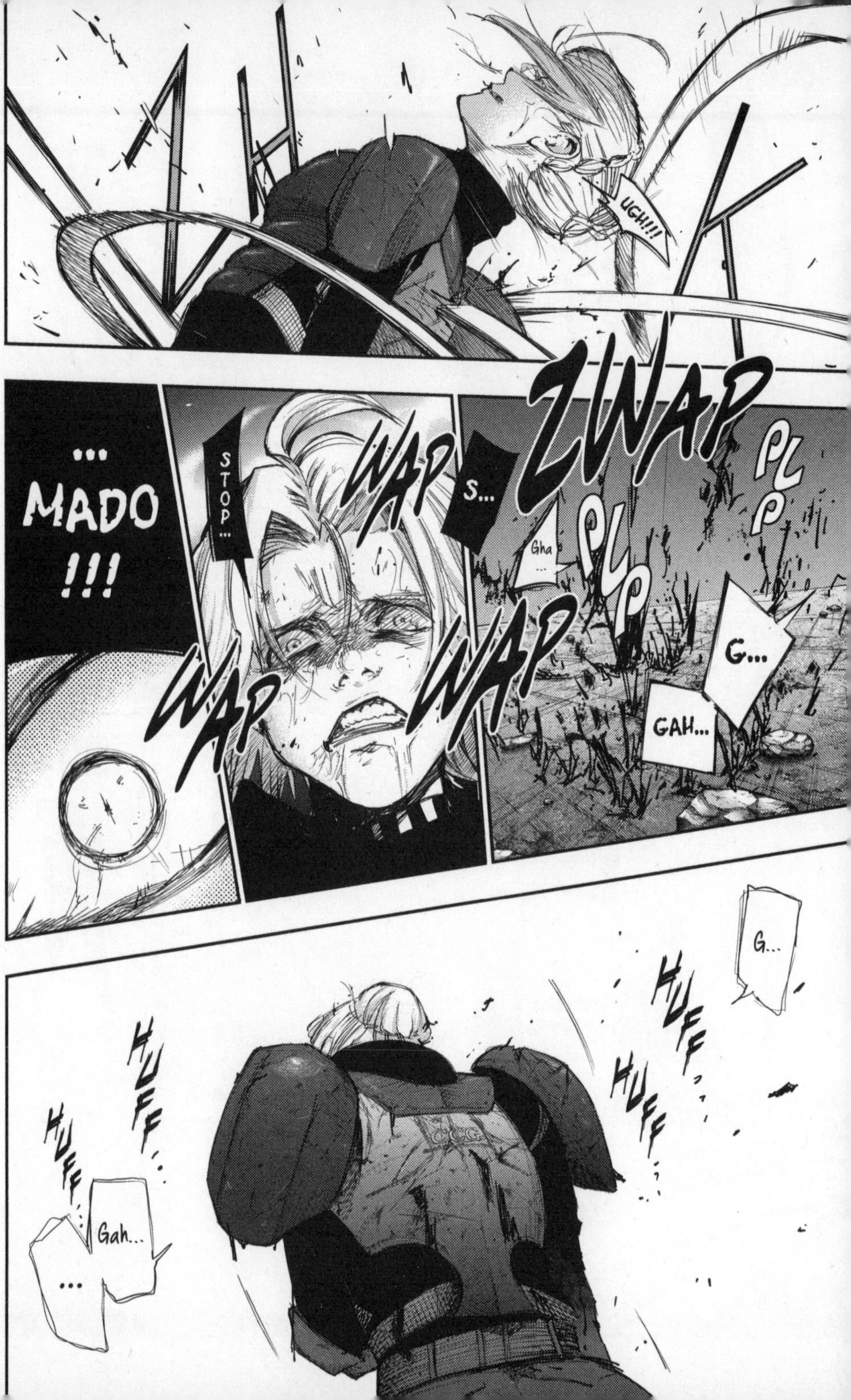
UGH!!!
ZWAP
PLP PLP PLP
Gha...
G...
GAH...
S...
WAP WAP WAP
STOP...
...MADO!!!
G...
HUFF HUFF
HUFF HUFF...
Gah...
...

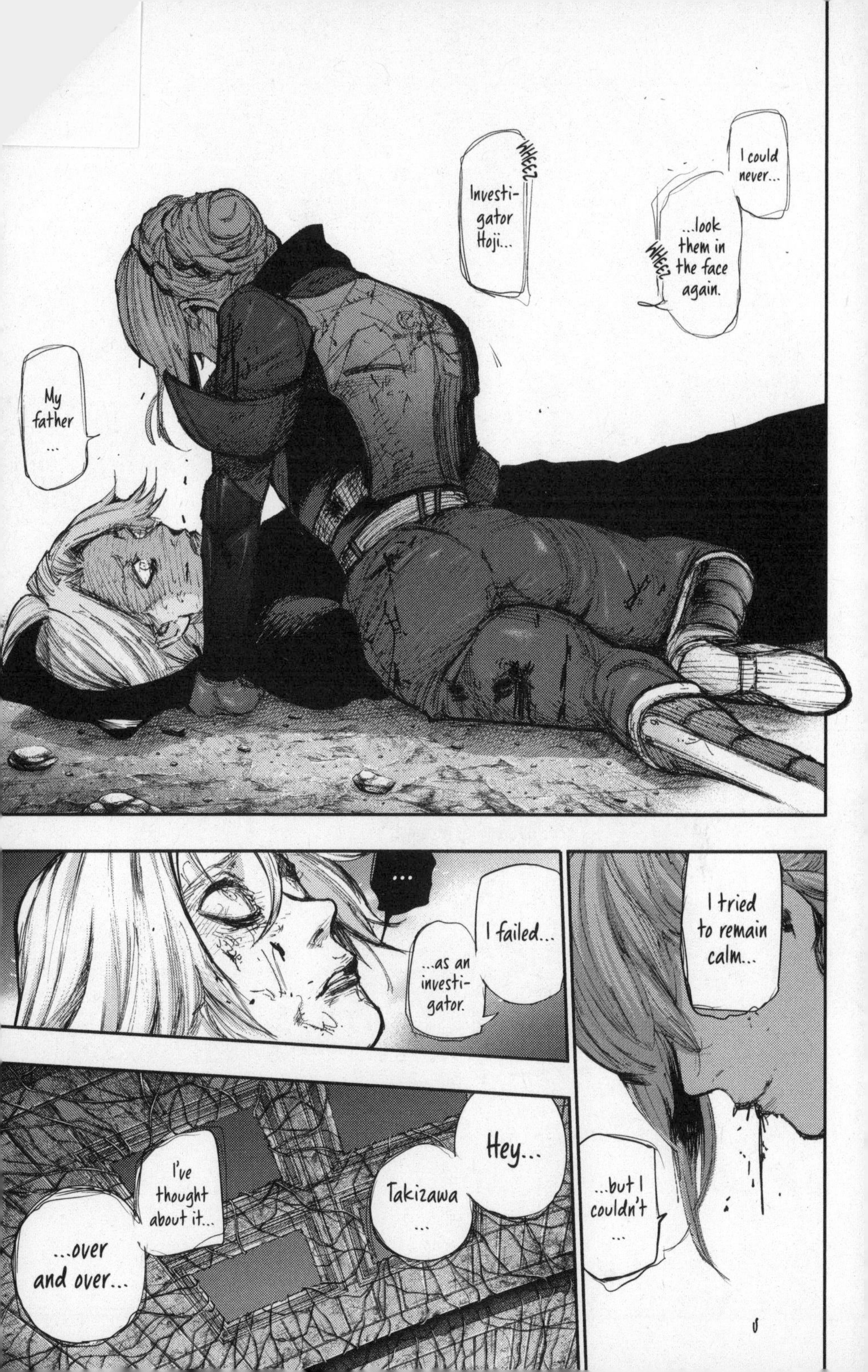
I could never...
...look them in the face again.
WHEEZ
WHEEZ
Investi-gator Hoji...
My father ...
I tried to remain calm...
...but I couldn't ...
...
I failed...
...as an investi-gator.
Hey...
Takizawa ...
I've thought about it...
...over and over...

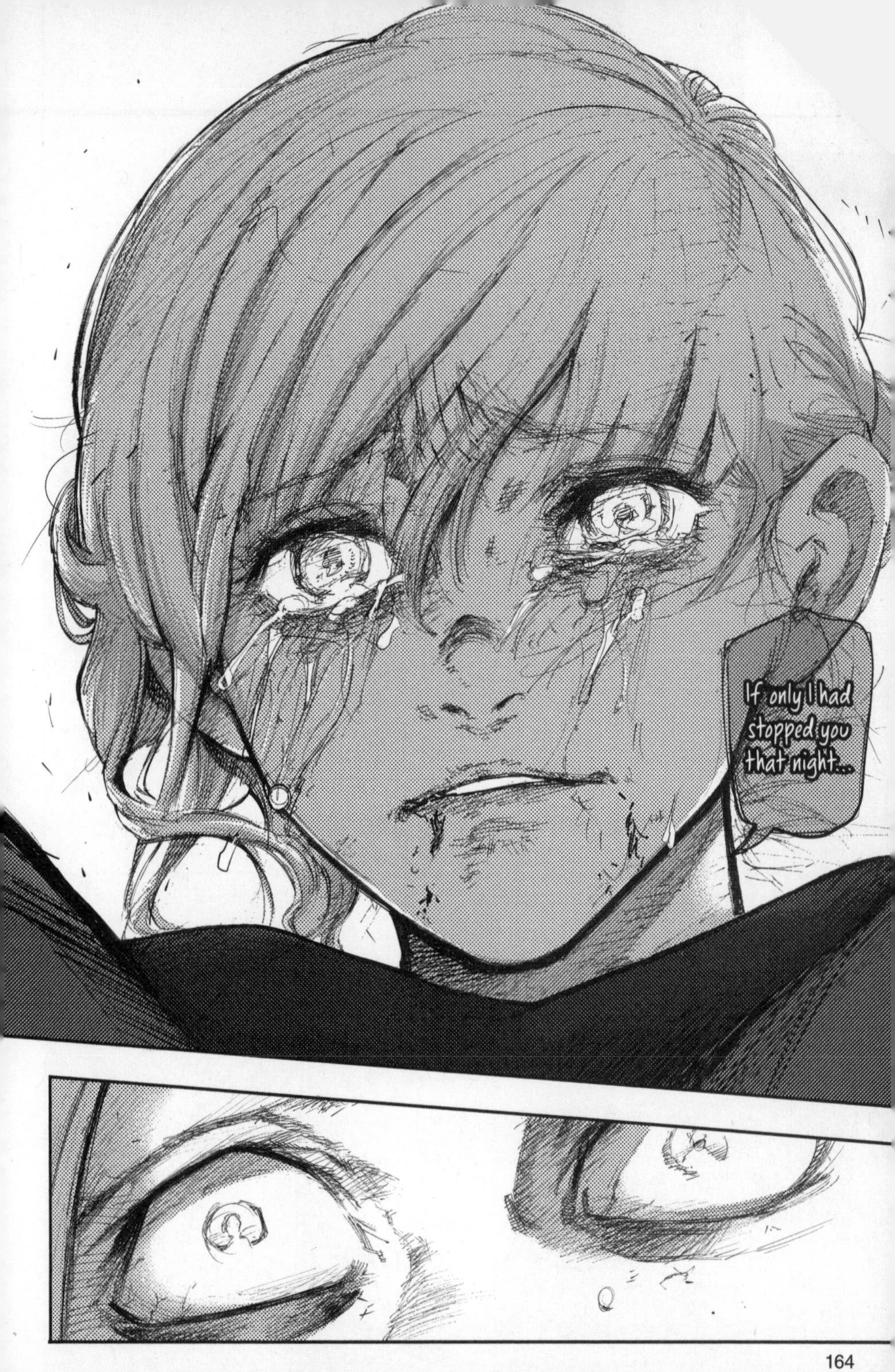
If only I had stopped you that night...

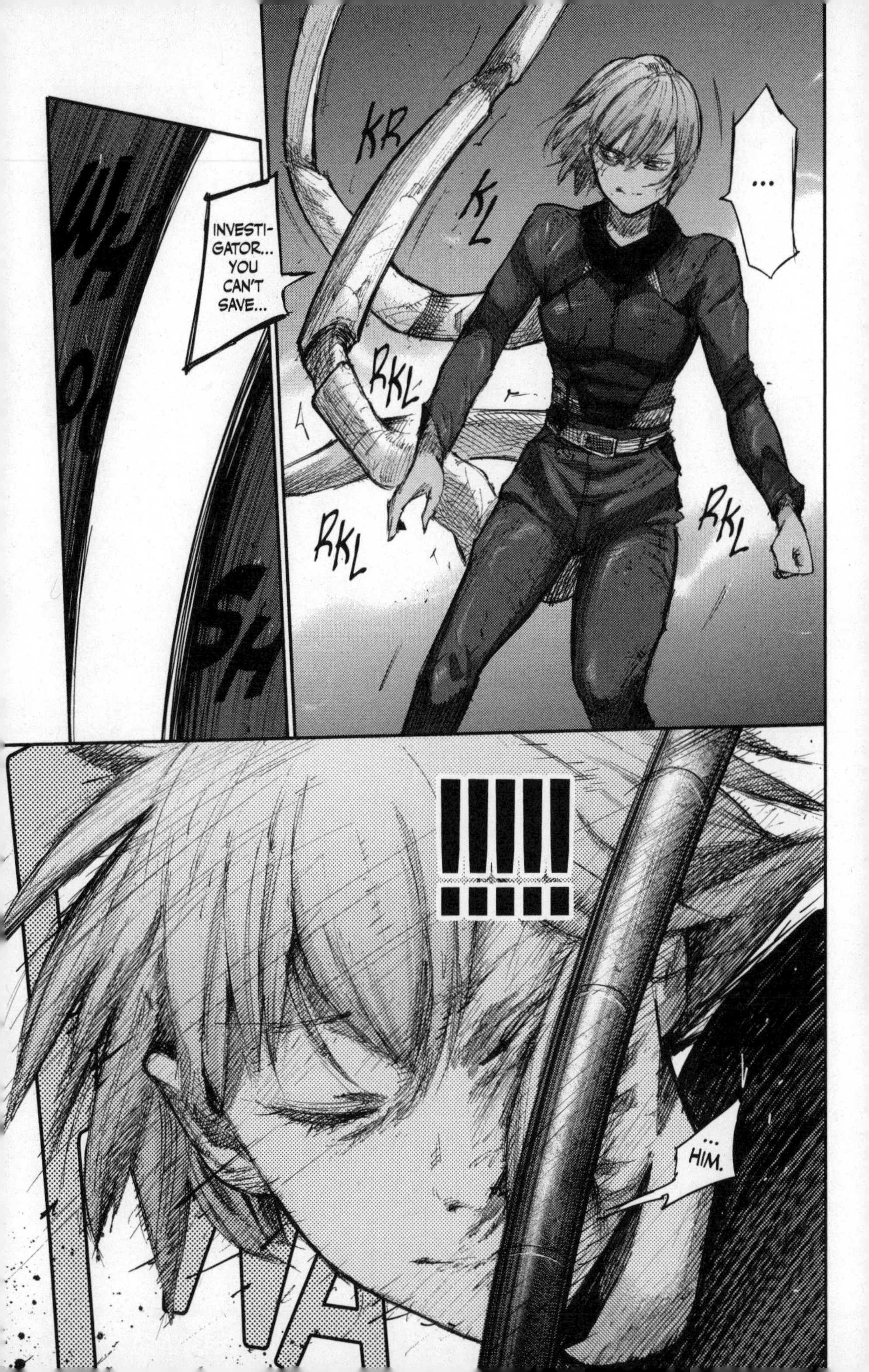
...
KR
KL
INVESTIGATOR... YOU CAN'T SAVE...
RKL
RKL
RKL
WHOOSH
!!!!!
... HIM.

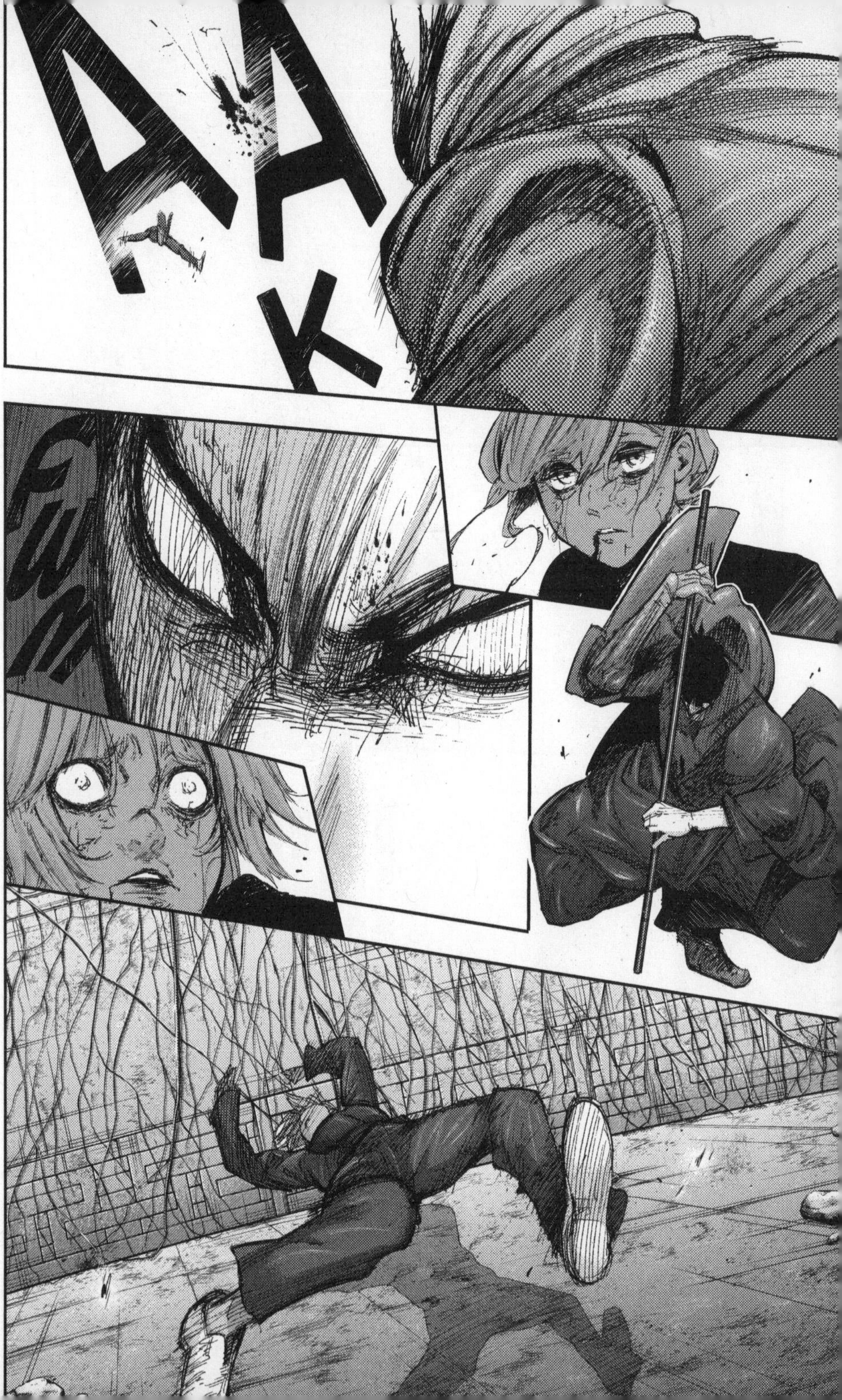
AAK
FWM

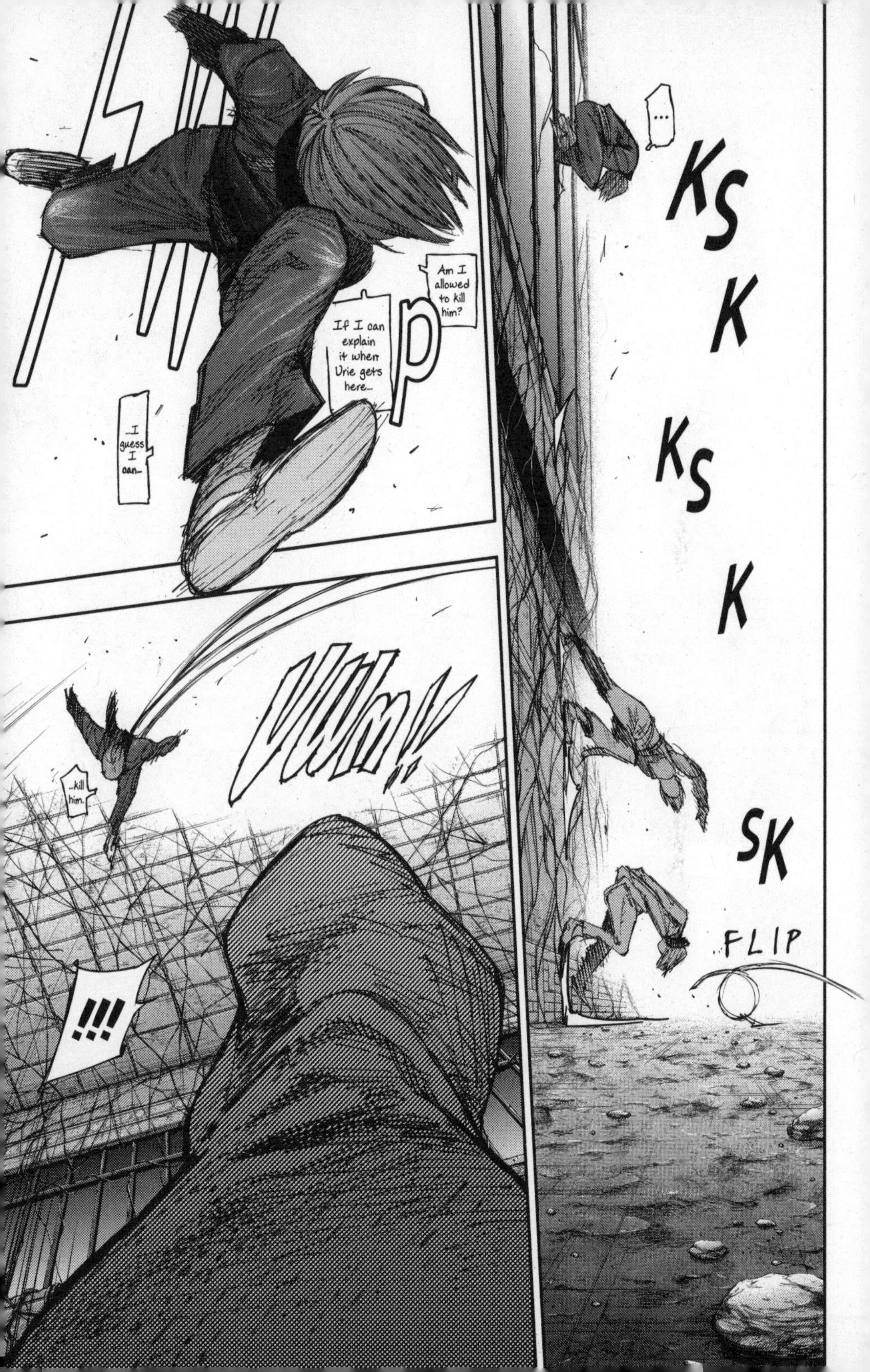
...
KSK
KSK
SK
FLIP
Am I allowed to kill him?
If I can explain it when Urie gets here...
...I guess I can...
...kill him.
!!!

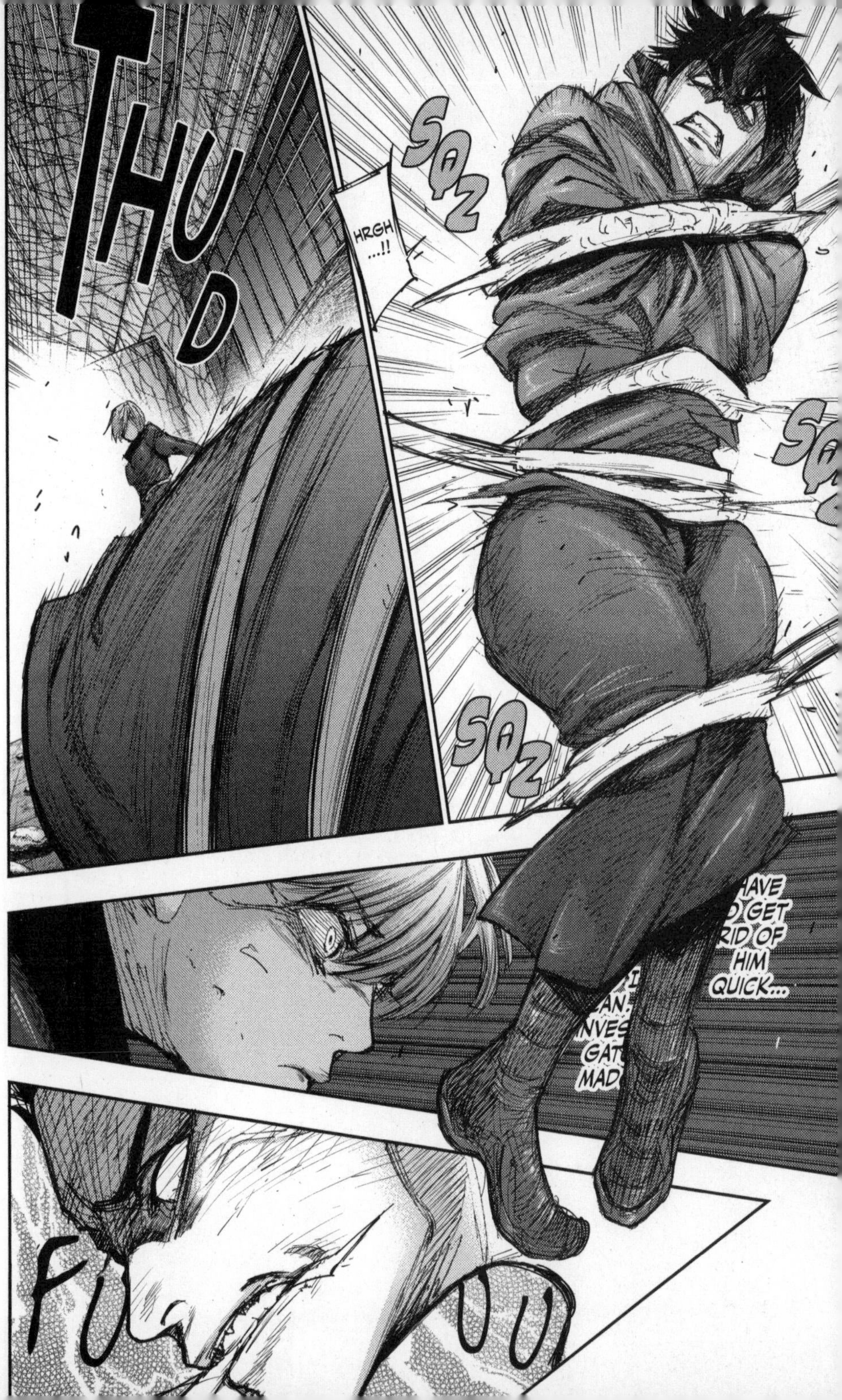
SQZ
HRGH ...!!
SQZ
SQZ
THUD
HAVE TO GET RID OF HIM QUICK...
FU OO

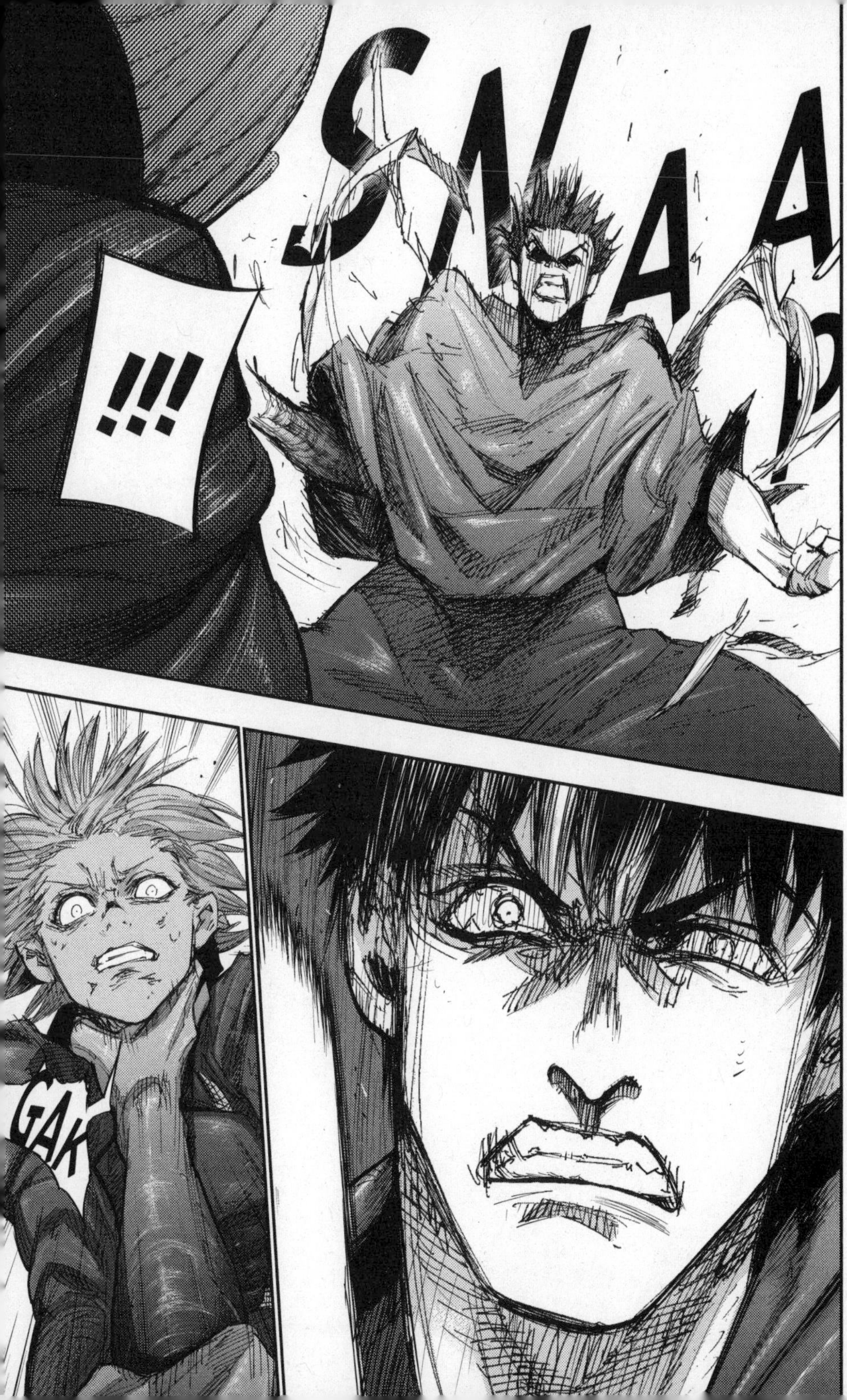
SNAA
!!!
GAK

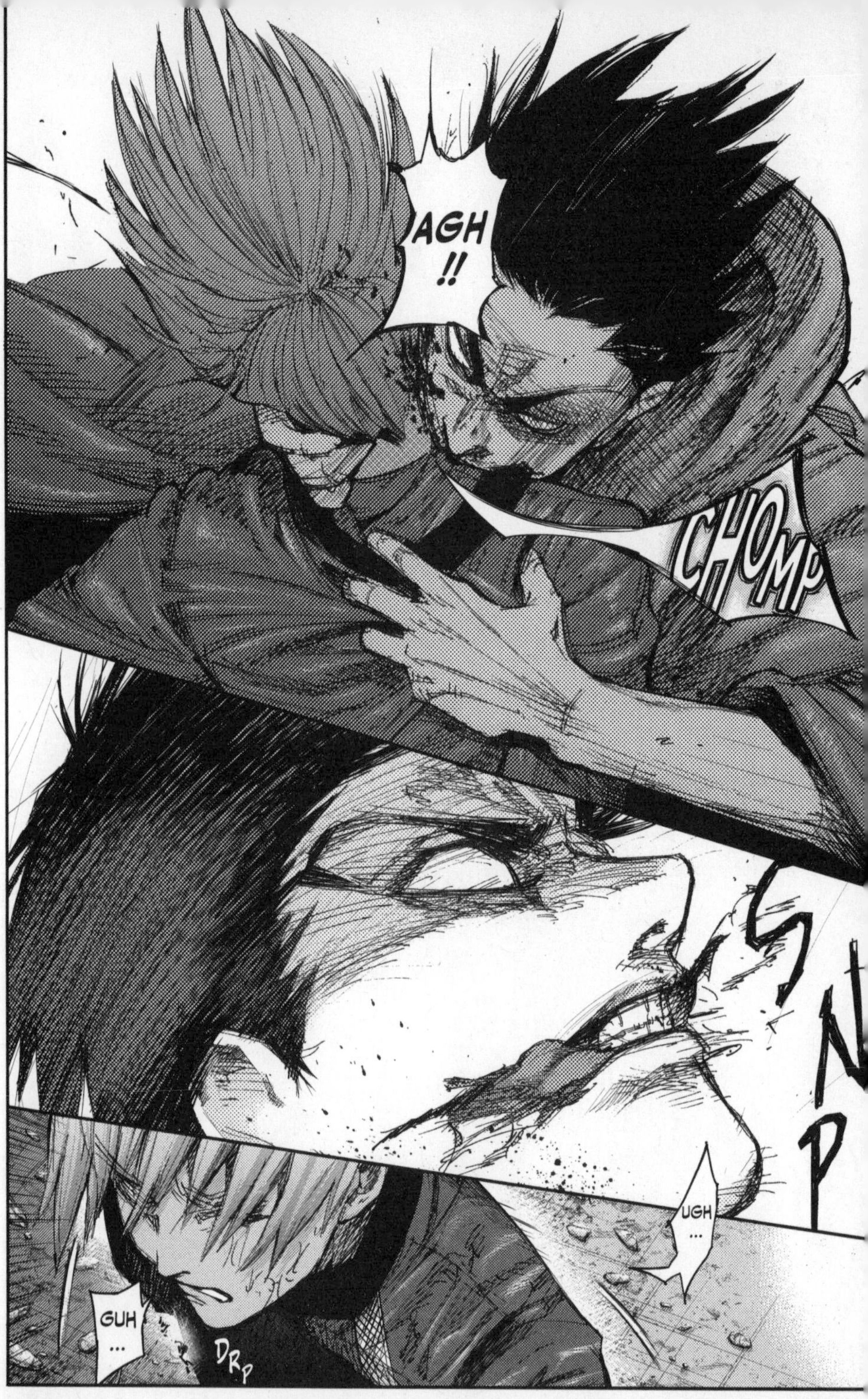
AGH !!
CHOMP
SNP
UGH ...
GUH ...
DRP

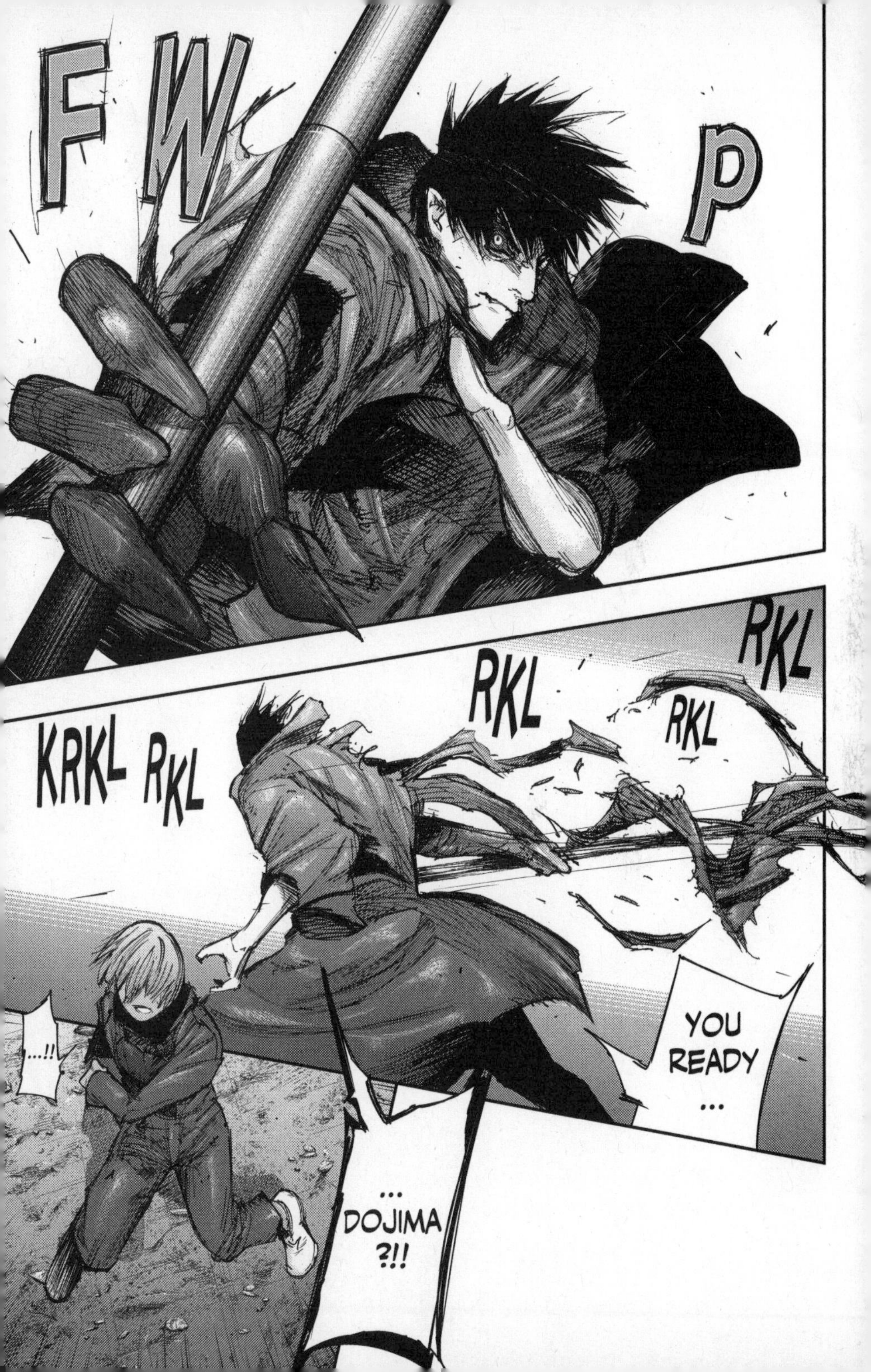
FWP
RKL
RKL
RKL
RKL
KRKL
YOU READY ...
... DOJIMA ?!!
...!!

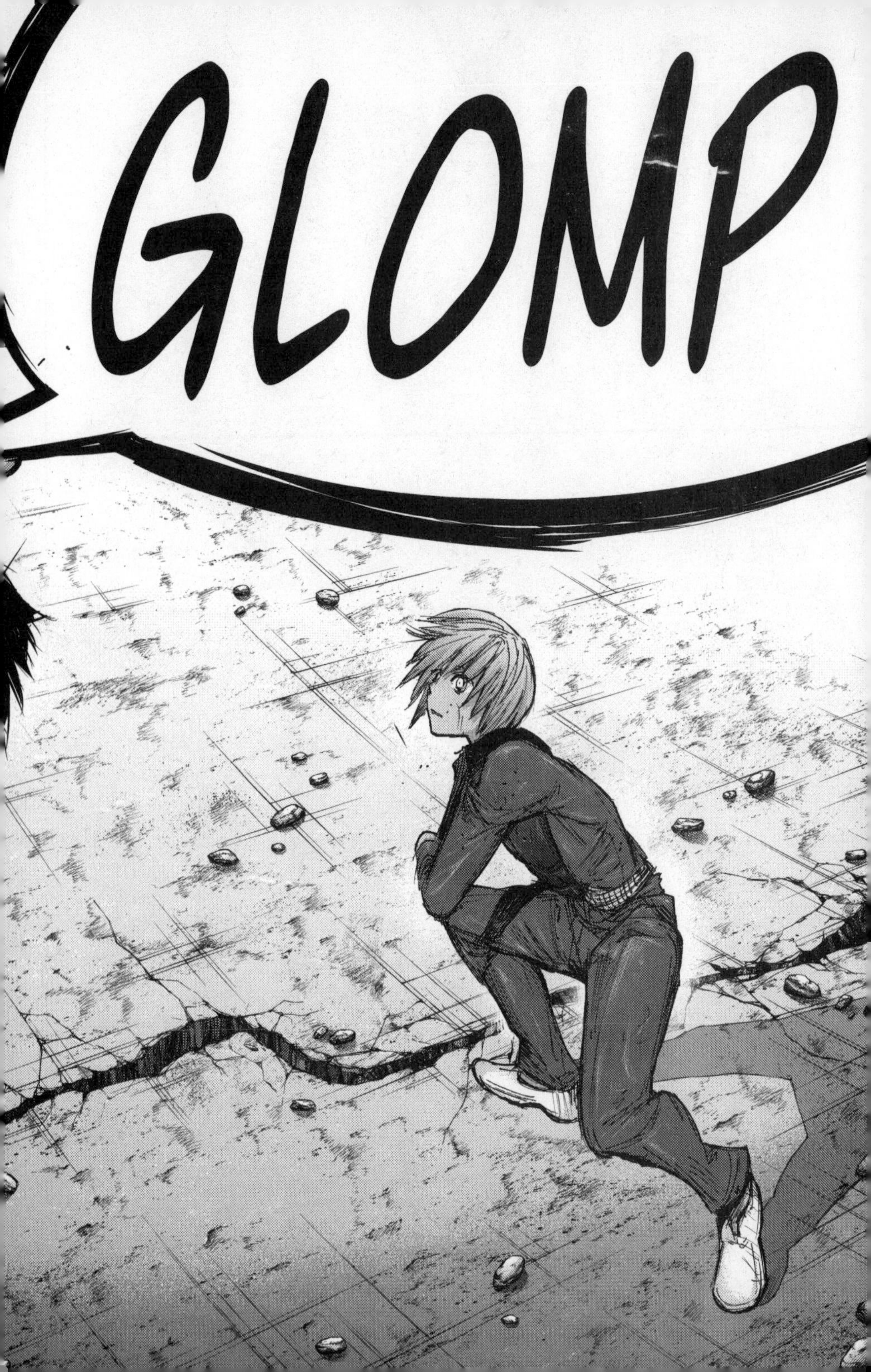
GLOMP

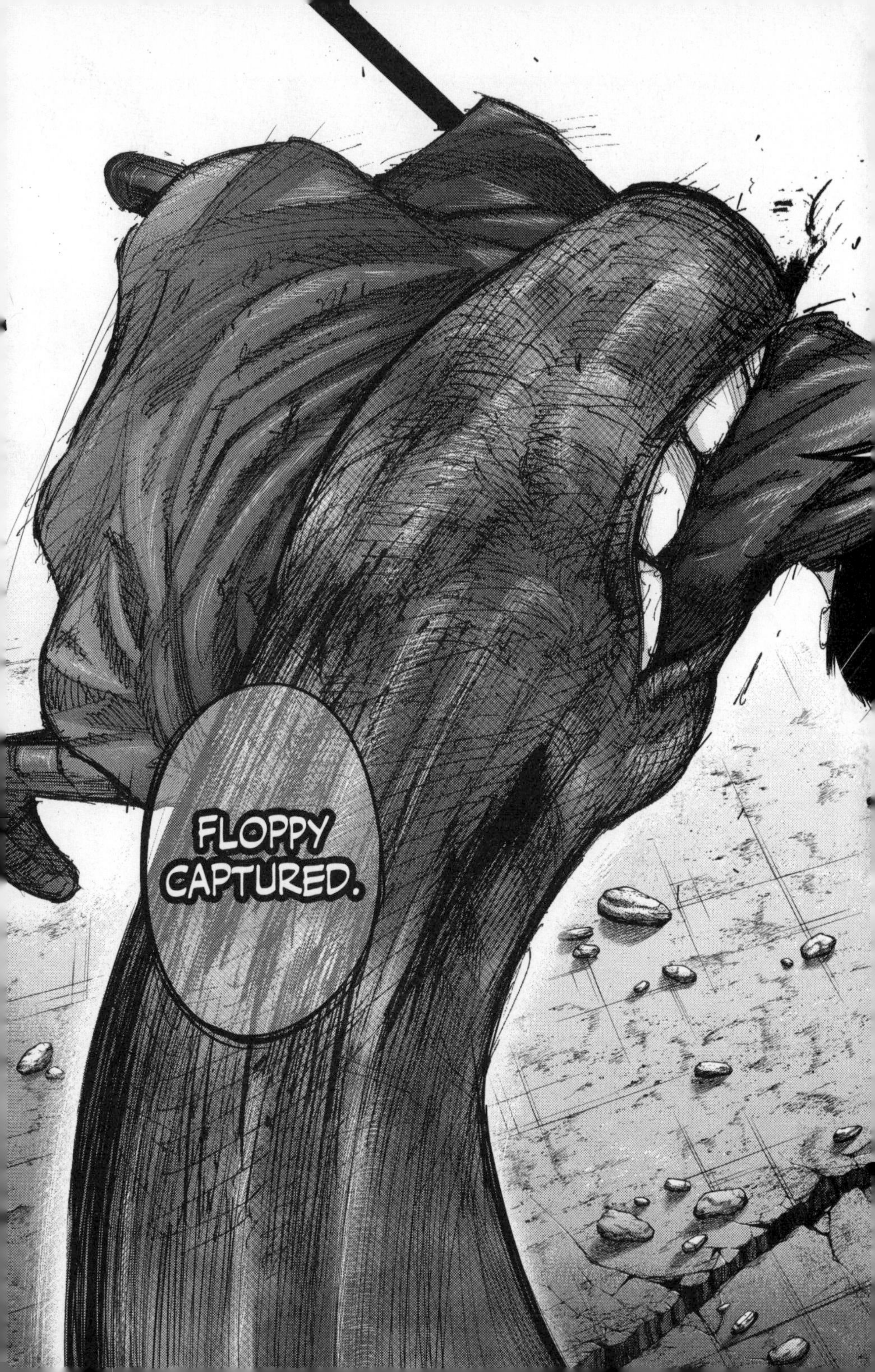
FLOPPY CAPTURED.

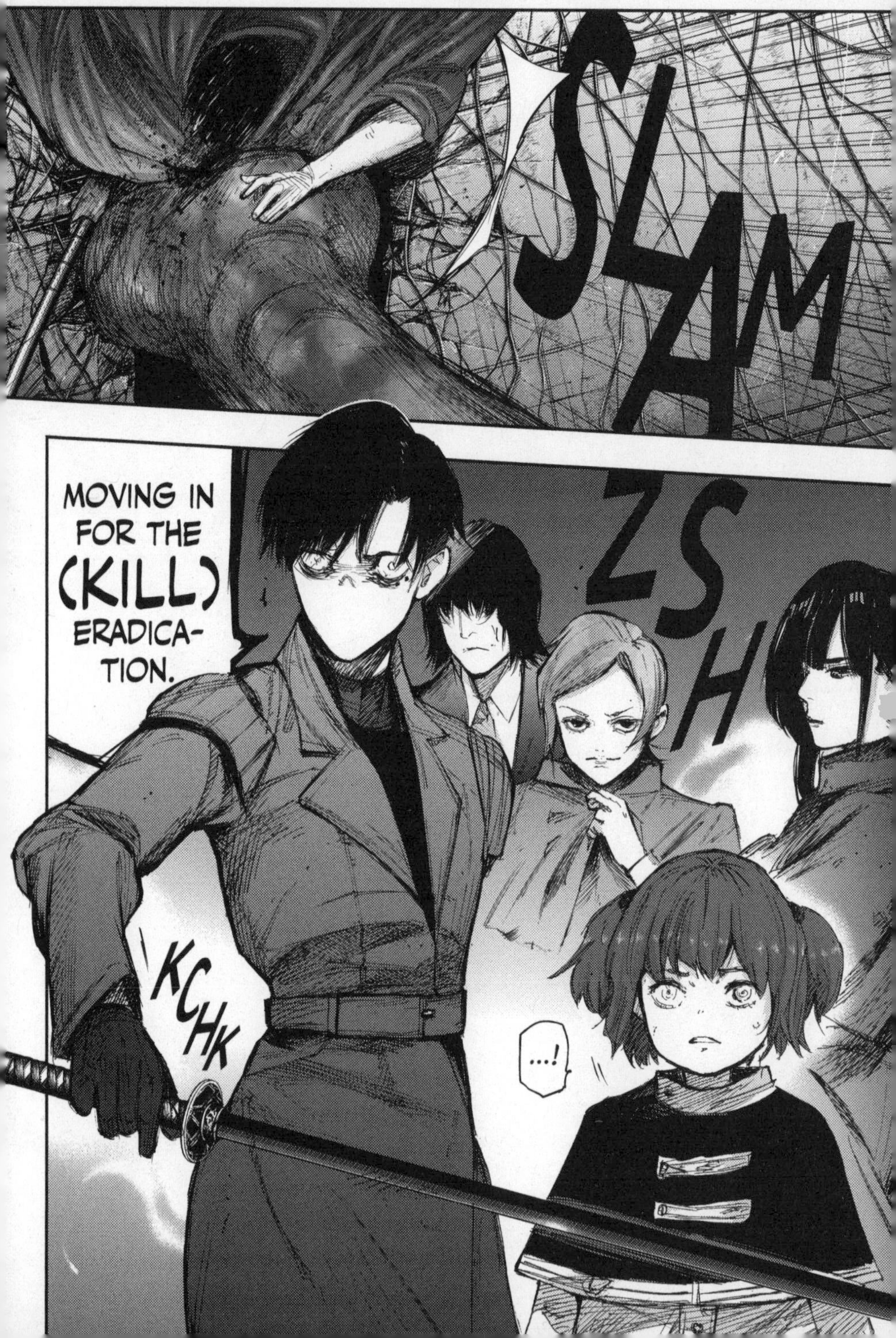
SLAM
ZSH
MOVING IN FOR THE (KILL) ERADICATION.
KCHK
...!

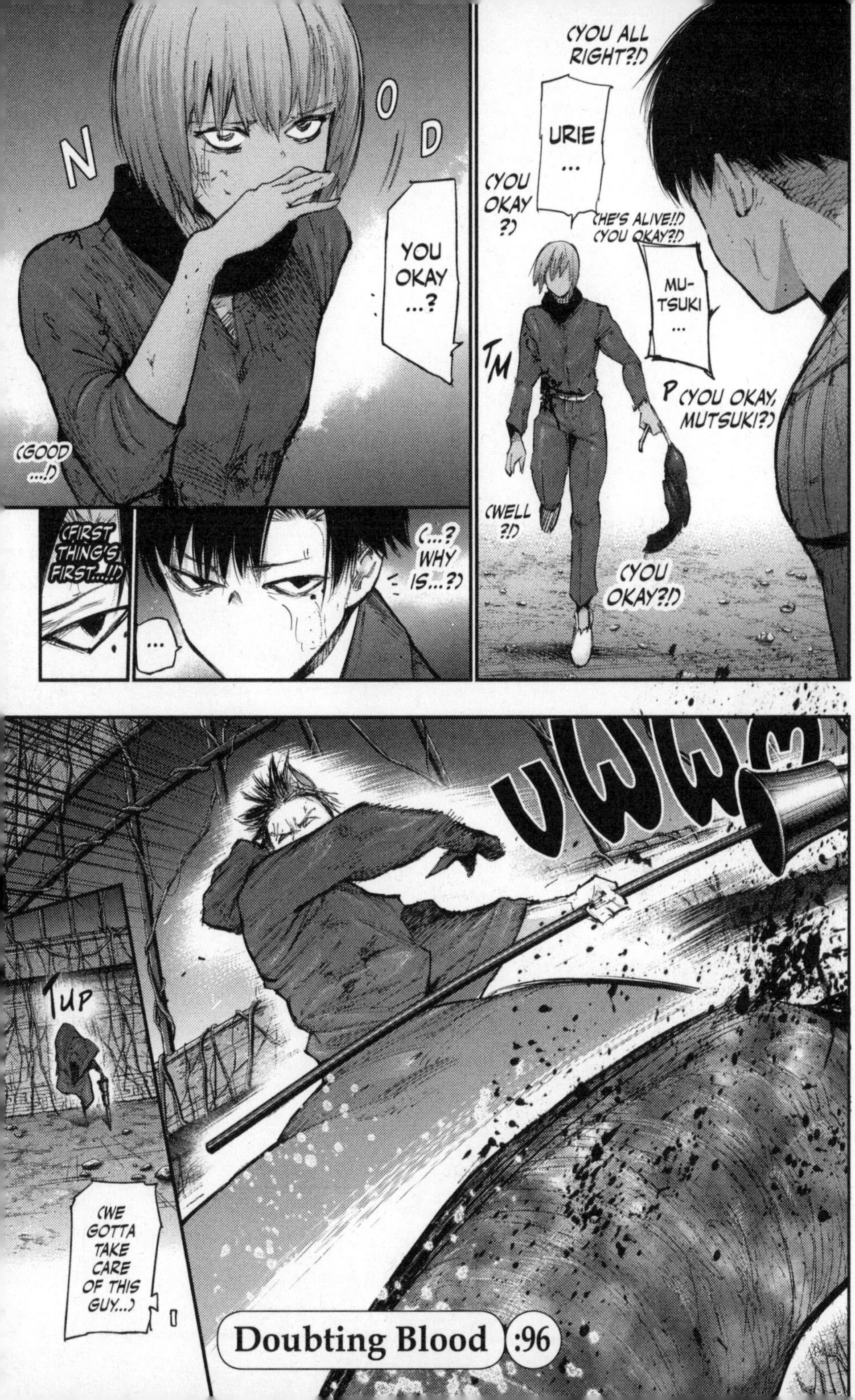
(YOU ALL RIGHT?!)
URIE ...
(YOU OKAY ?)
(HE'S ALIVE!!)
(YOU OKAY?!)
MU-TSUKI ...
TM
P
(YOU OKAY, MUTSUKI!?)
(WELL ?!)
(YOU OKAY?!)
NOD
YOU OKAY ...?
(GOOD ...!)
(...? WHY IS...?)
...
(FIRST THING'S FIRST...!!)
TUP
(WE GOTTA TAKE CARE OF THIS GUY...)
Doubting Blood :96

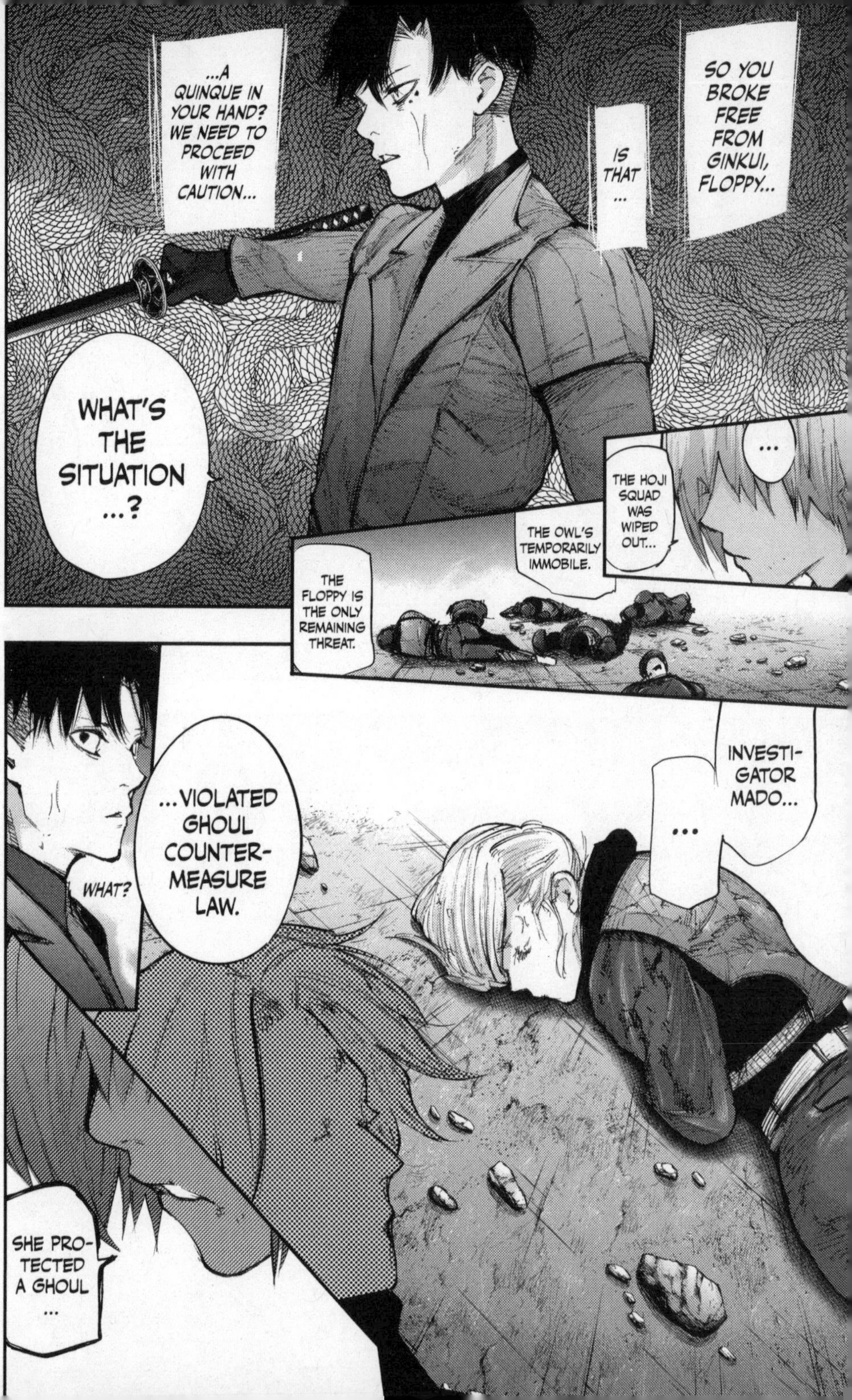
SO YOU BROKE FREE FROM GINKUI, FLOPPY...
IS THAT...
...A QUINQUE IN YOUR HAND? WE NEED TO PROCEED WITH CAUTION...
WHAT'S THE SITUATION...?
...
THE HOJI SQUAD WAS WIPED OUT...
THE OWL'S TEMPORARILY IMMOBILE.
THE FLOPPY IS THE ONLY REMAINING THREAT.
INVESTI-GATOR MADO...
...
...VIOLATED GHOUL COUNTER-MEASURE LAW.
WHAT?
SHE PRO-TECTED A GHOUL...

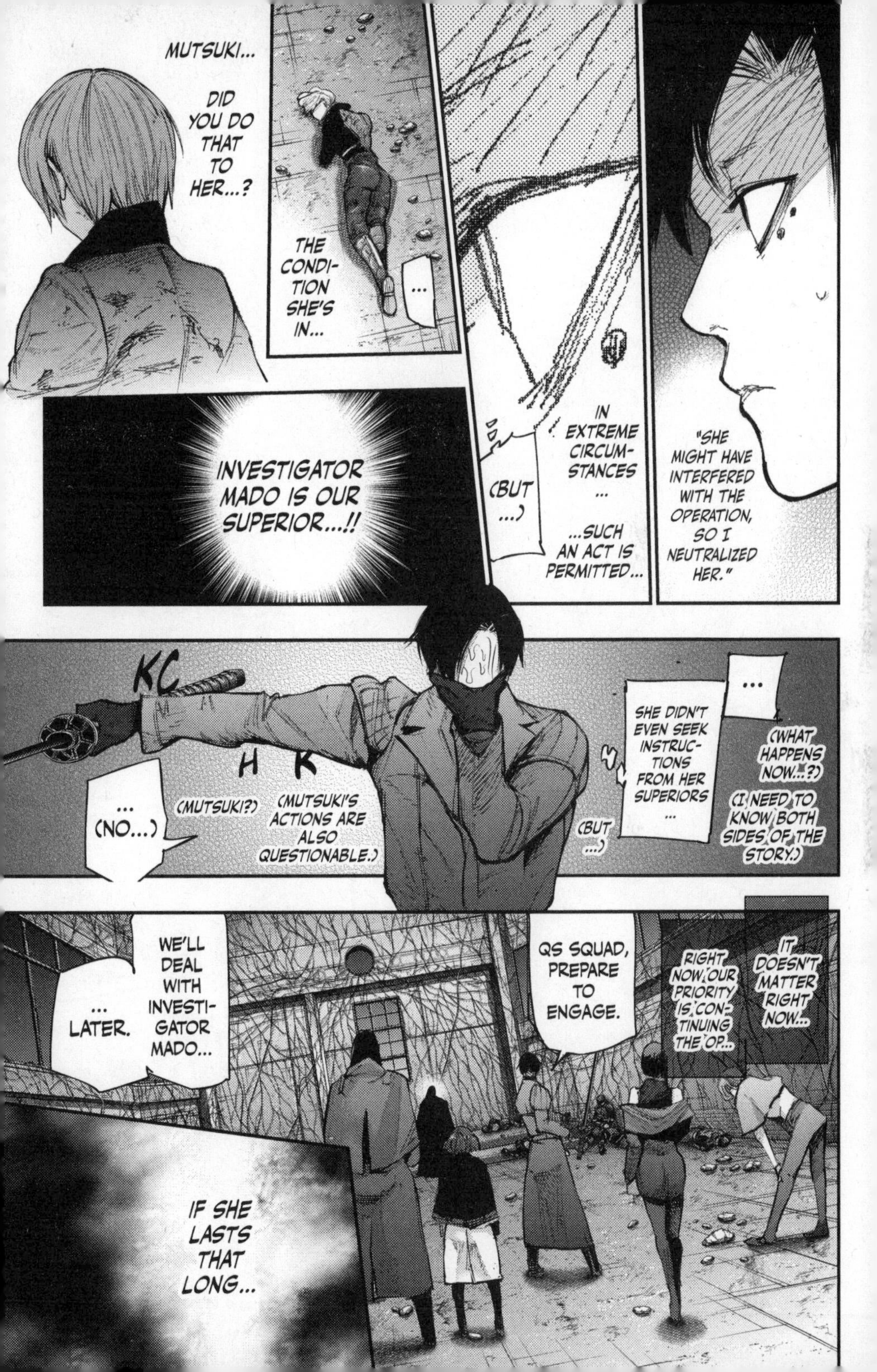
"SHE MIGHT HAVE INTERFERED WITH THE OPERATION, SO I NEUTRALIZED HER."
IN EXTREME CIRCUM-STANCES ...
...SUCH AN ACT IS PERMITTED...
(BUT ...)
THE CONDI-TION SHE'S IN...
...
MUTSUKI...
DID YOU DO THAT TO HER...?
INVESTIGATOR MADO IS OUR SUPERIOR...!!
...
(WHAT HAPPENS NOW...?)
(I NEED TO KNOW BOTH SIDES OF THE STORY.)
SHE DIDN'T EVEN SEEK INSTRUC-TIONS FROM HER SUPERIORS ...
(BUT ...)
KCHK
(MUTSUKI'S ACTIONS ARE ALSO QUESTIONABLE.)
(MUTSUKI?)
... (NO...)
IT DOESN'T MATTER RIGHT NOW...
RIGHT NOW, OUR PRIORITY IS CON-TINUING THE OP...
QS SQUAD, PREPARE TO ENGAGE.
WE'LL DEAL WITH INVESTI-GATOR MADO...
... LATER.
IF SHE LASTS THAT LONG...

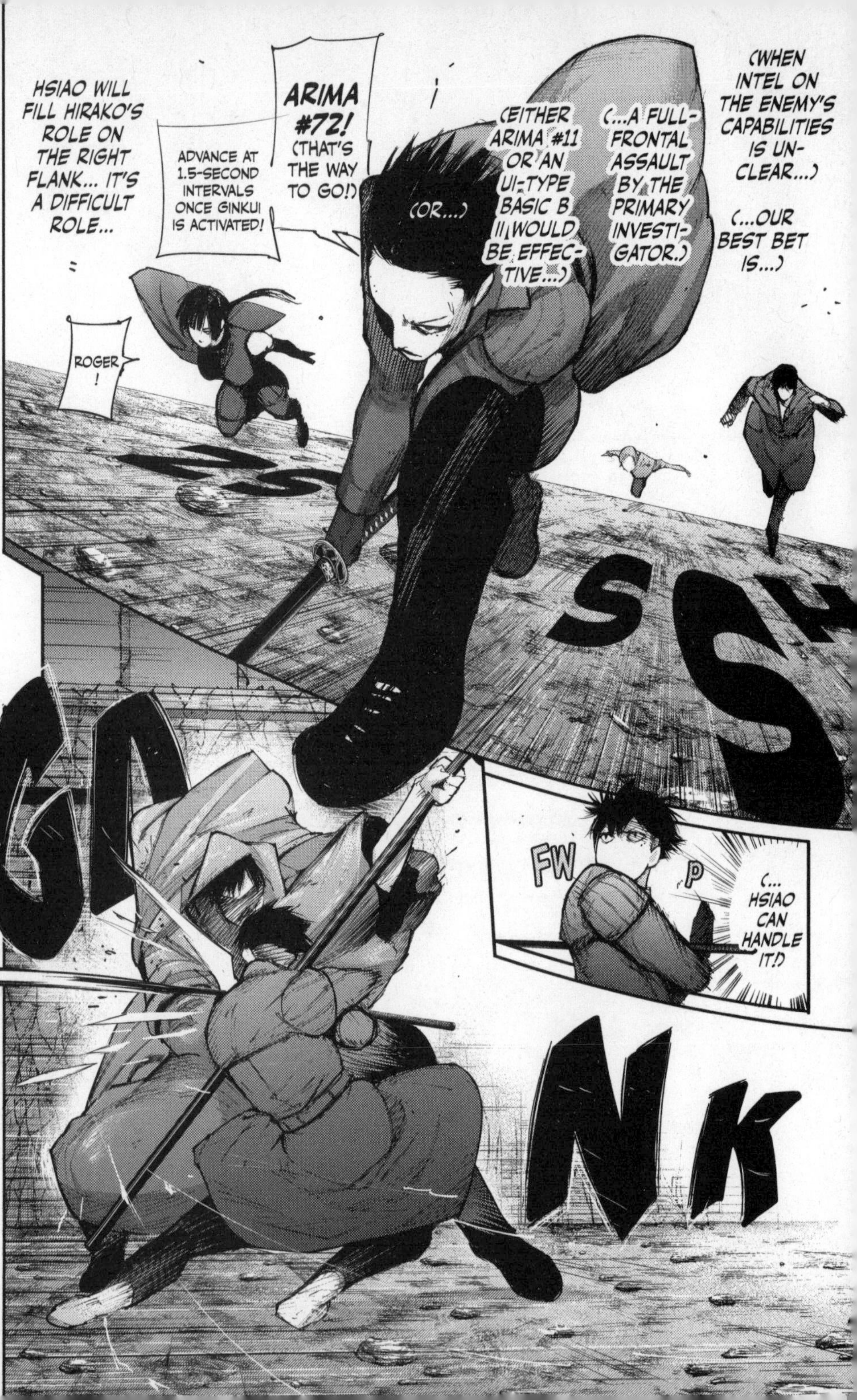
(WHEN INTEL ON THE ENEMY'S CAPABILITIES IS UN-CLEAR...)
(...OUR BEST BET IS...)
(...A FULL-FRONTAL ASSAULT BY THE PRIMARY INVESTI-GATOR.)
(EITHER ARIMA #11 OR AN UI-TYPE BASIC B II WOULD BE EFFEC-TIVE...)
(OR...)
ARIMA #72!
(THAT'S THE WAY TO GO!)
ADVANCE AT 1.5-SECOND INTERVALS ONCE GINKUI IS ACTIVATED!
HSIAO WILL FILL HIRAKO'S ROLE ON THE RIGHT FLANK... IT'S A DIFFICULT ROLE...
ROGER!
FW
P
(... HSIAO CAN HANDLE IT!)
GA
NK

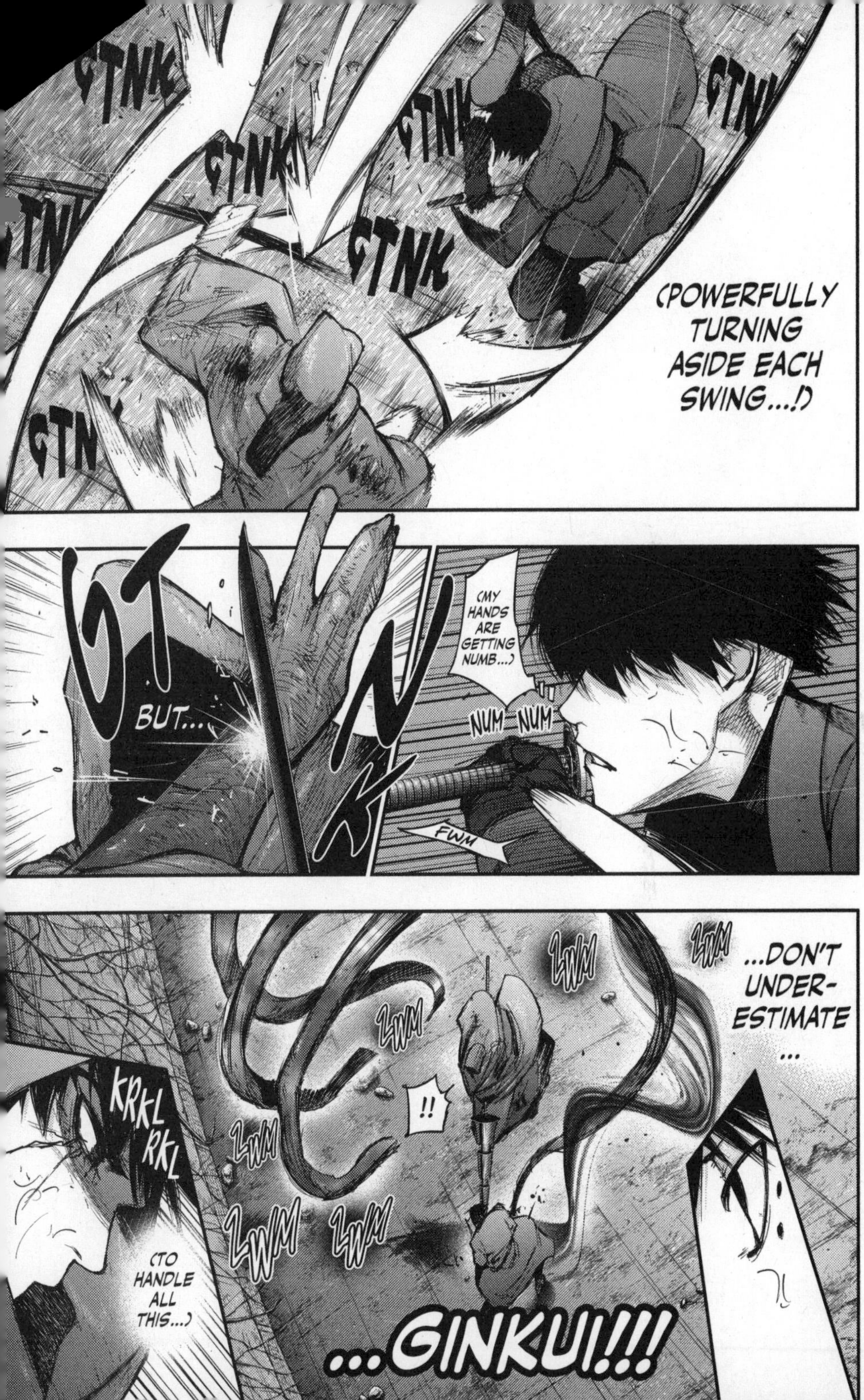
GTNK
GTNK
GTNK
GTNK
(POWERFULLY TURNING ASIDE EACH SWING...!)
(MY HANDS ARE GETTING NUMB...)
NUM NUM
FWM
GTNK
BUT...
...DON'T UNDER-ESTIMATE ...
ZWM
ZWM
ZWM
!!
ZWM
ZWM
ZWM
KRKL KRKL
(TO HANDLE ALL THIS...)
...GINKUI!!!

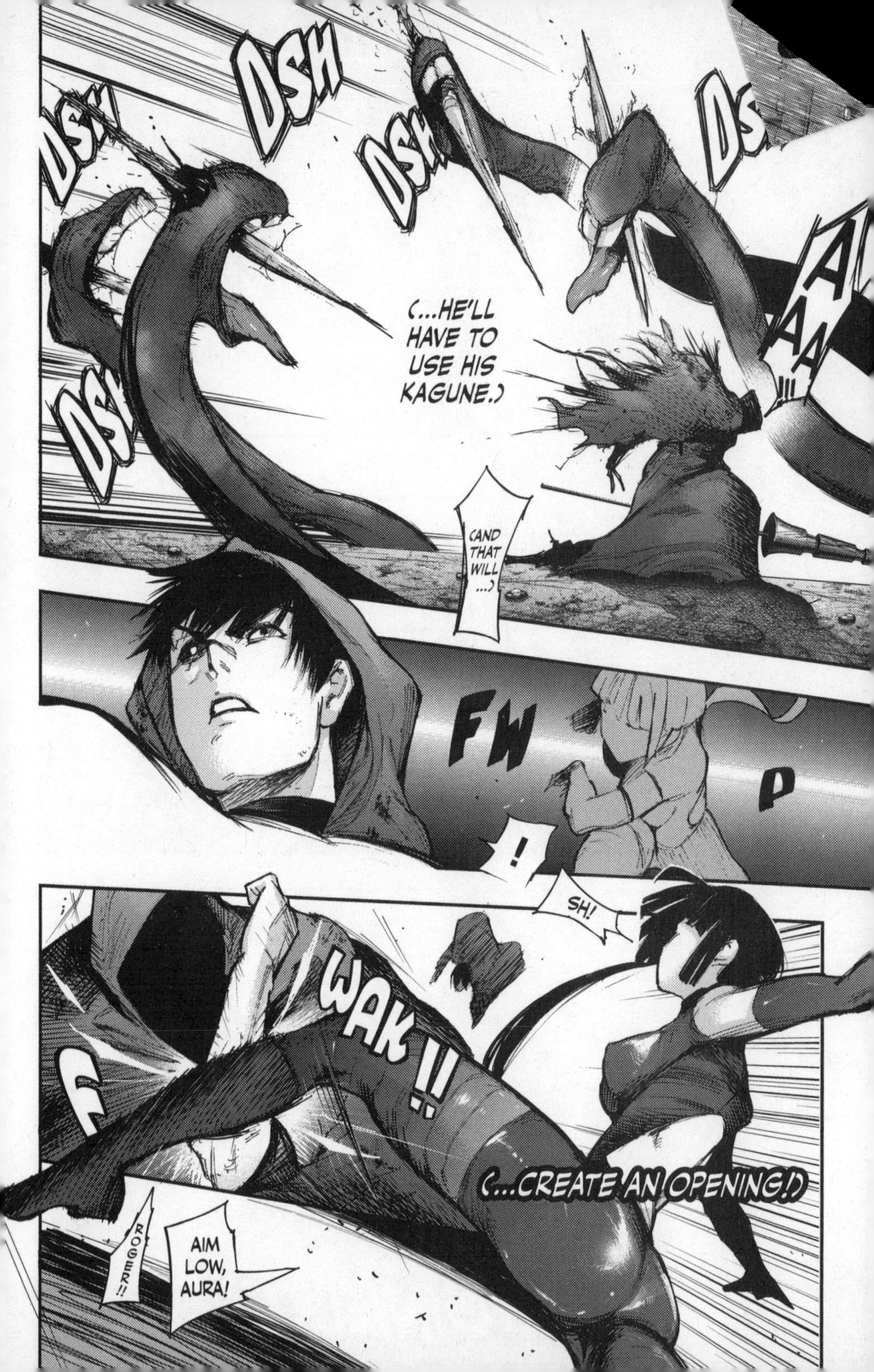
AAAA!!
DS
DSH
DSH
DSH
DSH
(...HE'LL HAVE TO USE HIS KAGUNE.)
(AND THAT WILL ...)
P
FW
!
SH!
WAK!!
(...CREATE AN OPENING!)
ROGER!!
AIM LOW, AURA!

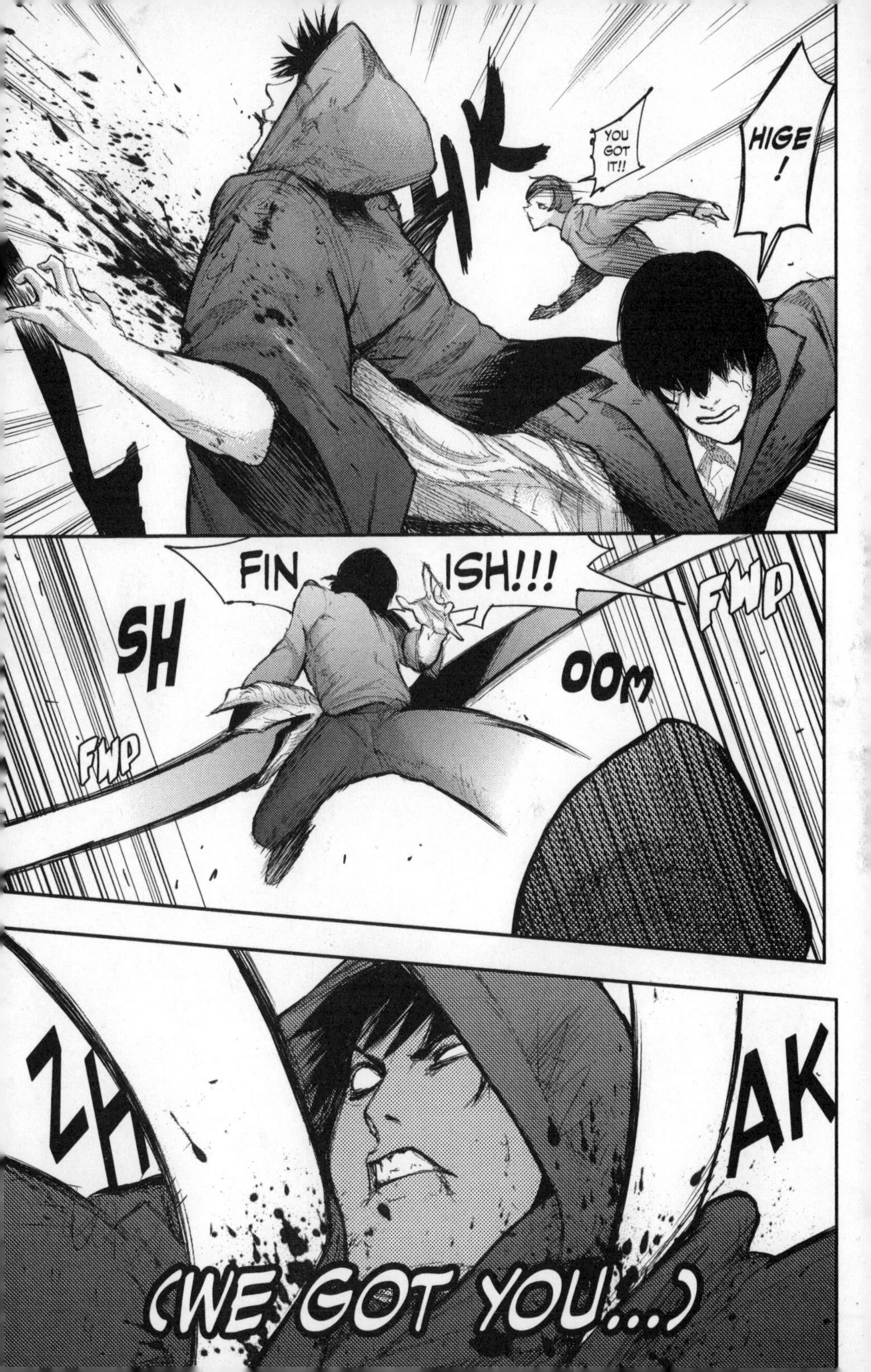
HIGE!
YOU GOT IT!!
FWP
FIN ISH!!!
OOM
SH
FWP
AK
ZH
(WE GOT YOU...)

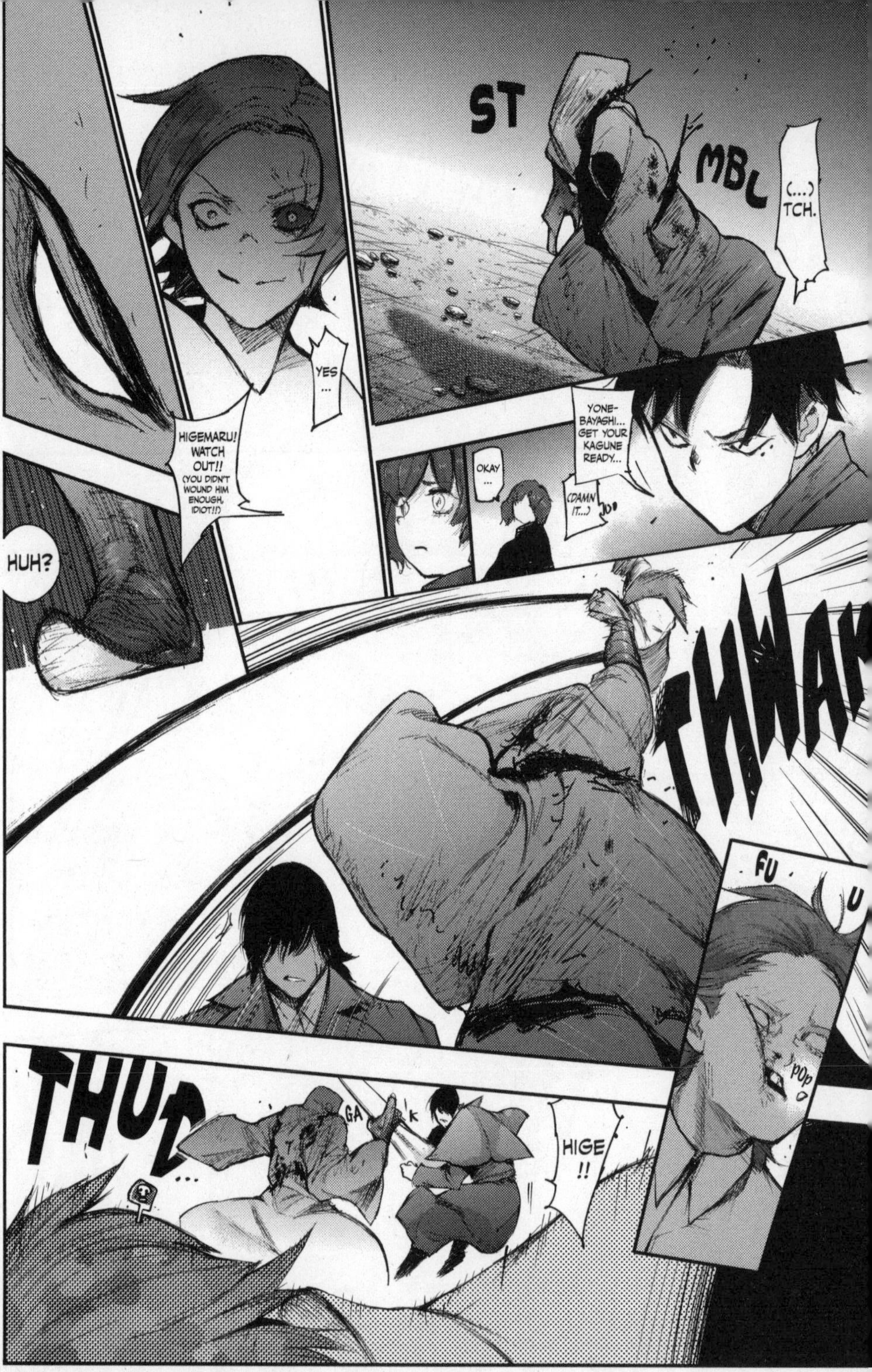

ST
MBL
(...) TCH.
YES ...
HIGEMARU! WATCH OUT!! (YOU DIDN'T WOUND HIM ENOUGH, IDIOT!!)
YONE-BAYASHI... GET YOUR KAGUNE READY...
(DAMN IT...)
OKAY ...
HUH?
THWAK
FU
U
pop
HIGE !!
GA
K
THUD ...

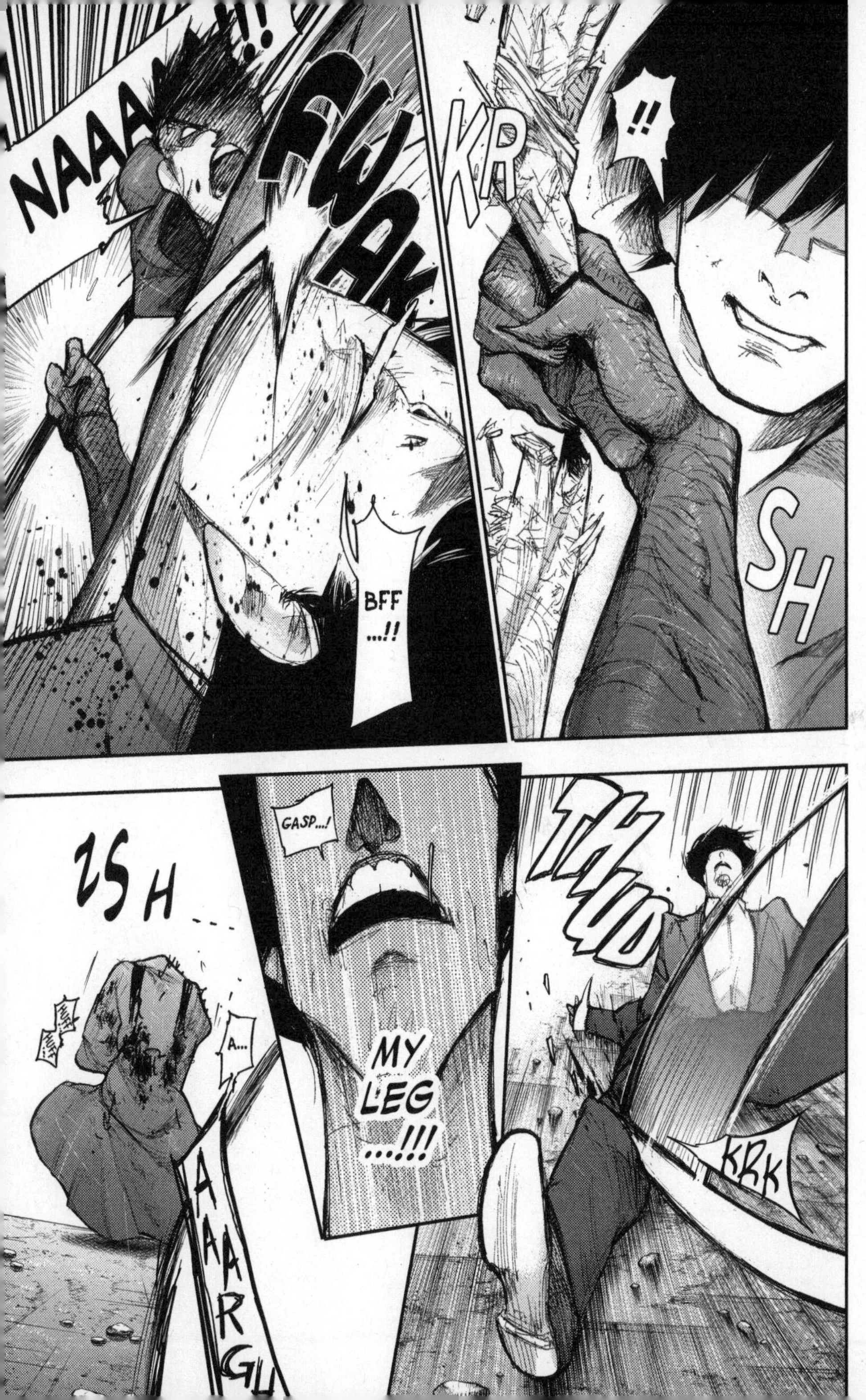
KR
!!
SH
NAAAAH!!
FWAK
BFF ...!!
THUD
KRK
GASP...!
MY LEG ...!!!
ZSH
HUFF HUFF
A...
AAARG

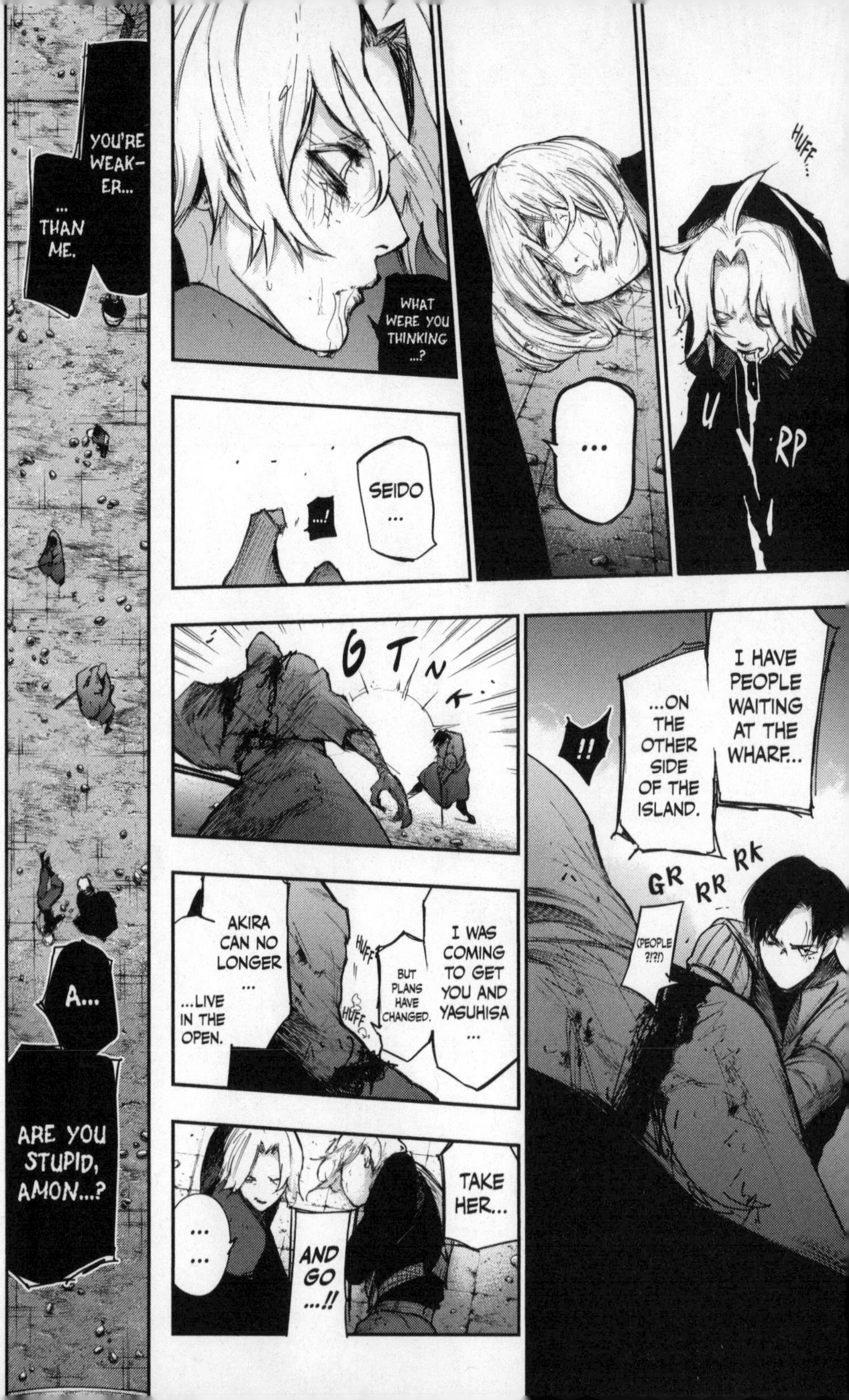

HUFF...
URP
...
WHAT WERE YOU THINKING ...?
...!
SEIDO ...
I HAVE PEOPLE WAITING AT THE WHARF...
...ON THE OTHER SIDE OF THE ISLAND.
!!
GRRRRK
(PEOPLE ?!?!)
GTNK..
I WAS COMING TO GET YOU AND YASUHISA ...
BUT PLANS HAVE CHANGED.
HUFF !!
HUFF
AKIRA CAN NO LONGER ...
...LIVE IN THE OPEN.
TAKE HER...
AND GO ...!!
... ...
YOU'RE WEAK-ER...
... THAN ME.
A...
ARE YOU STUPID, AMON...?

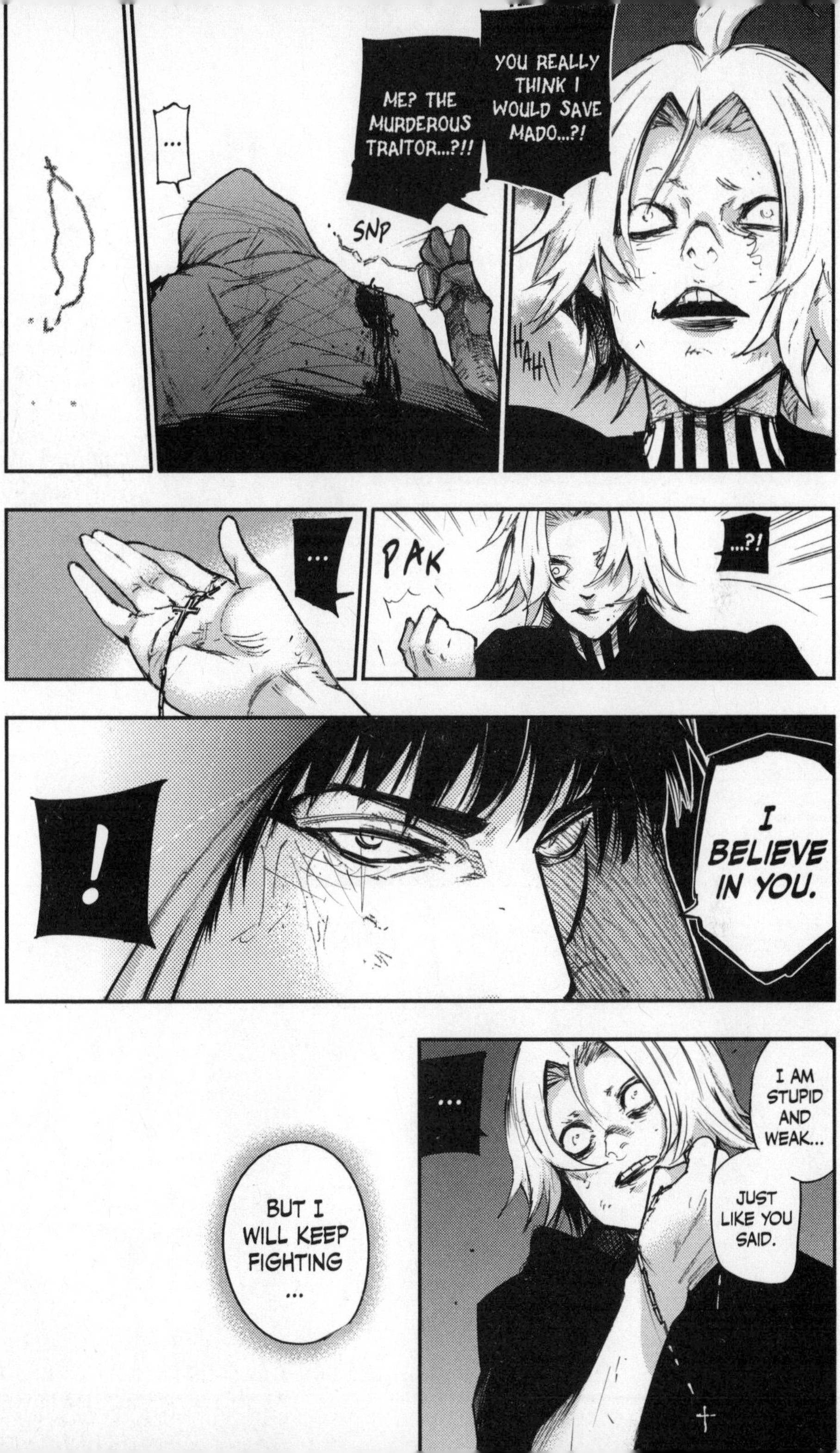
YOU REALLY THINK I WOULD SAVE MADO...?!
ME? THE MURDEROUS TRAITOR...?!!
HAH
SNP
...
...?!
PAK
...
I BELIEVE IN YOU.
!
I AM STUPID AND WEAK...
JUST LIKE YOU SAID.
...
BUT I WILL KEEP FIGHTING ...

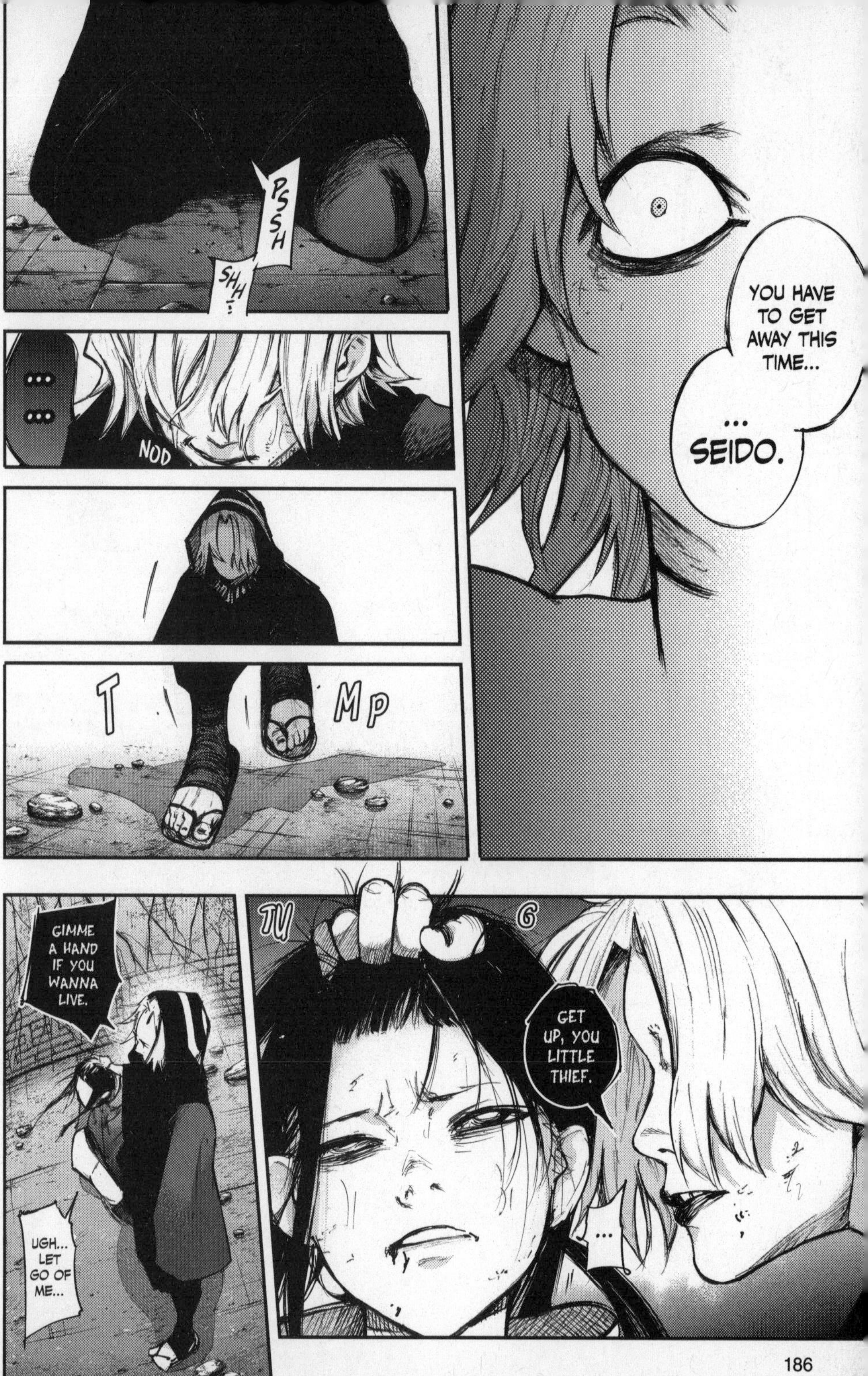
YOU HAVE TO GET AWAY THIS TIME...
... SEIDO.
PSSH
SHH
...
...
NOD
T Mp
TU G
GET UP, YOU LITTLE THIEF.
...
GIMME A HAND IF YOU WANNA LIVE.
UGH... LET GO OF ME...

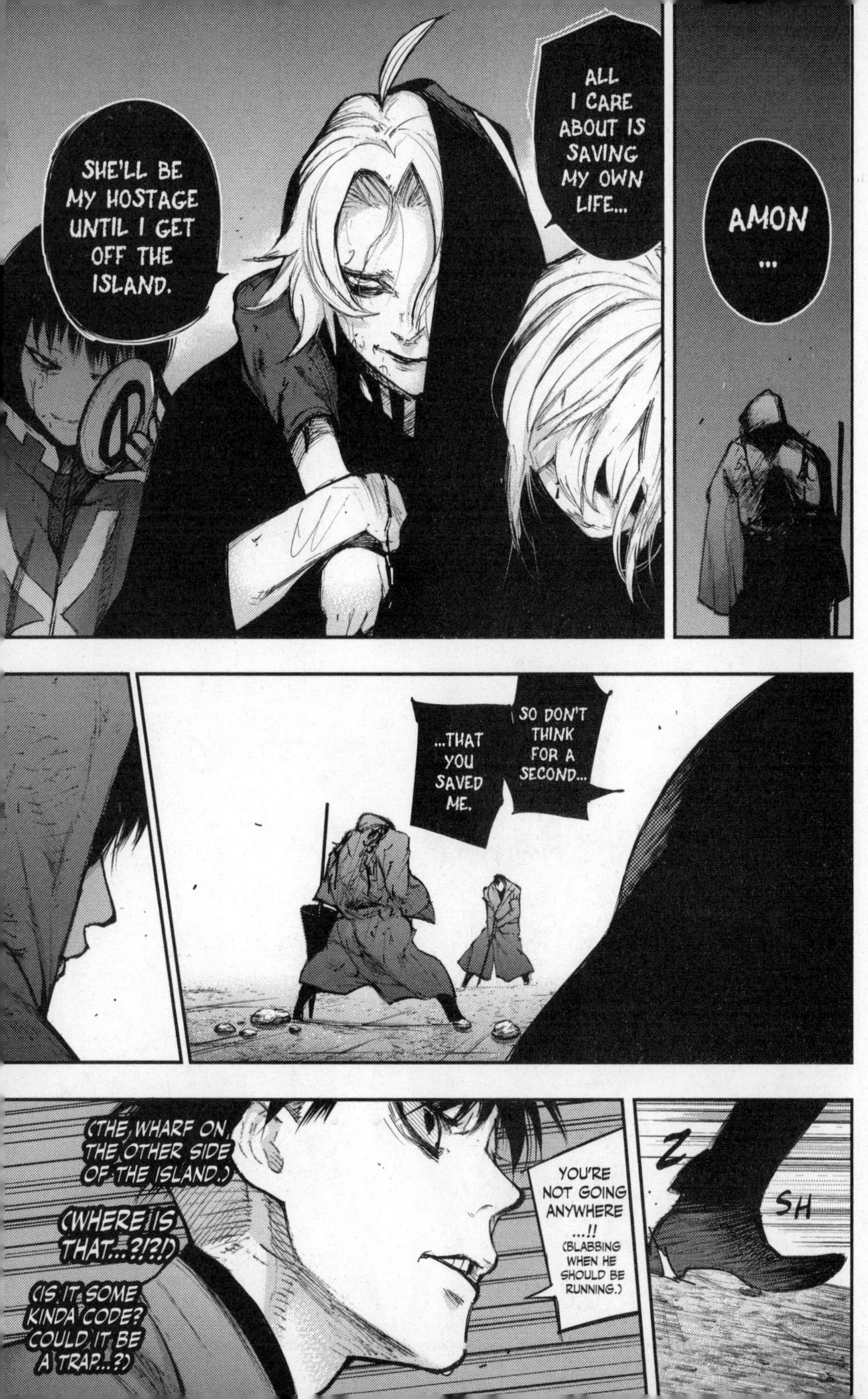
AMON ...
ALL I CARE ABOUT IS SAVING MY OWN LIFE...
SHE'LL BE MY HOSTAGE UNTIL I GET OFF THE ISLAND.
SO DON'T THINK FOR A SECOND...
...THAT YOU SAVED ME.
Z
SH
YOU'RE NOT GOING ANYWHERE ...!!
(BLABBING WHEN HE SHOULD BE RUNNING.)
(THE WHARF ON THE OTHER SIDE OF THE ISLAND.)
(WHERE IS THAT...?!?!)
(IS IT SOME KINDA CODE? COULD IT BE A TRAP...?)

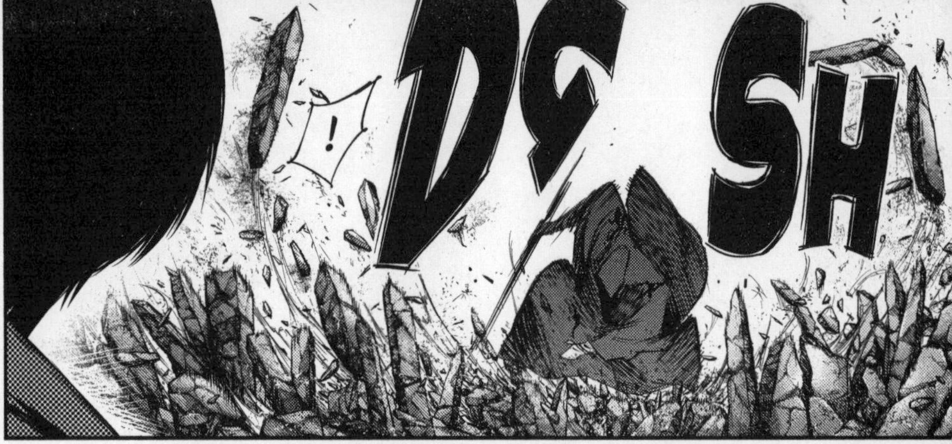
!

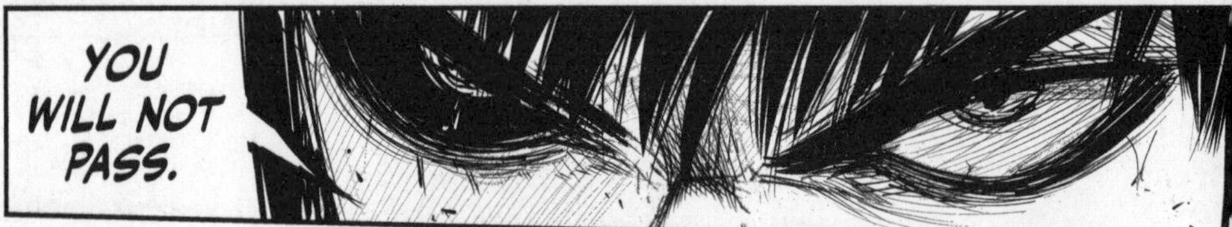
YOU WILL NOT PASS.

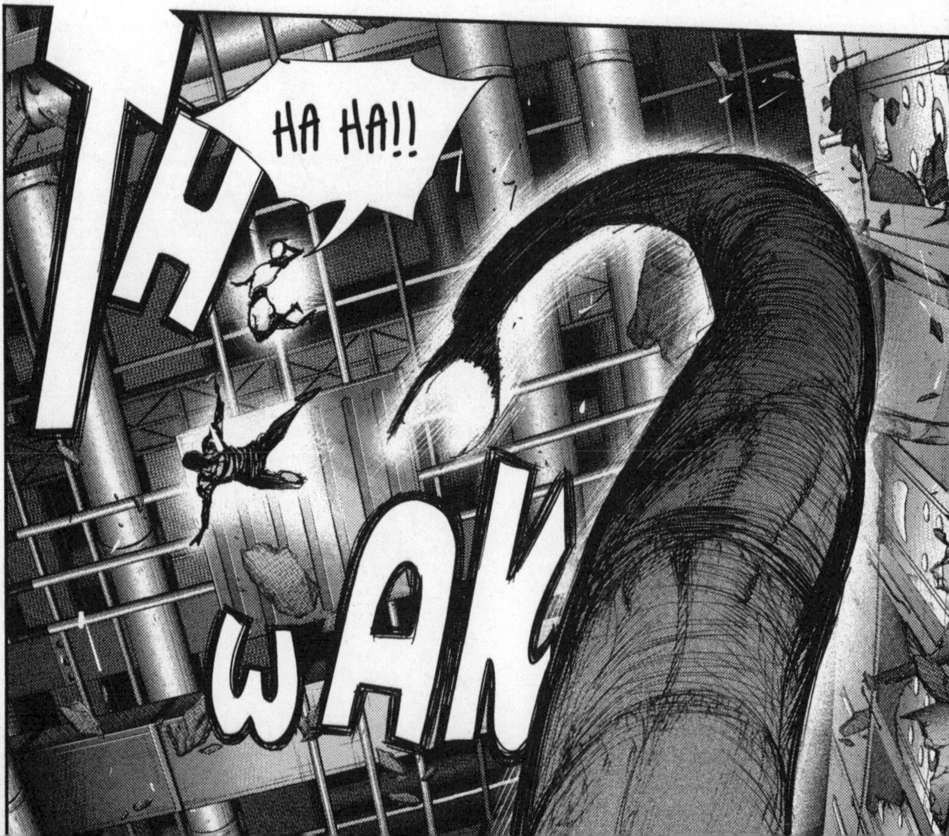
HA HA!!

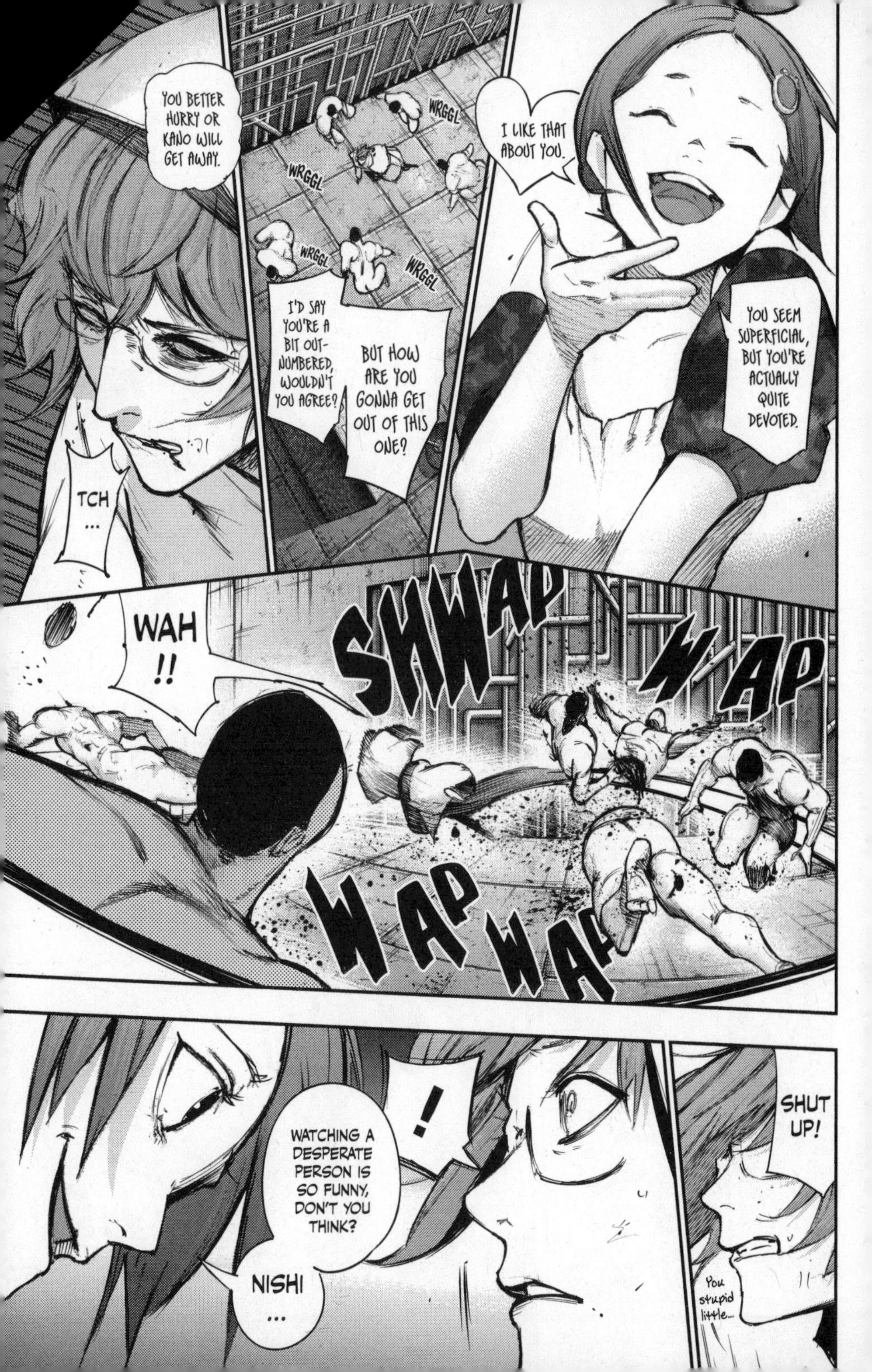
I LIKE THAT ABOUT YOU.
YOU SEEM SUPERFICIAL, BUT YOU'RE ACTUALLY QUITE DEVOTED.
WRGGL
WRGGL
WRGGL
WRGGL
I'D SAY YOU'RE A BIT OUT-NUMBERED, WOULDN'T YOU AGREE?
BUT HOW ARE YOU GONNA GET OUT OF THIS ONE?
YOU BETTER HURRY OR KANO WILL GET AWAY.
TCH ...
WAP
SHWAP
WAH !!
WAP
WAP
SHUT UP!
You stupid little...
!
WATCHING A DESPERATE PERSON IS SO FUNNY, DON'T YOU THINK?
NISHI ...

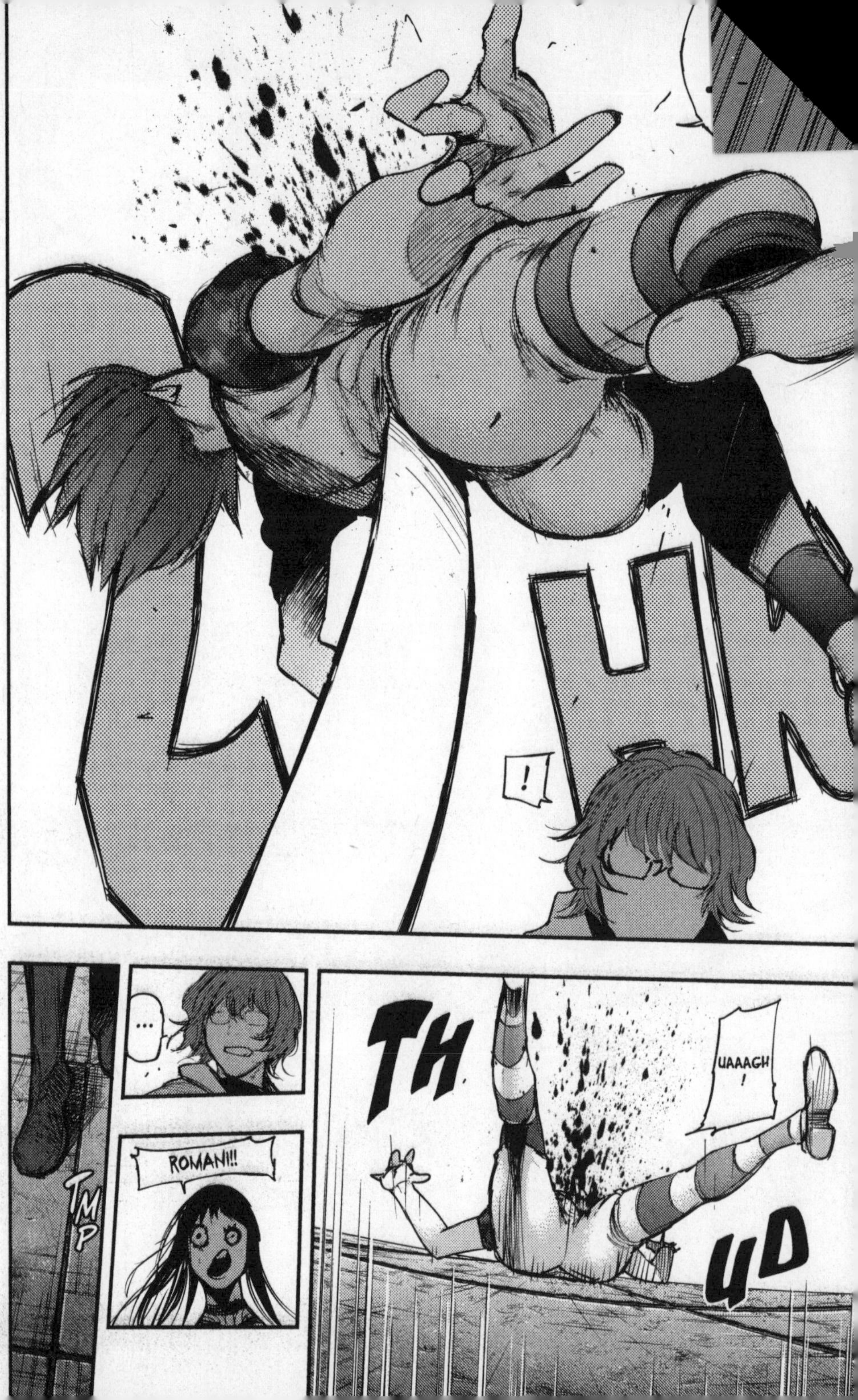
!
UAAAGH!
THUD
...
ROMANI!!
TMP

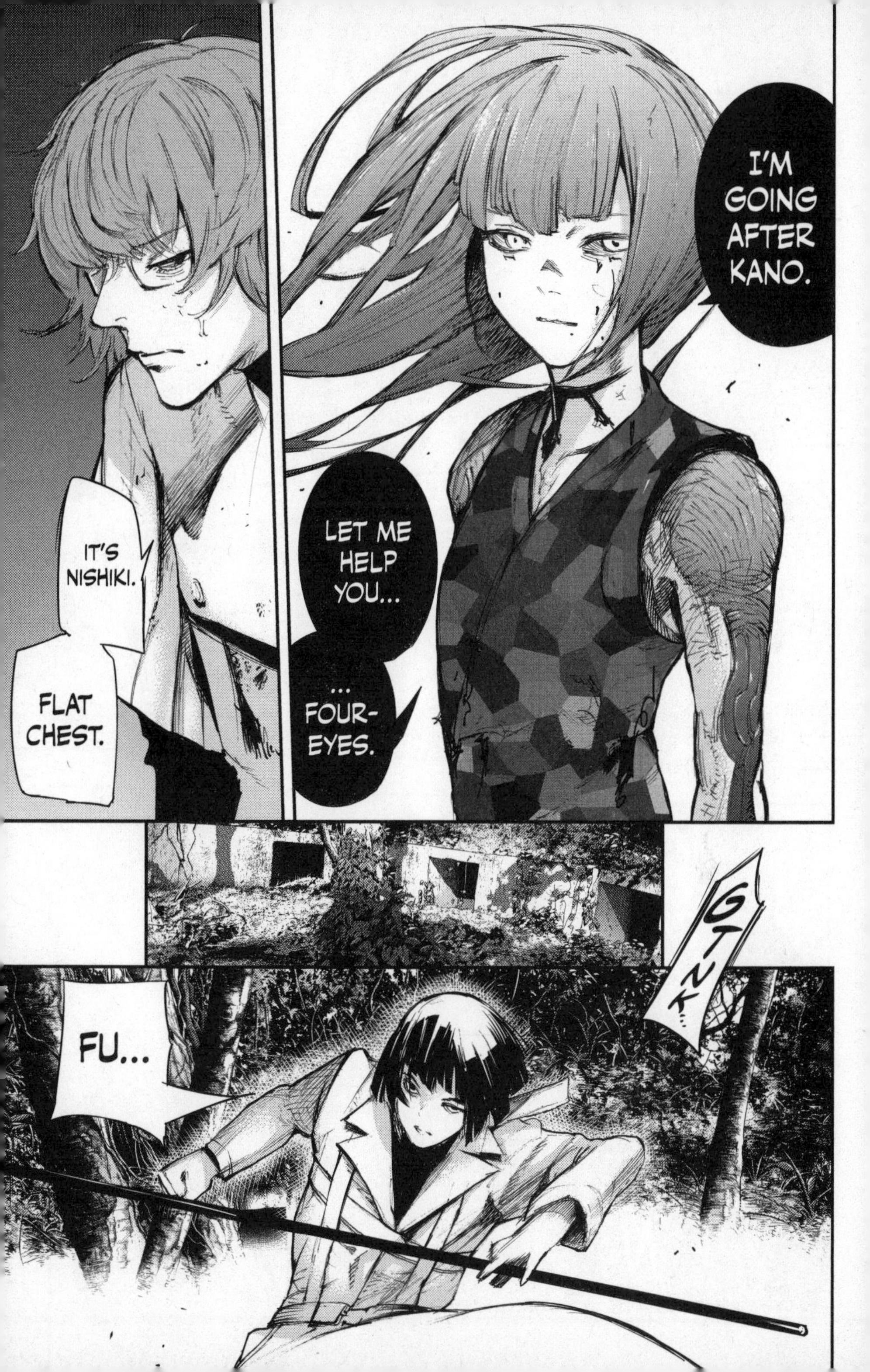
I'M GOING AFTER KANO.
LET ME HELP YOU...
... FOUR-EYES.
IT'S NISHIKI.
FLAT CHEST.
GTNK...
FU...

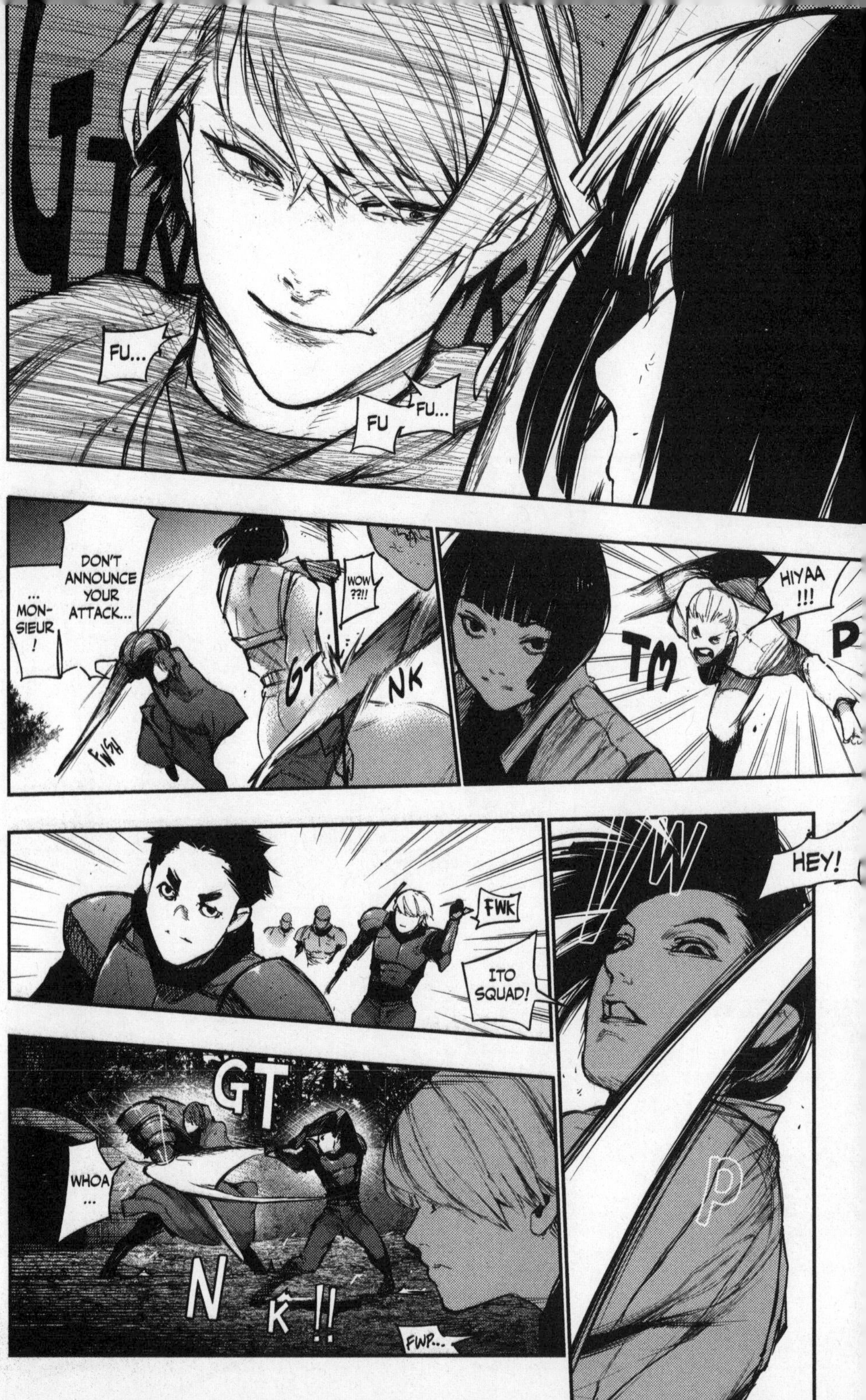
FU...
FU
FU...
HIYAA!!!
TMP
WOW??!!
GT
NK
DON'T ANNOUNCE YOUR ATTACK...
... MONSIEUR!
FWSH
HEY!
P
FWK
ITO SQUAD!
GT
NK!!
WHOA...
FWP...

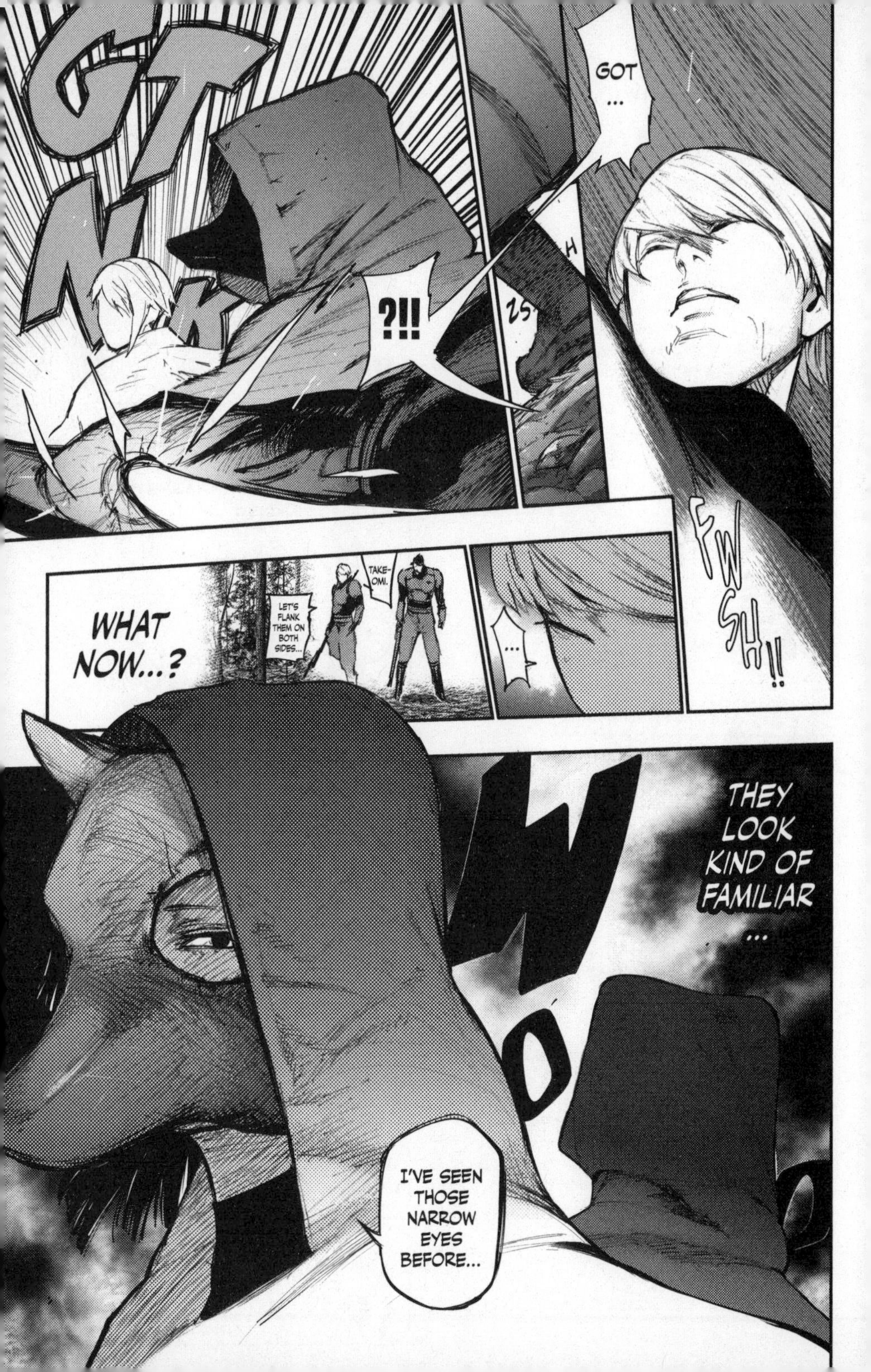
GOT ...
ZSH
?!!
FWSH!!
...
TAKE-OMI.
LET'S FLANK THEM ON BOTH SIDES...
WHAT NOW...?
THEY LOOK KIND OF FAMILIAR ...
I'VE SEEN THOSE NARROW EYES BEFORE...

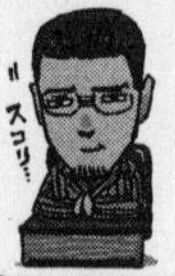

"Smrk..."

Matsuri Washu

Has recently been developing into a richer character.

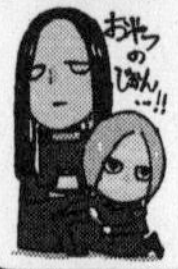

"Snack time!!"

Hanbeh Abara

Imported from a one-shot in *Shonen Jump*. I introduced him in the one-shot during volume 13 or 14 of *Tokyo Ghoul,* expecting him to be reintroduced.

Nakarai

Versatile character.

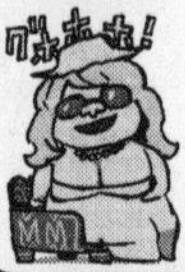

"Guho ho ho!"

Big Madam

Huge breasts.

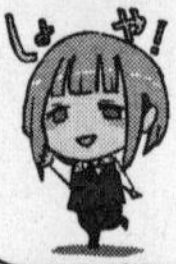

"Right?!"

Hairu

Right.

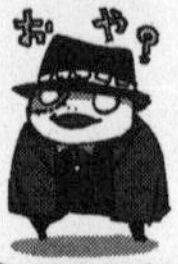

"Hmm?"

Kijima

Imported from "Jail."
I like him because he's like a monster.

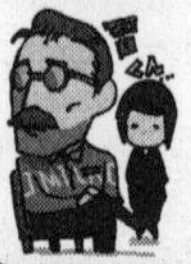

"Shu..."

Daddy Tsukiyama

You can tell he loves Shu.

Matsumae

An import from the novels.

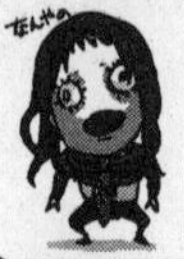

"What?"

Shikorae

Imported.

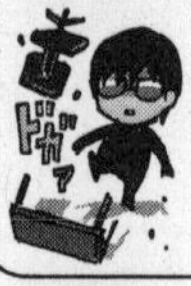

(Fwak)

Investigator SK

He must be going through a lot.

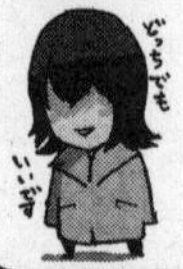

"Whatever is fine."

Shinsanpei Aura

"Sanshinpei," "Shinpeita," "Sanpeita."
His name can get confusing.

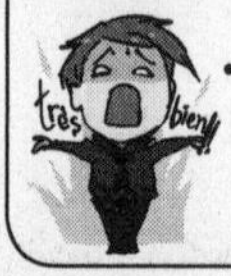
tres
bien!

"Tres bien!!"

Tres Bien

If you run an image search of "tres bien," you'll find Tsukiyama.

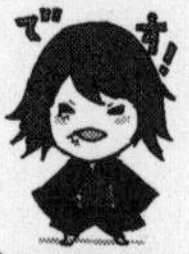

"Yes!"

Investigator Suzuya

Working hard.

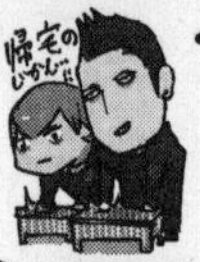

"Time to go home!!"

Mizuro

I wonder what he tells his hairstylist. Like, "Can you make me look like the guy in 009?"

Mikage

I really don't think he cares about the world.

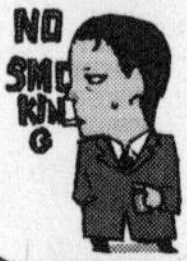

"NO SMOKING."

Fura

He's the same age as Arima, but he looks way older.

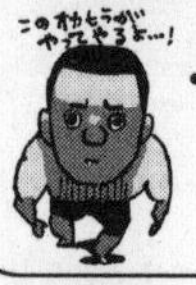

"I, Okahira, will take care of it...!"

Okahira

He'll take care of it.

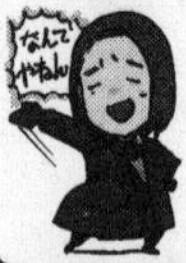

"What's up with that?!"

Furuta

He's meant to resemble a certain character.

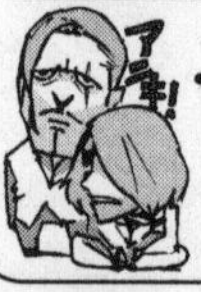

"Bro!"

Shosei

Hohgoro tore his ear off.

Hohguro

Actually quite tall.

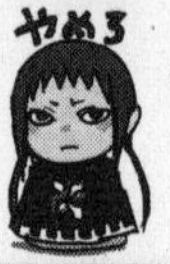

"Stop it."

Grave Robber

A Bin Brothers protegee. Her name 墓盗 can be pronounced "bo toru."
Bin=bottle.

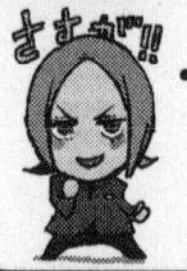

"I knew it!"

Higemaru

Drummer bobo called the new Qs second gen. I like that.

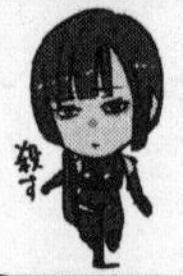

"You're dead."

Hsiao

The Chinese cuss words she uses aren't really used in Taiwan, but I think she uses them in her own unique way... Although I'm not sure.

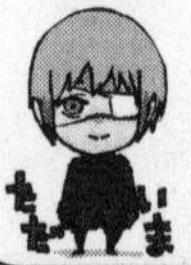

"I'm back!"

Kaneki

I messed up the eye patch for this one too, so I fixed it.

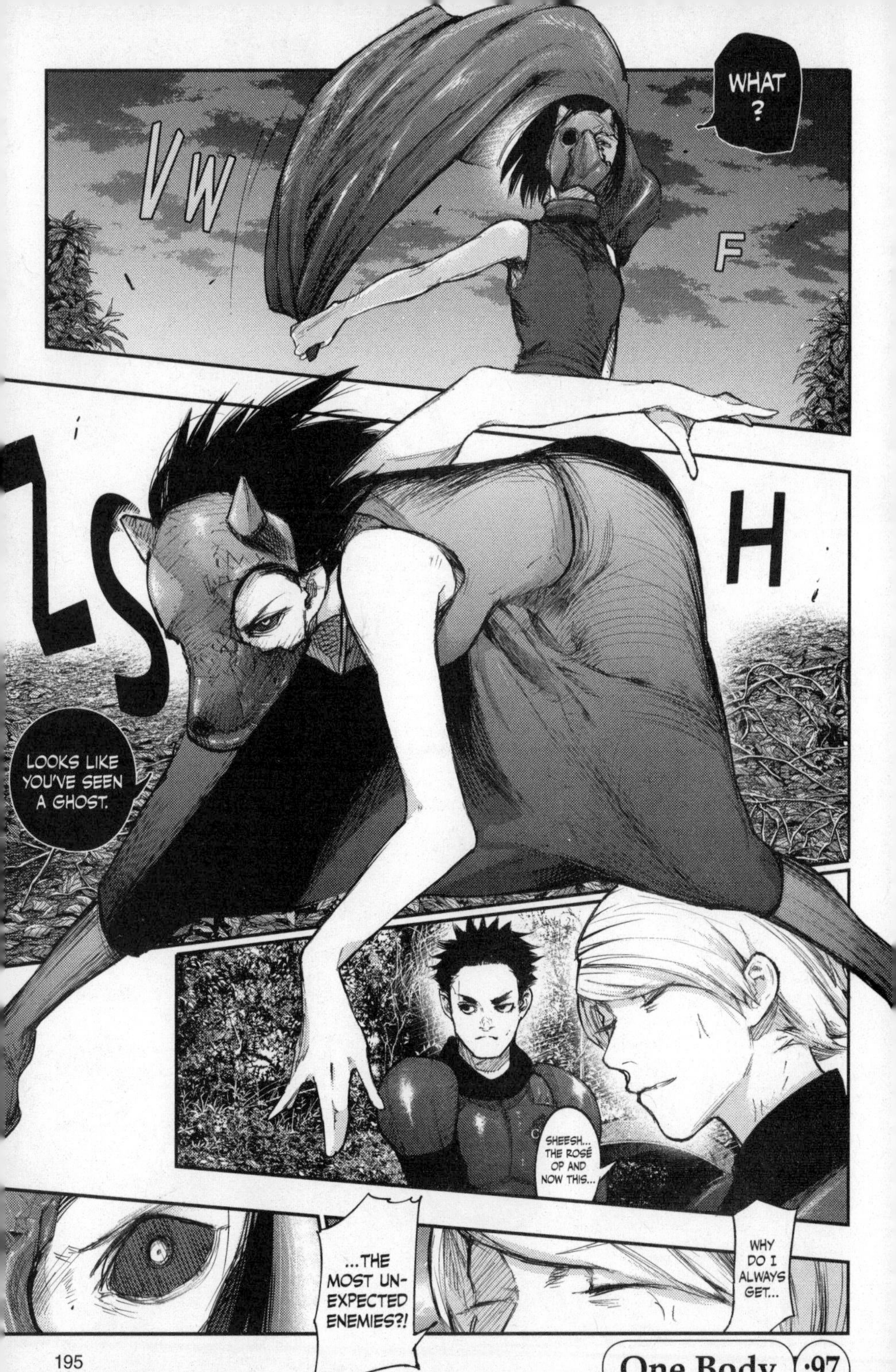
WHAT ?
F
VW
H
ZS
LOOKS LIKE YOU'VE SEEN A GHOST.
SHEESH... THE ROSÉ OP AND NOW THIS...
WHY DO I ALWAYS GET...
...THE MOST UN-EXPECTED ENEMIES?!

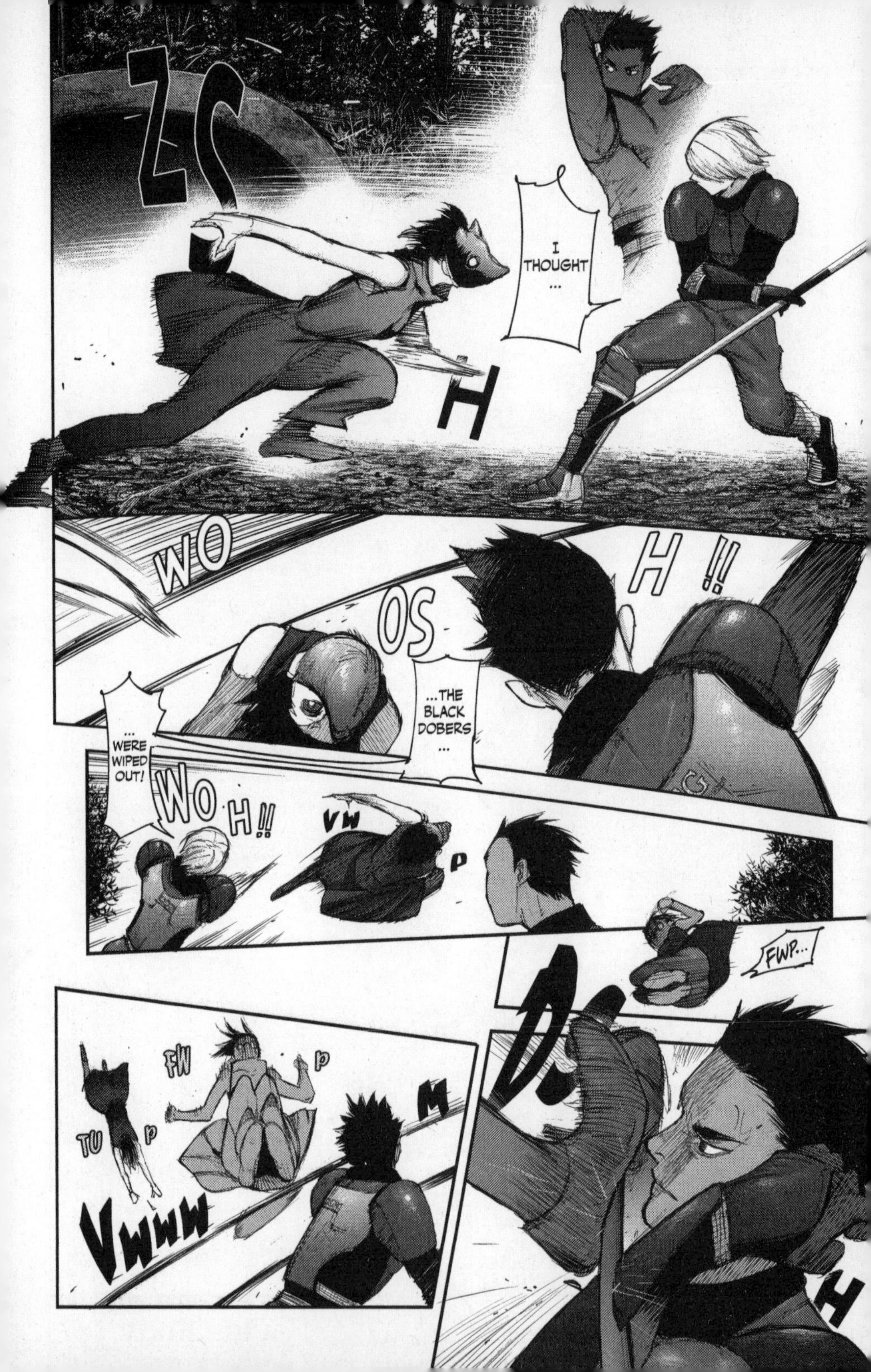
I THOUGHT ...
H
WO
OS
H!!
...THE BLACK DOBERS ...
... WERE WIPED OUT!
WO H!!
VW
P
FWP...!
H
FW
p
TU
p
M
VWWW

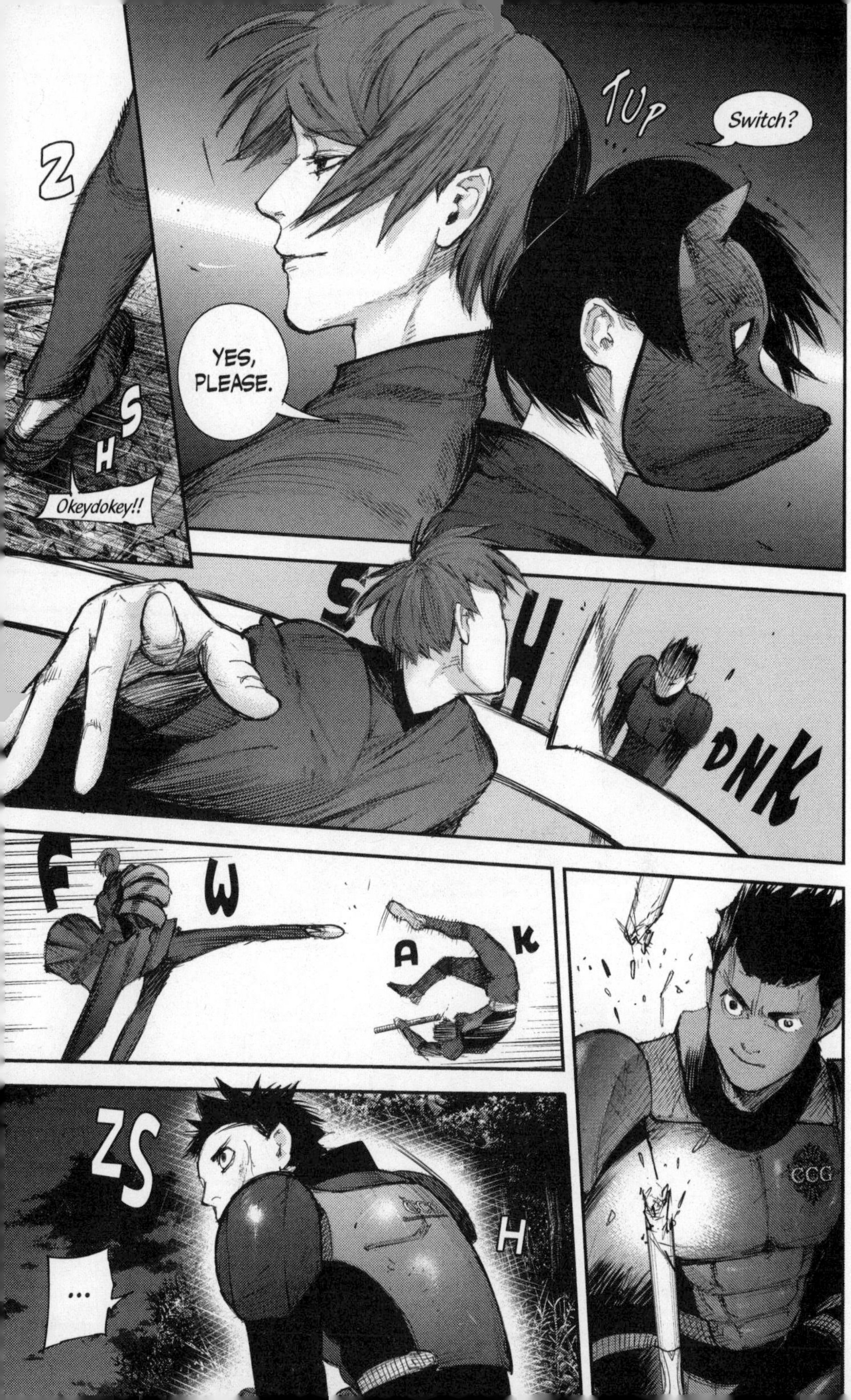
TUP
Switch?
YES, PLEASE.
Z
SH
Okeydokey!!
SH
DNK
FW
AK
ZS
H
...

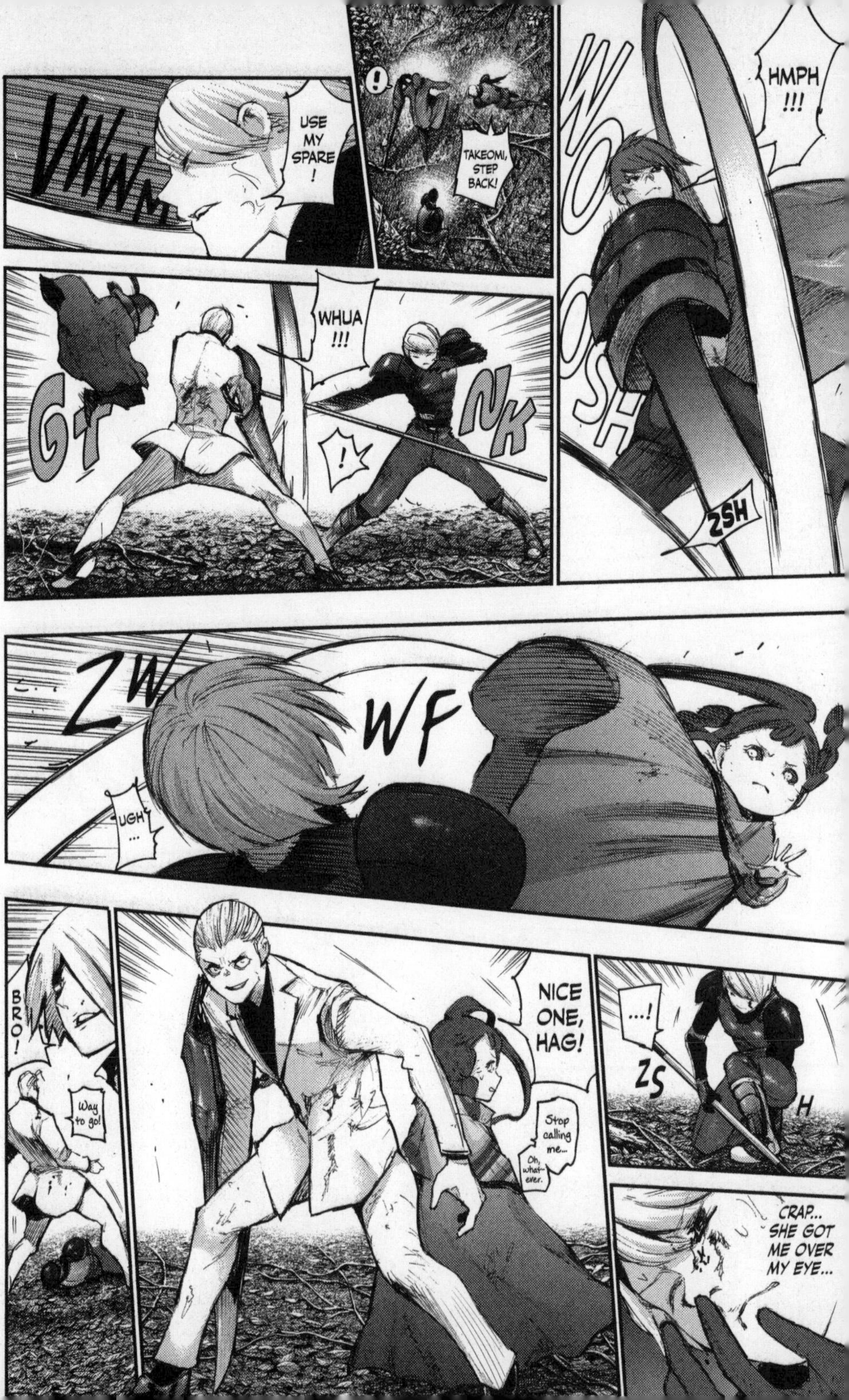
HMPH !!!
WOOOSH
ZSH
!
TAKEOMI, STEP BACK!
USE MY SPARE !
VWWM
WHUA !!!
NK
!
GT
ZW
WF
UGH ...
...!
ZS
H
CRAP... SHE GOT ME OVER MY EYE...
NICE ONE, HAG!
Stop calling me...
Oh, whatever.
BRO!
Way to go!

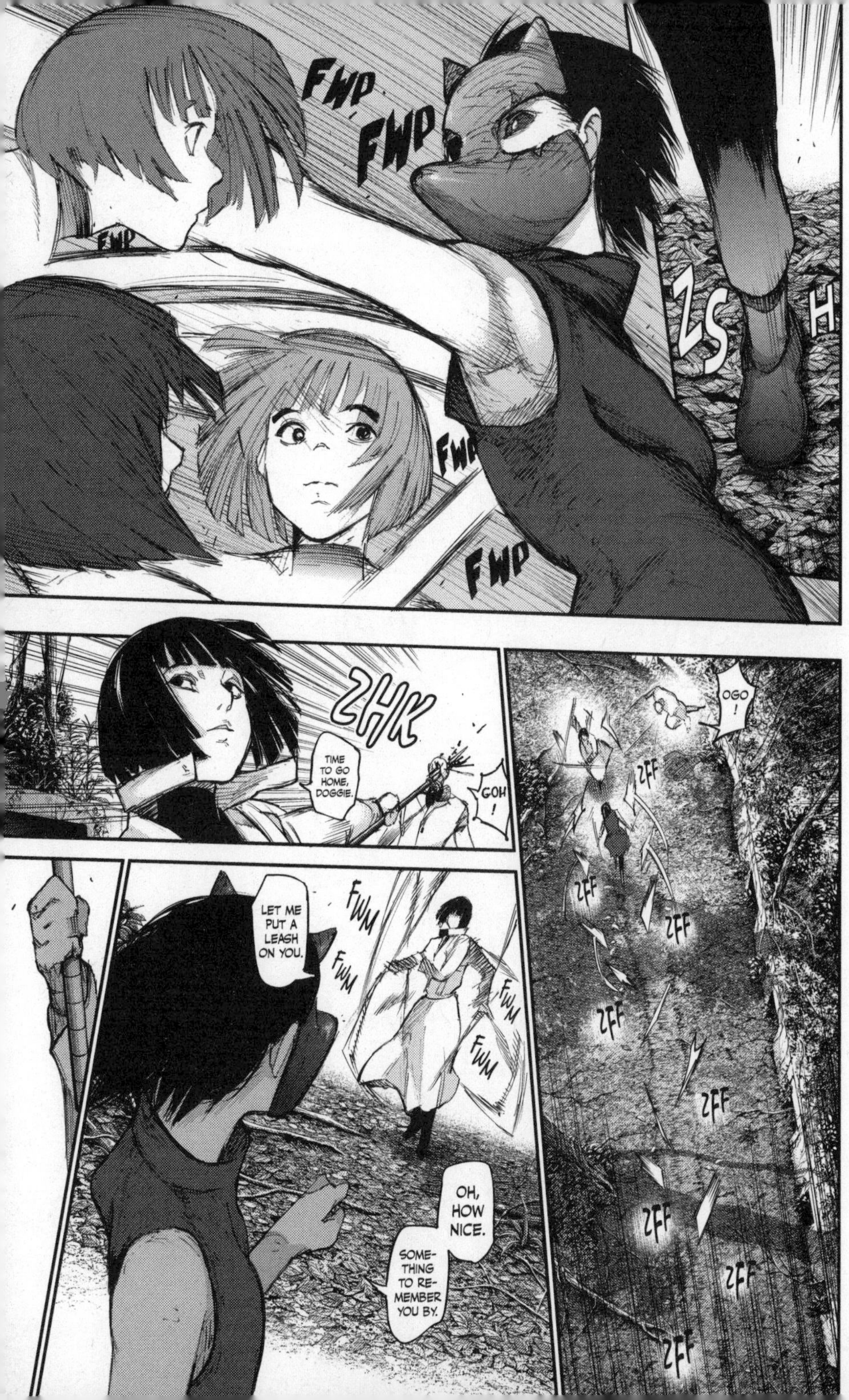
FWP
FWP
ZSH
FWP
FWP
FWP
OGO!
ZFF
ZFF
ZFF
ZFF
ZFF
ZFF
ZFF
ZFF
ZHK
TIME TO GO HOME, DOGGIE.
GOH!
FWM
FWM
LET ME PUT A LEASH ON YOU.
FWM
FWM
OH, HOW NICE.
SOME-THING TO RE-MEMBER YOU BY.

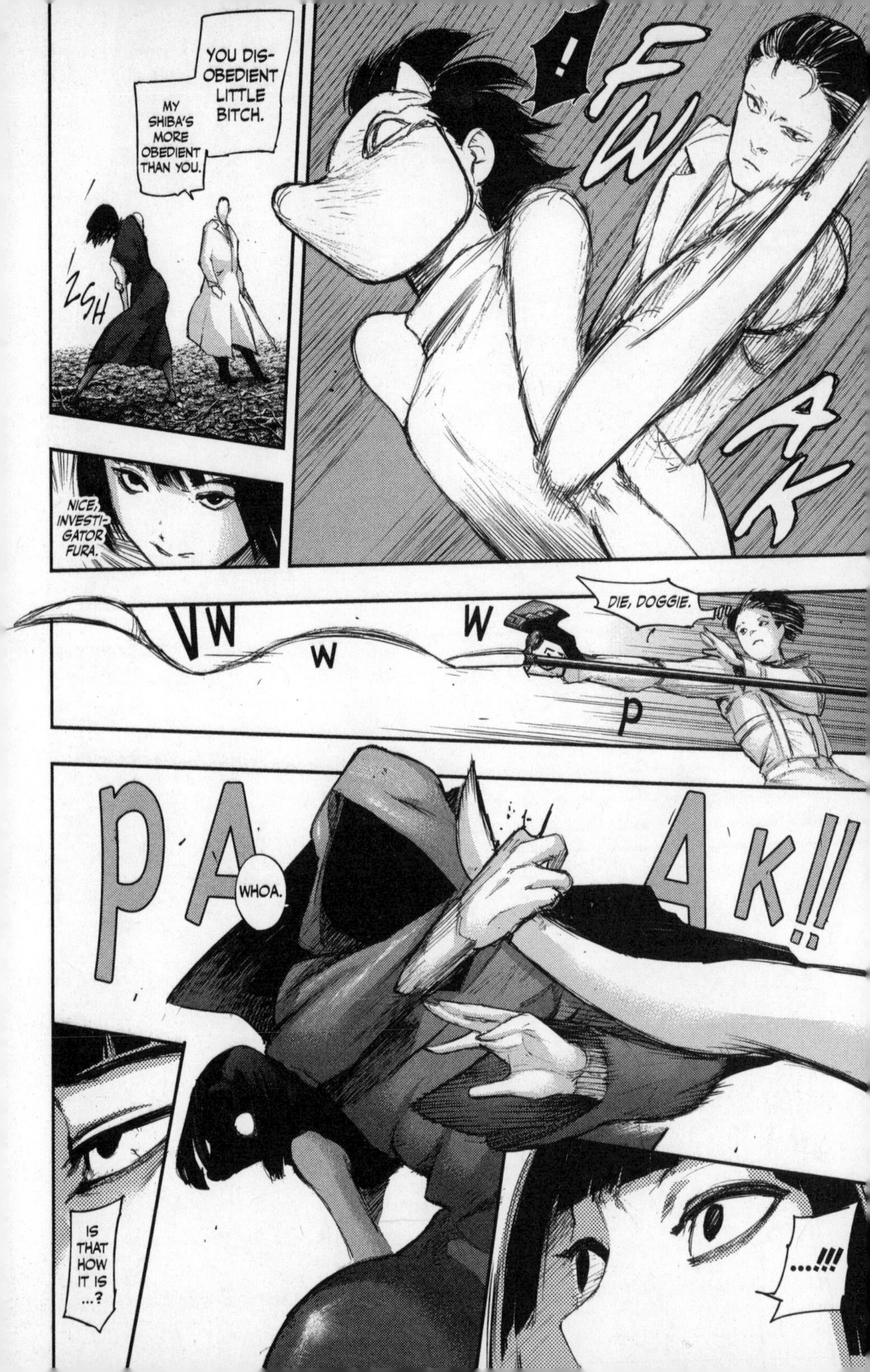
FW
!
AK
YOU DIS-OBEDIENT LITTLE BITCH.
MY SHIBA'S MORE OBEDIENT THAN YOU.
ZSH
NICE, INVESTI-GATOR FURA.
DIE, DOGGIE.
W
W
VW
P
PA
AK!!
WHOA.
...!!!
IS THAT HOW IT IS ...?

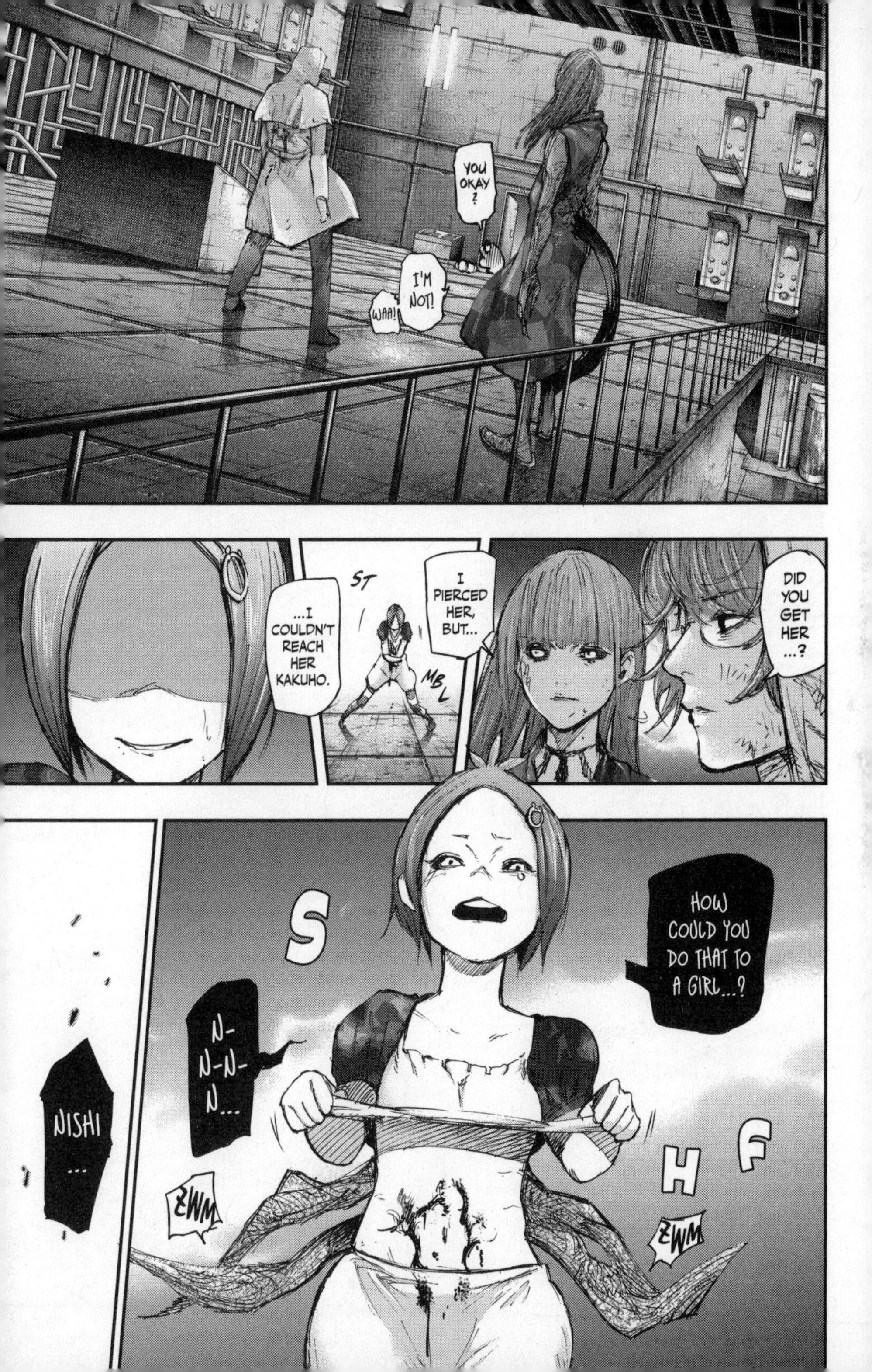

YOU OKAY?
I'M NOT!
WAA!
DID YOU GET HER...?
I PIERCED HER, BUT...
ST
MBL
...I COULDN'T REACH HER KAKUHO.
S
HOW COULD YOU DO THAT TO A GIRL...?
F
H
ZWM
N-N-N-N...
ZWM
NISHI...

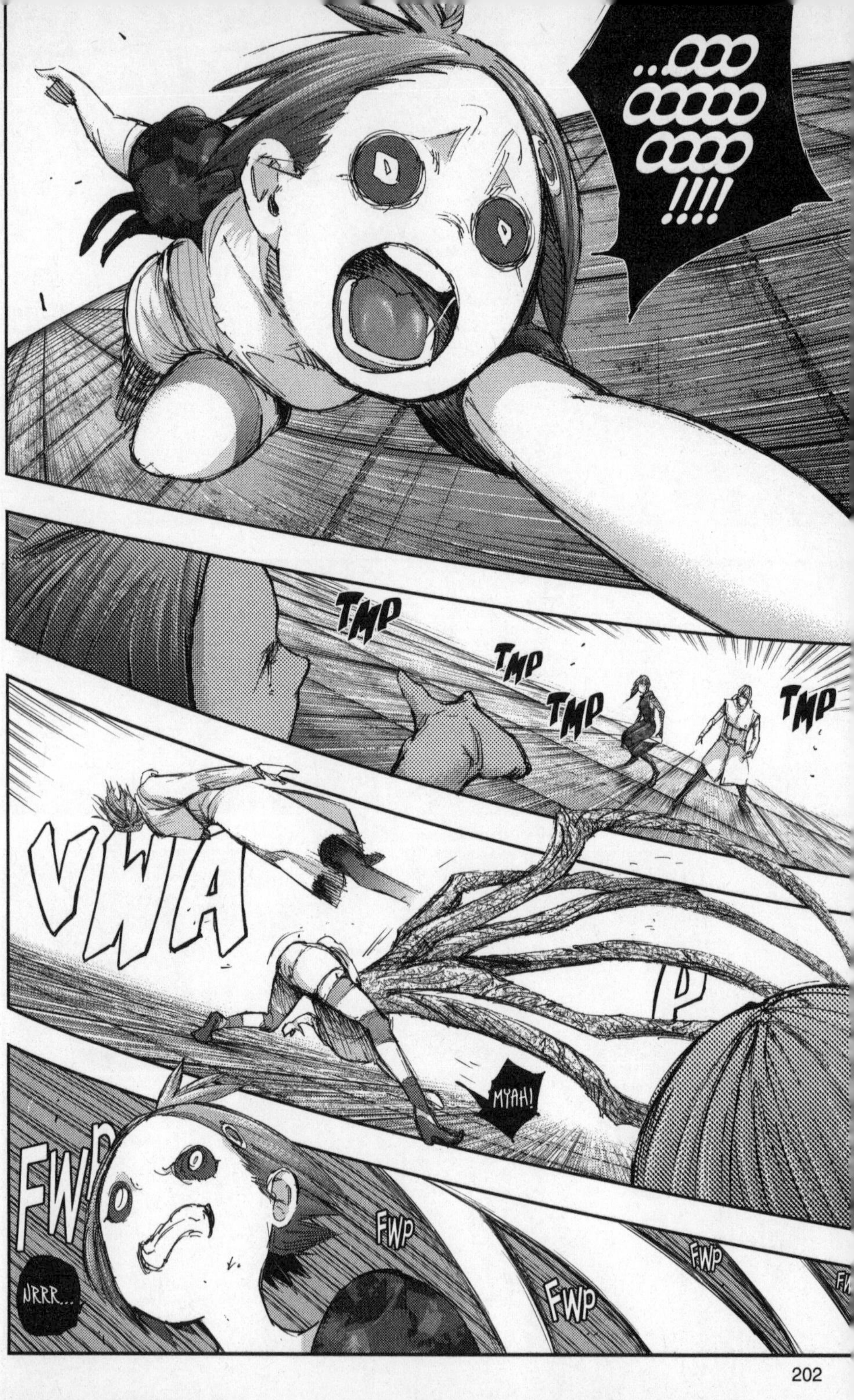

...OOO OOOOO OOOO!!!!
TMP
TMP
TMP
TMP
VWA
P
MYAH!
FWP
FWP
FWP
FWP
NRRR...

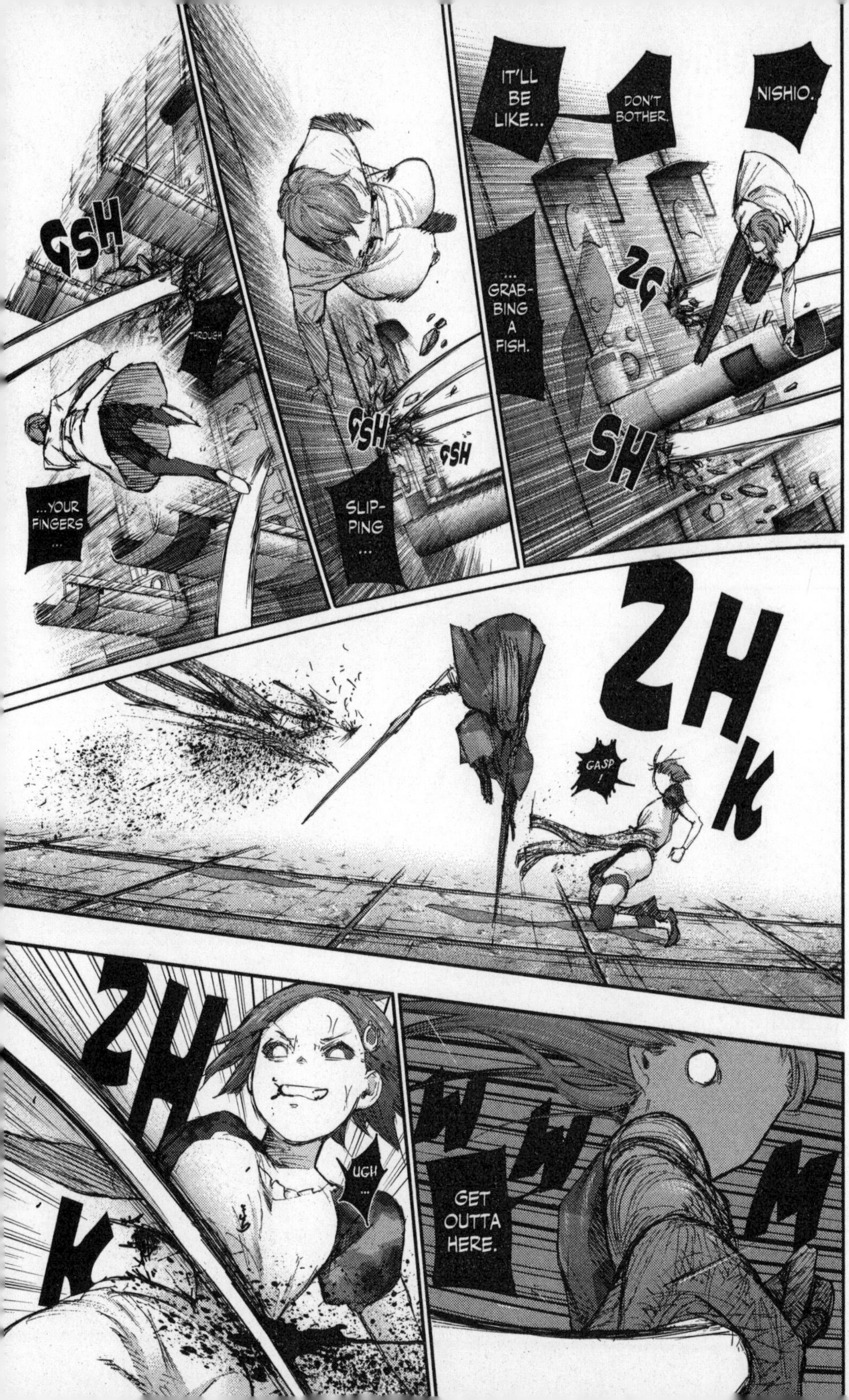
NISHIO..
DON'T BOTHER.
IT'LL BE LIKE...
ZG
...GRAB-BING A FISH.
SH
GSH
GSH
SLIP-PING...
GSH
THROUGH...
...YOUR FINGERS...
ZHK
GASP!
WWWM
GET OUTTA HERE.
ZHK
UGH...

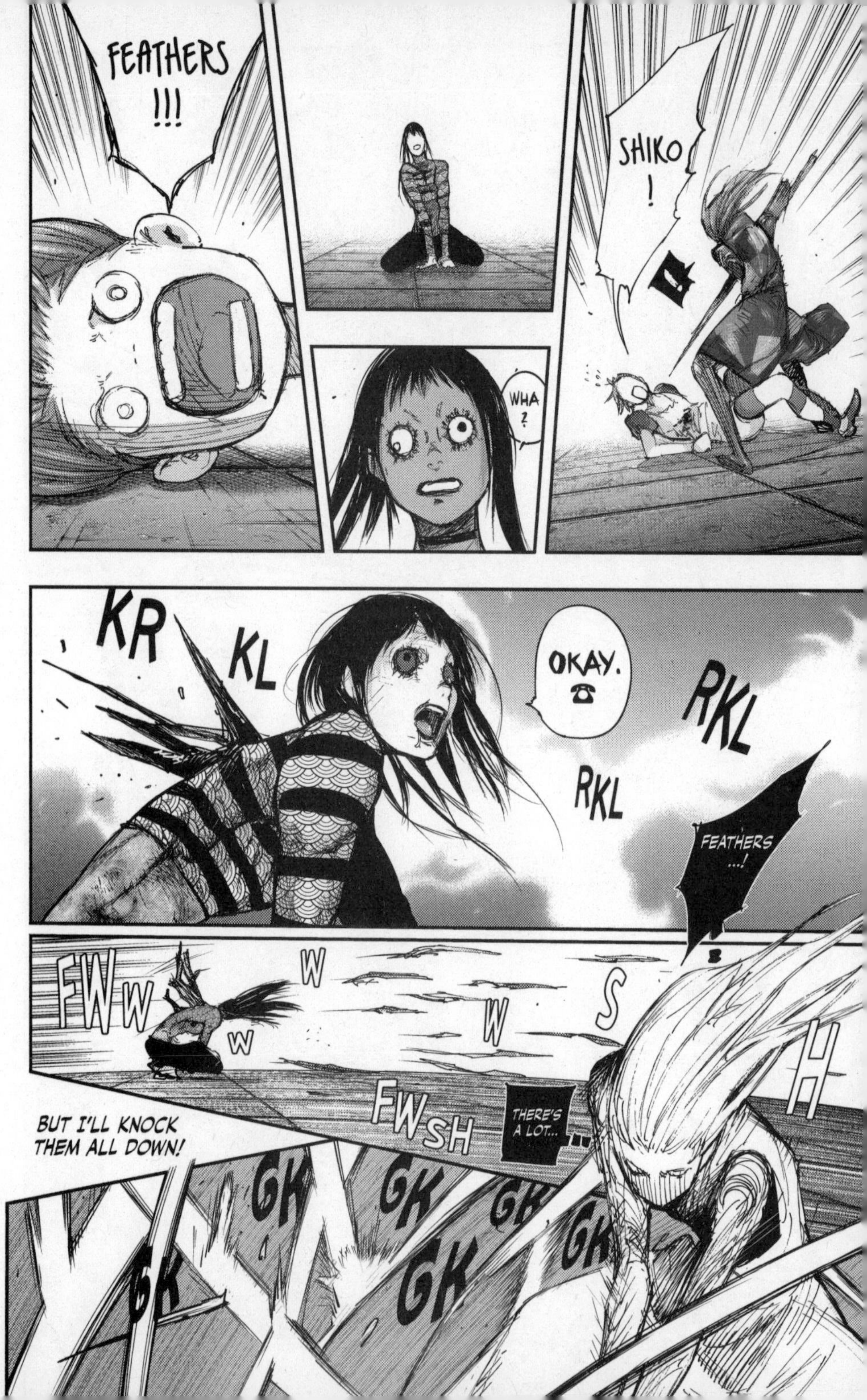

SHIKO !
WHA ?
FEATHERS !!!
RKL
OKAY.
KR
KL
RKL
FEATHERS ...!
SH
THERE'S A LOT...
FWSH
W
W
FWW
W
BUT I'LL KNOCK THEM ALL DOWN!
GK
GK
GK
GK
GK
GK

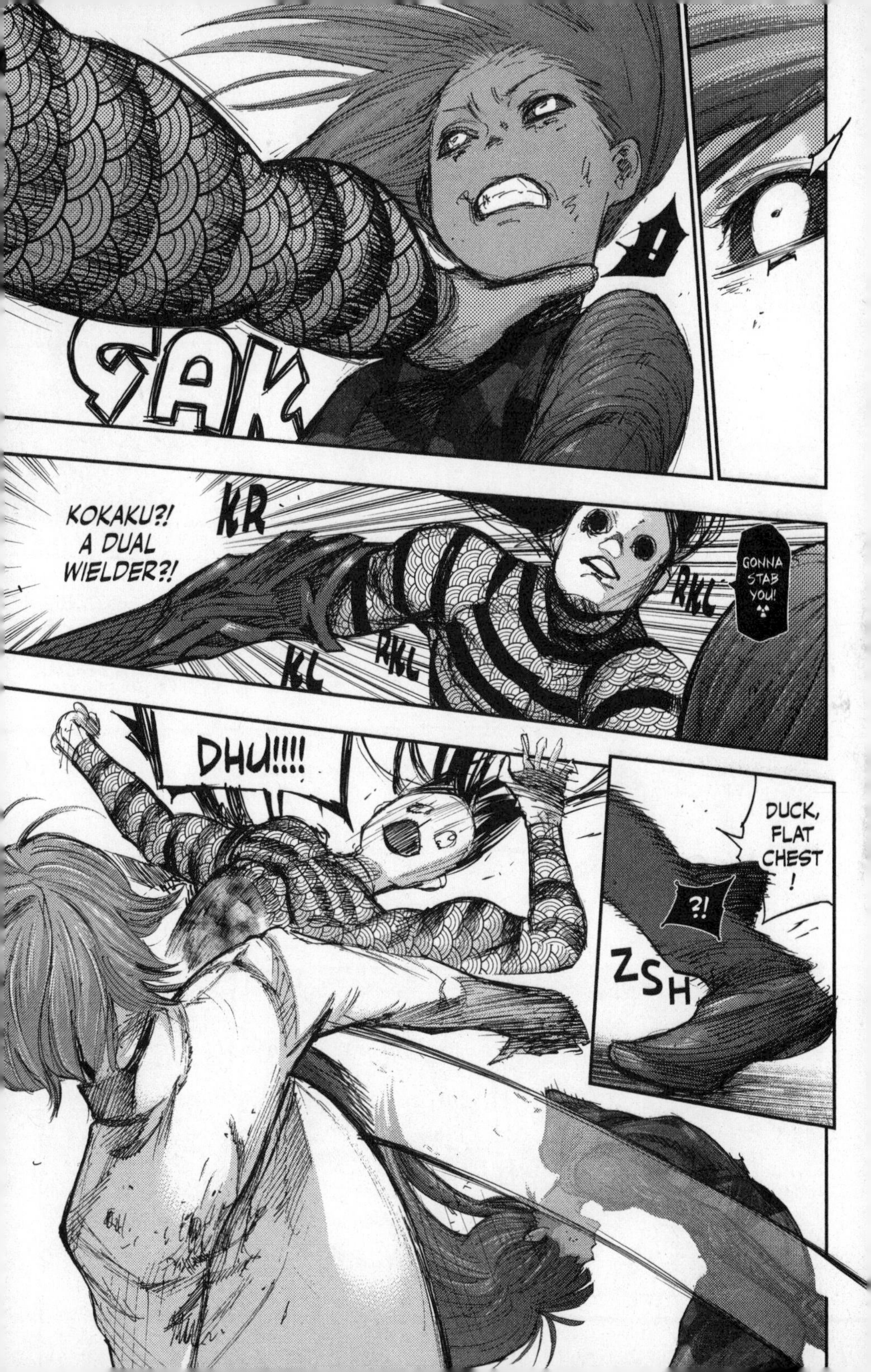
!
GAK
GONNA STAB YOU!
RKL
KOKAKU?! A DUAL WIELDER?!
KR
RKL
KL
DUCK, FLAT CHEST!
?!
ZSH
DHU!!!!

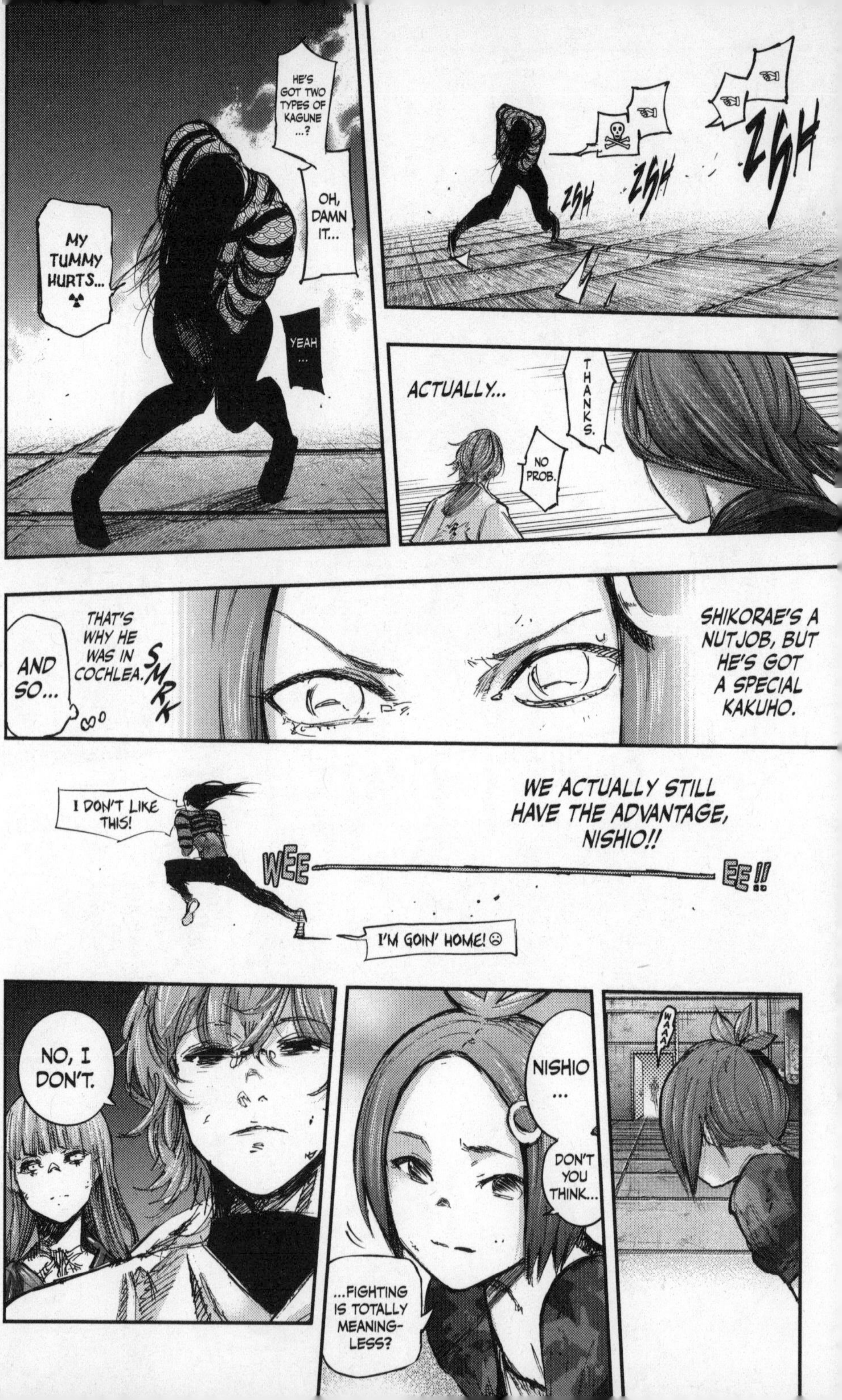
ZSH
ZSH
ZSH
ACTUALLY...
THANKS.
NO PROB.
HE'S GOT TWO TYPES OF KAGUNE ...?
OH, DAMN IT...
MY TUMMY HURTS...
YEAH ...
SHIKORAE'S A NUTJOB, BUT HE'S GOT A SPECIAL KAKUHO.
SMRK
THAT'S WHY HE WAS IN COCHLEA.
AND SO...
WE ACTUALLY STILL HAVE THE ADVANTAGE, NISHIO!!
WEE——EE!!
I DON'T LIKE THIS!
I'M GOIN' HOME!
WAAA
NISHIO ...
DON'T YOU THINK...
...FIGHTING IS TOTALLY MEANING-LESS?
NO, I DON'T.

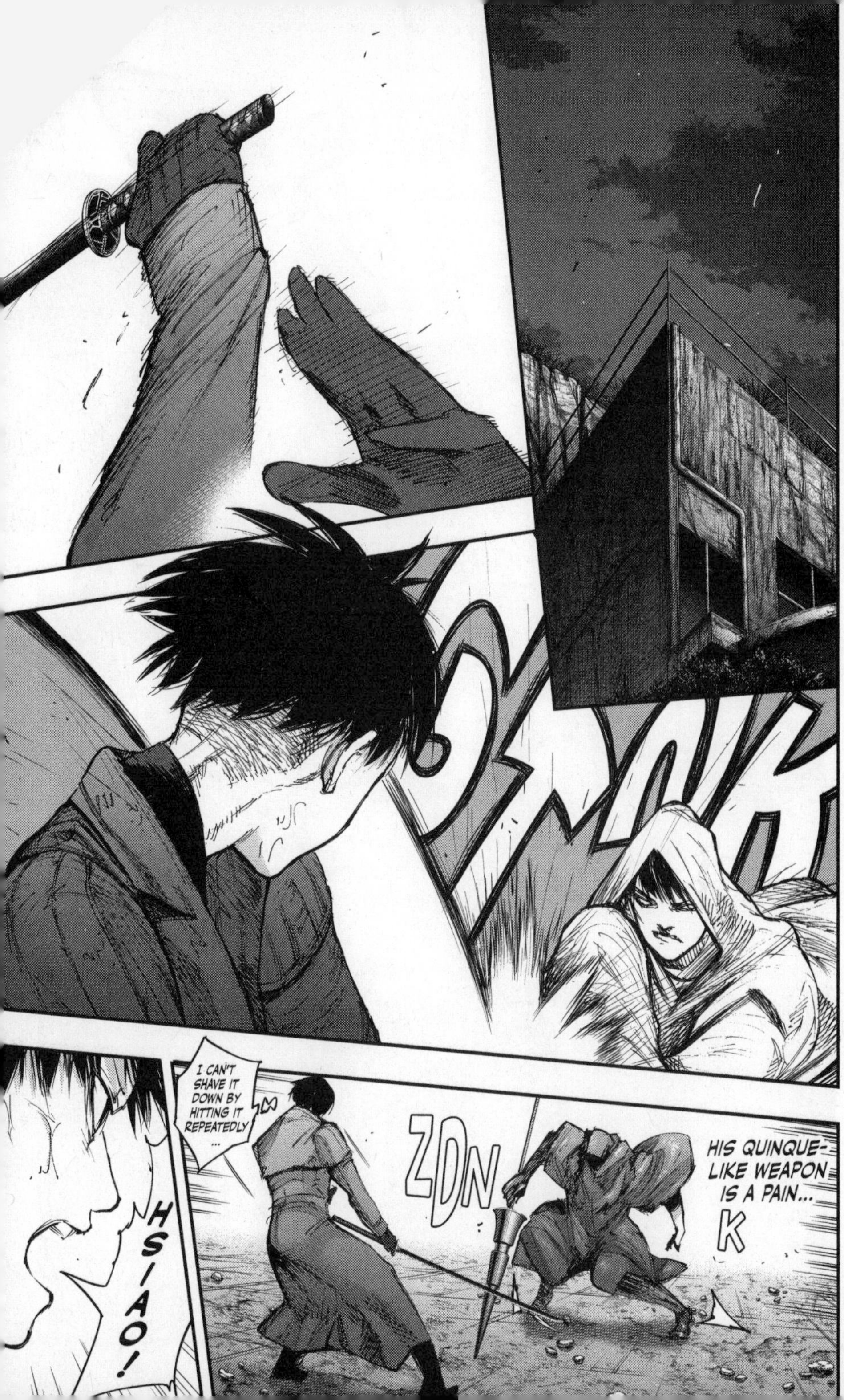
HIS QUINQUE-LIKE WEAPON IS A PAIN... K
ZDN
I CAN'T SHAVE IT DOWN BY HITTING IT REPEATEDLY ...
HSIAO!

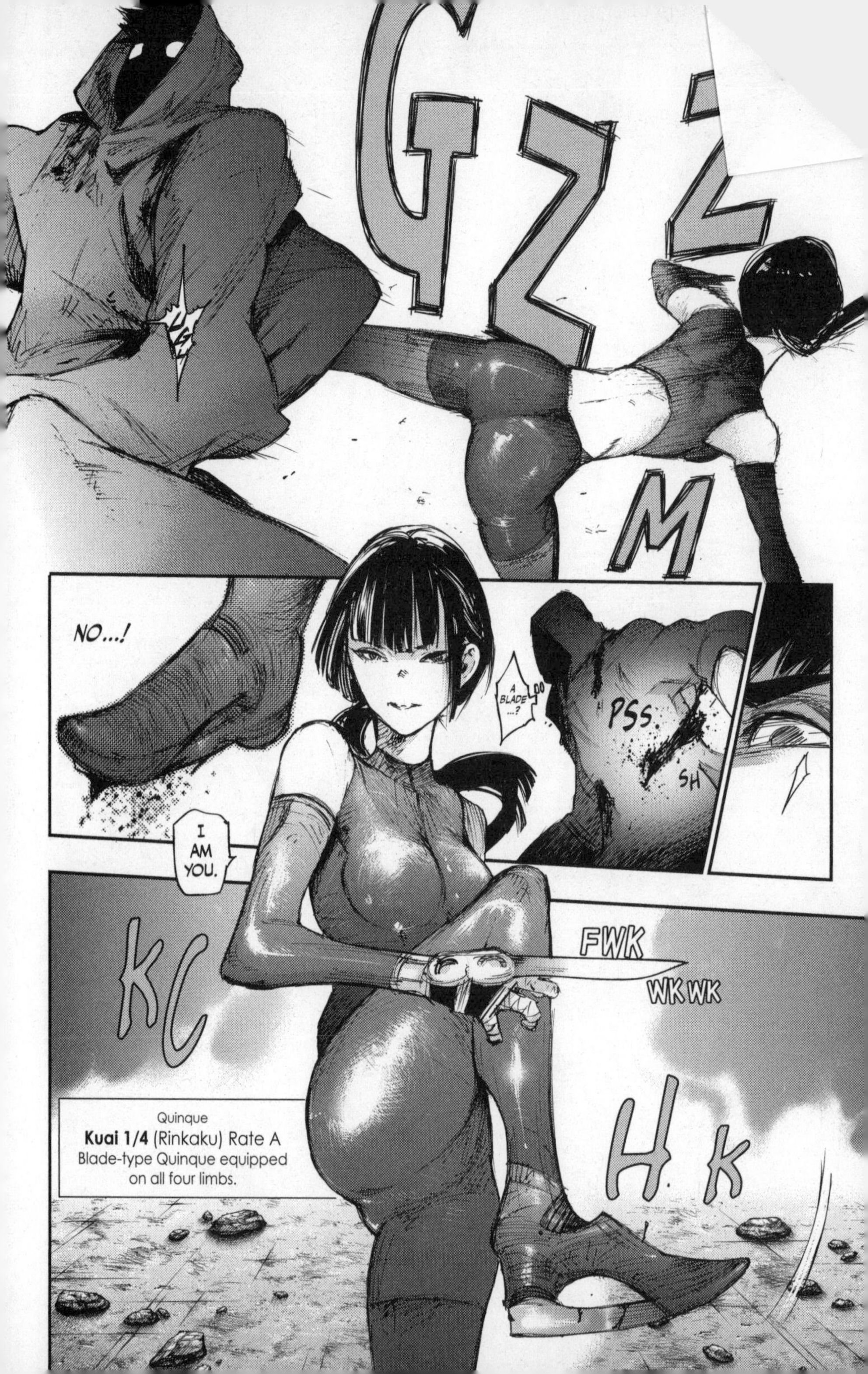
GZZM
A BLADE ...?
DO
PSS
SH
NO...!
I AM YOU.
FWK
WK WK
KC
Hk
Quinque
Kuai 1/4 (Rinkaku) Rate A
Blade-type Quinque equipped on all four limbs.

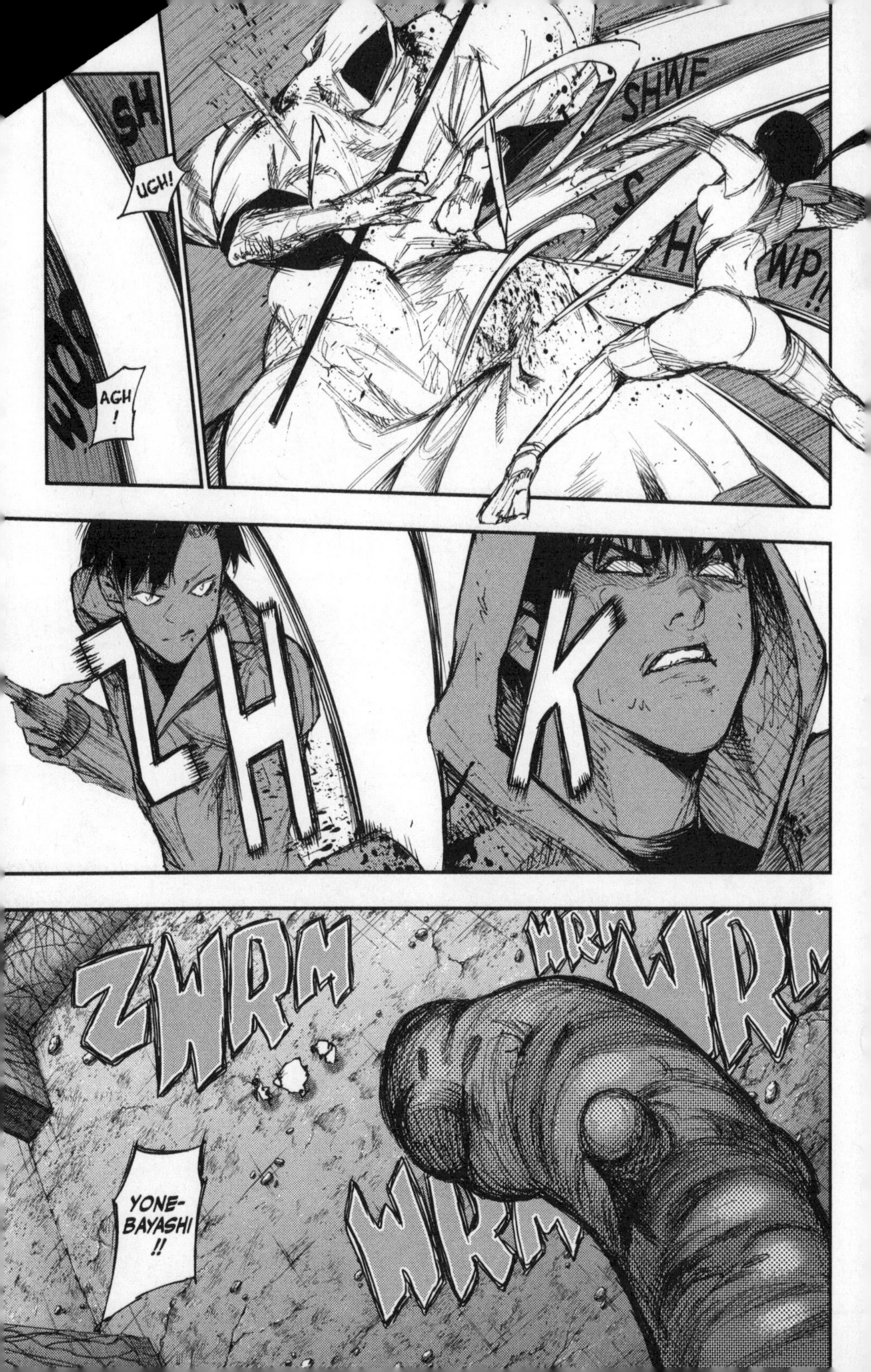
SHWF
SH
WP!!
UGH!
SH
AGH!
K
ZLH
WRM
HRM
ZHRM
WRM
YONE-BAYASHI!!

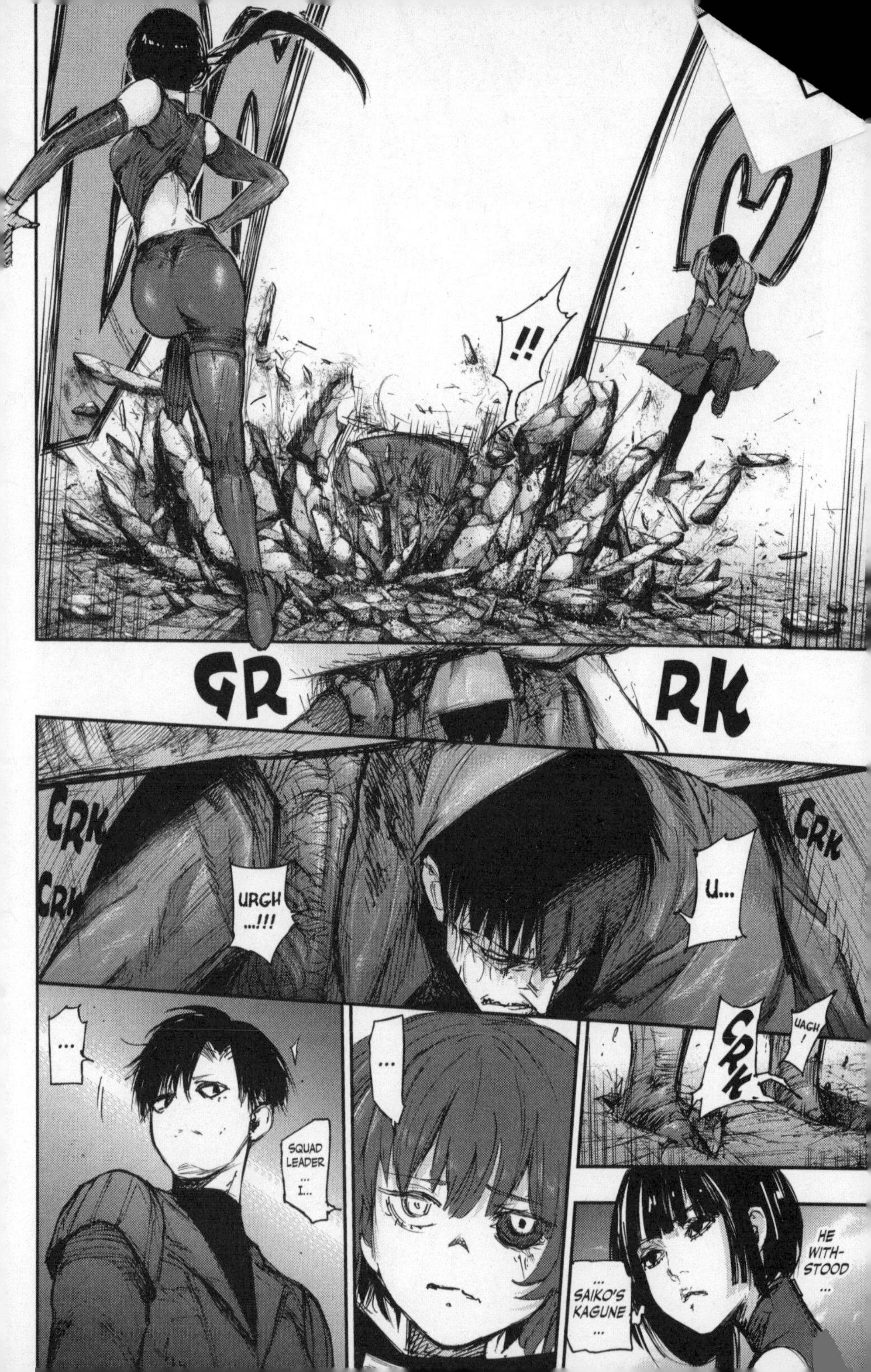
!!
GR RK
CRK
U...
URGH ...!!!
CRK CRK
UAGH !
CRK
HE WITH-STOOD ...
... SAIKO'S KAGUNE ...
...
...
SQUAD LEADER ... I...

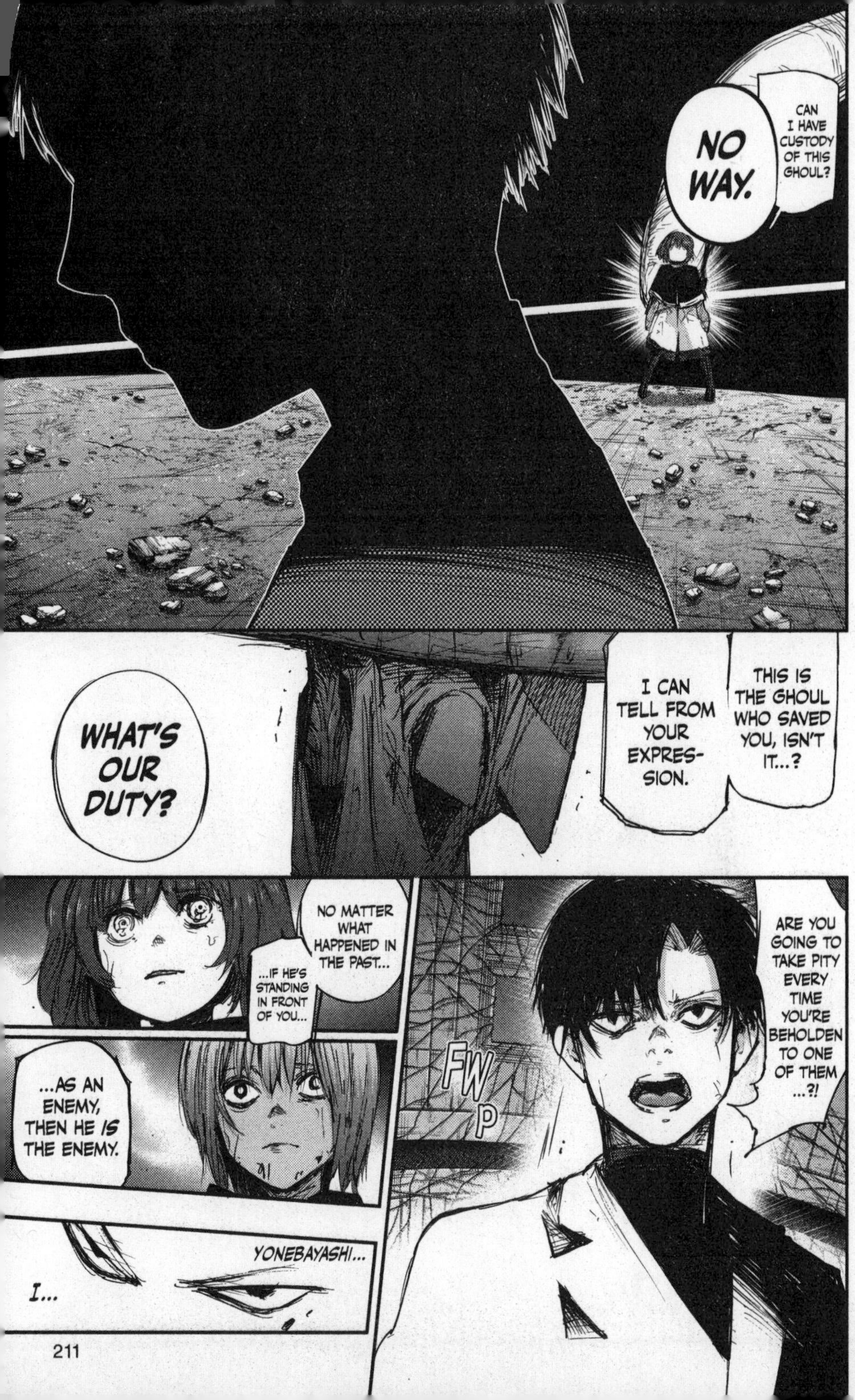
CAN I HAVE CUSTODY OF THIS GHOUL?
NO WAY.
THIS IS THE GHOUL WHO SAVED YOU, ISN'T IT...?
I CAN TELL FROM YOUR EXPRES-SION.
WHAT'S OUR DUTY?
ARE YOU GOING TO TAKE PITY EVERY TIME YOU'RE BEHOLDEN TO ONE OF THEM ...?!
FWP
NO MATTER WHAT HAPPENED IN THE PAST...
...IF HE'S STANDING IN FRONT OF YOU...
...AS AN ENEMY, THEN HE *IS* THE ENEMY.
YONEBAYASHI...
I...

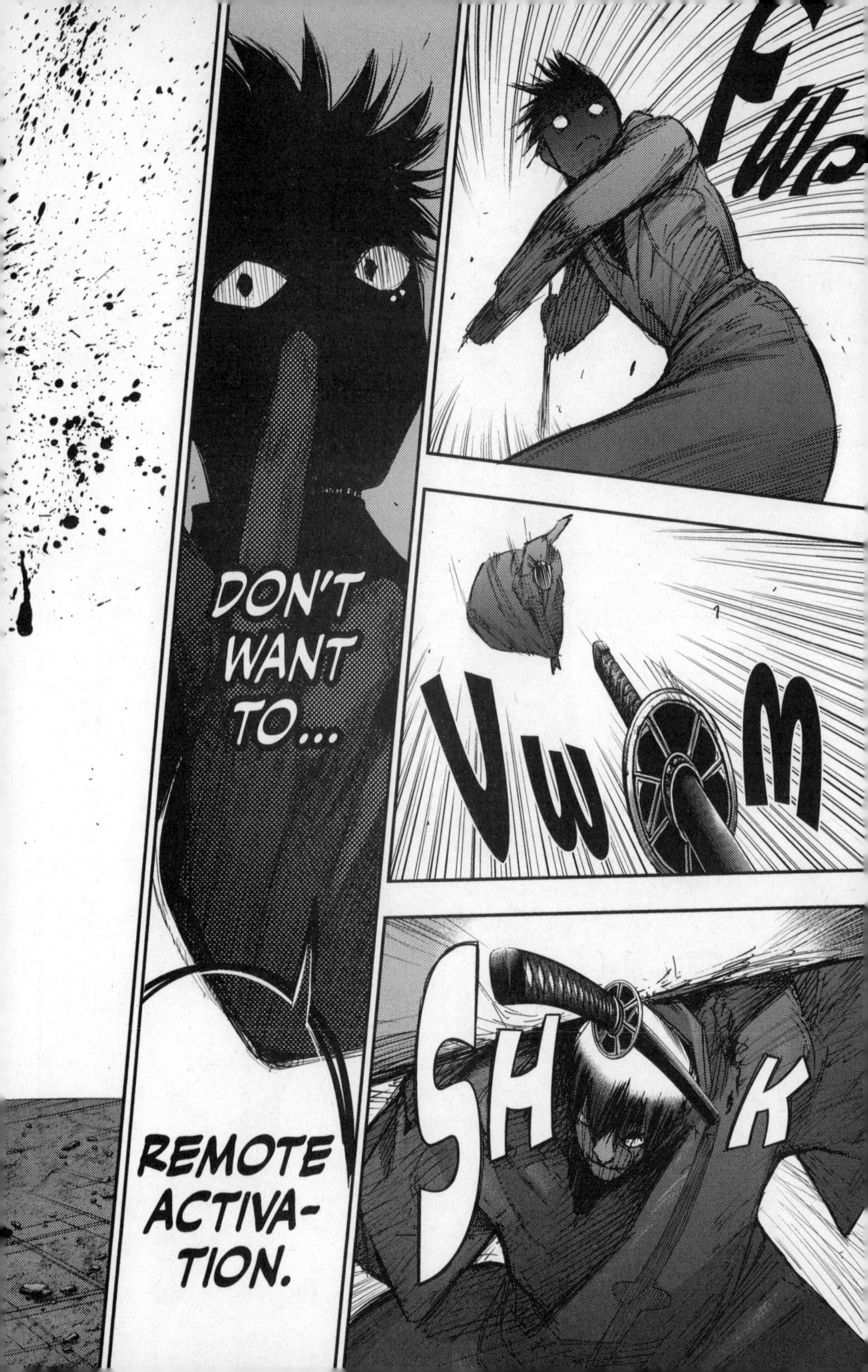
FWIP
VWOM
SHOK
DON'T WANT TO...
REMOTE ACTIVATION.

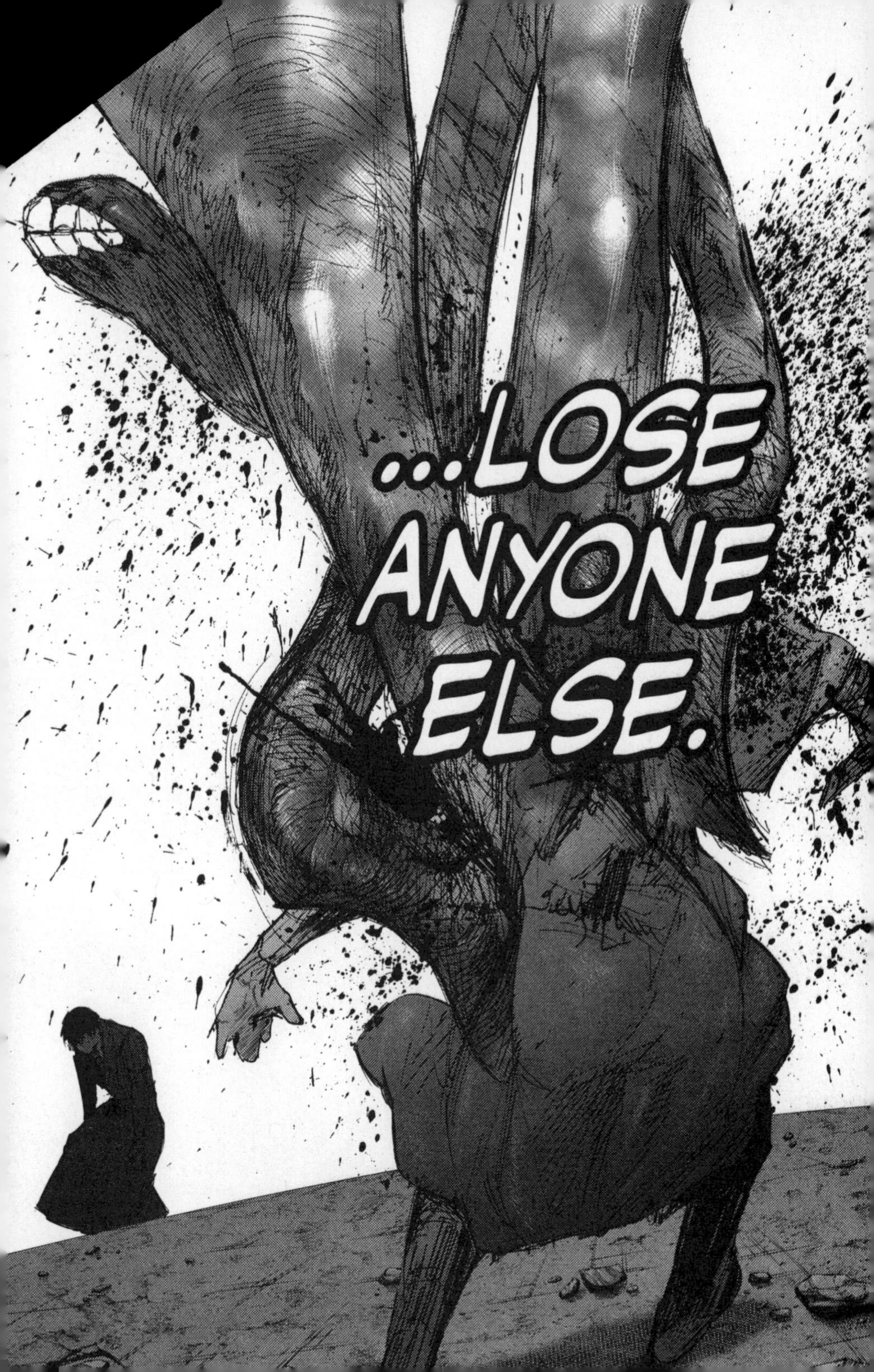
...LOSE
ANYONE
ELSE.

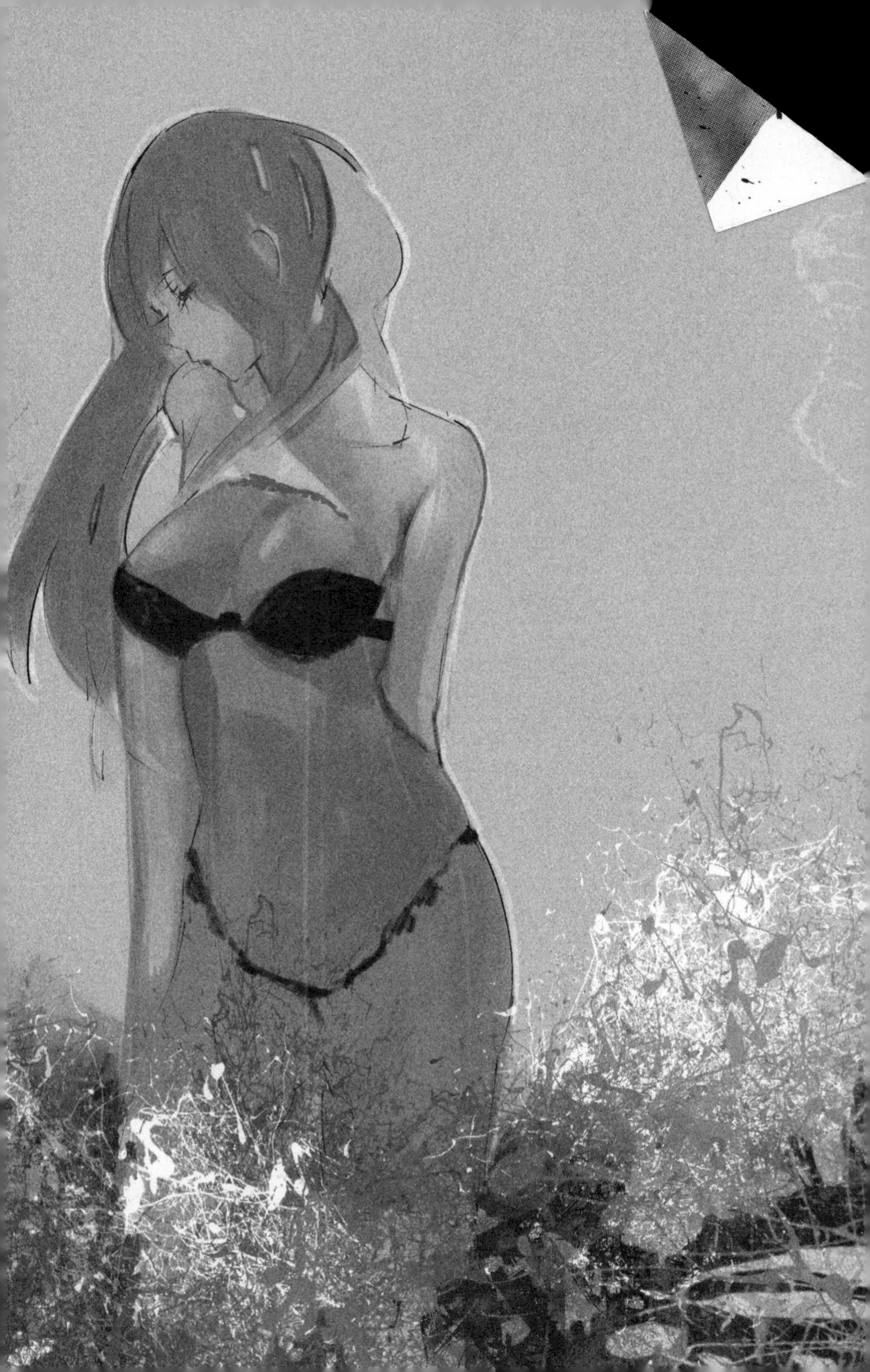

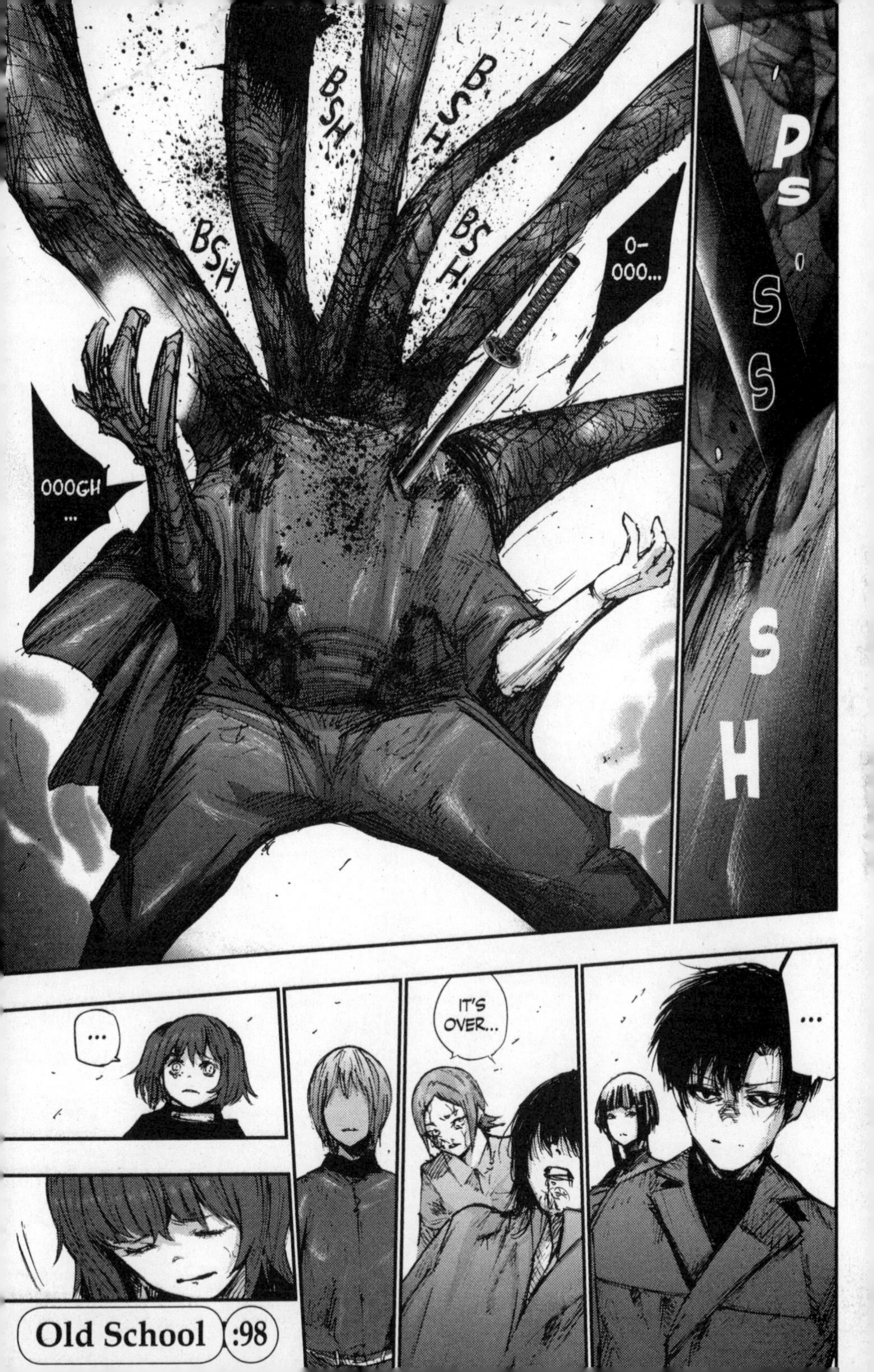
PS'SSSH
O-OOO...
BSH BSH
BSH BSH
OOOGH ...
...
IT'S OVER...
...
Old School :98

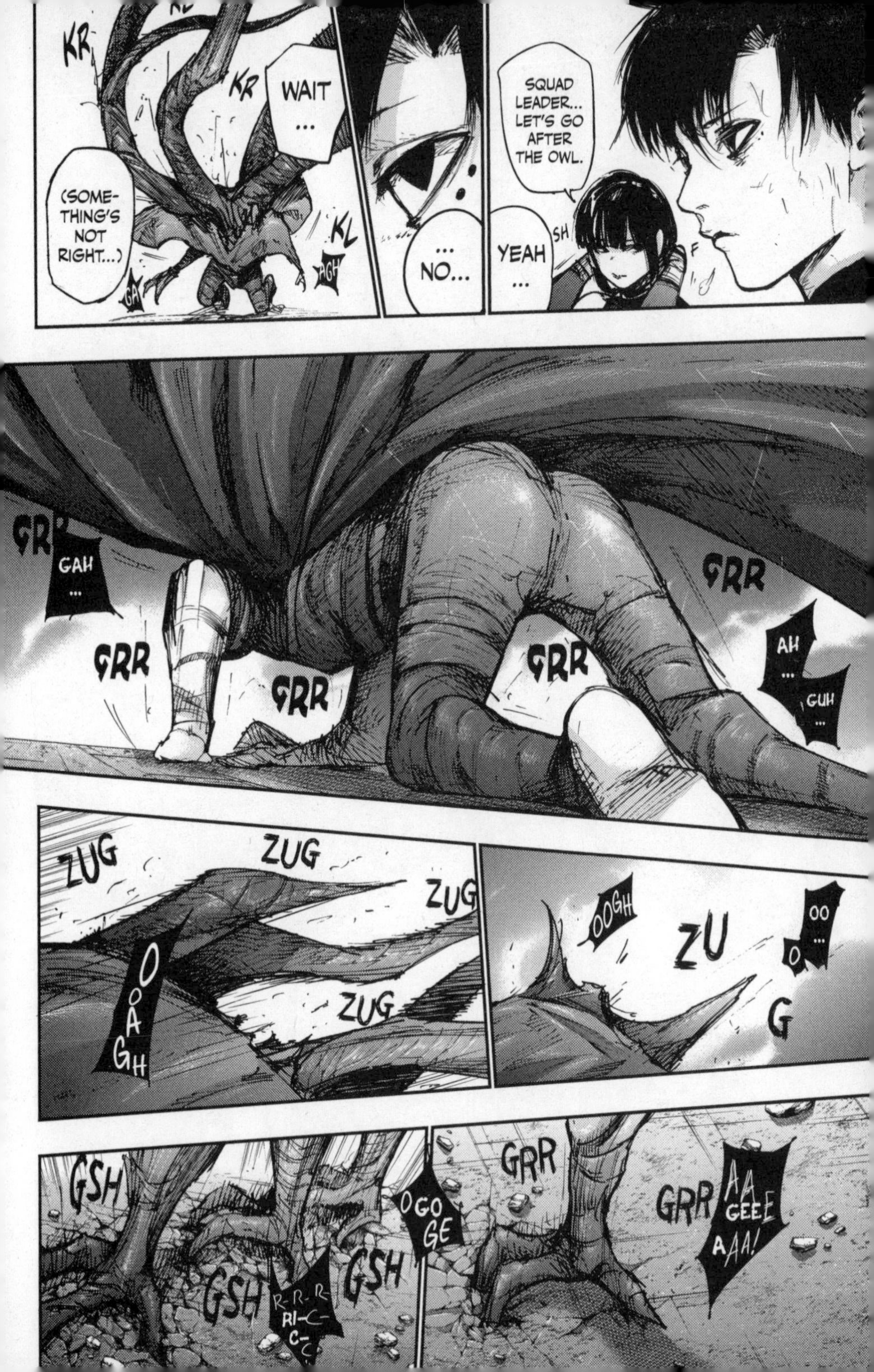
SQUAD LEADER... LET'S GO AFTER THE OWL.
YEAH ...
SH
F
... NO...
KR
KR
WAIT ...
(SOMETHING'S NOT RIGHT...)
KL
AGH
GA
GRR
AH ...
GUH ...
GRR
GRR
GRR
GR
GAH ...
OOGH
ZU
OO ...
O
G
ZUG
ZUG
ZUG
ZUG
OOAGH
GRR
GRR
AA GEEE AAA!
OGOGE
GSH
GSH
GSH
R-R-R-RI-C-C-C

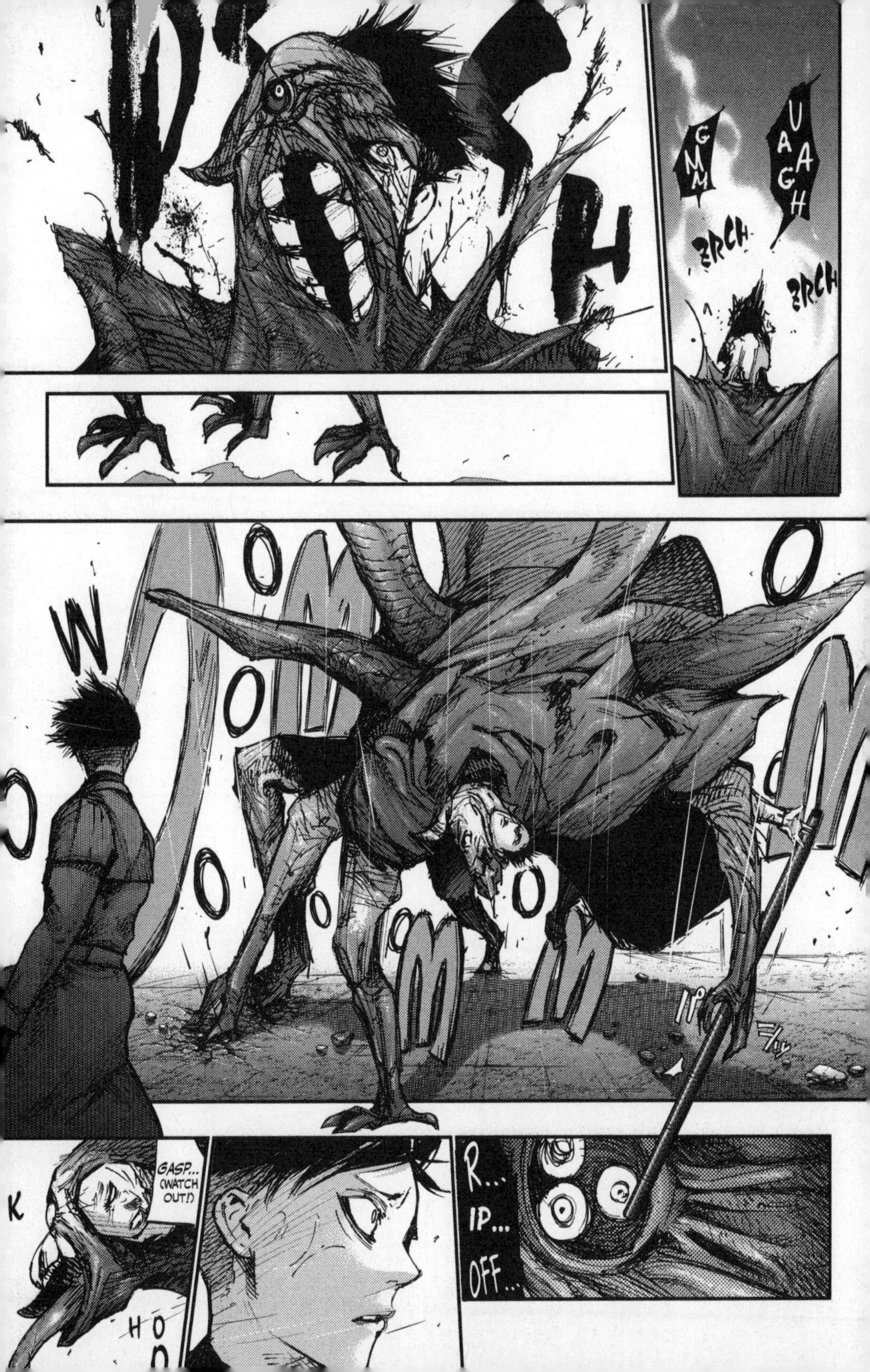
UAAGH
GMM
ZRCH
ZRCH
R... IP... OFF...
GASP... (WATCH OUT!)
K
HO

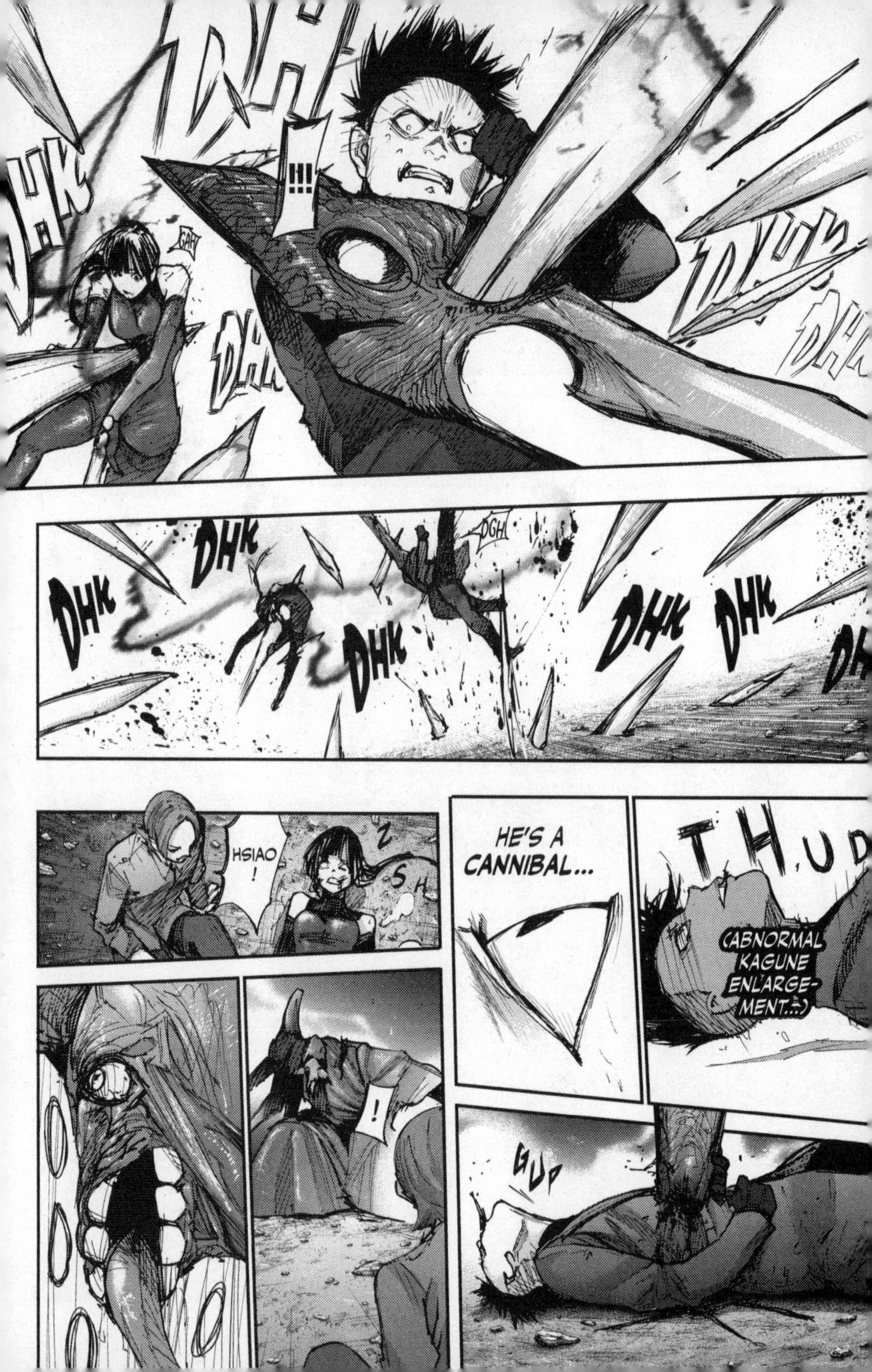
DHK
!!!
GAH
DHK
DHK
DHK
DHK
DGH
DHK
DHK
THUD
(ABNORMAL KAGUNE ENLARGE-MENT...)
HE'S A CANNIBAL...
HSIAO !
ZSH
GUP
!

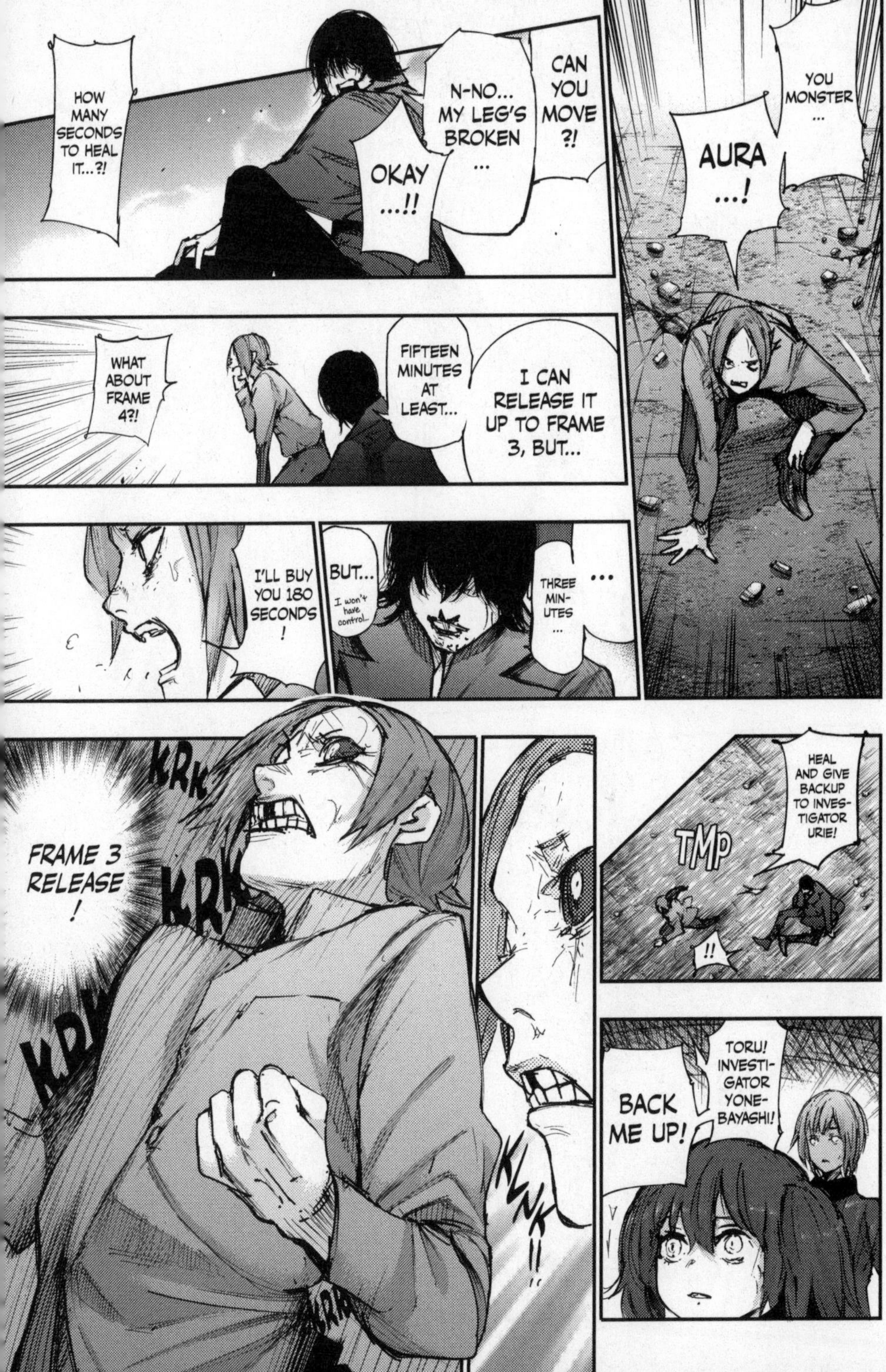
YOU MONSTER...
AURA...!
CAN YOU MOVE?!
N-NO... MY LEG'S BROKEN...
OKAY...!!
HOW MANY SECONDS TO HEAL IT...?!
I CAN RELEASE IT UP TO FRAME 3, BUT...
FIFTEEN MINUTES AT LEAST...
WHAT ABOUT FRAME 4?!
...
THREE MINUTES...
BUT...
I won't have control...
I'LL BUY YOU 180 SECONDS!
HEAL AND GIVE BACKUP TO INVESTIGATOR URIE!
TMP
!!
TORU! INVESTIGATOR YONEBAYASHI!
BACK ME UP!
KLUNK!!
KRK
KRK
FRAME 3 RELEASE!
KRK

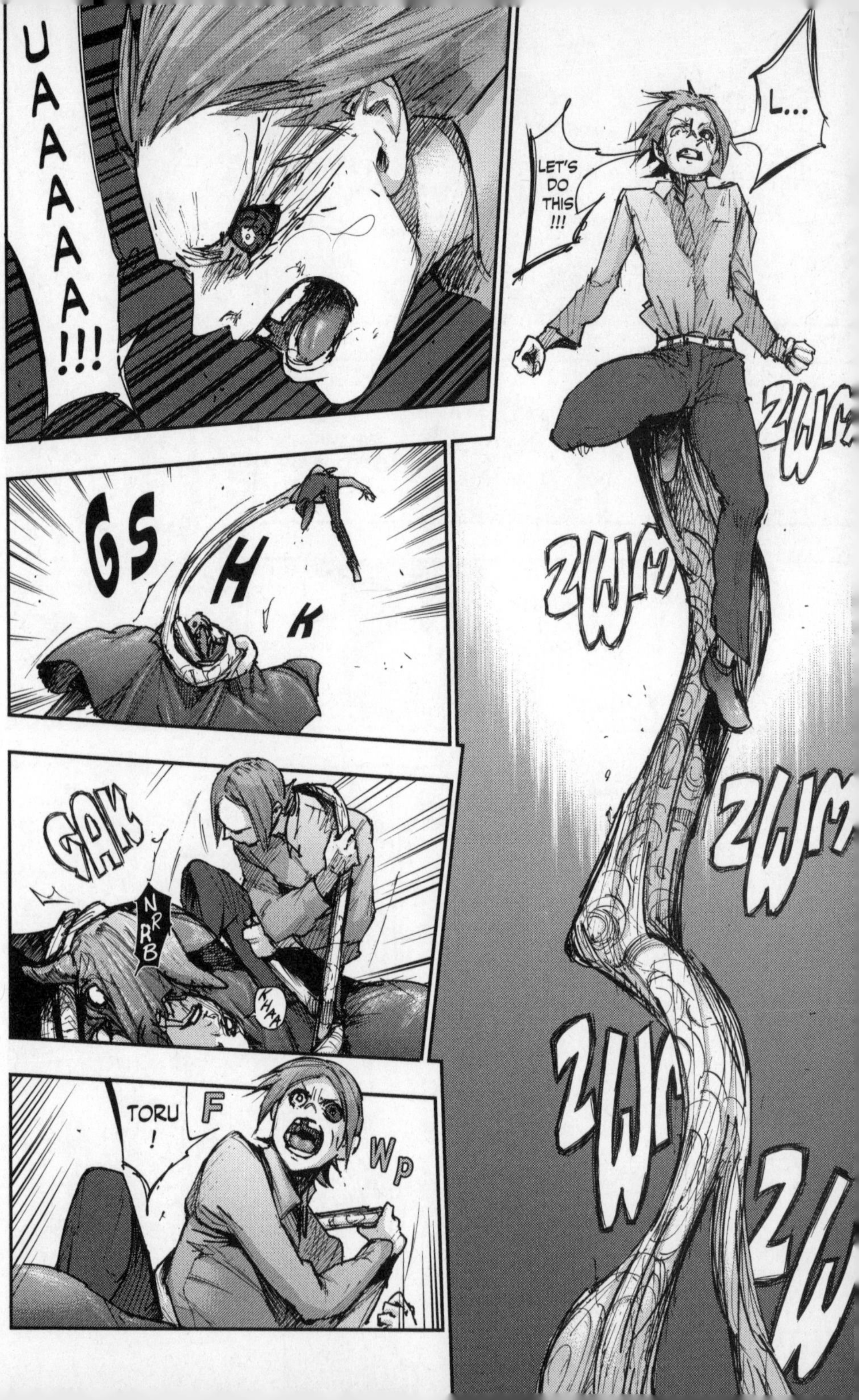
L...
LET'S DO THIS!!!
ZWM
ZWM
ZWM
ZWM
ZW
UAAAAAA!!!
GSHK
GAK
NRRB
KHAA
TORU!
F
Wp

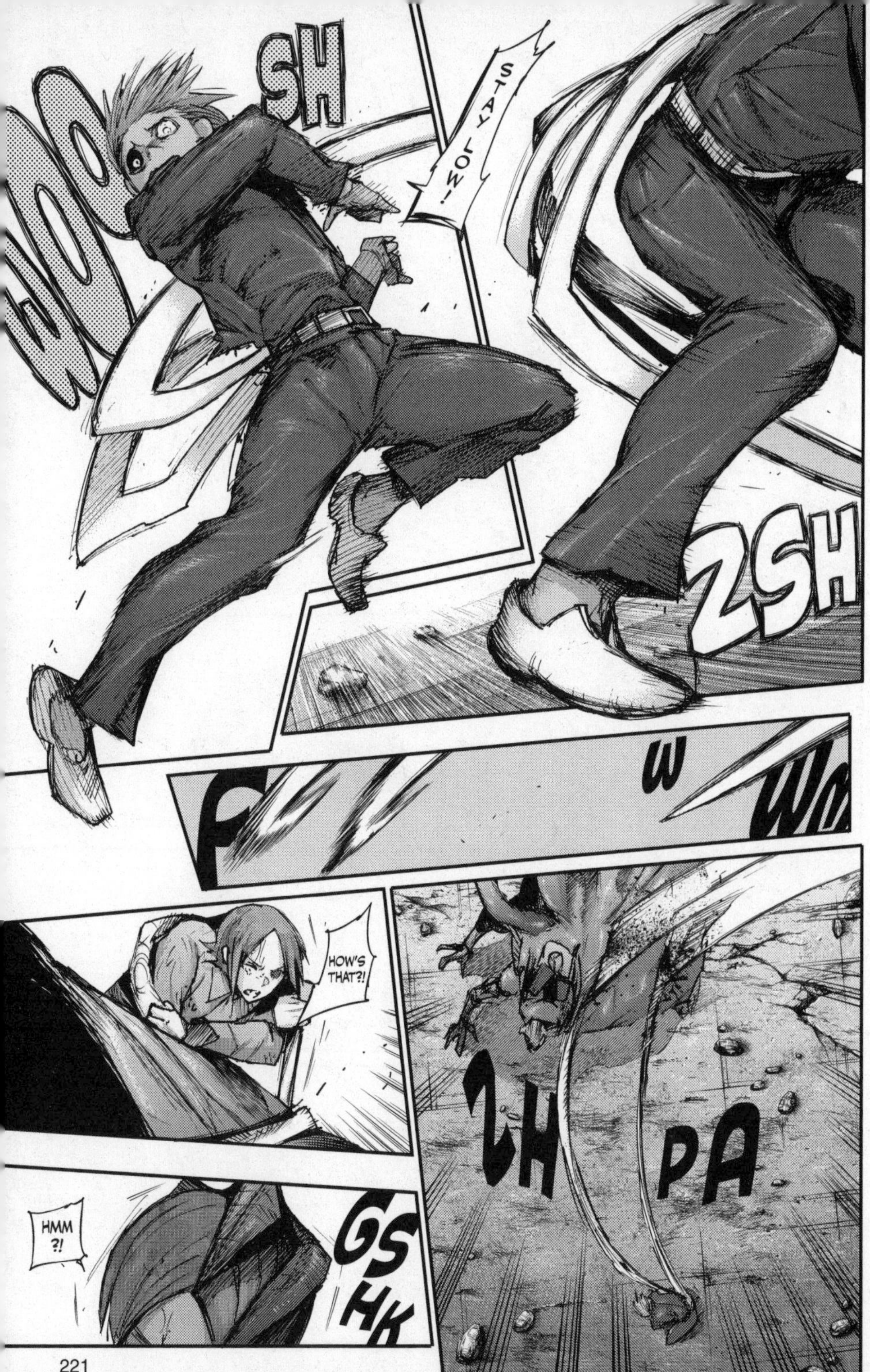
STAY LOW!
ZSH
WOOO
SH
WO
W
P
ZH
PA
HOW'S THAT?!
GSHK
HMM ?!

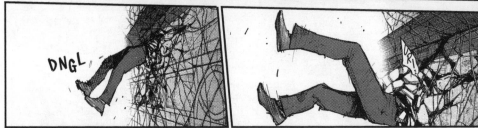

DNGL

KHA

HIGE
!!!

HIGE-
MARU
...!

CHOMP

!!

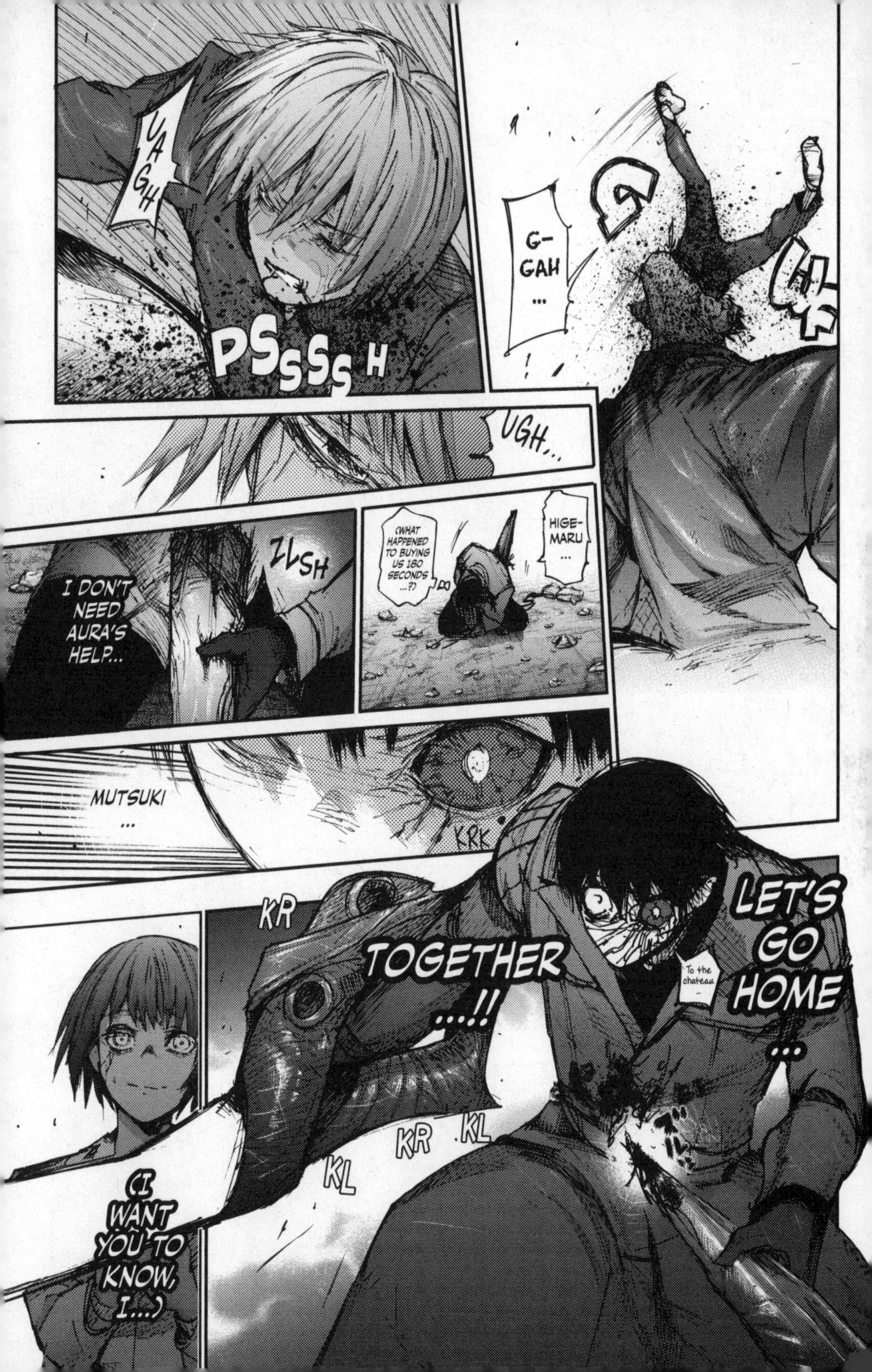

G-GAH ...
UAGH
PSSSSH
UGH...
HIGE-MARU ...
(WHAT HAPPENED TO BUYING US 180 SECONDS ...?)
ZLSH
I DON'T NEED AURA'S HELP...
MUTSUKI ...
KRK
LET'S GO HOME ...
To the chateau ...
TOGETHER ...!!
KR
KL
KR
KL
(I WANT YOU TO KNOW, I...)

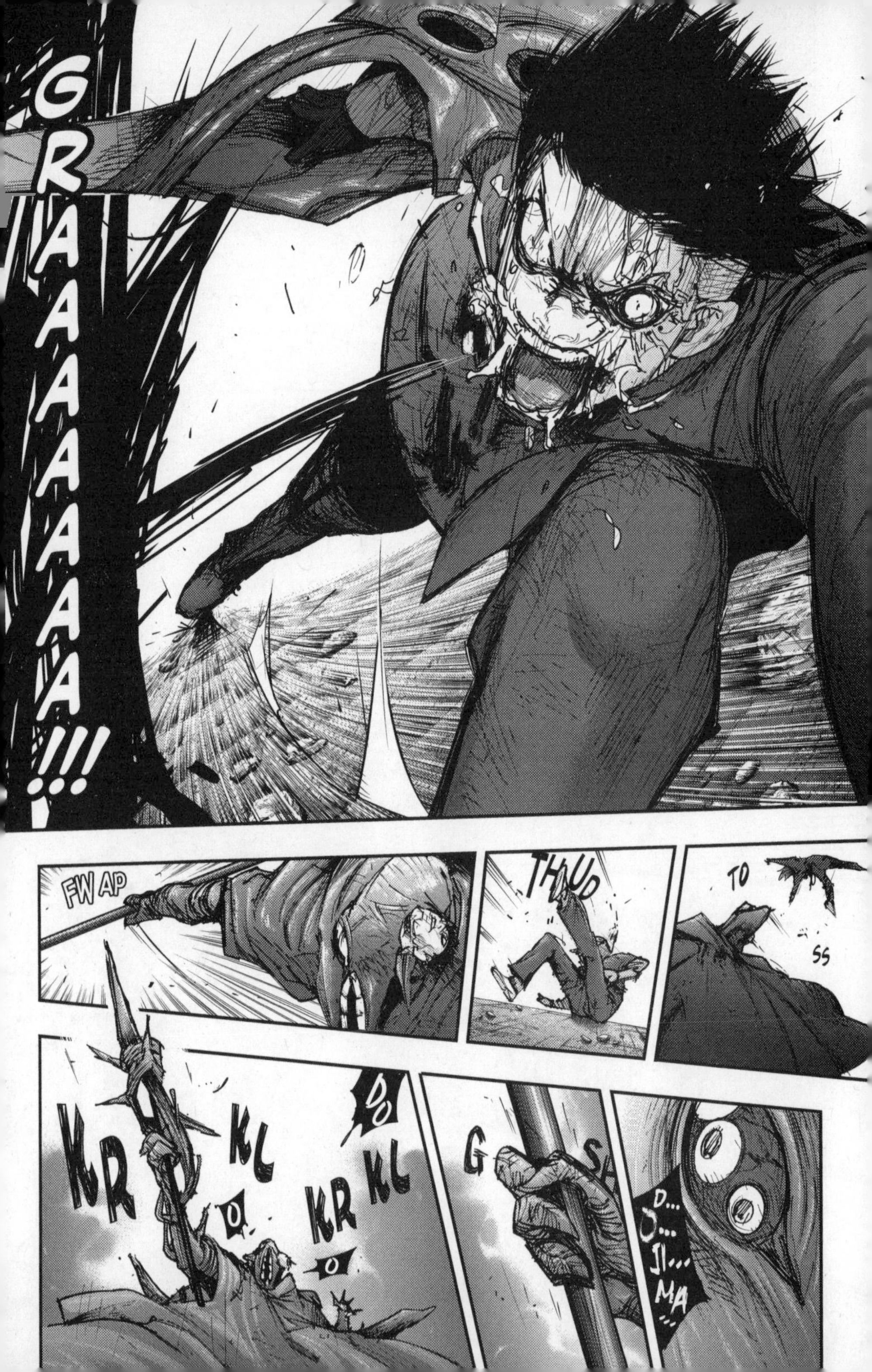
GRAAAAAAAA!!!
TO
SS
THUD
FW AP
D... O... JI... MA...
G
SH
DO
KL
KR
KL
KR
KR
O
O

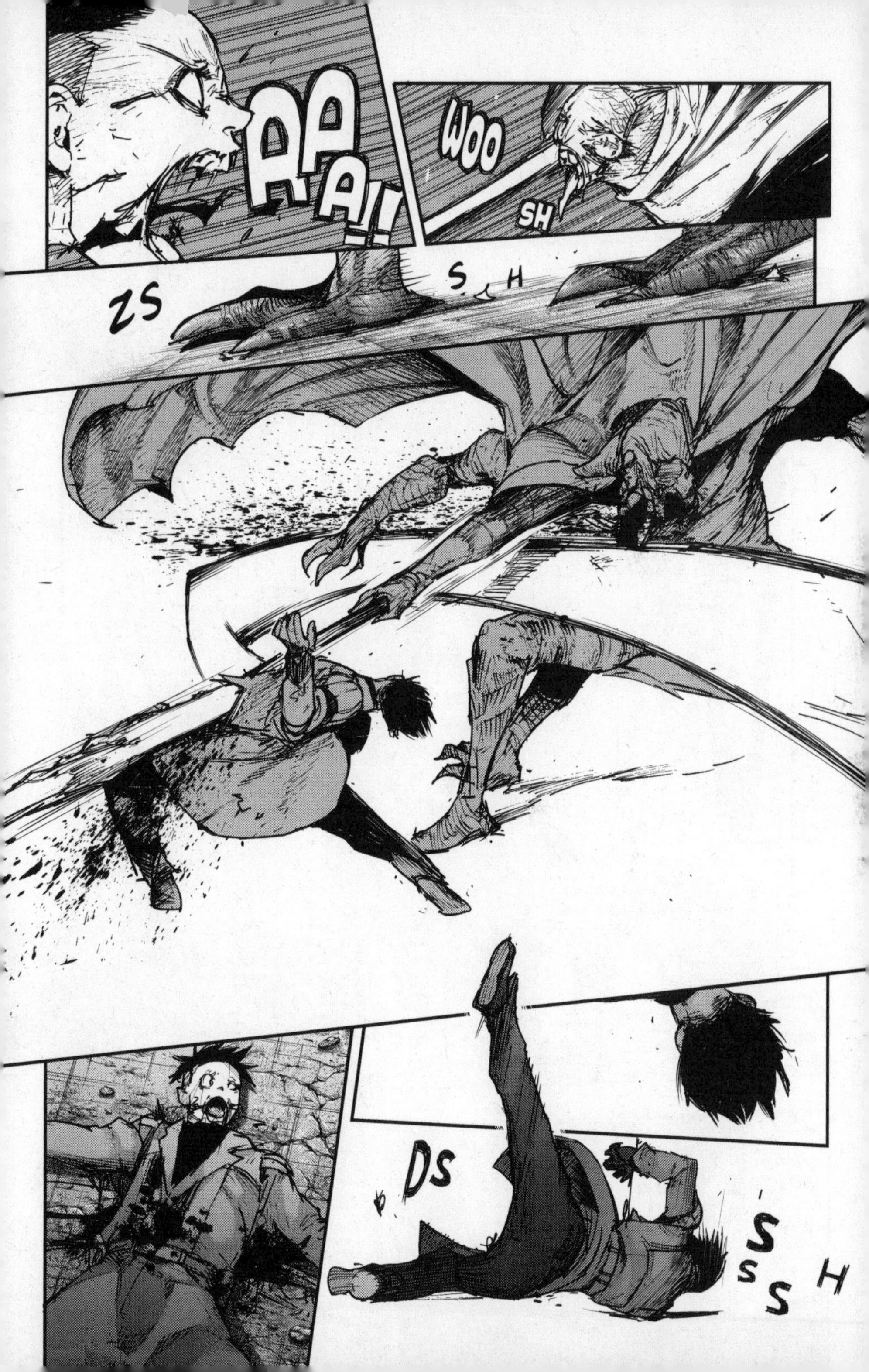
WOO
SH
AAA!!
S H
ZS
DS
SSSH

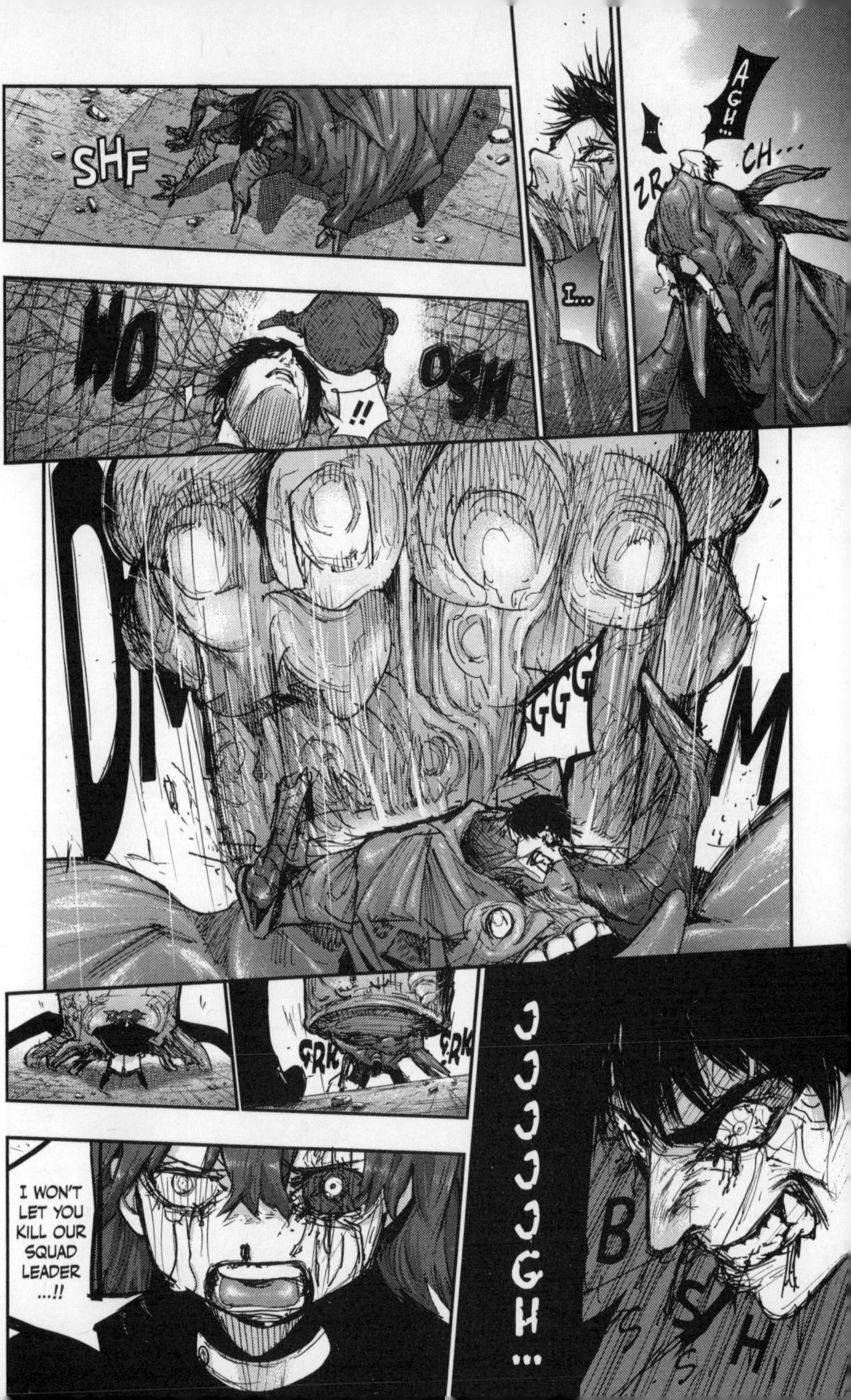

AGH!!
ZR...CH...
I...
SHF
WO OSH
!!
GGG
M
JJJJJJJGH...
BSH
SSS
GRK
GRK
I WON'T LET YOU KILL OUR SQUAD LEADER ...!!

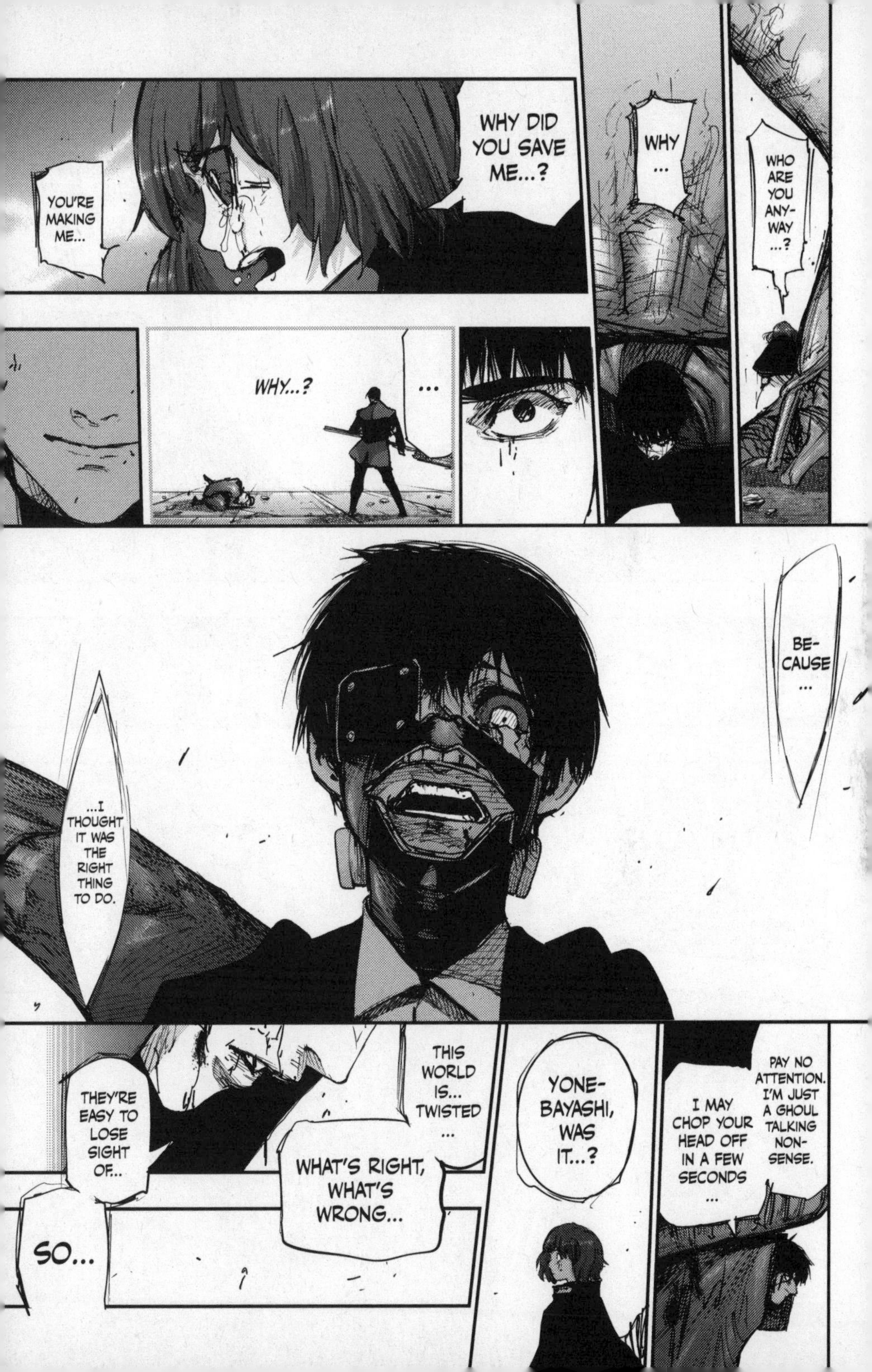
WHO ARE YOU ANY-WAY ...?
WHY ...
WHY DID YOU SAVE ME...?
YOU'RE MAKING ME...
...
WHY...?
BE-CAUSE ...
...I THOUGHT IT WAS THE RIGHT THING TO DO.
PAY NO ATTENTION. I'M JUST A GHOUL TALKING NON-SENSE.
I MAY CHOP YOUR HEAD OFF IN A FEW SECONDS ...
YONE-BAYASHI, WAS IT...?
THIS WORLD IS... TWISTED ...
WHAT'S RIGHT, WHAT'S WRONG...
THEY'RE EASY TO LOSE SIGHT OF...
SO...

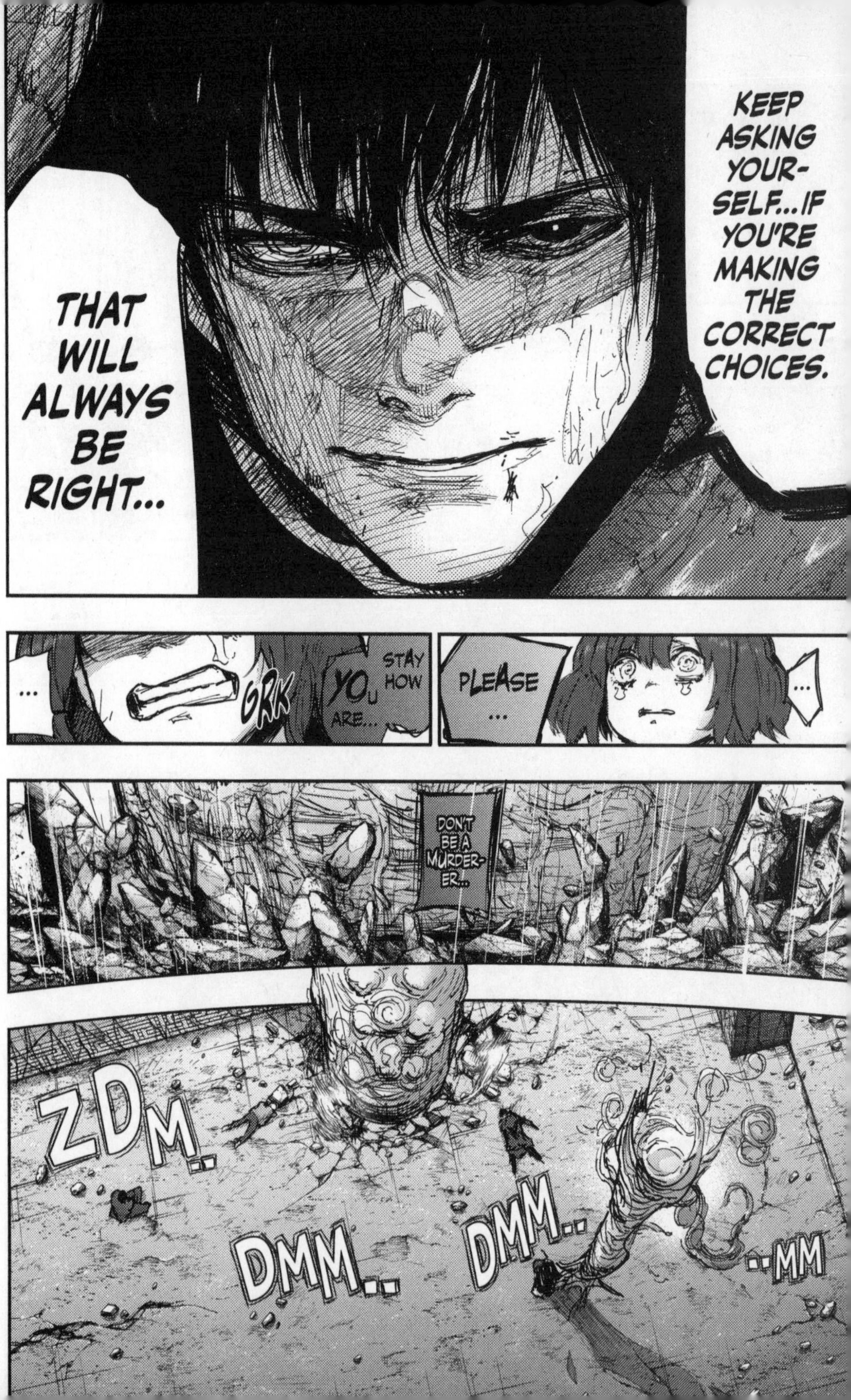
KEEP ASKING YOURSELF...IF YOU'RE MAKING THE CORRECT CHOICES.
THAT WILL ALWAYS BE RIGHT...
...
PLEASE ...
STAY HOW YOU ARE...
GRK
...
DON'T BE A MURDERER...
ZDM..
DMM..
DMM..
..MM

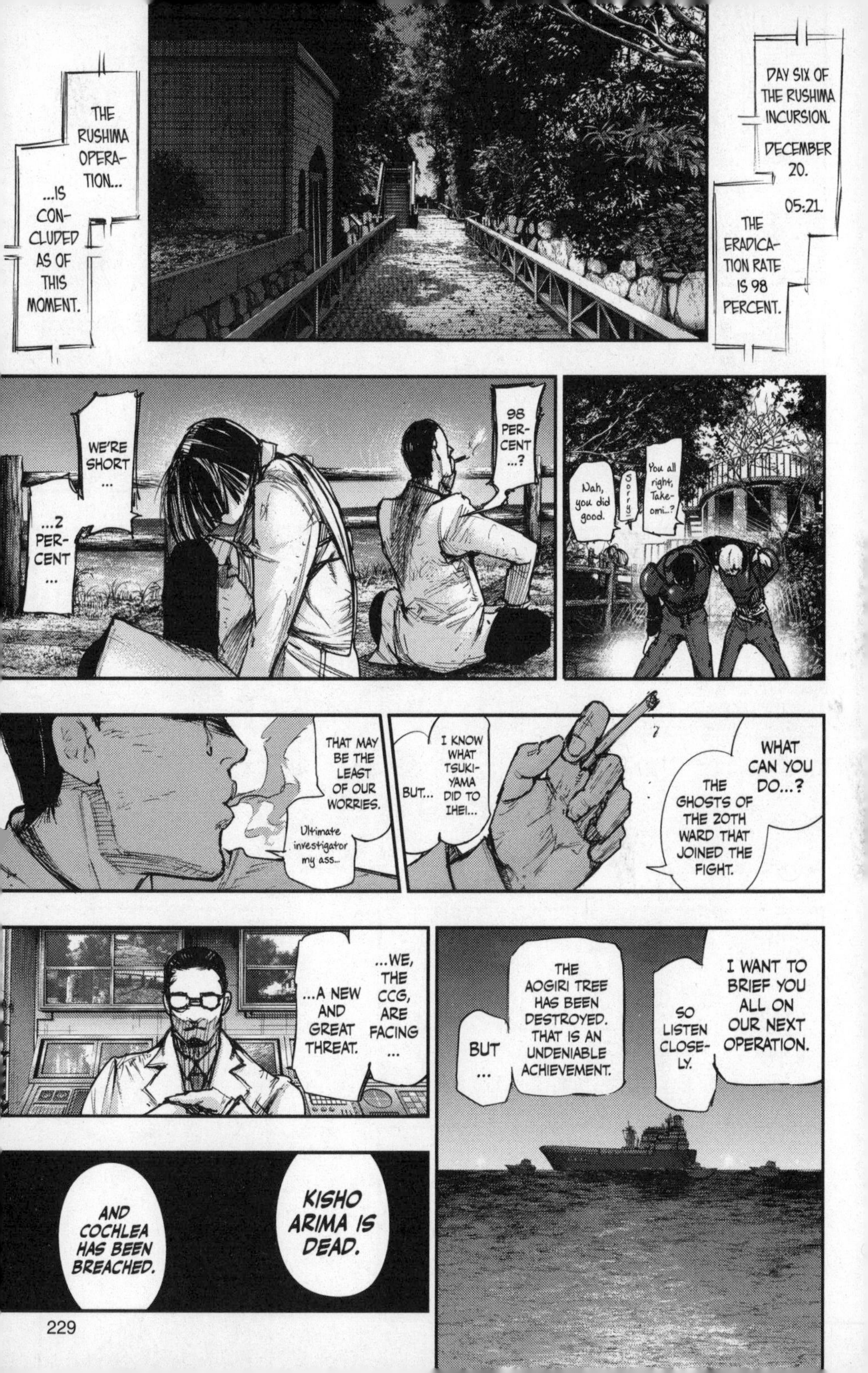
DAY SIX OF THE RUSHIMA INCURSION.
DECEMBER 20.
05:21.
THE ERADICATION RATE IS 98 PERCENT.
THE RUSHIMA OPERATION...
...IS CONCLUDED AS OF THIS MOMENT.
You all right, Takeomi...?
Sorry
Nah, you did good.
98 PERCENT...?
WE'RE SHORT...
...2 PERCENT...
WHAT CAN YOU DO...?
THE GHOSTS OF THE 20TH WARD THAT JOINED THE FIGHT.
I KNOW WHAT TSUKIYAMA DID TO IHEI...
BUT...
THAT MAY BE THE LEAST OF OUR WORRIES.
Ultimate investigator my ass...
I WANT TO BRIEF YOU ALL ON OUR NEXT OPERATION.
SO LISTEN CLOSELY.
THE AOGIRI TREE HAS BEEN DESTROYED. THAT IS AN UNDENIABLE ACHIEVEMENT.
BUT...
...WE, THE CCG, ARE FACING...
...A NEW AND GREAT THREAT.
KISHO ARIMA IS DEAD.
AND COCHLEA HAS BEEN BREACHED.

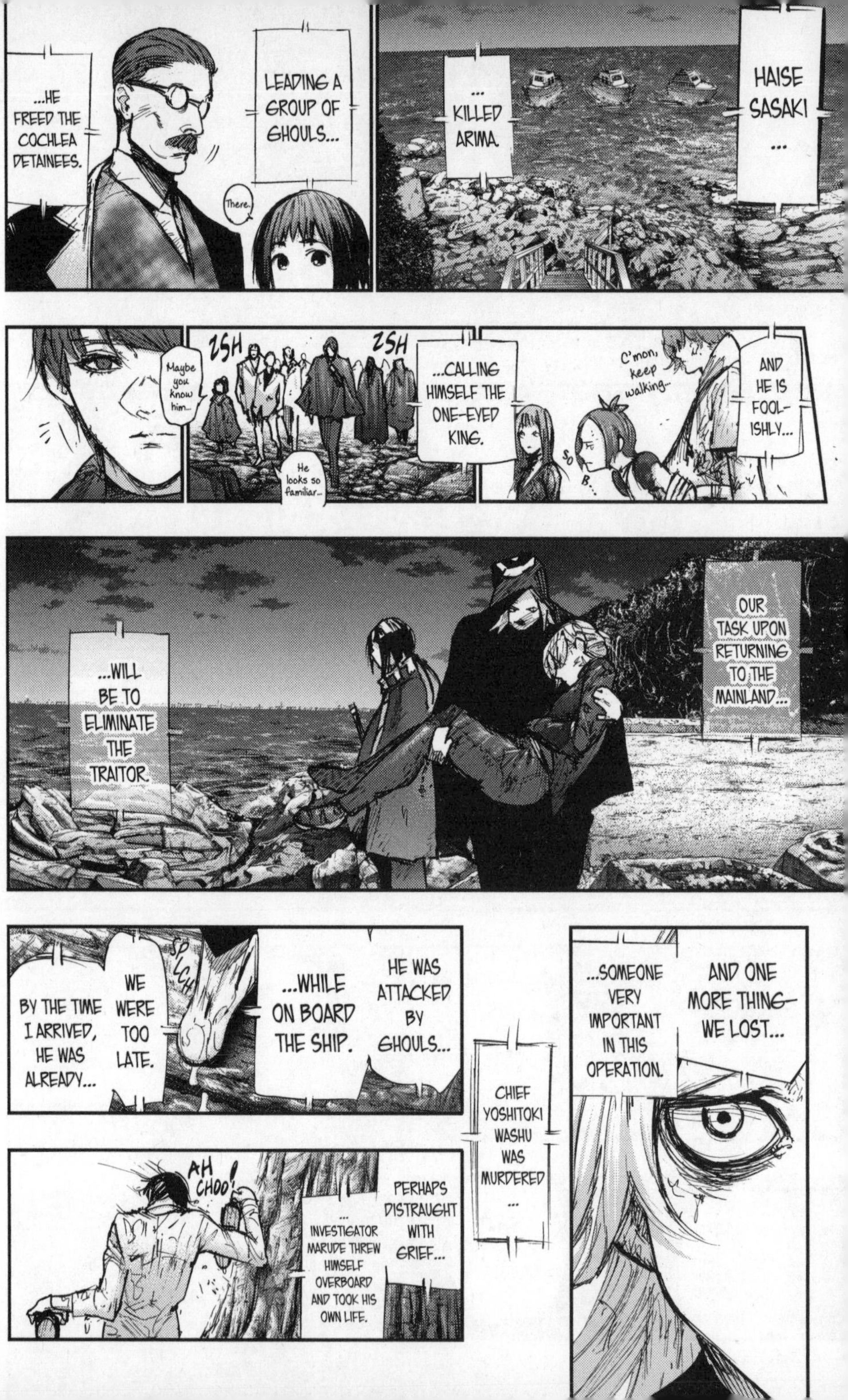
HAISE SASAKI ...
... KILLED ARIMA.
LEADING A GROUP OF GHOULS...
There.
...HE FREED THE COCHLEA DETAINEES.
AND HE IS FOOL-ISHLY...
C'mon, keep walking...
SOB...
ZSH
ZSH
...CALLING HIMSELF THE ONE-EYED KING.
Maybe you know him...
He looks so familiar...
OUR TASK UPON RETURNING TO THE MAINLAND...
...WILL BE TO ELIMINATE THE TRAITOR.
AND ONE MORE THING WE LOST...
...SOMEONE VERY IMPORTANT IN THIS OPERATION.
CHIEF YOSHITOKI WASHU WAS MURDERED ...
HE WAS ATTACKED BY GHOULS...
...WHILE ON BOARD THE SHIP.
SPLCH
WE WERE TOO LATE.
BY THE TIME I ARRIVED, HE WAS ALREADY...
PERHAPS DISTRAUGHT WITH GRIEF...
...INVESTIGATOR MARUDE THREW HIMSELF OVERBOARD AND TOOK HIS OWN LIFE.
AH CHOO!

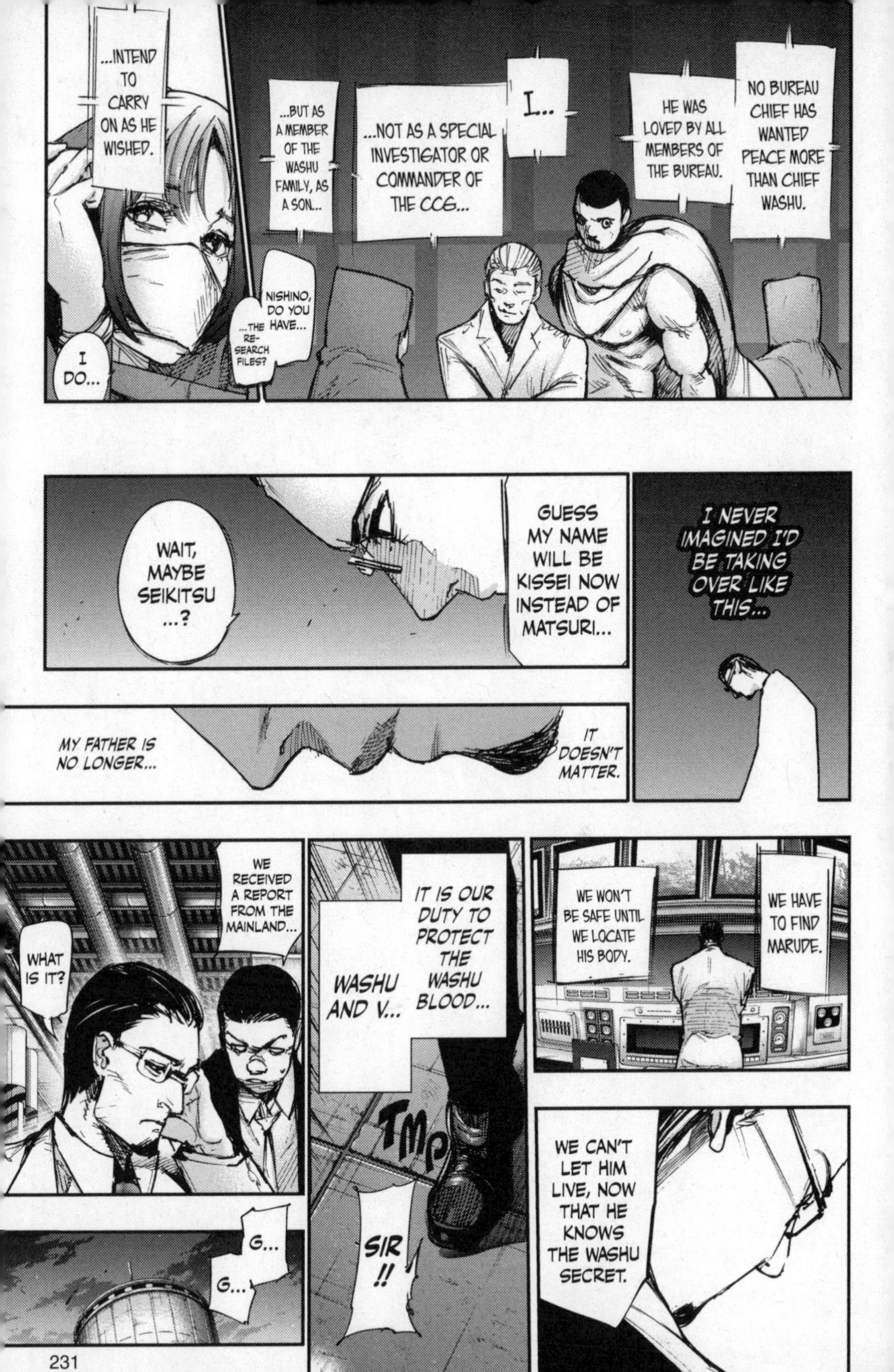
NO BUREAU CHIEF HAS WANTED PEACE MORE THAN CHIEF WASHU.
HE WAS LOVED BY ALL MEMBERS OF THE BUREAU.
I...
...NOT AS A SPECIAL INVESTIGATOR OR COMMANDER OF THE CCG...
...BUT AS A MEMBER OF THE WASHU FAMILY, AS A SON...
...INTEND TO CARRY ON AS HE WISHED.
NISHINO, DO YOU HAVE...
...THE RE-SEARCH FILES?
I DO...
I NEVER IMAGINED I'D BE TAKING OVER LIKE THIS...
GUESS MY NAME WILL BE KISSEI NOW INSTEAD OF MATSURI...
WAIT, MAYBE SEIKITSU ...?
IT DOESN'T MATTER.
MY FATHER IS NO LONGER...
WE HAVE TO FIND MARUDE.
WE WON'T BE SAFE UNTIL WE LOCATE HIS BODY.
WE CAN'T LET HIM LIVE, NOW THAT HE KNOWS THE WASHU SECRET.
IT IS OUR DUTY TO PROTECT THE WASHU BLOOD...
WASHU AND V...
TMP
SIR !!
WE RECEIVED A REPORT FROM THE MAINLAND...
WHAT IS IT?
G...
G...

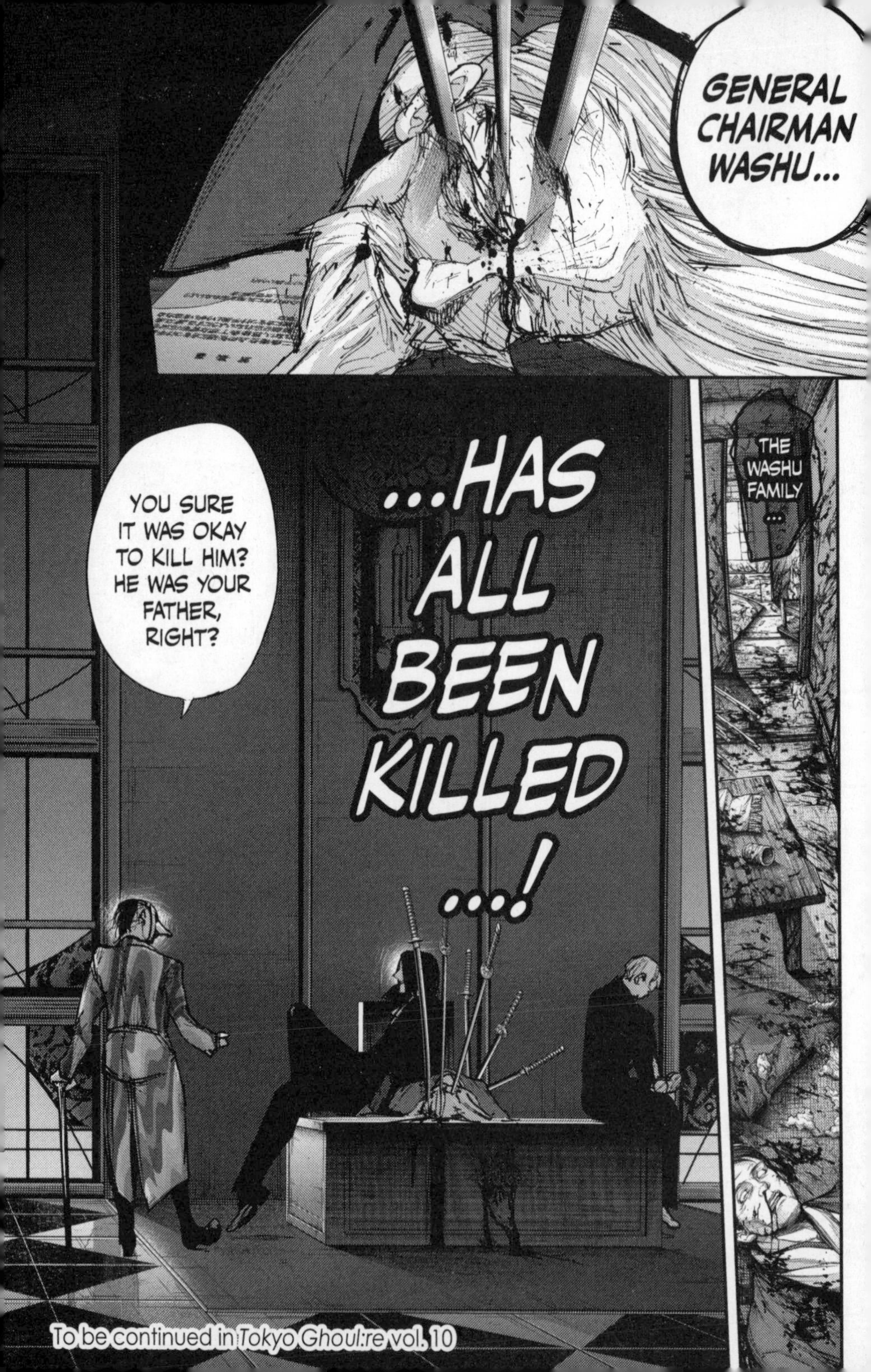
GENERAL CHAIRMAN WASHU...
THE WASHU FAMILY ...
...HAS ALL BEEN KILLED ...!
YOU SURE IT WAS OKAY TO KILL HIM? HE WAS YOUR FATHER, RIGHT?

To be continued in *Tokyo Ghoul:re* vol. 10

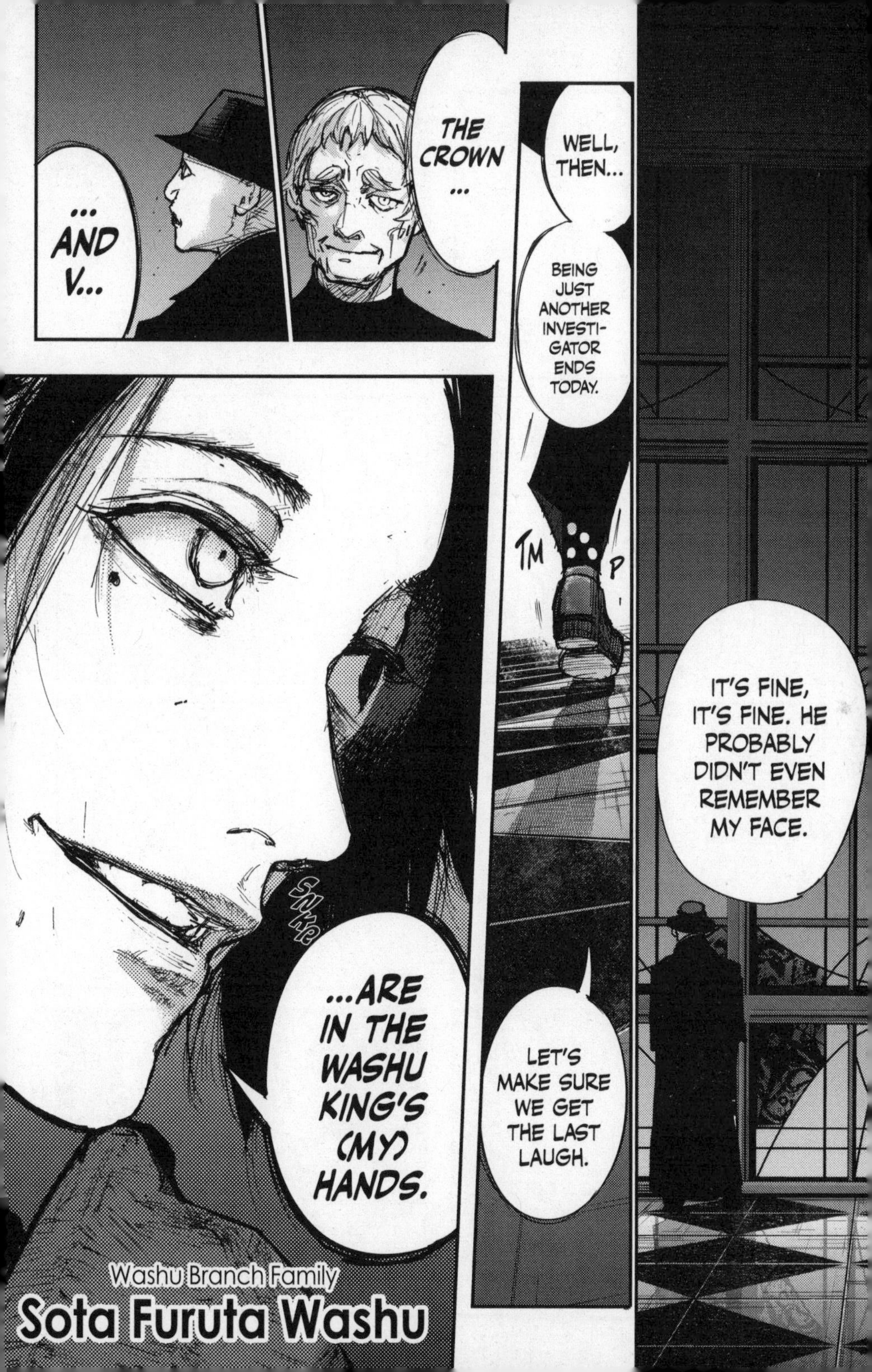
IT'S FINE, IT'S FINE. HE PROBABLY DIDN'T EVEN REMEMBER MY FACE.
WELL, THEN...
BEING JUST ANOTHER INVESTIGATOR ENDS TODAY.
TMP
LET'S MAKE SURE WE GET THE LAST LAUGH.
THE CROWN ...
... AND V...
SNKR
...ARE IN THE WASHU KING'S (MY) HANDS.
Washu Branch Family
Sota Furuta Washu

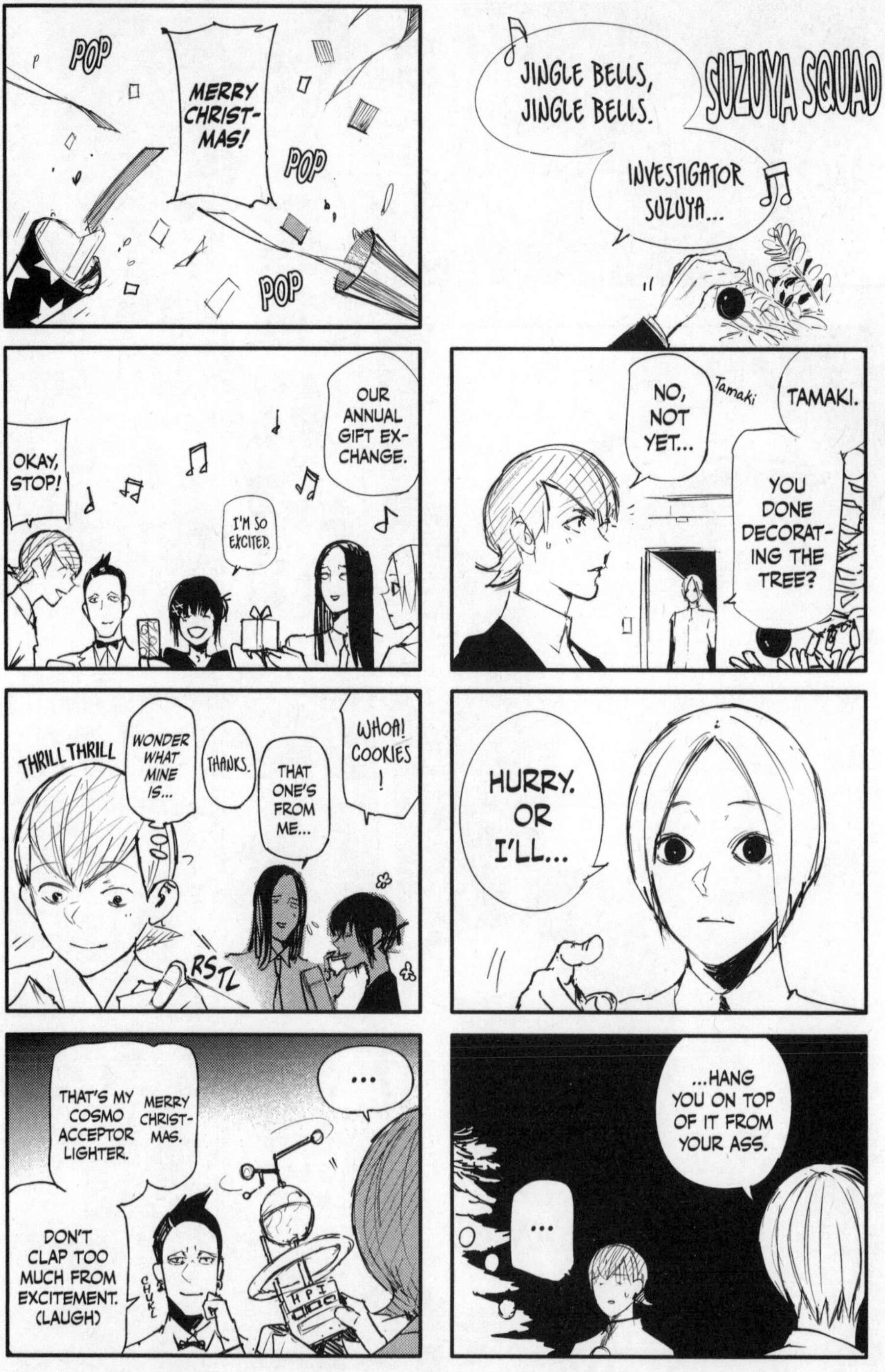
SUZUYA SQUAD
JINGLE BELLS, JINGLE BELLS.
INVESTIGATOR SUZUYA...
MERRY CHRIST-MAS!
POP
POP
POP
TAMAKI.
YOU DONE DECORAT-ING THE TREE?
Tamaki
NO, NOT YET...
OUR ANNUAL GIFT EX-CHANGE.
I'M SO EXCITED.
OKAY, STOP!
HURRY. OR I'LL...
WHOA! COOKIES!
THAT ONE'S FROM ME...
THANKS.
WONDER WHAT MINE IS...
THRILL THRILL
RSTL
...HANG YOU ON TOP OF IT FROM YOUR ASS.
...
...
MERRY CHRIST-MAS.
THAT'S MY COSMO ACCEPTOR LIGHTER.
DON'T CLAP TOO MUCH FROM EXCITEMENT. (LAUGH)
CHUKL
HPI

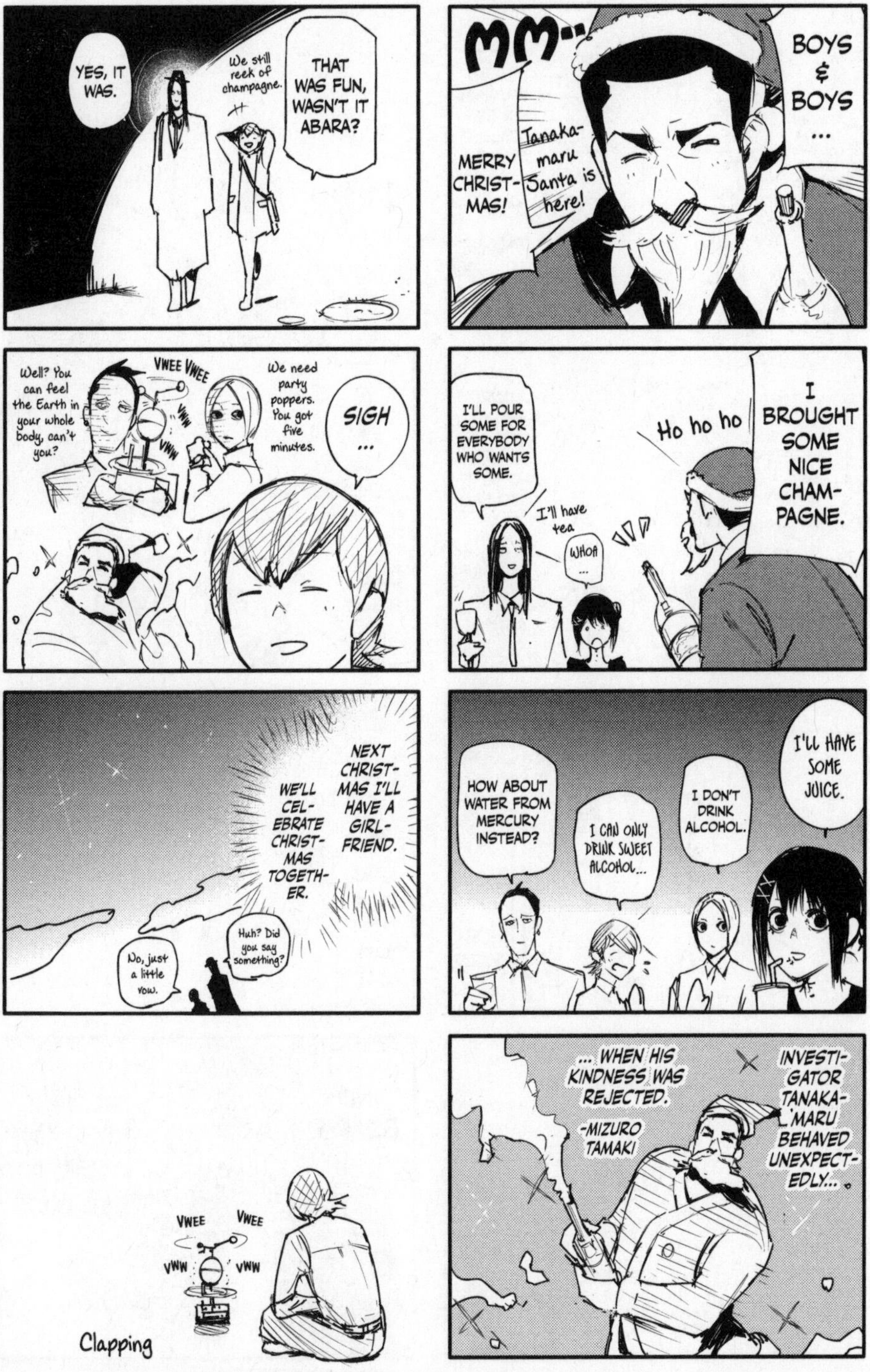
BOYS & BOYS ...
MM..
Tanaka-maru Santa is here!
MERRY CHRIST-MAS!
I BROUGHT SOME NICE CHAM-PAGNE.
Ho ho ho
I'LL POUR SOME FOR EVERYBODY WHO WANTS SOME.
I'll have tea
WHOA ...
I'LL HAVE SOME JUICE.
I DON'T DRINK ALCOHOL.
I CAN ONLY DRINK SWEET ALCOHOL...
HOW ABOUT WATER FROM MERCURY INSTEAD?
INVESTI-GATOR TANAKA-MARU BEHAVED UNEXPECT-EDLY...
... WHEN HIS KINDNESS WAS REJECTED.
-MIZURO TAMAKI
SIGH ...
We need party poppers. You got five minutes.
VWEE VWEE
Well? You can feel the Earth in your whole body, can't you?
VWW
VWW
NEXT CHRIST-MAS I'LL HAVE A GIRL-FRIEND.
WE'LL CEL-EBRATE CHRIST-MAS TOGETH-ER.
Huh? Did you say something?
No, just a little vow.
THAT WAS FUN, WASN'T IT ABARA?
We still reek of champagne.
YES, IT WAS.
VWEE VWEE
VWW VWW
Clapping

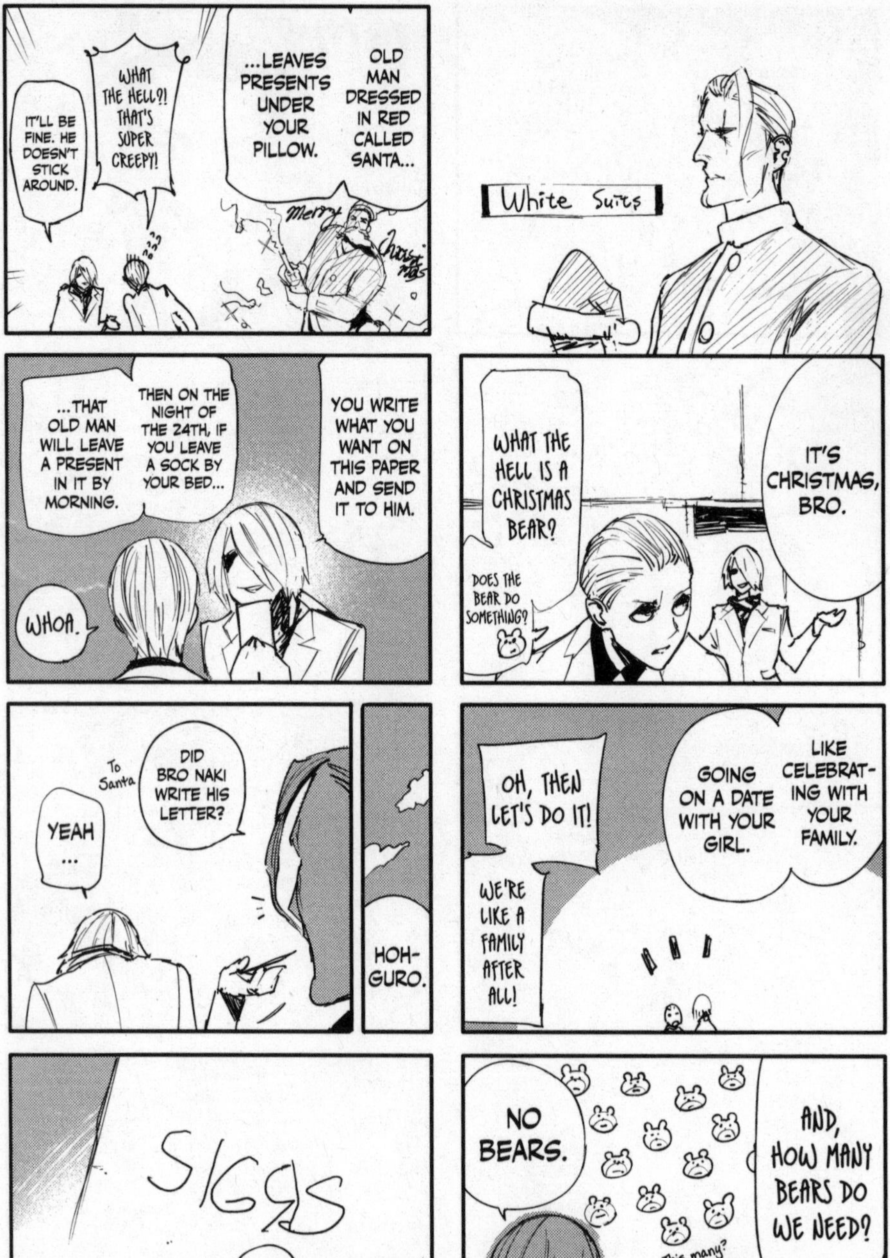
White Suits
OLD MAN DRESSED IN RED CALLED SANTA...
...LEAVES PRESENTS UNDER YOUR PILLOW.
Merry Christmas
WHAT THE HELL?! THAT'S SUPER CREEPY!
IT'LL BE FINE. HE DOESN'T STICK AROUND.
IT'S CHRISTMAS, BRO.
WHAT THE HELL IS A CHRISTMAS BEAR?
DOES THE BEAR DO SOMETHING?
YOU WRITE WHAT YOU WANT ON THIS PAPER AND SEND IT TO HIM.
THEN ON THE NIGHT OF THE 24TH, IF YOU LEAVE A SOCK BY YOUR BED...
...THAT OLD MAN WILL LEAVE A PRESENT IN IT BY MORNING.
WHOA.
LIKE CELEBRATING WITH YOUR FAMILY.
GOING ON A DATE WITH YOUR GIRL.
OH, THEN LET'S DO IT!
WE'RE LIKE A FAMILY AFTER ALL!
HOH-GURO.
DID BRO NAKI WRITE HIS LETTER?
To Santa
YEAH...
AND, HOW MANY BEARS DO WE NEED?
This many?
NO BEARS.
SIGRS
SUGAR?
I THINK IT MEANS SIGUR RÓS...
The correct answer is cigars.

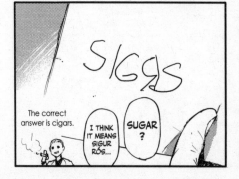

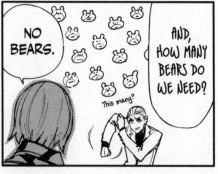

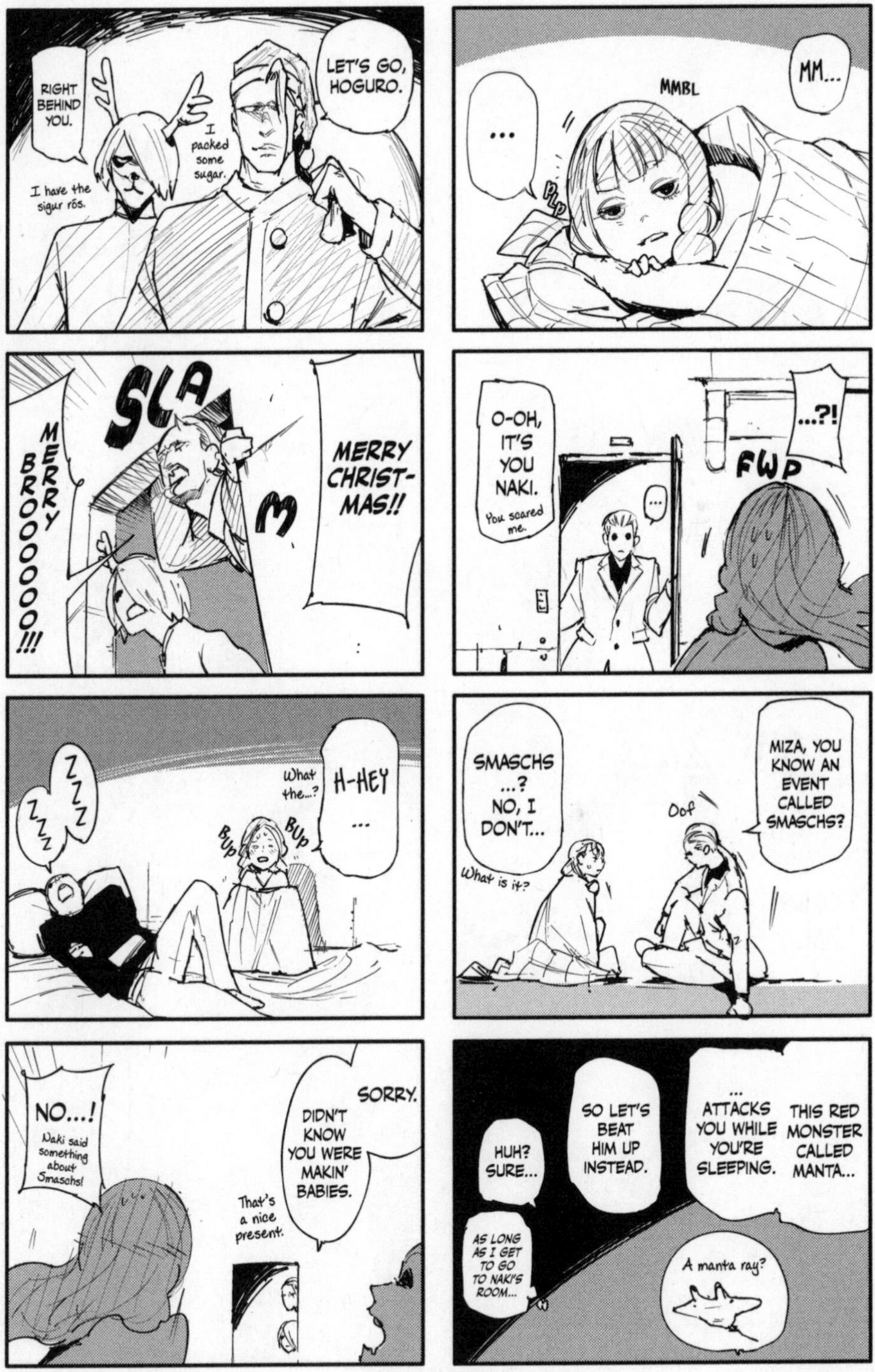
MM...
MMBL
...
PLp
LET'S GO, HOGURO.
I packed some sugar.
RIGHT BEHIND YOU.
I have the sigur rós.
...?!
FWP
...
O-OH, IT'S YOU NAKI.
You scared me.
MERRY CHRISTMAS!!
SLAM
MERRY BROOOOOOOO!!!
MIZA, YOU KNOW AN EVENT CALLED SMASCHS?
Oof
SMASCHS ...? NO, I DON'T...
What is it?
H-HEY ...
What the...?
BUp
BUp
ZZZ
ZZZ
THIS RED MONSTER CALLED MANTA...
... ATTACKS YOU WHILE YOU'RE SLEEPING.
SO LET'S BEAT HIM UP INSTEAD.
HUH? SURE...
AS LONG AS I GET TO GO TO NAKI'S ROOM...
A manta ray?
SORRY.
DIDN'T KNOW YOU WERE MAKIN' BABIES.
That's a nice present.
NO...!
Naki said something about Smaschs!

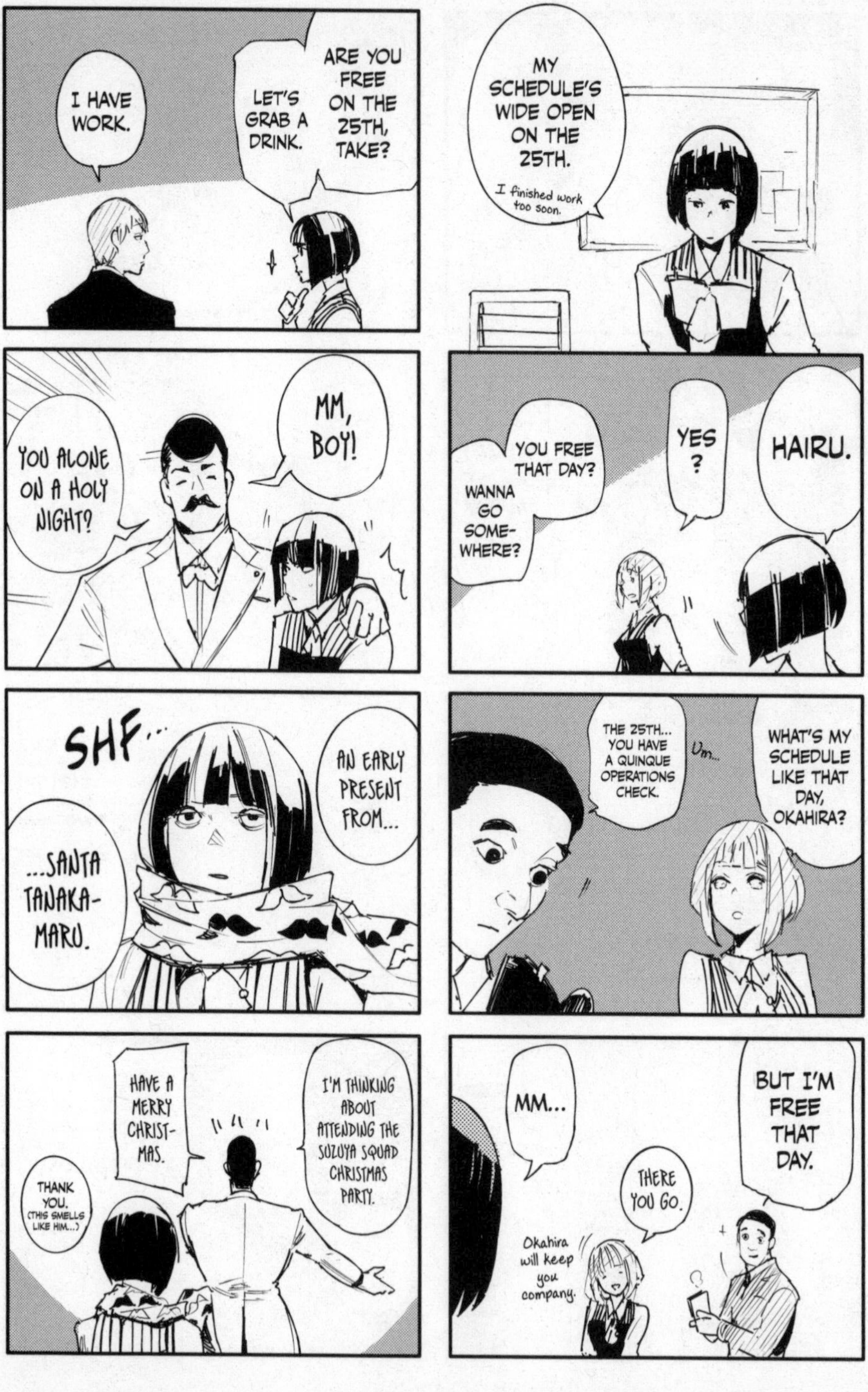
MY SCHEDULE'S WIDE OPEN ON THE 25TH.
I finished work too soon.
ARE YOU FREE ON THE 25TH, TAKE?
LET'S GRAB A DRINK.
I HAVE WORK.
HAIRU.
YES?
YOU FREE THAT DAY?
WANNA GO SOME-WHERE?
MM, BOY!
YOU ALONE ON A HOLY NIGHT?
WHAT'S MY SCHEDULE LIKE THAT DAY, OKAHIRA?
Um...
THE 25TH... YOU HAVE A QUINQUE OPERATIONS CHECK.
AN EARLY PRESENT FROM...
SHF...
...SANTA TANAKA-MARU.
BUT I'M FREE THAT DAY.
THERE YOU GO.
Okahira will keep you company.
MM...
I'M THINKING ABOUT ATTENDING THE SUZUYA SQUAD CHRISTMAS PARTY.
HAVE A MERRY CHRIST-MAS.
THANK YOU. (THIS SMELLS LIKE HIM...)

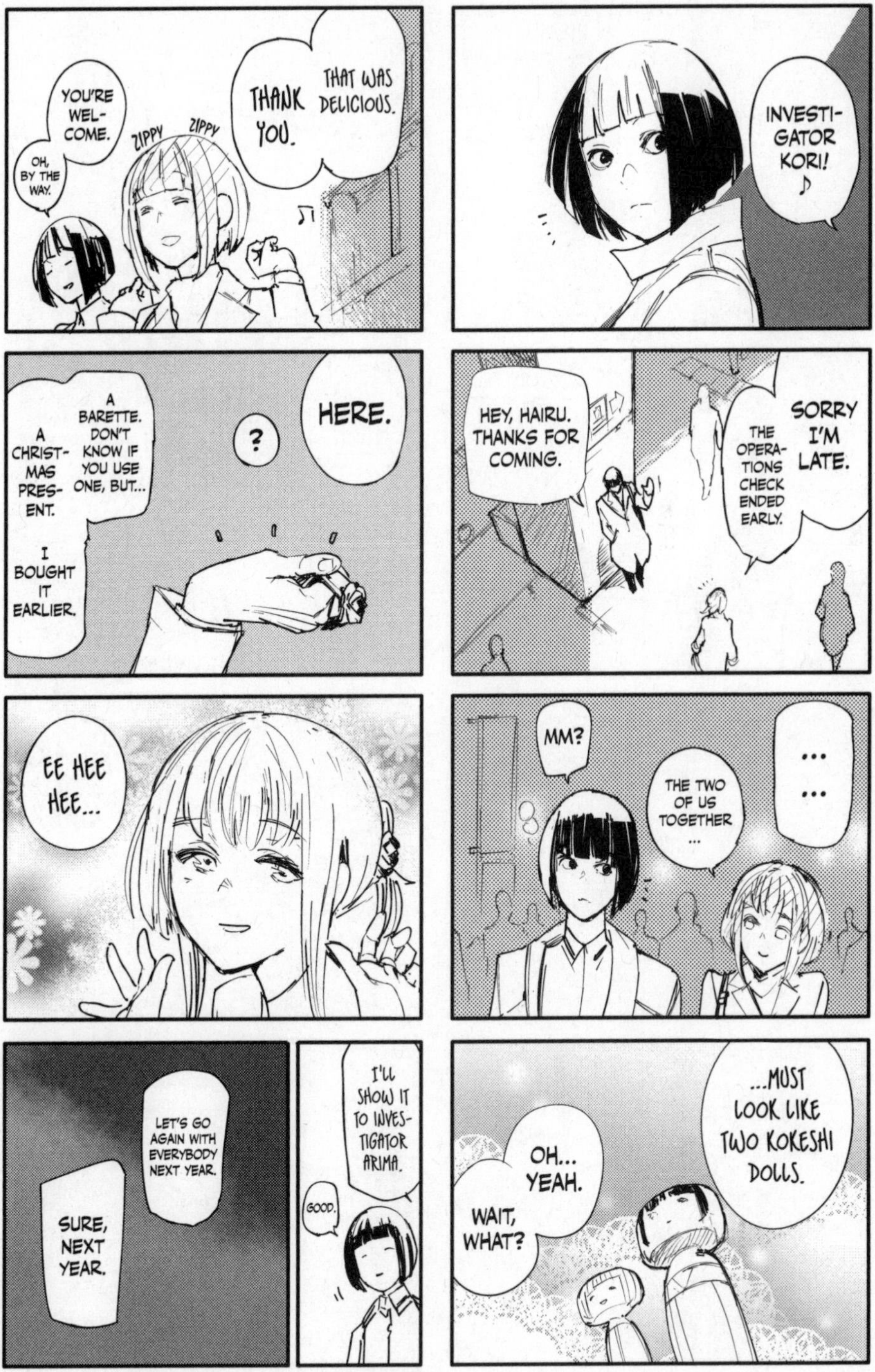
INVESTIGATOR KORI! ♪
THAT WAS DELICIOUS.
THANK YOU.
ZIPPY ZIPPY
YOU'RE WELCOME.
OH, BY THE WAY.
SORRY I'M LATE.
THE OPERATIONS CHECK ENDED EARLY.
HEY, HAIRU. THANKS FOR COMING.
HERE.
?
A BARETTE. DON'T KNOW IF YOU USE ONE, BUT...
A CHRISTMAS PRESENT.
I BOUGHT IT EARLIER.
... ...
MM?
THE TWO OF US TOGETHER ...
EE HEE HEE...
...MUST LOOK LIKE TWO KOKESHI DOLLS.
OH... YEAH.
WAIT, WHAT?
I'LL SHOW IT TO INVESTIGATOR ARIMA.
GOOD.
LET'S GO AGAIN WITH EVERYBODY NEXT YEAR.
SURE, NEXT YEAR.

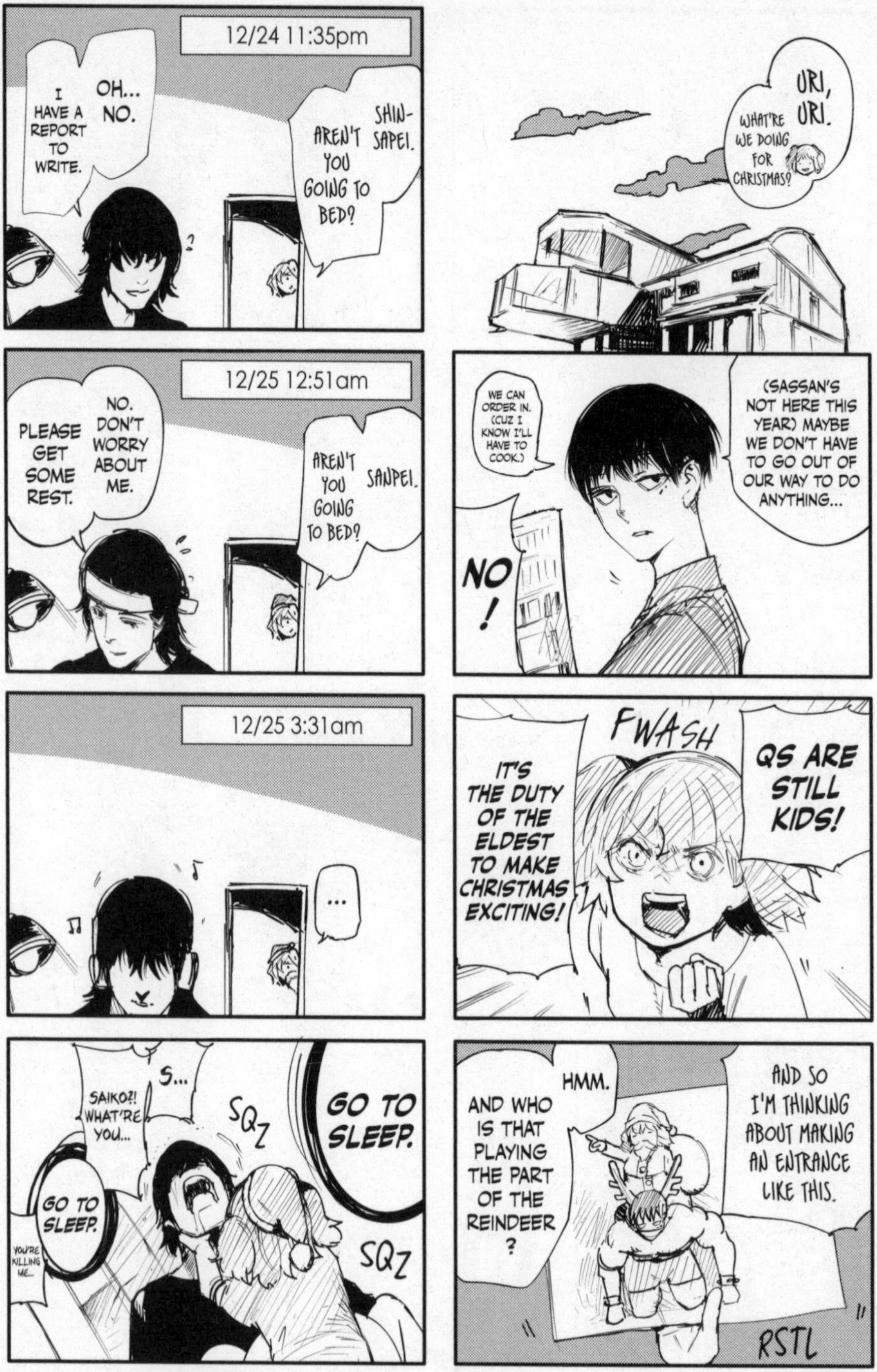
URI, URI.
WHAT'RE WE DOING FOR CHRISTMAS?
12/24 11:35pm
SHIN-SAPEI.
AREN'T YOU GOING TO BED?
OH... NO.
I HAVE A REPORT TO WRITE.
(SASSAN'S NOT HERE THIS YEAR) MAYBE WE DON'T HAVE TO GO OUT OF OUR WAY TO DO ANYTHING...
WE CAN ORDER IN. (CUZ I KNOW I'LL HAVE TO COOK.)
NO!
12/25 12:51am
SANPEI.
AREN'T YOU GOING TO BED?
NO. DON'T WORRY ABOUT ME.
PLEASE GET SOME REST.
FWASH
QS ARE STILL KIDS!
IT'S THE DUTY OF THE ELDEST TO MAKE CHRISTMAS EXCITING!
12/25 3:31am
...
AND SO I'M THINKING ABOUT MAKING AN ENTRANCE LIKE THIS.
HMM.
AND WHO IS THAT PLAYING THE PART OF THE REINDEER?
RSTL
GO TO SLEEP.
SQZ
S...
SAIKOZ! WHAT'RE YOU...
SQZ
GO TO SLEEP.
YOU'RE KILLING ME...

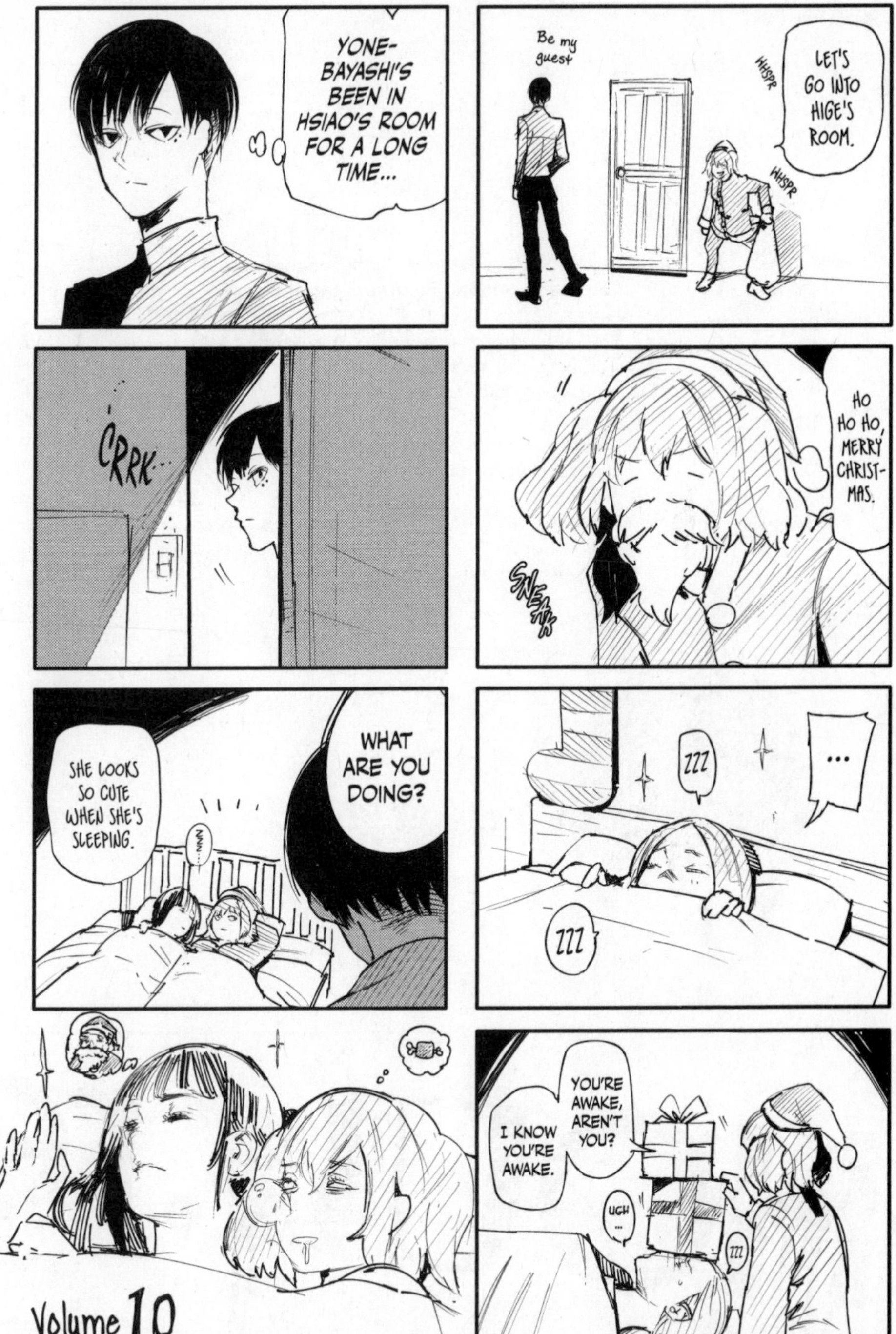
LET'S GO INTO HIGE'S ROOM.
WHSPR
WHSPR
Be my guest
YONE-BAYASHI'S BEEN IN HSIAO'S ROOM FOR A LONG TIME...
HO HO HO, MERRY CHRIST-MAS.
SNEAK
CRRK...
...
ZZZ
ZZZ
WHAT ARE YOU DOING?
SHE LOOKS SO CUTE WHEN SHE'S SLEEPING.
ZZZ...
YOU'RE AWAKE, AREN'T YOU?
I KNOW YOU'RE AWAKE.
UGH...
ZZZ

Volume 10 is out April 2019.

Staff ▶ Hashimoto, Kiyotaka Aihara, Niina/Nina, Ippo Yaguchi, Akikuni Nakao
Comic Design ▶ Hideaki Shimada (L.S.D.) Magazine Design ▶ Miyuki Takaoka Photography ▶ Wataru Tanaka
Editor ▶ Junpei Matsuo

Owl Project Report

● A-OWL

- Donor: Yoshimura
- Recipient: Kotaro Amon
- Change in Rc values: 230
                        970
                        5,820
                        10,181 (...)

Lab notes: Steady Rc Cell increase until second week.
                      Reached Kagune-generation threshold.

                      Rc Cells started to increase at an abnormal rate.
                      Administered Rc suppressant to calm subject when levels
                      passed 10,000.

                      Ceased administration of all medications. A-Owl will be
                      disposed of as a failure.

Kano's notes: It's very unfortunate. Theoretically this subject could
                      have become a Kakuja. If only we could have controlled
                      his development.

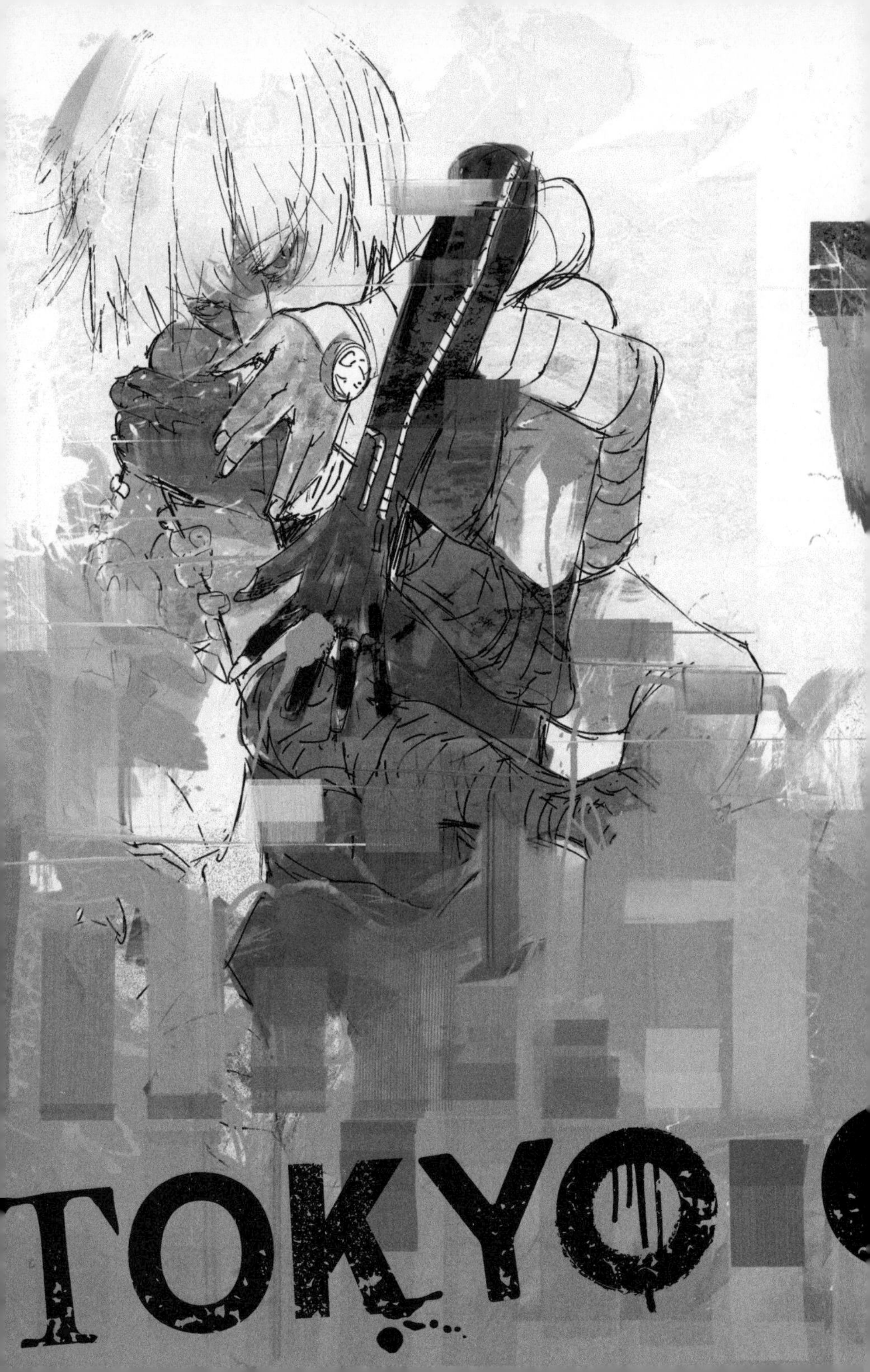
TOKYO

gHOUL:re

SUI ISHIDA is the author of the immensely popular *Tokyo Ghoul* and several *Tokyo Ghoul* one-shots, including one that won second place in the *Weekly Young Jump* 113th Grand Prix award in 2010. *Tokyo Ghoul:re* is the sequel to *Tokyo Ghoul*.

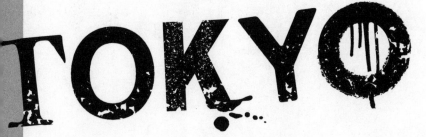

TOKYO G

Story and art by
SUI ISHIDA

First published in Japan in 2014 by SHUEISHA Inc., Tokyo.
English translation rights arranged by SHUEISHA Inc.

Translation Joe Yamazaki
Touch-Up Art & Lettering Vanessa Satone
Design Shawn Carrico
Editor Pancha Diaz

Printed in the U.S.A.

Published by VIZ Media, LLC
P.O. Box 77010
San Francisco, CA 94107

10 9 8 7 6 5 4 3 2 1
First printing, February 2019

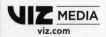

VIZ MEDIA
viz.com

VIZ SIGNATURE
vizsignature.com

ratings.viz.com
RATED T+ OLDER TEEN

PARENTAL ADVISORY
TOKYO GHOUL: RE is rated T+ for Older Teen and is recommended for ages 16 and up. This volume contains violence and gore.

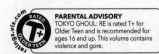

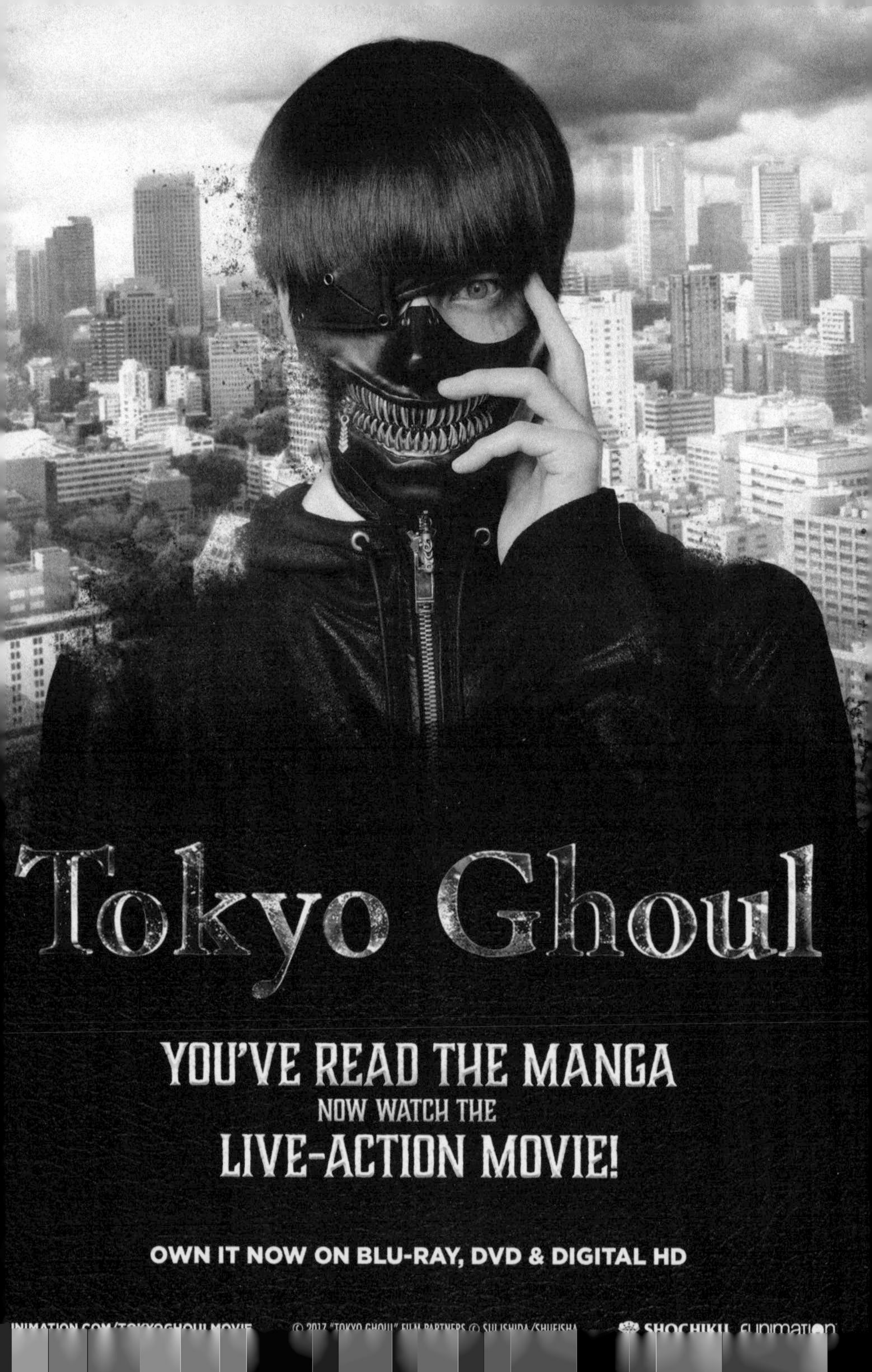
Tokyo Ghoul
YOU'VE READ THE MANGA
NOW WATCH THE
LIVE-ACTION MOVIE!
OWN IT NOW ON BLU-RAY, DVD & DIGITAL HD

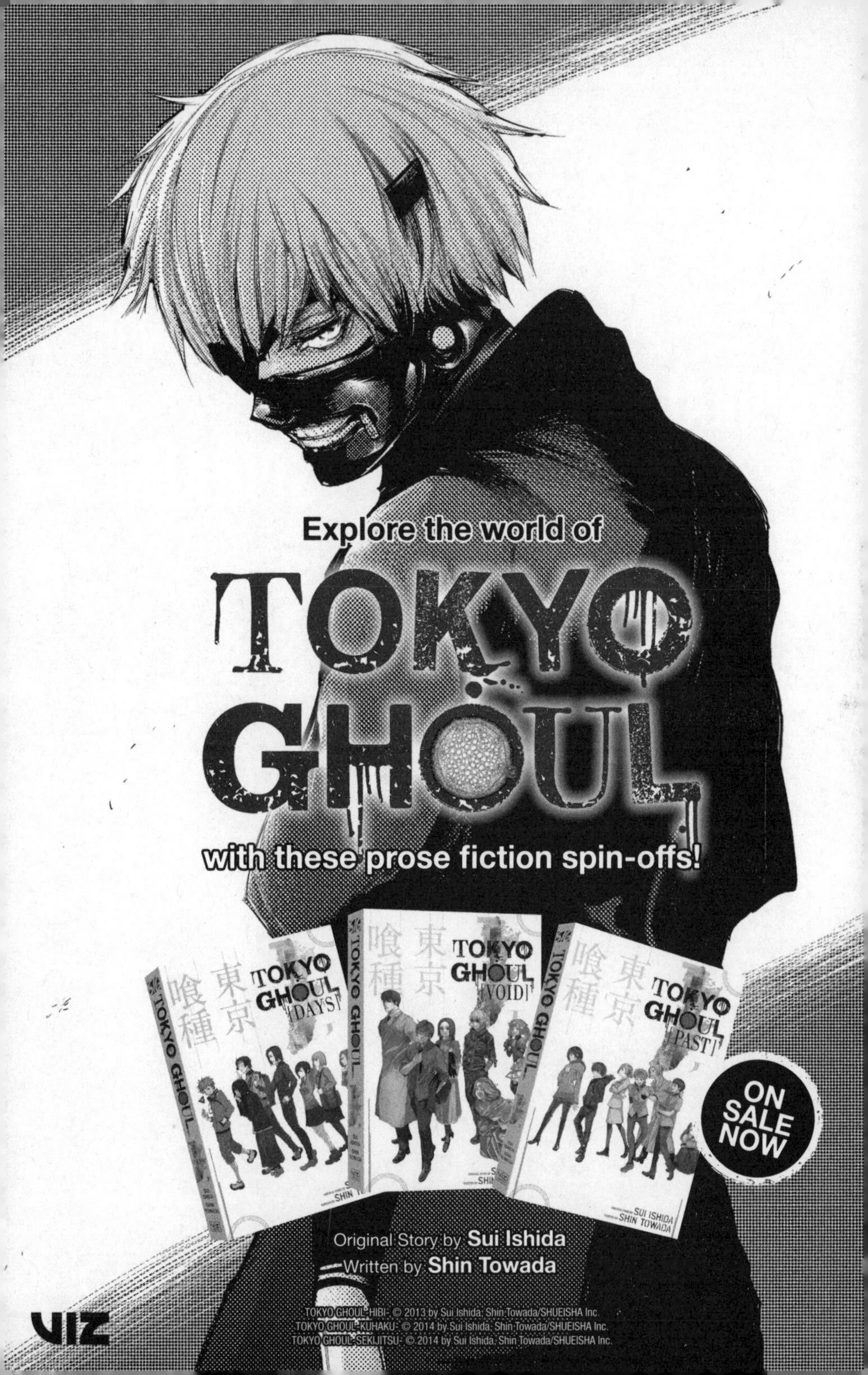
Explore the world of
TOKYO GHOUL
with these prose fiction spin-offs!
TOKYO GHOUL [DAYS]
TOKYO GHOUL [VOID]
TOKYO GHOUL [PAST]
ON SALE NOW
Original Story by Sui Ishida
Written by Shin Towada
VIZ
TOKYO GHOUL -HIBI- © 2013 by Sui Ishida, Shin Towada/SHUEISHA Inc.
TOKYO GHOUL -KUHAKU- © 2014 by Sui Ishida, Shin Towada/SHUEISHA Inc.
TOKYO GHOUL -SEKIJITSU- © 2014 by Sui Ishida, Shin Towada/SHUEISHA Inc.

UZUMAKI

Story and Art by **JUNJI ITO**

SPIRALS... THIS TOWN IS CONTAMINATED WITH SPIRALS...

Kurouzu-cho, a small fogbound town on the coast of Japan, is cursed. According to Shuichi Saito, the withdrawn boyfriend of teenager Kirie Goshima, their town is haunted not by a person or being but by a pattern: uzumaki, the spiral, the hypnotic secret shape of the world. It manifests itself in everything from seashells and whirlpools in water to the spiral marks on people's bodies, the insane obsessions of Shuichi's father and the voice from the cochlea in our inner ear. As the madness spreads, the inhabitants of Kurouzu-cho are pulled ever deeper into a whirlpool from which there is no return!

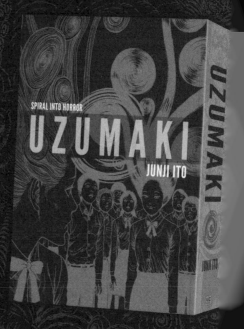

A masterpiece of horror manga, now available in a
DELUXE HARDCOVER EDITION!

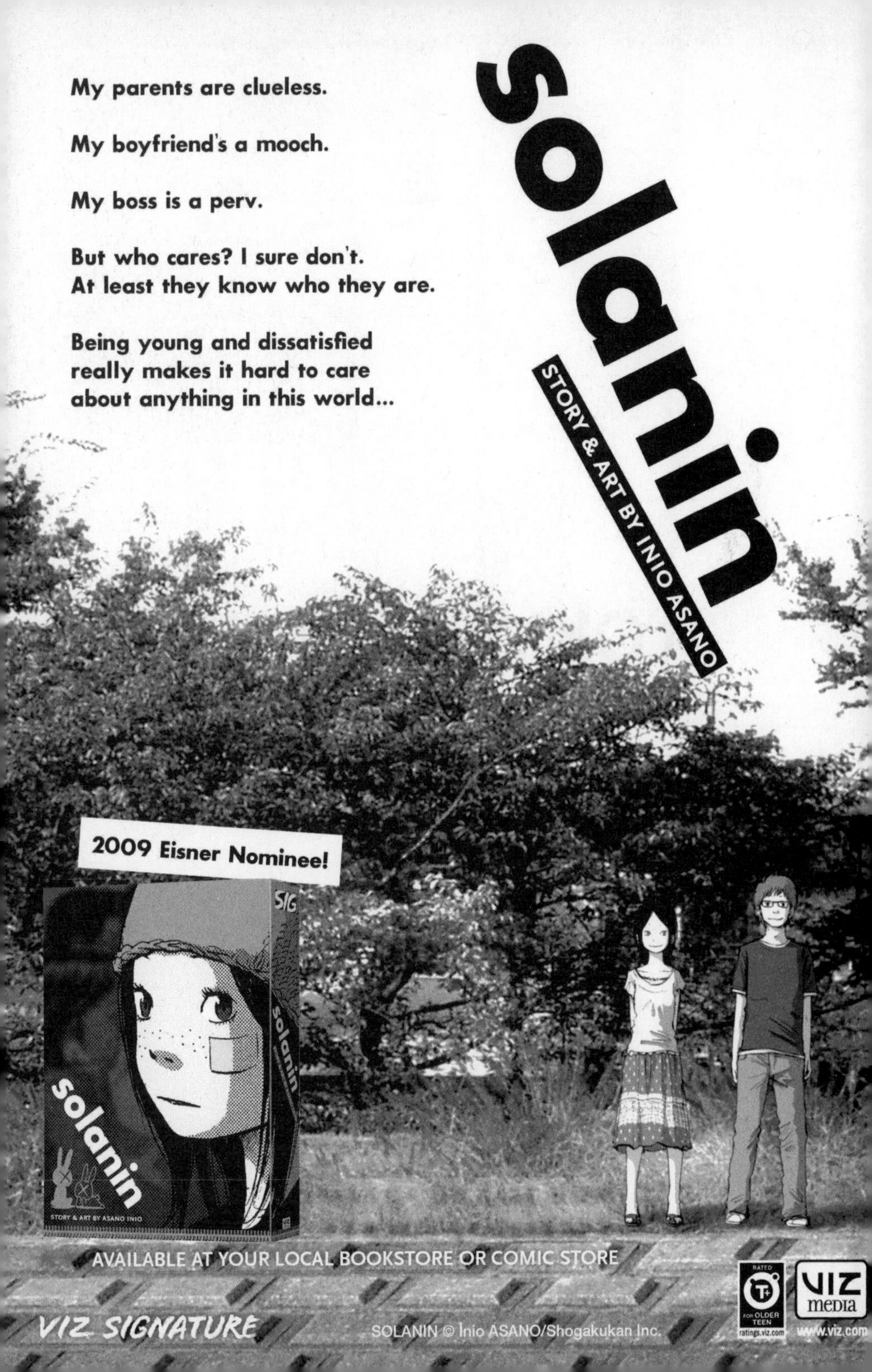
My parents are clueless.
My boyfriend's a mooch.
My boss is a perv.
But who cares? I sure don't.
At least they know who they are.
Being young and dissatisfied
really makes it hard to care
about anything in this world...
solanin
STORY & ART BY INIO ASANO
2009 Eisner Nominee!
SIG
solanin
solanin
STORY & ART BY ASANO INIO
AVAILABLE AT YOUR LOCAL BOOKSTORE OR COMIC STORE
RATED
T+
FOR OLDER TEEN
ratings.viz.com
VIZ media
www.viz.com
VIZ SIGNATURE
SOLANIN © Inio ASANO/Shogakukan Inc.

TOKYO GHOUL:re

This is the last page.
TOKYO GHOUL:re reads right to left.